SCENOGRAPHY AND STAGE TECHNOLOGY

From Le Rossignol (Stravinsky). Santa Fe Opera production. Courtesy of Woodfin Camp & Associates. Photograph by Adam Woolfitt.

SCENOGRAPHY AND STAGE TECHNOLOGY
an introduction

WILLARD F. BELLMAN

California State University, Northridge

Thomas Y. Crowell Company
New York   Established 1834

SCENOGRAPHY AND STAGE TECHNOLOGY An Introduction

Library of Congress Cataloging in Publication Data

Bellman, Willard F
    Scenography and stage technology.

    Bibliography: p.
    Includes index.
    1. Stage management.   2. Theaters—Stage-
setting and scenery.   I. Title.
PN2085.B43   792′.025   76-48992
ISBN 0-690-00872-4

Typography and cover design by William E. Frost

CONTENTS

This book has been written for all beginning students of theatre technology and the arts of the visual production. It is intended for the many courses that provide the student with a basic knowledge of the techniques of theatre production and introduce the artistic and aesthetic considerations which underly them. These considerations fall under the new label of "scenography," although they are often subdivided into such categories as scenery and property design, lighting design, costume design, and the like.

I approach the subject of stage technology and scenography from a foundation of modern theatre aesthetics. This seems to be the only reasonable way to connect art and technique in an area filled with increasingly complicated technology. Otherwise mechanics threaten to overpower the ultimate purpose of theatre, which must be art. Furthermore, the aesthetic foundations of theatrical production have broad implications for all students of theatre whether their ultimate interests are scenography, technology, acting, directing, or playwriting. Thus this text serves one of the basic requirements for a beginning course in theatre: it helps to establish broad foundations upon which later specialization may be built.

Of primary importance to modern theatre aesthetics is the concept of the tightly unified work of theatrical art. It is an almost unspoken assumption upon which most twentieth-century theatre is built. This text considers the many forms of theatrical organization that have been devised to achieve this unity, but focuses sharply on the organization utilizing the *scenographer* as the one most likely to produce a coherent work of art. While not typical of some current American theatrical practices, the concept of the scenographer is nevertheless the accepted mode of operation in much of the best of European theatre and is gaining acceptance in the more progressive theatre organizations in the United States. Furthermore, the basic aesthetic needs which the scenographer must satisfy are present even if the scenographer is replaced by a team of artists to whom the various artistic functions have been delegated. Thus the aesthetic of scenography remains valid even in those organizations that choose to do without the scenographer.

Contemporary theatre is far more than the peephole theatre. Although our technology and much of our architecture still reflect the heritage of the proscenium, new forms abound. These forms find expression in theatre architecture, in scenic styles, and most important of all, in challenges to the assumption that theatre is largely an interpretive art. Even unscripted theatre is no longer a fringe movement. It has implications for the scenographer and technician that cannot be ignored.

While aesthetic considerations are kept in mind, this text seeks to solve another more immediate problem evident in almost every educational theatre: if students are to be exposed to practical problems, they must work on productions. This means serving on crews. Since production crews have to meet deadlines that seldom jibe with the orderly sequence of lecture and laboratory, crew members find themselves asked to perform tasks that have yet to be mentioned in their classes. While no text can hope to solve this problem completely, this one does at least keep new crew members in mind. Careful study of those portions of the text devoted to their particular crew assignments should enable crew members at least to ask intelligent questions and to feel they have some grasp of the situation—thus allowing the crew supervisors to proceed more efficiently.

Theatre technology is ever-changing. New materials, new devices, and new requirements appear constantly. Perhaps one of the most important of these is the now federally reinforced concept of safety. A safe theatre has always been basic to continued artistic success, but recent federal legislation, the Occupational Safety and Health Act (OSHA), has eradicated much of the laissez-faire attitude of past safety enforcement. More stringent rules and more rigorous enforcement now affect the theatre as they do every other industry. With this new climate in mind, I have written a chapter on general safety considerations plus specialized treatments in each of the various technological areas.

Old established materials and ways of making things are being superseded. Changes result from both economic pressures and the demands of scenographers for greater freedom to devise three-dimensional elements whose shapes are not dictated by the limits of traditional materials. Thus wood increasingly is giving way to steel and light metal. And new materials bring new technologies. For example, electric welding, once an occasional specialty often "farmed out" by the scene shop, is now an everyday operation to be learned by all well-trained theatre workers. (Fortunately new machinery makes this possible.) Similarly, working with plastics is no longer confined to a few avant-garde workers and some property specialists—it is a standard part of any well-equipped theatre's shop procedures.

The very first implication of the word "beginner" is that such a person will progress to more advanced things. Such progression will be faster; and the drudgery of learning the many, often dull facts that must be mastered will be lighter if the student can have a glimpse of greater challenges to come. This text tries to offer some hints of advanced techniques, sophisticated machinery, and challenging experimentation. Beginners should certainly be aware of hydraulic and motor-driven stage devices and look forward to the day when they can try to work theatrical wonders with them. Similarly, computer-assisted lighting controls should serve to challenge students to reach the point where they can test their potentialities.

Of all the new areas of theatre artistry, scenic projection and laser technology are the most attractive. There is an almost irresistible impulse to delve into the intricacies of projections and to try to conjure a laser into producing fascinating images. But lasers and the exotic light sources used in scenic projection can be dangerous. The beginner, eager to work artistic wonders, may bring a theatrical career to a sudden end. Thus this text tries to sort out those areas of experimentation which are safely open to beginners from those which they should approach only with the guidance of an experienced supervisor. Given caution, there is no reason why beginners should not try to make magic with these strange and marvelous tools. Their very naïveté and enthusiasm may uncover artistic possibilities that more experienced minds might overlook.

Finally, since the academic world must somehow evaluate its work and is therefore apt to give examinations requiring definitions of terms, a glossary has been appended. It provides short definitions of most common theatrical terms. In many cases more elaborate definitions or treatments are available in the text. These should be sought via the index.

A book about the visual aspects of theatrical production must rely heavily on illustrations. Since hundreds of technical items must be shown, it is hard to avoid making some sections resemble pages from a manufacturer's catalogue. Showing many items in at least one of their uses helps, and the student is more likely to remember the tool or piece of equipment by associating it with its application. I am indebted to the many friends and commercial concerns who have made such illustrative material available. Without their help there would be fewer and less effective illustrations. Those illustrations not otherwise credited have been photographed by the author.

A particular debt of gratitude must be acknowledged to the many students of California State University, Northridge, who have generously contributed their time to help in setting up illustrations, to serve as models, and, at times, to act as friendly critics of material about to be photographed. They have added much to this text.

No book of this complexity could come into being without the assistance of a skilled editor. The present text has benefited from not one, but two editors, Marge Lakin and Phillip Leininger. Without their sharp eyes for stylistic improvements and their challenging minds, this book would have suffered.

The author is also indebted to the people who have by their contributions and astute comments helped to bring this text into being. They have done much to contribute to whatever merit it may have. They are certainly not to be blamed for its shortcomings. I am particularly indebted to my wife for her encouragement and rigorous editorial assistance. The following, necessarily incomplete list, will serve in a small way to recognize some of those who have made contributions to this book:

INDIVIDUALS

Richard Arnold   James Klain
Arthur Beer   John Knight
Nick Bryson   Andrej Majewski
Annelies Corrodi   Gary Minz
Ralph Duckwall   Van Phillips
Gary Gaiser   Richard Pilbrow
John Green   Ed Pruett
Helmut Grosser   John Rothgeb
George Howard   Bernie Skalka
Richard Johnson   Owen Smith
Kate Keleher   Josef Svoboda

FIRMS AND EDUCATIONAL INSTITUTIONS

Background Engineering
Berkey Colortran, A Division of Berkey Photo
California Institute of the Arts
California State University, Long Beach
California State University, Northridge
The Focal Point
H & H Specialties
Kliegl Brothers Lighting
Optical Radiation Corporation
Roscoe Laboratories
Siemens A. G.
Strand Century Lighting
Theatre Projects
Thorn Electric
University of California at Irvine
University of California at Los Angeles
Welton Becket and Associates, Architects

SCENOGRAPHY
AND STAGE
TECHNOLOGY

Modern theatre is a variable art. It seems to take new forms at every turn, and these often seem contradictory, even antagonistic to each other. The visual effects of modern theatre, which include scenography and the technology that supports it, share in this variability. Recent changes range from radical departures in theatre architecture to applications of laser and computer technology, and from experimental theatre groups that eschew the use of a playscript to abstract blends of theatre, art, technology, and sculpture that appear in modern art museums as "environments."

Yet the theatre, including today's theatre, has its aesthetic unity that comprises scenography and technology as well as all other aspects of our art. In spite of the contemporary ferment, however, most of the change will probably seem evolutionary, not revolutionary, to future students of the art. Interplay between innovation by playwrights and by other theatrical elements is an old and vital part of theatrical history. Playwrights and creative artists with new concepts pose challenges for production teams and for theatrical technology. New developments in technology and new concepts of production in turn stimulate the original artists. The interchange goes on and on, and the theatre profits.

If we are to understand fully the way in which scenography and theatre technology fit into modern theatre, we must recognize the theatre's *changing* nature, and its *evolving* aesthetic.

EDUCATIONAL THEATRE

Changes, apparent in all aspects of theatre, are of particular importance to the special kind of theatre with which we are most concerned: the educational theatre. If theatrical education is to be anything more than reiteration of current practices, it must not only recognize new developments in theatre, but be in the forefront of such developments. Moreover, the relative freedom from commercial pressures of the American

1

educational theatre makes it a superb milieu for research, experimentation, and testing of new ideas. Education aimed toward the future of theatre flourishes amid the new concepts and new procedures made possible by such a unique testing ground.

Nevertheless the theatrical past, traditional in methods and in art forms, still dominates our theatrical activities. Its techniques must be mastered and its technology learned. For example, although some may argue that the proscenium theatre is obsolescent, its terminology and machinery will certainly be a part of our theatre for that future we are able to predict. Theatrical aesthetics move even more slowly. In the 3000–4000-year history of theatre, its basic aesthetic has not changed, although much has been added. The educational theatre must of necessity work within that aesthetic.

It is important to recognize that the basic purpose of educational theatre is to teach the aesthetic, the arts and skills necessary to a student who wishes to become a future theatrical artist. One of the most important teaching devices must be the production of theatrical pieces of high artistic quality. This presents a contradiction in that a production organization composed of students cannot, by definition, have the necessary skills and highly developed talents to produce what the school needs — top-level art. This dilemma, inevitable in educational theatre, need not be a serious handicap if the school provides a sufficient number of artists and craftsmen of high quality who lend their abilities to the productions as a part of their teaching responsibilities. Such a combination of students, artists, and craftsmen should be able to produce theatre of very respectable artistic merit and thus provide quality artistic experiences for the student. This text is intended to assist the student's participation in this rather complicated educational process.

Educational theatre is also unique in its special methods of making effective the experience of participation in the creation of theatrical art works. Class work usually consists of three types of activity: lectures, structured laboratory sessions, and crew participation. It is the crew assignment that is unique. Unlike a set of educational experiences in a chemistry lab which move in carefully planned steps through the material, the crew experience is one of "total immersion." Students are assigned to a crew to assist in the preparation and presentation of a particular production not according to the schedule of materials being presented in their theatre production classes, but as the school's production program demands. Thus the students on a crew may be expected to perform sophisticated operations that have not been covered in class. One of the purposes of this text is to ease the trauma of such crew work. Although no text can be expected to answer all of the questions that will occur to students suddenly thrust into a crew, many things can be covered which will spare them the embarrassment of asking repeated naive questions, and spare the crew supervisors the necessity of explaining the same fundamentals over and over. Student readers are therefore strongly advised to study immediately those portions of this text applicable to their crew assignment. Ideally, they should have read the entire book by the time they become deeply involved in crew work, but this is a large order.

THEATRE AS MACHINE

Not only is the student called upon to do things that he has not yet learned, but he also may feel engulfed by a sort of four-dimensional monster that promises to swallow his entire academic life, including those hours he has set aside for sleeping. Still worse, he may be unable to find the slightest connection between the menial tasks to which he is assigned and the theatrical art work being created. The chaos in which he finds himself will probably seem to be populated by madmen who assume that since he is ''in theatre,'' he must automatically understand everything and be highly motivated to make any sort of sacrifice to ''his art.''

Students should think of the theatre plant and its occupants as a metaphorical ''machine'' whose purpose is the production of theatre art works. Each phase of the operation must fit closely into the others, all of them guided by a very complex artistic goal which we will discuss in detail in the following chapters. Ideally the architecture of the theatre building, the machinery within it, and the human organization that runs the plant are all bent on the common goal: the produced play. The study of the aesthetic of theatre production, which is the subject of the next chapters, is intended to assist students in relating their tasks to the process as a whole.

As we move through the discussion of the various phases of theatre production a stylistic problem arises. It should be manifestly obvious that any of the positions given can be effectively held by either men or women. However the structure of the English language would make the following material awkward if every ''he'' was replaced with ''he or she,'' or still worse, by ''the supervisor'' or whatever the term happens to be. Thus readers should understand that the male gender when used in the remainder of the text is a matter of grammatical convenience only.

PART ONE

A WORKING AESTHETIC OF SCENOGRAPHY

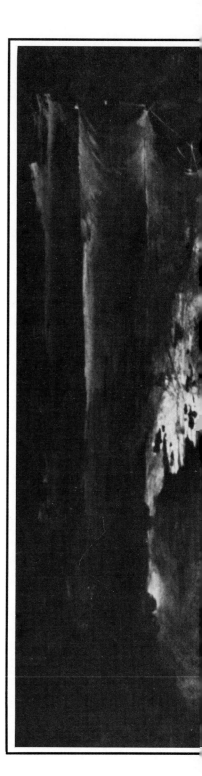

A rendering by Andrej Majewski for Macbeth.

1 THEATRE AS ART

INTRODUCTION Great theatre needs no defense as art in our present society. The major thrust of critical studies for the past fifty years has almost completely destroyed the once popular notion that theatre was a "mixture of the arts," some sort of hybrid composed of literature, dance, painting, and sculpture. Although materials and techniques from each of these arts appear with regularity in theatre, it has been well established that they do not do so within their own aesthetics, but as materials available to the theatrical artist who creates the unique aesthetic form known as "theatre."

But to say that theatre is an art is not to say that *all* theatre is art or that the *only* thing theatre can be is art. It would probably be stretching the truth to assert that all theatre even strives to be art. It often tries to be many other things and frequently succeeds. For example, the American professional theatre on Broadway often is described as "show business" with the emphasis on *business.* Under these circumstances, theatre must be judged as any other business: Can it make money?

There are still other kinds of theatre. For example, theatre may be psychological therapy, known as "psychodrama," considered a very legitimate kind of psychological treatment for its participants by some authorities.

Another type of theatre—also with certain psychological overtones—is what might be called "recreational theatre." If totally candid evaluations were possible, most community and "workshop" theatre would fall into this category. Such productions are almost never profitable at the box office, and their artistic success is almost always limited (exceptions are certain workshops conducted by highly talented professionals who create and maintain them to hone their already considerable talents). Nevertheless, recreational theatre is a legitimate type to which the rest of theatre owes thanks for the development of audiences.

Theatre is also an effective and legitimate educational tool. It can be used to teach many things, most particularly to develop cultural values as a part of a program in general education.

Of course a theatre organization can have more than one objective, and most do. It can seek to make money, create art, provide recreation, and teach all at the same time. Any or all of these purposes are valid and worthy of pursuit. However, it is neither honest nor psychologically healthful to claim theatrical art as our most important objective when recreation is obviously the chief purpose of our enterprise and artistic success really a hoped-for "plus."

At the root of much theatrical activity and closely related to the artistic impulses of all artists, including those in the theatre, is the ego. Probably one of the greatest ego satisfactions any human being can have is the acclaim that may come with *artistic* success. The acclaim that is given to *popular* success can be even louder—whether it is more or less satisfying is something only the individual can decide. The point is that the basic needs of the ego are strong motivations for most theatrical activity, and those sincerely interested in theatre as art must constantly take care that their ego needs and artistic impulses do not cancel each other to the detriment of the would-be artist. It is all too easy to confuse ego satisfaction with artistic success, particularly at curtain call time.

THE NATURE OF THEATRICAL ART

What is the aesthetic of this rapidly changing form to which we find ourselves attracted? What is its value in our modern world where the word "relevance" has almost become a cry of desperation?

Human activities do not neatly sort themselves out into categories; life tends to bump along in a manner which suggests that mere existence is somehow a triumph. Still, if anything separates humans from monkeys, porpoises, or whatever, it is the sensitive, questioning, organizing mind, particularly when that mind examines the self and the life we lead. When people seek to understand themselves, where they are, what they are doing, where they are going, they are most human.

DISCURSIVE AND NONDISCURSIVE EXPRESSION

In general, humanity's efforts to express the results of its searches take two forms. These forms grow out of two general ways of looking at a phenomenon in an attempt to understand it. The first way is *analytical:* one takes the phenomenon apart in some orderly manner and examines its components. For example, one might make a temporal examination of an event by taking it apart second by second, or a spatial examination of an object by separating it into its parts. What we are concerned with at this moment is the way in which we express the results of these activities. In the case of an *analysis*, the report will be in *discursive* form. This means that the "language" used will seek to present our findings in some sequential order that emphasizes interrelationships between individual parts. Such a report may be in language such as English or German, or it may be in the form of mathematics, scientific formulas, or whatever. The important point is that discursive expressions emphasize *parts* and *relationships among parts*. While discursive expression can handle hugely complex ideas (for example, vast scientific findings), the emphasis is on parts, their individual relationships, and the sequence formed by the analysis itself.

Many of the results of humanity's search for insight into its condition, however, are not suited to report by analysis. In such areas the findings take the form of whole experiences or whole concepts whose import lies in just that wholeness, i.e., the *complete pattern* that must be apprehended as a whole, not bit by bit. Art works are probably the most complex examples in this field. The intent of an art work is to produce a special combination of experiences, reflections, and insights *simultaneously*. That is, an art work demands that we both experience and contemplate the experience at the same time. Although the special analytical techniques of the science of psychology will reveal certain valuable things about the creative activity that went into making an art work, neither psychology nor any other form of analysis reported in discursive language can be of much value in getting at the central purpose of the art work itself. Only a special total experience known as an "aesthetic" experience can do this. Much of the remainder of our discussion will be indirectly aimed at making clear what an aesthetic experience is in regard to the theatre.

The general definition might be: *An aesthetic experience is a unique kind of human experience in which a special virtual world is created in which the observer simultaneously experiences and contemplates his experience.* ("Virtual" will be discussed in detail later in this chapter.) The result can be a unique kind of insight into human perceptions of life itself.

We are quite capable of comprehending a phenomenon as a whole, but our expression of such an experience must take a different form from that discursive "language" which works so well for analytical activities. The expression must be suited to the experience. It must be capable of presenting the experience as a whole, not merely bringing up a bit at a time. Such expression will be in *nondiscursive* form. A nondiscursive expression functions by *presenting*[1] to its recipient an entire

---

1. The term "presentational" also is used in this context.

complex of interrelationships usually involving both emotions and concepts. The nondiscursive expression always places the emphasis on the whole, not on the parts.

Both discursive and nondiscursive expression may at times use the same types of "raw material," such as the words and grammatical structure of language. The English language, for example, may be used discursively to write a careful analytical paper, or it may be used nondiscursively to write a poem whose entire thrust is toward a single but vastly complex expression of human feeling. In brief, an expression in language may be either discursive or nondiscursive depending on the motive and skill of the writer.

ART AS SYMBOLIC EXPRESSION

All art is a form of nondiscursive expression. Susanne Langer has described art as "The creation of forms symbolic of human feeling."[2] Note the purposeful character of art which implicitly underlies the definition: "human feelings" are recognized from the onset as something *needing* expression. Art is a necessary human activity, a part of striving to know oneself and one's destiny.

But if we are to function as working theatrical artists, a mere statement of the philosophical value of art will not suffice. What we need is a "working aesthetic," one that will help us to understand our art better and to solve artistic problems as we work. We can begin with the word "symbolic" as we find it in Langer's definition of art.

We start with sensory data. If, for example, you touch a live wire, you almost instantly draw your hand away from it. The sensory data are received and acted upon without taking time for contemplation. One does not think at all; one *acts.* This is Langer's point—if the human brain is to *think* about something, not merely react to sensory data by indicating some immediate action, some transformation of the raw data is required. What happens is called "abstraction," and the result is a *symbol.* Abstraction melds the raw data and the circumstances of its reception into a unit of thought capable of recall by means of an identifying "label." For example, the word "shock" can, in the context of the English language, become a symbol for the whole complex of pain, muscular contraction, and fear surrounding the experience of an electrical shock. In addition to these general experiences, each victim of a shock will include individual details filling in the "picture" of the experience. For the victim, the word "shock" evokes all of these things as a pattern. It has become a symbol.

The human mind works with symbols, not with raw sensory data. We can only respond to sensory data; we can think and feel using

---

2. Susanne K. Langer, *Feeling and Form* (New York: Charles Scribner's Sons, 1953), p. 40.

symbols. But we can do more than that with them; we can combine and recombine them into vast complexes of thought and feeling, and we can externalize them so that they may evoke similar complexes of thought and feeling in others. This is the root of human communication.

SYMBOLIC TRANSFORMATION

"Symbolic transformation" as a generic term refers to the transformation of sensory data into a form capable of being thought about by the mind. But it also refers to the final stage in the development of an artistic concept—that moment when the various symbols in the artist's mind suddenly are transformed and integrated. This is the "flash of inspiration" without which art cannot happen.

Thus the ultimate artistic symbolic transformation results in a single but complex symbol which may, if the artist successfully pursues the process to the end, result in an externalization which we call an "art work." There is a special quality about the art work: it symbolizes a concept so complex and so closely integrated that the art work and that which it symbolizes have become synonymous. Any change results in a change in the nature of the whole thing; its structure is *organic*. An organism is a living thing; anything that affects one part of it will affect all of it. One experience with a toothache is enough to convince most of us of the physiological truth of this statement. Metaphorically one may say that a structure is "organic" when it is so arranged that a change in any part will affect the whole. Art works are supreme examples of organic structures. We will have repeated occasion to remind ourselves of this as we consider the details of a theatrical production as they relate to the whole.

THEATRE AS INTERPRETIVE ART

The nondiscursive nature of artistic material causes many difficulties in the discussion of a completed art work. These difficulties multiply many times when the problem is the development of an art work from a previously prepared artistic "document" intended to guide the work to fulfillment by another artist or artists. This is known as an "interpretive art." For example, a playwright's script is intended to be produced by others, a musician's score to be played by other musicians. Such forms present more complex problems than the work of a painter whose art reaches the audience directly.

Interpretive art works place a special demand on intermediate forms (scripts, scores, etc.): there must be provided a special kind of nondiscursive guidance for the artist(s) who complete them. Discursive expression is of little value in this process, as most playwrights who have tried to depend on stage directions have discovered.

As if this were not handicap enough, the theatre (along with opera, and often dance) compounds its semantic difficulties even further by being so complex that it is nearly impossible for a single interpretive artist to take major responsibility for the fulfillment of the script. This must depend on a team of artists, dangerously near artistic creation by committee. Remember that the committees of the world usually are credited with the worst sort of compromises and mediocrity.

Having almost certainly guaranteed that it can never rise to the level of art (by being *both* interpretive and performed by committee), the theatre proceeds to confound the aestheticians by being one of the oldest viable art forms in human history, and one that continues to produce its share of artistic triumphs today. But it also produces some of the most dismal failures, frequently by talented people who, as they go down to failure, avow that they are hard at work on the artistic triumph of the decade.

The communicative process among theatre artists is far from perfect. Thus we will stress the potentials in the concept of the scenographer. It is the opinion of the writer that this concept rightly applied will produce a higher ratio of artistic success than most other organizational methods. An examination of some of the details of the communicative problems of interpretive art will clarify this.

COMMUNICATION IN INTERPRETIVE ART

What are the theatre's alternatives to discursive communication? Obviously nondiscursive (that is, symbolic) means will have to be used as the intermediary communicative devices if interpretation is to succeed. This is what any good playscript really is—an art work for interpretive artists, not a piece of discursive writing. Its poetry (in the broadest sense) is its essence. But this is not enough because several artists are going to have to deal with the script if it is to become theatre—and they are going to have to reach symbolic agreement. A meeting between director and actors, or between director and scenographer (or any other combination of artists of the theatre) is in fact an attempt at nondiscursive communication about an art work in process. It is fraught with potential for the worst kind of misunderstanding—that in which each party thinks he has communicated clearly and completely with the other, when in fact no communication at all has occurred. Since such "production meetings" eventually determine the form of actor movement, line delivery, settings, lighting, and such, the ultimate end of such misunderstanding can be wasteful, destructive to the egos of those involved, and can result in artistic chaos instead of success. Perhaps the ego hazard is greatest of all, at least in the environment of the American professional theatre world. Some who have been through many of these "wars" assert that it becomes instinctive to build protection for the ego from the very first moment of a production meeting by not taking any artistic positions at all (defensive pose), or by taking an absolute position that places everyone else on the defensive, such as, "The production will be done as follows!" (offensive pose). The very essence of non-discursive communication lies in sensitive perception of every innuendo used by those participating, and a willingness to "feed back" these perceptions to see if they are valid. Protective postures, whether offensive or defensive, are unrewarding.

Many varieties of theatre organization have been tried in an effort to create the one most likely to produce success. Some of these are listed and evaluated below.

FOUR "SOLUTIONS" TO THE COMMUNICATIONS PROBLEM

The Superartist

The superartist is probably what the theorist Edward Gordon Craig had in mind and is theoretically an ideal solution to the problem of communication. It in effect reduces the number of interpretive artists to one, a master theatre artist to whom all others — actors, dancers, craftsmen, and such — are totally subservient. The problem is that perceptive but totally subservient actors and craftsmen do not exist. Another problem is that the demands on the master interpreter are so numerous that practically no single person can meet them. Nevertheless, some giants of the theatre have succeeded in working this way. Their value to the educational theatre would be dubious since those working under them would learn little or nothing of the most essential artistic activities of the theatre.

Delegated Authority

In much of the American theatre today, a large number of artists are gathered together and each is given responsibility for a carefully defined area. There is a director, the actors, perhaps a choreographer, a music director to whom the actors may answer when they sing or dance, designers of scenery, lighting, sound, and costumes, and occasionally a special designer of masks or a special "creator of effects." The theory is sound on the face of it. Each does his bit under the aegis of the director who brings all of the pieces together. At times it works well, especially when the director is unusually aware of the communication difficulties accompanying this apparently logical division of labor. Several of the artists must be willing to function merely as craftsmen, resigning larger, more artistically satisfying responsibilities to others. For example, the lighting designer may defer in all but the most technical matters to the scenic designer who has, in effect, already designed the lighting in the process of designing the setting.

The system also works best in those productions that do not demand a high level of artistic integration in order to achieve some reasonable success. For example, a drawing-room comedy such as *Life with Father* may place few demands on lighting beyond the routine, thereby forestalling any deeply disturbing communications problems that might occur between a lighting designer and a set designer under more demanding circumstances.

With this delegated authority, however, theatrical efforts fail more often than they succeed. The failure is often the result of artistic chaos, the sort that causes critics to note that the action of the piece proceeded in spite of the setting, that the lighting was unrelated, or that the costumes, while gloriously beautiful, had little to do with the virtual characters wearing them. Furthermore, such failures often are suffered by production teams of highly talented, superbly trained artists. Clearly, such failures are caused by faulty aesthetic communication. Aesthetic matters never came together and the production did not achieve artistic unity. *Without unity there is no art; instead there is disaster.*

While aesthetic communication can be achieved using the delegated authority arrangement (otherwise there would be no successes at all), the system seems prone to generating failures. This is particularly true under the pressures of production deadlines and even more true under commercial pressures. Good aesthetic communication takes dedication and time—both commodities often in short supply at critical moments. The amount of time needed is increased, probably geometrically, as the number of participating artists increases. Dedication usually depends on the share of artistic responsibility delegated to each artist and, therefore, the potential ego satisfaction offered. The delegated authority system often reduces artistic responsibility to a minute amount, and occasionally even requires complete renunciation by some artists in favor of others. Add to this the ego-bruising potential of failure and it is no wonder that many professionals protect their egos first and worry about the artistic integrity of the show second. Ironically, of course, this almost guarantees failure.

Given talent, human dedication to art is the solution to this communication problem. Particularly in the educational theatre, however, other human factors enter the equation. Total involvement means total renunciation of much of the rest of the human world, something most people do not wish to consider as a permanent condition. Those who can dedicate themselves in this manner will appreciate the collective theatre group discussed below. But educational theatre workers have no choice. They work in two worlds by definition. Their responsibilities to the art of theatre are only a part of their responsibilities to education, and neither can be neglected at the expense of the other.

The Company as Collective Creative Artist

We will frequently refer to this organizational pattern of the collective creative artist[3] because it is responsible for much of the new, experimental theatre of our time. It is a form demanding the utmost human dedication. Actors and theatrical artists band together expressly to develop the highest sensitivity to each other's nondiscursive communications. They frequently live in the same quarters and always work together many hours each day. Such groups may include playwrights, or the group as a whole may create a script. Artists may specialize from time to time in such things as scenography, choreography, and the like. Artistic concepts are the mutual product of the whole group and are communicated, often with great precision, through a wide variety of nondiscursive modes such as pantomime, music, dance, poetry, drawing, sculpture, etc. Feedback is constant and highly developed to ensure that communications have in fact taken place.

Such groups can be said to have solved the problem of nondiscursive communications perhaps as well as any system so far devised. However the process is exceedingly wasteful of human resources, usually requiring an inordinately long time to put on a production. It is also only for those with a communal bent, since it totally consumes the lives of its followers.

Although no pattern of organization guarantees artistic success, it seems to this writer that the arrangement discussed next offers better odds than the all-too-common American theatre practice of widely delegated artistic authority.

Director-Scenographer Pattern

In a relatively recent development of European theatre, a *scenographer* is given almost complete artistic control over the matters usually assigned to set, lighting, and costume design. Moreover, since this organization has developed around unified productions often involving projections, masks, and moving scenery, the scenographer has extra responsibility for the totality of theatrical expression in space and time. He works very closely with the director; together they should complement each other's artistic efforts in unified productions whose parts blend into an inseparable whole (see for example Figures 1-1 and 1-2). This organizational pattern is based on the theatrical concepts of such early twentieth century theorists as Adolphe Appia and Edward Gordon Craig. Its most highly developed productions have probably been those at Bayreuth at the Wagner Festspielhaus, and in some of the work of Josef Svoboda, the Czechoslovakian scenographer.

---

3. Hereafter termed "collective theatre group."

With a scenographer instead of a number of artists whose duties overlap aesthetically (however seemingly clear the apparent delegation of authority) communications tend to be simplified—fewer artists have to interact.

In addition to ego satisfaction, working as a scenographer is also technically far more rewarding than working as one of many artists, particularly if one is interested in artistic unity in the theatre. In educational theatre the pattern offers a more reasonable way to alternate between creative efforts and educational duties.

THE BASICS OF ARTISTIC COMMUNICATION

The real issue in any artistic organization devised to produce interpretive art works is how well the artists succeed in their nondiscursive communications, whether their number be fifty or two. Given artistic talent and proper training, success will depend on two things:

1. The sensitivity of the artists to the symbolic communications of their co-workers.
2. The willingness and ability of each of them to "feed back," i.e., rephrase in other symbolic terms, the artistic information they have received. This is the only check against the *illusion* of communication without real communication.

If these conditions can be met, *any* organizational pattern is potentially capable of producing theatrical art. This text advocates the director-scenographer arrangement as the surest way to realize the potential.

Before we deal with the details of the artistic communication process in the theatre, we must clarify certain underlying aspects of art. Let us examine the terms "master symbol" and "virtuality."

MASTER SYMBOL

All art works, including the theatrical, are the result of a complicated process termed "creativity." The climactic moment in any creative process is sometimes called the "flash of insight"—often pictured by cartoonists as a glowing light bulb. The product of that moment (it may actually occur over a much longer time span) is a heretofore unrealized organization of symbolic material in the artist's mind that brings him to some new insight. If the artist manages eventually to externalize some substantial portion of this new perception, the result may be an art work that will somehow contain in symbolic form certain aspects, at least, of the artist's perception and communicate this to the audience.

FIGURE 1-1a

FIGURE 1-1b

FIGURE 1-1c

Figure 1-1. Scenography. Three examples of the work of Czechoslovakian scenographer, Josef Svoboda. (a) A rendering for Intolleranza by Luigi Nono, Theatro La Fenice, Venice. Direction: Vaćlav Kašlik, 1961. Courtesy of Josef Svoboda. (b) A production photograph of Gorki's The Last Ones, performed at the Tyl Theatre, Prague, Czechoslovakia, 1966. Direction: Alfréd Radok and Marie Radoková. This particularly illustrates the close relationship established by the scenographer between the environment and the actor; the projections in the background are images reflecting the thoughts of the character as he speaks. Photograph by Jaromir Svoboda. (c) A production of Loneliness by Macies Slomozyňski, Tyl Theatre, Prague, 1964. Direction: Miraslav Macháček. Photograph by Jaromír Svoboda. Photographs courtesy Josef Svoboda.

Figure 1-2. A setting for Moss Hart's Light Up the Sky. *Scenography: Van Phillips, Purdue University. Direction: Carl Williams. Photograph courtesy Van Phillips.*

The production artists enter the picture at this point (assuming traditional script-oriented theatre). In theatre we call the art work which is the product of the inspiration of the original artist, a "play-script" and the original artist a "playwright." As interpretive artists of the producing theatre, it is then up to us to examine that script and somehow apprehend the playwright's intention. From this apprehension we may proceed toward the production of the play.

We now need a term for the original artistic insight embodied by the script. Remember that the artist's original insight is nondiscursive; it remains nondiscursive in the script, and will exist as a nondiscursive element in the finished production. Any attempts to make it discursive contradict its special aesthetic quality and hence will be defeated. Giving it a "name," i.e., attaching a word to it, seems to suggest that it can then be described in words. This is patently untrue, but nevertheless it is a common error.

All that is possible is to attach a convenient "handle" to this completely nondiscursive central element of theatrical art. We will call it the "master symbol." Neither the label nor any other verbalization (discursive expression) can more than hint at the nondiscursive content. Other theatre workers have used the term "dramatic metaphor." For our purposes, we may treat these terms as synonyms although more sophisticated study will bring out differences.

The master symbol (for a concrete example, see the discussion below) is the unifying factor in interpretive art. In theatrical terms, this means that each of the interpretive artists (actor, director, scenographer) must use the master symbol as a means of determining what artistic elements will be included in the production and which of these need further development or change. It is the "touchstone," the ultimate test of all artistic material in our conventional theatrical aesthetic.

The problem raised by the discursive instruction that "everything must be tested against the master symbol" is that the entire creative process is nondiscursive. The simple statements we made above only describe what the creative artist does in an external way. Much of the remainder of this chapter and many further sections of this text will be devoted to this very process: gaining access to the master symbol, and devising symbolic devices in the various artistic modes of the theatre (scenery, lights, costume, etc.) that somehow meet the requirements of the interpretive artist's apprehension of the master symbol.

In the traditional theatre, as we have noted, the script is the source of the master symbol. Each of the interpretive artists must gain a perception of it by script study. Then the artists must share their perceptions through the process of what the theatre calls "production meetings." Out of this sharing must come some general perception of the master symbol that guides the production to its artistic conclusion.

A seemingly abstract example of a master symbol is "Real as only a dream is real." (See Chapter 2, What is a Production Meeting?) Its apparent abstractness is actually an advantage because it does not allow the scenographer or director to jump immediately to a visual concept. When visualizations are developed they can, however, be tested against the nondiscursive concept labeled "real as only a dream is real."

More apparently concrete examples of master symbols frequently occur. For example, a scenographer might find that the *idea* of a huge, somehow borderless Lucite wall symbolizes the alienation of a character in a dramatization of a story by Kafka. As long as the scenographer is careful to use the master symbol only as a "handle" for his perception of the script and the director uses it the same way, it will serve them well. If, however, the symbol is allowed to precipitate immediately the drawing of plans for a real wall of plastic, there may be serious artistic trouble. The most vital function of the master symbol will have been "short-circuited," i.e., its ability to govern what can or cannot be done within its artistic limitations will have been negated. It is all too easy for this to happen when the master symbol is expressed in such apparently concrete visual terms. Experienced and artistically cautious scenographers and directors will carefully avoid this trap by making a sharp distinction between the expression of the master symbol for purposes of artistic convenience and any visual implications in its wording. They will consider many visual concepts, evaluating each of them against the master symbol. For example, they might consider a sharp barrierlike demarcation in the lighting as a visualization of the "Lucite wall," or a laser beam repeatedly reflected might work. The solution could be as simple as a line drawn on the stage floor by the actors. Whatever the solution (and there are many more possibilities than these), it must be rigorously tested against the master symbol hiding behind the label, "Lucite wall." The ultimate result of this difficult artistic process may well be a staging that reveals nothing that could lead the audience back to "Lucite wall," but which does have good artistic unity.

THE MASTER SYMBOL IN NONSCRIPTED THEATRE

Nonscripted theatre operates somewhat differently. The group replaces the individual playwright as original creative artist; it evolves a master symbol out of symbolic material generated within the group itself. In this sense, such groups are original, not interpretive, artists. Having generated a master symbol, the group then goes through the externalizing process that somehow makes the master symbol available to others. Frequently a group may move without script to an externalization, a production. Occasionally a script will be created and then "interpreted."

In such groups the scenographer must be one of the artists; he cannot be external to the total creative process. More likely the scenographer will not only be party to these efforts, but will be a key element. His special interest in spatial expression and total view of the visual production fit well into this sort of work.

In either form of theatrical activity other artists and craftsmen such as scene painters, costume cutters, and mask builders must also have a share in the aesthetic processes. In fact it is probably safe to say that there are no jobs directly related to production of a play that do not in some way share in the aesthetic of the production. If such workers are to understand fully what artistic results are expected of them, they must share in the apprehension of the master symbol.

The expression of the master symbol can take place only in a special kind of "world," an atmosphere totally fee of the hampering realities of everyday existence. This is the world of the virtual.

VIRTUALITY

How is the life of an art work related to life itself? This is a question we must face clearly because of the special nature of theatrical art.

Unlike other arts, such as painting, the art of the theatre uses living human beings as its principal medium of expression. No one is likely to mistake a painted canvas representation of a human being for a living person, but it is not difficult to confuse the representation of a human being on stage, by an actor, with an actual person. The confusion that results from this fact is one of the things we must dispel if we are to construct a useful aesthetic of theatre.

The essence of all artistic representation is that the represented objects are *virtual,* that is, they exist only as art for the sake of their audience. Since this is a complicated concept, it may be worthwhile to examine the word "virtual" itself. While it is used in this discussion as a metaphor, its scientific meaning may help to clarify how this metaphor works. In the science of optics there are at least two kinds of images, *real* and *virtual.* The light rays forming a real image are so distributed on the image surface that the light energy on that surface varies with the details of the image. Thus we may make a chemical record of the image by placing a piece of photographic paper on the image plane, or we might scan the image to produce a television picture. An example of a real image is one formed by a slide projector on a screen. But there are also virtual images—for example, those seen in a mirror. An observer looking into a mirror sees an image of whatever is reflected in that mirror. If, however, we try to capture the image by placing a piece of film on the surface of the mirror where we "see" the image, the result will not be a picture, but a piece of film evenly exposed over its entire surface. This fogged film indicates that where the virtual image was seen there was no organized distribution of the light rays, hence nothing that the film could detect. Nevertheless, the image was clear to the observer. In the case of the virtual image, the observer's own optical apparatus (the lenses in his eyes) has done the organizing of the light into a real image. None existed at the mirror. This is the sense of our metaphorical use of the word "virtual" as it refers to artistic presentations. Just as a virtual image has its existence only in and for the human eye that sees it, the virtual elements in an art work exist only in and for the artistic audience.

As usual, there is a catch. Real objects, i.e., objects that exist in the world outside of art, are often brought into the virtual world of art to become part of its representational material. It is important to remember that when this is done the "real" object takes on a "virtual" character. If, for example, you bring a chair from your room to the stage as a prop for a play, you are making the chair virtual. At home the chair is something to sit in, chosen because of its special comfort and good looks. On stage it is a virtual chair, chosen to be part of the virtual environment of the scene. The conscious choice tells the audience something about the virtual people who use the chair. Anything on stage will tend to be viewed in this manner, whether it was actually chosen or brought there by mistake. Nothing viewed during a dramatic production will be understood as a "mistake" unless the theatrical context is destroyed by its obviously out-of-place nature. Thus we can say that in the theatre the chair can only have a virtual existence.

In a similar manner, an actor brings a body and emotional resources to the stage where they take on a virtual existence which becomes part of the virtual character being created. Note that the actor does not "become" that character; he carefully and consciously *creates* it using the body, emotional resources, the words of the playwright, and the assistance of the director. Just as the actor creates a virtual character, the director and the scenographer create a virtual environment for the play.

The beginning scenographer and technician (as well as actors and directors) should be certain to note the critical implications of this. Anything injected into the theatrical virtual world will become a part of it, being "read" by the audience as a further comment on the nature of that world whether so intended by the artists or not, unless the item is so glaringly out of place that it destroys the entire theatrical situation.

Virtuality confers a tremendous advantage, leading us to one of the most fascinating and satisfying aspects of the entire world of art. Virtuality confers freedom. The world of the virtual exists only for the sake of expression. It need not be bound by the limitations of real life nor even the logic that life imposes upon us.

The power of artistic freedom in the realm of the virtual was perhaps best understood by Adolphe Appia (1862–1929), a French-Swiss stage designer. He wrote "If the mystic yearns for heaven, the artist yearns for the dream, and his whole productivity bears its influence."[4] The dream Appia mentions is a metaphor for the vast freedom available once the creative artist enters the world of the virtual. Many artists have remarked how like a dream is the utter freedom of creative thought. Neither time nor space nor logical analysis have bearing. The contradictions of language and logic do not exist; there are no opposites and no laws. "Today," "tomorrow," and "yesterday" exist as separate times only if the artist so decrees. Black is not the opposite of white, and yes is no longer the contradiction of no. They are no longer mutually exclusive. Time and space are infinite. "Instantaneous" means whatever the artist wants it to mean. This freedom is almost terrifying in its power to express human feelings symbolically.

THEATRE AS VIRTUAL DESTINY

We cannot, however, enjoy the benefits of artistic freedom until we have mastered the aesthetic and the skills of our art. To this end, we

---

4. Adolphe Appia, *Music and the Art of the Theatre,* trans. Robert W. Corrigan and Mary Douglas Brooks (Coral Gables, Fla.: University of Miami Press, 1962), p. 99.

now begin an examination of the symbolic structure of the theatrical art from which we will move toward the particular aesthetics of the scenographer. Arts may be differentiated by the special kinds of symbolic processes that typify them. For example, music may be said to have its principal symbolic element, virtual time; painting, virtual space. Langer has written that the theatre is *virtual destiny,* and that the principal abstraction (symbolic device) by which this virtual destiny is presented is the "act."[5] The word "act," used in this sense, does not refer to the conventional divisions of a play. Instead, an "act" is any physical or mental activity performed by a character. It is anything indicating to the audience that something has happened (internally or externally in a virtual character) that forms a part of *a virtual history in the mode of dramatic action.*[6] Thus a completed play is a virtual history. An "act" is any bit of virtual history that moves the production toward its inevitable future. "Acts" have only one purpose — the development of a virtual future. Contrast this with the nature of acts in real life where, of course, they also take place. The future of real-life acts, i.e., their destiny, is anything but clear. In the purposeful virtual world of art the virtual destiny may be made clear (one of the freedoms of the virtual world) and such virtual destinies become potential insights into our own unrevealed destinies.

To clarify, take as an example the script of *Death of a Salesman.* One of the dramatic "acts" (in Langer's sense of the word) early in the play is the return of Willie Loman from a most unsuccessful sales trip. His description of that trip, particularly his lapses into illusion about it, are theatrical acts fraught with destiny, i.e., they contain within them much of the remainder of the play. *Death of a Salesman* is a complete world which has a definite ending, again in contrast to much human experience. The virtual world of Willy Loman and the other virtual human beings in the play ends with the curtain. The author's expression is, in that moment, complete; there is no more.

DISCUSSING THEATRICAL ART WORKS

As we move toward the specifics of an aesthetic of sceonography, it is necessary to reemphasize the hazards of using discursive language to discuss the nondiscursive elements of a script or play in production. To the extent that such a discussion is discursive — that is, analytical — it is by definition prevented from dealing with the essential wholeness or unity of the art work. As the discussion moves into the nondiscursive (symbolic or poetic mode), it will lose most of its outward specificity and clarity by depending, as any artistic expression does, on

---

5. Langer, *Feeling and Form,* pp. 306–307.
6. Langer, *Feeling and Form,* p. 307.

the personal emotional reactions of the recipient to bring it to completion. While this process works well when the goal is artistic expression, it is usually a gravely limited teaching device by itself.

Since it is our purpose to enter into this dangerous realm of discussion, and it must be the purpose of every student of theatre to spend much time there, some ground rules for avoiding the dilemma are hereby offered.

1. We must admit that there is no substitute for the art work itself, and never allow ourselves to get into the position of "explaining" any art work. Thus the student who says, "I know what *Hamlet* 'means,' but I cannot 'explain' it," is on solid aesthetic ground (although one could be using this valid position to hide a lack of preparation).

2. We must recognize the essentially symbolic nature of the art work, and *focus our discussion on the symbolic devices used to create the whole.* We must rigorously avoid any discussion of a specific art work except *in the presence of that art work.*

3. We must either ask questions of ourselves and others that can be dealt with in discursive language or consciously engage in the use of metaphor, artistic analogy, and symbolic devices. In theatrical terms this means orally interpreting lines, developing sketches or models, or referring to other art works such as poems. Then one must seek feedback from those to whom the communication is directed. For example, if you as scenographer, assert that the ending of *Macbeth* reminds you in some mysterious way of Beethoven's symphony, *Eroica,* and the director replies that you are exactly right—it reminds him of the *William Tell* Overture—you are both using nondiscursive techniques, but the feedback suggests that little artistic agreement has been found.

In the following discussion we will, as we have so far endeavored to do, try to operate by these precepts. In particular, we will attempt to concentrate on an analysis (in discursive terms) of the symbolic processes of theatre, especially scenography. Our examples will be most intelligible to those who have recently read, or still better, seen in production the play under discussion.

SYMBOLIC ANALOGY

In this discussion we will frequently refer to the "analogue relationship" that exists between an artistic symbol and life itself. The artist chooses a symbolic device because he feels that there exists between it and the human feeling which he is seeking to express some special relationship, an "analogous" relationship. An analogy between two things exists when they are similar in some ways, but different in others. An artistic analogy exists when these similarities and differences imply something about the human feeling expressed in the art work. Sometimes the analogue seems "natural," as when red light is used to symbolize fire. However art is seldom interested in such obvious and simple relationships; they are poor vehicles to carry the depth of human feeling the artist has in mind. Thus the choice of a symbol and the establishment of its analogous relationship to life is one of the most subtle aspects of artistic creation. The device and the analogue created by the artist function together to form what we will term a "symbolic device."

An example of a symbolic device (in this case, one that originates in literary form in the script) is the storm in *King Lear*. As the scene on the heath opens, the storm sets the mood. Tumult and chaos abound. But the storm evolves dramatically into a still more powerful symbol. We perceive that the important storm is not in the weather, but in Lear himself. One of the theatrical subtleties of staging this scene successfully is to make this perception clear to the audience, and to maintain a balance between the external storm (the effects) and the internal storm which the actor must create in his character.

Since the storm is one of the essential symbols that enable us to comprehend the human character of Lear, this symbolic device ultimately dissolves into the master symbol. It is a part of the virtual destiny which is *King Lear*.

Art and Virtual Space-Time

The virtual space of art varying in virtual time has an analogue relationship with the space-time of the real world.

The complex art of theatre utilizes both real space (the stage space visible to the audience) and real time (the playing time) plus a third and unique abstraction from reality. This is the use of human beings (actors) as the "raw material" for the creation of virtual beings (the characters).

Although it is an oversimplification, Figure 1-3 may help the reader to understand how the various artistic responsibilities usually are arranged in the theatre, and how the artistic analogue relationships with life exist in our art.

This figure shows the interlocking of artistic responsibilities and the relationships between the artists and their "raw materials." Note the dependent status of scenography. Its artistic effectiveness depends heavily on the work of the actors. The interrelationships shown in this figure remain essentially the same if the work of the author is replaced by a concept formed within a collective theatre group. Note also that much of the uniqueness of theatrical art lies in this arrangement of virtual elements. The result of this manipulation of abstractions is the virtual destiny Langer has described as the *theatrical mode*.[7]

---

7. Langer, *Feeling and Form*, pp. 306–307.

THEATRE CONSISTS OF:

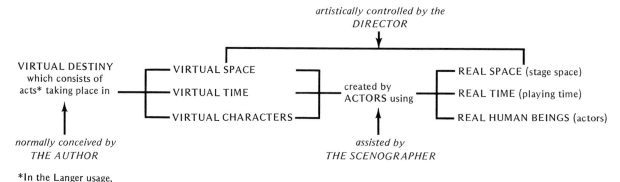

Figure 1-3. *This diagram shows the interlocking relationship that exists between theatrical artists and their materials. The comments in italics suggest the usual sources of the key elements.*

SPACE-TIME RELATIONSHIPS AMONG DIRECTOR, SCENOGRAPHER, AND ACTOR   As Figure 1-3 indicates in simplified fashion, the work of the scenographer and that of the actor overlap. First of all, the actor may be said to "create" virtual space. The mere conversion of the actor's body to that of a virtual human being (the character being played) creates virtual space in which this virtual character exists. The character then moves about, creating additional virtual space which the audience soon accepts. This is evident even in a classroom situation where an actor may "create a stage" simply by utilizing some of the space available at the front of the room. If one is at all skilled, the limits of this space will soon be apparent to the audience, and subdivisions within it may develop. "*Here* is the living room, and *here* the bedroom," the actor seems to be saying as he moves.

The scenographer also creates virtual space. When the curtain reveals a setting and/or a pattern of lighting on stage, or when the audience enters a theatre room to discover a portion of that room lit and prepared for the production about to begin, the scenographer has created virtual space.

As a production progresses, the scenographer and the actors jointly create and redefine virtual space almost continuously. It should be obvious that these manipulations of virtual space by both actors and scenographer must conjoin to form a part of the symbolic unity of the production as an art work. The person ultimately responsible for this symbolic unity is the director who, as Figure 1-3 indicates, maintains artistic control over the whole interpretive effort.

What is the nature of the expression in space-time that is wrought by the scenographer? How does it interrelate with the work of the actor? What is the real-life analogue that gives the expression its power and intelligibility? Note the differing way in which director, scenographer, and actor view virtual space. The director and the scenographer must take an overall view. They must be concerned with *all* of the virtual space created in a production and also with each subdivision of it and all relationships between subdivisions. The actor, on the other hand, focuses on the virtual space created by and related to his character. He will be secondarily concerned with space created by other characters with which he must interrelate. Last, or perhaps not at all, he will be concerned with the overall virtual space.

A production of *Romeo and Juliet* might illustrate these distinctions. The director and the scenographer must begin with the overall geography of the play—Renaissance Verona and its arrangement of jealous, rich families in close proximity. The swirl and flow of violent life through the virtual world is both fascinating and threatening. Beginning with such considerations and delving deeper and deeper into the movements that the characters of this play must make to express its tragedy to the audience, the director and scenographer will evolve a concept of space within which each actor, creating a virtual character, will operate. On the other hand, the actor playing Romeo, for example, will be most interested in those details of space that constitute Romeo's world: the distance from the ground to the balcony, measured not in feet and inches, but in the inaccessibility of Juliet; later, the dangerous space surrounding him and Tybalt; later still, the infinite space generated by what he sees as death separating him from Juliet. This actor may only occasionally consider that swirling space which encompasses the entire play.

Although they must start with the same overall view, the concerns of the director and those of the scenographer soon diverge. The scenographer focuses on the use of setting, lighting, and costume to create and vary space, while the director concentrates on moving actors, sometimes masses of actors, to give dramatic meaning to the space he and the scenographer are creating. For example, in the same production of *Romeo and Juliet,* the intimacy of the balcony must be carefully balanced with the infinity of the moonlit sky—a scenographic concern. However, the intimate balcony must not be so small that the virtual characters cannot move as they express themselves. This is a concern of both director and scenographer. Later in the production, the mechanical needs of the sword fight between Romeo and Tybalt must be reconciled with the minor role that "infinity" has at that moment.

SPACE-TIME ANALOGUES What in the general nature of human perceptions of reality makes expression in space-time such a powerful device? We live in a real space-time matrix. All of life is encompassed by the three dimensions of space, and by time. But our perceptions of space and time are abstractions, primary symbolic transformations that enable us to "think about" things. Like all such abstractions they become symbols that will probably be heavy with emotions. Anyone who has ever lain back on the grass staring into the stars on a clear night knows this. The difference between human perception and infinity is too great to be overlooked; the implications for our perception of the human condition are too powerful.

One such perception comes at the end of Walt Whitman's poem, "On the Beach at Night."

Something there is,
(With lips soothing thee, adding I whisper,
I give thee the first suggestion, the problem and indirection,)
Something there is more immortal even than the stars,

(Many the burials, many the days and nights, passing away,)
Something that shall endure longer even than lustrous Jupiter,
Longer than the sun or any revolving satellite,
Or the radiant sisters the Pleiades.

If infinite space is a human abstraction loaded with emotion, infinite time is doubly so. The limited span of human life is all too apparent when we confront infinite time. Such human perceptions are raw material for artists. The theatre, with its unique combination of virtual space and virtual time populated by virtual human beings is an ideal art form to express this material artistically.

Expression can take two general forms. The artist may directly confront these human dilemmas as Thornton Wilder does in *The Skin of Our Teeth*, or he may "insulate" us from the unpleasantness of such a confrontation as Noel Coward does in *Private Lives*. Much of the world of comedy and fantasy in the theatre uses this insulated approach, perhaps tinged with the ironic realization that real life is not so orderly and predictable.

The scenographer's manipulations of virtual space and time may ultimately be based on their analogue relationship with human responses to infinite space and time. For example, in the final moments of *Everyman*, illustrated in Plate VII, the scenographer has sought to place Everyman against a background suggesting infinite sky. The use of line and elevation on the jutting platform is intended to heighten this analogue situation by implying free movement through space.

A play in production may be thought of as an ever-changing and often vast sculpture in four dimensions: height, width, depth, and time. Its symbolic effectiveness rests on its analogue relationship to human perceptions of space and time. Change is of the essence since time is expressed through change, that is, *movement*. Movement may be first considered as a function of actors, but light must move with them if they are to be effective. Thus moving light, which varies space itself, takes on symbolic value of its own. Movement of images in projections and movement of the setting itself are often added by the scenographer. The result is a potential for creating a virtual world of incredible freedom for artistic expression.

2
THE SCENOGRAPHIC PROCESS

To accomplish his artistic task, the scenographer must maintain communication with the director, for together they develop and populate the virtual world of the play. Since the scenographer is an interpretive artist, neither his talent, which must be great, nor his training, which must be rigorous, can serve him except to the extent that he is able to establish successful rapport with the director (or with the collective artistic group), and to communicate his artistic needs to the many craftsmen and artists who will fulfill them.

We will approach the work of the scenographer in two ways. First we will create a hypothetical production meeting and abstract from it some typical dialogue. This will have the advantage of being concrete, but keep in mind that in "real" space-time a particular script and a particular set of personalities making up the production team might result in a rather different meeting—certainly one with much more dialogue.

After this, we will attempt a theoretical discussion of the work of the scenographer, which also will have its limitations. Discussing an artistic process in discursive language must present sequentially events that actually are simultaneous or may occur in a different sequence. Thus the abstract discussion will give the appearance of orderliness, when in fact no such orderliness exists. Logical development has little to do with the way in which the human mind evolves creative concepts—only the language of this discussion will appear to give logical sequence to events.

WHAT IS A PRODUCTION MEETING?

A production meeting may be viewed as any communicative situation in which artistic information is exchanged in the process of producing a play. Such meetings vary greatly in formality and structure as the process moves toward completion. The process actually begins with the tentative remarks and interchanges that precede the selection of a script or, in the case of collective theatre groups, the selection of a concept to be developed.

As the communicative process deals with more complex matters and begins to produce ideas that are sufficiently well developed to be communicated to others, the production meeting takes on its formal structure and appears on the production calendar. It usually is attended by key production personnel, particularly those from the business department of the theatre organization who must concern themselves with the budget. In the educational theatre, students often attend such formal production meetings. Because the student has no way of perceiving the great amount of work that has preceded these meetings, it may appear that artistic decisions of sweeping consequence are being made on the spot with remarkable precision and confidence. In reality, a summary of long, arduous, and often controversy-ridden discourse is being presented. The results may seem deceptively simple.

The format of such a meeting is much the same throughout theatre organizations. The director presents orally his view of the artistic nature of the production. The scenographer offers models or renderings which appear to meet the needs the director has outlined, and the discussion shifts to technical and budgetary matters. Unfortunately for the beginner, such meetings often are billed as though they represented the entire creative process involved in the artistic development of a script.

Later production meetings may seem even more technical, concerned mostly with details of mechanical arrangements, scheduling of crews, changes to meet the budget, scheduling of performances, and such matters. What will usually be invisible to the student attending such meetings is the vast amount of informal discussion that has been going on day and night between director and scenographer, and the research, study at the drawing board, trips to supply houses, consultations with engineering specialists, etc., which underlie such meetings.

If they carry out their intended function, the formal production meetings accomplish three things:

1. They serve to distribute artistic information efficiently among the crew members and the chief without the necessity of saying everything many times.
2. They offer every member of the production team a forum to raise questions, point out potential trouble areas, and compare one's understanding of the artistic information with that of others.
3. They serve as a formal feedback of information between the director and scenographer. Frequently the pressure of pre-

Plate I. **Don Carlos,** *An Impression. This painting represents an attempt to catch some of the nondiscursive elements in Verdi's* **Don Carlos** *through the medium of water color. It is not a stage design or even an idea for a stage design. It is instead an attempt at expression of nondiscursive material in another medium. Such an internal art work might figure in an early production meeting. Design by P. Messmeg, Vienna, Austria.*

PLATE I

Plate II. A Rendering. This plate is one of a set of renderings done by Andrej Majew-ski, a European scenographer, for **Die Zauberflöte** (The Magic Flute) *by Mozart.*

PLATE II

Plate III. A Rendering for Macbeth. This rendering represents a combination of a semicircular raked stage area, scenic elements, and projections. These elements would be later broken down into specific drawings for construction, and in the case of the projections, into hand-painted slides adjusted for distortion introduced by projection angles. Designs by Andrej Majewski.

Plate IV. Model. This is the model for a production of La Boheme (Puccini) performed at the University of Iowa, Hancher Auditorium. Director: Cosmo Catalano. Scenography: Kate Keleher. Photography: Bill Browning.

Plate V. **The Tempest**. *A production at Thiel College, Pennsylvania, designed by David Neighbor. Lighting and direction by Art Beer. Photo courtesy Art Beer.*

Plate VI. **The Country Wife**. *This plate shows a fully developed period setting and the closely related costumes. Note the care with which the various elements have been interrelated. Production at California State University, Long Beach. Director: David MacArthur. Sets: Ralph Duckwall. Costumes: Herb Camburn. Photography: Ralph Duckwall.*

Plate VII. **The Summons.** *This adaptation of* **Everyman** *in dance-narrative form was directed by Claudia Chapline Hood. Scenography by the author. Script adapted by James Brock. California State University, Northridge.*

Plate VIII. Spectacle in Musical Comedy. The production photo of the London production of Cabaret illustrates the large-scale use of light and color in such productions. This production was adapted from the original New York City production which was designed by Boris Aronson with lighting by Jean Rosenthal. Photograph courtesy Richard Pilbrow, Theatre Projects, London.

paring a more or less formal statement of artistic intentions (obviously a semantically difficult task) will bring out points of confusion which had previously been thought to be totally clear.

Dialogue taken from the transcript of a production meeting makes poor theatre. It is diffuse, often inconclusive, and usually seeks to establish private communications, not universal ones. It may be couched in metaphor. It may take the form of drawings, sketches, crude models, art works such as pieces of music or paintings brought into the discussion. In general, the wider the range of communicative devices, the greater the possibility that good artistic communication will occur. "Dialogue" is necessary as opposed to "edict" or "proclamation," otherwise no feedback will occur, and there will be no assurance that communication has taken place.

Since the most invisible parts of the production meeting are those in which the director and scenographer (and sometimes the actors) seek to express their artistic intent, the dialogue which follows concentrates on this kind of meeting. The reader should be aware that during the intervals between meetings in this dialogue, both the director and the scenographer have been almost totally involved in study, research, and artistic experimentation. Particularly in the case of the production of a period or realistic script, the scenographer will spend hours in research, abstracting stylistic material and checking his visual concepts for validity. The director must perform similar arduous research into such things as manner of movement, specialized gestures, weapons' handling, and other matters which set the style and lend historic validity to the production.

It is impossible to more than suggest in writing what amounts to perhaps half of the total communicative process in an early production meeting—the intonations, gestures, and bodily tensions of the participants. Thus the following excerpts must be treated as a sketch of the total communicative process. (It is absolutely essential that the student be familiar with the script of *Macbeth,* in order to understand the following dialogue.)

EXCERPTS FROM A HYPOTHETICAL PRODUCTION MEETING

The "cast" of this meeting consists of the director; the scenographer; and an actress who intends to play Lady Macbeth, and whose special interest in the total aesthetic development of the production makes her useful to our study.[2]

2. Those portions of the production meeting devoted exclusively to director-actor relationships have been deleted.

The script is Shakespeare's *Macbeth*. It was chosen in a discussion by the artists on the basis of mutual interest and apparent potential for generating artistic unanimity within this production team.

The theatre to be used for this production is a highly experimental structure combining many of the attributes of a theatre room with those of a proscenium theatre (see Chapter 3 for extended descriptions of these).

After the first sessions during which the script was chosen from a number of possible choices, the group agreed to allow three weeks for individual script study. Pressure of outside commitments made it impossible for the members to engage in any informal conversations about the play. Hence what follows is the first interchange since the script was chosen.

SCENOGRAPHER: How do you see the script?

DIRECTOR: I see it in flashes of color.

SCENOGRAPHER: Uh huh. (Long pause.) *What* colors?

DIRECTOR: Bright reds, oranges, and violets.

SCENOGRAPHER: Ahhh, yes. . . . (No confidence.) What shapes do these colors take? (By now he is patronizing the director as one would a delirious patient.)

DIRECTOR: Shapes? . . . . I haven't thought of them with shapes. [It is obvious that no communication is going to result from *this* line of conversation. The director has hit upon a metaphor so private to himself that the scenographer can find no "handle."]
[There followed some inconsequential conversation about non-production matters mostly as a face-saving device for the director, and then:]

SCENOGRAPHER: The colors aside, do you feel any movement in the play?

DIRECTOR: Lots of it. In and out. Up and down. It expands and contracts.

SCENOGRAPHER: That makes *some* sense to me. What do you mean, "expands and contracts"?

DIRECTOR: The more Macbeth's political control expands, the more his range of action contracts until finally he has all the power and none of the maneuverability. To put it another way, as Macbeth becomes isolated in emptiness, Lady Macbeth becomes isolated because her prospects have come to naught.

SCENOGRAPHER: (Now he has too many things to deal with at once.)

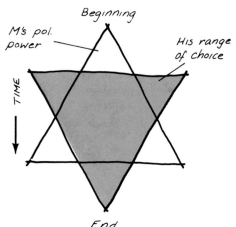

Figure 2-1. A quick sketch by the scenographer illustrating an understanding of the interrelationship between Macbeth's political power and his potential range for making choices affecting his future. This served as a kind of feedback for the director.

But. . . . back to the movements. Could we diagram it like this? (Shows sketch, Figure 2-1.)

DIRECTOR: Explain it.

SCENOGRAPHER: We move from top to bottom; I mean *time* moves from top to bottom. The back triangle represents Macbeth's power, the front one his potential for maneuverability. He can't move back in time, so once the process is started, the end is inevitable.

DIRECTOR: That's why I see it as an "up-down" play in disjointed time: "Time is out of joint," remember? [Feedback.]

SCENOGRAPHER: Yes, but this movement . . . the disjointed time . . . I can't quite put it together with this diagram . . . it doesn't do it. [Note that partial feedback is occurring. The scenographer has partially accepted and understood what the director is striving for. He needs help and the director provides it.]

DIRECTOR: Will this help? I see the up-down movement as a "fall." Macbeth falls from high places.

SCENOGRAPHER: (Facetiously while thinking things out.) How far?

DIRECTOR: (Understanding the tactics of the scenographer.) About 30 feet.

[Such dialogues seldom proceed for more than a few interchanges without some sort of break. The concentration is too intense. Remember that we have here only the lines. Scenographer and director are both paying as much, if not more attention to gestures, intonations, and muscular tensions.]

[During the laughter about the "30 feet" line the scenographer is scribbling something.]

SCENOGRAPHER: (Shows diagram, Figure 2-2.) Is the movement more like this?

DIRECTOR: Noooo . . . yes, it might be. Which way does it go?

SCENOGRAPHER: Top to bottom.

ACTRESS: (Finally entering in.) *The Wizard of Oz!*

SCENOGRAPHER: Not quite, but it *is* a vortex.

DIRECTOR: Cyclonic! Macbeth finds his "solution" in action; Lady Macbeth in retreat and inaction. It's a strange sort of reality. Dreamlike. Time and movement are all warped—out of joint. I've been thinking that the audience should see the play as real (consternation from the scenographer and actress) . . . real as only a dream can be real. (Neither the scenographer nor actress are ready to "buy" this, but they see possibilities.)

Figure 2-2. The "Vortex." This quickly scribbled diagram represents an attempt on the part of the scenographer to express the four-dimensional relationship (space/time) that exists in Macbeth *as the play moves toward its tragic conclusion. The drawing will be much more meaningful if the reader will imagine it as a diagram for a gesture made by the scenographer.*

SCENOGRAPHER: The cyclone idea fascinates me. Time accelerates as you go down. Macbeth's chances for altering the course of his fate get smaller and smaller. Lady Macbeth goes mad.

DIRECTOR: (To actress.) That brings up a big problem: *Why* does she go mad? I think it's a sexual thing. She's a very sensual lady who has a liaison with an equally sensual man. As he gains power, she sees her grasp on him slipping. She's losing all she has.

ACTRESS: But she eggs him on in the beginning. How about that?

DIRECTOR: Yes. I guess she thinks she can be queen and still have everything she already has.

ACTRESS: (Skeptical.) I hadn't thought of her that way. I see her as a grasping woman who wants power. She's in a world where women can't hold power directly, so she seeks it through her husband. When she gets it, it turns out to be nothing after all, and she goes mad.

SCENOGRAPHER: (Grateful for a chance to sort out his thoughts, and for the time structure that the actress has implied.) Time moves faster and faster for both of them for whatever reasons, and I see space somehow becoming more and more disjointed.

DIRECTOR: I've got it! The cyclone is really a boiling pot with a lid on it!

SCENOGRAPHER: (Dripping with skepticism.) A cyclone in a pot! (He's thinking back to "flashes of color.") (Long pause.) Wait a minute . . . you stir the pot and it goes round and round. . . . It might just work. [Time was running out on this session, and in spite of the strangely indirect dialogue, it was obvious that some kind of understanding was taking place. Most of it was hidden in the interplay of half-constructed metaphors. Evolving was a set of "interim symbols," symbolic devices of a private language that has meaning only to those few in the production group who have evolved them. The interim symbols form a sort of shorthand for the nondiscursive ideas being formulated. The most verbal interim symbol came to be, "real as only a dream can be real."]

DIRECTOR: Time is catching up with us. Have we gotten anywhere?

SCENOGRAPHER: I think so. I want to try to have something for you to look at next time.

ACTRESS: (To director.) I want to talk to you about Lady Macbeth soon. I don't think I agree with you about her motives.

Several days pass before the group can get together again. When they do, it is evident that the director and actress have had some private conversations about Lady Macbeth, but they are still far from any agreement about Lady Macbeth's madness.

SCENOGRAPHER: (Enters the room carrying a briefcase which rattles ominously with the sound of parts of a model, Figure 2-3.)

DIRECTOR: What's in the briefcase?

SCENOGRAPHER: (Dumps out case creating a pile of odd-shaped pieces of modeling clay.) There it is! (He also produces a plan of the theatre which, with intentional slowness, he places in the center of the table facing the director. Then he arranges the pieces of the simple model.) I have three triangles with their points cut off. You can arrange them in a lot of ways, and with the lifts on the forestage, they can go up and down.

DIRECTOR: (Already handling the model.) How far up and down?

SCENOGRAPHER: Farther than you will want.

DIRECTOR: Don't be so sure. How far?

SCENOGRAPHER: Ok, if you want complications this soon, you'll get them. The *total* up-down movement can be about 30 feet. If you want to go higher than 15 feet, you can't go lower than 30 feet from the topmost elevation.

DIRECTOR: How's that again?

[There followed some ten minutes of dialogue about the technical limitations of the lifts on the apron of the theatre. Eventu-

Figure 2-3. The First Model. This crudely sculpted model done in modeling clay was the first visualization produced. It is shown in one of the early arrangements that elicited some satisfaction from the director. Later in the discussion the model was reshaped and cut into progressively smaller pieces until it no longer existed. By then it had served its purpose. The blobs of clay represent actors approximately to scale of $\frac{1}{8}$ inch = 1 foot.

ally everyone got the idea of the limits of travel and realized that they were getting far ahead of themselves.]

DIRECTOR: I guess I know more than I need to know about that forestage. (Moving the triangles back into the stage area upstage of the lifts.) If we put these things up here, they can't go up and down, right? (Scenographer nods.) Well, I see the play close to the audience anyway so that will work. Let's try the sleepwalking scene on this thing.

SCENOGRAPHER: Where and how high do you want each level? (He is cutting odd-shaped pieces of modeling clay to raise the triangles in the air.)

DIRECTOR: I want Lady Macbeth to come from below, circle toward the audience with the doctor and nurse, and then exit downward at the end of the scene.

SCENOGRAPHER: Funny, I see her doing the same thing, but starting near the audience and circling upstage and away from the doctor and nurse for their comments on her. (Actress agrees with the scenographer.)

DIRECTOR: I could live with her entering down if I have to, but I want the three of them—doctor, nurse, and Lady Macbeth—all together. If Lady Macbeth is really asleep, they should be able to come right up to her without her seeing them, and I want them to form a single group. I want them all as close to the audience as possible for the main part of the scene.

SCENOGRAPHER: I get it, and it will work. How high up in the air should we play the scene? Like this? (Holds platform about 2 feet above stage level.)

DIRECTOR: Let's see. (Kneels at edge of table to view model as the audience might see it while lifting a platform up and down.) How about this?

SCENOGRAPHER: Ok, but how does she get up there? She's about 10 feet above stage level.

DIRECTOR: (Moving another platform.) Could this one be part way up?

SCENOGRAPHER: Yes, but we still need steps, and that breaks up the setting as I see it. Look here. (He adds some crudely modeled steps.)

DIRECTOR: I don't like that either.

(Long pause for coffee.)

ACTRESS: (To break the stalemate.) Could it lift up with them on it?

(Simultaneously.)

DIRECTOR: Yes!

SCENOGRAPHER: No!

SCENOGRAPHER: On second thought, it could, but I don't like it. We'd have a pause somewhere to get it back down again . . . those lifts are slow.

DIRECTOR: We're getting into technical details again. What if the levels were smaller and there were more of them? Then they could form steps leading up to the height I'd like to have. (He's already cutting up the model to demonstrate.)

SCENOGRAPHER: (Downcast.) There goes that idea! . . . but I see some possibilities. Especially if we run part of those levels below sight lines, at times changing the shape of the whole visible stage.

[Here followed a long session of cutting which gradually reduced the entire model to a pile of debris as endless possibilities were explored. It ended in a coffee break. Note that as soon as the model was brought out, an illusion of concreteness appeared although much less was being said in words.]

SCENOGRAPHER: I see a problem in this meeting. We thought we knew what we were talking about until I brought in this model. Now we're playing games with it, and I'm not sure I know where we are. For instance, what are we thinking of doing in all of that stage space upstage of the lift forestage?

DIRECTOR: I've one idea that may help you. I'd like to stage some scenes simultaneously. For instance, the killing of Malcolm's wife and son, and the part of Act IV, Scene III. I see one above and behind the other.

SCENOGRAPHER: . . . and the witches. They need to be above and around the whole play. Right? The regular stage space could contain levels for the witches and some of the scenes, and be a place for projections and effects, like the show of kings.

DIRECTOR: Great!

SCENOGRAPHER: (Not really listening—thinking how to relate the moving parts to this fixed staging.)

DIRECTOR: When do I see it?

Another week has passed. The scene opens somewhat like the last time. But this time the set is in a large corrugated cardboard box instead of the briefcase, and the scenographer has a roll of drawings and a tattered script. Director and actress have had several conferences about Lady Macbeth, and are now more nearly in agreement.

SCENOGRAPHER: (After the ritual of setting up the model, Figure 2-4.) Here it is.

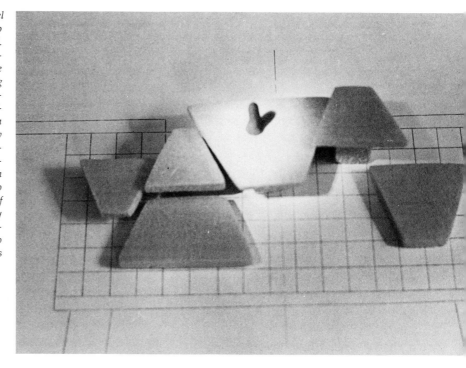

Figure 2-4. The Second Model. This model represents the reaction of the scenographer to the many changes made on the first model. Although he could have advantageously continued to work with clay on this model, he chose to use Styrofoam, a rapid-working material not quite as likely to be utterly destroyed during the discussion. The group suffered somewhat from the lack of pliability in the Styrofoam model which did not allow them to reshape the elements so easily. Therefore they concentrated on locating the existing elements with relationship to each other and at varying elevations. They also posited a great variety of arrangements of the modular elevator platforms, eventually agreeing on a down front entrance from below moving toward stage right. This was to be accomplished by adjusting the platforms to form a "staircase."

Let's try the sleepwalking scene.

They do. Several variations later they have arrived at a sort of spiral movement which brings Lady Macbeth out of the floor up right. She is followed by the doctor and nurse. They all circle toward stage center and up to a much larger level where the main scene takes place. They then circle downward toward the left portion of the apron, and Lady Macbeth disappears there. The group finally agreed upon this pattern of movement.

SCENOGRAPHER: This has got to be a dark scene—I see the witches faintly above it all.

DIRECTOR: I hadn't thought of them here, but it is a good idea. I want to see faces in the sleepwalking scene though.

SCENOGRAPHER: Of course. We can follow-focus them and increase contrast as the scene builds. On, "To bed, to bed, to bed," we can use a high angle key and then fade her out as she goes down out of sight.

DIRECTOR: . . . leaving the doctor and nurse to ride the platform down as the scene ends. You know, I think we see the whole play as though it were in some sort of labyrinth that contains a dream.

SCENOGRAPHER: The reality of the dream is the reality of a nightmare.

The meeting continued into a more and more detailed discussion of the production concept, and eventually a floor plan was sketched out and agreed upon. The model was refined after many interchanges between the director and scenographer, and a formal production meeting was called.

Thus ends our hypothetical production meeting. The most verbal interim symbol that came out of this series of meetings was, "real as only a dream can be real." It came to epitomize for this group of artists a complex concept of the master symbol that was growing more artistically complete as they moved into the later stages of production activities. Note that all of their verbalizations have a quality of indirection. Metaphor is combined with nonverbal forms such as sketches or models and with poetic elements from the script itself to form a complex communicative system whose only function is to facilitate the artistic effort. Such communications are never intended to be intelligible to those outside of the production group.

These fragments from a hypothetical production meeting portray fewer false starts and arguments than most such meetings contain in actuality. Nevertheless, they illustrate the sort of communication that must take place between director and scenographer. Note the important role that feedback plays in the process. Without it no communication can happen. The problem, of course, is that unless the artists take care, they may feel that they are getting feedback when they really are not. Therefore, argument and even open disagreement are desirable in a production meeting. Bland agreement, whether it is the result of friendship or awe at the towering artistic reputation of one of the participants, is of little value. Every participant should be eager to seek feedback by forcing paraphrasing and repetition from co-workers. Ideally the paraphrase should be in a different form of discourse. For example, if the director has offered an idea in word form, it will be better if the scenographer's restatement of it is in the form of a sketch.

As a crew member, the student may be lucky enough to be party to some of the early interchanges that form the beginning production meetings. More likely the student will enter the process at the more formal stages when a special production meeting is called for all crew members. This will almost inevitably consist of a formal presentation of the production concept. Such summary presentations tend to hide the vast amount of work and discussion already expended in their formulation. In the case of a director-scenographer team that has worked together on many productions, the communicative process may be said to be based on years of effort. This base may make the immediate interchanges between these artists appear deceptively casual and simple, leading the beginner to a totally inaccurate picture of the amount of work the development of a production concept requires.

Having developed the hypothetical production meeting as an example of the way in which the scenographer proceeds, we will now review this same work in more theoretical terms, developing some of the aesthetic implications of our example.

HOW THE SCENOGRAPHER PROCEEDS — TRADITIONAL THEATRE

At this point in the discussion, we will assume a conventional script-oriented theatre. Later we will concern ourselves with the special advantages and disadvantages for the scenographer who works with a collective theatre group.

The first step in the scenographer's procedure is to study the script. He must make the master symbol embodied in that script part of his artistic experience. Techniques for script study are rooted in the art of literature and can be learned only by the diligent study of many scripts. This is one of the reasons why the student scenographer should study extensively dramatic and general literature.

What does the scenographer seek while studying the script? No list of questions can more than hint at the artistic complexity of any individual script worthy of consideration as theatrical art. However, some examples may help to clarify the type of study the scenographer does. He may ask these questions about the script:

1. Where is the climax of the play?
2. What is its rhythmic structure? How does it proceed in time? What are its temporal patterns?
3. What kinds of movements do the characters seem to be making?
4. Where in the stage space does the climax seem to take place?
5. What elements from life are to be made part of the virtual world of the play?

Such questions and many more will have to be answered as the scenographer develops his concept of the master symbol of the script.

In addition to script study, but never as a substitute for it, the scenographer will hold frequent conversations with the director, such as those illustrated in the hypothetical production meeting. As he probes the artistic intent of the director, he may very well ask some of the above questions about the script, comparing the director's response with his own perceptions. He will also probably ask some of the following questions:

1. How do you see the play's spatial relationship to the audience? Close up? Well removed? Are the play and the audience in the same space?

2. How do you feel that the relationship between character X and character Y should be expressed on stage? (Refers to a specific scene under discussion.)
3. What is the relative importance of characters A and B as they play scene Z? And so on.

In addition to the aesthetic considerations of such questions, the scenographer and director may also address themselves to a set of more seemingly "practical" questions. Note that adequate answers to these questions must also deal with the aesthetic problems mentioned. If not, then these questions and their answers may merely conceal the fact that no real aesthetic communication has taken place.

1. What is the period of the play?
2. What are the minimum mechanical requirements if the plot is to work? This suggests the number of exits, essential properties, and the like.
3. How much playing space is needed?
4. Is the action to be violent, sedate, etc.?
5. What sort of virtual humans will exist in this space?
6. What is the mood of the play? (This is a deceptive question that should lead to much discussion of how the play changes with virtual time.)

Through such discussions, which take place in early production meetings, the scenographer seeks to develop a close artistic rapport with the director. This rapport must grow out of a set of almost totally nondiscursive communications that facilitate comparison of the perceptions of the master symbol by the director and the scenographer. Their combined perception will, of course, determine the kind of a theatrical production they will eventually create. They may possibly reach what they feel is genuine agreement on the master symbol, although agreement is more likely to be the result of incomplete communication. Most probably they will determine that they are close enough together in their perception of the master symbol to proceed, and that they will engage in a running nondiscursive dialogue on that subject as they develop the play. Occasionally it will be obvious that they are far from agreement concerning the master symbol. It would then be best if they agreed to abandon the project, thus allowing the theatre to form another production team if it is determined to produce that particular play. If this cannot be done and they must work together in spite of such serious artistic differences, it is almost inevitable that the artistic results will suffer.

Assuming reasonable agreement about the master symbol, the director and scenographer proceed with their discussions, seeking to produce a ground plan or "floor plan" which will, with the models and renderings growing out of the discussions, form the first tangible evidence of their intentions. A *ground plan* is a simple maplike diagram of the stage area showing the location of entrances and exits and of major scenic and property pieces which determine the movements of the actors (see Figure 2-5.) Such a plan, as simple as it may seem to those outside of the process, represents the "locking in" of many major artistic decisions. It will usually appear as part of one of the first formal production meetings in which others beyond the scenographer and director participate.

Although the agreement on a ground plan will lock many artistic decisions into final form, much work will remain. For example, moving into the details of lighting, the scenographer will need precise information about the movement of the actors and the rhythmic structure being developed by that movement. If the production schedule calls for blocking rehearsals early enough, these are an ideal source of such information. In a *blocking rehearsal* the director and actors work out the details of character movement. Such a rehearsal will give the scenographer a very clear picture of the temporal/spatial concepts the director has in mind. If previous communicative efforts between the scenographer and director have been successful, there should be no surprises, only further clarification that will make the detailing of the lighting easier. If communications have been unsuccessful, this should be painfully apparent to the scenographer who must then take immediate steps to rectify a situation almost too far developed for successful artistic unity to evolve. The scenographer may even have to change large portions of the drawings already in the shop, and alter orders already placed for materials.

Note that the blocking rehearsals represent a form of feedback devoid of the hazards of discursive communication as far as the scenographer is concerned. Thus they may have unique validity.

SCENOGRAPHY IN A COLLECTIVE THEATRE GROUP

If the theatre is engaged in the creation of a production without a conventional script, the scenographer will still have the same needs and may even ask many of the same questions, but under different circumstances. In one respect this will be an advantage; as a member of the collective theatre group, the scenographer will have been a party to the development of the script from the beginning. Thus, much of the aesthetic material needed will already be at hand. He will, nevertheless, have to transform this material into scenographic terms—something that should be second nature to him. His understanding of the movements of the actors should be clearer too, since much of the artistic communication that takes place in such a group comes via improvisations, i.e., scenes may be acted out to express the dramatic ideas that a member or members of the group wish to communicate to their col-

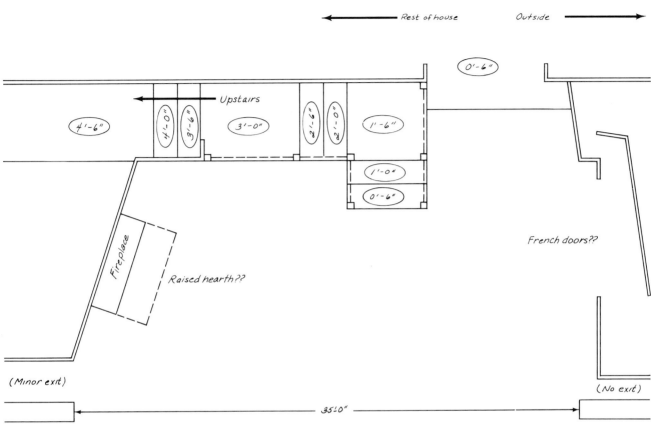

Upstairs

4'-6" 4'-0" 3'-6" 3'-0" 2'-6" 2'-0" 1'-6" 0'-6"

1'-0"

0'-6"

Fireplace

Raised hearth??

French doors??

(Minor exit)

(No exit)

35'-0"

Figure 2-5. A Sketch Floor (Ground) Plan. This is another form of feedback. It becomes useful when ideas have reached some degree of concreteness, and it is necessary for the scenographer and the director to fix agreement concerning the location of entrances, exits, and major scenic elements. It should be drawn roughly to scale although it is by no means a working drawing. When agreement is complete, this sketch can be turned into an exact floor plan—i.e., a working drawing.

leagues. Such improvisations will automatically contain material about character movement.

The communicative advantages the scenographer enjoys in a collective theatre group are somewhat offset by certain disadvantages that are apparently inherent in such groups. Probably the worst of these is the almost constant state of growth and flux that typifies the works of such groups. In an effort to maintain a maximum sense of freshness, and probably because of the continuous flow of creativity in such a group, there is a tendency to try to keep all elements of the production flexible. In some groups improvisation persists through the entire production process, and indeed throughout the performances themselves. This means that the movements of the actors and their interrelationships continue to change nightly. The scenographer and his craftsmen, therefore, must continually anticipate the upcoming shifts and be prepared to alter the scenography for them. Lighting, in particular, must remain in a highly flexible state.

Other, more theatrically conservative groups will terminate their improvisational experiments at some point in the production process, and allow the format to become sufficiently fixed to permit the scenographer to work from an established theatrical situation. However this point of fixation will likely be very late in the production calendar, leaving the scenographer little time to bring the work into focus and to accomplish the technical work. Unfortunately the medium of the scenographer is much less flexible than the human body when it comes to last-minute changes.

SUMMARY: THE SCENOGRAPHIC PROCESS IN BRIEF

The scenographer begins with symbolic material, including items from the script (if there is one), from the director, material from interaction of the collective theatre group (if he is part of such a group), research findings, and information gleaned from rehearsals attended before the work proceeds. From this diverse material he must create his own version of the master symbol—an almost totally nondiscursive process. This special apprehension of the master symbol, is the unique art of the scenographer: *he converts his individual perception of the master symbol into a visual space-time expression that is an organic part of the total production.* For example, from his perception of the movement planned for the actors, he creates a spatial expression that not only makes these movements possible but adds emphasis and heightens them. The result is the four-dimensional "sculpture" composed of moving actors, setting, lighting, costume, and other visual elements.

When the scenographer has grasped the master symbol the design process has started. His principle mode of expression from this point onward will be *visual*—he will produce sketches, models, and planlike drawings which externalize his concepts. Note that at this stage, these are visualizations intended as communicative devices, not as plans for future construction. Directors in particular must be aware of this in production meetings. Only after much communication and feedback will the scenographer move to the next step in the process: the preparation of specific plans, exact scaled models, and final renderings. Once this step has been taken, the communicative process is directed toward the various artists and craftsmen who must execute the work. At the same time, such plans and details may also serve as a final stage of feedback to the director who can read them—which all directors should learn to do.

FIGURE 2-6a

Figure 2-6. Examples of Scenographic Work. This series of pictures has been chosen to illustrate the close relationship that exists between scenography, acting, and directing. (a) and (b) Two views of a production of Don Carlos *by Verdi as produced at the Stadttheatre, Cologne, Germany. Scenography: Svoboda. Direction: Hengebauer. (c) and (d) A production of* Pelleas and Mellisande *by Maeterlinck at the Stadttheatre, Cologne, Germany. Scenography: Freyer. Direction: Hengebauer. Photographs courtesy Helmut Grosser, Cologne Stadttheatre.*

FIGURE 2-6b

FIGURE 2-6c

Communication between craftsmen and scenographer is also a two-way affair. Since the artists and craftsmen cannot be expected to understand fully the plans and specifications without a perception of the master symbol, they too must become a part of the aesthetic process. This is the purpose of formal production meetings, but such meetings should be supplemented by individual conferences.

One of the last steps in the scenographer's long process is the development and refinement of lighting cues. Lighting must be closely interrelated with the movement of the actors, one of the principal ele-

FIGURE 2-6d

ments in the entire scenographic process. The integration of the lighting with the movement should complete the scenographer's symbol and thereby bring the entire scenographic effort to fulfillment. (See Figure 2-6 for examples of scenographic work.)

This is as far as an abstract discussion of scenography can go. Only under the specific pressures of an actual production in progress can we be more specific. Therefore we now turn to the vast technology that has been developed to support the scenographer in the creation of space-time sculpture.

PART TWO

THE PHYSICAL THEATRE

Left: Ein Florentinerhut, *Labich; right* Die Frau Vom Meer, *Ibsen. Photographs by Stefan Odry*

**3
THE
PROSCENIUM
THEATRE**

GENERAL THEATRE TERMINOLOGY

Many general theatrical terms derive from what theatrical experimenters now consider an outdated form—the proscenium theatre. These experimenters challenge even the most basic premise of that theatre, the relationship between play and audience. We will examine these new ideas, but we must start by making traditional definitions clear. The following working definitions are subject to later variations.

The *audience* consists of those human beings who are the recipients of the theatrical art work, who view it, hear it, aesthetically experience it at the end of the process by which it came into being.

Actors are human beings who use their bodies, voices, and their personalities as raw material for the artistic presentation of virtual human beings, the *characters* they portray. In this sense, "playing a role" means the conscious creation of a virtual human being in a particular situation. Thus actors, unlike audience members, are in a conscious state of creative activity during the presentation of the production; it is this creative activity that most distinguishes them from audience members.

The *script, drama,* or *book* is the work of the playwright. It is a special kind of literary form which is not completed by the author's writing, but by players' acting in a theatre. It provides the words that the actors speak, the basic organization of their activities, and a large share of the emotional and intellectual content of their production. Some scripts have literary merit on their own, i.e., they may be read to oneself for literary pleasure (Shakespeare), but this is a different kind of aesthetic experience only obliquely related to our experience of the same play in production.

THEATRE PLANT

Literally, the physical theatre is the building in which theatre production takes place; it is a piece of architecture. This edifice may be a valuable piece of real estate, a matter of civic pride, a center of community activity, or even (to those of Puritan persuasion) an abode of the devil—but most important, it is a structure for the production of art works, i.e., plays. Of course, not all will attain that standard; only a few of the many plays produced rise to the level of art.

A play in production exists in both time and space and *only* when there is an audience to behold it. No dress rehearsal, however carefully organized, is quite like a performance. Consequently a great deal of theatrical organization and activity is devoted to the audience, looking after its comfort and safety, and facilitating its participation in the artistic ritual of play production. The craft of theatre management is devoted to making this part of the theatre work. Audiences must be ticketed and seated; provided with refreshments during intermissions, with washrooms, telephones, and many other conveniences necessary to their happiness. Their safety must be rigorously guarded. Exits must be provided and they must be lighted under almost any circumstances, stairs must have railings, and fire laws must be obeyed.

All of these things and more are for the care of one-half of the theatrical phenomenon—the audience. The rest of the physical theatre is devoted to the other half—to the production of the play the audience has come to see. The central element of this section is the "stage." Conventionally this is a well-defined space clearly separated from the audience and surrounded by working spaces on every side except that occupied by the audience. Ignoring convention, the "stage" may be any space devoted to the production of the play for the audience and visible to that audience, whether separated from it or including it. The same physical space might conceivably contain both audience members and play, the only distinction being in the minds of those persons involved.

But space is not enough except in rare cases. The space must be organized, i.e., "designed," and supported by working and storage spaces around it which make possible the required appearance and disappearance of persons and things. Modern theatre space uses much machinery to be maximally effective. The interrelationships among these working spaces, the devices, and the supporting spaces that surround them, signify the idea of the theatre as a production machine. Each space and each device within that space should be directed toward one primary goal: the production of the play. Any architectural, mechanical, or organizational defect will tend to make that job harder and the machine less effective.

The theatrical machine makes possible some of the major expressive elements in theatrical art, for example, the way things are related in time. Thunder follows lightning and reaction follows stimulus. The theatrical machine must make these sequences, and others still more sophisticated, not only possible but amenable to subtle adjustment. In the subtlety lies the expression. For example, after a character exits the timing and tone of a door slam effect off stage tells us much about the mood and dramatic meaning of that exit. The degree of machinelike efficiency of the theatre determines the degree of control we have over that sound effect.

The machinelike efficiency of a well-run theatre is wonderful to behold and thrilling to be a part of, but it is really a metaphor. The theatre is ultimately the people in it, not the cold walls nor the machinery. People, not machines nor architecture, make art works. Nevertheless the metaphor is useful; it reminds us of interrelationships without which the theatre can never come close to art. It helps us to measure the degree to which our planning and organization are paying off in "machinelike" efficiency which will make it possible (never certain) that art can be achieved.

THEATRICAL GEOGRAPHY

Since the actor is the central figure in all forms of theatre, it is his view that determines the manner in which locations are described. As the actor stands on stage facing the audience, his left is called "stage left," his right, "stage right".[1] If he moves away from the audience we say that he is moving "upstage"; going toward the audience is moving "downstage." These terms date back to the days when the floor sloped upward toward the back of the stage, an architectural device used to aid the illusion of great depth when combined with painted perspective. Stage floors are almost always level these days, but the terms persist. Since left and right and upstage-downstage are not accurate enough to describe positions on large stages, the playing area is divided further as shown in Figure 3-1. The "playing area" is the floor space occupied by actors when they are in view of the audience. Note that all of the locations refer to the *actor's* left or right. The terms applied to the areas surrounding the playing area are derived from the proscenium theatre, originally conceived as a stage house for "wing and drop" settings. The wing and drop theatre was perfected in the eighteenth and early nineteenth centuries. All settings consisted of flat painted elements. Those at the sides were known as "wings." They were moved on and off stage in sets on special tracks, making rapid change possible. At

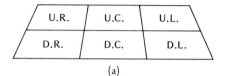

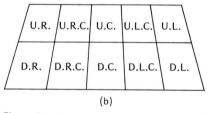

Figure 3-1. *Designation of Stage Areas. (a) The division system used on most stages of small or medium size. (b) The system used when the stage is large. Abbreviations: "U," up; "D," down; "L," left; "R," right; and "C," center.*

---

1. The British theatre often substitutes the terms, "prompt" and "opposite prompt" for stage right and stage left. These are abbreviated "P." and "O.P." The word "prompt" refers to the prompter, a person charged with the task of calling cues to those actors who forget their lines. This function, if it is needed, now is usually given to the stage manager.

the same time "drops" were raised or lowered closing the upstage portion of the setting. Few such theatres still exist. The modern stage seldom uses the wing and drop technique, although the terms have persisted. The spaces at the sides of the playing area, once occupied by sets of wings, still are called "wings." Occasionally modern scenic elements somewhat like eighteenth-century wings are used and are also called "wings."

In addition to left and right and up and down, the student of theatrical geography must distinguish between those parts of the theatre building devoted to the audience and those used by players and technicians. The dividing line is the special wall that gives the proscenium theatre its name. The word "proscenium" refers to the opening in the stage house wall through which the audience views the play. Originally the audience and its functions were found on one side of this wall and the stage and players on the other; this strict division of areas has long since been altered. The "house" is the large room fitted with seats where the audience gathers to watch what is occurring on stage. The "lobby" is the area through which the spectators pass on the way into the house and where they get refreshments during intermission. Adjacent to the lobby is the "box office," a small room (or rooms) with a window through which tickets are sold.

At the front of the house between the audience and the proscenium there may be two items more related to actors than audience—the "orchestra pit" and the "apron." The orchestra pit (abbreviated "pit") is properly a depressed area in the floor at the front of the seating area. It should be low enough to keep the musicians and their instruments from blocking the view of the stage. The pit is usually concealed from the audience by a low curtain. It may extend back under the apron to accommodate more musicians. The apron is really a part of the stage, extending forward from the proscenium into the house. It is sometimes used as a separate playing area in which scenes are acted in front of the closed main curtain. While such a scene is playing, the setting is being changed behind the curtain. This makes a very convenient format for musical productions which thereby alternate large scenes involving spectacle with small scenes. These small scenes are "in one." If a second curtain, perhaps 10 feet upstage of the main curtain is added, the area thus created is "in two." This system of designation ignores stage left, stage center, or stage right.

PROSCENIUM THEATRE IN DETAIL

Over the several hundred years of its development, the proscenium theatre has evolved into an incredibly efficient theatre machine capable of handling vastly complicated productions in a tight repertory schedule with ease and safety. A visit to any of the major opera houses of the world—the Metropolitan, the Salzburg Festspielhaus, the Berlin Opera, to name three of the most famous—should convince anyone of the capabilities of the form. Such theatres can handle the demands of as many as three separate operas in one working day with ease. It is no wonder that almost all of the theatre machinery of the present has developed within the format of the proscenium theatre.

As we already know, the proscenium theatre (sometimes called the "peephole theatre") allows the audience to view the production through an opening in the wall of the stage. This neat separation makes it possible to devote almost all architectural elements on one side of this wall to the needs of the production. In a fully equipped proscenium theatre the area devoted to production may be three times that devoted to the audience. The production area comprises the *playing area,* or *acting space,* and the *backstage space,* or *working space,* which supports the activities in the playing area. In this working space are found the machinery and the people who operate it. The great flexibility of the proscenium theatre comes from the fact that scenery, actors, and properties can move in and out of the playing space from left and right, the rear, above and below. This movement usually is assisted by machines that push, pull, lift, or lower things as they are needed, and take them rapidly and quietly away when they are no longer necessary. Most of this chapter is devoted to this machinery and those who operate it. However, there are certain details of the house that we must understand if our knowledge of the proscenium theatre is to be complete. We will deal with these next.

AUDIENCE AREA

Seats for the audience in a proscenium theatre may be arranged in several patterns. The oldest is the *ring theatre* (Figure 3-2), the traditional opera house format. Seats on the main floor are said to be in the "orchestra" in the United States and in the "parquet" in some parts of Europe. Above and around these seats, which are usually the most costly, are the horseshoe-shaped balconies which are divided into boxes, i.e., groups of several seats each enclosed in a separate room opening into the main auditorium space to allow a view of the stage. The view afforded by some of the seats in the boxes is restricted. However the view from box to box is usually excellent and this was the original rationale in designing box seats. Those who sat in them came to be seen by those who sat in other box seats. It was and is a social occasion with some theatre thrown in for good measure. A by-product of this ring or horseshoe theatre was that the shape produced remarkable acoustics, particularly for music. Some of the most famous opera houses in the world are of this type, now more valued for their acoustic

Figure 3-2. A ring theatre. This theatre is typical of the many ring theatres built during the nineteenth Century. It is still in use in Schwetzingen, Germany. The house has been carefully restored in its original style but the stage has been completely modernized and its working space extended. This view from the stage shows how the "rings" of boxes surround the orchestra providing those in the box seats with a good view of each other at the expense of a reduced view of the stage for those in the side boxes. Note the high, profusely ornamented proscenium arch which is partially visible in the foreground. Courtesy Staatliches Hochbauampt, Mannheim, West Germany. Photograph by Thome.

excellence than their social function. However the ring theatre is no longer considered ideal. Its more modern adaptation, the balcony theatre, has superseded it. In this theatre the main floor remains about the same, but the balconies are designed for a much better view of the stage (see Figure 3-3). Several balconies are common in larger houses. Acoustics vary from excellent to terrible.

American Seating Plans

The main floor and even the balconies can be adapted to two variations in seating arrangement. This decision must be made when the building is being erected or undergoes a major reconstruction, because the flow of the audience to and from the seats must be adjusted accordingly.

Figure 3-3. A Modern Proscenium Theatre. Compare this theatre with the one shown in Figure 3-2. Note that the rings of boxes have given way to balconies designed to provide the best possible view of the stage. This theatre also features continental seating on the main floor. Note the generous back-to-back spacing between the rows of seats, allowing audience members to pass in front of seated spectators as they move to or from their seats. Each group of two or three aisles ends in a wide exit door at either side of the house. These doors lead to a wide side foyer, and in case of emergencies, directly to the outside. The window-like openings in the second and center of the third balconies are built-in positions for balcony-front lighting. Dorothy Chandler Pavilion, Los Angeles, California. Photograph courtesy Welton Becket and Associates, Architects.

In "American plan seating" the audience enters and leaves the seating area from the rear, proceeding down vertical (as related to the proscenium line) aisles. It enters each row of seats from an aisle and sits in relatively closely spaced rows of seats. Safety regulations require that no seat be more than six seats (not counting the one you are sitting in) from an aisle. This limits rows to fourteen seats between aisles. Aisle width must vary according to a safety formula to allow everyone a safe exit in case of fire or panic. Emergency exits are provided at the front left and right of the house, but these do not figure in the normal flow of traffic. Such theatres tend to have large lobby areas at the back of the house to accommodate the entering or exiting audience, but may have no side-of-house space. The down-front emergency exits must open either to the outside or (in the New York City code) to a fire-safe area large enough to hold the audience comfortably.

This form of seating has become almost standard throughout the United States (hence its name) because of the replication of New York

City building codes which originally specified it. It is efficient in handling crowds but dedicates a lot of valuable space near the center of the house to aisles, and separates the audience into distinct groups. Also the long vertical aisles produce other safety problems when an attempt is made to *rake* the house (i.e., slope the floor) to improve the view of the stage.

Continental Seating Plans

In the continental seating plan, which first appeared in Europe, the audience enters the auditorium area from the sides. Each row of seats forms its own aisle; the seats are spaced far enough apart so that a person can walk comfortably in front of a seated audience member without requiring him to rise (See Figure 3-3). Seat rows can be any length as long as the side entries can accommodate the occupants of the row. There are no vertical aisles. Floor slope can be as steep as needed. Tests have shown that such houses can be emptied of occupants at least as fast as those seated according to the American plan, and sometimes faster. A bonus is more comfort for long-legged audience members. If reasonable comfort standards are applied, both plans allow for equal audience density. Ignoring comfort, the American plan will probably put more people into less space.

Many other variables in both seating plans considerably affect the audience's comfort and how well it can see the production. For instance, seat width can vary considerably. The floor slope that gives a view over the person ahead of you, the presence or absence of seat arms, air conditioning, auditorium lighting, and many other things influence the mood of the audience member who encounters the staged work.

STAGE AREA

As we move from the house to the stage, we enter the area that should be most familiar to the technician and the scenographer. Figure 7-1d, page 122, shows a cross section of a proscenium stage. We will examine stage parts and stage machinery beginning with the apron (or forestage) and working upstage. After a study of the wings and the area immediately upstage of the acting space, we will study the space above the stage, and finally, that below it. Not all proscenium theatres will have all of the equipment mentioned, but a well-equipped one should have most of it. We begin with the apron area including the orchestra pit.

Forestage or Apron

In its pure, late nineteenth-century form, the proscenium theatre had little use for an apron or forestage. The curtain line represented an

Figure 3-4. A Modern Forestage. This shows the evolution of the apron from a miniscule space for utilitarian use to a major playing area. Note that the curtain line is well upstage of the playing space provided, and that the sides of the apron have been extended to produce still more playing space. This particular apron includes two elevators, one of which is visible (note the joint in the floor). The other carries the first rows of seats visible in the lower right corner of the picture. This theatre also features an adjustable proscenium opening, shown here at its narrowest setting. When opened to its maximum, the side-stage areas become part of the main stage. The theatre is MacGowan Hall, University of California at Los Angeles.

invisible "fourth wall" of the scene being played on stage. The tradition of the fourth wall required that the curtain line never be crossed by the actors. Of course, the earlier form of the proscenium theatre with its wing and drop staging had used the proscenium line as a point of demarcation. Actors delivering "asides" (speeches written to be directed to the audience) would cross down to the tiny apron to make their speech. Stepping back behind the fourth wall brought them back into the virtual world of the play and rendered their speech again dramatically audible to the other characters. When in front of the fourth wall, their lines were for the audience only, and were "not heard" by the characters on stage.

Because modern drama no longer observes the tradition of the fourth wall, proscenium theatres usually are provided with a considerable forestage and even with side stages (see Figure 3-4). These extend the playing area toward the audience leaving the main curtain as a set-changing convenience rather than marking the downstage limit of the dramatic space of the play.

The apron area includes the orchestra pit because it may become a part of the apron. In many houses the orchestra pit is really an *elevator* or *lift* (see Figure 3-4). Its floor is moved (often hydraulically) up or down, enabling the theatre to have a larger apron when it is raised to stage level, more seating in the house when it is lowered to the level of the house floor and equipped with seating, or an orchestra pit of varying depth. In most cases, the pit elevator also doubles as a freight elevator because it is arranged so that it may be lowered completely to the basement floor to move heavy objects in or out of there, making it a highly versatile device. In some still more elaborate installations, the pit elevator is divided into two or even three elevators, enabling the apron to be adjusted in increments or even to be stepped. Such installations may cost hundreds of thousands of dollars, but are highly desirable.

The apron itself (or an edge of the pit elevator) usually is equipped either with *footlights* or a footlight trough. These provide light from below and in front of the actors—something that is occasionally desirable even with modern lighting, and was once the very trademark of the theatre. This same location usually is fitted with outlets for special lighting instruments as they may be needed, and for microphones. Occasionally other devices for special effects also are included. Examples are: a trough to catch water from a "rain curtain" (pipes above the apron), a prompter's box for opera, and special retracting microphones for musical comedy.

In many theatres the apron purposely is made large enough so that it can be used for "acts in one." This means acts that take place in front of the *act curtain* (which closes the proscenium opening) while settings are being changed backstage. The apron often is occupied by speakers, lectern, and the like, for nondramatic uses of the building.

The apron, especially the all-purpose sort described above, frequently is floored with hardwood and finished like a fine floor. This adds a certain elegance to the theatre as a meeting hall, but causes no end of troubles for theatre workers. The glossy floor reflects light where it is not wanted, is sharply demarcated from the regular stage floor at the curtain line, and resists efforts to attach theatrical devices to it by being too hard and too highly valued by the owners.

MAIN CURTAIN   The main curtain also is called the "act curtain," the "rag," the "grand drape," and many other confusing names. It is sometimes a complex of two or more curtains and an assortment of related devices. Its basic function is clear: to close the proscenium opening. It is also the symbolic device that signals the beginning and end of theatrical action. Thus the word "curtain" means "end of act" even when no curtain is used. In fact the word "curtains" is synonymous with "the end" in and out of the theatre.

The main curtain may be moved into or out of the proscenium opening in a variety of ways: (1) It can be drawn to the sides ("draw"). (2) It may lift upward as a unit ("lift"). (3) It may draw sideways and diagonally upward to drape at the sides of the opening ("tab"). (4) It may lift in a predetermined pattern to form a shaped opening within the architectural opening of the proscenium ("profile" or contour). (See Figure 3-5.) An old form (now seldom found) was the roll-up curtain that opened from the bottom up by rolling around a cylindrical device ("drop curtain" or "olio"). The most common forms are the draw curtain and the lift curtain, which frequently are combined giving the director the alternative of either type of motion.

VALANCE AND TEASER   The valance and the teaser must be considered together because they often are combined into one item or the terms are applied indiscriminately to both. Strictly speaking, a *valance* is a short, often highly ornamental piece of drapery within the top of the proscenium opening. It serves to lower permanently the effective height of the architectural opening known as the proscenium. As such, a valance is often permanently mounted in position ("hung dead") and only occasionally removed for cleaning or replacement. A *teaser*, again strictly defined, is a separate curtain from the valance and is hung from a batten so that is may be used to adjust the height of the proscenium opening from show to show or even from act to act.

However, the functions of valance and teaser may be combined by hanging a single piece of drapery (either ornamental or plain) from a movable batten, thus allowing adjustment of the proscenium opening. Unfortunately valances often are viewed with suspicion by theatre workers. If they are highly ornamental, they tend to be distractions.

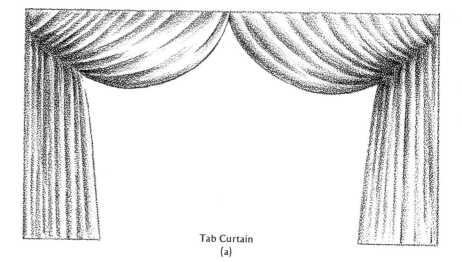

Figure 3-5a. Tableau (Tab) Curtain. This curtain is drawn into its open position by two ropes which pull it diagonally upward and outward. Such an arrangement can be worked into a draw-lift curtain if desired.

Figure 3-5b. Contour (Profile) Curtain. This curtain is operated by multiple lines that may be adjusted to provide a wide variety of contours.

Tab Curtain
(a)

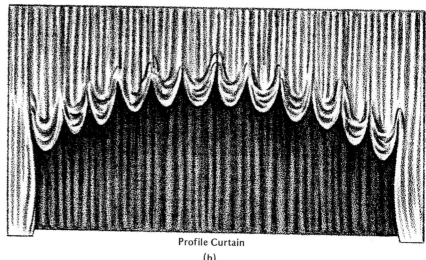

Profile Curtain
(b)

Worse still, they may be used by theatre builders to adjust for the fact that not enough space was built above the stage. In such a situation, the only choice may be the installation of a valance that *permanently* lowers the effective height of the stage opening and provides needed space to hide curtain tracks, lighting equipment, and other paraphernalia. Such cost-cutting procedures, though deplorable, often are found in theatres.

TORMENTORS   At the sides of the proscenium opening and just upstage of the main curtain one usually finds *tormentors* or *portals.* These are devices to regulate the effective width of the proscenium opening. If they are simply curtains hung from whatever overhead structure has been provided, they usually are called "tormentors," a name said to derive from their tendency to impede entrances and exits at these important points. If they are solidly built scenic elements, even including built-in lighting positions on their upstage side, they are called "portals." In either case, they are usually movable horizontally to allow adjustment of the width of the proscenium opening.

INNER PROSCENIUM   Instead of, or in addition to, the teaser and tormentors, the stage may be provided with an inner proscenium. This often is devised for a particular production and forms a part of its scenic design. It is exactly what the name implies, a structure of wood and canvas designed to appear to be an architectural device framing the proscenium opening. Inner prosceniums frequently are used with traveling shows to adjust the size of various theatres to the needs of the setting. They can also be used to bring an oversized proscenium down to more workable dimensions, thereby gaining backstage space, in a theatre with a stage larger than necessary or economically useful. Sometimes this results in cutting off some seats in the house because they no longer enjoy a good view of the stage, but the house may be too large for good dramatic purposes anyway.

ASBESTOS   Any completely equipped proscenium theatre must have some provision for controlling a stage fire at least long enough to clear the house of people. The standard way of doing this in the United States has been to provide a "fire curtain" made of woven asbestos which slides up and down in tightly fitting steel slots worked into the proscenium arch. These are known as "smoke slots," or "smoke pockets," and are intended to prevent smoke from leaking rapidly around the asbestos curtain and into the house. The asbestos curtain itself must be provided with several automatic and manually operated devices which will lower it in an emergency. The automatic device usually consists of heat sensitive metal links high in the rigging system which melt when a predetermined temperature is reached, and thus allow the asbestos to lower of its own weight. The fall is controlled to keep the heavy asbestos from smashing through the floor. The automatic system is supplemented by rope rigging at either side of the stage which may be activated simply by cutting a tie-line in case of emergency. Thus, at the sides of the stage on the back of the proscenium wall, you will find a sign reading, "Cut rope in case of fire." Alongside the sign will be found a sharp knife and the rope that must be cut. *Do not tamper with this apparatus.* In case of fire, if the asbestos does not lower automatically, this rope should be cut.

The asbestos also is provided with a normal means of raising and lowering it so that it may be used to cut off the stage from the house whenever needed. In fact, in some localities it is required by law that the presence and working condition of the asbestos be demonstrated to the audience by lowering and raising it while they are in the house. This usually means that the asbestos is discovered to be in lowered position when the audience enters, and that it is raised some time before the beginning of the first act to reveal the act curtain. When such display of the asbestos is required, some effort generally is made to make it into an attractive device.

IRON CURTAIN   Although the term "iron curtain" has taken on political meaning in our contemporary vocabulary, it was originally, and still is in Europe, a stage term, referring to the European equivalent of the asbestos curtain. This is a very heavy but movable wall of steel plates which can be lowered into the proscenium opening in case of fire. It usually is provided with a small door so that one may step through it when it is down. It serves the same function and is operated according to about the same procedures as an American asbestos curtain. It is, however, more durable. One fault of asbestos curtains is that as they age, the asbestos gradually disintegrates and falls away. Many old asbestos curtains are nearly transparent, making them useless against fire.

FAN AND DELUGE SYSTEM   Recent revisions in the New York City building code have resulted in new modes of protecting audiences from fire on stage. As a part of the revision, the proscenium theatre has itself been challenged. Previously most professional theatres, which sought the workable advantages of the proscenium stage, were locked into the proscenium-asbestos curtain/small apron pattern because nothing else would pass fire laws. The new devices do not depend on closing an opening in a wall to protect the audience.

The new system consists of two major parts: a powerful emergency fan arrangement designed to sweep smoke and fumes up and away from the audience area and out of the building, and a "deluge" system of sprinklers designed to drown any fire on stage in a matter of moments. This new fire protection system has encouraged the development of theatrical architectural forms that make use of the overhead machinery of the proscenium theatre but are not limited by the necessity for a proscenium. (See the section "Thrust Stage Theatre" in Chapter 4.)

Upstage of the Proscenium Wall

As we move away from the proscenium wall, our discussion is complicated by the multiplicity of parts. To clarify this we will concern ourselves first with those parts directly related to the stage floor, then with those hanging above the floor, and finally with those parts below floor level.

STAGE FLOOR   The stage floor is a working surface, not just a decorative surface to be walked upon. Thus it should properly be a soft wood floor finished in a dark, nearly nonreflective surface. Any stage with a varnished floor, whether hard or soft wood, cannot be said to be properly equipped. It is desirable that the part of the stage floor that forms the acting surface be *trapped,* that is, divided into removable sections which can be taken out to allow the installation of steps, lifts, etc., leading to the basement. It is still more desirable that the stage floor itself be divided into a series of lifts which can descend far into the basement or even rise well above stage level to form platforms. The lift floors may occasionally have traps in them. Another variation in the stage floor is the *revolve.* This is a circular platform, the larger the better, built into the floor and turned by motors to enable the operators to change settings rapidly. It is possible to combine all of these variations into one theatre (New York's Metropolitan Opera House, for example), but at huge cost.

In any event, the stage floor should be wooden and so arranged that it has some spring or "give" to it for the benefit of dancers who will otherwise be apt to injure their leg muscles. It should be strong enough to drive a truck over, if necessary, in loading a production in or out.

The stage floor, whether movable or not, is fitted with electrical outlets known as "floor pockets," and microphone outlets known as "mike pockets." These may also double as loudspeaker outlets, or there may be separate "speaker pockets."

BACKSTAGE AREAS   To the left and right of the acting area are located the *wings.* The term originally referred to the scenic elements hiding these areas from the audience, but today it refers to the space itself. In a well-designed proscenium theatre, the wing areas will each be at least as large as the acting area, thus making it possible to move a complete set to either side via a *stage wagon,* a large rolling platform with a set riding on it.

Upstage of the acting area there may be considerable working space. This is simply referred to as "backstage" in most American theatres. In Germany, where this area is expanded to allow the operation of a full stage wagon, it is known as the *Hinterbühne,* which may be translated as "the rear stage" rather than the confusing "backstage." Actually the *Hinterbühne* is a separate stage area upstage of the usual acting space. It is often elaborately equipped with wagons, perhaps including a revolve within a wagon. Large American opera houses have

Figure 3-6. Stage Manager's Station. An illustration of one of various arrangements made for stage manager functions. A stage manager's station at the Desert Inn, Las Vegas. Actually, in the large review show organization used in Las Vegas, there is no stage manager in the original sense of the term. Instead there are "cue callers" who concentrate on cuing a carefully defined group of functions. Coordination is achieved by closed-circuit television and close intercommunications. This particular station is built into the stage left inner proscenium which remains in place for the entire run of a show, perhaps two years.

followed this German pattern. For example, the stage at the Metropolitan has a *Hinterbühne* equal in size to the main playing area, with a full-sized wagon on which a large revolving stage is mounted. The entire assembly can be motor-driven to the downstage area where it fits over the space normally occupied by large stage elevators. Thus an elevator stage can be converted into a revolving stage.

Stage Manager's Desk   The stage manager is the most important single person backstage during the time that the curtain is up. In most theatres he is provided with a desk in the wings, usually located near the tormentor left or right where he has a clear view of the acting area. This desk is elaborately equipped with communications gear; emergency equipment controls; secondary controls for lighting, sound, and stage machinery; and the like. The desk is the nerve center of the theatre machine while a production is being presented (see Figure 3-6).

Space Above the Stage

The movement of scenic elements horizontally across the stage floor into the wings may be either a hand operation or mechanized. It is more often mechanized in Europe than in the United States. However, lifting scenery into the space above the stage almost always requires machinery.

The original proscenium theatre style used scenery ideally suited to lifting and, hence, early development of scenery-lifting machinery. Figure 3-7 shows a cross section of a modern rigging system.

Since scenery "flew" into the space above the stage, this space soon became known as "the flies" or "fly loft." Shipfitters were hired to fit out the stage for lifting scenery and bequeathed their terminology to the theatre. The equipment was thus called "the rigging," and the device used to tie off the lines (ropes) to hold the scenery in place was given its seagoing name, the pin rail. The wooden "pins" inserted into holes in this rail were "belaying pins"—the same device used aboard ships for this purpose. See Figure 3-8 for some examples of these applications as they are still in use today.

The rigging is one of the most important aspects of the proscenium theatre. Therefore, we will examine it in detail.

RIGGING   The basic principle of stage rigging is extremely simple: Pulleys are attached to a very strong structure at the top of the stage building and ropes are run over them (see Figure 3-9). One end of the line is attached to the scenery and the other is pulled to raise the scenery. It is the simplest of hoists. Since it was desirable to be able to pull the lines from the wing areas while raising scenery over the acting space, two or more pulleys were used to direct the line to a convenient place for pulling. Once pulled, the line was tied to the rail to keep the

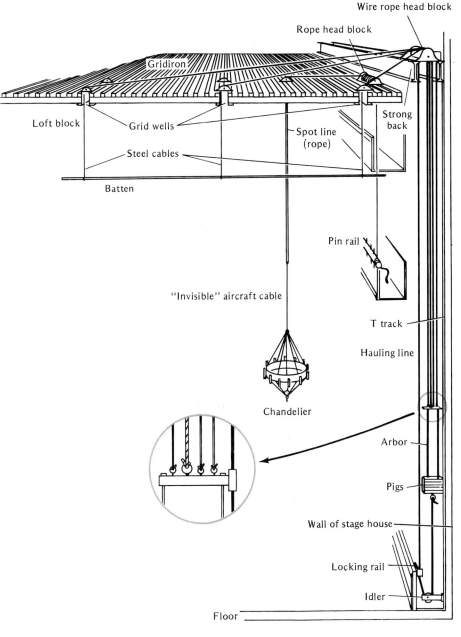

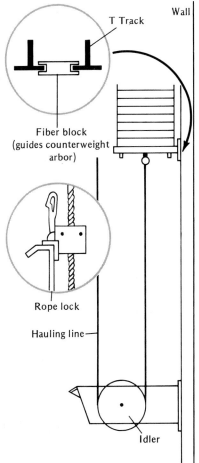

Figure 3-7. Modern Rigging System. (a) This drawing shows a portion of a typical five-line counterweight rigged stage with rope sets available for spot lines. For simplification, only three of the five grid wells have been shown. The location of the pin rail and the distance from floor to gridiron are arbitrary; there would actually be much more space below the pin rail in most theatres. Also, the sizes of the arbor and locking rail have been increased to clarify them. The loading gallery is shown directly above the pin rail. (b) Shows in detail the T-track and the locking rail.

scenery from dropping. The rail had to be strong enough to take the combined upward pull of all the lines attached to it, and the overhead structure had to be strong enough to take twice the downward pull of everything hanging from it.

FIGURE 3-8a

Figure 3-8. Pin Rails. (a) A double pin rail with removable wooden belaying pins. The lower rail, visible near the bottom of the picture, allows the low trim of a set of lines to remain tied off and thus set while the drop has been hauled out of sight to high trim and tied off at the upper rail. Although this is a rather old pin rail, the earliest form would have been made entirely of wood. (b) A more modern rail made of steel with the pins permanently welded into place. Since it is seldom necessary to suddenly release a piece of scenery and let it fall to its lowered position, permanently installed pins are safer and just as satisfactory.

FIGURE 3-8b

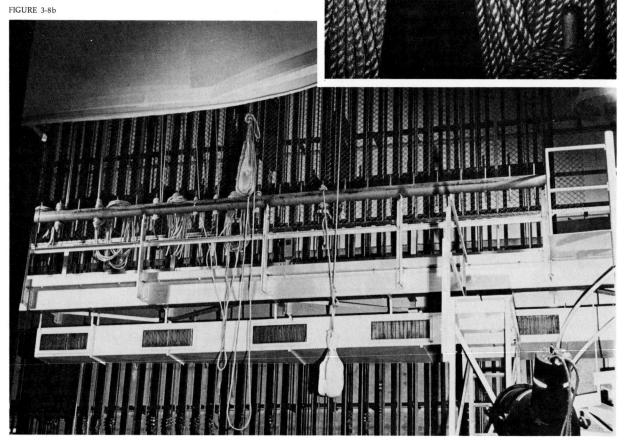

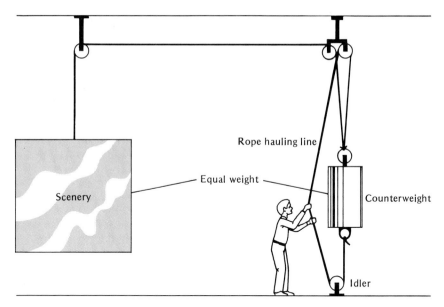

Figure 3-9. This simplified sketch illustrates the principle of the counterweight system. The stage-hand moves the scenery up or down by pulling on the rope called a "hauling" or "operating line." If things are in proper balance little effort will be needed to move a heavy piece of scenery.

Scenery

Equal weight

Rope hauling line

Counterweight

Idler

Gridiron Undoubtedly the first rigging was simply attached to the underside of the roof of the theatre. This is still done in simple installations. It became obvious that a stronger structure than the roof was needed, and that installing and rearranging the lines would be easier if one could walk about on it. The result was a special structure installed just below the roof called the "gridiron" (grid) because this is precisely what it usually was—an open gridwork of iron (Figure 3-10). It is a scary place for those not used to heights. The pulleys are arranged over slots or openings in the gridiron to allow the ropes to fall where they are needed. Other pulleys direct the lines to the side of the stage and downward. One walks on the openwork with an all-too-clear view of the stage floor far below. It is usually more of a psychological hazard than a real one because there are few grid openings that would allow one to fall through accidentally.

Usually the chief slots for pulleys (more properly called "loft blocks") are arranged in upstage-downstage rows to support the devices underneath. These slots are known as "grid wells." It is possible, however, to install a loft block almost anywhere on the grid. The pulleys at one side of the stage that direct each line downward to the rail are known as "head blocks." They are supported by a *strongback*, a heavy beam designed to take the tremendous pull that all of the lines will exert when the stage is full of scenery (see Figure 3-11).

Line Sets Lines are normally arranged in "sets" consisting of three, five, or even seven lines in a row parallel to the proscenium opening.

Figure 3-10. Gridiron. This photograph should be related to Figure 3-7 to determine how the gridiron fits into the structure of the proscenium theatre. This figure shows a typical gridiron arrangement for a combination wire rope and hemp rigging. Most of the battens are permanently supported by wire rope line sets. Spot lines, two of which are visible in the foreground, are rigged with hemp and used to carry short battens or single objects. Note the grid wells arranged to handle the wire rope sets. They are spaced to accommodate the five lines composing the standard rigging for this medium-sized theatre. See Figure 3-11 for details of the pulleys.

Figure 3-11a. Loft Block. This single steel pulley with its grooved sheave directs the line downward toward the batten below. It is attached to the gridiron by a hook at the end away from the head block and a bolt-operated clamp at the end near the head block. Thus the hook holds against the tug of the weighted line even if the clamp is not completely tight. Such blocks seldom need maintenance, although oil may be needed if they develop a squeak.

Figure 3-11b. Head Blocks. These multiple sheave pulleys are secured to the "strong back," a very heavy steel beam firmly attached to the frame of the building. This beam must carry the entire angular force exerted by the many lines which turn downward toward the counterweights over the sheaves. Note that each head block sheave contains a groove for each wire rope in the set plus a larger groove for the operating line.

Figure 3-11c. Rope Set Head Blocks. The center head block contains a complete five-line rope set. A bolt holds the head block in place; the other end of this piece of angle iron terminates in a hook which is held in place by the tension on the ropes. The head block at the right of the picture has a single rope for a spot line.

The on-stage ends of these lines are attached to a *batten* which is usually a long piece of $1\frac{1}{2}$ inch pipe. On old stages it was made of laminated wood. This pipe makes the lines work as a set, and whatever is to be lifted is attached to the batten by means of short lengths of chain equipped with snap hooks. These chains are known as "trim chains" because adjusting the snap hook into various links of the chain will level the scenery with the floor. This is called "trimming it"—seagoing talk again.

A head block for a line set will have as many *sheaves* (pulley wheels) as there are lines in the set, and probably one more whose purpose will be evident shortly.

A well-equipped stage will have line sets arranged continuously from just upstage of the proscenium wall to the back of the stage house at close intervals. Intervals of 6 to 12 inches usually are considered adequate.

Pin Rail A *pin rail* is a heavy piece of wood or metal set in a heavy framework to hold it in a horizontal position like the rail of a ship. This rail is drilled vertically at intervals to accept wooden or metal belaying pins around which ropes may be fastened (see Figure 3-8). It forms the tie-off point for the simplest of flying systems. The ropes, usually in sets, are hauled downward until the scenery is in the proper position and then tied off with the figure-eight knot shown in Figure 3-12 to hold the scenery in place.

In a stage using the pin rail as the sole means of holding settings in the flies, the rail will usually be situated on a balcony well above

Figure 3-12. The Pin Rail Knot. The knot on the left has been simplified to show the arrangement of the rope needed to make it hold. Note that the weighted rope passes under the lower part of the pin and then forms a figure-8 as it passes around the upper portion. The upper loop has been twisted a half turn to make the free end of the line pass under the weighted portion. This twist and friction hold the load. The knot on the right shows how the figure-8 usually is repeated once before the twist is made. This makes a more secure knot and allows the operator to control the weight on the line(s) easily even before he makes the twist. The knot is tied using several lines at a time unless there is a special reason for separating them. See also Figure 3-8.

FIGURE 3-13a

the stage floor and so arranged that the operators of the lines face the stage as they work. This arrangement saves floor space and gives the flymen or riggers a better view of the stage as they raise and lower scenery. Most modern stages are equipped with a pin rail as an auxiliary to the counterweight system described below. As an auxiliary device, the rail serves special rigging problems and *spot lines* (special ropes for such things as chandeliers). It may be located either on the stage floor or on a balcony, whichever is convenient.

Counterweight Systems Even in the earliest proscenium theatres devices were used to increase the pulling power of the men operating the lines. One of the earliest of these was the *sandbag,* a heavy canvas bag weighted with sand and attached to the lines to equalize the weight of a heavy piece of scenery. An attachment device that held all of the ropes together and provided a secure ring to tie on the sandbag was known as a "clew." They are still used (see Figure 3-13). The sandbag helped move heavy scenery but created problems. It swung freely about backstage often tangling (fouling) other line sets and even striking people. If it broke free, it was a deadly hazard. Furthermore, it had to be hoisted by brute force into position every time it was installed. The strain on the ropes was increased by the addition of sandbag counterweights because heavier equipment could now be handled. Clearly, a better system was needed. This system was the *guided counterweight system* using wire rope (cable) instead of hemp rope to support the scenery. With this device tons could be handled safely. It is still in use today with only minor improvements.

The basic pulley system remains although it must be built stronger to take the heavier loads. The lines are usually $\frac{1}{4}$ inch steel cable with a breaking strength measured in tons. The offstage ends of the lines are no longer directly pulled by hand but are attached to an *arbor.* This is a heavy metal framework designed to hold chunks of iron known as "counterweights" (or "pigs"). (See Figure 3-14.) These counterbalance the weight of the scenery, leaving the operator only the task of overcoming the friction in the system plus any slight unbalance. The counterweight arbor is pulled up and down by means of a *hauling line* or *operating line* that runs from the top of the arbor up and over the head block and down to the stage floor. This line runs on the extra sheave in the head block. At the floor it passes around still another sheave known as the "idler" and runs upward to the bottom of the

Figure 3-13. (a) Sandbag Counterweight. A pair of sandbags used to counterweight a heavy object hanging from spot lines. Note that the bags have been attached to the lines by means of a clew. (b) A close-up of the clamping devices inside the clew that grip the lines when the tightening screw is operated. These clamps are so arranged that an increase in the strain on the ropes causes the clamps to pull tighter. Clews must usually be installed while the weight of the scenery is being held by riggers. Care must be taken to make sure that they are properly installed and tightened.

FIGURE 3-13b

FIGURE 3-14a

Figure 3-14. Counterweights in an Arbor. (a) Shows a wire-guided counterweight system. This old system depends on two tightly stretched wires, one of which is visible near the center of the picture, to keep the weights from swaying excessively. The arbor consists of a metal bar that passes through the center of the stacked weights and a cross-piece to which the lower operating line is attached. (b) A modern T-track system. The arbor is held firmly in position by the sliding guides which engage the T-track at the back of the arbor. Weights are held in place by the vertical rods that form the arbor's sides. These engage the slots in the ends of the weights. Weights are tilted to add or remove them. The small weights that weigh about 20 pounds are called "wafers." The large weights, about 40 pounds each, are called "pigs."

FIGURE 3-14b

arbor. Thus it and the arbor form an endless loop, allowing the operator to haul the arbor and its attached line set either upward or downward (see Figure 3-15). The operating line is hemp, usually $\frac{3}{4}$ inch or more to allow the operator to get an easy grasp on it. He never need pull on the wire rope itself.

Before the operating line passes around the idler and back upward to the underside of the arbor, it passes through the *locking rail* that serves the same purpose as the pin rail, but without the heavy load (Figure 3-15). It prevents the line sets from moving unexpectedly. This is accomplished by passing the operating line through a friction clamp that can be set or released by means of a lever. When locked, an additional safety device—a metal ring—is slid down over the line and lever handle to prevent the lock from popping open under tension. When the lever is released the line moves freely and the set can be operated. The locking rail clamps are designed to hold only minor unbalances and should under no circumstances be expected to hold against a major imbalance.

Since the locking rail is the operation center of the flying system, it usually is provided with special lighting and with identifying markers to enable the operators to identify each line set quickly. Trim marks will have to be established by taping, or otherwise marking each operating line as it passes through the lock to indicate *high and low trim*, i.e., the position of the operating line when the scenery is stored and when it is in use.

Figure 3-15. Locking Rail, Idler Pulley, and T-Track. This view shows how the operating line passes downward from the arbor (above, out of view), through the idler pulley, and upward through the rope lock. Also note the T-tracks at the rear of idler pulley. These extend all the way to the gridiron and guide the arbor.

If the counterweights were kept on the stage floor (as they are in simple setups) it would be necessary to raise each piece of scenery into the flies the first time by brute force in order to get the arbor down to where it could be loaded with iron—a dangerous operation. The reverse would be necessary when it was desired to remove the scenery, and this is even more dangerous. To avoid this work and hazard, a sturdy metal bridge—the *loading platform*—usually is installed just below the gridiron within reach of the arbors when they are in their up position (see Figure 3-7). Obviously, when the arbors are up, the battens are down, and this is where they will be when being loaded with scenery. After the scenery has been attached to the batten, someone climbs to the loading platform and, after cautioning everyone to stand clear of the area under the loading platform (or *gallery*), loads the arbor until the scenery is balanced. It may then be raised with ease and safety. Unloading follows the reverse procedure.

Some readers may have noticed that there is a flaw in the above description: it assumes that the scenery to be loaded onto the batten has little height and that the batten will be near floor level. This is untrue of much scenery, which may stand perhaps 15–20 feet high while resting on the stage floor. In this case the batten will be well up in the air and the arbor far below the loading platform. The scenery must either be "muscled" into its up position and the arbor loaded from the floor, or a second loading gallery must be available at some convenient distance below the first. A large proscenium theatre may have several such galleries to accommodate various loading situations. A less well-equipped theatre will need more muscle.

It is obvious that tons of pig iron swinging above the backstage area as they move up and down with the scenery would constitute a hazard and threaten to tangle lines. The arbors must be guided in their paths. The simplest way to do this is to stretch iron wires, two to an arbor, between floor and gridiron, and provide sliding rings on the arbors to engage the wires (see Figure 3-14a). This works over relatively modest heights, but still allows too much swing for high gridirons. The proper solution is to borrow from the devices used by the elevator maker, who faces a similar problem when controlling the counterweight for a heavy elevator traveling many stories. The *counterweight guide* track, a T-shaped iron bar, is run from floor to gridiron and a lubricated matching device slides up and down on this track, holding the counterweight securely in its proper path (see Figure 3-14b). These T-track guides usually are fastened to the side wall of the stage house. Such a system will suffice for almost any height of stage house. Some of them range up to 100 feet.

As flexible as the counterweight system is, it still requires manual operation from the stage floor adjacent to the locking rail. Furthermore, overcoming the inertia of exceedingly heavy loads may be more than one person can easily accomplish. Electrical hoists often are used. The commonest system is simply to substitute the hoist for the person pulling on the operating line. The counterweight remains to balance the load, but the operating line becomes a chain driven by an electric motor with proper limit switches and reversing mechanisms. Speed control can be added to these *motorized line sets* at moderate extra cost. The result is a counterweight set that can be operated from any location equipped with the electrical controls. For example, a motorized main curtain can be raised or lowered from the stage manager's desk, the projection room at the back of the house, or from wherever control is necessary. Similar systems usually are provided for movie screens, and for the asbestos curtain, which is always a very heavy device. If there is a lighting bridge, it is often motorized.

Recently the entire concept of the counterweighted line set has been challenged. It is pointed out that this system originally was devised for handling flat scenery positioned parallel to the footlights. This is essentially true; the installation of any set pieces that hang in an upstage-downstage direction will seriously impede if not eliminate the use of those line sets between the ends of the angled piece. This problem has often been alleviated by the use of *spot lines* — rope sets or single lines positioned within such settings and operated without the batten which locks the lines into horizontal patterns.

Modern engineers have asked: Why not eliminate the line sets entirely, using nothing but motorized spot lines which can be electrically linked into sets as needed without the limitations of the battens? This resulted in the development of *synchronous grid winches*. These might be thought of as electrically operated spot lines. They are capable of being electrically interlocked into sets consisting of as many lines as are needed in whatever configuration is desired. The electrical interlock makes all lines operate together, just as the old batten-and-arbor system did, without necessitating a predetermined arrangement of the lines.

The substitution of an electric motor for human hands on the operating line has led to some difficulties. Where a human being can be expected to recognize unusual conditions (such as more than usual strain or an unusual noise) and stop hauling, an electrical motor will continue to operate. Thus fail-safe systems are needed. These are sensing devices which gather information about the location of parts of the system and about unusual stresses, and relay this to the motor in a form that will cause it to stop or reverse before harm can be done. Without such systems it would be very easy for a motor to hoist a set up against the grid and continue pulling, breaking the fastenings and dropping the set to the stage floor. Several varieties of grid winch systems are now on the market.

EQUIPMENT LOCATED IN THE FLIES Whatever the suspension system,

Figure 3-16. "Border Light." The typical arrangement of lighting equipment found in many American theatres. The heavy, permanently mounted borderlights for the principal light source, spotlights, may also be mounted on the same pipe. Photograph courtesy University of California, Los Angeles.

there are a number of theatre parts that will be standard in any fly loft.

1. The asbestos safety curtain has already been discussed. It is the first line set counting upstage from the proscenium arch because it must run in the smoke slots that seal it to the proscenium opening. Very modern theatres built according to the latest New York City building code may not have an asbestos curtain. Instead there will be a special "deluge system" that is designed to douse any fire.

2. The teaser or a combination teaser/valance that is movable.

3. The main curtain is usually just upstage of the teaser although some theatres may have a movie screen hanging just downstage of the main curtain ("the main") to allow the showing of movies while a set is on stage. If such a screen exists, it will usually be equipped with its own draperies to mask it top, bottom, and sides. If the movie sheet (another term for screen) is not located down of the main, it will be somewhere in the downstage portion of the flies.

4. The light bridge or first electric (batten). An older term is "first borderlight," or "border." This is the first set of hanging lighting apparatus. In its most elaborate form it consists of a bridge, moved by a heavy winch that can support tons of lighting instruments and operators if necessary. In some European theatres the bridge is actually an inverted U-framework surrounding the top and sides of the proscenium opening and carrying tons of equipment and personnel. It has even been made to roll upstage on a craneway to allow alterations in the size of the proscenium opening (in the Frankfurt Opera House). In older, simpler stages the first electric is simply a heavy-duty line set equipped with a pipe batten and a set of electrical circuits fed from above via flexible cable. In many old theatres or those equipped mainly for concerts and the like, the term, "first borderlight," still applies. In these cases the unit is a row of lighting fixtures as in Figure 3-16. Usually additional space for lighting equipment is provided above this borderlight strip. In any case, the first electric is an exceedingly heavy line set and, for this reason, frequently is motorized.

5. Tormentors (if they are not hung downstage of the electric) are mounted on the ends of a regular batten, or if necessary, an extra long one.

6. Drapery settings are used if the stage is a multipurpose one where concerts, lectures, and other auditorium functions take place. A drapery set provides a tasteful background with minimum effort on the part of the stage staff. For theatrical purposes a drapery set will provide a neutral "limbo" background when this is needed and aid in masking. ("Masking" consists of preventing the audience from seeing what it should not see.) The ideal fabric for such draperies is cotton velour, a velvetlike material which, although fairly expensive, is durable, easily flameproofed, and has good acoustic properties.

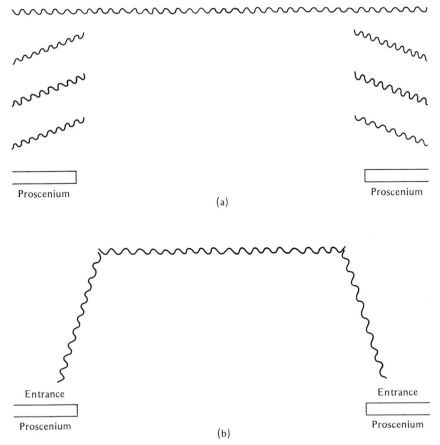

Proscenium

Proscenium

(a)

Entrance

Entrance

Proscenium

Proscenium

(b)

Figure 3-17. Drapery Setting. (a) The typical arrangement of draperies hung in wing and drop style to dress a stage for general use. Such an arrangement commonly is found on stages used for a variety of functions such as concerts, meetings, dance recitals, etc. (b) Another arrangement of draperies for general-purpose settings. This provides fewer entrances but offers a more continuous surface of drapery. Neither of these drapery settings provides much in the way of acoustic advantage to performers, but they do offer a neutral background appropriate for a variety of occasions. Parts of these same drapery settings are often useful as masking for stage settings made up of scenic elements.

Drapery settings consist of enough pieces to completely enclose the playing space and to mask off the lighting equipment and other apparatus overhead. They may take the form of wing-and-drop arrangements, or form an enclosure around the acting space. This latter arrangement is sometimes mistakenly called a "cyclorama." In either case the material is hung in "fullness." This means it is arranged in heavy folds using about twice the cloth that would be needed if it were stretched flat. The result is a rich, deep surface. See Figure 3-17 for simple floor plans of the two common arrangements. Unfortunately for theatrical use, which requires black, concert and lecture applications usually require the drapery to be some light-but-neutral color such as pearl grey or buff. This can lead to doubling the already considerable demands that a drapery setting makes on the flying system, or to frequent sessions during which the draperies are rehung for either concert or for theatrical use.

The average drapery setting will consist of two or three sets of *legs*,[2] usually hung from the ends of batten sets, but sometimes hung on special lines. There will be as many cloth masking borders as pairs of legs. These borders will hang from line sets. There will also be at least one *close-in curtain*. This is a curtain the full width and height of the stage opening or more, whose purpose is to mask the upstage area. It often is fitted as a *traveler*.[3] Obviously this takes a line set. Thus seven to nine line sets may be almost permanently assigned to a drapery setting, a large share of many theatres' resources.

7. Additional electric pipes or borderlights may be used. Originally there was one borderlight for every 5–6 feet of distance from the proscenium. This may still be the case if the theatre is "fully equipped" with borderlights. Actually this is needlessly extravagant and wasteful of space in most theatres today. "Electrics" are more apt to be found at about 10 foot intervals and consist only of circuitry and hanging facilities for spotlights until you reach the proper position for lighting the cyclorama. Here a more specialized setup will be found and it will usually result in another very heavy pipe. Of course, any batten can be converted to lighting use by running in temporary electric lines and installing equipment.

8. The cyclorama is a special curtain devised to give the illusion of open sky or horizonless staging.[4] It is made of muslin or canvas, preferably seamless. It hangs in a U-shape around the acting space totally enclosing it except near the tormentors. This special line set is provided with loft blocks at strategic points over the U-shaped pipe and special pulleys to guide the lines to the head block. This technique of changing the direction of lines running over the grid is known as "muling" and results in extra friction. The cyclorama set will usually be harder to operate than most of the other lines.

The remainder of the lines are left open for various uses as each show is installed or removed. Line sets are numbered from downstage to upstage, counting *all* lines in most theatres. Thus a theatre may have sixty lines, although only forty-five of them are available to any given show.

9. It may be both wasteful and undesirable to use an entire line set to support such a thing as a chandelier in the middle of a setting. For this purpose *spot lines* are rigged. These consist of hemp (rope) lines run

---

2. A leg is a narrow curtain hung at the sides of the stage to mask off the wings.
3. A traveler is a heavy track that carries the supports for the curtain, and allows it to be hauled horizontally to open or close the space it hides.
4. A cyclorama is the ideal way to satisfy this frequent need. Theatres without cycloramas usually try to achieve the same results by using simple flat drops of muslin or even smoothly finished, carefully painted back stage walls. The word "cyclorama" should be interpreted to include such make-do substitutes throughout this text.

over the grid into special loft and head blocks installed for this purpose. These blocks are quite easily movable and are set for each use. The working (offstage) end of the spot line is fastened to a pin rail if one is available. If not, or if floor operation is more convenient, it is often equipped with a sandbag and operated from near the locking rail.

This completes our discussion of the machinery and theatre equipment hanging above the stage floor. The operation of this equipment is the province of the rigger. The reader is referred to the discussion of the duties of the rigger in Chapter 15 for details concerning the operation of the flies.

The reader may have noted that the entire concept of flying depends on the stage house (the building that encloses the flies) being large enough and high enough to allow scenery to be lifted completely out of sight of the audience for storage. If such height is not provided, the theatre is crippled and cannot be called a complete proscenium theatre. Generally two and one-half to three times the working height of the proscenium is necessary.

It should also be evident that the system of lifting things out of sight above the stage is not dependent on the presence of a proscenium; the system is applicable to other theatre forms such as thrust stages and theatres in the round.

Equipment Beneath the Floor

The space below the stage floor of a proscenium theatre is also a potential scenery-handling area. At the very least, the floor should be equipped with traps, and it should be possible to arrange entrances and exits through these. The addition of elevators (lifts) converts the entire region under the floor into a major scenery-handling system. This system can easily equal the flies in capability and has the particular facility of handling bulky, three-dimensional elements with ease. While the stage at the Metropolitan Opera in New York City was very expensive to construct, and therefore not typical of American proscenium theatres, it does illustrate the tremendous flexibility of the fully developed elevator system. We should examine this carefully because of the possibilities such systems offer to more experimental theatrical forms.

The Metropolitan's stage is equipped with elevators from the curtain line to the back of the normal acting area. In addition, there is a very short travel-equalizing elevator on the apron that makes it possible to raise the entire stage floor about 1 foot to accommodate full stage wagons without the otherwise inevitable step up at the curtain line. The orchestra pit also is equipped with elevators.

The flexibility of the Metropolitan's stage is enhanced further by the fact that two of the stage elevators are double-deck units. For example, the top level might carry the set for Scenes I and III, while the lower level carries Scene II. After Scene II, while Scene III is playing, Scene IV can be set on the lower level. When combined with the great flexibility of the plant, this offers a wide variety of speedy scene changes.

Such lift systems are not cheap. The Metropolitan's system cost upward of $2 million. They also require considerable maintenance and can, if not carefully engineered and operated, constitute a great safety hazard. After all, huge amounts of energy are needed to move such heavy equipment. Also it is possible to create a hole in the stage floor that is several stories deep—no place for careless wanderers.

COMBINATIONS OF LIFTS AND REVOLVES   It is quite feasible to combine the shifting capabilities of the revolve with those of the lift. It has been done in many European installations with success. The revolve becomes a steel structure several stories high that runs on circular tracks, much like railroad tracks deep in the subbasement. Drive systems resemble those used to drive heavy cranes along their tracks at a factory. The entire revolving assembly carries the lifts, machinery and all, within it. The result is an extremely flexible theatre.

TERMS   The under stage space is known as the "trap room," if the stage is trapped, and the "lift space," if lifts are installed. It is important to know that the fire department will enforce rather rigid rules about what may or may not be stored in these areas. They are, after all, directly under the playing space and may very likely be opened into it. The use of such space for storage (especially in theatres with limited access to this area, which are likely to treat it mainly as a storeroom) should be cleared with the fire inspector.

Other Work Areas

A fully equipped proscenium theatre may or may not have shops for the construction of all of the various settings, props, electrical devices, etc., that are used in it. In many city locations real estate is too expensive to justify the installation of such shops on the premises. However, they must be located somewhere. Since this book is written with the educational theatre in mind, and since the student is expected to be familiar with these shops and to work in them, we will list them without regard for their proximity to the stage itself. Student crews will quickly sense the difference between having the shops adjacent to the stage and having them elsewhere. The amount of hauling about, and motion wasted running back and forth to remote shops, will add hours to their working days.

The following shop areas are essential to the operation of a fully equipped proscenium theatre:

1. Scene shop. This is where much of your time will be spent. It will be detailed in Part Four, "Scenery."

2. Paint shop. Although this is frequently a portion of the scene shop set aside for painting scenery, a large well-equipped theatre will have a separate paint shop. It will provide adequate space and light for painting scenery, and will have facilities for mixing paint and the necessary tools for the scene painter. A paint shop is discussed in detail in Chapter 21, "Scene Painting."

3. Property shop. In many theatres this is simply a corner of the scene shop. However, new plastics techniques and the necessity for special ventilation have separated the property shop more and more from the scene shop. This will also be studied in detail in Part Five, "Properties."

4. Metal shop. This often is combined with the lighting and special effects department because these areas have much need for metal-working equipment. If the theatre follows conventional all-wood construction practices, scenery and property construction crews will have only occasional use for the metal shop. If the theatre is using welded steel or other metal materials for its three-dimensional scenery, the metal shop will be the source of most of this work. Such a metal shop is discussed in Chapter 12, "Weight-Bearing Three-Dimensional Scenery."

5. Costume shop. Costuming is beyond the scope of this text. The costume shop is an area equipped with sewing machines, cutting tables, dye vats, laundry facilities, etc., for preparing and decorating stage costumes. Those working on scenery and properties will occasionally have need to use costume shop facilities for such things as seaming fabric for large drops, mending draperies, and so on.

6. Electric shop. This is a function of lighting, and will be discussed in Part Seven of this text.

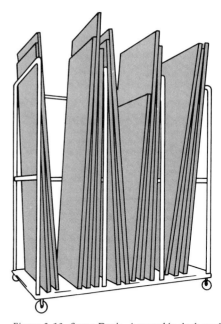

Figure 3-18. Scene Dock. A movable dock made up by building a framework of heavy pipes on a rolling platform. Note the frames that separate the storage area into narrow sections to prevent too many flats from leaning against each other, and to facilitate the removal of flats without moving the entire contents of the dock.

Storage Areas

No theatre, proscenium or otherwise, ever has enough storage areas. You will be mainly concerned with those storage areas for scenery, props, and lights. The *scene dock* is a special rack for the storage of flats. It consists of a series of metal or heavy wooden supports arranged so that the flats can be stored standing up, and so that they will not form impossibly heavy piles (see Figure 3-18). It should be possible to "leaf through" the flats much as one might go through books on a shelf. All projections that might puncture or tear the fabric of adjacent flats must be removed before storage.

Storage will usually be by categories such as height, width, openings, age, and the like. There will often be a *flat file*, a card file with a 3 by 5 inch card for each flat. The card should bear a sketch of the flat, its dimensions, notes as to its condition, and any other data that will aid in identifying it. If the flat is altered, the card should be changed accordingly. As flats are placed in a show, it is common to pull their cards from the file and hold them out until the flats are returned to the dock. Thus the file should represent a running inventory of available flats for upcoming productions.

The *prop room* serves as storage for furniture, assorted hand props, and almost anything else that the minds of designers and directors can devise. It is frequently also the repository for three-dimensional scenic units such as platforms, rock walls, trees, step units, etc. These items are bulky and hard to store, but represent a sizable investment in materials and time and often are stored for possible future use. They may also serve the needs of rehearsals and class projects.

Like the scene dock, the prop room should be equipped with a catalogue. Some theatre organizations go as far as to photograph each property (a Polaroid camera is fine for this) and fasten the photo onto the reference card. In any event, the prop should be well identified and evaluated as to its probable use. A dollar value may also be established, if this will aid the business end of the theatre. (Props often are rented out.) The operation of the prop room and its inventory is frequently one person's full-time job. This person is the one to seek out if you are requested to get a list of props out of the prop room. He will know where things are and will aid you in properly checking out the props and charging them to the right show. Returning props should follow the same procedure. If there is no prop room attendant, you must follow whatever arrangements have been made to keep the props in a secure, orderly way. A chaotic pile of junk is not a prop room; it is only a fire hazard.

The *light room* is the storage place for lighting equipment not stored on lighting battens. It may also contain a small electric shop for the repair of lighting equipment. It is discussed in Part Seven, "Lighting."

4
NEW THEATRICAL FORMS

INTRODUCTION The proscenium theatre, now several hundred years old, reached its peak during the late nineteenth and early twentieth centuries in the great ring theatres of Europe with their tiered balconies and grand decor. Today more democratic and stage-oriented thrust balconies are the norm in such theatres as the Kennedy Center and the Dorothy Chandler Pavilion, as well as many European theatres. They all have a proscenium, but they do not hold to the aesthetic of the fourth wall. The apron, no longer limited to occasional announcements, is a valuable playing space, often provided with extensive elaborations.

But this new flexibility has not satisfied those who reject the basic aesthetic of the proscenium. All variations of the proscenium theatre have one thing in common—the clear separation of play and audience. The proscenium itself is an architectural expression of this idea. Using the apron as playing space does not close that gap very much. Now there has arisen a more fundamental challenge to the basics of the traditional theatrical aesthetic. In order to understand its significance and implications we must review some fundamental aesthetics.

PURPOSEFUL THEATRICAL EXPERIENCE

The aesthetic of modern theatre implies purposeful creative activity. The virtual destiny of successful theatrical art is intended by its creators to affect every human being caught up in it. The artists express human feeling to evoke human responses from their audience. Perhaps one can say that *art, including theatrical art, results in the broadening of human experience, an increase in sensitivity, and greater awareness of human nature.*

The roots of the modern challenge to traditional theatre may be found in two questions:

1. How far may the purposeful nature of theatrical art be carried? That is, how far can and should the theatre go in the direction of having an *immediate* effect on human behavior? The answer that many modern experimenters give to this question is, "Very far indeed!" "Purposefulness" may even be extended beyond the normal boundaries of art to include the rhetorical purposes of the propagandist or the sense-indulgent purposes of those who seek "total experiences."

2. How can this best be accomplished? When such experimenters consider this question they soon come to the conclusion that the proscenium aesthetic is far too mild an artistic "tool" to get the results they seek. Moreover, much of its freshness has worn off, and the aura of the "new" or the "experimental" can be generated better with new staging forms.

The sharpest break with the aesthetic of the proscenium theatre comes whenever the psychological separation of play and audience, sometimes referred to as "aesthetic distance," is challenged. In a proscenium theatre, audience members normally find themselves psychologically more outside than inside the dramatic action of the play. However, the duality of being emotionally involved with the virtual destiny being played out on the stage and the awareness that it is indeed *virtual* is an essential part of all theatrical experience. But what if the members of the audience are physically surrounded by and engulfed in the action of the play? What if the actors physically touch them and treat them as part of the dramatic environment? What if they are not only invited into, but physically compelled to participate in the virtual action of the play?

Many will question whether such audience experiences are within the realm of theatre at all; others will insist that such experiences are in fact the *only* realm of the theatre, and that all of the past pales by comparison. Still others will wonder whether audience members who find themselves propelled into the action of a play can, in fact, still maintain a certain distance from this experience. Can they still treat it as a *virtual* experience, knowing that it has been contrived for their perception, that it is not a part of life itself? If it is possible for aesthetic distance to exist under these conditions, would not then such aesthetic experience far exceed the intensity possible in a proscenium theatre? Can this intense aesthetic experience have an even greater ultimate social effect?

While generalized answers to these questions may be impossible, judgments can be made concerning individual experiments that challenge conventional audience-play relationships. This is what is being done within many experimental theatre groups in the United States and Europe. Audiences and critics must make these individual judgments as productions appear. Experimenters must evaluate the results as they see them and continue experimentation.

THEATRE WITHOUT PLAYSCRIPT

Some theatre groups use no authored script at all. Instead they improvise lines along with action as they develop a theatre piece before an audience. This makes them original, not interpretive artists. Two justifications may be offered for eliminating the script: First, these groups feel that this gives them nearly total control over their material. If "control" means responsibility for all parts of the art work, this cannot be denied. Secondly, such groups feel that improvisation provides the ultimate artistic freshness—they present the material at the very moment of its creation. There is never the sense of "going through the motions" that sometimes pervades other productions.

Although such groups spend endless hours working to achieve intergroup communications and developing a general format for a production, each presentation will differ depending on actor inspiration and interaction with the audience.

Unfortunately the control and freshness felt by the performers are not always communicated to the audience. The inward concentration required by the improvisation may obscure communication. Moreover the style of language developed under this system seldom reaches great heights of expressiveness. In spite of these and other difficulties, such groups have produced more than enough intensely moving theatre to justify serious consideration.

AUDIENCE-ACTOR INTERMIXING

Another area of experimentation, often combined with script variations, challenges the traditional distinction between audience members and actors. Instead of *witnessing* a theatrical event, audiences are invited *to participate in* such an event. While, however, "actors" and "audience" are then participants, the actors are a constant from performance to performance and control the structure of the event. Audience members are transient; they participate in only a single version of the event. A "happening" is a structured experience of this sort. An event is staged, i.e., caused to happen, by the "actors" and an audience is invited to participate in it. The distinction between such an event and life itself is that all concerned are aware that it has been contrived—it has been *made to happen* because the producing group feels there is merit in participating in it. Note the key word, "participation"; merely being there is not enough.

Many argue that "participation" need not be defined as extremely as some groups have done. They maintain that such groups have lost sight of the essentially dual nature of an aesthetic experience. Nevertheless this intermixing has produced intense theatrical experiences.

The role of the scenographer in such theatre is central because much of the event is visual. It involves careful manipulation of space and time—the province of the scenographer. In fact, his role is expanded by such an approach because the design now embraces the total environment of the event. What bothers these experimenters about the proscenium theatre is its ready-made generalized environment with built-in separation of audience and play—the very thing these workers are trying to break down. Scenography in experimental theatre, however, envelopes the entire space that contains the event, thus becoming a major challenge to the sensitive scenographic artist.

THEATRICAL TERMINOLOGY FOR NEW FORMS

As we have seen, technical theatrical terminology evolved out of the architecture of the proscenium theatre and the seagoing riggers who first brought their trade to the theatre. Almost all presently available theatrical machinery was invented for the proscenium theatre and named accordingly. These names were transferred to other forms of theatre wherever they were workable. Thus one finds rigging, line sets, and even a "fly gallery" in a theatre without a proscenium. Seats on the main floor of a thrust stage theatre near the stage may be ticketed "orchestra" although there is no balcony above and behind them. Similarly, seats farther away and higher on the steeply raked floor may be labeled "balcony." A "borderlight" may be found in a theatre that has not the slightest hint of any borders.

But there are cases where proscenium terminology simply will not work. Where is "stage left" or "stage right" in a theatre-in-the-round? Is "up left center" an adequate designation? Arbitrary area numbers, compass points, or "clock" points (go from 8 o'clock to 1 o'clock) may be used. The problem is even greater in houses in which the entire structure is used for either audience or players as the needs of the production dictate. Map grid systems such as, "move from A-3 to D-10," may be the only possibility.

THEATRE ARCHITECTURE AND THE INNOVATIVE THEATRE

Practically every architectural form of theatre that can be thought of has been tried at one time or another in the long history of our art. Various aesthetics have been derived from those forms, or shaped them, in the particular society of the period. Our "new" theatres evolve out of our times and our world and have their own aesthetic.

We will discuss innovative theatre in three broad catagories: thrust stage theatre, theatre-in-the-round, and theatre rooms. This is only a matter of convenience; every permutation and combination of form that modern theatre workers can think of probably can be found operating somewhere. The categories are merely to help to place these theatres into some manageable arrangement.

BREAKING THE FOURTH WALL

You will recall that in the traditional proscenium theatre the curtain line was an invisible "fourth wall" of the room represented realistically on the stage. Actors observed this tradition by remaining inside the curtain line and treating it somewhat as though it were opaque. Even in the days of utmost realism, this did not preclude such theatrical devices as increasing voice level above that which would have been required had the wall been real and the audience not present, or blocking the movements of the actors so that the audience could more clearly understand what was happening. Thus the fourth wall was always a stylized theatrical convention—more of a metaphorical representation of a theatrical style than a strict rule.

It did have important architectural and technical implications. Fourth-wall theatres were built with little or no apron and few facilities for lighting it unless it was planned that the theatre might occasionally serve as a public auditorium and that speakers might work from the small apron. In that case, a few front-of-house (FOH) lights were provided for the apron. The rest of the FOH lighting instruments, if any, lit the area just upstage of the curtain line. Acoustic arrangements in a fourth-wall theatre assumed that all action would take place upstage of the curtain line. The only sound of significance that originated in front of the curtain would be from an orchestra in the pit.

In the 1930s a "revolutionary" event took place. The production of Thornton Wilder's *Our Town* required that the actor playing the "stage manager" repeatedly step "through the fourth wall" and address the audience directly. Other characters were also asked to do this on occasion. This was no mere revival of the nineteenth-century tradition of the aside; it was the beginning of the end of the tradition of the fourth wall. From this beginning, the aesthetic rapidly developed and theatre architecture followed suit. Aprons of playable size appeared in new theatres and old theatres were renovated to provide playing space where there once had been either seating or an orchestra pit. New lighting positions were devised and new acoustical considerations were introduced into the design of theatres. The evolution of this idea has taken two forms. One is the now almost standard construction of a usable apron in front of proscenium stages. The other is the thrust stage.

The addition of a workable apron to a proscenium theatre does not present many architectural problems in a new building, but it may be difficult in an old one. If funds are available, the installation of an orchestra pit elevator or elevators (Figure 3-4) may make possible the production-to-production alteration from pure proscenium theatre to thrust stage proscenium theatre. Given enough money and machinery, even more diverse changes can be wrought.

As far as the scenographer and technician are concerned, the working apron offers few handicaps and many advantages if the theatre has been equipped with these playing areas in mind. More lighting positions in the house are necessary and, ideally, the forestage (apron) should be provided with shifting facilities. Since working forestages are almost standard format in newly built proscenium theatres today, they need no further discussion here.

Thrust Stage Theatre

The thrust stage theatre (Figure 4-1) is one logical development of the idea of breaking the fourth wall. In this theatre the apron has become the entire playing area—the proscenium no longer exists. Thrusting the apron into the area once occupied by the audience leads to wrapping the audience around three sides of that apron. This creates a fan-shaped house that has the advantage of seating a large number of spectators relatively close to the acting area. Although members of an audience will have widely divergent views of the stage, all will have a sense of intimacy because of their short distance to the stage. This intimate feeling is believed essential by those seeking an aesthetic impact greater than that offered by the proscenium theatre.

There are also economies in building a thrust stage theatre when cost is computed on a per-seat basis. The removal of the stage house makes it possible to eliminate the fly loft which is an expensive feature of a proscenium stage. Recent experience indicates that this may be an economy that disregards aesthetics, but it does result in less expensive construction.

Production costs may also be reduced on a thrust stage because less scenery tends to be used. Without a fly loft and often without large side stages or upstage working areas, single sets or simple unit sets tend to be standard.

AESTHETIC OF THE THRUST STAGE THEATRE   The thrust stage theatre imposes its aesthetic on a production just as surely as does the proscenium theatre. The closeness of the audience combined with the wide disparity in sight lines (Figure 4-1) affect acting and directing styles and the work of the scenographer. Actors and directors must be especially

aware that the audience is spread over a wide angle and no part of that audience may be slighted. If the actors play toward the front, as is their habit in proscenium theatres, those audience members on the sides of the house will be constantly subjected to profile views of the action. Whenever an actor plays to one side, the opposite side is getting a view of his back. Blocking thus is complicated by mechanical factors that may tend to take precedence over the needs of the drama. In spite of the fact that most members of the audience will be within less than 70–80 feet of the stage, acoustical problems may plague the actors and director.

The thrust stage, as it is usually designed, is not apt to be very popular with scenographers and technicians. The removal of the proscenium arch generally has been treated as an excuse to economize. Shifting facilities and backstage work space tend to be reduced to unworkable minimums. This is not an inherent characteristic of the thrust stage format, but it seems to be the natural consequence of designing an "intimate" theatre. Apparently "intimacy" translates into "economy" all too readily.

Actually the aesthetic imposed by the divergent sight lines and the increased sense of the presence of the audience multiply the scenographer's problems. Furthermore, the loss of facilities for changing and storing settings has the effect of reducing the scope of theatrical illusion to what can easily become stultifying monotony. All settings tend to be architectural units, built into place for the production and remaining unchanged except for lighting and decorations, no matter what the locale of each act may be.

Theatrical illusion is often associated with the proscenium stage because it separates the audience from the play. However, the proscenium theatre does not have sole rights to illusion; witness, for example, an ice show.

Given the space and the equipment, the thrust stage can generate its own elaborate aesthetic including varieties of theatrical illusion and theatrical spectacle that combine intimate audience relationships with richness. The sparse, aesthetically limited approach that many poorly designed and equipped thrust stage theatres offer to the scenographer need not be the rule. The 180-degree sight lines that seem to be such a limiting factor when combined with lack of working space, can actually be an aesthetic challenge. Lighting too appears at first to be limited by the wide sight lines. This is especially true if lighting is responsible for almost all visual change because the scenery is a single, rigid architectural setting. But, given the chance to move scenery about, to fly items in, and to shift sets into offstage working areas, effective lighting can begin to evolve.

Up to the present the thrust stage theatre has seldom been given a chance to develop its aesthetic. It has been tied to the need for economy instead. Yet the thrust stage theatre is inherently capable of more theatricality, of involving its audience intimately, and of spatial expressions unique to itself.

Theatre-in-the-Round (Arena Theatre)

One of the more discernible early, experimental forms in the United States, which arose in the 1930s, is theatre-in-the-round. The format is simple (see Figure 4-2). A stage is placed in the center of a room and seating is arranged all around it, thus bringing a maximum number of people to within a minimum distance from the stage. Only recently, however, has this format been applied to create large-capacity houses. Early forms were all devised to exploit its intimate, very theatrical quality, many seating less than 100 people. In this size, audiences find themselves so close to the actors that they feel the intensity of the virtual situation strongly. At the same time they are acutely aware of the

Figure 4-2. Theatre-in-the-Round (Arena Theatre). A typical arena arrangement of seating and playing space. Note how audience members are always placed so that they look across the playing area at other audience members. Space is more than usually generous in this particular theatre-in-the-round because it is only one of several audience-playing space configurations possible. Many small arena theatres make do with much less space. Theatre at California State University, Long Beach; Frank Homolka & Associates, Architects. Photograph by Larry Frost. Photograph courtesy California State University, Long Beach.

theatricality or virtuality of the situation because they constantly have within their field of view other members of the audience seated around the playing area. Entrance aisles and even the aisle space surrounding the house may be used as acting space, thereby surrounding the audience with action. Nevertheless theatre-in-the-round makes a strong distinction between actor space and audience space, although both of these spaces are enclosed in a total "theatre space." Its essence is that the audience surrounds the players. For this reason, such theatres also are called "arena theatres."

PROBLEMS OF THEATRE-IN-THE-ROUND   It is obvious that theatre-in-the-round presents the problems of the thrust stage in radical form. Since the audience surrounds the playing area, there is no horizontal direction in which to shift scenery or properties. Unless an elevator takes the entire space vertically to a level where sets can be changed (a very expensive arrangement), the only way to make changes is to haul everything down the aisles by hand. This problem is somewhat alleviated by the second difficulty with this form; sight lines. The audience views the stage from nearly every angle. Only the aisles are unoccupied. Therefore scenery and properties must be low and/or transparent so that all may see the action. Directors must arrange the blocking so that each segment of the audience gets its fair share of the action.

Since there can be no vertical surfaces of any consequence in the acting area, illusion, as we know it in the proscenium theatre, is nearly impossible. Some attempts have been made to treat the entire room as a "setting," decorating the perimeter walls or casting projections on them. This has limited value because these walls are removed from most of the action. Actors will only occasionally use the outer aisles because a part of the audience must turn completely around in their seats to see them there. Most audiences will not do this for long; they merely listen. Lighting also is complicated by the audience's encirclement of the playing area. One man's side light becomes another's back light and still another's front light, with the added risk that someone will see only the glare from the instrument itself.

THEATRE-IN-THE-ROUND AESTHETIC Those who work successfully in theatres-in-the-round manage to turn the handicaps mentioned above into virtues. Given the proper script, this is quite possible. If the script depends upon close audience-actor contact and needs little in the way of theatrical illusion, it may work very well. As long as multiple settings can be represented by fragmentary bits of scenery and a few properties that can be brought in and out of the aisles rapidly, multiple scene shows work well. Since houses tend to be small, the vocal demands on actors are minimal and they can concentrate on subtle characterization. The nearness of the audience renders extreme subtlety and naturalism in acting possible. In this regard, acting for the theatre-in-the-round is somewhat like cinema or television acting; it is a close-up art.

The scenographer must have much the same attitude as the actor; a few details meticulously worked out must replace large scenic effects. Interesting experiments with "total environments" using scenery at the perimeters of the theatre can be made, but relating these to the actors may become difficult.

Lighting presents special problems that the scenographer must consider from the beginning of the production's conceptualization. Perhaps the greatest advantage is the nearness of the audience. Tiny subtleties almost never visible in a proscenium theatre may be counted on to "read." Since the actors will be within a few feet of much of the audience, the usual concerns for plasticity are minimized. The audience can see three-dimensional forms at these distances with almost completely flat lighting. This leaves the way open for working with light and shade as an expressive device but with the considerable restriction that high vertical lighting angles will be the only ones seen as somewhat the same by the entire audience. Usual side lighting and 45-degree key lighting will not be seen consistently from all angles.

In summary, the aesthetic of theatre-in-the-round might be described as cameolike. It is a form suited to detail in both acting and scenography. It provides the intimacy of a cameralike view of the production with the clear theatricality of a situation where the audience cannot quite forget that it is in a theatre because it is always looking at itself.

ECONOMICS AND TALENT   The simplicity of its architecture and the minimal need for scenic devices make theatre-in-the-round an ideal form for theatres with small budgets. Since it also places minimum demands on the vocal apparatus of actors and upon their ability to project characterization over a great distance, this format is much loved by small amateur groups of limited funds and experience. Some groups that have started on such "shoestring operations" have grown in artistic stature to become major theatrical influences in their areas.

LARGE THEATRES-IN-THE-ROUND   In recent years a number of large theatres-in-the-round were constructed in dome-shaped structures adapted for the production of musical theatre. The idea seemed to have considerable merit. A large audience could be seated within remarkably little distance of the playing area and production costs could remain relatively low because of the minimal demands for large expensive settings. A repertoire of musical theatre was presented (for example, such productions as *Oklahoma!, South Pacific,* and *The Music Man*). Early results were good; audiences flocked to the productions to sample the "new" style and benefit from the reduced prices made possible by the economical productions. The production companies flourished. Then the limited aesthetic of the form began to take its toll. Audiences soon discovered that each production had an uncomfortable resemblance to the previous one because it was nearly the same visually. They missed the splendor of the illusions possible in the proscenium theatre. They also became more than ever aware of the artificiality of the heavily amplified sound that had to be used in most of these theatres because of the acoustically unfavorable characteristics of the domed ceiling. Finally, producers soon ran out of scripts that they could force into this limited format. The result has been the decline of these theatres; many of them are now serving other purposes such as boxing arenas or churches.

The point of this rather sad discussion is that the theatre-in-the-round format seems to have built-in limitations that are serious even for an intimate theatre, but almost overwhelming when the structure is magnified to accommodate large audiences. Because little theatres, such as community and educational theatres, seldom try to make a profit, they have been able to experiment with the theatre-in-the-round form to aesthetic advantage. Commercial enterprises have had poor luck trying to make money with the format.

Theatre Rooms

This form of theatre has been given a variety of names such as "black box theatres," "multiform theatres," "flexible theatres," etc. No matter what the name, the form is simply a space dedicated to the production of plays. Permanent architectural features are purposely kept simple and/or flexible in order to impose a minimum of architectural preconditions on each individual production. In general, there are two ways of doing this: (1) The room may be almost empty of theatrical accoutrements, these being built in as needed for each production and removed and rebuilt for the next. (2) The room may be provided with an extremely flexible floor arrangement which can be rapidly rearranged for each production or even during a production. Such a room should also have a flexible grid.

Remember that theatre rooms are intended to hold *both* audience and play, and the arrangement of these two key elements is subject to constant change. No permanent seating is provided, no designated "stage area" exists, and no "backstage" area is predetermined. In the design of a theatre room, flexibility is the foremost consideration.

Probably the only consistently desired architectural element for theatre rooms is some type of overhead gridwork strong enough to be walked upon and from which a variety of lighting equipment, scenic elements, and even actors may be suspended to meet the needs of the productions. Other than such a gridiron, the requirements of theatre rooms are mainly adequate space (there is almost never enough), a very strong floor to take heavy construction, large loading doors, and front-of-house facilities for the audience.

FLEXIBLE FLOORS   A more heavily mechanized and architectural approach to the theatre room idea is the modular floor theatre (see Figure 4-3). These theatres strive to maintain the complete flexibility of a theatre room while eliminating some of the need for expensive and time-consuming construction for each show. They also strive toward the idea of a theatre which is flexible from moment to moment to fit the needs of the production. However such a goal has seldom been reached because of safety considerations and cost.

FIGURE 4-3b

FIGURE 4-3a

Figure 4-3. Flexible Floor Theatre Space. The photographs show the flexible theatre at California Institute of the Arts near Los Angeles. (a) Shows details of some of the individual lift units. These lifts are individually operated to arrange the floor design and then locked into place with steel pins run through holes in the supporting columns, Photograph by Tom Bronsterman. Photograph courtesy California Institute of the Arts. (b) A production in the above theatre. This catches some of the spatial variety available in this theatre. The production is The Incredible Rocky, which was created and directed by Denny Stevens and Steve Friedman. Lighting: Gary Mintz. Setting: John Kallapos. Photograph courtesy Gary Mintz.

The reasoning for this type of theatre is simple but costly: If the floor of the room can be divided into a sufficiently flexible set of modular lifts, its "topography" may be altered at will by operating the lifts. The platforms, steps, and ramps thus created can carry either players or audience, and ideally should be amenable to change while the production is in progress. It would indeed be a powerful stroke of theatricality if the topography of both the setting and the house could change to meet the aesthetic needs of the moment.

Practicality militates against such pie-in-the-sky aesthetics. Any reasonably possible modular form will impose its lines on the design to the dissatisfaction of the scenographer. Note that the theatre in Figure 4-3 follows a square or rectangular module. Angles or curves that cut across modules become harder to execute and require expensive construction—one of the things the modular approach intended to avoid. If the lifts are to work while people are on them, they must meet rigid safety standards. Hydraulic lifts or screw jacks, the two most common means of moving such heavy objects, are powerful devices. They can mash or mangle anything that obstructs their movement. Also equipping each of 50 to 100 or more lifts with its own hydraulic system is exceedingly expensive. The theatre illustrated was not able to raise the necessary money to meet the safety requirements. Therefore it may be altered only between performances by means of movable jacks that lift or lower modules which are then locked into place for the duration of the run.

Audience access to theatre room areas, especially those equipped with lifts, is complicated; the path the audience must take to their seats will vary widely from show to show. The ring lobby represents one approach, but at the expense of providing staircases to nowhere whenever the lifts at those points are at their low setting. These must have safety rails and be carefully guarded.

Overhead arrangements are also difficult. If the gridiron is high enough to change scenery and properties, it may be too high for lighting. The open gridwork directly over the audience makes difficult the masking of sounds from power winches and similar machinery.

The totally rebuilt theatre room that is stripped to the bare walls before each performance is mounted, is by far the most flexible. No modules or prearrangements beyond those set by the main structure of the building stand in the way of the scenographer. But this too has its disadvantages. Complete rebuilding is costly, particularly when modern fire laws determine every choice of material. Shifting is also difficult. Theatre machinery does not adapt well to continuous rebuilding and expense may be enormous. The result is that most settings in theatre rooms are unit settings where some portions are changed to "shift" the scene.

In spite of all of these problems, the theatre room probably offers the experimental theatre group interested in trying out new audience-play relationships the greatest flexibility. Such theatres as Richard Tschechner's "Garage Theatre," the theatre at California Institute of the Arts near Los Angeles, the "Theatre Room," at the University of Texas, and the *Schaubühne am Hallschen Ufer* in Berlin are good examples.

SCENOGRAPHY FOR THEATRE ROOMS Just as the aesthetic of theatre rooms varies with each production, so will the approach of the scenographer. He will find himself designing a total environment for actors and audience. It will begin to have its effect the moment the audience members pass into the space especially constructed for their use during the production. Similarly, the totally revised spatial arrangements for each production will have their effect on the actors as they go about learning to work within it.

The scenographer and the technicians will find themselves engaged in work commonly left to the structural engineer and the architect. They must consider such things as audience circulation into the room, the combined weight of the seated audience, and what thrust will be placed on the seating platform if everybody on it stands up at once. Safety and fire codes need constant scrutiny to be sure that expensive construction can pass inspection.

Designing in a theatre room is a process of creating complicated interrelationships. There are interrelationships between audience and actors, between actors and actors, and within the audience. Although these relationships are not unique to the theatre room, they are fixed by the architecture of the building in most other theatres. In the theatre room, however, they await the fresh approach of the scenographer for every production.

Theatre rooms, like the thrust stage theatre, often suffer from misdirected economy. They tend to be secondary production areas added to theatre plants as a frill. As a result they contain production space and little else and their aesthetic is still in the exploratory stage.

SUMMARY

The real challenge to students may well lie in the application of the techniques of the now about-to-be-outdated proscenium theatre to new, more vital forms. Our ultramodern, even innovative theatrical technology seems to be thus rooted in the past. However, the apparent irony is only superficial—the living interplay between technology and aesthetic development results in a constant growth of both. Take as an example scenic projection which developed out of the need for more "realistic effects" in the nineteenth-century illusionistic theatre. Its terminology and basic machinery remain the same but its application to three- and four-dimensional expression in modern theatre often far removed from the proscenium style offers some of the most aesthetically rewarding moments of our art.

Much of art consists in taking old forms and old techniques (with their old names) and casting them into new arrangements, thereby producing new modes that may eventually initiate their own forms and techniques readying the cycle for a renewed movement.

PART THREE

ORGANIZATION AND SAFETY

From I and Albert, *Book: Jay Allen; Music: Charles Strauss.*
Photograph courtesy of Theatre Projects, London

5
HOW THE PRODUCING THEATRE IS ORGANIZED

INTRODUCTION In every theatre there are two levels of organization—an administrative overstructure and a production group. In small theatres the same persons may serve at both levels, but their jobs are nevertheless separate. The purpose of this chapter is to examine the way in which the producing level operates.

Unlike the administrative overstructure, the production organization or team exists only for the duration of a single production, although the same people may reorganize themselves over and over again to do many productions. (This highly desirable situation is typical of European repertory theatres.) Nevertheless, each production requires a unique organization because of its special technical and artistic problems. Figures 5-1 and 5-2 diagram typical artistic and production organizations. Since these tend to intermingle in a manner not easily diagramed in two dimensions, the reader will have to imagine each variation in Figure 5-1 as a sort of transparent overlay of Figure 5-2.

The first figure shows a number of ways in which artistic responsibility may be shared. As we noted in Part One, talent and dedication are the most important elements in successful theatre. Thus it should be obvious that no particular organizational arrangement can, by itself, guarantee artistic success. Nevertheless, it is the opinion of this writer that the director-scenographer scheme offers talented and dedicated theatre workers the best possibility of artistic success and makes the most reasonable demands on their personal lives.

DETAILS OF THE PRODUCTION ORGANIZATION

Figure 5-2 represents a typical organization in a theatre of moderate size. Note that the artists, near the top of this organization, provide artistic guidance to the technical staff below them. In turn, the artists are dependent on this staff for both technical proficiency and artistic responsibility within the limits of the jobs assigned to them. Figure 5-2 will clarify how technical decision-making works. When a problem is encountered, it tends to move up through the hierarchy until it reaches a person who knows how to solve it, and who initiates a decision which then moves downward. If, for example, the rigging crew runs into a question about the exact low trim (location) for a piece of scenery, they consult their chief, who, in turn, passes the problem upward. It could conceivably go all the way to the scenographer if only he knows how high the scenery should hang.

Many theatres will not have a large enough staff to handle all of the positions shown in Figure 5-2. This means one person may hold two or even three positions, a normal condition which merely emphasizes that this person must know and accept all of the responsibilities of each position.

Other theatres, particularly large repertory houses, or educational theatres seeking to give the maximum number of students production experience, will subdivide responsibilities even further. For example, each major crew may be divided into two groups: a crew in charge of the preparation of the area and another in charge of running the show.

CLEAR LINES OF AUTHORITY

One of the keys to successful organization is that clear areas of responsibility are marked out, and these must not be violated by people higher in the chain of command. If, for example, the property chief is responsible for the security of all properties (as is usually the case), it is unwise for the director, in the absence of the prop chief, to issue props to the cast. This erodes a clearly established role, leaving the prop chief with responsibility but without the necessary control. If, in the prop chief's absence, the director must have access to props, responsibility must be shared, not placed on the prop chief alone. It is important for you to observe such rules. As a crew member, you may need materials or access to certain areas. Your impulse will be to go to anyone with authority. You should and probably will be told to seek out the person directly in charge of the area even if the person you have asked has the keys available. You must understand that this is the only way an organization as complicated as a production group can operate. When you work up to positions of responsibility, you will want the same kind of support yourself.

Figure 5-2 depicts a two-way relationship. Decisions tend to move downward from the top, while problems move upward from the bottom.

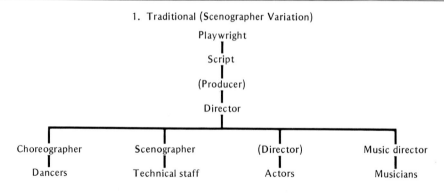

1. Traditional (Scenographer Variation)

Playwright
Script
(Producer)
Director

| Choreographer | Scenographer | (Director) | Music director |
| Dancers | Technical staff | Actors | Musicians |

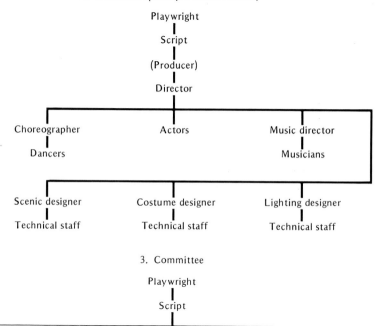

2. Traditional (Multiple Artist Version)

Playwright
Script
(Producer)
Director

Choreographer   Actors   Music director

Dancers   Musicians

Scenic designer   Costume designer   Lighting designer

Technical staff   Technical staff   Technical staff

Figure 5-1. Some Variations in Artistic Organization. The two traditional variations are by far the most common. The collective theatre group organization is the most demanding. Note that while the playwright heads each of the first three diagrams, his authority is almost always entirely transmitted via the written script. He is seldom present in person during the production process.

3. Committee

Playwright
Script

| Choreographer | Scenographer | Director | Music director |
| Dancers | Technical staff | Actors | Musicians |

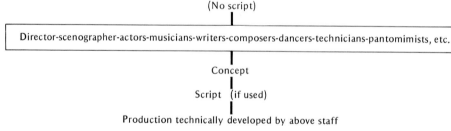

4. Collective Theatre Group

(No script)

Director-scenographer-actors-musicians-writers-composers-dancers-technicians-pantomimists, etc.

Concept
Script   (if used)
Production technically developed by above staff

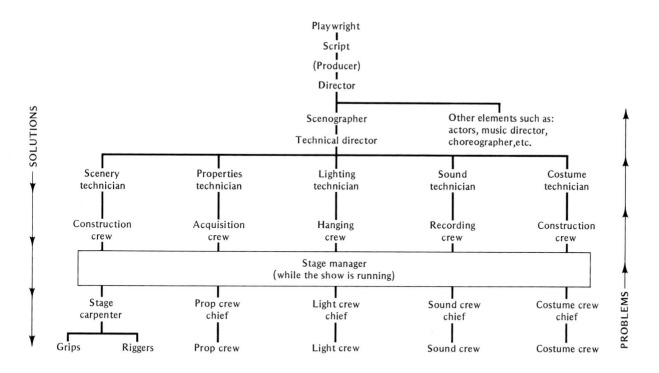

SOLUTIONS

PROBLEMS

Playwright

Script

(Producer)

Director

Scenographer

Technical director

Other elements such as:
actors, music director,
choreographer, etc.

Scenery technician	Properties technician	Lighting technician	Sound technician	Costume technician
Construction crew	Acquisition crew	Hanging crew	Recording crew	Construction crew

Stage manager
(while the show is running)

Stage carpenter	Prop crew chief	Light crew chief	Sound crew chief	Costume crew chief
Grips Riggers	Prop crew	Light crew	Sound crew	Costume crew

Figure 5-2 The Production Organization. This drawing shows a typical production organiza-
tion for a moderately large educational theatre. Smaller organizations will normally combine
the duties of the preparatory and the running crews. Large organizations may subdivide even
further.

SPECIAL PROBLEMS OF TRANSMITTING DESIGN INFORMATION

The source of all design information (What color is the setting? What is
the nature of each prop? How is the lighting arranged?) is the scenographer. This artist, in careful cooperation with the production's director, makes all the design decisions. He or his assistants make the working drawings that stipulate what must appear on stage and how it is
to be built or adapted from stock. He also prepares property lists and
will frequently choose the props. He will probably provide samples
of base coats of paint for the setting, check the mix before it is applied,
and be closely involved in the application of textures, shading, and
other finishing steps. He also prepares the light plot, including selection of color, devises the lighting cues, and creates the art work for
any scenic projections that might be used.

This means that you, as a crew member, will sometimes get your
instructions directly from the scenographer. Ideally, these instructions
should be limited to design matters, which get special consideration

because it is very difficult to describe an effect in words. Only the scenographer can demonstrate precisely what is wanted.

Transmitting Technical Information

Mechanical details are another matter. For example, the manner in which a run of flats is to be supported will usually be worked out by the technical director. He may delegate this authority to the shop chief, who may hand it on to a reliable assistant. You may get the information directly from that assistant as the two of you install supports for the flats.

This should be clear: If you have a question that is clearly related to design (for instance, the choice of a piece of period furniture), you must expect to hear either directly or indirectly from the scenographer. If you have a question about something mechanical, your crew chief will either have the answer, or know who does.

Production Meetings

The many communications problems that come into focus at production meetings have been discussed in Part One. As a crew member, you will undoubtedly attend a number of such meetings, and you should carefully prepare yourself. If you have been instructed to read the script and witness a run-through rehearsal before the meeting, do so. No amount of talk in the meetings can be a substitute for experiences, and much that is said will make little sense without them.

Production meetings are also times for pinpointing problems. If you have a problem, or if you see one developing, ask a question. Although there are many pairs of eyes and ears on every production staff, theatre is so complicated that it is easy for things to get overlooked until they provoke a crisis. However, you should distinguish carefully between problems and matters of interpretation. As a crew member, it is doubtful that the director will want to hear that you feel the leading lady should be dressed in red instead of blue. On the other hand, if you know from experience that the dye in the blue fabric will run when wet, and the script calls for it to get soaked, you can help by sharing your knowledge.

DESCRIPTIONS OF CREW JOBS

The following are general descriptions of the usual duties of crew members filling each of the postions in an elaborate breakdown of jobs as shown in Figure 5-2. If two or more positions are combined, the duties are accordingly lumped together.

SCENERY CONSTRUCTION—
CARPENTER

Hauls in carpentry supplies (lumber, nails, hardware, etc.) and stores them in shop for use

Measures, cuts, and fits wooden parts of flats

Fits joints, squares and fastens them

Applies fabric to flats and trims in readiness for flameproofing/base coating

Builds all three-dimensional objects made of wood.

Does simple metal work with pipe, strap iron, wire, and the like as needed on scenery

Operates table saw, pull-over saw, band saw, jointer, lathe, nailer, power stapler, electric handsaw, electric jigsaw, router, etc.

Is familiar with all carpenter's hand tools

Occasionally sharpens blades and maintains tools

Performs repairs on settings during run of show

Works with plastics and other wood substitutes

May work with welder to make steel set pieces

SCENERY CONSTRUCTION—
PAINTER

Mixes flameproofing and paint to color samples

Applies flameproofing, size, and base paint

Patches flat covers with fabric

Lays out and paints detail on flats and other elements

Applies special spray paints, oil paints, etc.

Flameproofs draperies and drops; paints same

Handles touch-up during production runs if detail work is needed

Maintains and repairs painting equipment—brushes, rollers, sprayers, mixers

PROPERTY ACQUISITION CREW

Gets prop lists from director and designer; coordinates these lists

Checks availability of props at stores, rental houses, and other sources

Aids designer and director in final choice of props

Makes purchases and handles funds and/or paper work involved in process

Buys materials for property construction, if necessary

Handles details of hauling, storage, and return of props rented or borrowed

PROPERTY CONSTRUCTION CREW

Builds props as specified

Decorates and "animates" props

Aids in the construction of effects—magic wands, flaming torches, etc.

Works with all tools of carpenter plus such things as jigsaws, welders, metal drills, glue guns, heat guns, etc.

Works with wood, metal, papier-mâché, plastic, fabric, asbestos fiber, etc.

GRIPS

Assembles and shifts scenery, including heavy props and set pieces

Handles wagons, outriggers, trip and lift devices, jacks, lashing, hinging, and all fastening techniques

Aids in spiking stage and maintains spikes during run

Does minor repairs on setting during runs

Stacks and stores scenery in wings; checks it for security and readiness for each performance

Often works with property crew in placing set props and striking them

Works with riggers in hanging scenery

Works with carpenters in original assembly of settings on stage

Operates power-driven stage equipment—revolves, lifts, wagons, etc.

RIGGERS—FLYMEN

Mounts and operates all hanging elements

Operates locking rail and pin rail

Works with grips in hanging set pieces from battens

Devises special rigs such as flying setups for actors

Tests and repairs rigging as needed

Operates motor-driven line sets, grid winches, etc.

Operates mule

Is a specialist in knots, cable fasteners, etc.

PROPERTY RUNNING CREW

Has responsibility for handling all properties during run of show except those permanently fastened to setting until strike

Stores props securely off stage and checks them before each performance

Has properties ready to hand to actors as needed, and takes props from actors as they come off stage

Installs and removes set dressing during shifts with help of grips

Makes minor repairs on props during run

Provides expendable props (food, etc.) and stores them before and after show; often buys such props during run if this is not done by acquisition crew

LIGHTING CREW

Often called "electricians" ("controlboard operator" may be a special category within this heading)[1]

SPECIAL EFFECTS CREW

The duties of the special effects crew overlap with the property crew. If treated as a separate crew, they perform such things as scenic projections, appearances and disappearances, magic tricks, rain, lightning, smoke, etc. These special skills are not covered in this text for beginners.

Costume Crew and Sound Crew

Costume and sound crews are vital to the production organization, but are not covered in this text.

Each of the crews mentioned above will have a crew chief, who is the immediate administrator and is responsible for such things as dividing work, supplying tools (from the tool room) not owned by crew members, arranging breaks, and other matters relating to the crew's needs.

---

1. See Part Seven, "Lighting."

SUPERVISORS

If the theatre in which you are working is moderate to large in size, there is a good possibility that each of the several areas (scenery, properties, lights, sound, and costume) will have a supervisor who takes long-term responsibility for his area, the equipment used in it, and those who work with it. In some cases these supervisors will be permanent employees of the theatre; in others, they may be graduate students who earn their way through school doing these jobs. In either case, a supervisor is very important to crew members. He will be their chief source of technical information—a combination teacher and administrator. The chances are great that he will be evaluating your work. He may also be the best spokesman for the entire crew if trouble develops.

Supervisors in areas outside of your crew assignment can also be helpful. If you are on the property crew, for example, and have just finished making a property lamp that must light up, it will probably be the lighting supervisor who will aid you in getting it wired.

SCENE SHOP FOREMAN

As far as scenery and property crews are concerned, the person who can be most helpful is the scene shop foreman. He will usually be a specialist, a woodworker with the skill and experience to make almost anything that the designer can contrive. He will know his power and hand tools well, and keep them in the finest condition. He will inevitably be responsible for the safe, dependable operation of the shop, including the enforcement of safety rules. If the shop is large, he may have one or more assistants who are learning the trade. When you work in the shop, you will be under his supervision via your crew chief. His word is law in the shop because he is responsible for it. You will find him to be a storehouse of information—he will know the best and easiest way to do things. Seek out his help and advice.

In many small theatre organizations the duties of all of these supervisory personnel will be combined with those of the "technical director." In even smaller setups the director of the play will also be the technical director and bear all of the other responsibilities as well —a nearly impossible task!

TECHNICAL DIRECTOR

In terms of the development of all technical materials for a given show, the technical director stands above all shop foremen, crew chiefs, and such. He answers only to the scenographer, director, and budget officer. His job is to coordinate all technical elements of the production and to engineer them if this is necessary. He is concerned with setting, lighting, costume, makeup, sound, props, projections, effects, etc. Thus his influence extends over all elements of the production.

The technical director works with the director and the scenographer to form the "committee" that puts on the production. If he is also the scenographer, he may be "engineering" his own designs — that is, making the device work reliably and safely. For example, sets of stairs must not only look the way the scenographer wants them to look; they must withstand the strain of actors moving, perhaps violently, over them. This involves an engineer's knowledge of the strength of various wooden and metal parts and the methods of putting them together to take advantage of that strength.

Unless the designer has already made them, the technical director and his staff will produce the drawings from which you will work as you construct the settings. In any event, the technical director takes the responsibility for seeing that the drawings will lead to safe, workable scenery that meets design specifications. He must also see that the plans are carried out within the various shops' time schedules and capabilities. He will concern himself as well with the cost of the materials being used, and will help the entire staff to stay within their budgets.

His authority over crews is absolute. If a crew is not performing well, he may do whatever is necessary to complete the job. While he will not exercise this authority unless necessary, he may replace the crew chief, change crew membership, or do anything else to improve crew performance. If the technical director does have to reorganize a crew, something has gone very wrong, and a number of lesser authorities have failed in their tasks. Remember, the technical director is charged with the responsibility for every element of the show except the actors.

STAGE MANAGER

As Figure 5-2 indicates, the duties of the stage manager cut across the entire technical chain of command. Once the show is running, he is the chief administrator. As the principal representative of the artistic staff on a night-to-night basis during the run of the show, his duties go beyond the areas of scenography and stagecraft. They range from providing coffee for the director to comforting stage-frightened actors and assisting in middle-of-the-night repairs of the stage machinery. As a crew member, you will find the stage manager to be your highest authority during the run.

The following is a list of the stage manager's duties:

Assists in tryouts, keeping data on candidates, addresses, etc.

Puts up all call sheets, call-back lists, etc.

Assists in scheduling rehearsals

Arranges for rehearsal space and props

Spikes set in rehearsal space and later on stage

Assists in preparation of paper work, e.g., duplicates floor plans, rehearsal schedules, etc.

Prepares and keeps up-to-date cast and crew lists, including addresses, phone numbers, etc.

Prepares book—all lines, cues, warns, calls, etc.

Checks rehearsal attendance and calls tardy members

Opens and closes rehearsal space

Handles valuables for cast while rehearsing, and later on stage

As the show approaches technical rehearsal week, the stage manager adds to his already impressive list of duties the following:

Plans shifts using information from scenographer, technical director, and working drawings for the show

Assists in checking on arrival of properties, special effects, etc.

Takes over the stage manager's console backstage, and conducts technical rehearsals under the direction of the technical director and the director

Rehearses shifts until they are perfected

Times rehearsals and reports times to director

Instructs cast and crew in safety procedures

Opens and closes theatre for these rehearsals

Gradually takes over complete charge of run of show as technical rehearsals merge into dress rehearsals, including working out calls for the actors from the green room in time for their cues

Enforces safety rules backstage and is responsible for backstage discipline

During the run of the show, the stage manager is in complete charge. His duties include the following:

Opens and closes the theatre for each performance

Authorizes opening the house to let in the audience when all is in readiness, and has authority to delay the show if necessary

Has responsibility for all emergency decisions including one to stop the show if an emergency threatens

Checks attendance (sign-in sheets) and calls missing or tardy cast and crew members

Authorizes the substitution of understudies

Continues to enforce all backstage rules

Gives cues as necessary to all elements of production; may delegate many of these if the theatre is equipped with a light and sound booth at the back of the house

"Holds the book," i.e., he gives cues to the actors as needed (although this may actually be done by an assistant)

Times each part of the show

Orders the beginning of each shift and checks its progress (See Chapter 14, "Shifting Scenery.")

Serves as administrator for the troop in dealings with the fire inspector, the theatre owner, etc.

May call brush-up rehearsals

May be the sole administrator of a touring company

May authorize payrolls

6

SAFETY IN THE THEATRE

INTRODUCTION All theatre workers, from the newest beginner to the most experienced veteran, must place one consideration above all others including the artistic: Safety. Safety is a matter of moral obligation, self-preservation, and the law. Common sense dictates that a theatre should be operated in such a way that no one gets hurt. We invite an audience to view our work in the theatre; they are our guests. They deserve every consideration necessary to ensure that no harm comes to them. Since humans are prone to carelessness and misdirected enthusiasms that may cause them to place other considerations (e.g. ''the show must go on'') before safety, laws have been written and enforcement procedures worked out to minimize the chances of an accident happening. Many theatres, especially those working under the strictures of a reduced budget, may come to feel that they are being persecuted by over-enthusiastic or erratic safety inspections. This may be so, but it does not argue that we should seek the abolition of safety laws or try to find ways of circumventing them. Such a policy misses the fundamental point that the safety laws and their enforcement officers are the best assurance we have of a safe theatre.

LAWS DEALING WITH THEATRE SAFETY

At present, the United States is in the midst of one of the most comprehensive revisions of its safety laws in its entire history. Until 1970 safety was the exclusive concern of state, country, and local law. Now the Occupational Safety and Health Act of 1970 (abbreviated OSHA) provides the overriding authority of federal law. The impact of this law is widely felt throughout the country. OSHA is really a set of laws designed to bring state safety standards up to minimum federal standards. As long as state law meets

BACKSTAGE SAFETY RULES

1. Do not smoke backstage at any time.

2. Do not tamper with safety equipment.

3. Know how to operate:
   a. Fire extinguishers
   b. Asbestos
   c. Emergency ("panic") lighting
   d. Panic exit doors and fire doors

4. Know where the emergency exits are. Plan what you would do if the asbestos came down in an emergency.

5. Know where the first aid kit is and how to use it.

6. Know where the emergency phone is and be sure the proper numbers are available.

7. Observe all warning signs, barriers, and lights.

8. Keep your calm; do not run backstage—if you plan properly, you should not need to.

9. Do not allow visitors backstage during performances; unsupervised small children should not be allowed backstage at any time.

10. At the cry, "Heads," take shelter from falling objects.

11. Stay clear of any stage machinery, ropes, electrical gear, etc.

12. Do not tamper with electrical equipment. If something is wrong with the electrical apparatus, call the electrician.

---

the federal standards and sets up sufficiently effective enforcement organizations, the federal law defers to state law, remaining in the background as a "watchdog." Twenty-six states have already achieved this goal and in these states safety is again a matter of state law and state enforcement. The other states are attempting to bring themselves into compliance with OSHA and thereby regain control over their safety programs. It is probable, however, that it will be a long time before all states are able to comply. Thus theatre workers in each state will have to determine whether they are under federal or state jurisdiction concerning safe working conditions. If they are under state law, it may be that state standards are even stiffer than OSHA standards.

OSHA and state laws meeting its minimum requirements apply only to the conditions imposed on employees. Since a condition that is unsafe for employees may also be unsafe for audiences, there is a relationship between OSHA and audience safety. State and local codes, however, have a more direct relation to audience safety. A *code* is a carefully organized set of laws, often interrelated in a complicated manner.

TWO IMPORTANT CODES

State and local building and safety laws are derived from many sources, but the two most important to the theatre are the *National Fire Code,* and the *New York City Building Code.* The National Fire Code (commonly called "the code") is the product of the nonprofit National Fire Protection Association. This organization annually publishes a ten volume edition of the code, including recommended practices and other data. This is a recommended model rather than a set of laws. OSHA itself adopted segments of the National Fire Code. States or cities frequently enact segments of the code, usually with local additions. These may have the effect of making the code much more stringent than the National Code. Local theatre workers must know local rules and abide by them even though they may be much more strict (and may seem much more arbitrary) than the National Code.

The New York City Building Code has served as a model for hundreds of municipal building codes throughout the country, particularly as it pertains to theatre seating arrangements. However, local problems and local history do cause variations that theatre workers must be aware of. For example, the laws regarding exit lights and asbestos curtains are unusually strict in the Chicago area because of that city's history of fires, particularly the disasterous Iroquois Theatre fire.

NATIONAL ELECTRICAL CODE

Actually the electrical code is a part of the National Fire Code. Electricians refer to it as "the code" as though it were a separate document. (It may be printed separately for convenience.) The electrical code is probably more frequently altered to meet local conditions than most other sections of the National Fire Code. Large municipalities commonly rewrite large sections of it to require special wiring techniques. Most of these requirements are aimed at residential and commercial structures and only incidentally refer to the theatre. Most frequently the theatre falls under a "catch-all" phrase written into local law which says that the provisions of the National Code shall apply wherever local law does not stipulate. This often works to the advantage of the theatre worker who knows the code well and can point out to a local electrician that the theatre is a special case falling under the more generous national law rather than the restrictive local law.

WHO ENFORCES THESE LAWS?

The Occupational Safety and Health Law is enforced by either federal inspectors or their state counterparts, if the state is in compliance with federal law. Building and safety laws are enforced during construction periods by local building inspectors who are alerted to the need for inspection when a construction permit is filed. After that, the local fire inspector is the chief enforcement officer, at least in the theatre. His major interest is in fire hazards, but anything that might hinder the flow of an audience from a building in case of fire or other emergency is also in his domain. He is the inspector most often seen in the theatre.

WHAT IF WE FAIL INSPECTION?

The fire inspector, or any other safety enforcement officer may issue orders for changes, close the show and/or building, or issue personal citations that can result in large fines and even jail sentences. Usually he will write out an order for compliance or give an oral warning and then return to verify that the required changes were made. If they have not been made, he may resort to stronger measures.

See Appendix II for additional information on prevention and control of fire in the theatre.

WHAT OTHER SERVICES DO INSPECTORS PERFORM?

Although some theatre workers take the misguided position that the fire inspector is their natural enemy and do everything to get him out of the building as soon as possible, they are missing a chance to get some much-needed help. Experienced fire inspectors are excellent resource people who will almost always take the time to answer questions about safety equipment. They are usually glad to conduct either formal or informal classes in fire safety, the use of fire-fighting equipment, and perhaps even in such sophisticated things as how to work safely with plastics. In addition to these safety-related matters, the inspector is often a walking treasurehouse of how-to-do-it information on such things as the way to get a fire effect on stage, how to make lightning, and much more. This is particularly true of inspectors in large metropolitan areas who may frequently encounter theatrical problems.

Actually this is the clue to successful relationships with inspectors. If they are brought into the theatre from the beginning to help solve and prevent problems, they are unlikely to storm in just before opening night and close a show. If the attitude toward inspection is positive and the inspector is treated as a helpful friend, not a mortal enemy, the theatre will be not only safer, but probably better.

OTHER BACKSTAGE SAFETY RULES

1. *Exit signs* must be visible and must lead to safe *fire exits*. There are rules governing the brightness and often the color of these signs. There are also rules governing their wiring, the provision for emergency power, and in some places even for the presence of a gas light. Alterations on or tampering with exit signs is both illegal and unwise. If they are too bright, seek the advice of the inspector.

2. *Emergency illumination* must be provided for both the audience and those backstage. Strangely enough, the second part of this proviso is often ignored. The very minimum would be the presence of working flashlights in the hands of key personnel instructed to use them to light the way out in an emergency.

3. Every person in the crew and cast should know where there is a telephone that will reach the fire department, police, or other emergency personnel, and procedures for making such calls. The usual location is at the stage manager's desk.

4. While the inspector will check *fire extinguishers* for proper type and operating condition, they will do little good if no one knows how to use them. *Every crew member should read the instructions on each type of extinguisher in the backstage area and be ready to explain what type of fire each should be used on and how it is operated.* The fire inspector will usually be glad to provide safety lectures and demonstrations if he is asked.

5. *Overhead safety* is most important to the riggers, who work overhead, but everyone should be aware of the heavy weights hanging above the stage and the hazards of carelessness. No one should be allowed to work the counterweight system without adequate training and supervision. Every crew member should be conscious of the system and concerned about who is running it. If there are electrically operated sets, controls should be in secure places and not subject to curious, "I wonder what this button does," tampering. All crew members should assist in keeping working areas clear while the lines are being operated and in clearing the area under the loading galleries while they are in use. Climbers working in the grid or on a lighting bridge should empty their pockets of any loose objects that might fall. A ball point pen dropped from 50 to 80 feet can be deadly. Needed tools should have lines on them tied to a belt or part of the rigging so that if they slip, they cannot fall. While work is being done on the grid, the stage should be kept clear.

It should be obvious that anything that is raised into the flies should be securely fastened to the line set holding it and that all of its parts should be securely fastened together. A good test is to imagine what might happen if two pieces of scenery, one going up and the other down, were to swing together. Would anything be knocked off and fall? Such overhead collisions do happen; sets should be built to withstand them.

All working parts of the rigging system should be periodically inspected by someone familiar with this equipment to make sure that it is safe and reliable. This is particularly true of rope lines that age rapidly and lose strength before they look worn. Such lines should be replaced on a regular schedule as recommended by the rope manufacturer.

All ties and fastenings should be safe. You will be tying a lot of knots and hooking a lot of trim chains. Be certain that you would be willing to stake your life on each tie; you will be doing so every time you work under it. If you have any doubts about anything that is to go into the flies ask your supervisor for an inspection. Be particularly suspicious of ties made with wire. Baling wire is a common commodity backstage, handy for tying things together, but it kinks easily and is then apt to break. It should be used sparingly and with much care. Snap hooks are another common device. You should know their working strength and the proper way to fasten them. Be conservative in your application of this knowledge. For example, a snap hook may have a safe capacity of 200 lbs on a straight pull, but a twist or angular strain may exceed this capacity even though the load itself is well under 200 lbs. When in doubt add extra fastenings or ask your supervisor.

Examine parts as you use them. Previous strains may have bent or even partially cracked them reducing their strength to a fraction of what it would be if the part were new. Hanging hardware is a good example of this; look it over as you install it and get rid of faulty pieces.

6. *Safety Lines*. In many areas the law requires that all lighting and similar equipment hanging over the audience or over the stage be equipped with a "*safety chain*." This may be either a piece of chain or stout metal cable equipped with snap hooks. It should be fastened around the yoke of the instrument or to a special ring on the instrument, and then wrapped around the batten so that the instrument cannot fall free even if its C-clamp breaks (a rare but possible happening) or slips loose. See Figure 6-1. Good sense dictates that safety chains should be installed whether or not the law requires them whenever human beings must work under equipment. This is supremely important in the case of special effects machines which vibrate from motor drives, clock works, or the like.

Although not always required by law, it is also a good idea to make sure that no gel frames, barn doors, or hoods can come loose from their lighting instruments and fall. Although such things are much lighter than an entire lighting instrument, they may still be deadly if they fall from a considerable height.

Figure 6-1. Safety Line. This photo illustrates one type of safety device used to prevent the fall of any heavy object hung over the heads of workers or audience. Although this device is made of aircraft cable, similar devices made of chain are also common.

7. Safety On The Deck. The stage floor (deck) can be hazard-ous, particularly in the half-darkness that is usual during the time the curtain is up. Cables, ropes, protruding parts of settings, piles of props, and stored set pieces are some obvious hazards. It will be necessary to provide dim, downward-directed safety lights backstage. This is the job of the electrical department, but it is also your job to help to main-tain these lights and keep them properly directed. Access areas and passageways are a problem. They will almost inevitably be narrow and

cannot be well-lighted without spilling light onto stage. Sometimes during very dark scenes, even the safety lights (but not the exit lights) must be dimmed or extinguished. Backstage personnel should plan their activities so it is not necessary to move around during periods of total darkness. To aid visibility the leading edges of steps and lead-on platforms should be painted white wherever they are invisible to the audience. Sometimes phosphorescent paint that will glow in the dark if it has been well-illuminated previously (a bright flood of light from a lighting instrument just before the show starts will help) is painted over the white paint. Another method involves the use of ultraviolet sources (see Part Seven, "Lighting") to cause fluorescent paints to glow in unsafe areas. This process has the advantage of a brighter glow and the disadvantage of the extra lighting apparatus.

Any openings in the stage floor should receive careful attention. These are particularly hazardous if they contain machinery such as a man-lift for sudden appearances.

If there are lifts, revolves, or other motor-operated equipment on or in the stage floor, special hazards exist. Even a small effects revolve can develop enough power to smash a foot or a hand. A larger unit has the power of a huge shear and can sever limbs with ease. All operations involving the use of such equipment should be supervised and operated by well-trained people who are aware of the risks involved. When working a lift or revolve be sure you know exactly what you are to do and plan in advance what you would do if something went wrong. Caution others, especially emotionally charged actors, to stand clear when things are moving or about to move. Know how to stop and reverse the machine and be sure that it is completely shut off and in a safe condition when you close it down.

SUMMARY

Ensuring safety in the theatre is a never-ending task. Theatres are dangerous places; people are working under great tension, using huge amounts of electricity, using powerful machines, and working under heavy objects hanging in the air. Audiences are crowded into restricted spaces without natural light and often into high balconies. Panic is always possible. We must remember that no production, however artistically important, is more important than the safety of the human beings in the theatre.

PART FOUR

SCENERY

From Frühlings Erwachen, *Frank Wedekind. Photograph by Stefan Odry.*

INTRODUCTION

In this part we will deal with scenery from its beginnings with the scenographer to the point where it is ready for painting. In the process we will consider the drawings, models, and other means used to communicate the scenic needs to the scenery construction shop; the shop itself, its equipment; the materials needed in construction; and the various categories of scenery. Because metal has become so important a scenic material, it will be treated separately. In order to understand this vast body of material, we must first discuss the categories of scenery.

Scenery in the modern theatre can be said to date back to the eighteenth-century era of wings and drops devised for the early proscenium theatre, where the audience was far removed from the setting and accepted as satisfactory the painted detail on flat canvas. The lightweight nature of the scenery, which was either roll-up drops or framed wings with painted details, fitted beautifully into the shifting techniques of the eighteenth-century theatre. The acoustic properties of this scenery were poor, but this made little difference because the actors were well downstage of the settings.

During the twentieth century, audiences came closer to the stage, although they were still clearly separated from the players by the proscenium. Lighting, now electric, became brighter and painted detail fell out of favor. Today, however, this same type of scenery made of wooden frames carrying canvas or muslin covered with painted details remains in use. It is still standard in many theatres because its advantages may outweigh its disadvantages. It is reasonably cheap to build, shifts easily, can be reused many times, and stores in a small space.

However, the proscenium itself has been challenged; many theatres now bring their audiences within touching distance of the setting, having abandoned the proscenium in favor of more intimate styles such as thrust or theatre-in-the-round. Under these conditions, the scenery made of a framed piece of fabric loses much of its original advantage. Convenience and low cost no longer offset its obviously fake nature.

Meanwhile, a much different approach to scenery was taking place in the film industry. If intimate theatre is a close-up art, film is even closer. The camera is quite capable of magnifying detail; it can even make it much larger than life size. With the addition of sound to the motion picture, acoustic reality became as important to the cinema as visual reality. More recently the requirements of the television camera have been proving even more demanding (if this is possible) than those of the movie camera. The result has been the development of a much more lifelike type of scenery. These two movements have now come together, and the present definitions of the categories of scenery in this text reflect the results.

Scenery that is soft to the touch has the acoustic effect of a piece of cloth. It may consist of fabric hanging in folds (drapery), of fabric hanging flat from a batten and capable of being rolled up to remove it from sight (roll drop) or being lifted into the flies (normal drop), or of fabric supported by a wooden framework and capable of standing by itself on the stage floor (flats). It is important to note that this represents a departure from earlier definitions of "soft scenery," which referred *only* to those pieces of fabric that had to be supported from above such as drops and drapery. "Framed scenery," i.e., flats, was known in this context as "hard scenery." Since this was the only other type of scenery that existed at the time, the definition made sense.

SOFT SCENERY

The term "flat" is used in connection with both soft and hard scenery. Usage suggests that the clearest distinction between these types of flats is made by using the word "flat" to refer to a unit of soft scenery, and the phrase "hard flat" to refer to the analogous piece of hard scenery.

Hard scenery, by our modern definition, does not give to the touch and reflects sound in much the same way as a regular building wall. It is inevitably made of a framework of wood covered with some nonflexible material such as plywood, very heavy cardboard, or Masonite. Unlike soft scenery, the surface of hard scenery can be treated to resemble any common construction surface such as brick, plaster, or stone. It will seem just as hard to the close-up camera or eye and will reflect sound much like the real article. Obviously hard flats are more durable than soft flats. They are also heavier and more expensive, but this is the price that close-up scrutiny exacts.

HARD SCENERY

Soft scenery includes the following subdivisions: draperies, hanging drops, roll drops, framed drops, and flats. All of these have in common a fabric surface that is "soft" to touch and to sound.

SUMMARY OF DEFINITIONS

Hard scenery includes only hard flats and larger pieces (not common except in the film industry) made in the same manner. The surfaces of hard scenery are unyielding to the touch and reflect sound more nearly like a solid wall.

Given these definitions, we will now proceed with our study of the entire category of scenery.

7
PLANS FOR SCENERY CONSTRUCTION

INTRODUCTION This chapter deals with the information that comes to the scene shop from the scenographer.

WHAT INFORMATION COMES FROM THE SCENOGRAPHER?

The visualization of a setting by a scenographer may begin either in the form of casual sketches on paper or as three-dimensional sketches executed in cardboard or in modeling clay. As the form of the setting takes more definite shape, these sketches, whether two- or three-dimensional, become more exact and detailed. Ultimately, after approval by the director, the information is transmitted to the shop for execution. In some cases, the scenographer merely prepares a floor plan, longitudinal section, and renderings or a scale model (see Figure 7-1 and Plates II and III). The rest of the drawings are done by the technical director or assistants. In the majority of cases, however, all of the drawings will be done by the scenographer. Beginning scenographers should prepare themselves to do all drawings so that they can gain the knowledge of scene construction necessary to create stageworthy settings.

However many drawings, sketches, and models there are, and whatever their source, their most important function is to transmit an artistic concept! The abstractions that the scenographer has developed into a special master symbol and then into the models, renderings, and working drawings, are the guiding principle for it all. As a student, it is not enough to study these materials only to determine how you would build, for example, a doorway for the Act III setting; you should study their relationship to the model and renderings, asking questions if necessary, until you understand the artistic concept being brought to the stage.

FIGURE 7-1a

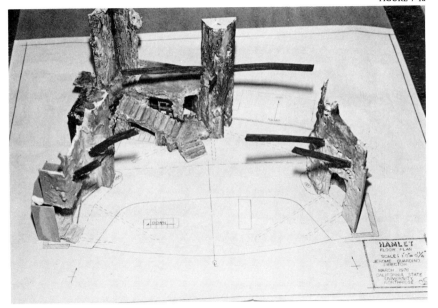

FIGURE 7-1b

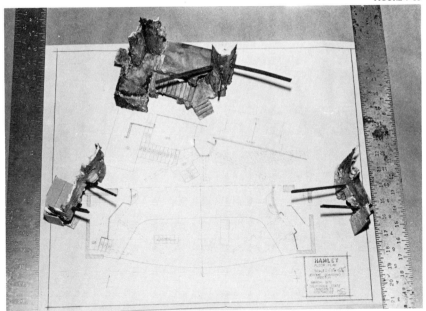

FIGURE 7-1c

Figure 7-1. Shop Plans. The various illustrations indicate the usual types of information communicated by the scenographer to the shop. They are samples of what will be an extensive set of drawings. Each production is unique and will generate its own special kinds of plans devised to solve its problems. The reader should particularly note the first series of illustrations (a, b, and c) which refer to the same production of Hamlet *(Shakespeare). A production photograph of this set is shown on page 375. The remainder of illustrations refer to other shows. (a) This figure shows how the floor plan relates to the model. Here the model has been superimposed over the floor plan to enable the reader to visualize how the orthographic projection (no perspective) is derived from the three-dimensional model. Some details have been left out for simplicity. (b) Here the model has been moved back off the floor plan to reveal the lines representing the model. Note that the lines have been simplified. This finished floor plan will serve a variety of purposes during the development of the production, including guiding the spiking of the setting on the stage floor, developing the light plot, working out shifts, and aiding the director in working out blocking. However, its most important function, one which demands that it be accurately scaled, is to serve as the master sheet in the shop's full set of working drawings. (c) This model built in exact scale and installed in a scale model of the stage house provides the shop and the director with an exact impression of the final setting. In this regard a model is preferable to a rendering such as those shown in Plates II and III. Care must be taken to view a model at angles resembling those from which the audience will view the finished setting.* Hamlet *staged at California State University, Northridge. Setting: Owen W. Smith. Director: Jerome Guardino. (d) Shows a longitudinal section (rigging plot). This drawing is of great importance when parts of the setting must be moved in and out of the flies. It also is used for determining vertical sight lines. Note that the drawing may be more than a strict orthographic projection; items in planes other than that of the "cut" may be shown if this clarifies rigging problems. (e) These drawings of details provide the shop with complete instructions for building and painting. (f) The front elevation is part of the detail drawings. Its purpose is to give exact information about the fronts of scenic elements, often including painting information.*

121

FIGURE 7-1d

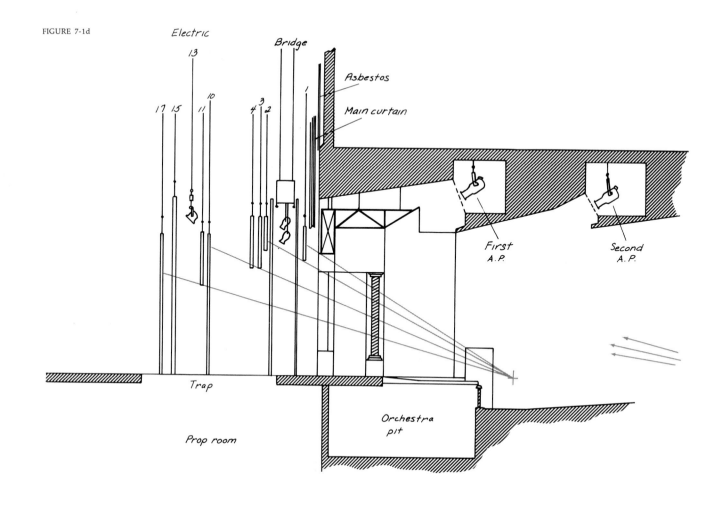

Electric
13
17 15 11 10
4 3 2
Bridge
Asbestos
Main curtain
First A.P.
Second A.P.
Trap
Prop room
Orchestra pit

SCALE

All drawings and models, even the most preliminary, must have some sort of scale. This means that all parts of the model or drawing must bear the same ratio to real life. A model, for example, might be scaled to a crudely sculptured "actor" about $\frac{3}{4}$ of an inch high. If we assume that this crude figure represents a 6-foot tall actor, we have a sense of the size of the proposed setting. The scale must be consistent throughout the model. Steps cannot be scaled as though the actor were 12 feet tall while doors are scaled as though he were 6 feet tall.

122   7 PLANS FOR SCENERY CONSTRUCTION

FIGURE 7-1e

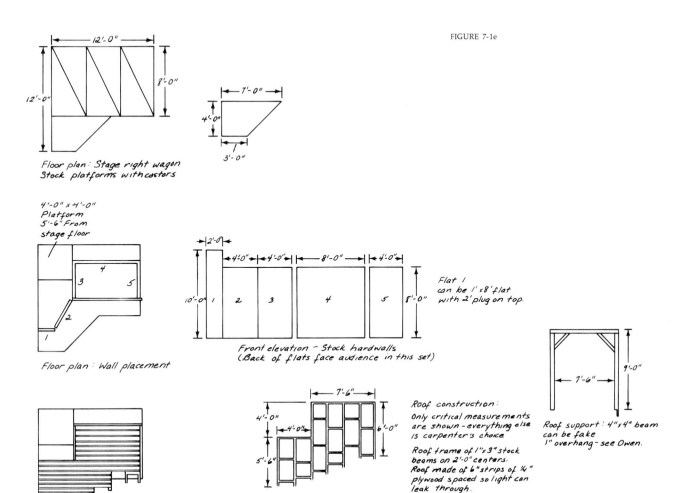

Floor plan: Stage right wagon Stock platforms with casters

4'-0" x 4'-0" Platform 5'-6" From stage floor

Floor plan : Wall placement

Front elevation - Stock hardwalls (Back of flats face audience in this set)

Flat 1 can be 1'x 8' flat with 2' plug on top.

Roof construction: Only critical measurements are shown - everything else is carpenter's choice

Roof frame of 1"x 3" stock beams on 2'-0" centers. Roof made of 6" strips of ¼" plywood spaced so light can leak through.

Roof support : 4"x 4" beam can be fake 1" overhang- see Owen.

Floor plan: Roof placement

Although a simple "actor scale" will suffice for beginning sketches or models, something much more precise must be used to indicate the exact size of the finished scenery. An exact scale must be chosen and drawings or models made precisely to it. It might, for example, be $\frac{1}{2}$ inch = 1 foot if we are working in English scale or 1:25 (centimeters) if metric scale is being used. Presently English measurements are in use throughout the United States building trades. The metric system is being used more and more, however, and scenographers and technicians should be able to work in either system. Ironically, the "English system" of measurement is now no longer used in England; the metric system has already taken its place there.

SCALE   123

FIGURE 7-1f

THE SCALE RULE

Although it is possible to compute the number of eighths of an inch (assuming that $\frac{1}{8}$ inch is equal to 1 foot) in any dimension given in feet and inches and to then count off this number of eighths to indicate the dimension, this tedious process is unnecessary. A scale rule, a rulerlike device (Figure 7-2) used to measure off distances in scale, will do the job for you. One simply selects the proper scale and measures with the ruler. There are two types of scales available in the English system and one in the metric system. Of the two in the English system, the architect's scale is the one used in theatrical work. It is so divided that dimensions may be scaled off in feet and inches. The other type, the engineer's scale, allows measuring in tenths of feet—a system of little use in the theatre. Metric scales are designed to work on a direct proportion such as 1:25 or 1:50, etc. Some idea of the comparison between metric and English scales may be gained by noting that 1:25 is roughly the equivalent of $\frac{1}{2}$ inch = 1 foot, while 1:50 is roughly $\frac{1}{4}$ inch = 1 foot. These relationships are close enough for quick approximations but not exact enough for conversion of details. Pocket calculators, which make very close equivalency calculations in a matter of seconds, are available at reasonable prices.

The first thing a technician does when reading a drawing is to note the scale, which will generally be shown in the lower right-hand corner along with the title and other data. In some cases the notation will read, "Scale varies." This means that some of the several drawings on that page are scaled differently from others. Be careful to note the scale on each part of the page as you read it. Some may be unscaled. Sketches, for example, often are included to show how some part fits another or how something works; these may be marked, "Not to scale." They are not to be used to determine dimensions. In many other cases a drawing will be marked, "Do not scale." This means that, although the draftsman has been as accurate as possible, he has computed the dimensions and entered them on the drawing. These dimensions are the correct ones, even though a measurement of the lines on the drawing with a scale rule ("scaling") does not agree. It is a general rule in shops that indicated dimensions take precedence over scaled dimensions. In fact, many carpenters will not scale from a drawing unless specifically instructed to do so. This is the opposite procedure of that of the scenographer who frequently draws sketches until he has what he wants, then scales the sketches to get the dimensions for the working drawing.

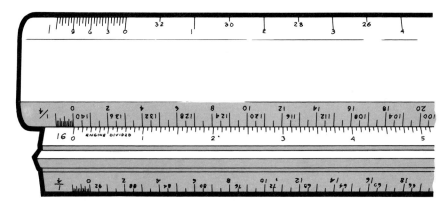

Figure 7-2. The Scale Rule. This shows two types of scale rules adjacent to each other to enable the reader to compare the normal inch scale with the $\frac{1}{4}$ inch = 1 foot scale. Note how the $\frac{1}{4}$ inch scale has been marked so that one can read off dimensions directly in feet and inches instead of counting $\frac{1}{4}$ inch increments. For example, one would measure off 7 feet 6 inches by placing the 6 inch mark of the $\frac{1}{4}$ inch scale at one end of the space to be measured and going to the 7 foot mark (opposite the $1\frac{3}{4}$ inches mark on the rule) to find the other end of the distance. Metric scales are also available. Similar operations may be performed in a variety of scales found on the triangular rule.

ENLARGING FROM SCALE DRAWINGS

It will frequently be necessary to enlarge a scenographer's sketch or detail to full scale. One method of doing this is to divide the drawing into squares representing 1 foot in scale and to divide the flat or drop into full 1-foot squares. Then each foot is drawn carefully using the guide lines to keep the drawing in proportion. A faster method is to use an opaque projector to project the image optically at full scale onto the surface, where it is traced in chalk or charcoal. This method may also be used to transfer designs directly out of a book or magazine when making historical or realistic replicas (see Figure 7-3).

WORKING DRAWINGS

Working drawings are plans sent to the shop to indicate how the setting (and properties) are to be constructed. They consist of four categories:

1. Floor plans (ground plans)
2. Hanging plots (longitudinal sections)
3. Elevations
4. Details

These are organized into a packet of drawings with the floor plan(s) on top. In addition to giving the layout of the settings, the floor plans serve as an index to the other drawings. For example, a fancy balustrade may be merely sketched in on the floor plan, but there will be a notation "D-1, a," which tells the shop workers to look at detail drawing 1, part a, to find out how the balustrade is to be built. In some cases, this method of reference is carried further by referring from one detailed drawing to another.

ORTHOGRAPHIC PROJECTIONS

Most working drawings will take the form of orthographic projections. This means that they show the items in the drawing to scale but *without perspective*. Such drawings have the advantage of showing all parts of the scenery to the same scale. The disadvantage of orthographic projection is that depth (three-dimensionality) cannot be shown. Thus the reader of a set of orthographic drawings must construct a three-dimensional object in his mind from the various orthographic views—usually front, side, and top. To aid the unskilled plan reader, the scenographer will normally provide sketches in perspective and/or a model of the setting.

All beginning scenographers and technicians should at least be capable of reading a floor plan and a longitudinal section. A typical floor plan is shown in Figures 7-1d, e, and f. Note that only general information is shown in a floor plan. It is too small in scale to carry much detail. It must also be used as a starting point for more drawings by

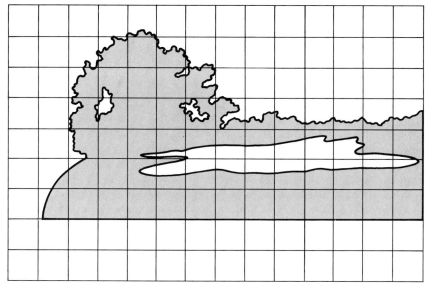

Squares equal 1 foot

Figure 7-3. Enlargement. This figure shows one of the common methods of enlarging a drawing. Note how the drawing has been overlaid with a grid of lines representing squares 1 foot in real size. This grid then is reproduced full scale on the surface to be painted and the details of each square are drawn in carefully. See Figure 10-4d from which this drawing was made.

others who will want it as uncluttered as possible. For example, the light plot will be developed from the floor plan. A light plot contains so much information itself that even the simplest floor plan may seem crowded. The floor plan gives the necessary information for *spiking* the set. Spiking is the process of taping or painting lines on the stage floor to indicate where the walls, doors, windows, etc., will be when the set is in place. This enables rehearsals to take place without the scenery. The set may also be spiked in a rehearsal room.

SIGHT LINES

You will note in Figure 7-1b that the location of the seats farthest right and left at the front of the house are shown. These represent the two seats farthest from the center line of the particular theatre illustrated. The view from these seats, known as a sight-line helps the designer plan the backings for his setting, and the riggers to set up the *masking*. Masking is dark-colored drapery or scenery installed to keep the audience from seeing around or over the setting into backstage areas. It is a particular problem when shows tour and the sight lines are very different from house to house. Accurate floor plans of each stage will assist in solving this problem.

HANGING PLOT (LONGITUDINAL SECTION)

The hanging plot provides vertical information in much the same way as the floor plan provides horizontal information. It is a vertical section (a "cut" through) of the stage house at a 90 degree angle to the curtain line showing the location of all hanging objects (see Figure 7-1d). The drawing may also include a cross section of the house showing most extreme seats in the balconies, if the scale is small enough. If not, sight lines from those seats may be indicated. The hanging plot provides the scenographer with the information necessary to determine who in the house will see what portions of the setting. For example, such a drawing might tell the designer that the people in the second balcony will be able to see part of the floor of a balcony. He will, therefore, have to specify that the floor is to be painted. If the scenographer plans to fly tall pieces of scenery, a hanging plot will tell him how high these must be lifted to take them completely out of sight. Having established this height, he may then have to face the fact that the top of the proposed set piece extends 3 feet above the gridiron! As unpleasant as this news may be, it is better to find it out while drawing the hanging plot, than to be told the same thing by the riggers as they are trying to mount the show.

Like the floor plan, the longitudinal section will be useful to other areas, particularly lighting. Working from it and the floor plan, the scenographer will be able to locate instruments with considerable accuracy once he has determined the angle at which he wishes the light to strike the actors.

Unless it is clearly evident in the floor plan and longitudinal section, the scenographer must also provide schedules or shifting details to make clear to all concerned how the set works. This means that crew members should be able to determine which pieces work together to form each separate setting, and how the parts move in relationship to each other. Such information is especially vital when working out details of lighting because moving objects, although out of sight of the audience, may interrupt light, causing unwanted shadows.

FRONT ELEVATIONS

Elevations are views drawn from the front, sides, or back of an object. Although a designer's perspective sketch gives a great deal of information about the general layout and appearance of a setting, it cannot be used to take measurements for construction because three-dimensional objects in a perspective drawing appear to get smaller as they recede from the plane of the drawing. A front elevation (without perspective) drawn from the same point of view as the sketch would not add much information. Although heights would now be accurate, widths would be true only in those pieces of scenery sitting parallel to the curtain line. For this reason, a front elevation of a setting normally consists of a series of head-on views of each flat wall section, starting from stage right. Where there are gaps or openings, space is left between the drawings. One might imagine this as looking like a view of the entire setting folded out onto a flat surface.

Actually such a front elevation may run across two or more sheets of drawings, if the stage is large. Backings also are included so that the shop personnel know the size of each surface that they must provide. However joints between flats making up continuous walls are not usually shown unless the scene shop personnel must be instructed on how to break a long run of flat wall into conveniently sized units for shifting.

A considerable amount of front detail is shown on front elevations, including such things as the location of any hanging devices that will be needed for pictures, mirrors, and the like. These locations tell the shop where to install extra toggle rails to support such objects. Three-dimensional trims (made up of moldings) or cornices are drawn in. If the painting of the scenery is simple, it too may be indicated on the elevation in lieu of a separate painter's elevation. Front elevations often are coded to direct the reader to detail sheets for specific information on trim, cornices, plate rails, etc.

Rear Elevations

A rear elevation is analogous to a front elevation. It shows the back of the walls with construction details. Since flats are a standard item, most scenographers only show rear elevations of those requiring some special construction, such as a deeply recessed archway or a trick panel. Beginners in the shop should study the rear elevation of a typical flat to memorize construction details. They cannot expect to find them on every working drawing.

Elevations of Three-Dimensional Objects

Unfortunately for the beginning student of scenography or stage technology, modern stage settings tend less and less to be made up of simple flats arranged to represent the walls of rooms. The more scenography involves itself with the moving actor, the more completely settings become related to sculpture.

Therefore, many of the drawings that the student technician may encounter will represent three-dimensional objects, often of great complexity. It is probable that several rather complicated drafting techniques will be used to make these objects clear. At the very least there will be orthographic projections of all sides, and very probably at least one section through the object. Frequently these basic drawings will be supplemented by additional details and by sketches designed to show the reader what the finished object will look like, how it fits into another object, etc. Such drawings are known as "details," whether they refer to two- or three-dimensional objects. The draftsman will provide whatever number of details are necessary to assure proper construction of the object. Hence there may be enlargements of parts, even up to or over real size, cutaway views showing interior construction, and the like.

A number of techniques have been devised to show what a three-dimensional object will look like within the limits of the two dimensions of a drawing. The most realistic of these is the *perspective drawing*. It applies the rules of visual perspective that ultimately derive from the way our seeing apparatus works, to produce a two-dimensional representation of three dimensions. Unfortunately, perspective drawings are tedious to make and almost impossible to use to indicate the exact size of objects.

A number of pseudoperspective systems have been devised to approximate perspective without these difficulties. The simplest is the *isometric drawing*. Instead of using the converging lines that perspective drawing uses to represent parallel lines receding from the observer, an isometric drawing allows the lines to remain parallel, and always views the object in such a way that lines at right angles to the vertical in the real object are represented along angles 120 degrees to the vertical. While this distorts the figure, it makes scaling possible. Reference to a book on mechanical drafting will reveal many other systems. Since they appear only occasionally in theatrical drawings, they are not detailed here. The beginner should seek the help of the instructor or supervisor when he encounters a set of drawings that include details using advanced techniques. He will not find them difficult to read once they have been explained. Making such drawings is, however, more of a challenge.

8

THE SCENE SHOP

INTRODUCTION The scene shop is the center of construction activities in most theatres. In many cases it is the *only* shop in the facility and must serve all construction functions—scenery, props, electrical, metal, effects, plastics, and sometimes even maintenance of stage and classroom equipment. However, for our purposes, we will assume that the scene shop is dedicated only to the construction of scenery using conventional woodworking methods.

A well-organized scene shop will be arranged to facilitate an orderly flow of work. Raw materials are stored close to places where they will be needed and power equipment is located near the working areas supported by these tools. There is sufficient working space to allow several operations to go on simultaneously.

MATERIALS USUALLY STORED IN A SCENE SHOP

Traditionally scenery has been made from wood and woodlike materials, and from fabric. Scene shops are mostly a variation of regular carpenter shops and their tools and techniques are merely specializations of standard techniques used in carpentry.

Although bulk quantities of many materials used in scenic construction may be stored elsewhere, day-to-day working quantities of the following should be on hand in the shop.

LUMBER

Lumber is a natural product cut from the trunks of trees. The wood obtained will vary depending on the species of tree from which it was taken, how it was cut, and how the lumber has been further treated before being used. The following discussion is based on the standards set forth by the West Coast

131

Lumber Inspection Bureau (WCLB), which sets most of the grading standards for lumber products in the United States.

Wood generally is divided into hardwood and softwood. Actually these terms have more to do with the general categories of trees from which the lumber is cut than with the actual hardness or softness of the wood itself. If the wood comes from a conifer (a tree that has needlelike leaves such as pine or fir, and bears cones carrying its seeds), it is termed "softwood." If the wood grew as part of a broadleaf tree such as maple or oak, it is known as "hardwood." Almost all wood used in scenery construction is softwood—most of it is pine. There is one exception: some very thin plywood (a material made by gluing together thin slices of wood to form a wide, thin sheet) is made from basswood, a hardwood.

The kind of wood in lumber usually is designated by the species of tree from which it was cut, with certain modifications. Several varieties of trees that produce substantially the same wood are grouped under one name. For example, the label, "yellow pine," refers to wood obtained from several varieties of pine trees; since the wood is about the same as far as construction is concerned, it is all called "yellow pine."

Lumber Dimensions

Dimensions are traditionally given in even inches in this order: thickness, width, and length. Thus one might say, "1″ × 12″ × 10′ yellow pine." This would refer to a piece of yellow pine 1 inch thick, 12 inches wide, and 10 feet long.

The thickness and width dimensions, however, represent the original thickness of the boards when they came from the sawmill. As lumber comes from the mill, it is heavily laden with water and sap from the tree and the cut surfaces are a mass of slivers. It is heavy, prone to warping, and very hard to work. Therefore, before it is sold, most lumber is cured by drying and is then planed. As it dries, it shrinks. The planer takes off an additional bit as it removes the splinters. The result is that the original dimensions are considerably reduced. Nevertheless, you designate (and pay for) the original dimension. Once lumber has been planed it is described as "surfaced," and our piece of 1″ × 12″ pine (now about $\frac{3}{4}$″ × $11\frac{5}{8}$″) might be further described as "S4S," meaning "surfaced four sides." However, this designation is frequently left off because so little unsurfaced lumber is sold that lumber is understood to be surfaced unless otherwise designated.

Lumber normally comes in even number lengths such as 10′-0″, 12′-0″, etc. Actually the pieces will often be somewhat longer than these dimensions to allow the carpenter to cut a bit off to square each end and still have a full dimension piece of lumber. Although good quality lumber will be exactly square as far as the sides are concerned, there is no assurance that the ends will be cut exactly square unless the mill so designates. Some mills use this feature as a selling point.

How Lumber Is Sold

In small quantities at retail stores, lumber is often sold by the lineal foot. Thus one might buy 100' of 2" × 4" white pine. When lumber is sold in quantity at wholesale prices—and this is the way a theatre should buy it—it is sold by the thousand board foot. A *board foot* is any combination of dimensions that multiplies out to 144 cubic inches. Thus a piece of board 6 inches wide, 1 inch thick, and 24 inches long would contain 1 board foot. Similarly, 18" of 2" × 4" stock would equal a board foot. Note that the nominal dimensions are used, not the actual dimensions of the finished lumber. A thousand board feet (abbreviated MBM) is the standard unit for pricing purposes. For example, a theatre might order 1000 MBM of 1" × 3" yellow pine. Since it takes 4 lineal feet of 1" × 3" lumber to equal 1 board foot, $(1 \times 3 \times 48)$ the order would contain 4000 lineal feet of 1" × 3" lumber.

The complete formula for calculating the cost of an order of lumber, without mathematical simplification is:

$$\frac{T \times W \times L}{144} \times n \times \frac{\text{Cost per MBM}}{1000} = \text{Total cost}$$

where T = thickness in inches; W = width in inches; L = length of each piece in inches; and n = number of pieces.

A simplification is possible that makes the formula easier to apply to normally given dimensions. Since the divisor 144 represents the number of square inches in a square foot, and since one must multiply the normally given length of the pieces by 12 to convert to inches, it is possible to simplify by leaving the length in feet and altering the divisor to 12. Thus the practical formula becomes:

$$\frac{T \text{ (in inches)} \times W \text{ (in inches)} \times L \text{ (in feet)}}{12} \times n \times \frac{\text{Cost per MBM}}{1000} =$$
$$\text{Total cost (in cents)}$$

It is also frequently convenient to compute the cost per lineal foot of commonly used dimensions since this figure will be useful in estimating the cost of materials for a production. This formula, simplified, is:

$$\frac{T \text{ (in inches)} \times W \text{ (in inches)}}{12} \times \frac{\text{Cost per MBM}}{1000} = \text{Cost per lineal foot}$$

Lumber Grades

Wood cut from a log may vary from perfectly clear (free of knots and blemishes) to knotty, laden with pitch (partially dried tree sap that is about as sticky as soft tar), ridden with worm holes, or even partially rotten. Lumber grades determine the quality of the wood and, of course, the price. The top grade is labeled "A." It is seldom seen in lumber yards and rarely sold other than to furniture manufacturers and makers of doors, window frames, etc. The next lower grade is "B & Better," lumber that is almost completely free of knots and blemishes. This is the top grade commonly found in most lumber yards. Usually this grade is needed by the theatre for flat construction. It is relatively expensive but produces little waste if properly used. The next lower grade is "C" which contains a few small tight knots and other blemishes. Below grade "C" are a number of "construction grades" ranging down to lumber fit for nothing except the crudest use. The theatre finds a great deal of use for the higher construction grades of lumber to build weight-bearing structures. However, these grades are not normally useful for building flats.

Plywood

Plywood is a special material made by slicing logs up into thin layers and gluing these slices together at right angles to each other to make a sort of sandwich of wood. The result is large sheets of wood (much larger than could be cut in one piece from most logs) that have considerable strength and are economical to make. It is also possible, although not often useful to the theatre, to make up plywood with cheaper materials in the inner layers and rare hardwoods on the surface.

Almost all of the plywood made in the United States is made from Douglas fir wood, the source of most construction materials in the American lumber industry. Thousands of fir logs are sliced spirally into thin sheets of wood for plywood. Although Douglas fir is too heavy and too splintery to be used as lumber for flats, it is quite satisfactory in the form of plywood.

Plywood is usually sold by the sheet, a standard sheet being $4'\text{-}0'' \times 8'\text{-}0''$. Sheets are also made in 10 and 12 foot lengths. Plywood comes in a wide variety of thicknesses beginning at about $\frac{3}{32}$ inch. Usual thicknesses for theatrical purposes are $\frac{1}{4}$, $\frac{3}{8}$, $\frac{1}{2}$, $\frac{3}{4}$, and 1 inch. The $\frac{3}{32}$ inch thickness, sometimes known as "bend board," is used to cover curved surfaces.

Plywood also is categorized as to the type of glue used in its manufacture. "Marine" plywood uses the best quality glue that affords almost total immunity to separation from immersion in water. It may be used occasionally in the theatre where conditions necessitate. The next most durable type is "exterior," which has been glued to resist moisture but not total immersion. Exterior type sometimes is used in the theatre. However, the most commonly used type is "interior." This plywood is glued with relatively cheap glues that have only limited resistance to moisture and are sufficient for most theatrical uses.

Plywood is graded according to the quality of the outer plies. A sheet designated "A-A" would be top quality (whether exterior, interior, or marine) and would have both surfaces completely free of any blemish that might prevent its use as a varnished surface. "A-C" grade would have only one surface of high quality. The other would be satisfactory for painting. A grade "C-C" sheet would have both sides of paint quality. Grade "C" will commonly have "plugs" in the surfaces. These are places where knots or blemishes have been punched out of the sheet before gluing and replaced by a piece of good wood the same size. The result is much like an inlay, producing a smooth surface satisfactory for painting but not as strong as a completely blemish-free piece of wood. Grade "C" surfaces are adequate for most theatrical applications. In some areas lower grades of plywood are available, such as "shop grade." This is plywood from which the blemishes have not been removed, but the sheet has been sanded to dimension. "Shop grade" sheets must be 90 percent usable. It is a good buy when available.

Although plywood is usually bought by the sheet, a better method, if storage space is available, is to buy it by the unit. A "unit" of plywood is a stack of sheets conveniently sized for handling by a forklift. Units run from about 35 sheets of $\frac{3}{4}$ inch plywood to as many as 130 sheets of $\frac{1}{4}$ inch material. They normally come baled together. A shop should be prepared to have units loaded directly into the storage area when delivered (the dealer will usually bring along his forklift) unless facilities for handling such heavy packages are available.

Storage

Both dimension stock and plywood need to be available. Lumber is best stored in a rack that allows for separation of sizes and types. A bin for short pieces should be nearby to encourage workers to use them instead of cutting up long boards. Plywood should also be stored on a rack and it should be kept flat to prevent warping. Since it is very difficult for one or two workers to lift part of a stack of plywood to get at a sheet of a different thickness, the rack should make each thickness directly available (see Figure 8-1). Masonite and heavy cardboard, two shop staples, may be stored on the same rack because the sheets are the same size.

Since the most critical application of lumber in the theatre is in the construction of flat frames, further details concerning lumber types and varieties will be discussed in Chapter 9, "Soft Scenery."

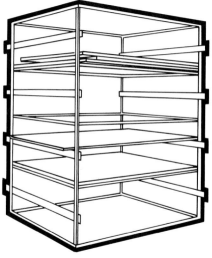

Figure 8-1. Plywood Rack. This rack is useful for storage of sheet material such as plywood, masonite, cardboard, and the like. Since these materials are very heavy when stacked in quantity, and the rack must be quite sturdy, welded steel construction is preferred.

HARDWARE

A wide variety of nails, screws, bolts, nuts, hinges, special stage hardware, and the like must be easily available. These are best stored in bins and drawers such as those shown in Figure 8-2. Note the labels on the front of each storage space. If parts are replaced in the bins, care should be taken to get these items back in their proper place. An odd mixture of bolts in the $\frac{1}{4}$ by 24 by 2 inch bolt drawer will only confuse everyone.

Nails

Nails come in a variety of types, including "common," "box," and "finish." Common and box nails have moderately large heads, while finish nails are nearly headless (see Figure 8-3). Box nails are the most frequently used type for theatrical construction because their slender shanks are less likely to split the wood commonly used in the theatre. The heavier-shanked common nails are used where heavy construction lumber is being nailed together. Finish nails have occasional theatrical applications where the heads might show. A variation on the common nail, "the double-head" (Figure 8-3) is much used for theatrical construction that must be disassembled later. A special nail, the "clout nail" is often used in flat construction. It is made of soft iron and has a wedge-shaped shank (see Figure 8-3). It is designed to clench (curl over on itself) when driven through a piece of wood and against a piece of iron. Clout nails must be specially ordered from a wholesaler or theatrical supplier.

Nails also come in a wide variety of sizes that are designated by the word "penny." This once indicated the cost of a nail in British pennies, but now if refers only to size. (See Figure 8-3 for sizes common to the theatre.) Note that "10 penny box nails" are about the same length as "10 penny common nails" although the shanks of the box nails are thinner.

Screws

A variety of joints used in the theatre require a fastening less susceptible to pulling out than a nail. Wood screws commonly are used in these places. They are designated by length, a number referring to their shank diameter, the type of head, and the material from which they are made. Some stage sizes are shown in Figure 8-4. Note that flat head iron screws are the common theatrical type.

Figure 8-5 shows a variety of other types of hardware that are commonly found in the scene shop.

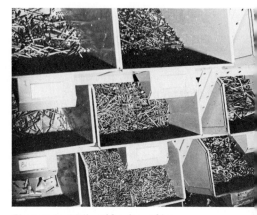

Figure 8-2a. Nail and hardware bins.

Figure 8-2b. Small parts drawers.

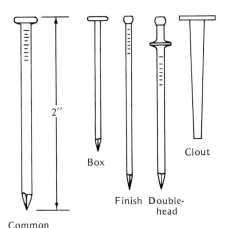

Figure 8-3. Nails. Some of the most commonly used nails are shown. Note the double-head nail, used wherever it will later be necessary to disassemble the construction, and the appearance of the head will not cause problems.

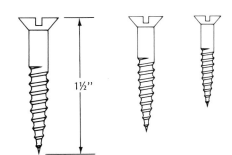

Figure 8-4. Screws. This shows some of the most commonly used wood screws. Although they are made in a variety of finishes such as chrome and even galvanized, theatres normally use plain steel screws with no special finish.

PAINT AND GLUE

If a theatre is still operating on the now nearly obsolete method of mixing paint from dry pigments, these will be stored in large bins equipped with scoops for handling the pigment. If modern, premixed paint is used, the cans of paint will simply be shelved. Dry carpenter's glue is stored like bulk pigment. White glue is kept in 1- or 5-gallon containers or in barrels. Since there is a large price advantage in buying white glue by the barrel, a barrel rack such as that shown in Figure 8-6 often is used. Day-to-day quantities of glue are tapped from the barrel and kept in 5-gallon plastic containers.

FABRIC STOCKS

Although the scene shop will have occasion to use many types of fabric, it will generally only stock fabric for covering flats and making drops (usually muslin), and gauzes or scrims for making transparencies. Other materials will either be bought as needed or obtained from the costume department, which will inevitably have a wide selection.

Muslin (or canvas if the shop can afford it) will be either stored on large rolls or shelved in bolts. Gauzes and scrims will come in bolts or rolls. The shop should also have storage space for used materials, especially gauzes and scrims, which should be stored in dust-resistant bags kept in a clean, dry place. Details concerning the choice of muslin for flat-covering applications will be discussed in Chapter 9, "Soft Scenery."

SHOP INVENTORY

Computing the real cost of a setting is a challenging matter under the best of conditions. Keeping adequate stocks of building materials also is difficult if no one knows how much of an item is on hand. Therefore most shops maintain some type of running inventory system, usually in the form of a check sheet to be marked when materials are taken from stock for use. Such a sheet may be found in the paint storage area, for example; when a can of paint is removed for use on a show, the sheet is checked to tell the person in charge of inventory at a glance just how much is left. There may also be a list indicating each item used on a specific show. It is to the advantage of everyone in the theatre to follow inventory instructions meticulously.

SHOP EQUIPMENT

To the beginner, a scene shop may seem to be an array of mechanical monsters, but to the experienced shop worker, it is a familiar place

Figure 8-5. (a) Hooks and Eyes. These items are commonly stocked in shops. They offer a handy way of fastening scenic items together when only a moderately secure joint is needed which must be rapidly fastened and unfastened. (b) Fastening Devices. These are some of the more common fastening devices used in the theatre. All require that a hole be drilled through the items to be fastened, but they offer a secure joint. The device at top left, known as a "tee nut," is used to make a smooth attachment for a bolt inserted through a piece of wood and screwed into the nut which has been driven into the back of the material flush with the surface. (c) Assorted Stage Hardware. A few of the many items necessary to the operation of a properly equipped stage.

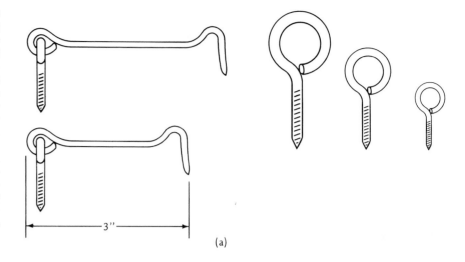

(a)

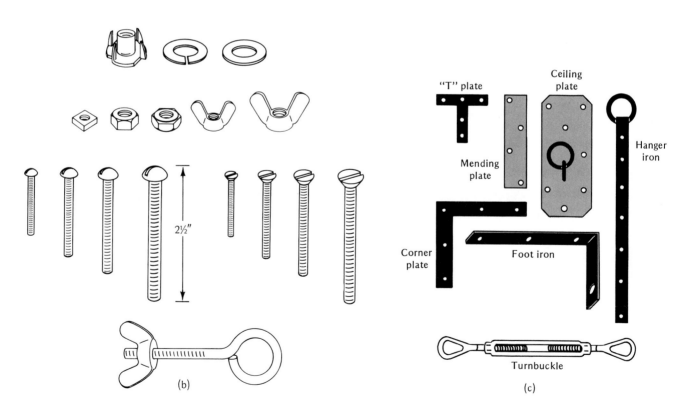

(b)

(c)

equipped with machines that enable him to get his job done. The following discussion of the tools found in a shop is not intended to be a substitute for careful instruction in their operation, but it should aid the student in identifying each piece of equipment and its function.

LARGE POWER EQUIPMENT

Large power equipment, the workhorses of the scene shop, multiply the effectiveness of human hands many times over. They are expensive and often more delicate than they look. They can also be dangerous if not properly operated and maintained.

Table Saw

One of the most essential shop tools is the table saw (Figure 8-7). This machine is especially good for cutting boards lengthwise to make narrow strips (ripping), and it should be so located that long pieces of lumber can be passed through it in ripping operations. It can also cut at angles, make wide grooves, and if necessary, cut across the grain of a board. The rapidly rotating blade can tear through wood at a fast rate. Thus, it is dangerous. Keep clear of it, and make sure that no clothing or hair get near it. When pushing a board through the saw, use a push stick instead of your hand—push sticks can be replaced.

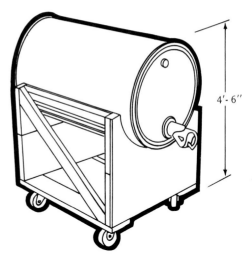

Figure 8-6. *Bulk Glue Storage. The advantages of quantity purchase of white glue make such a device worth having. Note that it is movable to allow shifting about the shop. Since a full barrel of glue may weigh nearly 200 pounds, the structure must be sturdy.*

Figure 8-7. *Table Saw. Table saws come in a number of sizes. A good scene shop should have at least a 2-horsepower size. Small home craftsman sizes are not adequate.*

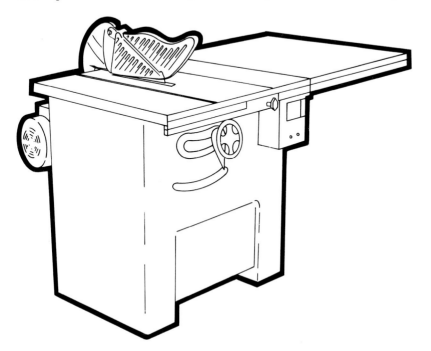

Radial Arm Saw

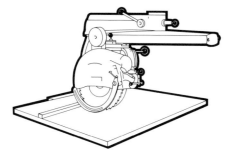

Figure 8-8. Radial Arm Saw.

Although crosscut work can be done on a table saw, the radial arm saw is much more convenient. This machine sometimes is called a "pull-over saw" because that is how it works. The rotating blade is moved across the work to make the cut. Therefore a radial arm saw is ideal for cutting long boards to length. The table extensions are about 16 feet long on either side of the saw to support the lumber while it is being cut (see Figure 8-8). The unwieldy board need not be moved once it is placed against the back support of the saw table. Since the blade is in clear sight rather than under the work as it is in the table saw, it is easy to see exactly where the cut will be.

Radial arm saws can cut a wide variety of angles, and can, if necessary, be used to rip boards—a dangerous operation if not done properly. They are versatile machines although most of the time they are the "cut-off saw" in a scene shop. They can throw chips and even pieces of lumber if not properly handled.

Band Saw

Compared to the two saws discussed above, the band saw (Figure 8-9) seems a gentle machine. It produces little of the screaming sound of whirling blades, nor the roar of wood being rent. This is an illusion; it can cut flesh just as fast as the others. It is absolutely necessary if smooth curves are to be cut in wood or metal. (It can also be equipped with metal-cutting blades.) The narrow, continuous band blade makes it possible to follow rather sharply curved lines accurately; the narrower the blade, the sharper the curve. This tool should be installed with clear space around its table to allow for swinging large pieces of material as they are cut.

Jig Saw

The jig saw (Figure 8-10) cuts still sharper curves than the band saw. It has a very fine blade that is moved up and down to make it cut. It is designed to do relatively light cutting with precision, and can cut complicated curves in light material.

Jointer (Planer)

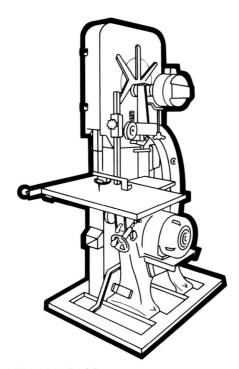

Figure 8-9. Band Saw.

The jointer (often called a planer) smooths the surface of a piece of board by taking off a thin layer of wood (see Figure 8-11). This noisy, quite dangerous machine is also used for reducing a board to an exact dimension. It requires space at either end to allow passage of long pieces of lumber.

Wood Lathe

The wood lathe (Figure 8-12) is designed to allow the operator to make various round shapes such as lamp bases and stair spindles, out of wood. Of all the shop tools, it is one of the most satisfying to operate. Reducing a roughly square piece of wood to a graceful spindle or newel post is fun. However this rather expensive tool should not be operated by a beginner without supervision and instruction.

Sander

The sander (Figure 8-13) makes rough wood smooth and can adjust dimensions to a very fine tolerance. It cuts more rapidly than most beginners realize and can ruin work instead of finish it if you are not careful. Also, the sandpaper disks and belts wear out quickly, so it should be used only for fine finishing. The jointer is better for larger cuts.

Shaper

A handy tool, the shaper may not be found in any but the best-equipped shops. It can make any straight piece of soft wood into a decorative molding, thus saving many dollars. The shaper cuts plain pieces of wood into intricate moldings by means of rapidly rotating knives. It is a dangerous machine if carelessly used.

Drill Press

Equally good in working on wood or metal, the purpose of the drill press is to make accurate holes (Figure 8-14). It is more dangerous than it looks and sounds because work can easily catch on the whirling bit and injure the operator's hand.

Air Compressor

An air compressor may not even be visible in the scene shop, but its product, compressed air, will be much in demand. It produces power to spray paint, to drive staples and nails, and to do many other things necessary in scenic construction.

HAND-HELD POWER TOOLS

Smaller tools operate electrically or by compressed air, but they are held in the hand while in use, thus limiting their power and accuracy. For example, it is far easier to make an accurate cut on a board with a radial arm saw than with a portable electric handsaw.

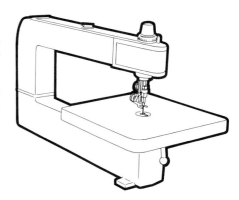

Figure 8-10. Jig Saw.

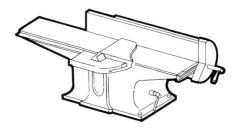

Figure 8-11. Jointer (Planer).

Figure 8-12. Wood Lathe.

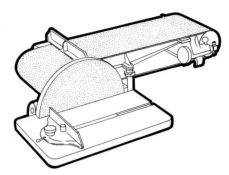

Figure 8-13. Sander.

Figure 8-14. Drill Press.

Figure 8-15. Electric Handsaw.

Electric Handsaw

The electric handsaw, a miniature radial arm saw without the guiding apparatus, is a rapid-cutting tool useful for rough cuts on the job (see Figure 8-15). It cannot, however, equal the accuracy of a table or radial arm saw. Poor quality electric handsaws with inadequate guards can be very dangerous.

Sabre Saw

The sabre saw (Figure 8-16) is a hand-held version of the jig saw. It can cut a wide variety of curves in either wood or metal, depending on the blade used, but does not cut as smoothly as a band saw. Also, it is only as accurate as the hand holding it. Blades are easily broken unless the saw is used properly.

Electric Drill

A highly versatile tool whose original purpose was to drill holes, the electric hand drill comes in a variety of sizes. The $\frac{3}{8}$ inch size is most common and is satisfying for light-duty hole drilling in wood or metal. With speed control and reversal mechanism, it can also drive screws, operate a variety of rotary files to ream out holes, and do many other things.

Power Stapler and Power Nailer

Two devices found only in more sophisticated shops are great labor savers. The power stapler (Figure 8-17a) can revolutionize flat construction. By far the fastest, most economical way of attaching corner blocks and keystones, it must have compressed air to operate. The power nailer (Figure 8-17b) is a tremendous time saver if much heavy construction involving the driving of 6- to 10-penny nails is necessary. It too must have compressed air and uses specially packaged nails.

Cutawl

A Cutawl is used to turn out fine filigree work from thin plywood or cardboard. It is operated by moving the cutter over the work so that the cutting tool goes through the material from the top. No starting hole is needed, and inside cuts can be made with ease. Use care not to overload; it is for delicate work only.

Router

A relatively heavy-duty tool that can be used much like the Cutawl, but on heavier stock, the router (Figure 8-18) consists of a very rapidly rotating cutter attached directly to a small but powerful motor. It is used also to form decorative edges on paneling, table edges, around the inside or outside of cutouts, etc. The powerful cutter gouges easily and throws chips; use it with care.

HAND TOOLS

Tools that have no power operation work only at the speed of the human hand. Just a few of the more common are listed here because there are so many types, depending on the sophistication of the scene shop and the desires of the shop foreman. Note that many of these tools can be replaced by power-operated equipment such as those mentioned above.

The following types of hammers (Figure 8-19a) are common. A regular carpenter's hammer is used for driving nails and pulling partially driven nails. The ripping hammer is also used for driving nails, but is adapted for tearing apart nailed materials by driving the wedge-shaped claw between the parts to be separated. The tack hammer generally has one magnetized face and is used for holding and driving tacks. The ball peen hammer is used to shape metal parts and to "rivet" the ends of bolts to prevent the nut from coming off.

Squares (Figure 8-19b) are used to make or check right-angle joints. A framing or carpenter's square can be used to check right-angle joints and to compute angle markings for cuts. A tri-square can be used on smaller parts to mark and check for squareness. A combination square is used like a tri-square, but has the additional capability of marking 45 degree angles. A bevel guage is used to accurately transfer from one angle cut to another.

There are many varieties of saws (Figure 8-19c). The following are the types you are most likely to encounter in the scene shop. The coping saw is used to make curved cuts in delicate materials. The hacksaw cuts metal and can be fitted with different types of blades depending on the metal to be cut. Handsaws are fitted with either rip or crosscut teeth. The ripsaw is used to cut with the grain of the wood; the crosscut saw to cut across the grain. A back saw is used with a mitre box (Figure 8-19d) for cutting exact angles in wood for picture frames, cornices, etc.

The nail puller (Figure 8-19e) is much handier than the claws of a hammer when the nail has been driven completely home.

The level (Figure 8-19f) is used to determine if something is exactly horizontal or vertical. The combination square also has a small level built into it.

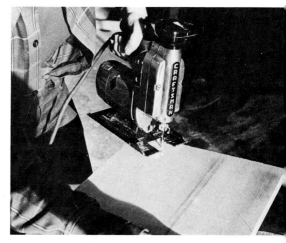

Figure 8-16. Sabre Saw.

Figure 8-17a. Power Stapler.

Figure 8-17b. Power Nailer.

Figure 8-18. Router.

The brace and bit (Figure 8-19g) is convenient for drilling holes where a power drill cannot reach.

The ratchet screwdriver (Figure 8-19h) works by pressing on the handle rather than by twisting. It is faster than a regular screwdriver, but is more apt to slip, and takes some practice to use properly.

The plane (Figure 8-19i) is used for smoothing wood and for making minor size adjustments.

The staple gun (Figure 8-19j) has almost succeeded in making the tack hammer obsolete. It is used for fastening thin wood, cardboard, cloth, or other thin materials, to wood or cardboard.

Figure 8-19a. Hammers. Left to right: regular carpenter's hammer, ripping hammer, tack hammer, ball peen hammer.

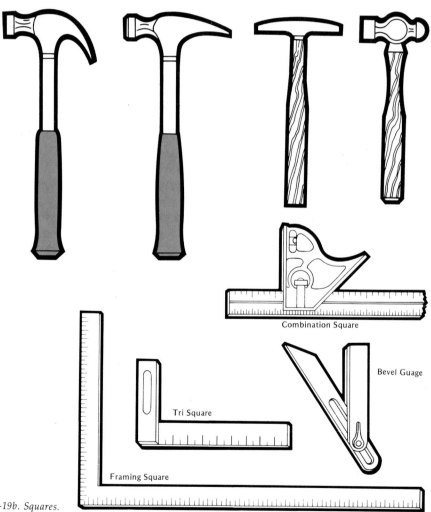

Combination Square

Bevel Guage

Tri Square

Framing Square

Figure 8-19b. Squares.

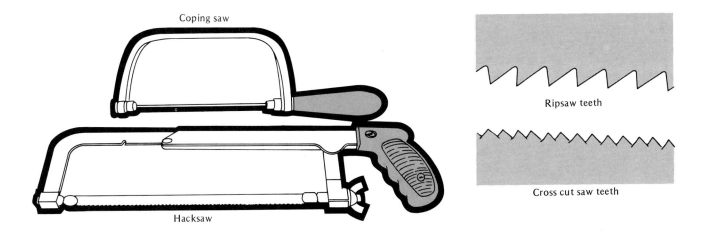

Coping saw

Ripsaw teeth

Hacksaw

Cross cut saw teeth

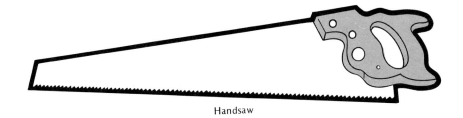

Handsaw

Figure 8-19c. Saws.

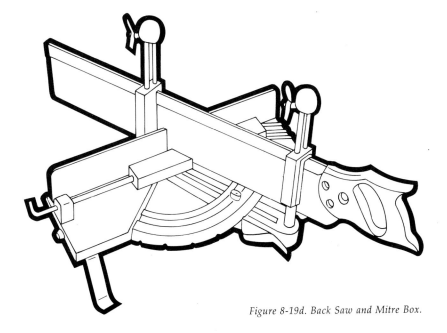

Figure 8-19d. Back Saw and Mitre Box.

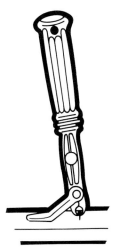

Figure 8-19e. Nail Puller.

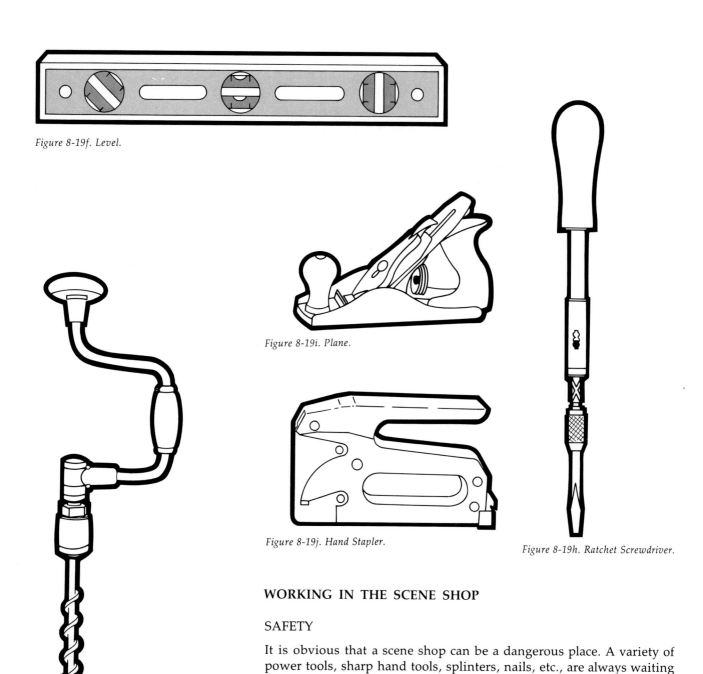

Figure 8-19f. Level.

Figure 8-19i. Plane.

Figure 8-19j. Hand Stapler.

Figure 8-19h. Ratchet Screwdriver.

Figure 8-19g. Brace and Bit.

WORKING IN THE SCENE SHOP

SAFETY

It is obvious that a scene shop can be a dangerous place. A variety of power tools, sharp hand tools, splinters, nails, etc., are always waiting for the careless or unwary. Shop rules must be stringently enforced.

Safe Use of Power Tools

Power tools should be used only by those who have been properly trained and authorized to use them. It is not enough to be familiar with a table saw, for instance, in your home shop. You must be checked out on the scene shop table saw before using it, since it may have some quirks you have not previously encountered.

When operating power tools avoid distraction. If someone calls you or comes up to talk, turn off the machine until you can give it your undivided attention. Never wear clothing or unbound hair that could become tangled in the machine. Protective eye shields or goggles should be worn whenever operating equipment that may throw off bits of material in the direction of the operator.

Dull, out-of-adjustment power tools are both dangerous and inefficient. Blades should be kept sharp and the entire machine maintained in good adjustment. Be careful not to overload equipment; feed heavy boards very slowly.

Get help when you need it. For example, it is risky for one person to try to handle an entire sheet of $\frac{3}{4}$ inch plywood on a table saw. Similarly, it is a good idea for a second person to clear ripped pieces from the back of a table saw.

All workers in the shop should beware of sudden noises, such as the shriek of a saw blade that has been twisted in the cut of a large piece of board. Give help at once. Such mistakes usually result from having insufficient help to handle the material or overloading a too small saw.

Keeping the Floor Clean

Much work will be done on the shop floor in spite of all modern conveniences. Sawdust, small cuts of wood, nails, etc., will accumulate. Therefore bare feet or thin-soled slippers are forbidden in shops. Puncture wounds are dangerous. All flammable waste should be swept up and placed in a safe container for disposal. The fire inspector will enforce this rule if shop personnel do not.

Organizing Shop Work

A job can be done best in less time if you plan ahead. You should understand what to do before you start cutting up expensive wood. Make sure you have adequate space in which to work and have gathered the proper tools for the job. Plan your trips to power tools. If you find that you will need ten pieces all of a size, cut them all at once using a stop block on the saw table instead of measuring each one individually.

As you plan the job, allow not only time to do the job, but time to put away the tools, store the finished product, and sweep up the work areas.

**9
SOFT
SCENERY**

INTRODUCTION The definition of soft scenery has already been given in the introduction to this part. However it may be worth emphasizing that soft scenery, by our modern definition, includes unframed fabrics such as draperies and drops, and framed fabrics such as framed drops and flats. Draperies have already been discussed in Chapter 3, "The Proscenium Theatre," because they ordinarily are purchased as part of the original stage equipment, and are in any event, seldom made in the local scene shop. Framed and unframed drops will be covered in the following discussion. However, the staple of theatres using soft scenery is the flat, which will be discussed in considerable detail in the chapters that follow. Although it is something of a holdover from the nineteenth century, it is still the most common single scenic item in the American theatre.

WHAT IS A FLAT?

It is possible that future texts on stage technology will omit much of the material in this chapter. New staging techniques make the simple flat less and less common on many stages. The cost of conventional materials may result in entirely new methods of constructing whatever form of soft scenery replaces the flat. Nevertheless, at this stage in the theatre's history, it is necessary to study in detail the construction of flats.

A *flat* is a sturdy wooden frame covered with tightly stretched fabric which may be painted to resemble any surface commonly found in building construction and many of those found in nature. It is termed "soft scenery" because the surface "gives" when pressed. The flat has several advantages:

1. It is light in weight and easy to move about on the stage.

2. It is relatively inexpensive to build, particularly if it is possible to use it repeatedly.
3. It fits the standard procedures in a scenic construction shop.
4. There is readily available a well-designed line of fasteners, interconnecting and hanging hardware, and other devices intended to work with the flat.
5. Much of the machinery on the proscenium stage is designed to handle the flat.

PARTS OF A FLAT

The parts of a typical simple flat, identified in Figure 9-1, should be learned by every student of technical theatre. Note that certain parts get their names from their function. The *rails* are so named because it is common practice to slide flats around on the stage floor, and the rails are designed to facilitate that movement. Imagine what would happen if the *stile* was carried through to the floor so that sliding action tended to pull the grain of the stile apart as the flat moved (Figure 9-2). Since flats frequently are inverted, both rails are installed in the same way. The *toggle rail* is placed near the middle of the flat to serve as a brace to prevent the tension of the covering fabric from bowing the stiles. It also serves as an anchor for pictures, etc., that may be hung from the front of the flat as they would be on the wall of a house. When it serves this anchoring purpose, the toggle rail is placed wherever it is needed, or an additional toggle rail is installed. Flats taller than 10–12 feet usually have two toggle rails, simply for purposes of bracing.

There is wide variety in the types and locations of corner braces. Many theatres which use only small flats, perhaps 8 feet tall, may not install corner braces at all unless they are on very wide flats. On the other hand, professional practice, which anticipates the rigors of touring productions, requires corner braces on nearly every flat except those less than 18 inches wide.

The remaining wooden parts of a simple flat frame are the corner blocks and the keystones, which we will discuss below as we examine the joints in a flat. Metal parts, other than nails, screws, and the like, vary with the means employed in fastening flats to each other, and will be discussed later.

LUMBER USED IN CONSTRUCTING FLATS

Frames of flats presently are made of wood, although this may not be true much longer because lumber of the quality needed for good flats is getting to be as expensive as metal. Aluminum extrusions seem to be a logical replacement for wood in flats, but have not yet appeared

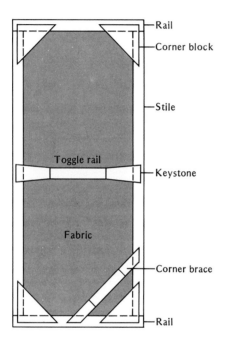

Figure 9-1. Parts of a Flat. This drawing should be memorized by all theatre workers.

Labels: Rail, Corner block, Stile, Toggle rail, Keystone, Fabric, Corner brace, Rail

FIGURE 9-2a

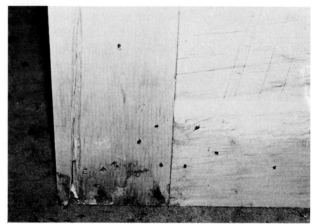

FIGURE 9-2b

Figure 9-2. Proper Installation of Rails. Note that sliding it across the floor (running) will destroy a flat with an improperly installed rail. (a) A properly installed rail. (b) An improperly installed rail. Note the splintered stile.

in that application. The following are the requirements for lumber to be used in building flat frames:

1. It must be strong and light.
2. It must not split or splinter under the stresses of joining or handling.
3. It must be relatively inexpensive; a requirement that is getting harder and harder to satisfy.
4. It must be generally available in constant supply and reliable grade.

Grades of Wood for Flat Frames

Stock 1 inch by 3 inches in grade "B & Better" meets most of the requirements listed above with one exception: it may not be sufficiently straight-grained. The tension of the tightly stretched fabric places a strain on flat frames beyond that anticipated by "B & Better" grade lumber. Stage carpenters, therefore, like to select straight-grained boards from the lumberman's stock of 1 by 3 inch "B & Better." This may cost extra if the carpenter is not a treasured customer known for his steady purchases over the years. Another method of assuring that the 1 by 3 inch stock for flat construction is straight-grained is to purchase 1 by 12 inch stock from the lumberyard and sort the boards before ripping to 1 by 3 inches. Only straight-grained boards are ripped. Those rejected are saved for use in wider cuts where the somewhat crossed grain will not be a problem. Since most theatres use a considerable amount of wider 1 inch stock, this is an economical way to proceed.

Types of Wood for Flat Frames

Ideally and traditionally, "B & Better" Idaho white pine is the ideal flat-building lumber. It meets every requirement except price and availability. Thus you will find it in use only in the most expensive professional scenic studios, and not always there. The next best species is yellow pine, often called Ponderosa, which is the common name of the tree from which most of it is cut. This lumber is not quite as good as white pine but it is available and is more reasonably priced. A bit more brittle than white pine and a little heavier, it is quite satisfactory when in proper grade. A third good choice—Sitka spruce—is available only in some areas. This is the lumber from which old-fashioned wooden airplanes were made. It is light and tough although a bit more flexible than pine. In the lumber areas of the Northwest it may turn out to be more economical than pine, but in the rest of the country it is not usually available.

The species mentioned above are reasonably satisfactory for flat frames; those listed below are poor substitutes to be used only under conditions of desperation and poverty:

1. Western red cedar and redwood. Both of these species split too easily, have low strength, and usually are too expensive.
2. Douglas fir. This is the standard lumber of the construction industry. It is strong, cheap, and moderately light, but splits and splinters too easily for good flat framing. It is also apt to be pitchy and knotty. You will use lots of it in larger sizes for weight-bearing structures, but it is not recommended for flats.

Generally, if the proper grade of pine is not available or is too expensive, it is better to move down a grade than to use another species. The only exception to this may be the case where Sitka spruce is available at a low price and proper grade.

Lumber Sizes for Flat Frames

The traditional lumber for flat framing is nominal 1 inch by 3 inches. However, where flats are subject to heavy use or where the construction of tall flats (over 14 feet) is common, a better material is "four quarter" (4 quarters of an inch thick [i.e., a full inch] stock, ripped to about 3 inches wide from full 12 inch stock. The lumber for ripping these boards may cost more than nominal 1 by 12 inch board, although the difference may be small or even nonexistent in large orders. The increase in strength will be considerable.

It will usually be economical to buy lumber in the length most commonly used for making flats or in a length that will allow the carpenter to cut a stile and a rail out of one piece with little or no waste. Specified lengths may cost a little more than "random lengths" of the same grade, but they will make up their extra cost and more by allowing for economical cutting. Anyway, the theatre shop will generate enough short pieces, some of which can be used to make corner braces, which can be cut from 1 by 3 inch or even 1 by 2 inch stock if this is handy.

Keystones and Corner Blocks

Keystones and corner blocks are small pieces of plywood used to make the butt joints that hold the flat frame together (see Figure 9-1). In the professional theatre they may be specially made up from basswood plywood, neatly beveled and sanded. Such blocks make a neat, strong joint, but an equally good joint may be made by using blocks cut from $\frac{1}{4}$ inch fir plywood. Scraps left over from other construction often are used, although it will occasionally be necessary to cut up a whole sheet of plywood to get enough blocks for making a number of flats. Grade "C-C" $\frac{1}{4}$ inch plywood is adequate, and "shop grade" may be used if funds are low. See Figure 9-3 for cutting dimensions. Note that the grain must run parallel to one of the two sides of the triangle, not to the hypotenuse. Reject any corner block that has been cut from an obviously flawed portion of plywood.

FABRICS USED IN COVERING FLATS

The standard professional theatre material for covering flats used to be heavy "duck," a canvaslike cotton material of high durability and cost. It is still used, but is becoming prohibitively expensive. In its

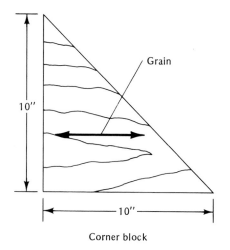

Corner block

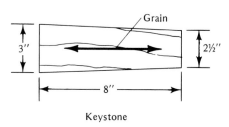

Keystone

Figure 9-3. Keystones and Corner Blocks. Be sure to note the way the grain runs.

place most theatres use heavy *muslin*, the same cotton material from which cheap bed sheets are made. A good, heavy grade (140 threads per inch) makes a very satisfactory covering for flats. It should preferably be unbleached because this material is both stronger and cheaper. It also shrinks more when first moistened, an advantage in getting smooth surfaces. Muslin is bought most cheaply in large wholesale rolls from a cotton fabric wholesaler. Such rolls are heavy and hard to handle unless mounted on a special rack, but the savings are well worth the trouble. Next best, though considerably more expensive, is to buy muslin by the bolt from fabric houses. The most expensive way to buy it is in small retail quantities, or as preflameproofed material from a theatrical supplier. Buying a grade with less than 140 threads to the inch will save money, but this thin material will not take paint as well nor will it be as durable. Whatever grade of muslin is purchased, it should be at least 72 inches wide, so there will be no need to seam it for ordinary flats. Muslin is also available, although at higher prices per square yard, in special 30 foot widths. Such widths are used for seamless drops, cycloramas, and other special applications. This material usually is bought by the running yard (each running yard equals 10 square yards) as needed. It may be purchased either preflameproofed (and shrunk) or untreated.

HOW IS A FLAT ASSEMBLED?

A flat is simply a sturdy wooden frame with fabric stretched tightly over it. The stretching is achieved by shrinking the fabric after it has been firmly attached to the frame. This makes a smooth surface but also puts considerable strain on the frame, which must be constructed with this strain in mind. Flats are not intended to support heavy weights, either hanging from them or sitting on top of them, but they can be expected to carry such moderate loads as pictures, cornices of light wood, or part of the weight of a ceiling made of wood and muslin. They also have to take the considerable stress of handling, stacking backstage, and perhaps shipping. Under all of these conditions, they must not only hold together, but also remain square and true so there will be no noticeable gaps between them.

JOINTS FOR FLAT FRAMES

There are two standard joints: (1) the *mortise and tenon* joint used in professional scene shops, and (2) the *butt* joint (see Figure 9-4). The first is the stronger *if* it is properly made, but it takes a professional carpenter with the right machines to do the job. A poorly made mortise and tenon joint is worthless. The only alternative for shops without

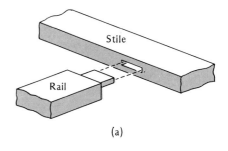

(a)

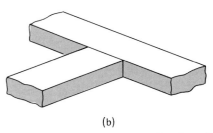

(b)

Figure 9-4. (a) Mortise and Tenon Joint. A wood joint made by making a hole in one part and a tight-fitting insert in the mating piece. This is an excellent joint for scenery construction if done by an expert in a well-equipped shop. It is seldom used in amateur or academic theatre. (b) Butt Joint. A simple joint between two pieces of wood, made by cutting the parts to fit against each other tightly, that uses a fastening device (nail, corner block, screw, etc.) to hold the parts in place.

experts and machines is the butt joint. Properly made, the butt joint is nearly as strong as the mortise and tenon. With reasonable care, it can be properly made by student technicians using simple tools. Cuts should be square, which is not much of a problem if a power cutoff saw is available. If a handsaw or electric handsaw must be used, the cut should be marked with a tri-square or carpenter's square and the saw should be carefully operated. Next the rail and stile must be held precisely square while the joint is being fastened. A carpenter's square will do this adequately, although a *template* (a carefully squared frame) can be made to speed up the work.

Attaching Keystones and Corner Blocks

Three-layer plywood is twice as strong in one direction as the other. The strength is in the outer layers, and lies across the grain of these layers. Students should test this strength difference for themselves by trying to break a scrap of plywood first across the outer grain and then with it. Even the weakest student can usually break a small piece of plywood if it is bent across the outer grain. This is why the blocks should be applied so that the outer grain runs *across* the joint.

Corner blocks and keystones are fastened in a variety of ways, depending on shop facilities and preferences of the technical director. The oldest and still one of the strongest ways is to use $1\frac{1}{4}$ inch clout nails. The shank of these nails is wedge shaped. The nail should be driven with the wedge cutting *across* the grain of the 1″ × 3″ (*not* the grain of the plywood) to lessen the chance of splitting (see Figure 9-5). A proper nailing pattern is shown in Figures 9-6a,b. This places two nails strategically on either side of the joint. Note that the nails are staggered to avoid splitting the 1″ × 3″. If the nails are driven home against a piece of smooth iron (a clinch plate), they will clinch automatically, making a solid joint. Nevertheless one should turn the freshly nailed flat frame

Figure 9-5. Clout Nail Joint. If clout nails are being used, they must be installed so that the chisel point of the clout nail is driven across the grain of the 1″ × 3″. Note the grain of the corner block.

over and check to see that no nail ends protrude above the surface of the wood. If they do they will probably snag your fingers while you are covering the flat.

A clout-nailed joint is perhaps the most nearly permanent of common theatrical joints. It is possible to use a nail puller to remove the nails, but this is tedious work that also destroys the corner block. Therefore, mistakes should be caught before driving the nails home. Start three or four nails, enough to hold the joint in position. Then double check with a square before driving them. After four nails have been set, the remainder can be driven without fear that the flat will go out of square.

One thing to be avoided is clout nails so short that they do not clinch, about the worst holding device that could be devised. Their wedge shape makes them work back out after they have been driven into the wood. The result is a flat that literally falls apart during use.

Some technicians place glue under the corner block before nailing it in place. This makes a somewhat stronger joint, although the plywood is still the only weight-bearing "bridge" between rail and stile. Undoing a glued joint after the glue has set is nearly impossible. One usually saws them out and tosses the now-too-short lumber into the scrap bin.

Another method of fastening blocks is to use blued shingle nails just short enough to avoid having them pass through to the other side of the rail. They should be about $\frac{3}{4}$ of an inch long. Since these nails do not clinch, they do not make quite as secure a joint as clout nails, but they are cheaper and easier to find. Glue can, of course, be used with shingle nails as well as with clout nails.

A third way to fasten corner blocks and keystones to flats is to use a power stapler. This is by far the fastest method yet devised. Although the initial cost of the power stapler and the air compressor to run it is high, the long-run dividends in time saved are remarkable. The staples must be chosen to come just short of passing completely through the plywood and the 1" × 3", or staple ends will form a hazard. Operators must be well trained in the use of the staple gun and must know the hazards of incorrect use. Removal of stapled corner blocks requires about the same amount of effort as that of blocks nailed with shingle nails.

Perhaps the most tedious way of fastening corner blocks is to apply them with $\frac{3}{4}$ inch screws. This method does have the minimal virtue of enabling one to remove the corner block for a second use at some later date. However, the time it takes is seldom worth the effort, with the exception of temporarily installed toggle rails for purposes of supporting a special picture, cornice, or the like. In this case, the fastening between the two keystones and the rails of the flat to which the rail is being applied, may advantageously be done with wood

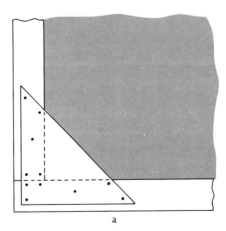
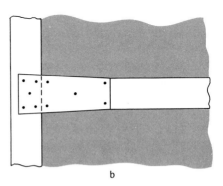
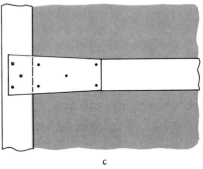

Figures 9-6a and b. Nailed Joint. This shows a typical nailing pattern for applying corner blocks (a) and keystones (b) with either clout nails or blued shingle nails. Note that two nails are strategically placed at either side of the joint. Staples are applied in the same pattern. (c) Screw-attached toggle. Note that screws have been used only to attach the keystone to the rail. Such a toggle may be installed for special purposes, such as supporting a picture on a wall, and then removed without serious damage to the flat.

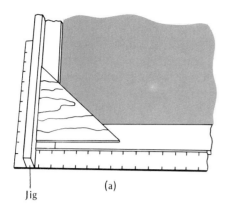

Jig

(a)

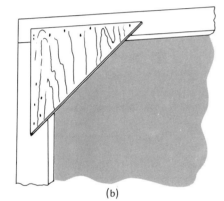

(b)

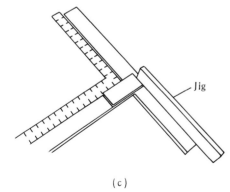

Jig

(c)

FIGURE 9-7d

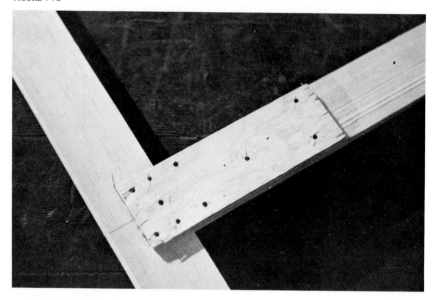

FIGURE 9-7e

Figure 9-7. (a) Spacing a Corner Block. This must be done while the rail and stile are held securely in square. Note the standard $\frac{3}{4}$ or 1 inch framing stock used as a "jig." (b) A Properly Installed Corner Block. Note that the top grain of the plywood runs across the joint and the spacing is even. (c) Spacing a Keystone. This is done in the same manner as the corner block except that the square must be held inside the joint instead of outside. (d) A Properly Installed Keystone. Note the nailing pattern. (e) Finished Frame. Note set back of all blocks.

FIGURE 9-8a

screws. This will enable you to remove the special toggle rail without much injury to the flat (see Figure 9-6c).

All corner blocks and keystones should be applied $\frac{3}{4}$ of an inch from the outer edge of the flat to accommodate the edge of flats placed at right angles to the first flat (see Figure 9-7). If full inch stock is being used throughout the theatre, the allowance should be a full inch. The easiest way to make this adjustment is to use a small piece of the proper thickness 1" × 3" as a "jig" to set the distance (see Figure 9-7a and c). Note also that corner blocks and keystones must be set back from door and window openings in flats just as they are at the outer edges.

COVERING A FLAT

After the flat frame has been completely constructed, and checked for square and for protruding nail ends on its front surface, it is ready for covering. Figure 9-8 shows the covering process. Note that the muslin is normally cut to fit some 2–3 inches beyond the edges of the flat, and door and window openings are ignored unless the shop is trying to save material by piecing the cover. The muslin is laid evenly over the flat allowing for shrinkage. The exact allowance depends on the quality of the muslin and the binder to be used in the size coat to come. It is usually about right to allow the fabric to just touch the floor at the center of a flat 3–5 feet wide (see Figure 9-8a). You should have your supervisor check the amount of slack until you are sure of this. After placing the fabric, it is common practice to set tacks or staples near the inside edge of the rails and stiles as shown in Figure 9-8b. The tacks or staples should be driven lightly into the wood to facilitate their removal after the glue has dried. (Experts will probably omit tacking.)

Adhesives for Covering Flats

The traditional adhesive for attaching fabric to flat frames is a mixture of carpenter's glue (also called "animal glue"), wheat paste, and cheap pigment. Carpenter's glue comes as a yellowish meal or as flakes of amber-colored material. The glue is covered with warm water, allowed to soak until it forms a heavy gel, and then cooked in a double boiler to make a thick, syrupy liquid known as "strong glue solution." (See Chapter 21, "Scene Painting," for full details of this process.)

Strong glue solution then is diluted with warm water, wheat paste (follow directions on package), and enough cheap pigment to avoid "glue burns" (spots that show through the finish paint on a flat, have a smoother than normal surface, may be stained brown from the color of the glue, and are very difficult to obliterate). Exact

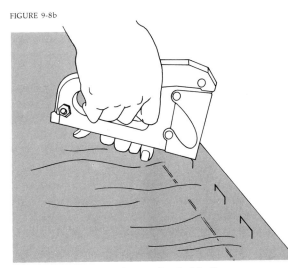
FIGURE 9-8b

Figure 9-8. (a) Cutting and Arranging the Muslin. The amount of slack shown here is about correct for a good grade of muslin. Note the overlap at the edges of the flat. Either staples or tacks may be used to hold the muslin in place. (b) Tacking the Fabric with a Stapler. This is the most convenient method of holding the fabric in place until it can be glued. Note how the operator is holding the stapler away from the rail so the staple will be only lightly driven into the wood, and can be easily removed later.

proportions of wheat paste, glue, and pigment will vary over a considerable range, depending on the quality of the glue, shop practice, and other variables. Sufficient paste and pigment must be present to give the glue a gray color and to assure that no burns will form where glue has been applied too generously.

The modern adhesive for attaching fabric to flat frames is white glue. If it is adopted along with modern premixed scene paints, there will be no need for a glue pot in the scene shop. Although white glue does not usually stain like carpenter's glue, it can glaze the fabric, producing a permanent change in texture that is hard to hide. There are two methods of avoiding this problem. One is to dilute the white glue 2:1 with water and add pigment (usually whiting). The glue mixture then is applied in the manner described below. The other method is to use glue straight from the container, but to apply it under the fabric only.

Carpenter's glue or diluted white glue is used to adhere fabric to flat frames by applying a layer to the surface of all wooden parts outlining the finished flat. Thus all perimeters, whether around the outside of the flat or around window or door openings, are glued. Rails or braces not outlining a perimeter should be scrupulously clean of glue or they may show through the finished flat surface. (The only exception to this rule is if lack of funds makes it necessary to piece together flat covers to use up every scrap of muslin.) After the glue has been spread on the wood, the fabric is pressed down into the glue taking care that no wrinkles are formed. Remember that the fabric must remain slack to allow for shrinkage later.

When the fabric is in place, a coat of glue paste is applied to the top of the fabric being careful to glue only those parts that contact the glue underneath. Then the glue-coated surface is hand rubbed causing the still-soft glue to penetrate the pores of the fabric completely, thus assuring good adhesion. This rubbing process is best done by bare hands—a method that will be sure to find any protruding nail ends or splinters. After the glue has been rubbed in, the covered frame is allowed to dry at least overnight—always long enough to allow the glue to completely harden. Any attempt to size or flameproof a flat before the glue is completely dry will probably result in the shrinking fabric pulling away from the frame. Tacking may help to hold such pulls, but they will seldom be invisible in the finished scenery.

The above method can be altered to allow the use of white glue direct from the container and to save time. Because of the superior strength of white glue over carpenter's glue, undiluted white glue can be applied to the wood as described above and the fabric pressed into place, without applying glue to the front surface of the fabric (Figure 9-9). The flat is allowed to dry thoroughly and is then trimmed and treated just like any other flat.

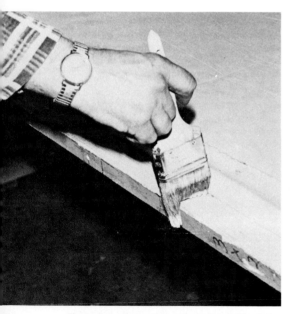

Figure 9-9. Gluing Down the Fabric. This photograph shows the simplified process that involves applying the strong white glue only to the surface of the wood.

TRIMMING AND FLAMEPROOFING

After the flat has dried, it must be trimmed (Figure 9-10) and the tacks must be removed with a tack puller. The trimming is done with a very sharp knife; commercial grade single-edge razor blades are often used with a holder for this process. The idea is to cut the fabric down into the grain of the wood very close to the outer edge of the rails and stiles. The same process is used to cut out the muslin covering any openings in the flat. A quicker way to trim is to simply cut around the flat very close to the wood, but this tends to leave frayed bits of fabric that may eventually pull loose from the frame and show. The trimmings often are saved to make patches over joints between flats (known as "dutchmen"), so do not toss them out unless you are told to do so.

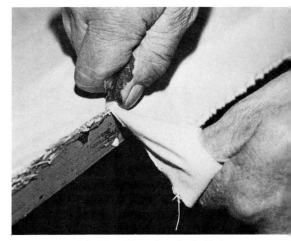

Figure 9-10. Trimming. Note that the knife is pressed into the wood, not merely drawn along its edge.

Flameproofing is required by almost every fire department in the country and should be employed whether required by law or not. It is a simple operation that shrinks the fabric and coats the fibers with chemicals to prevent flames from spreading if fire comes into contact with the fabric. Note that it will not prevent the fire from burning a hole in the flat where flame or heat contacts it; it only prevents the flames from spreading.

The prescribed chemicals are mixed with hot water and applied to the flat by either brushing or spraying. You should not attempt to flameproof those areas of fabric glued to the wood. This is apt to loosen the glue and will have little effect anyway. The areas of the fabric not backed by wood and glue should be well dampened with the flameproofing but should not be dripping wet. You will note that the muslin or canvas shrinks as soon as it gets wet. It will shrink still more as it dries. Since flameproofing is somewhat caustic, avoid getting it into your eyes or mouth, and wash out containers, sprayers, and the like immediately after use.

Size Coating

Sometimes time may be saved by combining the flameproofing with what is called a "size coat," a thin coat of glue solution intended to shrink the fabric, flameproof it, and fill the pores of the fabric so it will take paint better. Old-fashioned size water was made from the same carpenter's glue that was once used to glue down the fabric. It was much diluted (sixteen parts of warm water to one part glue) and colored with some pigment, usually white, to prevent glue burns. A size coat made up from white glue is less likely to present this problem and is made the same way: glue, warm water, and some pigment, plus the flameproofing if this is not applied as a separate first coat. It may be sprayed or brushed onto the fabric. Your supervisor will make the decision to combine steps depending on his experience with the pigments, flameproofing, and the equipment at his disposal. Chemical reactions occasionally take place when combination is attempted which could result in a gluey mass instead of a paintlike mixture.

At the same time you flameproof the flats, you will probably be asked to prepare a sample of fabric for the fire inspector. This is simply a piece of the same muslin used to cover the flats treated with each step of the process and allowed to dry. It is then tested and the remainder retained for the fire inspector. The inspector has the right, of course, to test a sample from one or more of the flats if he thinks it necessary. However, if he feels that the shop is trustworthy, he will usually be satisfied with the prepared sample and will make his test on it. If it passes, he will approve the setting (assuming everything else is satisfactory). If the sample does not pass tests, it will be necessary to add more flameproofing to the back of the flats until it does pass, or even in desperate circumstances, to use special and expensive "high penetration" flameproofing. If the process still does not pass, the fire inspector can forbid use of the setting or require that it be treated by a professional flameproofer—a very expensive step.

VARIATIONS IN FLAT CONSTRUCTION

Ordinarily, no set can be made from only plain flats with no openings. Doors, windows, or openings of some sort are almost always a part of settings. Although the basic construction techniques are the same for all soft flats, there are some special steps the student should learn concerning the construction of flats with openings in them.

Doorways and Doors

The location and operation of doorways is a design matter that must be decided by the scenographer and the director. Many of these decisions are made early in the scenographic process when the floor plan is being discussed. Since entrances are a major factor in the design of actor movement, their location and arrangement become a concrete expression of the total concept of stage movement designed by the director and the scenographer. Although crew members will have little to do with this design process itself, it may be instructive to review some of the considerations that go into it. Observant crew members may be able to understand the rationale behind what may otherwise seem to be an arbitrary arrangement.

Entrances and exits are major concerns in each scene ("act" in the Langer sense[1]) that the actor plays. If these can be arranged so that the actor can easily face the audience and thereby take the scene

1. Susanne K. Langer, *Feeling and Form* (New York: Charles Scribner's Sons, 1953).

(be the primary focus of attention), the actor will usually be more effective. Thus major *entrances* tend to be in upstage positions which allow the actor to come into the playing area face forward and upstage of other actors. Major *exits* are often designed downstage for the same reason. Of course, exceptions abound, but the principle of providing the actor with a strong entrance or exit is almost always a primary consideration. Note how closely the construction of the scenery relates to the expressive movement and thereby to the artistic goals of the production.

Like the location of doorways, the operation of the door shutters (that part of the door that hangs on the hinges—commonly called simply a "door") themselves is a matter of artistic concern. Stage doors usually open offstage, although exterior doors in most homes open inward. Thus stage doors defy realism. However, the advantages of offstage and upstage movement are both artistic and practical. Artistically, the offstage movement brings the actor on stage clear of the shutter and in a more favorable position to command attention. Technically, swinging the door offstage and upstage moves the shutter toward the bracing that holds the door flat up, reducing any tendency toward jiggling. Since only one side and the front edge of the door are even revealed to the audience, construction is simplified. Furthermore, the door shutter will often serve as its own masking piece, reducing the need to install a two-fold (two flats hinged like a folding screen) behind the opening.

BASIC DOOR FLAT   A flat to accommodate a door is framed as shown in Figure 9-11. Standard framing techniques are used with one exception. The two "legs" forming the parts of the flat at either side of the door opening will be relatively weak. They will tend to bend when the flat is moved, and may spread under pressure, making the door fit poorly. To avoid this a *sill* or *foot iron* is installed across the bottom of the flat as shown in Figure 9-12. This sill iron is simply a piece of strap iron recessed into the lower edges of the two bottom rail pieces. It is held in place with wood screws. Once the door flat has been built, a door may be installed in it in either of the ways mentioned below.

BUILT-IN DOOR   The simplest method of installing a door in a flat is to build it into the flat opening by nailing a thickness piece (a piece added to the edge of a flat to give it the appearance of having the thickness of a wall) to the 1″ × 3″ surrounding the door opening and installing the casing on the front. Be sure that no joints are arranged in such a way that the audience could look through them at light operating behind the set. After such a casing is installed and a sill iron has been fitted to the flat, the door shutter is hinged to the casing. This is done while making sure the shutter will not hang up on the sill iron. Door

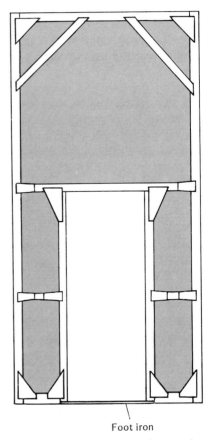

Foot iron

Figure 9-11. Door Flat. Note the use of non-standard corner blocks to achieve special strength.

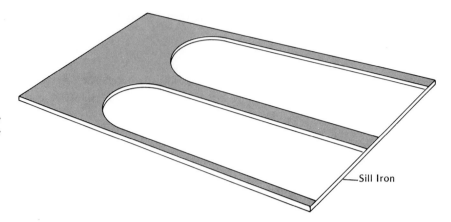

Figure 9-12. Sill Iron. More elaborate irons are available from supply houses although this simple strip of iron will be adequate for most purposes.

Sill Iron

shutters are often hinged to the back of the thickness pieces to minimize the risk that the door will hang up during action. If for reasons of design this cannot be done, the door shutter must fit quite loosely inside the door opening.

The best time to install the door stops is after the door has been mounted and tested to make sure that it does not drag. Simply hold the door in its proper closed position, mark the stop location, and then nail it into place. After the door flat is completed, it should be raised into vertical position and tested again to make sure that the door moves freely over its entire swing. It should not have a tendency to swing to either the open or the closed position when the flat is vertical; if this happens, move the hinges slightly. The final step will be the installation of the latch and decorative hardware.

INSERT SYSTEM   As its name implies, the insert system consists of building stock flats with standard-sized window and door openings in them. Then a number of artistically varied door and window units are prepared and installed in these standard flats as needed. Such changes can even be made between acts.

Many theatres that constantly use flats as their major scenic elements find this system useful for a number of reasons:

1. It aids in the economical alteration of scenery from show to show by allowing interchange of doors or windows within the same stock flat frame.
2. It lightens handling problems for traveling or for shifting. Some units such as double doors may be so heavy that this is the only practical way of moving them.
3. If the shop is somewhat remote from the stage, the insert system may solve an otherwise almost impossible transport situation.

All flats with door and window openings for inserts must have the openings built somewhat larger then the finished dimensions planned for the doors and windows. The exact amount will be determined by construction practices but will work out to somewhere between 2 and 3 inches. This will allow for the thickness pieces of the frame and some clearance to aid the insertion of that frame. The frame itself (door or window) is a separate unit which simply slides into the opening and is temporarily locked there. If the insert is a door unit, it carries the sill iron. Whether it is door or window, the insert carries all of the working parts, thicknesses, special casing ornamentation, and the like. The flat provides the opening and the support. Considerable accuracy is required in the construction of these units so that the parts will be completely interchangeable and so that they will fit securely into the various openings.

Latching the inserts into the openings can be accomplished in a variety of ways. One of the fastest is to use a couple of hinges as shown in Figure 9-13. The loose flap of the hinge is held flat against

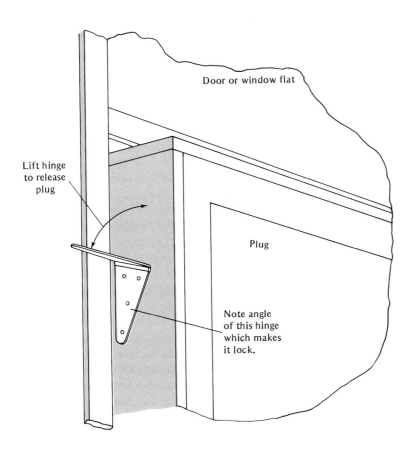

Door or window flat

Lift hinge
to release
plug

Plug

Note angle
of this hinge
which makes
it lock.

Figure 9-13. Strap Hinge Latch for Plugs. This drawing shows how a simple iron strap hinge can be installed to form a latch for a door for window plug. The sketch shows a rear view of the upper corner of a door or window plug. The hinge is screwed to the thickness piece so that it falls and jams against the stile of the opening in the flat. It must be angled slightly so the loose flap cannot fold down against the fixed portion.

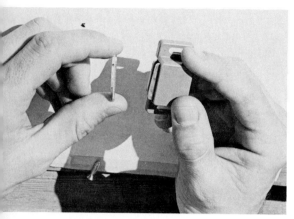

Figure 9-14. Magnet Door Latch. The latch must be installed so that the striker meets the magnet squarely.

Figure 9-15. Rim Latch.

the vertical portion of the insert and the assembly is slid into the opening. The hinge flap drops down to lock the insert into place. Two people are needed to remove the insert, one in front, and one behind the scenery. The person behind unlatches the hinge fasteners and the one in front pulls out the insert. Other methods involve the use of screen door hooks, temporary wooden blocks nailed to the back of the insert, barrel bolts, etc.

The insert system also has its drawbacks. Construction is somewhat more complicated by the fact that each door or window frame must exist as a solid structural unit without the bracing afforded by the flat frame. A special storage area must be allocated for the door and window units although some of this will be compensated by more compact storage of the empty flat frames. Unless the latching system used to hold the units into place is well made and properly operated, there will be a greater tendency for jiggling, fouling of shutters, and the like.

LATCHES   The appearance of the doorknob and the decorative plate (escutcheon) if any, are a matter of design. The actual mechanism that holds the door shut is a technical matter. Usually the knob and latch handle that are seen by the audience are not "practical" (this means they do not actually operate the door). Regular door latch mechanisms require much thicker doors and door casings than most theatre sets provide. When installed on makeshift arrangements they do not work well. A reliable door is absolutely essential on the stage. Actors may panic if they cannot open a door, and have been known to tear doors off hinges or even force them to open in a direction opposite to that intended.

There are two common solutions: (1) the use of rim locks, and (2) the use of magnet latches. Magnet latches (Figure 9-14) are the most immune to actor panic in that all they take is a push in the right direction and they will release. However, they do not always hold if the actor slams the door. They also make no sound resembling that of a normal latch. Rim latches (Figure 9-15) are extremely simple surface mounted door latches. They must be operated by pushing a lever to open the door. The latch catches firmly when slammed. Neither system is totally foolproof. Actors should rehearse with the doors complete with latches to make sure they know how to work them.

Archways

Archways are openings in a wall without a shutter. They are simply made up of flats and thickness pieces. The short flat across the top of the opening is known as a "header" or "plug." The apparent thickness of the wall in which the archway is installed is a design consideration. If the wall is to appear to be thicker than about 1 foot, flats are used as thickness pieces; for narrower thicknesses, lumber usually is used (see Figure 9-16).

Windows

Although there is a variety in the types of windows that the scenographer may desire, the same two basic construction techniques mentioned above can be used. Windows may be built into flats or inserted as needed. Since a window opening does not run to the floor, sill irons are not needed. However another problem will present itself: the weight of the window and casing tend to make the flat unwieldy. Extra bracing will be needed to make the flat stand upright if the window unit is heavy, and the crew will have to handle the flat with caution during shifting.

Window designs offer even wider variety than doors. The simplest is the window that is never opened. The proper framing is nailed to the back of the thickness pieces and the opening closed with whatever the designer specifies. It is a common practice to close window openings with galvanized screening such as that found on a screen door. This provides some of the illusion of glass at a distance and prevents actors from inadvertently passing a hand through the "glass" and destroying the illusion. It also adds some strength and provides a base for some shortcuts to imitating fancy window paning. For example, a square window can be closed with screening, and diamond-shaped panes can be outlined with friction tape run over the screen. This will "read" rather well from a distance and is both fast and cheap. If filigree work is required in the window, the screening will provide a good support for it.

If the "glass" must be broken on cue, perhaps by the fist of an actor, special soft plastic can be obtained from theatrical supply houses. It is expensive and very fragile. It should be avoided unless really necessary. Under certain circumstances regular single-strength window glass can be used and even broken (for example, by a tossed rock in sight of the audience). This must be carefully controlled because of the danger from broken glass. It is desirable that a well-trained and trusted stagehand actually break the glass in a controlled and rehearsed manner instead of depending on the movement of an actor. A mousetrap can be rigged to strike the glass in a predetermined place and direction *every time* to give the illusion of breaking by a thrown rock.

"Stained glass" windows are often required. They can be simulated in several ways, depending on how far away the audience is and what degree of realism is sought. If the window is to be back-lighted and viewed from some distance, it may be completely covered with thin muslin which can then be painted with dyes to produce a realistic

Figure 9-16. A Deep Archway. Note the cut of the sweeps (the curved portions) and the way the archway has been used to brace the flat and the adjoining wall. This archway has been constructed using hard flat techniques. Thus the vertical arch walls are of plywood, and the sweep is covered with bendboard.

Figure 9-17. Casings. These casings are part of a set of door plugs. They are decorated with 3-D trim.

effect. If much light strikes it from the front, the texture of the muslin will be revealed, spoiling the effect. A still more realistic but arduous method of simulating stained glass can be produced by using acetone (beware of fumes and highly explosive vapors) as a cement to join pieces of acetate color medium to form the appearance of such a window.

Backings

A *backing* is a scenic element seen through an opening in the setting. Its purpose is to give the illusion that the setting extends off into other mostly unseen portions of the structure, and to prevent the audience from looking through openings directly into the backstage areas. In the case of a doorway, it may represent part of a hallway or another room supposed to be adjacent to the one seen on stage. Window backings suggest exteriors or the exterior walls of other structures. While the exact nature of the backing is a matter for the scenographer, the mechanical arrangement is a technical matter. Backings can also be arranged to solve purely technical problems of bracing. For example, most door flats require additional bracing to prevent the flat from swaying when the door is operated. Arranging the door backing so that one of the backing flats intersects the door flat at some angle near 90 degrees and fastening the door flat and backing firmly together will often solve the bracing problem. In the case of an archway, it is often possible to tie the archway to the backing across the top, making a sturdy, free-standing unit. Window backings may need to be farther from the window flat to allow lighting equipment to be installed. This makes it more difficult to use the backing as a brace.

Bracing and Design

As we have just seen, backings can be used to solve many bracing problems. Good design will solve many more. The shrewd scenographer will plan jogs at either side of a doorway or a large window unit that may present a bracing problem. Such jogs break up the monotony of an otherwise too-flat wall, and they make the setting brace itself. Such design features are especially important in a setting that must be shifted rapidly.

VIOLENT ACTION   None of the methods mentioned above will suffice if the play calls for violent door slamming or violent action around a window. Soft scenery will not maintain the illusion under such conditions. The only recourse is to use hard flat construction techniques in the area where this violent action is to take place. Regular door or window hardware can also be used. See Chapter 10, "Hard Scenery."

Modular Flat Dimensions

A theatre that seeks to make the soft flat system work to its top efficiency will settle on one or more standard heights for its flats, and will try to build flats in widths that follow a 6 inch module. This means that there will be flats 1'-0", 1'-6", 2'-0", 2'-6", etc. Odd dimensions such as 1'-9" will be avoided if possible. Seldom will such differences as 3 inches be important since the location of the setting on the stage can vary enough to make up this difference, and it will not be noticed by the audience. If an exact dimension must be provided, part of a flat can be allowed to protrude at a rear corner, unseen by the audience.

JOGS   Note that flats narrower than 1 foot are seldom built. If they are needed a board will provide the narrower sizes at less cost and trouble. Flats from 1 to 2 feet are often called "jogs" because they usually serve to put a jog in the wall line. Jogs in a setting wall are desirable both for variety and because they make the setting stand more securely. Jogs not seen by the audience are seldom installed.

In a stock scenery situation there will always be the need for special units, such as deeply recessed archways, grand castle doors, etc. These are built as needed and may be retained in the hope of finding further use for them. They present a constant storage problem and may cost more to store than their possible second or third use will justify.

CASINGS   Most windows and doors are finished off by some kind of casing, consisting of a piece of wood which frames the opening, concealing the edge of the door jamb and usually providing a decorative element (see Figure 9-17). In the case of door and window inserts, the casing is an essential part of the insert. It helps to hold the unit in place. Casings usually are installed on built-in doors to give the proper style. They are made up of lumber and molding arranged to the specifications of the scenographer. Moldings may be bought in a wide variety of cross-sectional designs from commercial lumberyards or specialty shops, or they may be made up in the scene shop on the shaper. Small quantities may even be made with a router. Another way to make moldings is to form them from foam plastic with a hot wire cutter. See Chapter 18, "Plastics in the Theatre."

THREE-DIMENSIONAL (3-D) TRIM   Three-dimensional trim includes most door and window casings and any other materials fastened to the front of a piece of scenery to give style and depth to the setting (see Figure 9-18). Sometimes elaborate cornices consisting of a combination of moldings and stock lumber will be specified. Such cornices are often temporarily held to the flat's surface with wing bolts and removed for shifting or storage. Paneling of more modest dimensions is usually more permanently fastened in place by nailing to temporary toggle

Figure 9-18. 3-D Trim. This figure and Figure 9-17 illustrate the use of solid trim instead of painted detail. Note that even in a photograph the effect is more realistic because the shadows are exactly a function of the lighting; 3-D trim makes a setting heavier to shift and harder to store.

Figure 9-19. A Framed Drop. This drop is framed like a gigantic flat. It would not stand without support from above without sagging. The bar near the top is a stiffener that has been added to reduce bending.

rails located especially to support it. Such 3-D trim is usually placed on the flats after base coating, but before detail painting (if the trim will pass through the paint frame well or is otherwise capable of being handled).

DROPS

Drops are another category of soft scenery. A *drop* is a large fabric surface intended to be hung from a batten. It may be completely or partially framed depending on need and available material. A framed drop is an oversized flat designed to hang. Its frame is made of 1 by 3 inch lumber using regular butt joints. Bracing consists of stretchers to keep the rails from warping inward from the tension of the fabric (see Figure 9-19). A framed drop can also be made up by battening together a number of stock flats and covering the joints with fabric strips (dutchmen). If the detail to be painted on the surface is sufficient to cover the joints, a drop made up of flats is just as effective as a one-piece drop. It will be heavier, but it will be easier to work openings into the drop.

Unframed drops are large pieces of painted fabric, usually muslin, hung from battens (see Figure 9-20). In some cases, a batten is built onto the top edge of the drop by sandwiching the fabric between two long pieces of 1 by 3 inch lumber. Since a drop may be 30 to 50 feet wide, the 1" × 3" must be joined by overlapping the joints. In other cases, drops are fitted with webbing and grommets like a drapery and tied to existing battens.

The bottom of a drop may also be fitted with a batten made up of 1 by 3 inch stock like the top, if the drop has an even bottom and is intended to hang to the floor. If it is a "partial drop," hanging only part way to the stage floor, no bottom batten will be installed and the bottom edge will be cut to whatever outline the scenographer requires, often weighted at strategic points to make the drop hang better.

There is a wide variety of possibilities in the construction of drops. For example, a drop may be a "cut-out" made by cutting away part of the fabric to make an outline—perhaps part of a tree. This cut-out area may be filled with black-colored netting (invisible to the audience) upon which fabric "branches" with leaves may be glued. A framed drop may have doorways or other openings built into it. There have even been "drops" made to support a chorus of dancers on an elaborate iron frame which descended from the flies complete with occupants, although such a drop hardly falls into the category of soft scenery.

SCRIMS AND GAUZES

Scrims and gauzes constitute a special kind of drop. These thinly woven materials have the properties of being nearly transparent when the only lighted objects on stage are behind them, almost opaque when their front surface is lighted and there is no light on the objects behind them, and seemingly hazy or foglike when there is light on both their front surface and on the objects behind them. Thus they make appearances and disappearances possible.

Since much of the optical quality of these materials comes from the fuzzy threads from which they are woven, any colorant must be carefully chosen and applied. Anything that tends to mat down the fibers will make the scrim more transparent and therefore less capable of making an object disappear. Thus scrims are usually treated with dyes or very thin washes of scene paint except for those portions that are intended to be opaque. Such portions may be heavily loaded with opaque pigment or even covered with painted muslin or some other highly opaque material.

There is a wide range of scrim and gauzelike materials that may be selected by the scenographer depending on what degree of opacity he wishes and how great a change he needs. The thinnest of these are the *nettings* such as bobbinet. Some are so thin that they can be used to suspend more opaque objects in space without visible support. This is often done in cut-out areas of foliage drops or borders as noted above. Purely abstract bits of scenery can be similarly suspended from thin nettings.

Gauzes are somewhat more opaque than nettings. They are almost never totally invisible on stage. The commonest gauze used in the theatre is made from linen and has about twice the opacity of a single layer of cheesecloth. This theatrical gauze comes by the roll in 6 foot widths. Its natural color is a medium brown which can be bleached to near-white or dyed to almost any color. It takes flameproofing well. However it has one disconcerting trait—it does not shrink when dyed, sized, or painted; instead, it stretches. Therefore any painting, dying, or other treatment involving moisture must be done while the gauze is temporarily stretched on the paint frame. After it has dried, it must be mechanically stretched over any frame that it is intended to cover. Medium and large drops of theatrical gauze are often made by seaming the 6 foot widths.

The standard material for theatrical disappearances is known as "scrim," occasionally called "sharkstooth scrim" or Hansen cloth. It is woven of cotton to form an open rectangular weave, comes in widths of about 30 feet, and is sold by the yard. It is thus ideal for making up large seamless drops. The material takes dye and flame retardant easily and shrinks considerably as it dries. Properly treated with dye or thin scene paint and lit with care, it can appear completely opaque at one moment and almost invisible the next.

There are a wide variety of other materials available that offer varying textures and opacities, such as the many fabrics available for

Figure 9-20. *Unframed Drop. Since this drop may be rolled or folded, it should be painted with flexible paint. Such drops usually are installed so that the sides are not visible. This conceals the natural curve of the fabric edge. Photograph courtesy California State University, Long Beach.*

home curtain and drapery applications. The costume department can usually provide samples and extensive advice on such fabrics.

Although gauzes and scrims and their many similar relatives are commonly made up as drops, the scenographer may specify that they be applied to flat frames, used to cover certain openings in flats, or even used as multiple layers of drapery to surround an entire setting. Such materials offer a tremendous variety of textures, and can provide the scenographer with entrances and exits in which characters magically "dissolve" into or out of the scene.

ROLL DROPS

Obviously a drop is most useful in a theatre with a complete fly loft. However it is possible to design a roll-up drop in the manner of an old-fashioned "olio curtain." Such drops must be painted with extra flexible paint to prevent flaking from repeated flexing of the surface. A small amount of glycerin may be added to some scene paints to make them flexible.

CEILINGS

A ceiling is usually a framed drop made to be hung face down over the setting, its edges resting lightly on the tops of the flats making up the set. Since the ceiling hangs face down, there must be enough tension on the fabric to prevent it from sagging visibly. Bracing should be designed accordingly. Partial ceilings can be made up from stock flats.

10 HARD SCENERY

INTRODUCTION Hard scenery has already been defined in the Introduction to Part Four. It is the most realistic of presently used scenic techniques in the theatre. Since it is relatively new to the theatre and does not have the long-time acceptance of soft scenery, it is important that we weigh its advantages and disadvantages.

ADVANTAGES OF HARD FLATS

Hard flats have better acoustic properties, lend themselves better to realistic surfacing, and are more durable than soft flats. Although the acoustic properties of a hard flat vary with its surface material, any type of surface used for a hard flat is many times more reflective of sound than painted fabric. Furthermore, their solidity makes a door slamming or a window being closed sound more like real life. In an intimate theatre this is apparent to the audience's ears. On a sound stage or on a television set, the microphone makes these differences even more noticeable.

Fabric can be painted to resemble almost any real-life wall surface, but the operative word is "resemble." Resemblance is not enough for an intimate theatre audience that can reach out and touch part of the setting. A hard flat can be surfaced exactly like the wall it is to represent. If, for example, we wish to reproduce a brick wall (Figure 10-1), an exact duplicate of this rough surface can be built up on a hard flat.

Obviously hard flats are more durable than soft ones because the materials are inherently stronger. Only in a movie studio situation can the long life of these flats be fully exploited. Durability may also be measured by the ability of scenery to stand up under violent action. A fight scene involving a doorway may almost destroy the set if soft scenery is used, and door slamming

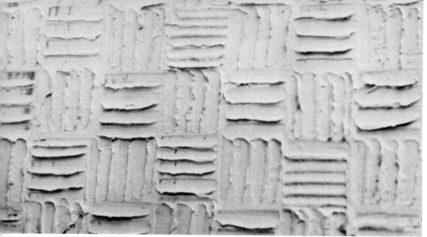

FIGURE 10-1a

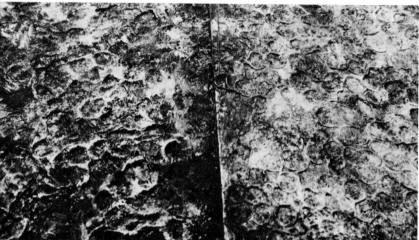

FIGURE 10-1b

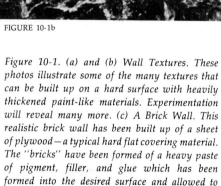

FIGURE 10-1c

Figure 10-1. (a) and (b) Wall Textures. These photos illustrate some of the many textures that can be built up on a hard surface with heavily thickened paint-like materials. Experimentation will reveal many more. (c) A Brick Wall. This realistic brick wall has been built up of a sheet of plywood—a typical hard flat covering material. The "bricks" have been formed of a heavy paste of pigment, filler, and glue which has been formed into the desired surface and allowed to dry. A similar surface can also be formed by vacuum forming panels of "bricks" over a master mold and carefully mounting the sheets together.

will not sound convincing. The obvious answer, even in a setting otherwise made of soft scenery, is to use hard flats at the points of most stress.

DISADVANTAGES OF HARD FLATS

The most obvious disadvantage of hard flats is that they cost more to build, but this can be offset by their long life if the scenographer is willing to restrict wall surface treatments to those easily covered for repeated use. Handling and storage problems also are aggravated by hard scenery, which weighs more and is bulkier than soft scenery. This is particularly true of large pieces that are really practical only on motion picture lots where they are built in place and remain there until destroyed or reworked.

CONSTRUCTION OF HARD FLATS—FRAMING

The framing of a hard flat must approximate the type of support given to a real wall by its frame of 2 × 4 inch lumber. This is done by making up a frame out of 1″ × 3″ or 1″ × 2″ stock set perpendicular to the wall surface as in Figure 10-2. This places the strongest dimension of the framing stock at right angles to the surface of the wall, making the wall more rigid. Note that the strongest dimension of the framing in a soft flat must oppose the stress of the shrinking fabric. The hard flat frame is jointed using ordinary butt joints and nails. No corner blocks are needed because the surface will serve to brace the frame. Rails and stiles are arranged to overlap as in soft flat construction because handling conditions will be the same. Toggle rails are installed at 3 to 4 foot intervals depending on the surface material to be used. A 4′-0″ module is often used because most surface materials come in 4′-0″ × 8′-0″ sheets.

COVERING HARD FLATS

There is a considerable variety of material available for covering hard flats. Choice will depend on the degree of hardness needed for acoustical effect and strength, available budget, and availability of material. The following list is arranged roughly in order of cost and hardness:

1. *Corrugated cardboard must* be the preflameproofed variety, since it is nearly impossible to flameproof cardboard from boxes. The double corrugated variety is by far the best.
2. *Cardboard* varies from paper material $\frac{1}{8}$ inch or less in thickness, which is nearly useless, to heavy, durable material $\frac{1}{4}$ inch thick. There are a variety of trade names for this material, and one of the most common is Upsonboard. The heavier varieties may not need flameproofing. Check with local authorities.
3. *Cellotex*, a trademarked material made of corn fiber pressed into a relatively loose sheet, is low in strength and relatively low in flammability. Test it and flameproof if necessary. It is a good acoustic absorbent, and is much used to suppress excess reverberation. Note that this does not mean that it has much effect on sound transmission. It is rather weak for hard wall applications, but makes a fine imitation tile or heavy shingle over some harder material.
4. *Masonite*, another trademarked material, is made of wood fiber that has been compressed into thin sheets. There are two varieties, tempered and untempered; the latter is cheaper but not as strong. It comes in a number of thick-

Figure 10-2. Hard Flat Construction. Note the sturdy structure. The $\frac{1}{4}$ inch A-D plywood has been installed with its good surface facing the audience, hence the knots are visible on the back.

nesses beginning at $\frac{1}{8}$ of an inch. The tempered variety is somewhat waterproof. It is quite low in flammability.

5. *Plywood* is sufficiently strong for almost any hard wall application and is usually the most expensive material used.
6. *Wallboard or Gypsum board* is really a standard wall-building material that is used occasionally for very heavy theatrical purposes. It has the advantage of being very heavy, giving it the best acoustic value of any of the materials in this list. It is also flameproof. However, it is brittle and expensive. It is available in $\frac{1}{2}$ inch and thicker sheets in dimensions of 4'-0" × 8'-0", or 4'-0" × 12'-0".

SURFACE TREATMENT OF HARD FLATS

The choice of hard scenery over soft scenery almost always implies some special surface treatment. Often this will be done to imitate a surface found in regular construction such as brick, or in nature such as rock surfaces (see Figure 10-1). Since these and many other surface treatments require some very heavy texture technique that will give deep relief, hard scenery is almost a necessity if the surface is to be well supported.

Many materials are used for these purposes. Perhaps the most common in the motion picture industry is plaster. Unfortunately it is very brittle and quite heavy, characteristics that make it less applicable to the theatre. Nevertheless, some other materials that can be worked much like plaster to get the same results are sold in paint stores as texture paints. They consist of pigments mixed with large amounts of extenders to give them a pastelike consistency. If they are mixed to the consistency stipulated on the package, they may be too thin for heavy relief work. Try using less water or thinner.

Masonite, which has already been mentioned as a surface material, is probably still better as a material to be attached to the actual hard flat surface and then carved into relief. As long as it is not subject to abrasion or pressure, it is strong enough for this purpose.

There are a number of latex materials available in European markets and to some extent in the United States that can be mixed with pigments, extenders, and the like, and troweled onto a surface to produce a wide variety of durable heavy textures and designs. The various papier-mâché materials mentioned in Chapter 11, "Nonweight-Bearing Three-Dimensional Scenery." are all applicable to texturing and building up hard wall surfaces.

Still another approach is to appliqué vacuum-formed plastic (see Chapter 18, "Plastics in the Theatre") objects to the surfaces. Some that are commercially available are imitations of brick walls. There is also a line of molded ornaments made from a special nonshrinking mix-

ture of sawdust and glue. These, while expensive, are excellent reproductions of carvings and filigree work from period décor. They are very
effective at close range.

Foam plastic may be glued or fastened to a hard scenery surface
or may be sprayed in place. This can then be carved or surfaced by a
wide variety of techniques. Again refer to Chapter 18.

In some instances, where it is advantageous to have a textured
surface that is actually soft to touch, foam rubber or foam urethane may
be applied and carved.

OPENINGS IN HARD FLATS

Construction of doors and windows is actually simpler in hard flats
than in soft flats. The structure of the flats is strong enough to support
standard home construction practices if desired, or the plug system
may be used. In either case, acoustic properties will be superior.

FASTENING HARD FLATS TOGETHER

Most standard methods of fastening soft flats will work with hard flats.
However, the fact that the rails and stiles are at right angles to the surface opens new possibilities. For example, adjacent stiles may be
fastened together with bolts and wing nuts. C-clamps or patented pinch
clamps (much like an oversized clothespin) may also be used (Figure
10-3).

SHIFTING HARD SCENERY

Because of its weight, hard scenery is not apt to be lifted into the flies,
although this is possible. Similarly, its weight will tend to minimize
piece by piece hand movement of sets. The most practicable methods
involve the use of wagons, lift jacks, and similar devices. The extra
rigidity of the hard flats makes this type of shifting easy to arrange.

COMBINING HARD AND SOFT SCENIC TECHNIQUES

It is frequently necessary to begin with a conventional soft flat frame
and attach to it materials that fall in the category of hard flat surfacings.
For instance, one may need to create a profile of foliage or an architectural cornice. This is usually done by constructing the wide areas
using standard soft scenery methods and attaching pieces of ''profile
board'' (thin plywood) to the edges. The same technique can be ap-

Figure 10-3. Fastening Hard Flats Together. Hard
flats may be bolted together with a $\frac{1}{4}$ inch bolt
and wing nut, or fastened with a large pinch
clamp (upper), or a C-clamp (lower). Bolting or
clamping with a C-clamp is the most secure.

FIGURE 10-4a

FIGURE 10-4c

FIGURE 10-4d

FIGURE 10-4b

Figure 10-4. Profiling. Note how hard flat materials have been worked into the edges of these profiled flats to give strength to the irregular edges. Such profiles are normally covered with muslin before painting. (a) Stock flats profiled. (b) Profiled doorway. (c) Finished set pieces. (d) Ground row. The profiled piece of scenery is intended to be placed upstage near the cyclorama to suggest distant objects. This professionally painted ground row is almost a theatrical curiosity; it dates back to the early 1930s.

plied to a wide variety of construction problems such as cut-out arches with no thickness, ground rows (silhouettes of foliage and such to suggest a horizon line), or even completely abstract forms (Figure 10-4). Such profiling usually is added to the flat frame before it has been covered and the covering muslin carried over the profile. In some cases final cutting of the profile is done through the muslin after it has dried onto the flat.

11
NONWEIGHT-BEARING THREE-DIMENSIONAL SCENERY

INTRODUCTION Flats, hard or soft, can give the illusion of solid walls. They even make good "garden walls" and "stone archways" if properly painted and textured. However, there are many scenic elements that do not lend themselves to flat construction. For example, one can frame a flat in the silhouette of a tree. This will work in certain kinds of stylization, but if the audience must see the tree as a three-dimensional object with the lighting so arranged that shadows are cast, flat construction will not work.

This leads us to a wide variety of construction techniques aimed at satisfying just such demands. Three-dimensional construction is time consuming and may require expensive material. Moreover, the finished pieces are highly specialized and difficult to store even if the piece can be useful later. The expense is compensated for not only by the potential for realism but also by the fact the three-dimensional scenery works better with the actors who are, of course, also three-dimensional. It can offer the actor scenery that he can play on, in, over, and under. The director will find that planning of movements for his actors has now become a much more satisfying and expressive art. Ever since the writings of Adolphe Appia became known in the theatre near the year 1900, three-dimensional settings have been gaining prominence. Today, some theatres depend so much on them that they almost never build or use a flat.

Three-dimensional scenery is divided into two categories: (1) nonweight-bearing elements, and (2) weight-bearing elements. The distinction is that the nonweight-bearing elements are never asked to do more than support their own weight and perhaps that of a few other lightweight pieces. Weight-bearing elements are built to hold up actors, often while they are running, jumping, or falling. Occasionally the categories are

Figure 11-1a. This figure illustrates the framing of a large cylindrical element. The structure eventually was covered with lightweight cardboard, making it quite sturdy.

mixed. For example, a stage tree may be entirely nonweight-bearing except for one portion of the trunk and one limb, or a mountain may be equipped with a path of weight-bearing elements. The categories simply refer to the specific construction techniques used in each portion and need not be applied to entire settings.

Nonweight-bearing scenery consists of a broad category of three-dimensional objects. They are designed to be as light in weight as possible to aid in shifting, but rugged enough to stand the rigors of backstage handling. Occasionally portions will follow standard flat building methods, but for the most part construction techniques will be devised to fit the needs of the moment. If the object is of some considerable size — and many will be huge — the construction process must take into consideration the need to shift the object. This may be done by providing a wagon base, lifting points, or other means of handling.

It is impossible to make an exhaustive list of construction techniques, since scenographers and theatre technicians are constantly devising new methods and revising old ones. The remainder of this chapter deals with some of the conventional methods of construction of nonweight-bearing scenery. Some new construction techniques will be discussed in Chapter 18, "Plastics in the Theatre."

FRAMING

Most methods of building three-dimensional settings — both weight-bearing and nonweight-bearing — begin with the construction of some sort of frame or mandrel on which the structure is built up. In non-weight-bearing scenery, the frame simply serves to hold the piece together and frequently to support the outer surface until it reaches its full strength. If, for example, the outer surface is to be papier-mâché, the frame will have to support the wet material until it dries and hardens. After that, the skin may be stronger than the frame underneath.

Frames are usually made of wood such as scrap lumber because the scene shop is accustomed to working with it. Fastenings may be nails or power-driven staples. Most designers will find it difficult and unnecessary to draw the framing details of these structures, therefore sketches or models are provided and the construction chief is left to devise the framing as he builds it. The exact nature of this "ad-lib" framing is determined by the availability of usable wooden parts. Pieces are cut and fitted in until the right shape develops (see Figure 11-1).

If for some special reason the frame is made of metal (welded iron rod, for instance), the same procedure is followed — cutting, welding, and bending until the results are satisfactory. A hammer and a conduit bender may figure prominently in this process. It will be helpful if the frame can be built on some sort of base, such as a piece of plywood. The frame may also be built atop a standard wagon which will form a permanent base for the unit.

COVERING THE FRAME

Perhaps the most common way of covering three-dimensional objects is to enclose the frame in wire netting (1 inch No. 16 or 18 diamond mesh wire is good). The netting is then molded to the approximate contour of the finished article and eventually covered. Working with the wire netting can be hazardous business. It must be cut with heavy tin shears or a wire cutter, and its ends will be razor sharp. As it is cut and modeled, it is tied in place with pieces of soft iron wire ("baling wire") or with hog rings. It is also nailed or stapled to the wood frame wherever possible. As work progresses, the sharp ends of the cut wire should be pushed into the interior of the object to protect workers during the remainder of the process.

Although wire is probably used most frequently for frame covering, some other materials are sometimes desirable. For example, thin strips of wood or cardboard make the construction of a stage log easier because they form the contour more readily. Glue-impregnated fabric will serve the purpose when the outer covering is to be plaster or plastic foam.

Once the frame has been constructed and covered with wire or other material to approximate roughly the shape of the finished object, the outer covering material may be applied.

FINISHING THE OUTER SURFACE

PAPIER-MÂCHÉ

Papier-mâché is a material made up of paper fiber (originally wood fiber) bonded with glue and wheat paste. If it is bought ready-mixed at art supply houses, it is necessary only to add water. The prepared material is handy but may be more expensive than some theatre budgets can stand, and may not be available in quantities on short notice. Homemade papier-mâché is easy to make, and it is cheap, particularly if student labor is available. There are two methods: strip and pulp.

Strip Method

The strip method consists of dipping strips of newspaper into a mixture of paste, glue, and warm water, and draping the wet strips over the

Figure 11-1b. Back of a large cornice. Note the combination of wood framing and bendboard used to achieve the concave curve of the cornice. Further 3-D detail was added to the front.

wire-covered frame. Several layers may be built up before the weight of the wet paper causes sagging. At this point the object must be dried before more dipped paper can be added. Ultimately objects of considerable strength can be built up if enough layers are added.

The paste-glue solution is obtained by making up a batch of regular wheat paste following the directions on the container. Wheat paste powder is a standard commodity at paint and wallpaper stores. It is so cheap that no substitution is necessary. Once the paste has been mixed and the lumps stirred out, white glue is added. The proportion of glue to paste may vary from pure paste to about 25 percent glue. The more glue, the greater the strength of the finished object and the greater the cost. Carpenter's glue may also be used if the shop keeps this as its standard adhesive.

As layers are being built up on the object, it will be advantageous to use newspapers of differing color so that the workers can determine when the object has been covered entirely with a given layer. Use care; the wet object tears easily until it has dried.

Pulp Method

The pulp method consists of making paper pulp out of various soft cardboard objects such as old paper egg cartons. Newspapers can be used but it is a tedious process to soak and stir them until a pulp is created. Unsized paper products—anything that resembles blotting paper—can also be used. Heating and stirring will help to break down the structure and return the paper to the pulp state. Once pulped, the paper is mixed with glue and paste and applied to the foundation wire or surface to be treated. The amount of glue used will depend on the necessity for adhering to the base and on the amount of strength needed in the finished product. If the paste is to be kept in a moist state for more than a day or so, a few drops of antibacterial disinfectant should be added.

In spite of the fragile nature of the raw paper, papier-mâché can be a very strong material. Paper furniture, which has been manufactured and finished with lacquer by the Chinese for centuries, endures as well as wooden furniture. As first applied, papier-mâché is not impervious to water. It can, however, be painted with waterproof paints or lacquers to build up a water-resistant surface. Such pieces can even be used as the statuary in practical fountains.

Normally papier-mâché is so dense that it is flame resistant, and this property can be reinforced, if necessary, by adding flameproofing solution to the wet mixture or spraying the finished and dried parts with flameproofing solution.

In addition to making up three-dimensional scenic elements, papier-mâché is a common material for building up what is known as three-dimensional trim. Baroque filigree, for example, can easily be molded onto plain paneling by using papier-mâché. After it has dried, it can be highlighted with gold paint to produce a rich, heavy effect.

DRYING PAPIER-MÂCHÉ   Drying speed for papier-mâché will be in proportion to its thickness. Pieces over $\frac{1}{2}$ inch thick may take weeks to dry in some climates. Wherever possible such thicknesses should be avoided by imbedding small blocks of wood under the mâché to fill in the thicker parts. Drying time can be improved by the use of fans and the application of commercial infrared heat lamps. Although they produce more visible light, stage lamps are also efficient at producing infrared. The only problem is that they have a shorter life. In spite of this, shops often use 1000–2000 W lamps in stage floodlights as drying lamps. The lamps are efficient, low in cost, and easily available. However use caution; they can set fire to dry objects placed too close to them and left long enough to build up heat.

SHREDDED ASBESTOS

This material has frequently been used in the theatre as a more durable substitute for papier-mâché. However, recent strict regulations governing the use of asbestos in any way that might result in the breathing in of the fibers make it unlikely that any theatre shop will want to use the protective equipment and other precautions necessary. It has been shown that minute asbestos fibers may cause cancer. The only practical recommendation concerning this material is that it be avoided by theatre workers, since much safer substitutes are available.

CLOTH AND PLASTER

A technique using cloth and plaster is excellent for simulating sculpture because the surface texture will be completely realistic. The technique is simple: strips of muslin or gauze are dipped into a paste of plaster of paris and water, and draped over the frame of the object. The wet mass is worked into shape as the plaster sets, and further coats are added to finish the object. A certain amount of color can be worked into the finish coat if desired (Figure 11-2).

Regular plaster of paris will probably set too rapidly for convenience. A little white vinegar added to the mix will slow this process down. Experiment with small portions until you get the right setting speed for your job. Another solution to this problem is to buy prepared "patching plaster" at a building supply house. This is already mixed with inhibitors to slow the hardening process.

Although cloth and plaster work rapidly and produce a finish like that of many sculptured objects, the material is somewhat brittle

Figure 11-2. Fabric and Plaster Statue. This realistic statue was made by molding fabric dipped in plaster of paris. It then was dried, painted, and highlighted.

when dry. The cloth will tend to keep it from coming to pieces, but the plaster will break.

FABRIC AND WHITE GLUE

A slower but more durable process than cloth and plaster is the use of fabric and white glue. Strips of fabric, usually muslin or gauze, are dipped in a solution of white glue and whiting, and draped over the frame of the object. These are allowed to dry and the surface built up to the desired thickness. Flameproofing may be added if this is needed.

The process will proceed more slowly than that using plaster because the glue takes longer to set. However, the results will be more durable under heavy use.

JUTE RUG PADDING

Simulation of tree bark over wide areas of a large stage tree can be a time-consuming task if papier-mâché is used. A better method is to make up a wooden frame; contour it with either wire, thin strips of wood, or strips of heavy cardboard; and cover it with jute rug padding. This smooth-surfaced padding, which is also cheap, should be purchased in a natural brown color that may eliminate the need for more than a few streaks and stains of paint. The padding should be worked onto the tree in folds and irregularities imitating tree bark (Figure 11-3).

Jute is flammable and must be flameproofed. Standard fire-retardant chemicals such as those used for muslin work well, but they should be forced into the jute using a high-pressure sprayer. If it is necessary to apply the retardant by brushing, both surfaces of the padding should be treated before the material is installed. After installation, tests should be run to see if it is necessary to add still more retardant to make up for that dislodged by handling.

DRAPED MUSLIN

Another technique for imitating tree bark, which is more tedious than using rug padding but less apt to wear off on costumes, is to build up the texture of bark by loosely draping folded muslin while wet with a thin glue solution. Final shaping can take place as the glue sets (see Figure 11-4). Color can even be worked into the glue to save a step in the painting process. Flameproofing should also be added.

Both of these processes depend, as do most techniques in scenery, upon the willingness and ability of the individual crew members to study the type of tree bark to be imitated and then to execute it skillfully. Simple mechanical application of the material will not do.

Figure 11-3. Rug Padding Tree. This fantastic tree and root system has been sculptured from jute rug padding. The material was heavily flameproofed after installation, and then highlighted with color.

Figure 11-4. Fabric and Glue "Log." This log was made by applying a formed layer of fabric dipped in glue to an inner core to suggest the bark. The texture of the tree to be simulated should be carefully studied and imitated in the still-soft fabric. After the glue has dried paint can be applied to add to the effect.

PLASTICS

The introduction of plastics into the theatre has made available such materials as fiberglass and foamed plastics. Since these are also applicable to a variety of theatrical uses, and since they require special safety precautions, they are discussed separately in Chapter 18.

12
WEIGHT-BEARING THREE-DIMENSIONAL SCENERY

INTRODUCTION "Weight-bearing structures" is a large category, involving every sort of built-up device used to get actors above floor level. The following list of subdivisions will assist the reader to understand these important scenic elements:

1. Wood scaffolds and rigid platforms
2. Modular systems using wood
    a. Parallels
    b. Platform and leg systems
3. Other weight-bearing structures
4. Systems using metal
    a. Commercial scaffolding
    b. Pipe and slip-on fittings
    c. Punched metal angles
    d. Welded square steel tubing
    e. Other welded steel materials

Since metal weight-bearing structures have become such an important part of theatrical scenery, they are discussed in detail in Chapter 13.

WOOD SCAFFOLDS AND RIGID PLATFORMS

A wooden scaffold is probably the simplest approach a theatre can take to the problem of providing a large rectilinear area elevated some distance off the stage floor. A *scaffold* is a crude wooden framework of heavy lumber topped with a plank floor. Outside of the theatre, scaffolds are used by construction workers to enable them to work efficiently at a height. Since the scaffold is a temporary structure, to be removed when the work is finished, no effort is made to improve its appearance—the only concern is safety. The more cheaply this can be done and the more of the material that can be salvaged for later reuse, the better. Because scaffolds are so common in the building industry, the techniques used in their construction are well known, and suppliers of building materials provide a special "scaffold grade" of lumber for this particular purpose. Such lumber is chosen for its strength, not its appearance. Metal scaffolding systems are also provided for the building trades; we will return to these later.

A theatre can use standard wooden scaffold-building techniques when it is necessary for a rather large floor area to be raised to a considerable height, and this structure need not be shifted. In some instances the framework of the scaffold itself will become a part of the design. In this case the scenographer plans the location of each post and brace, concerning himself with the engineering of a solid, safe structure, and with the lines formed by that structure. The way to keep the structure strong is to break rectangular forms into triangles so arranged that the weight of the actors atop tends to pull or push on the braces forming the triangle.

If the scenographer plans to hide the front faces of the scaffold (behind a skin of flats, for example) he will often leave the construction of the scaffold up to the stage carpenter who will know exactly what to do. Student carpenters should observe how scaffolds are built on construction sites. Note how advantage is taken of the strong dimensions of the heavy timbers used as horizontal supports. They are always placed so that the weight is at 90 degrees to their thickness. The only exception to this is the flooring of the scaffold. Here the width of the material is walked upon although the boards are more limber in that position.

Scaffolds are relatively cheap and easy to build but they are almost impossible to shift. If a scaffold is needed and shifting is necessary, the solution is to break the structure down into shiftable small scaffolds or *rigid platforms*. A rigid or "permanent" platform is a small-sized scaffold built to stand solidly and safely by itself. A number of rigid platforms may be used repeatedly in different combinations to make up a more flexible scaffoldlike structure than could be built in one piece. Thus rigid platforms are more often found on stage than are scaffolds.

FLOORING FOR WOOD SCAFFOLDS AND RIGID PLATFORMS

The normal flooring used in construction scaffolding is 2 inch planking laid on top of the supporting *joists* (the beams that are directly under the floor). Although such a floor is satisfactory for workmen, it is seldom adequate for actors whose movements must be governed by the nature of the character they are trying to create. Furthermore, actors are not as familiar with high places as the average construction worker and may feel insecure on a crude plank floor. The standard material for flooring stage scaffolds is plywood. Normally the $\frac{3}{4}$ inch thickness is used, but 1 inch or even $1\frac{1}{4}$ inch plywood can be used to advantage. The $\frac{3}{4}$ inch material must be supported at least every 4 feet. The heavier thicknesses make it possible to space the joists further apart, thus saving materials. If the scaffold must support very heavy loads or the stresses of dancers leaping about in unison, the supports must be much closer together, generally on 16 or 18 inch centers for $\frac{3}{4}$ inch plywood. Figure 12-1 shows a flooring arrangement for a structure that must support all kinds of action including the weight of a full-size grand piano. Note the joists.

It should be obvious that the scenographer must be certain of the load to be imposed on the scaffold when he specifies its construction. Directors must be aware that they cannot make large increases in the load and/or the violence of the action taking place on a structure after it has been built, without checking with the scenographer to make sure these increases fall within the safety factor that has been engineered into it. Neither should other organizations—for example, a dance group—make use of existing scaffolds for rehearsals or experimentation without first checking with its designer. It is not feasible to build every stage scaffold to take any stress that might be placed on it.

MODULAR WEIGHT-BEARING STRUCTURES

A *module* is a unit of measure used as a standard guide in determining design dimensions. Ideally, this unit should allow for economical use of materials because parts can be used as they come from the factory, or cut in such a way that no waste results.

Modules save both construction time and money by allowing the use of factory-cut material and tending to standardize the dimensions of braces, joists, etc. which are used with the material. Unfortunately over use of modules may reduce a good design to monotony.

HORIZONTAL MODULES

The standard factory dimension of plywood manufactured in the United States is 4 by 8 feet. The module dimension is 4 feet, making it possible to use half sheets with no waste or full sheets of plywood without cutting them. This also works out to be a reasonable maximum span for $\frac{3}{4}$ inch or 1 inch thick plywood, depending on the load. The designer will therefore seek to make as many of the dimensions as possible be multiples of 4 feet. Even fractions of the module will prove helpful because parts can be cut from a sheet of plywood leaving a useful remainder. Framing lumber for platforms, scaffolds, etc., comes from the lumberyard sized in 2 foot increments because this fits the modular needs of the construction industry. The scenographer can take advantage of this also. Another advantage comes with the use of full-sized sheets of plywood. These come from the factory trimmed and

Figure 12-1. Flooring for a Heavy-Duty Platform. This platform is used to fill in an orchestra pit and must be able to support a grand piano. Note how the heavy 4 by 6 inch beams have been placed to carry the load. To support the plywood, 2 by 2 inch steel has been added. If steel were not being used, 2 by 4 inch timbers would be needed.

squared with far greater accuracy than most shops can accomplish. Platforms, topped with full sheets of plywood, will fit together with great precision. The basic 4 foot module can be applied to parallels, rigid platforms, stage scaffolds, and even to segments of irregular structures. It will result in a considerable saving in time and money.

Obviously the module concept should not be allowed to force a designer into shapes that do not fit artistic needs. Nevertheless, a realistic appraisal of what dimensions can be perceived from the audience will often reveal that the difference between a 3 foot 9 inch dimension and a 4 foot dimension is unimportant as a design matter, but offers the carpenter the opportunity to use a modular unit.

VERTICAL MODULES

Although horizontal modules are quite easily established around standard building industry modules with only minor restrictions on the artistic needs of the scenographer, vertical modules tend to have to meet artistic requirements first and then satisfy whatever modular requirements they can. This is because steps or ramps that must be negotiated by actors will have an important effect on the manner in which they move. The design of movement is always a predominant consideration before any such nonartistic concerns as gaining advantages from the use of modules.

Fortunately, some of the most useful step dimensions (risers 6, 8 or 12 inches in height) can also be fitted into the common material module (48 inches) with ease. The 6 inch is perhaps the most common. This produces an easy step for actors to negotiate and results in even dimensions which intersect the 4 foot module evenly. A 4 foot high platform is a good height for many stages. Note that the 8 inch step module also intersects the 4 foot module. It produces a slightly steeper run of steps which will take up less floor space and still play well. The 12 inch step is rather high and plays awkwardly for most actors. But it gets a great deal of height in a relatively short run of steps.

PARALLELS

The idea of using modular techniques in the theatre is not new. One of the first "standard" platform units in the theatre was devised as a modular unit. This was the *parallel* — a folding platform base that could be fitted with standardized top units. Early parallels were topped with a floor made up of regular softwood flooring nailed to cross pieces which held it together, i.e., "cleated" together. Such tops could be any convenient size because flooring was bought by the board foot and cut to fit. Frequently theatres would settle on a 3 by 6 foot module for parallels if this size fitted well into the width of the theatre proscenium — for example, five such parallels would exactly fit into a 30 foot proscenium. Furthermore, such parallels were easy to handle. Presently, wood flooring has increased in price, making it nearly prohibitive as platform topping. Meanwhile the cost of plywood has decreased. There is also much less labor involved in the preparation of a parallel top from a sheet of plywood; one needs only to nail on the cleats (now serving as stiffeners) and the top is finished. The result is that most parallels are now built on a 4 by 8 foot module using sheets of $\frac{3}{4}$ inch plywood just as they come from the mill, but with cleats added, to make up tops (see Figure 12-2). Such tops are usually more accurately squared than any that can be cut in a scene shop. They make superior parallels.

The framework of a parallel is made from 1 by 3 inch lumber of high quality using standard shop joining methods. There is con-

FIGURE 12-2a

Figure 12-2. Parallel. (a) The complete parallel frame and the top with its cleats. Note that two faces of this parallel have been completely covered with $\frac{1}{4}$ inch plywood, providing strength and facing at the same time. (b) The rear of the same parallel with typical framing and corner block construction.

FIGURE 12-2b

siderable economy in using parallels because there need not be as many tops as folding frames. The tops should be completely interchangeable, and since they are full sheets of $\frac{3}{4}$ inch plywood, they can be returned to stock if necessary.

Unless parallels are constructed with great precision and properly maintained after construction, they may produce shaky, noisy platforms. It is also necessary to face those sides that are in view of the audience because the frames are open, scaffoldlike structures. A large set of parallels represents a considerable investment in materials and building time, and will take up a sizable amount of storage space. It is practical to use parallels only in a theatre whose designers tend to use many weight-bearing structures, and are willing to work largely within the established module. If odd sizes and shapes are the routine thing, neither parallels nor any other modular system will pay for themselves.

There are several ways of framing a parallel, but the one shown in Figure 12-2 is probably the best. It has the advantage of providing a flush, framed surface on every side of the parallel upon which facing is easily installed. Parallels of this sort can be clamped together at their frames for a more rigid setting. The weakness of this design, however, is the way in which the hinges must be fastened to the wood at two of the corners. Either a hinge must be specially bent or one side of each of these hinges must be fastened to the edge of the wood—not a very strong joint. Carefully note the hinging pattern shown in Figure 12-3. If the hinges are not properly applied, the frame will not fold. Also note the hinging pattern must be anticipated when the corner

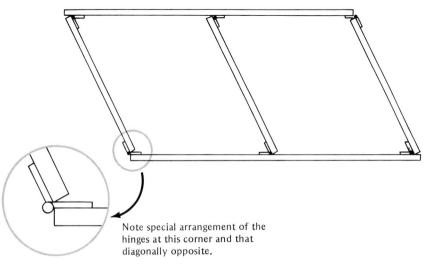

Note special arrangement of the hinges at this corner and that diagonally opposite.

Figure 12-3. Hinging Parallels. This hinging pattern allows the frame to fold flat, providing the hinges have been accurately placed. It also allows the parallel to have square corners with no indentations due to overlap. It requires that hinges on two of the outside corners be specially bent or bolted. See detail.

blocks and keystones are applied to the frames. *All* hinges must be mounted in such a way that the thickness of the plywood corner blocks will not serve to lever the framework apart when the parallel is folded up.

Building parallel frames is not work for beginning carpenters. The frames must be exactly square and the joints must be extremely secure. Hinging the frame together is also a tricky job since any slight error in placing the hinges will result in strains that add up as the platform is folded and will tend to pull the hinge screws out of the wood.

See Figure 12-2a to determine how the top holds the entire framework in open position. Note that the cleats drop into place alongside the cross-frames of the parallel and keep the framework from closing while in use. If all the parallels are framed the same, all cleats should fit into place the same way and parts should be interchangeable. Note that the top goes on *only one way*. The procedure in assembling parallels for a production is simple: open the frame to a square position, note the relationship of the cleats to the frame as you lower the top into place, and jiggle the base slightly to allow the cleats to seat. If the platform is in good shape, no other fastening should be necessary. If the result is noisy because the top does not fit tightly, and exchanging tops or frames does not remedy the situation, you may have to nail the top into place. Use only a *few* 6 penny or 8 penny nails, and drive them accurately to avoid splitting the frame. This should be done *only* if requested by the crew chief because it tends to ruin the frames. Some carpenters use wood screws instead of nails. This makes a tighter joint but takes longer and leaves larger holes in the wood.

Regular frames are normally built for parallels over 1 foot high. Below that height, it is easier and stronger to simply hinge pieces of lumber together to make up a solid wood frame than to try to build a frame out of 1 by 3 inch lumber. Such frames may be made either of regular stock or of $\frac{3}{4}$ inch plywood cut to size.

Storage of Parallels

When parallel frames are stored, they should not be piled so that the weight of a large stack of frames bears heavily on those at the bottom. Even the best-built frames will not usually fold all the way without some strain. The best storage arrangement is to rest each frame on edge, loosely folded but not forced. Although the entire parallel, when assembled, is a very strong structure for its weight, the frames are fragile and should be handled with care.

Fastening Parallels Together

In many cases several parallels will be assembled into a unit that must be fastened together to avoid jiggling and noise. Two systems work

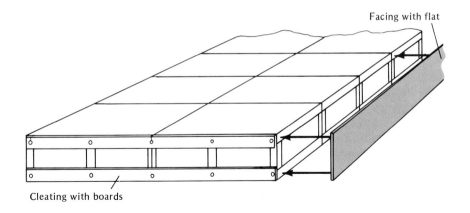

Facing with flat

Cleating with boards

Figure 12-4. Cleating Parallels Together. This sketch shows how a large solid platform may be made by running 1 by 3 inch or wider stock around the entire platform to tie the parts together. If the platforms are to be faced, this facing may serve the same purpose.

well: (1) The entire unit may be framed together by running boards along the top and bottom (if necessary) as shown in Figure 12-4. Sometimes the facing will serve this same purpose on the front side. (2) C-clamps can be installed underneath the platforms to hold the frames together. This system has the advantage of being completely concealed within the structure and it avoids making any holes in the wood. However, it is not quite as sturdy as the first system.

THE PLATFORM AND LEG SYSTEM

Another approach to the problem of modular weight-bearing scenery is the platform and leg system. In this case, basic platforms are built at a minimum height. This is usually 6 inches, 8 inches, or 1 foot. These basic platforms are rigidly built and stored as fully assembled units. When greater height is needed, legs are bolted to the platforms (see Figure 12-5). If an accurate job is done in drilling the bolt holes, the legs will be interchangeable with no additional drilling. To do this, a *jig* (a simple but accurate drilling guide) must be used. Legs are provided in a variety of heights and used as needed.

This system takes about the same amount of storage as the parallel system, but has the advantage of providing very rigid platforms at the most-used heights. The basic platforms are constructed as shown in Figure 12-5 using high-quality stock and $\frac{3}{4}$ inch plywood in full sheets for tops. Parts should be securely nailed together after being carefully squared. Cement-coated nails (nails with a special adhesive on them which makes them very hard to pull) are often used to decrease the chance of joints opening under severe use.

Although the experience of this writer indicates that the platform and leg system results in more durable structures than the parallel system, there are some disadvantages that must be considered:

Figure 12-5. Legging Up Solid Platforms. To increase the height of stock risers, 2 by 6 inch legs have been used. The riser, which has been legged up, is still upside down.

1. Each platform will have visible holes in all four corners when no legs are used and visible bolt heads when legs are installed.
2. The bolt holes enlarge with use, making old platforms jiggly.
3. At heights over 3 feet, the legs tend to be unstable unless temporary cross-braces are added or several platforms are tied together. Parallels do not exhibit the same problem to this extent.
4. Facing is more of a problem because the legs are recessed from the faces of the basic platforms.
5. Although storage problems are less acute than for parallel frames, the stock of legs may be mistaken for a stock of short lumber and used up.

Either parallels or rigid platforms with legs work well at heights up to 4 feet. Between 4 feet and about 6 feet the rigid platforms usually perform better if well made and braced. Above 6 feet neither type works as well as the steel structures discussed in Chapter 13.

OTHER WEIGHT-BEARING STRUCTURES—STEPS

Step units for the stage fall into two categories: *carry-off* and *onstage*. Carry-off steps are out of sight of the audience and serve mainly to provide actors with an access to the setting. This utilitarian purpose can be served by any step unit that is safe and will fit into the space at hand. Generally old step units from stock are adapted to this purpose, sometimes fitted with handrails for safety if the rise is more than 4 feet. In cramped quarters a special, extra-steep run of steps may be designed and built (Figure 12-6). In still other cases where space is not at a premium, stock platforms may be assembled into a set of access steps or even into a runway leading well off stage and then provided with steps. Such runway entrances are a great advantage to actors who must come on "on the run," "exit fighting," and the like. Off-stage edges of such steps are frequently marked with white paint for better visibility in near-darkness.

Steps onstage are a very important part of the designer's work. As he designs the steps, he is literally designing the movement of the actors who must use them. He can produce steep, hard-to-climb steps that will force the actor to appear to be laboring, or he can design a gentle flowing run of curved stairway, down which an actress can float. Movement cannot be the only consideration; the flatter the steps, the greater the amount of floor space they will take up getting to the required elevation.

STAIR PARTS

There are three basic parts to a step unit: *treads*, *risers*, and the *carriages*. Treads are the part one's foot rests on; the risers are the vertical

Figure 12-6. Carry-off Steps. This is typical of most backstage stairs. Note the safety rail both on the stair and on the platform at its top. Such stairs often are stocked for repeated use.

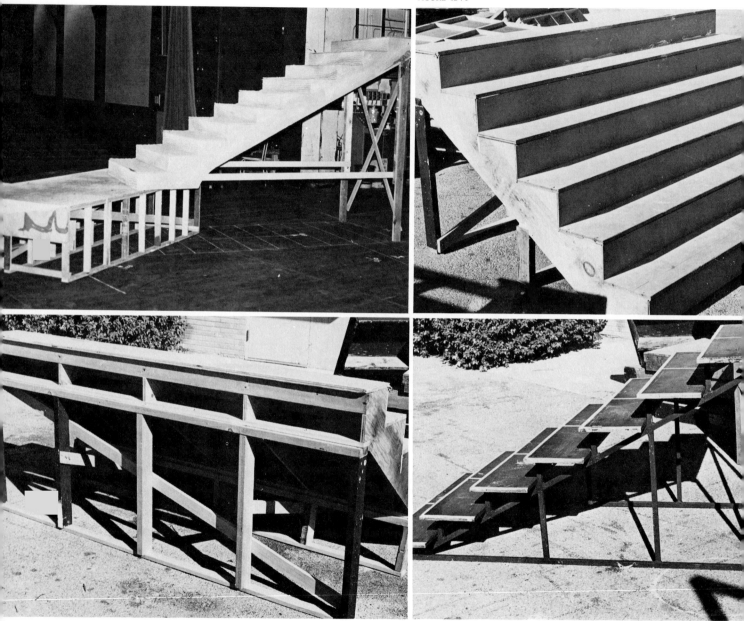

FIGURE 12-7a

FIGURE 12-7b

FIGURE 12-7c

FIGURE 12-7d

194   12 WEIGHT-BEARING THREE-DIMENSIONAL SCENERY

Figure 12-7. Step Units. These are some of the many ways of providing steps on stage. (a) A run of stairs and a platform. Note how the stairs have been separately legged to allow independent shifting. The platform is extra heavy for violent action. (b) and (c). A wide run of Stairs shown from both top and underneath. Construction is typical. (d) Steel framed step unit. This unit is useful as a carry-off step, a part of an audience entrance system for a flexible theatre, or as a part of a setting.

parts; the carriages hold up the entire run of steps. Carriages must be strong and well braced. Several ways of building step units are shown in Figure 12-7.

Free-standing step units are common in most theatres. They are liked because they carry their load independently of any other structure and provide their own bracing. They are usually heavy for their size, being built of $\frac{3}{4}$ inch plywood with bracing where it is needed (Figures 12-7b and c) and with smooth surfaces on all sides. Long runs of steps are made up in modular units to make them easily compatible with existing platform structures.

Construction of stair units calls for good carpentry (joints must be square and true) and is costly in both time and materials. For this reason stairs are usually kept in stock as long as they remain in good condition.

CIRCLES AND RAMPS

Circles and ramps, which provide special problems, are usually built for specific shows. Occasionally, pieces will be considered valuable enough to add to stock. One stock element often found is the modular ramp. It should be built to meet the modular platforms being used in the theatre at some common dimension (2 feet or 3 feet). It is possible to construct a parallel frame to support a ramp if the repeated use of the ramp will justify the effort.

Circular platforms or platforms representing parts of a circle frequently are used. One of the most useful setups is to construct four quarter-circle platforms of modular height that may be legged up as needed. The quarter-circles can then be used in a variety of applications. Similarly, triangular pieces called "pies" are often stocked as part of a platform and leg system. These angular pieces make possible a 30 or 45 degree change of direction in a run of platforms. Such angles occur sufficiently often to justify the pies as stock items. Unfortunately, parallels constructed in the shape of pies tend to be unstable.

A series of pies or segments of circles of varying dimensions may be stacked up to make corner stairs of either angular or circular outline. Both patterns will be repeatedly useful.

13
METAL AS A SCENIC MATERIAL

INTRODUCTION Wood has been the traditional material of theatrical scenery for centuries. This is now changing for several reasons:

1. Wood is becoming increasingly expensive and hard to get in grades suitable for scenic construction.
2. The present trend away from flats and drops and toward three-dimensional scenic elements is making the superior strength of metal desirable.
3. Because fire safety laws are becoming stricter, the nonflammable nature of metal makes it highly desirable.
4. Scenographers are becoming more aware of the many opportunities for new forms and otherwise impossible structures that the great strength of metal provides.

Thus the theatre is undergoing a technological change in scenery construction that may well prove to be as revolutionary as some of the recent changes in lighting control.

The European theatre preceded the American theatre in this change because the cost of wood rose in Europe earlier than it did here. European theatres are routinely equipped with metal shops; some are even subdivided, segregating welding operations into a separate area. Few American theatres have moved farther in this direction than to set aside a corner of the scene shop as a metal shop and provide a few special tools. Most theatres find it necessary to move some of their woodworking equipment in order to temporarily set up for metal working. This brings the risk of mixing highly flammable wood and sawdust with sparks from welders and grinders—something safety officials will not long tolerate. Since a complete metal shop seems a future necessity, one is described.

METAL SHOP

The metal shop area should be well ventilated, to remove welder fumes, and well lighted. The floor should be of concrete or other nonflammable material. Tables with sturdy heatproof tops should be provided. Ideally, one table should be covered with a very heavy iron top that can be used for welding. No flammable materials should be stored in or even near the metal-working area. Special care should be taken that greasy rags and waste are stored in nonflammable containers, and that these materials are not allowed to accumulate. Fire extinguishers should be handy and well maintained. A first aid kit is necessary. Minor burns and cuts from sharp metal will be the usual hazards.

Of course, not very many theatres will have complete metal shop facilities and a separate room in which to operate them. The necessary equipment for a metal shop is mentioned below in order to acquaint the student with the tools (wherever he may find them) and to supply reinforcement to those theatre administrators who are seeking to modernize their plants.

LARGE TOOLS FOR THE METAL SHOP

Some large tools may be found in the woodworking portion of the scene shop. If a separate shop for metal working is to be established or if extensive work is to be done in both wood and metal, such tools should be duplicated with special blades, bits, or other parts for each application.

Electric Welding Equipment

Electric welders are essential metal-working equipment. There are several types, of which only the wire welder is useful for beginners:

1. The AC welder. This relatively simple machine for use with welding rods is occasionally termed a "buzz box." It is quite adequate for small shops where occasional welding will be done by those skilled in operating such a machine. This skill takes considerable practice to learn and maintain. The AC welder can also double as a power supply for a hot wire cutter for foamed plastics.

2. The conventional DC welder (Figure 13-1a). This is a more expensive but more flexible variation of the AC welder. If funds are available for a DC welder, they may be better spent for the wire welder mentioned below. However, if a conventional DC welder is available at little cost, perhaps from surplus, it will be a very useful tool for the experienced

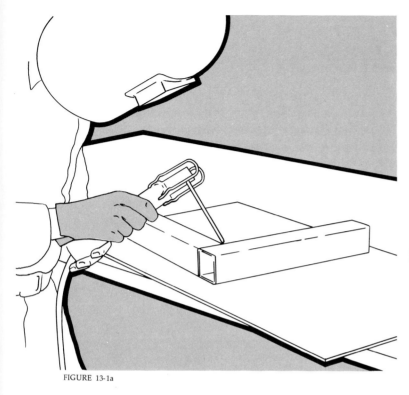

FIGURE 13-1b

FIGURE 13-1a

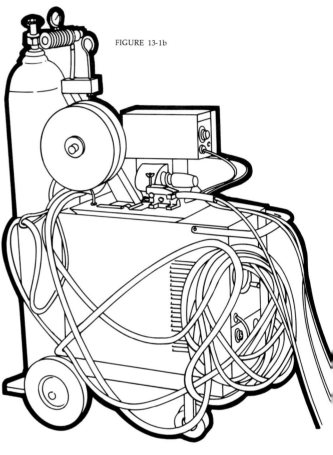

Figure 13-1. (a) Conventional Electric Welder. The electrode of a conventional electric welder showing how the operator must maintain the arc distance. This takes considerable skill. The power supply for such welding electrodes may vary from a heavy AC transformer to a very heavy-duty DC generator powered either by an AC motor or a gasoline engine. Such welders are common in professional metal shops. (b) DC Wire Welder. The gas tank provides inert gas which shields the arc and makes flux unnecessary. The spool contains the welding wire which feeds through the gas hose to the electrode. See Figure 13-10 for the electrode.

worker. Beginners can be taught to use it, but only with considerable instruction.

3. The DC wire welder (Figure 13-1b). This expensive but highly desirable machine is discussed in detail later in this chapter. It is an ideal tool for beginners.

Oxyacetylene Cutting and Welding Equipment

Oxyacetylene cutting and welding equipment (Figure 13-2) can be used either to cut steel or iron materials or to weld a variety of materials together. Actually it is the standard auto or machine shop equipment.

Although it can be dangerous in the hands of the completely un-initiated, its use is easily taught. Cost of operation is quite low if the gas is properly turned off after use. The torch may also be used for flame-sculpturing foamed plastics, but the work must be done outside where ventilation is excellent, since the fumes may otherwise be dangerous.

Power Hacksaw

The power hacksaw is almost essential if much work is to be done with square steel tubing (a highly useful commodity). This simple-to-operate machine is a large rugged motor-driven version of the hacksaw.

Drill Press

The drill press (see Figure 8-14) is similar to the machine specified for wood working. It should be equipped with a good set of high-speed bits and a drill vise.

Bench Grinder

The bench grinder, often found in wood shops, is useful for cutting, shaping, and sharpening operations. Goggles or a face shield are necessary to protect the operator's eyes from flying grit and are required by OSHA.

Figure 13-2. Oxyacetylene Cutting and Welding Equipment. The set consists of a bottle of oxygen, one of acetylene, and the regulators and hoses necessary to feed these gases to the torch. Either a cutting torch or a welding torch may be fitted to the system.

Figure 13-3. One-half Inch Electric Drill. Note that this rather powerful tool must be securely held with both hands when operated.

Metal-Working Lathe (Machine Lathe)

The very expensive machine lathe may not be available in any but the best-equipped metal shop. Its advantages are many because it can be used to manufacture innumerable items that require round metal or hard plastic shapes. Those working with scenic projection equipment will find such a lathe highly useful, and it should be located so that its use can be shared. It is not a tool for the beginner although simple operations are easily learned.

Sheet Metal Brake

The full commercial version of the sheet metal brake is a huge unwieldy piece of equipment beyond the needs of most theatre shops. A smaller unit is sufficient. It is used for forming sheet metal by bending, and is also useful in the lighting shop.

SMALL TOOLS FOR THE METAL SHOP

Obviously a variety of hammers, chisels, files, and pliers will be needed. Vise-grip pliers are especially useful. Discussed below are some of the more useful electrically operated tools and some special hand tools.

$\frac{1}{2}$ Inch Electric Drill

The heavy-duty version of the common hand-held electric drill is the $\frac{1}{2}$ inch electric drill (Figure 13-3), used for drilling wood and light metal. It should be equipped with a set of good-quality bits, some of which will also fit the drill press. Note that this machine is not a substitute for a drill press or vice versa.

Electric Hand Grinder

Figure 13-4. Electric Hand Grinder.

The electric hand grinder (Figure 13-4) is used for smoothing welded joints and rough cut edges of metal, and for fitting whenever the work cannot be taken to the bench grinder. Goggles or a face mask are absolutely required to protect the eyes. Flammables should be removed to a safe distance.

Electric Impact Wrench

The electric impact wrench (Figure 13-5) is commonly found in auto shops either in the electric or compressed air version. On stage it is exceedingly useful for assembling and disassembling structures of metal lumber or any other structures that are held together by bolts and nuts.

Jacks

Automotive jacks of the hydraulic variety or screw jacks will be used for forcing welded metal parts into exact shape when the heat of welding has warped them. They are also useful for lifting heavy wagons to repair casters.

Pipe Cutter and Pipe Dies

The pipe cutter and pipe dies are absolutely essential for making up metal devices for the stage. The pipe cutter is a tool that will accurately cut common sizes of steel pipe by rotating it around the pipe. With each turn a screw is tightened to drive a hard steel cutting wheel deeper into the steel until the pipe wall is cut through. A pipe die is a specially shaped piece of very hard steel which is forcibly screwed onto the end of a piece of pipe to form threads. They are delicate. Use with care.

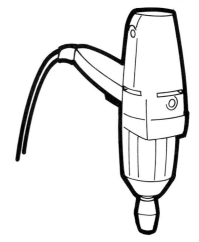

Figure 13-5. Electric Impact Wrench. This tool may be replaced by an air-driven impact wrench in some shops.

Anvil

The anvil is needed for pounding heated metal into shape. It can be combined with a large bench vise but will serve better as a separate item. It is indestructible.

Heavy-Duty Bench Vise

This bench vise should be firmly bolted to a heavy bench. It is used for all manner of bending and shaping operations. If fitted with pipe clamps, it will also serve for pipe work.

STORAGE OF METAL SUPPLIES

Steel tubing and other metal forms are best stored on a metal rack similar to those on which pipe is stored. Such racks allow the steel to be categorized by cross section and length, making choice of materials easy. These racks may be built in the shop at a great saving if the steel tubing itself is used. They should be capable of holding a large stock of metal in various sizes if the theatre is to take advantage of large-scale buying.

SYSTEMS USING METAL

Unlike wood, which is sold as a stock material for use in the theatre, metal may be obtained in a variety of organized systems, each devised to satisfy certain needs adaptable to the theatre. We will consider a number of such systems in addition to techniques that use stock metal materials.

COMMERCIAL SCAFFOLDING

Commercial scaffolding, which you have probably seen on a construction site, consists of welded framework units, made of steel or aluminum alloy tubing that fit together with several varieties of patented clamps and fasteners. The result is a flexible, enormously strong, and easily assembled system. Most commercial builders rent the scaffolding as needed, but the rental system will not always work well for theatres. Rental stocks of scaffolding tend to be encrusted with plaster, old paint, and rust that reduce their usefulness for theatres. Perhaps the best plan is to rent for a couple of times while trying out the system. (Rent clean scaffolding if at all possible.) A basic stock may then be purchased. Occasional special pieces can be rented or purchased as needed. The renter or seller can also provide the theatre with engineering details on the scaffolding. In most cases the strength will far exceed anything the theatre might need. The only exception may be long spans which might be loaded to capacity. Renters will also often provide instruction on the proper method of setting up the scaffolding and handy tricks to speed up the process. See Figure 13-6 for an example of the application of commercial scaffolding.

Adapting commercial scaffolding to the theatre results in a variety of difficulties because theatrical needs are quite different from those of the construction industry. Commercial users need heavy planks for flooring; $\frac{3}{4}$ inch by 4 foot by 8 foot plywood will be the usual theatrical flooring. Since scaffolding is not made in 4 foot modules, heavy joists will usually have to be installed on top of the scaffold and the plywood laid over them. Facing commercial scaffolding will also present problems. No fittings are readily available for fastening flats or other wooden structures to the faces of steel scaffolds. If the theatre owns the scaffold, special plates with drilled and tapped holes can be welded to the vertical portions of the scaffolding. Otherwise the facing may be temporarily wired to the scaffold with iron wire. Finally, commercial scaffolding is not usually made for rises less than 4 feet. The standard vertical module is more likely to be about 6 feet.

The result of all these difficulties is that commercial scaffolding is not a substitute for parallels or legged platforms. It is instead a valuable supplement when greater heights and greater strengths are needed. It is an excellent medium for temporarily filling in a large orchestra pit to extend the apron of the stage (Figure 12-1). It is also fine for large on-stage or carry-off structures and is especially good for shows where its structure can serve as a design element.

As a crew member, you may assist in the assembly of commercial scaffolding. Once you master the patented clamps, you will find the

Figure 13-6. Commercial Scaffolding. This setting is made of regular commercial steel scaffolding. This material is also useful for many concealed applications on stage. The photograph shows the Painters Theatre production, In Praise of Falling. *Book and lyrics: Shirley Kaplan; music: Bill Obrecht; direction: June Ekman. Photograph by Marton Brown.*

work goes rapidly. Most parts can be easily handled by two people, since the scaffold is designed to provide its own support as you build it up. Ladders may be built into the side panels for convenience. It becomes a sort of jungle gym for crew members as they build it. (Actors may use it the same way, as in Figure 13-6.) There will usually be screw jacks provided at the bottom of the lowest section for the purpose of leveling the scaffold on an uneven floor. Check carefully with a spirit level as you set the first sections.

PIPE AND SLIP-ON FITTINGS

There are a number of systems marketed that provide a variety of joints in ordinary water pipe without the necessity of threading joints. The pipe is simply sawed or cut with a pipe cutter to the proper length, any burrs removed, and slipped into the patented fittings where it is held in place by a set screw or similar locking device. A variety of angle-joints, clamps for fixing pipes at crossing points, and flanges for attachment to wooden surfaces are available. Although these fittings are moderately expensive in initial cost, they have a long life. Pipe, of course, is a standard commodity in the theatre and is usually purchased in wholesale quantities. Such systems can be quite economical over a long period of time because parts are almost completely salvageable.

One such system, devised at Northern Illinois University, is based on the use of 1 inch pipe and patented fittings which may be used to attach the pipe to reinforced $\frac{3}{4}$ inch plywood platform tops as shown in Figure 13-7. Cross-bracing is added to the platform as needed by the use of clamps and 1 inch pipe to produce strong structures. A particular advantage is that unlike most of the other systems using prefabricated metal parts, this one does not force the scenographer to use rectilinear shapes. Curves, ramps, or other irregular shapes may be supported by the pipe legs as needed. Furthermore, as Figure 13-8 and

Figure 13-7. (a) An isometric drawing of a stage platform using standard steel water pipe and special fittings. (b) A detail of such a platform.

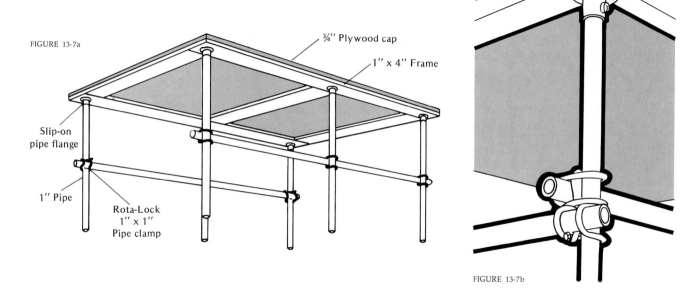

FIGURE 13-7a

¾" Plywood cap

1" x 4" Frame

Slip-on pipe flange

1" Pipe

Rota-Lock 1" x 1" Pipe clamp

FIGURE 13-7b

Figure 13-8. Drawing showing how the steps shown in Plate XII were supported. Note how the pipe supporting the upper steps passes through and also supports the upstage portion of the step below. Courtesy Richard Arnold, Northern Illinois University, DeKalb, Ill.

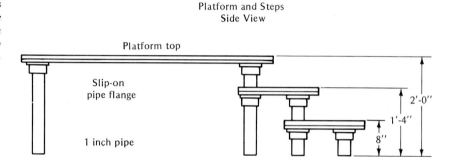

Platform and Steps
Side View

Platform top

Slip-on pipe flange

1 inch pipe

2'-0''

1'-4''

8''

Plate XII show, settings can be devised in which the supporting structure is nearly invisible, creating a light, airy quality impossible to achieve with wooden substructures.

As an additional bonus, this same system of pipe fittings has a set of elbows, tees, and similar parts that enable the shop to make up very satisfactory handrail systems for seating areas in flexible theatres where permanent rail systems are impractical.

PUNCHED METAL ANGLE

Another approach to weight-bearing structure, the use of the punched metal angle, will remind you of your childhood erector set. It is manufactured by several steel companies and sold in bundles consisting of a number of feet of the metal together with the nuts, bolts, and washers needed to put it together. It comes in stock lengths. The manufacturers also sell a patented cutter that makes square cuts and 45-degree cuts easy. They provide engineering instructions designed for nonengineers and helpful hints for assembly.

This material was not designed for the theatre; it was designed as a relatively cheap, strong, fire resistant system for building up storage units in stockrooms and the like and works best on rectilinear structures. The following are its advantages:

1. It is strong for its weight.
2. It is relatively cheap because of the possibility of reuse.
3. It works rapidly in the hands of experienced workmen.

There are disadvantages:

1. It is not self-squaring in spite of any claims on the part of dealers. It must be carefully squared at every joint.
2. It tends to loosen up under the vibration of walking or running actors. This can be alleviated by setting the nuts and bolts tightly with an impact wrench.
3. It has sharp corners that are dangerous.
4. The bolt heads make it impossible to install wood parts flush with the metal frames.
5. Odd angles are rather difficult to execute.

To get the maximum economic advantage out of metal lumber, large quantities must be purchased at one time. Thus a theatre planning to try it out must invest in a sizable order. A couple of bundles will not be a fair test. The material comes in a variety of strengths depending on the thickness of the sheet steel from which it is made. The temptation will be to use the lightest type available because the loading charts provided indicate that this is strong enough. This could be a mistake since theatre loads tend to be "live loads" (actors move,

FIGURE 13-9a

FIGURE 13-9b

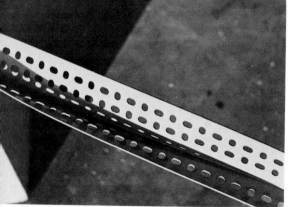

Figure 13-9. (a) Punched Metal Angle. This material is strong when installed so that the wide portion of the angle is perpendicular to the load. A platform top could be attached to the horizontal portions of the material as shown. (b) Overstressed Member. This piece of punched metal angle shows the effects of applying a stress at an angle to the wide portion. Once the material has been deformed by a stress such as this, it presents little resistance to further stress, and will fail under an otherwise properly sized load. Such pieces should be immediately replaced in a structure.

jump, and fall), and these are much harder on material than the "dead loads" encountered in storage applications. This problem is compounded by the fact that metal lumber has most of its strength in those directions at right angles to the two metal surfaces. It is quite weak if it is loaded in a way that causes twist or stress on the diagonal (see Figure 13-9). Therefore braces have to be carefully planned. Even temporary stresses in weak directions should be avoided. The writer has seen otherwise strong platforms weakened by workers climbing the framework and twisting the braces. The ultimate result was failure. The implication of this is that braces and parts located in vulnerable or high-stress areas should be of heavy-duty material. In most cases identical punching of holes makes the light-duty and heavy-duty material mechanically interchangeable.

Another approach to the problem of live loads and high stress areas is to fabricate T-bars by bolting two of the L-shaped pieces back to back, following the manufacturer's directions for bolt spacing. The result will be a member considerably stronger than the two parts used separately.

Given the willingness to be careful about construction details, and the purchase of a cutter and an impact wrench to speed fabrication, metal lumber can be an economical construction material. It salvages well and lasts a long time in the theatre. The short scraps that gradually accumulate find many uses—they make good corner reinforcements, for example.

Stage crew members will find that metal lumber is easy and rapid to work with provided they take the precautions mentioned and work from well-thought-out plans. They must beware of the sharp edges. Once the pieces are assembled, most of these edges will be concealed, no longer presenting a hazard.

WELDED SQUARE STEEL TUBING

It is more and more obvious that wood is becoming so expensive that other materials may prove to be more economical for construction of weight-bearing scenery. One of the most likely possibilities for this is square steel tubing. Given the shop tools for working steel, several studies have shown that steel tubing construction can often be at least as cheap as wood construction when moderately heavy loads are encountered. This saving will be evident not on one show, but, rather, over a period of several productions where the reuse of the same steel will effect economies.

Not only does steel tubing seem likely to become more and more a standard item in scenic construction, it also opens up new opportunities to the scenographer. The great strength of steel makes possible the design of structures that would be out of the question in wood. Previously these structures were possible only to the scenographer who worked in theatres with huge production budgets, such as those in Las Vegas or on Broadway. This is no longer true because of new price structures and advances in welding techniques.

The adoption of steel as a basic material for use in the theatre will work major changes in the scene shop. Where it was previously almost exclusively a woodworking shop, it must now deal with metal cutting and welding, operations that are not entirely compatible with woodworking. Ideally a separate shop or at least a separate area should be devoted to metal work. However, it is possible to economize by utilizing some existing shop tools (equipped with metal cutting blades) and adding welding apparatus. In a single-shop operation, careful discipline will have to be exerted to make sure that tools are not misused and that no fire hazards are created by welding.

DESIGNING WITH SQUARE STEEL TUBING

Once the transition has been made, the scenographer will find that steel tubing offers many design advantages over wood. Most of these derive from the great strength of steel in relation to its cross-sectional area. Also, welding makes possible a wide variety of joints that would be very hard to execute in wood. A joint need be no thicker than the stock material itself, and may be made at any angle with equal strength. Wood does not offer such flexibility. Bends and curves are possible in steel that would be nearly impossible in wood. However the scenographer should be aware that the intricacies of decorative wrought iron can probably be better achieved with plastic than with steel.

One of the first great design advantages that will occur to the scenographer working with steel is the possibility of very thin structures that support heavy loads. For example, a cantilever capable of supporting hundreds of pounds is possible with a thickness of less than 3 inches. A balcony or a "bridge" from one support to another may be almost fantastically thin for the length of the span.

There is also a safety factor in steel construction that is not available in wood. Because it is brittle, wood tends to fail completely when it is overloaded. Thus, if a cantilevered balcony is overloaded, it is apt to break off suddenly. Steel structures gradually deform under overloads, giving those on them a better chance to get off, and usually merely bending slightly, allowing workers to jack the structure back into place and add bracing.

The scenographer using steel will probably consider the possibility of constructing fantastically airy "jungle gymlike" structures which actors can climb through, over, and under with complete confidence. Many such structures have been used in the professional theatre with great success. The possibilities opened to the director for actor movement are almost infinite. Such structures can also be portable: It is simple to break welded steel structures into easily handled units which bolt together or fit together by telescoping one piece of tubing into another to make a strong joint.

Because steel is inherently fireproof, the scenographer need not concern himself about flameproofing it. It resists wear much better than wood, and is repaired easily by welding if bent or broken.

Solving Stress Problems

Rules of thumb for working with wood have been used for many years in the theatre in lieu of engineering formulas. Similar rules of thumb can be worked out for steel. The designer need not compute the deflection of each beam as he designs it. A general approach is to evaluate the flexibility of the square stock to be used by applying stress to it and noting the *deflection* (how it bends). Bridging a piece of tubing between two solid supports and standing on it will give some idea of its strength. Remember that the addition of flooring over the steel will increase the strength of the entire unit. Once some norms for spacing of braces have been worked out, the structure can be built and tested. If it appears too weak at some point, it is a simple matter to weld in additional bracing.

WORKING WITH SQUARE STEEL TUBING

Square steel tubing comes in a wide variety of sizes and in several qualities of steel. Unless available in surplus at very cheap prices, the more exotic kinds, such as stainless steel, should generally be avoided by theatre workers. They will probably present unusual welding problems. Of course, if the look of stainless is what the scenographer wants and the budget can stand it, the technicians should get the necessary tools and learn how to handle the material.

Tubing, like most other theatrical materials, is most economically bought in quantities. If storage can be arranged, steel can easily be bought in bulk and kept on hand for a long period of time. It stores well. Costs are rising as this text is being written, so stockpiling is becoming more attractive all the time. Producing groups may be able to combine their needs into a single large order and reap an advantage in price and delivery costs.

Cutting

Steel must be cut to size before welding. There are two general methods: *sawing* and *burning* (cutting with an oxyacetylene torch). Sawing is by far the more accurate and presents fewer fire hazards, but it is much slower. If the shop has a band saw, it can be equipped with a metal cutting blade to cut tubing. A still better solution is to purchase a power hacksaw. It is not an expensive or bulky tool and will do a good job. Occasional cuts can be made by a hand-operated hacksaw, but this is tedious and usually inaccurate.

If an oxyacetylene torch is available, tubing can be rapidly "burned" into two parts—by far the fastest way to disassemble a steel setting. Burning, however, leaves edges that are rough and hard to fit together to make a good joint. Care must always be taken that the sparks and bits of molten metal do not set fire and that no one is burned. The torch operator should be carefully instructed and the equipment should be in first-class condition. However, operation of an oxyacetylene torch is not a difficult skill to learn. The gas for running the torch is inexpensive if bought as part of the supplies for a large institution. Many school shops will already have this equipment and be engaged in instructing operators.

Gas Welding

There are two general categories of welding: *gas* and *electric arc*. Both may be used with success on steel tubing. Gas welding is done with the same basic equipment used to cut steel, an oxyacetylene torch. The difference is in the structure of the torch itself and the addition of a wirelike rod of material into the flame. This fills the joint to make the weld. Like cutting, gas welding is an easily learned skill that good theatre technicians should know. However, the beginner should not attempt it without adequate training and supervision. Special goggles are absolutely necessary and protective clothing is desirable. There should be no flammable materials near the welding area, and any volatile combustible solvents should be removed completely from the room. Check local fire regulations and observe them carefully.

Electric Arc Welding

Electric arc welding is done by generating an electrical spark between a rod of material (electrode) used to fill the joint and the metal to be joined. The control of the spark with ordinary welding apparatus is a matter of considerable skill. A certified welder, qualified to make all manner of complicated welds capable of holding up under severe stresses, is a highly skilled, well-paid specialist. Most theatrical welding can be done with a much lower degree of skill since it need not meet such rigorous standards. Special machines that take much of the skill out of this routine welding are also available. These machines are known as "automatic self-feeding DC wire welders" (Figure 13-1b

Figure 13-10. Welding with a Wire Welder. This operation is simplified by the machine shown in Figure 13-1b. The spacing of the electrode from the work is automatically set when the outer portion of the electrode is touched to the work. This electrode is out of operation. Note how the wire feeds through the center. The inert gas flows out around it, protecting the arc.

and 13-10). Most are portable. They are so designed that any one can do a satisfactory weld on simple materials such as steel tubing with a small amount of instruction. It is quite possible that beginners in well-equipped theatre shops will find themselves on the welding crew.

These advanced welding machines are moderately costly. As this book is being written, a complete set of machinery costs between $1200 and $1500. However, this is not much more than the cost of a good table saw for a wood shop. The machine uses welding wire instead of rod as the electrode. The wire is automatically fed as the electric arc melts it away. A flow of carbon dioxide prevents oxygen from the air from interfering with the welding process. The design of the welding electrode holder (Figure 13-10) determines the spacing from the work, and thereby the length of the arc. The operator need only guide the holder over the joint to be welded.

Electric welding produces an intense flare of bluish-white light rich in ultraviolet rays. This light is dangerous; it will produce severe sunburn and badly irritate an unprotected eye. Therefore everyone witnessing the welding process must use a protective mask and protective clothing to prevent the light from striking the skin. If the observer is close to the arc itself, he must wear a heavy protective leather apron to prevent being burned by the flying sparks. Close observation is one of the best ways to begin the process of learning to weld. The room where welding is being done should be well ventilated because the fumes are objectionable, and, of course, no flammable materials should be nearby. All volatile inflammable liquids, such as acetone, should be completely removed from the premises.

Shaping the Welded Object

Unlike wooden construction, welded steel objects are subject to considerable adjustment after they are put together. This is a good thing because the heat of the welding may warp the steel. Such warps or any minor errors in setting angles of joints can usually be corrected by pounding or by using a jack to force the object into shape. Of course, this is best done before any wooden parts have been attached.

FASTENING WOOD TO STEEL

Obviously wooden objects cannot be nailed to the steel framework; therefore bolts or self-tapping screws are used. The steel is drilled to accept the fastener and the wood bolted or screwed into place. If it is necessary to glue fabric to a steel structure, it is better to attach narrow strips of $\frac{1}{4}$ inch plywood and glue to them. This makes the salvage of the steel easier, and obviates the necessity of finding a glue that will hold the fabric to the steel. (Contact cement would do this but it is not a regularly stocked shop item.) If the steel must be painted, it will have to be cleaned with a solvent such as paint thinner to remove the oil on its surface. Once this has been done, regular scene paints will adhere.

FLYING STEEL OBJECTS

Although they tend to be heavy, many steel objects can be flown if desired. Attaching hanging apparatus is much simpler than when using wood. Rings may be welded into place or eyes passed through holes drilled in the steel and bolted. If welds are used for hanging, they should be thoroughly tested by placing several times the normal stress on them and jolting them severely.

SALVAGING A STEEL SETTING

Unlike wood, steel is salvageable down to very short lengths. It can be welded back together to make a piece about as strong as new material, and the weld will hardly be visible from the audience. Therefore, steel settings are usually stripped of all wood and fabric and then cut apart with an oxyacetylene torch to produce straight pieces of stock.

This stock is then stored until needed. The amount of steel lost in this process will be exceedingly small. When the shop has gathered a large amount of steel parts too small to justify welding them together, they may be sold to a scrap metal dealer to recover a good share of the original cost. If this practice of cutting apart and salvaging is followed, welded steel tubing will prove to be an economical material for the theatre. Of course, it is not a general substitute for wood, but it will solve many weight-bearing problems economically and open the way to new design possibilities for the scenographer.

OTHER WELDED STEEL MATERIALS

Square steel tubing is by far the easiest lightweight steel form to work with in a theatre shop. Joints are relatively simple because of the square cross section of the stock. Round steel tubing or iron pipe are also frequently welded to make weight-bearing structures. The tubing is lighter for a given strength; the pipe is more commonly available. Both have the advantage of providing a round shape, easily grasped by actors who may swing from a horizontal part of the framing; and offer a somewhat simpler line to the design. The disadvantage is in making joints. Since one cylindrical shape must inevitably intersect another, each joint must be ground to fit before welding. This tedious process slows construction and increases cost. Pipe can, of course, be threaded and joined in the usual manner, although this is also slow work and produces more noticeable joints.

Other standard forms of structural steel such as bar stock, channel, angle, and I-beam can be welded by the shop welder into occasionally useful forms for settings. More often these materials will be used to construct machinery needed for the theatre.

14
SHIFTING
SCENERY

INTRODUCTION The plans for changing the settings begin with the scenographer. As he works out his design concepts he must keep in mind the limitations of the theatre in which the production is going to take place. For example, he will have to rule out large three-dimensional set pieces that must be stored backstage during part of the show if there is little backstage space available. Architecture thus determines the ultimate limitations placed on the scenographer and thereby determines the limits of all productions done in the building.

But these are negative factors against which scenographers and technicians match their ingenuity and artistry, while focusing their attention on the positive elements in the movement of scenery, props, and lighting. In modern theatre the scenic elements are becoming more and more a part of the rhythmic structure of the production. Movement of scenic elements in sight of the audience has become a powerful design factor aiding the moving actor in a spatial expression of the production.

Both the most utilitarian and the most artistic shifts must be done with finesse, and it is the job of various specialists to do this. This chapter details the work of these people and explains how they operate the machines that assist them.

JOB DESIGNATIONS RELATING TO SHIFTING

In the highly unionized professional theatre the jobs involved in shifting and handling settings, props, and lighting are strictly defined. Some of these definitions grow out of logical division of labor and some out of the necessity for union job distinctions.

The *stage manager* is the leader of the production team, both professional and non-professional. His general duties are discussed in Chapter 5, "How the Producing Theatre Is Organized." Here we are only concerned with his control over scene shifts. The stage manager orders the shift to begin, times it, makes all final checkouts, then orders the actors to return to the stage and the next scene to commence. In many cases the stage manager also organizes the shift, assigns jobs, and designates where various items will go. In these matters he must be in close communication with the scenographer and the technical director who originally worked out these details.

The *chief carpenter* or *stage carpenter* is in direct charge of the *grips,* the stagehands who handle the setting. He is usually responsible for all scenic elements that are handled on the stage floor by grips, and indirectly responsible for set pieces that fly. These lines of responsibility vary from place to place.

The *property chief* and the *property crew* handle the furniture, set decorations, and such, working under the general control of the stage manager.

If scenery is flown either from hand-operated lines or power-driven equipment, it is the responsibility of the *riggers,* who are specialists in the mechanics of rigging systems. They will be discussed in the following chapter.

The *chief electrician* is responsible for all electrical equipment backstage including properties such as table lamps. However, electrical props are normally placed in the proper position by the prop man and then connected by the electrician. Similarly, lighting equipment mounted on the setting which must be moved during a shift, is handled by stagehands and connected by electricians.

These sharp designations vary somewhat from one part of the country to another even in union houses. They blur almost completely in nonunion theatres, whether professional or not. Generally speaking, the educational theatre will divide up backstage jobs on the basis of the needs of the immediate production, the degree of capability and reliability of the students, and the need to give students varied experiences in their educational theatre careers. Thus there is likely to be a "stage crew" whose responsibility includes that of the professional grip, property man, and often that of the rigger. Lighting crews tend to remain separate entities although there are no arbitrary distinctions to designate who carries in a property lamp and who hooks it up.

However the backstage crew is organized, the shifting must be done safely, efficiently, and with artistic sensitivity. In the discussion that follows we first investigate the various types of scene shifts, then discuss methods of moving scenery and properties, and finally detail the individual jobs of crew members.

TYPES OF SCENE SHIFTS

The complexity of a scene shift can vary from none at all in the case of a single-setting show with no property changes, or a production in an architectural setting in which changes are only a function of the action, to hugely complicated productions with a large number of full-stage changes executed in sight of the audience. Scene shifting is often further complicated when a show tours from one theatre to another. This requires that the setting not only shift rapidly but that it be demountable to pass through too-small doorways, to survive the rigors of repeated loading into trucks, railway cars, and even aircraft, and to be stored backstage in areas almost too small to accommodate it.

Although the special requirements of moving the show from theatre to theatre are not exactly a part of the usual definition of scene shifting, they do condition the way in which the scenery will be handled and are usually performed by the same crews. Thus we will consider such actions as haul-ins and strikes as a part of our discussion of scene shifting.

HAUL-IN

Whether a show tours or not, there will be some form of haul-in unless the setting is actually built on the stage itself. A haul-in consists of bringing the setting, properties, lighting equipment, and other paraphernalia from the shops or storage areas, and assembling this equipment on stage. In the case of a show built in an adjacent shop in an educational or community theatre, the haul-in may be almost imperceptible. Pieces will be placed on stage and given over to the cast for use as they are finished to the point where they can be safely used for rehearsal. There will frequently be much hauling back and forth of partially finished pieces that are used in rehearsals, and then returned to the shop for further work. At the other extreme is the Broadway situation where the entire finished setting, properties, and lighting equipment are brought into the theatre in one huge effort. This is usually the first time the cast will have the use of any parts of the setting, which was built and painted in a studio and delivered to the stage in its completed form. Lights are installed and technical rehearsals begin almost immediately. The situation is about the same in the case of a touring show except that the cast already has used the setting at some other location.

Touring calls for special construction techniques that make it possible to break the setting and properties into transportable pieces without damage. Special joints are used for this, which are not a part of the scene-to-scene shifting operations. While these joints are demountable, they are designed to produce maximum rigidity when assembled but not to facilitate rapid, quiet joining and unjoining under between-scenes conditions.

STRIKE

There are three varieties of strike. The first consists of taking the setting apart in preparation for moving to another location or for temporary storage pending reopening of the production. The second consists of destroying the setting at the end of the run. It may be sold, salvaged for parts, or hauled to the dump, depending on union regulations and future plans for more productions. The third consists of tearing down a setting between scenes in preparation for building up the next scene. This happens when the command, "Strike it!" is given as a shift begins.

REPERTORY SCENE SHIFTING

Scene shifting is a way of life in a repertory theatre, which plays a different show every night over a period of time often repeating the cycle at set intervals. Things are complicated further when one production is scheduled for the matinee and another for the evening performance. Theatres designed for repertory are often equipped with expensive revolves, wagons, lifts, and such, to facilitate the movement of complete settings, or large sections of settings, at the push of a button. European opera houses are examples of this sort of organization. The presence of three productions on the same stage in the same day is not uncommon, nor does it present impossible shifting problems. Adequate machinery, skilled workers, and careful planning make such a schedule work.

DARK-NIGHT PROBLEMS

In a typical educational or community theatre the production may play for a night or two, be dark for several days, and then play again. During the dark nights other groups will use the stage, requiring that the setting be completely removed to safe storage backstage or even to special storage areas during these intervals. Such shifting somewhat resembles touring. Settings must be made with joints that allow the set to be demounted to pass through doors or to store in tight quarters although these joints may play no part in the between-scenes changes. There is often the further complication that properties may mysteriously disappear and lights may become reangled during these breaks. To catch these unplanned changes, crews must be cautioned to check every item thoroughly each time the production has been dark.

BETWEEN-SCENES SHIFTS

The most precise work of the stage crews involves between-scene shifts. They are almost always done under pressure of time and usually in dim light with restrictions as to the amount of noise that can be made. This is where the organized skills of the crew chiefs and their superiors and the planning of the theatre consultant and architect will be severely tested.

OPEN CURTAIN SHIFTS

We noted in the introduction to this chapter that while scene shifts are often utilitarian, taking place behind a closed curtain, there is an increasing tendency to make movement of the scenery an active part of the entire production. In today's theatre it is often possible to speak of "choreographing the setting." Such movements of scenic elements may take place at designated scene changes or may occur as required by the dramatic development, giving the illusion of almost continuous movement. However they are done, each movement becomes a part of the virtual world of the drama and must be handled as carefully as the most important character movement. If the movements are operated mechanically using offstage controlled motors, lines, and such, they must fit into the overall rhythmic structure of the production. If the moving force is provided by crew members costumed to fit into the visual world of the production, these members must move with the precision of dancers. Obviously rehearsals are just as important to such shifts as they are to any other part of the production.

There are endless possibilities for complications in scene shifting. Changes will range from the almost casual rearrangement of a few properties to a complete change of setting, properties, and even rearrangement of lighting instruments between scenes. Perhaps the worst situation is the dreaded "dead cue," where a complicated shift must take place in a time span clearly delineated to the audience by a piece of music or action in front of the curtain. Such shifts must be "dead right" or the lapse will be painfully obvious to the audience. Most theatre workers strive to avoid these situations whenever possible.

Although it will not cover all contingencies, a review of the procedure to be followed in the change from one complete "box setting" to another with complete property change will illustrate the kind of organization required in complicated scene shifting. A "box set" is one made up of flats that form the illusion of three sides of a room, usually topped by a ceiling. It offers a challenge to the crews, especially when backstage space is limited.

SHIFTING BOX SETTINGS

There are no mysteries about successful scene shifting. Efficiency will be the result of careful organization and much practice. The chief will usually be the stage manager, who will seek continually to refine the operations until he has made the shift in well under the stipulated time. This will give him spare time to accommodate emergencies which his forever pessimistic intuition tells him are bound to occur.

There should be no wasted motion. No one should enter or leave the stage empty-handed. Things should be worked into reasonably large loads rather than carried individually. Where possible, wheels are better than backs. Talking should be minimal, and disagreements over who is to do what should be nonexistent. No one should be over-worked and things should never be hurried to the point of danger; safety is even more important than efficiency.

As we describe our hypothetical shift, we will assume that the first-act setting is in place and the properties are in whatever location they were as the curtain came down on Act I. Curtain calls, if any, have been completed and the house lights have come on. The stage manager knows that the setting and properties for Act II are stored in their planned places backstage, and that those for Act III are also in their storage place. As he turns on the work lights he commands, "Strike it!" and notes the time. The actors have cleared the stage as rapidly as the curtain calls would let them and will remain off the stage until called by the stage manager. If there is a "green room" (a waiting room for actors where they can talk, smoke, and relax) they will go there, or to their dressing rooms for costume changes, etc. The actions of the various crews will proceed in approximately the following manner.

1. The ceiling will be raised to clear the top of the setting. If there is a chandelier it will be lowered into the waiting arms of the property crew who will guide it into its storage box, and the electrician who will disconnect it. Its now-empty line will be readied for the Act II chandelier or weighted and taken out of view. If the "ceiling" consists merely of false beams, these will be lifted clear of the top of the setting, and any light fixtures either taken to the flies or struck, depending on the needs of the remainder of the play.

2. The moment the work lights come on, the property crew enters the setting bringing with them any carts or carrying baskets they are using. Ideally these will contain some of the properties for Act II which will be stored in a clear place for later installation. (No empty hands, if possible.) The property crew begins to clear the walls of the setting of pictures, bric-a-brac, etc., at the predetermined place where the scenery crew plans to start to disassemble the setting. This point or points will be determined by the most efficient path to and from the

storage areas for Act I and Act II. Meanwhile the setting crew has been taking down backings outside of the setting proper, moving carry-offs, and preparing to "break" the setting the moment the property crew has cleared all the bric-a-brac. As it is being cleared, the rest of the property crew moves the large furniture downstage to form a clear working area at the points where the set is about to be broken.

3. The scenery crew opens or "breaks" the setting in the planned location(s), and the pieces are carried to their storage location. The crew members return with parts of the Act II setting that have been stored in the order of their assembly on stage. These parts are set in the clear working area pending installation. This haul-out and haul-in operation is continued until the whole Act I setting has been removed and the entire Act II setting is on stage. As this process progresses, part of the scenery crew begins to assemble the new setting on its "spike marks" (dabs of paint or pieces of colored tape on the floor) as soon as space is available to do so. However they must not close off the opening in the setting until all scenery and props have been exchanged.

4. As the above operation is proceeding, the property crew is carrying off Act I props and returning with Act II props. The properties have been arranged into predetermined loads, stacking small chairs atop sofas and small props atop tables, into drawers, etc. As soon as space is available they begin to place the properties in their spiked locations. As soon as parts of the Act II set are in place, pictures and bric-a-brac are installed on these. As the shift progresses, each crew member consults his checklist to make sure that nothing is forgotten or put in the wrong place. Crucial properties, such as the gun which *must* be in the desk drawer, are double-checked by the crew chief. Checklists are often made up on cards and hung around crew members' necks so they have both hands free.

5. As the last piece of the setting is lashed into place, the stage manager orders the ceiling to be lowered. If a chandelier is part of the new setting, this will have been hauled into place by the property crew and attached to its spot line. The electrician will have hooked it up and tested it. It will then be hauled into place against the ceiling.

As the change progresses, the various crew chiefs report to the stage manager: "Set ready!" "Props ready!" As he monitors the change, the stage manager will have issued a call for the actors at the point where he knows they will appear on stage just as the change is finished. He then double-checks the setting himself, giving special attention to crucial items. If all is in readiness, he calls, "Places!" and the actors take their places in the setting for Act II. After a quick check of the running crews, he calls, "Curtain!" He notes the time; and the shift has been completed.

Ideally, as each item is carried off stage it is placed in its predetermined storage location where it will be in readiness when needed again and where it will not block the next scene shift. However, it will often be necessary to quietly continue the storage process after the curtain has gone up on Act II. It is also important to be sure that properties that reappear in a subsequent act are placed in readiness for that reappearance.

During the progress of each act, the property crew will man the property tables, handing out and retrieving properties as the actors use them and bring them off stage.

HELPFUL HINTS FOR SCENE SHIFTS

While the above process seems straightforward as one reads it, you will find that it can be achieved only after many grueling rehearsals. The stage manager will often sit at the center of the stage calling off the seconds during shift rehearsals as he works for his goal of a shift well under the time the director has required. The following hints will help you in making shift rehearsals as short as possible.

1. Make out a written list of your duties as they develop. Write it on a card and carry it in a pocket or hang it on a string so you will have both hands free.

2. Do not be helpful at the wrong time. As shifts are being worked out by the stage manager, do exactly what you are told and nothing else. Do not volunteer help to others unless an emergency occurs that may cause damage—then help quickly. The reason for this is that the stage manager is trying to find out how many people are needed and how long it takes for each job. If you try to help by offering assistance to others, you complicate the process. When the stage manager sees that a job is too large for the crew assigned to it, he will either assign more help or find a better way of getting the job done. Ideally everybody should be working to capacity all the time.

3. Contrary to the above, once the jobs are assigned and the shifts begin to smooth out, if you find you have time to be of assistance outside your own work, do so, but let the stage manager know. Almost all shifts continue to get more efficient each time they are done. This added efficiency will serve you well when someone becomes ill and fewer people must do the job. To this end, you should become familiar with the jobs of others, so you can do them in an emergency. Occasionally, this will be done on an assigned basis much like understudying a role.

4. Stay out of jobs you do not know how to handle. This is especially true of handling electrical apparatus. If you are not a member

of the lighting crew, keep hands off. Although you may know electricity and stage lighting, there are so many special hookups used backstage that it is dangerous for those not familiar with all the details to handle the equipment.

5. Have patience; do not rush things to the point of danger. Moving settings so fast that they are in danger of being destroyed or of injuring someone is not good theatre. It is far better to lengthen a shift a few seconds than to get hurt, leave out an essential item, or place something off spike mark. Greater speed will come with more experience.

6. Check and double-check is the rule. Heroic efforts to undo mistakes make good after-theatre talk, but it is far better to avoid the emergency in the first place.

SHIFTS USING THE FLY LOFT

Historically, the use of the fly loft is much older than the box set shift described above. The proscenium theatre was originally devised around the concept of entirely flat scenery that was either lifted into the flies or moved horizontally into the wings. The famous wing and drop setting of the eighteenth-century theatre was one of the fastest systems of scene change ever devised, making it quite possible to change the entire stage during the delivery of a single line. A few such stages still exist, such as the one at Drottningholm, Sweden. The wing and drop concept is still much used, particularly in the musical theatre. The original aesthetic has changed; no one now seeks to create the illusion of three-dimensionality with paint and canvas on drops and wings. Wing and drop settings are now a form of stylization in which the very two-dimensional nature of the paintings (once so vigorously fought by Adolphe Appia) has become an element of theatricalization suggestive of another era in theatre.

Although the sliding wings of the eighteenth-century stage are seldom used today, the painted drop is much in use, often with rolling three-dimensional units. The result is a very fast, highly theatrical method of shifting, often performed in sight of the audience and "choreographed" as part of the action. Organization of such shifts is complicated. Frequently, drops move in or out as wagons roll to carefully preplanned locations, and actors move with the scenery. A miscue could injure actors or result in a collision of major proportions. Successful shifts are the result of careful planning on the part of the scenographer and close cooperation between riggers and grips. The riggers raise and lower the drops and other flying pieces while the grips operate the rolling units. Since the latter are often electrically or hydraulically driven, great amounts of kinetic energy are being expended and everything must work with precision.

ELEVATORS

On elaborately equipped stages such as the Metropolitan Opera House or the MGM Theatre in Las Vegas, still another possibility is available for handling scenery. These stages are equipped with huge elevators that enable the scenographer to plan to move whole settings vertically from the below-stage area. These elevators may also be equipped with revolves or wagon stages to further assist changes either at stage level or below stage. When elevator stages are combined with a fully equipped fly loft, the possibilities for elaborate shifts are immense. Operation of such a system becomes a study in theatrical ingenuity; men and machinery cooperate to accomplish dazzling changes.

However the crews are organized and however complicated or simple the shifts, the basic skills of the various crew members will determine how well the job gets done. Since the nature of the skills depends on the kinds of machinery available to help the crew members, we will discuss their skills in relationship to the tools they use, starting with the simplest — hand movement of scenery.

MOVING FLATS BY HAND

A flat, especially a large one, is an awkward thing to move about until you know how. If it falls in an uncontrolled manner, it may be ruined and cause damage to some valuable properties. If it is handled in the wrong way or gripped in the wrong place, it may be badly damaged. The idea in shifting flats is to keep them in a vertical position, moving them quietly and efficiently by touching only the wooden parts, and to avoid handling the painted front surface as much as possible. The first step is to get the flat into the upright position. If the flat is small enough and the grip is strong enough, it can be simply lifted into the vertical position by picking it up. But remember that this takes considerable room; do not poke the moving flat through another one nearby.

GETTING FLATS INTO A VERTICAL POSITION

In general there are two methods, depending on size and fragility, used to raise a flat to a vertical position. Smaller flats with little three-dimensional decor may be "edged" up by one person (two makes the work easier) as shown in Figure 14-1. The trick is to make the entire operation in one smooth motion taking advantage of the inertia of the flat once you have started it moving. Large flats or runs of flats stiffened together cannot be edged; they must be "footed" and "walked" up while one person "foots," as shown in Figure 14-1. Note that at least one person "foots" the flat by placing a foot against the part which is to become the bottom when the flat has been raised. If this is not done, the flat will skid across the floor while being walked up, and may even tip over those walking it, causing them to lose control of it. Those walking up the flat must get under it and push upward on it at solid places such as rails and toggles. If the flat is very tall, still another stagehand pushes and steadies the top with a pole or stage brace. Use care; if the flat slips, the pole may go right through the covering.

Figure 14-1. (a) Edging Up a Flat. This simple process enables one stage crew member to move a flat to vertical position. Care must be taken that the flat does not fall sideways. (b) Walking Up a Flat. While one person "foots" the bottom to keep it from moving, two (or more) helpers lift the flat and push it to a vertical position.

223

RUNNING FLATS

Once a flat is in a vertical position, it can be moved about the stage floor by "running." This is done by seizing the edge, lifting slightly, and dragging the rail along the floor as you move the flat (see Figure 14-2). Since you are in front of the flat, you will be able to see where you are going. Two flats of medium size can be run at once by placing them face to face. Running flats takes advantage of the construction technique that requires the rails to be extended past the stiles. If the stile ran through to the floor, it would splinter as it was dragged along.

STACKING FLATS

Flats are usually stored backstage by stacking, that is, they are leaned against a wall or other support in a near-vertical position. Thus they are ready to run to the on-stage position without the necessity of standing them up. They also take up less floor space this way. If possible, flats should be stacked in pairs, face to face and back to back (see Figure 3-18). This provides the maximum protection for the painted surfaces. Flats with protruding parts, such as cornices, must be stacked alone to avoid poking the protrusions through other flats. One should be especially wary of small items such as nails driven into rails to hold pictures, etc. A "picture hook" is the proper hardware for this job because it will not poke holes in other flats while stacked.

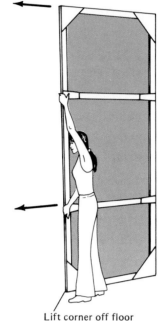

Lift corner off floor

Figure 14-2. Running a Flat.

FLOATING FLATS

Whenever it is necessary to lay a flat down on the floor, the easiest and safest method is to "float" the flat down (Figure 14-3). More than one flat can be floated at one time. Floating requires a clear floor space somewhat larger than the flat, preferably clean of dust. If the space is rather limited, it is a good idea to foot the flat from the back. The flat is simply tilted slightly to make sure that it falls on its face, and it then is allowed to fall freely to the floor. Surprisingly, it will fall slowly because of the resistance to the air offered by its large surface. It will settle gently to the floor with a gust of air from underneath. In even the cleanest shops it will be a good idea to shield your eyes from this air, which will contain dust particles. Obviously one should not expect an uncovered flat frame to float to the floor.

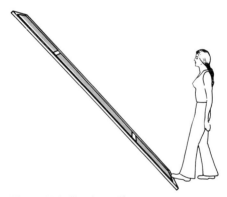

Figure 14-3. Floating a Flat.

HOW ARE FLATS FASTENED TOGETHER AND WHAT MAKES THEM STAND UP?

Flats will stand by themselves just as a screen will, if they are held together in such a way that they brace one another. For example, a "two-

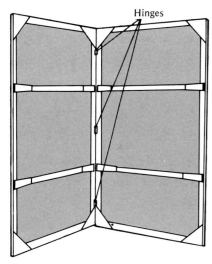

Hinges

Figure 14-4. A Two-fold.

fold'' (Figure 14-4) will stand easily as long as the flats are not parallel to each other or nearly so. Completely folding the two-fold or opening it up will make it unstable. A shrewd set designer will often create an entire setting completely supported by repeated application of this simple principal. A jog at either side of a doorway may be particularly helpful if the door must be violently slammed shut.

LASHING FLATS TOGETHER

One of the oldest and still one of the fastest ways to fasten flats together and/or take them apart again, is *lashing*. This consists of "lacing" the flats together with pieces of rope passed over special hooks attached to their backs (see Figure 14-5). Each flat has a piece of "lashline," actually light cotton rope, attached to its top right-hand corner (as viewed from the rear). Along the sides are attached *lash cleats* and/or hooks to engage the rope as it is flipped over the cleats and drawn tight. Properly done, lashing will not only hold the flats together but even pull slight warps into line. Lashing works best on flats that are in line with each other or form less than a straight angle on their on-stage side. When the flats meet in such a way that the less-than-straight angle is on the back, substitution of lash hooks for cleats will improve the joint. Lash hooks are simple metal hooks installed in place of lash cleats where tension at an odd angle might cause the lash line to slip off the cleat. When flats must meet at right angles, the addition of stop blocks and stop cleats (see Figure 14-5) will aid considerably.

There are several ways to attach the lash line to the top of a flat. The most common one is to install a *lash line eye* (see Figure 14-5). A more economical way is to drill a small hole in the upper right-hand corner block, insert the lash line and tie a knot to keep it from pulling out. Still another method is to install a small metal eye in the inner edge of the stile. Under no circumstances should this eye or anything else protrude from the back of the flat or it will puncture adjacent flats when they are stacked. Lash lines should just clear the floor when hanging free.

Lash cleats are usually bought from a theatrical supply house. If economy requires it, you can make your own out of strap iron. Be sure to grind off all sharp edges. Homemade hardware is economical only if you have free labor, such as in a school or volunteer theatre group. In a state of complete desperation, 8 penny nails can be substituted for lash cleats by driving them part way into the inner edges of the stiles. This is strictly a makeshift arrangement that should be replaced as soon as possible because the heads of the nails will hamper the lashing operation. The nails also bend under pressure.

Flipping the lash line over the cleats, tensioning, and knotting it require a knack which only practice can confer. Note in Figure 14-5

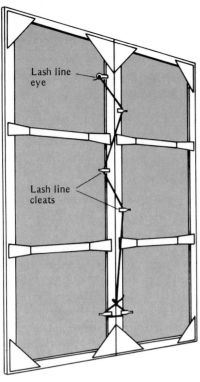

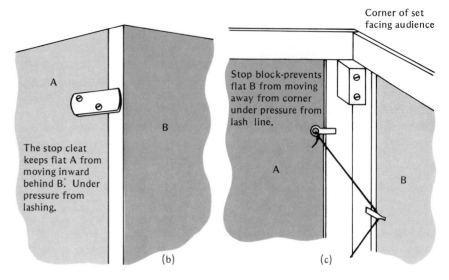

Figure 14-5. (a) Lashing Flats Together. Note the hardware. The eye at the top and the cleats are all of the single screw variety. There are several other types available. The knot is a slip knot that enables the crew to disassemble the setting quickly. (b) Stop Cleat. (c) Stop Block.

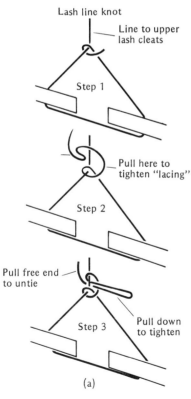

(a)

how the grip has allowed slack in the line to enable the rope to flip over the cleat. Final tension will be applied as the knot is tied after hooking the line around the two bottom cleats.

HINGING METHODS

Hinges in the theatre are used as fasteners almost as much as they are used for their pivoting properties. There are two kinds.

Loose Pin Hinges

Hinges known in the hardware trade as "loose pin back flaps" are common theatrical hardware items (see Figure 14-6). Ordinarily they are sold in ungalvanized iron, which is cheaper and satisfactory for almost all theatrical uses. Unlike door hinges, they are not sold by the pair, but by the piece. They are shipped with a regular hinge pin that has not been riveted into place and can be pulled out to separate the two parts of the hinge. Some theatre workers promptly remove and discard the pin, which is hard to get hold of during a fast scene change, replacing it with a bent nail or piece of heavy wire. Some hinge manufacturers are now supplying back flaps with proper theatrical pins.

Tight Pin Hinges

Tight pin hinges (Figure 14-6) are identical to the loose pin type above except for the pin, which is riveted into place. In an emergency one can

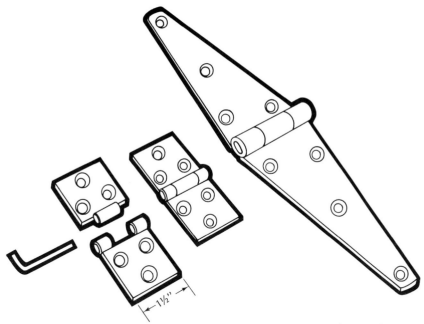

Figure 14-6. Hinges. This shows three of the most commonly used hinges. At the left is a loose pin hinge or "back flap." Next is a tight pin hinge. Upper right is a strap hinge.

grind off this riveted end of the pin and convert it into a loose pin type. There is seldom the need to reverse this process.

HOW ARE HINGES USED? Hinges may be used either to allow two parts to move with respect to each other, or as fastening devices. When used as fasteners, hinges are so installed that they hold the parts together without allowing movement, but the removal of the loose pins allows the parts to be separated. Whole runs of setting walls are sometimes done in this fashion. However, it is more likely that the setting will be broken down into two- and three-folds which are in turn held together by loose pin hinges. In fact, sometimes lashing can also be inter-mingled into this setup to advantage.

HINGE FRONT OR BACK? Obviously the decision to hinge front or back depends on which way the unit is to fold. Once installed, hinges can work in only one direction. However, the theatre worker must also worry about the appearance of the resulting joint. He always seeks to conceal the fact that the setting is really a group of separate units. Thus he laps the flats so that light cannot leak through a joint from the back. He also often hinges on the front to make his two-folds fold together so that he can conceal the joint with a piece of cloth known as a "dutch-man," which is glued over the hinges and painted to match the rest of the flats it joins. This hinge-and-dutchman combination makes a very strong, neat joint. However, it can only be made as a two-fold unless a special piece of wood called a "tumbler" is installed to allow the flats to fold over each other (see Figure 14-7). Incidentally, it makes little difference whether tight or loose pin hinges are used in a dutchmanned joint, provided the pins do not show. The dutchman will hold the pins in if they are loose.

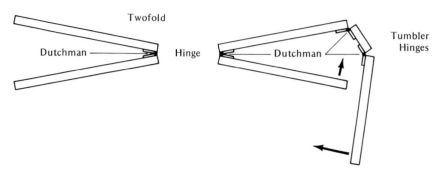

Figure 14-7. Dutchman and Tumbler. This figure illustrates how a tumbler allows a three-fold flat to be folded. Note where the dutchmen have been glued.

Loose pin hinges installed on the backs of flats make a good joint, but a slow shift. They are particularly slow during set up. If the designer can arrange to have the hinge-fastened joints assembled before the show or during a long intermission, it will be possible to disassemble the settings quite rapidly during short breaks. This is because it is easier to pull pins than to align the flats to insert them. Hinges above the reach of a stagehand on the floor can have their pins flipped out with a short stick during disassembly. A ladder and careful alignment by two people are required for set up. The pins are often attached to the rear of the flats by a short piece of string so they will always be handy during shifts. Stagehands should carry extra pins in any event. In addition to fastening flats together, you will find loose pin hinges in use for everything from holding up a cornice on a wall to holding together "breakaway" props. They are standard throughout the theatre. The tight pin hinge is indicated whenever hinging action is required, and there is no need to take the joint apart. However, it is often used simply as a fastening device by installing hinges in such a way that they work against each other and merely hold the parts together.

Other Hinges

You will find several other types of hinges around the theatre, both stronger and lighter than the back flaps. These are used for conventional door-hanging and property-making applications, and should not be substituted for back flaps. They are too expensive and often poorly designed for the job.

MISCELLANEOUS FASTENING TECHNIQUES

1. *Hooks and eyes.* These are the common screen door hooks one finds around the home, or their larger cousins. They are used when the designer needs something stronger than lash lines but faster to work than loose pin hinges. They are also used by theatres unable to get standard theatrical hardware. Hooks and eyes are available at any hardware store. Their disadvantage is that they seldom hold the flats precisely in place. They cannot apply the tension of the lash line or the rigidity of the pin hinge. But they are fast, have no loose parts, and are readily available. Hooks and eyes are popular with hard flat workers who need only a slight but quickly worked fastening to hold their heavy scenery in place.

2. *Clamps.* All theatres will find that a stock of C-clamps is a good investment, since they will do jobs that nothing else will do. For example, they can be used to pull together two badly warped flats. Or they can fasten a flat securely but temporarily to a platform. If you are using hard flats, a number of small C-clamps will hold the flats rigidly together and present no installation problem at all. In fact, the ease with which C-clamps can often be installed at the last moment makes them a good addition to the stage manager's emergency gear.

3. *Nails.* Flats may be nailed together if the set does not have to be shifted during the run, and if you do not mind nail holes in your flats. Many theatres do nothing else, particularly community theatres that confine their activities to single-set productions. *Double-headed* or *scaffold nails* (see Figure 8-3), which cannot be pounded flush with the wood, make disassembly easier but show more than conventional nails. The one thing to be avoided if at all possible is the sound of hammering backstage while the audience is in the theatre — a mark of rank amateurism.

If you are nailing flats together, use the minimum number of nails that will do the job. The beginner often feels that if a few nails are good, many more will be better. Too many nails, however, make a weak joint by splintering the wood so that none of them hold well. They also tend to rapidly destroy the flat frames.

STEADYING SCENERY — STAGE BRACES

Even after the flats have been properly fastened together, one cannot always be sure that the setting will stand solidly, particularly if doors are to be slammed or a "fight" is to make contact with the scenery. In such cases, bracing and/or stiffening must be used, although it will add minutes to setup and strike time. The standard unit for this is the *stage brace,* an adjustable device that braces against the stage floor and the back of the setting as in Figure 14-8. There are two types: wood and

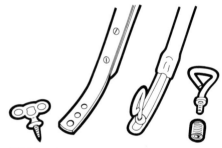

metal. Most experienced stagehands prefer the wooden braces because they have always used them, and because they are probably less apt to come out of adjustment. The effectiveness of a stage brace usually depends on one end being firmly attached to the floor. There are two standard ways of doing this:

1. Using the regular stage screw or "stage peg," an oversized wood screw with a large handle. It is pressed into the soft wood floor and screwed in securely, leaving a hole. After many such operations, the stage floor is damaged and must be resurfaced.
2. Using the "patented" stage screw, a two-part device consisting of a socket set into the stage floor and a threaded screw that runs in and out of the socket. Once installed, the socket is often left in the floor for future use. This is practical because stage screws tend to be used over and over in certain parts of the stage. Installation is done by drilling a hole in the wooden floor and carefully screwing in the socket with a large screwdriver, so that it is flush with the floor or slightly below the surface (see Figure 14-8b).

Either of these devices makes a very secure link with the floor. The foot of the brace is simply placed in position and screwed down. The tops of stage braces are fastened to the flat stiles (or wherever else they are needed) by means of a *brace cleat* (Figure 14-8c). The special hook device in the top of the brace is placed over the eye face down, and rotated as it is inserted into the hole in the cleat. A 180 degree rotation locks the brace into place so that it pushes against the flat portion of the brace cleat, not the fabric. The brace is extended by means of the length adjustment until it reaches the floor in a position favorable to bracing. It is then fastened to the floor. The last step is to adjust the length of the brace to make the setting stand upright, and the lock the brace at that length. This operation can be done rapidly during a shift if the sockets are already in the floor. If pegs are in use and the holes have already

Figure 14-8. Stage Brace. (a) A modern metal stage brace in use. Note how the brace has been hooked into the brace to cleat in such a way that it pushes on the cleat, not on the flat or fabric. (b) The bottom of the brace shown in (a) including a portion of an old type wooden stage brace plus the two types of stage screws commonly in use. The stage screw with the conical threaded portion has been the standard device in theatres for many years. It holds well but it rapidly ruins stage floors. It is impossible to set in any but a softwood floor. The "patented" stage screw (right) requires that a metal insert be placed in the stage floor before it can be used. Once in place, the insert is usually left for future use. Such inserts may be installed in hardwood floors, although with difficulty. (c) The top of a brace and cleat. Note how the brace hook is installed into cleat to avoid pressure on fabric.

been made during rehearsals, they need only be found and reused. Crew members often mark these holes for easier location. Be sure to keep track of the pegs and braces. They are easy to lose backstage in semidarkness.

Although no stage should be equipped with a highly finished hardwood floor, many are. It is also occasionally necessary to arrange stage facilities on floors not intended for such use, which must not be marred with stage pegs. Figure 14-9 shows a device designed to solve this problem. This is not as secure as a properly pegged stage brace, but it will sometimes suffice. Generally, if the stability of the setting is in doubt and pegs may not be used, it is better to use one of the methods described below.

Figure 14-9. *Bracing on a Finished Floor. This arrangement consists of a combination of the adjustable function of a stage brace (note the middle of the brace) and that of a jack. Stability is attained by placing stage weights in the metal tray at the back of the horizontal bracing. Note that the entire unit rides on casters, making shifts simple. Lighter scenic elements could be supported similarly without casters, thus making them less apt to move during a production. Photograph courtesy University of California, Los Angeles.*

Other Methods of Steadying Scenery

Most bracing methods are associated with shifting devices in order to combine the two functions. For example, a section of a setting can be made to stand up by building it against the front of a low platform. If this low platform also has retractable wheels, the whole unit can easily be moved when necessary. There is one other device which may or may not be associated with shifting techniques. This is the *jack* (Figure 14-10). In its simplest form the jack is a triangular brace fastened to the back of a flat and extended outward to make the flat stand, much as a picture or calendar is made to stand up on a desk. Hinges commonly are used to attach jacks to flats. If it is desirable that the jack fold against the flat for storage, the hinges are applied to one side only as in Figure 14-10a, to allow folding. If a rigidly fixed jack is desired, the hinges are applied on both sides to eliminate movement. In either case, the jack may be removed completely if loose pin hinges are used.

Although jacks can be attached to the floor by installing a foot iron at their outer end, they are usually weighted instead (Figures 14-10b and c). This makes them useful where floors must not be marred.

Stage braces steady the scenery by attaching it to the stage floor. *Stiffeners* are designed to hold the parts securely together in relationship to each other. They keep a run of flats from bending and swaying under stress.

Although considerable stiffening can be acquired in the process of installing jacks and by angling the wall surfaces to each other, more is often needed. The usual solution is to install a piece of 1 by 3 inch (or larger) lumber against the back of the flats so that the strongest dimension of the lumber (the 3 inch width) resists any bending that might occur (see Figure 14-11). Stiffeners may be installed at whatever angle will best resist bending, but most are installed either horizontally or vertically (see Figure 9-19). If the set is to be built into place, stiffeners are often nailed in place. A better method is to install them with tight

FIGURE 14-10a   FIGURE 14-10b   FIGURE 14-10c

Figure 14-10. Jack. This simple bracing device comes in a wide variety of shapes. (a) The simplest form consists of a wooden framework either hinged or permanently fastened to the back of the scenic element it must support. (b) A more elaborate type of jack made to carry weights to balance the scenery. Such jacks are kept in stock and nailed or bolted to the scenery when needed. They usually are fitted with casters as shown. (c) A welded metal jack intended to be stocked and used repeatedly. Note how the jack has been made to fit the dimensions of the counterweights standard to the theatre. It is easily attached to wooden construction by means of double-headed nails or screws. Two or more of the jacks shown in (b) and (c) may be used together to handle a large piece of scenery, perhaps even an entire wall.

pin hinges. If the stiffener must be removed, the tight pin hinges may be replaced by the loose pin type, or if speed in shifting is needed, special hooks may be used. In other cases a stiffener may be pivoted, allowing the set to be shifted rapidly by turning the stiffener. Although the various hooks and pivots for stiffeners facilitate rapid shifting, they do not make as efficient use of the stiffness of the lumber as a firm attachment made with hinges, nails, or screws.

Occasionally the bottom of a piece of scenery will have a tendency to move. This often happens to a door flat in which the shutter must be slammed. In such cases, the flat can be fastened directly to the stage floor by use of a *foot iron* (see Figure 8-5c). Of course this slows down shifts. It will be helpful if the stage screw is attached to the back of the set with a short length of cord so it cannot be lost.

SHIFTING LARGE SCENIC ELEMENTS—WHEELS

If you work a hand-operated scene shift—and many theatres do this season after season—you may wonder if the theatre has yet to discover the wheel. Everything is dragged or carried. Wheels can help a lot, but the problem with wheels in the theatre is that they may roll when they should not. If the director must choose between an easily shifted setting that may also shift under the actor's feet, and a hard-to-shift setting that is solid, his choice will be the latter. Therefore, about as much time is spent locking rolling set units into place as is spent making them roll in the first place.

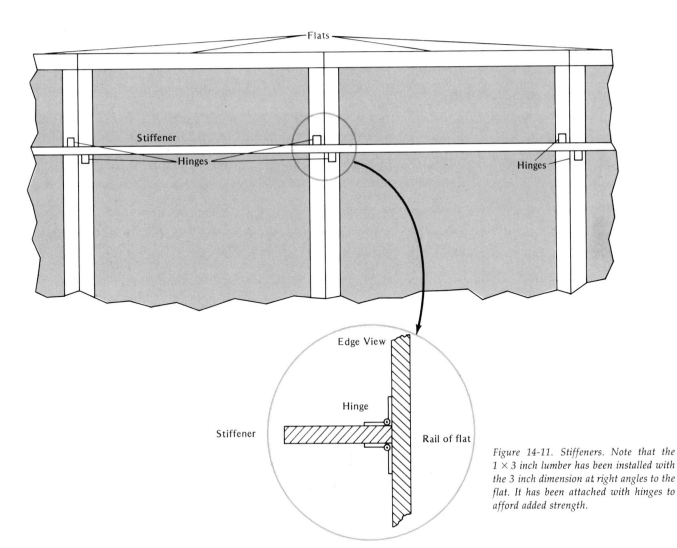

Figure 14-11. *Stiffeners. Note that the 1 × 3 inch lumber has been installed with the 3 inch dimension at right angles to the flat. It has been attached with hinges to afford added strength.*

CASTERS

Casters are the wheels placed under set pieces, large furniture, props, and the like. They may be as small as the tiny casters under a Louis XIV desk, or as large as the 8-inch monsters that carry a large stage revolve. They come with wooden wheels, steel wheels, plastic wheels, and rubber wheels. There are two general categories: (1) fixed, which run in a straight line unless skidded, and (2) swivel, which turn easily unless heavily loaded. They have a variety of bearings, and unfortunately, the simpler ones often squeak. The best casters have costly ball bearings.

A basic fact about casters is that the larger the wheel, the easier they roll. This is why baby buggies have large wheels. Unfortunately, large wheels take up a lot of space, and theatre casters need to be as small as possible. When they are small, they roll with difficulty and tend to dig into the floor.

WAGONS

The simplest application of casters in the theatre is the *wagon,* a rigid platform on casters. Parallels are not suited to this use because the frames cannot accommodate casters. A rigid platform for use with casters must be built with the knowledge that the entire weight on the platform will be supported only at the points where casters are installed. A 4 by 8 foot platform, 6 inches high will usually be equipped with six casters with wheels about 3–4 inches in diameter. Such a wagon should handle about as much weight as it would sitting solidly on the floor without casters. A number of wagons can be fastened together with bolts or cleats to make up larger units.

Platforms for use as wagons may be constructed of either wood or metal. Slotted metal angle works well; welded square steel tubing works even better because it is stronger and the wagon can be much thinner if this is needed. Welding will allow mounting plates for the casters to be securely fastened into corners in the steel frame instead of under the supporting member, as would be necessary if wood were used.

Moving Wagons

Stage wagons loaded with settings are heavy. The scenery on the wagon will seldom be able to take the push necessary to move the wagon. Therefore, the rule is, push or pull the wagon, *not the scenery.* While this can be done by bending over and shoving on the wagon itself, it is far easier to pull on a short length of rope or chain attached to the wagon. For this purpose, iron plates with heavy rings in them, known as *ceiling plates,* are installed at strategic points on the wagon. They must be placed where they are invisible to the audience and where the pulling will do the most good. Short lengths of rope or trim chains are attached to these by snap hooks. The pulling rope or chains are not usually left on the platform because they form a hazard backstage.

Holding Wagons in Place

Small wagons can often be locked into place by wedging them on the upstage and offstage sides. This simple method will work well if the action on the wagon is not violent. Wedges can be attached to the wagons by short lengths of line to avoid losing them in a fast shift. If wedges are not practical, the next best method is to use a barrel bolt or two inserted into holes in the stage floor (see Figure 14-12a). This produces a more secure wagon but requires more shift time because the wagon must be aligned accurately with the predrilled holes in the floor. The barrel bolts also have to be lifted and locked in their upward position before moving the wagon.

The specially constructed platform lock shown in Figure 14-12b can be used to hold wagons quite securely in place and still allow for quick shifting with no loose parts to harass the crews. This lock can be fitted to the perimeter of a wagon anywhere that it will not show, or if wagons must fit closely together (or every side will be seen at some time), the lock may be mounted inside the framework of the wagon and operated through a hole cut into the wagon's floor. Note that although these locks operate on the principle of the commercially available foot-plunger door stop, they are much heavier. They are capable of lifting the wagon completely off the casters. Because of this, they must be securely fastened to the frame. The frame should be built so that each lock-mounting point is strong enough to carry a large share of the load placed on the platform.

A still more secure method of fixing a wagon in position is to use one or more foot irons fastened to the upstage or offstage sides of the wagon high enough to clear the floor during movement, and secured to the floor with stage pegs or patented stage screws. Foot irons require accurate alignment and therefore additional shift time. They are also a hazard during shifts because they protrude from the backs of the wagons. The wagons, however, will be about as secure as possible.

Air Bearings

Air bearings (Figure 14-13) are a relatively new product that offer the opportunity to move extremely heavy loads—far heavier than the theatre will usually encounter—with great ease, and to allow them to sit solidly on the floor between moves. An *air bearing* is a thin disklike device (a few of the very large ones are rectangular) that is installed under the scenery to be moved. If it is properly installed, the scenery will rest partially on the air bearing and partially on its substructure until the bearing is activated by a large volume of compressed air at moderate pressure. When the air is turned on, the bearing lifts the load a fraction of an inch on a cushion of air. This reduces friction to a phenomenally low level, making it possible for one person to move objects weighing tons.

The advantages of air bearings are obvious; objects of any weight found in the theatre can be moved with ease. In fact, all commercially available air bearings have a rating far exceeding anything to be commonly found in a theatre. (Engineers have designed air bearings to move an entire sports stadium.) Since the bearing is actually a cushion of air, the object can be moved in any direction with equal ease.

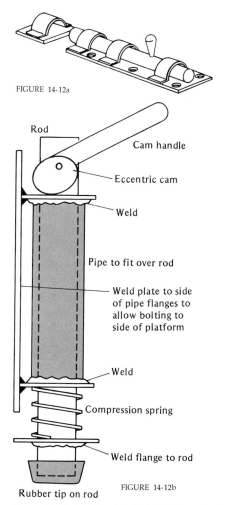

FIGURE 14-12a

Rod
Cam handle
Eccentric cam
Weld
Pipe to fit over rod
Weld plate to side of pipe flanges to allow bolting to side of platform
Weld
Compression spring
Weld flange to rod
Rubber tip on rod

FIGURE 14-12b

Figure 14-12. (a) Barrel Bolt. (b) Platform Lock. This shop-made lock can be used to hold stage platforms in position and then quickly released to allow shifting. It is based on the design of commercially made door holders, but is much heavier. This simple lock is made from a steel rod that fits through a piece of pipe. A heavy compression spring forces the rod downward until the cam handle is operated forcing the rod upward and releasing the lock. The lock is simply bolted to the side of a wagon or installed inside the wagon and operated through a hole in the deck. Courtesy Richard Arnold, Northern Illinoise University, DeKalb, Ill.

FIGURE 14-13a

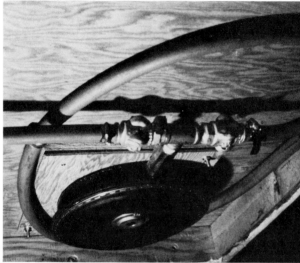

FIGURE 14-13b

Figure 14-13. (a) Air Bearing. This commercially made air bearing is about 12 inches in diameter and can easily handle 1000 pounds. It is shown upside down here to allow a view of its working parts. When it is in operation, air is forced into the bearing through the pipe fitting and the regulator which adjusts the flow of air. The air then passes into the housing of the bearing and inflates the rubber diaphragm. The air escapes through the four holes near the center of the diaphragm and forms a film between the diaphragm and the floor. It is this nearly friction-free film of air that actually supports the weight of the load and makes the bearing work. As the air escapes from under the diaphragm, more air takes its place as long as the supply lasts. When the air is turned off, the weight of the load is carried by the heavy metal post in the center of the bearing. Mounting arrangements are provided on the top of the housing. A piece of plywood has already been bolted to the bearing, making attachment to wooden structures easy. Such bearings are available in sizes from 1000–60,000 pound loads. Still larger sizes can be made if needed. (b) Solving Air Supply Problems. Manufacturers recommend that air line runs to each of the air bearings used on a wagon be approximately the same length to aid in equalizing pressure and volume of delivery. This photograph shows how extra loops in the air lines were arranged to accomplish this. Photograph courtesy Richard Johnson, School of Fine Arts, University of California, Irvine.

The disadvantages of air bearings have prevented them from being generally accepted in most theatres. First, they require a substantial air supply. If the theatre is equipped with a 5-horsepower air compressor, there will be no problem. Smaller compressors (e.g., 3 horsepower) will be marginal. The air supply problem is aggravated further by the necessity to use more than one air bearing in order to balance the load. The two or three air bearings will be working at a minute fraction of their capacity but will still require a sizable volume of air.

The amount of noise produced by air bearings can be considerable, particularly if the floor is not tight and devoid of cracks or scars. They work best on very smooth, sealed concrete. On most stages the normal irregularities of the floor will make the bearings noisy and further increase their air demand. The noise can be quite noticeable unless the scene shift is covered by rather loud music or sound effects.

It is possible that the bearings will chatter if they are improperly adjusted and the load is far out of balance. This leads to what is perhaps the greatest handicap of air bearings. To keep the load in balance and to cut down on the number of bearings needed, it is necessary that the scenery be built to be supported from below (while moving) at only two or three points. This means that the understructure must be engineered carefully and the bearings located with some accuracy, thus adding substantially to the cost and difficulty of construction of the scenic unit.

In spite of all of these problems, air bearings offer what may ultimately be the ideal solution to the "caster problem" on stage. They are movable only when activated, solving the locking problems so common to castered scenery. Since they move equally well in any direction, it is possible to track a piece of scenery in a complex movement pattern that would be out of the question with casters.

It seems reasonable for a stage shop equipped to do advanced iron work to make air bearings suitable for theatrical use. This could bring the cost down to the point where as many bearings as are necessary could be installed. Air demand might not be much greater because each bearing could be quite small compared to the commercially available units.

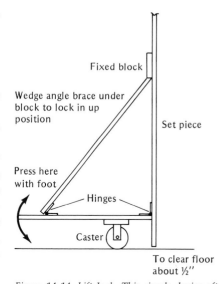

Figure 14-14. Lift Jack. This simple device often is used in sets of two or more. The set piece sits firmly on the floor while in use and is lifted onto the caster for shifting. Note floor clearance. Such jacks may either be installed at the back of a set piece or inside a wagon setting.

LIFT JACKS

An ideal way to combine the ease of movement of the wagon with the solidity of the platform sitting on the floor is the lift jack. With this device the scenery is on wheels *only* while it is being moved; it sits on the floor when in position. The problem is that lift jacks take space and special construction.

There are several variations on the lift jack, but they all depend on mounting the casters on a lever device which can be used to lift the set piece off the floor, placing its weight on the caster, and then reversing this process when the scenery has been positioned (see Figure 14-14). Note that the hinge must carry all of the weight of the object during lifting and hauling operations, and that this weight is a live load, susceptible to sudden jerks.

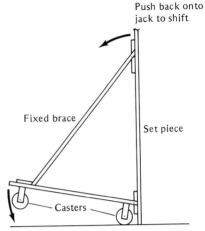

Push back onto
jack to shift

Fixed brace

Set piece

Casters

Figure 14-15. Tip Jack. Like the lift jack, the tip jack usually is used in sets to handle a relatively heavy piece of scenery. In this case the set piece is tilted back onto the casters to move it. It is stored off stage in tilted position. Such jacks work only when the structure of the set piece is such that its center of gravity is close to the front caster and can be shifted to a position between the casters by tilting.

Several lift jacks are usually provided for a single unit. Since they may be operated one at a time, a twisting strain will be placed on the entire piece of scenery.

Lift jacks are seldom applied to stock stage wagons. They are much more practical for large pieces utilizing specially built wagons framed for the lift jacks. Note that there is no sharp distinction between a wagon and a piece of three-dimensional scenery on wheels. The term "wagon" tends to be reserved for stock rectangular rolling platforms, but this use is not consistent. Thus a technical director may speak of "wagoning" a piece of scenery, whether he intends to put stock wagons under it or to frame it for casters or lift jacks.

TIP JACKS

Another method of providing ease of movement and solid positioning while in use is the tip jack (see Figure 14-15). Tip jacks are especially well adapted to heavy pieces such as fireplaces with mantelpieces whose weight is downstage of the flat that provides the wall surface. Such units can be tilted back to roll with ease.

JACKKNIFE WAGONS

When moderately large wagons are used, the problem of alignment with other parts of the setting becomes more acute. One solution is to permanently pivot one corner of the wagon—usually the downstage corner in the left or right wing area—and swing the entire wagon on this pivot (see Figure 14-16). This resembles the movement of the blade of a jackknife. Such a wagon can be shifted much more rapidly than a totally free wagon. It can even be driven by a motor, if this is desired. The pivot itself is often demountable making it possible to mount such a wagon for a single act within which there may be several rapid shifts, and then to remove it completely once that act is finished. Settings can be changed while the wagon is in its offstage position if this is done quietly.

REVOLVES

There are two types of revolves: (1) those built permanently into the stage, and (2) those mounted temporarily on the stage floor. The first type is enormously expensive if it is full-stage size, and must be planned into the initial construction of the building. The temporary type is often devised for a single production, although some theatres carry revolves as stock items. These are made to be taken apart for storage.

A temporary revolve is a wagon that is made to revolve around a pivot at its center instead of running across the stage in a linear movement. It need not be circular; some revolves are octagonal or hexagonal, if this suits the needs of the designer. Small revolves are often driven by hand in much the same manner that platforms are moved. Trim chains or short lengths of rope are attached to heavy rings mounted on the structure for pulling. More elaborate methods include rope drives operated from backstage, rim drives using motors if the outer perimeter is built as a true circle and braced properly, and friction motor drives bearing on the floor under the revolve.

Settings mounted on a revolve must be fastened securely, especially if it is a motor-driven revolve. The centrifugal force of the movement plus the jerking of starts and stops tend to loosen fastenings.

HAZARDS OF ROLLING SCENERY

Any piece of scenery that is heavy enough to need wheels to move it can be dangerous while in motion. If hands or feet get between the moving object and any stationary object, they can be crushed or cut off. Motor-driven apparatus is particularly hazardous because it can be operated at a distance and must be shut off by an operator; it has no built-in stop mechanism when someone screams. The wedge-shaped space where a straight edge of a platform is tangent to a revolve is especially dangerous, and should be covered up. Actors and crew members should be cautioned about such areas.

Whenever wagons or revolves are to be used in a setting, it is vitally important that the stage floor be kept free of anything that might jam a caster, including nails, tacks, splinters, hairpins, scraps of cloth, bits of costume jewelry, etc. One nail can bring an entire show to a stop by locking a wagon so that it will not move. Daily sweeping and frequent checks of the casters should be routine practice.

PROPS ON WHEELS

Large properties are as likely to be moved on wheels as are pieces of scenery. A real cookstove or refrigerator, for example, may be equipped with a small wagon and lift jacks just as a piece of scenery might be. The same cautions prevail. The prop must be securely locked into position on stage so it will not move when the actors use it.

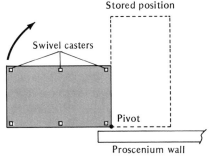

Figure 14-16. Jackknife Wagon. This simple shifting device guarantees that the wagon will follow exactly the same path each time it is moved and thus that it will exactly align with other set pieces. Such wagons can even be motor driven if this is desirable. Since the wagon is on swivel casters, it may also be completely removed from the wings by releasing the pivot point and rolling it off as a free wagon. Reattaching the pivot takes time; it must be aligned exactly.

15
FLYING SCENERY

WORK OF THE RIGGERS

Being a grip or property person is a responsible job, but it does not usually involve danger to life and limb unless powerful motor-driven wagons or revolves are being used. In contrast, the work of the rigger always involves potential danger to all on stage. Normally the flies are full of heavy objects often weighing a total of many tons. All of this weight is the responsibility of the riggers. It must be safely hung and must move safely and surely on cue.

As we examine the tasks assigned to the riggers and the machinery they use, you may have occasion to refer to Chapter 3, "The Proscenium Theatre," for details of the rigging system as it is found in a well-equipped theatre. Although some rigging operations are exceedingly complex, involving a considerable knowledge of physics and engineering, we will confine our discussion here to those simple operations commonly performed by student crews.

WHAT GETS FLOWN?

Almost anything can be flown if the necessity is great enough. Such bulky and heavy objects as practical setting bridges may occasionally be lifted out of sight. However, most of what goes into the flies of a proscenium theatre is scenery particularly adapted to flying. Stage draperies, drops, borders, flat sections of walls, ceilings, chandeliers, etc., are the usual things rigged and flown. Most of these are flown for the following reasons:

1. They must be supported from above anyway. Thus support and shifting become one operation.
2. They run parallel to the footlights and fit neatly into the existing batten system.
3. Their weight is relatively slight, making them easy to lift.

4. Their shape and structure make them hard to handle otherwise.
5. They must be seen hanging in front of the audience.
6. Flying is the only way to get the piece in or out in the time available.

Unless special arrangements are made, or the stage is equipped with very modern grid winch equipment, pieces running on upstage-downstage angles are not usually flown. Or if such pieces must be flown, they are flown parallel to the battens and angled only when down. If a piece of scenery must be angled across several battens on a conventional stage, those battens crossed are effectively taken out of service until the piece is removed. Since this destroys much of the utility of the system, it is seldom done. Even flying pieces of more than nominal thickness may cause trouble. Line sets may be as close as 6 inches on centers, which means that any scenery more than about 3 inches thick may foul the piece next to it.

Modern grid winch systems are designed to overcome these problems. (See Chapter 3.) Because they do not have battens as a permanent part of their equipment, pieces may hang at angles without blocking other lines.

COMMON RIGGING PROCEDURES

The basic machinery of the rigger is the entire fly loft system described in Chapter 3. In a modern theatre this means that there will be a set of counterweighted lines at frequent intervals from the proscenium to the back wall of the stage house, a number of motorized sets, provisions for hemp spot lines, or even full hemp sets as needed, and the necessary weights, clews, sandbags, sheaves, etc., needed to make these things work.

Knots and fastening devices are another basic part of the rigger's equipment. He must be prepared to attach either rope or wire cable to a variety of objects with utmost security. Common rigger's knots are shown in Figure 15-1. The student should obtain a piece of rope and practice these knots until he would be willing to stake his life on their security. Although rope can be safely knotted, wire rope (cable) requires something more sophisticated. It carries much heavier loads and needs metal-to-metal fastenings. Since one or two cable clamps may often hold the entire weight on a set of lines, such fastenings must be secure. Note in Figure 15-2 that multiple clamps are the usual procedure. Small aircraft cable is extremely strong and almost invisible on stage. Thus it is often used in sight of the audience. The most critical application of this sort, although not for beginning riggers to work out,

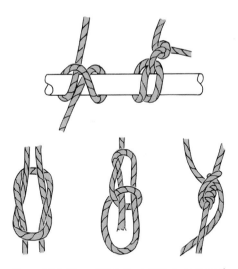

Figure 15-1. Clove Hitch (top). This knot is used to tie rope to battens. Note that it is finished by adding a common half hitch. Bottom: Square Knot (left). This is used for tying two lines of the same size together. Bowline Knot (middle). This makes a loop that will not tighten or loosen without untying. It is used wherever a fixed size loop is required. Stopper Hitch (right). Used for snubbing lines at the locking rail, it is also used wherever it is necessary to tie a small line to a larger one.

FIGURE 15-2a

Figure 15-2. (a) Wire Rope Fasteners. These clamps, also called "Crosbys," are used wherever it is necessary to make a loop in wire rope. They are commonly used to fasten wire rope lines to battens as shown. (b) Pressure Fasteners. These patented devices are used to make up loops in small-size wire rope for flying objects, including human beings, when the support must be invisible to the audience. Small diameter aircraft cable, such as that shown, commonly is used. Note that double fasteners are the rule. The fasteners are installed by crimping them on with a special tool.

FIGURE 15-2b

is the cable made for flying actors. Special crimp-on fasteners are used for securing aircraft cable. They must be carefully installed in multiples and tested to well beyond the weight they are intended to carry. A good test is to hang sandbags from the made-up cable equal to several times the weight of the planned load. Allow the weight to hang overnight to straighten the cable and to allow any slow slippage to reveal itself. Then hoist the load up several inches and allow it to drop, throwing a sudden jolt on the fastening. The fastener should withstand several such jolts with no visible slipping or distortion. If any does occur, cut off the fasteners and install new ones.

MUSCLES AND COUNTERWEIGHTS

"Muscling" is the riggers' name for the heavy, sometimes dangerous work of lifting something into the flies by brute strength. It can never be completely avoided although a well-equipped stage reduces it to a reasonable minimum. In most cases counterweighting is the answer to muscling. Once a unit is properly counterweighted, only minimum effort is needed to overcome inertia and to move it. On rope sets, sandbags are the normal counterweights (see Figure 3-13). With wire-cable systems, pieces of cast iron commonly are used. These come in two sizes referred to as "pigs" (about 40 pounds) and "wafers" (about 20 pounds). They will vary in width and thickness depending on the spacing of the line sets (Figure 3-14). Occasionally lead counterweights are used where arbor space is limited. There are also square counterweights designed for more primitive wire-guide systems.

Counterweights require no maintenance but they should never be stored at the edge of a loading gallery (Figure 3-7) where they might fall. Sandbags are more treacherous. As they get old the stitching weakens, especially at the point of greatest strain where the hanging ring is attached. They are also susceptible to damage from swinging into sharp objects. An old or even slightly damaged sandbag is dangerous. It may suddenly drop or it may merely leak sand, gradually getting lighter in weight and lowering something unexpectedly. Therefore, sandbags should be inspected at every use and replaced often. Unfortunately, they are expensive and usually cannot be made on the lightweight sewing machines in the costume department.

MOTOR SETS

Motor sets fall into three categories:

1. *Motor-driven lines* for light pipes, movie screens, etc.
2. *Grid winch systems* designed to replace conventional counterweight systems
3. *Portable winches*

Almost all modern theatres with completely equipped counterweight systems will have one or two motor-driven line sets. Usually one is installed on the grand drape to enable it to be operated remotely for motion picture projection. Another usually is required to operate the movie screen. Since these are not very apt to be worked on by the student riggers, they will have little contact with them, although they may be the only examples of motor operation in the theatre. Other, luckier theatres may have several of the heavy electric pipes motorized or even have a motor-driven light bridge. A few modern theatres may have grid winch systems.

MULE

A movable electric winch for hauling lines is commonly known as a "mule" (see Figure 15-3). This machine consists of a heavy-duty gear-motor equipped with a spindle around which a rope may be wrapped. The framework carrying the motor and its controls is on wheels and has a special bracket that fits under the frame of the locking rail. This holds the machine down and places the front pulley directly in position to accept a rope tied to the underside of the arbor at the hauling line eye. When this rope is wrapped around the spindle and pulled while the motor is operating, it cinches down on the spindle allowing the motor to haul the arbor, no matter how underweighted it may be. If the operator wishes the arbor to rise, lowering the setting, he simply loosens the tension on the free end of the rope, allowing the rope to slip over the spindle. An experienced operator can achieve fine control over a very heavy load this way.

Normally the mule is used to haul exceedingly heavy loads into a position where the arbor can be loaded or unloaded. Once balance has been achieved, the mule is removed and hand operation takes over. Occasionally the mule will be used for complicated rigging problems involving changes in the weight of a piece of scenery during the run of a show. Such rigs are beyond the scope of this text.

Although the mule is a great work saver, it is also dangerous. It is powerful enough to tear scenery apart by pulling the fastenings loose, or it can pull a heavy rope in two, dropping settings to the floor. The mule should never be operated by beginners, although they may help an experienced rigger operate it.

Figure 15-3. Mule. This heavy winch is used for a variety of hauling operations on stage. A loop at the end of the heavy rope is attached to whatever is to be hauled, and the line snubbed around the steel drum as shown. When the operator pulls on the free end of the rope, the line tightens around the moving drum, and the machine pulls the load. The drum may be powered either forward or backward.

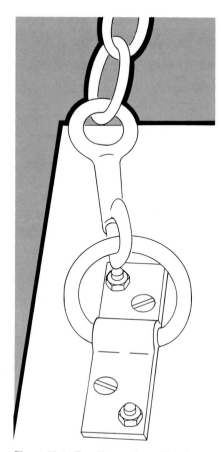

Figure 15-4. Top Hanger Iron. This hanger is part of a special rig; it was not possible to run the supporting line to the bottom of the scenery.

SOME TYPICAL RIGGING SITUATIONS

Each rigging problem will have its special details. Experienced riggers pride themselves on their ingenuity in solving each problem as it comes up. There are, however, certain operations that are common to many productions and that will introduce the beginner to some of the basic techniques required.

MOUNTING A FRAMED DROP

A framed drop may be a specially made unit consisting of a large piece of cloth, framed on its outer edge and braced, or it may be made up of a number of stock flats, battened together to form a large flat surface. The latter is probably more common because stock elements can be used and salvaged for reuse, and because it is quite easy to work openings into such a drop.

Although the procedures below can best be learned by doing them on stage, the following steps for installing a framed drop are given to provide the reader with a sense of the complexity and constant concern for safety which typify the work of riggers.

1. Place the drop face down on a clean stage floor, its top under the line set on which it is to hang.
2. Lower the batten to about 3 feet from the floor and release the trim chains. Install more chains if necessary. Distribute the chains so that they will be over the principal stiles as determined by the chief rigger.
3. Install hanger irons (Figure 15-4). Normally two will be required for each hanging point—one at the top rail, and one on a stile near the bottom of the drop. Hangers *must* be both bolted and screwed to the wooden frame and the frame must be sound. Use washers under bolt heads and nuts. Check carefully.
4. Attach hanger wires. Normally the wire will pass through the top hanger iron and be attached at the bottom. (This means that the bottom hanger iron takes most of the load.) Aircraft cable makes the best hanger wire. It must be tightly clamped with multiple cable clamps and carefully tested for holding strength. Any kinked wire should be rejected. If turnbuckles or other trimming devices are to be installed, these must be rated to handle loads well above the weight of that part of the drop carried by each line. Such devices should be thoroughly inspected for bends or signs of cracking, and any suspicious ones should be discarded.
5. Upper ends of hanger wires are attached to the trim chains. Observe same safety precautions used for fasteners.

LIFTING A FRAMED DROP

After all of the hanger wires have been fastened and checked and their upper ends attached to the trim chains, the drop is ready to be lifted into vertical position. The following steps are used for a drop too heavy to be easily lifted by one person.

1. The operating line is snubbed firmly to the locking rail. See Figure 15-1 for the knot.
2. A rigger is sent to the loading gallery, and the area below that gallery is cleared of people.
3. The arbor is loaded with iron up to the estimated weight of the drop. Accurate estimates are a source of pride among riggers. Since the drop is still resting on the floor, the entire weight on the arbor will be held by the snub line. Use care.
4. Several riggers cautiously release the snub and allow the arbor to lower, taking the weight of the drop as it moves. This is accomplished by holding the hauling line firmly and operating the rope lock slowly to control movement.
5. As the batten moves upward, it will begin to lift the top edge of the drop with it. Crew members hold the drop by its *bottom*, guiding it slowly forward as the top rises. The idea is to guide the drop into a vertical position without bending it unduly and without having it sway when it lifts clear of the floor. If the drop is at all weak, it will be necessary for crew members to "walk it up" from underneath to prevent it from bending too much.
6. As the drop reaches the vertical position, the accuracy of the adjustment of the trim will be evident. If a large error has been made, one or two of the supporting lines will try to take all of the weight of the drop, and may warp it or even break it. Unless the weight is distributed rather equally on all hanger lines, the drop should not be lifted clear of the floor. Once a reasonably close trim has been established, the drop can be raised into the flies for storage or it may immediately be trimmed.
7. Final balancing of the load must take place after the drop is completely supported by the counterweight system. If the riggers have been almost exactly right in their estimate of the weight of the drop, the arbor is pulled all the way down and weight added or removed to get exact balance. If the estimate has been well under the weight of the drop, a problem may be encountered. When the bottom of the drop is resting on the stage floor and cannot be easily raised because the drop is still much heavier than the arbor, riggers will find that the arbor is out of reach of the loading platform but still

far from accessible from the floor. The arbor must either be muscled into an accessible position, or if the theatre is extra-well equipped, loading may be accomplished from an intermediate loading gallery.

There are a number of variations in this procedure depending on the theatre's equipment and the wishes of the technical director. For example, if the theatre has no loading platform, it will be necessary to muscle the drop into upright position, rough trim it, and raise it into the flies before it can be counterweighted. This process is much like that which must be followed when rigging a framed drop on a rope set. A mule is a great help in such operations. It can be used to raise the drop into the vertical position and hold it until it is trimmed. Then the drop can be lifted into its high trim position and the counterweight attached, whether it is a sandbag or a loaded arbor. However, great care must be exercised while using the mule because a mistake may allow the drop to fall—a dangerous and costly accident.

RIGGING UNFRAMED DROPS OR DRAPERIES

Unframed drops are actually easier to rig than framed ones. An unframed drop usually is rolled around its batten when it is stored. The rolled drop is carried to the stage and unrolled in a position that places the batten which forms its top directly under the pipe batten of the counterweight system. If the drop is fitted with tie cords instead of rolled, or if a set of draperies is being rigged, the material is unfolded on a clean floor. The center of the drop or curtain is found (the center usually is marked on the top webbing), and tied to the pipe batten on its center. If drapery is being hung, the outer ends are tied. Then each half is tied at its center point, and the process of subdividing the drapery by tying the center of each segment is continued until the slack has been evenly distributed. Note the knot in Figure 15-5. If a flat drop is being hung, it is tied from the center outward toward each side, making sure that it hangs flat.

In either case, the weight of most of the material will still rest on the floor when the drop is completely tied. If the drop is fairly light in weight, it is muscled up and the arbor loaded from the floor. If it is quite heavy, the arbor-loading procedure mentioned for framed drops is used.

Draperies and drops are allowed to "hang out" for several days to allow the weight of the material to stretch out wrinkles. Trimming is not a problem on counterweight sets if the pipe battens are level. On rope sets, trimming will have to be accomplished at the pin rail. See Figure 3-12 for the belaying pin knot. If the drop is to be counterweighted with a sandbag, trimming must be done at the clew (see Figure 3-13b).

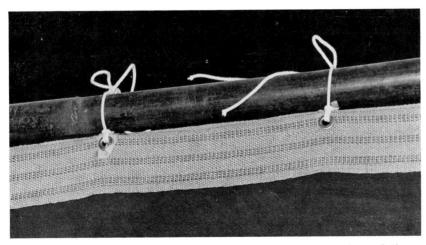

Figure 15-5. Batten Tie. This knot, which is exactly like tying shoestrings, is the standard way of tying drops or draperies to battens. It allows the drapery to be removed rapidly by pulling a loose end of each knot.

RIGGING A SPOT LINE

A spot line is a single line especially located to support an object that cannot be hung from the counterweight system or the permanently installed rope sets. Occasionally spot lines will be rigged in pairs.

In a properly equipped proscenium theatre there will be a gridiron which may be walked on. The first step in rigging a spot line is to install a loft block (see Figure 3-11a) at a point on the gridiron directly above the spike mark on the floor. This work should be done while the stage floor is kept completely clear of all workers not wearing hard hats. Only necessary tools should be carried to the grid, and these should preferably be tied to short lines attached to the worker's belt. The sheave is bolted into place and then a line is dropped through the sheave to reach the stage floor. This will check the location of the sheave. Hold the other end of the rope firmly; if it slips, someone will have to retrieve it from the floor making the long climb back to the grid. The other end of the rope is lead across the floor of the grid avoiding other equipment which may be in its path, and fed downward through a head block to the pin rail. It is not necessary that the head block be exactly in line with the loft block, but large angular errors should be avoided. If there is no head block available where one is needed, one must be installed. This process is much like the installation of a loft block. Usually the head block will have multiple sheaves of which you will use only one or two for spot line applications. Once the rope is installed, a small sandbag is tied to its on-stage end to make it descend from the flies when needed. Then the operator at the pin rail hauls the spot line out of the way, and ties it off at the rail.

The spot line may eventually be equipped with aircraft cable if it is to carry an object that must hang within the sight lines. This cable can, if necessary, be spliced to the spot line so that it will run through the loft block, allowing the object hanging on it to be pulled high into the flies.

TRIPPING

A large drop or cyclorama may be too long to be raised completely out of sight on a stage with a rather low grid. Soft, unframed drops or sky drops may be "tripped" by attaching a second line set to the bottom of the drop which is used to lift the bottom level with the top. This reduces the stored height of the drop by one half. Tripping should be a temporary measure. If a sky drop is left tripped for any great length of time, it will develop a permanent dust line in the fold.

A scene from Antigone. *Photograph by Stefan Odry*

TRAVELERS AND TABS

Riggers will often be called on to rig various kinds of drapery which will control the stage opening. The most common is the *draw curtain*. The draw may also be a *lift curtain* if it is mounted on a counterweighted line set. In some cases either lift or draw, or both, will be motorized. Motor installations normally are done by the supplier's professional riggers when the draperies are installed. Hand-operated sets are often rigged by student crews.

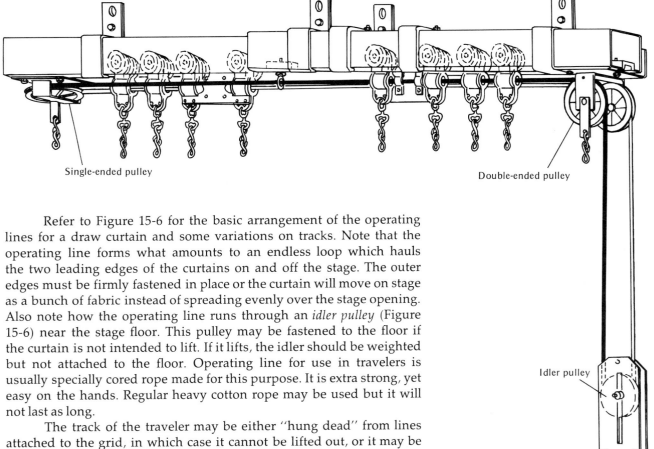

Single-ended pulley

Double-ended pulley

Idler pulley

Refer to Figure 15-6 for the basic arrangement of the operating lines for a draw curtain and some variations on tracks. Note that the operating line forms what amounts to an endless loop which hauls the two leading edges of the curtains on and off the stage. The outer edges must be firmly fastened in place or the curtain will move on stage as a bunch of fabric instead of spreading evenly over the stage opening. Also note how the operating line runs through an *idler pulley* (Figure 15-6) near the stage floor. This pulley may be fastened to the floor if the curtain is not intended to lift. If it lifts, the idler should be weighted but not attached to the floor. Operating line for use in travelers is usually specially cored rope made for this purpose. It is extra strong, yet easy on the hands. Regular heavy cotton rope may be used but it will not last as long.

The track of the traveler may be either "hung dead" from lines attached to the grid, in which case it cannot be lifted out, or it may be mounted on a counterweight set. If the track is hung dead, it should be mounted with turnbuckles so fine trimming can be accomplished.

Large stage draperies, particularly main curtains, are heavy objects. Riggers will find a mule useful in rigging them. If one is not available, a block and tackle may be needed.

Figure 3-5 shows some of the other possibilities for rigging main or special curtains. The tab curtain (tableau) is perhaps the most com-

Figure 15-6. Traveler Rigging. This drawing shows the "endless rope" arrangement used to haul curtains horizontally. Courtesy H & H Specialties.

mon after the draw curtain because it makes a pleasant stage opening shape and can be easily rigged on an existing draw curtain. Note that weights must be installed to make the curtain close properly.

MARKING TRIMS

Whatever is hung from the counterweight system, it will usually be necessary to mark the hauling line to indicate the proper positions of the object. "Low trim" is most important because this marks the position of the object when it is in sight of the audience. "High trim" is the storage position. There may also be intermediate positions.

One method of marking trims is to insert brightly colored flags of fabric between the strands of the hauling line. These are easy to see and will clear the idler pulley if they are narrow strips of fabric. However, their insertion is hard on the hauling line and takes considerable time. Another method is to ring the hauling line with colored tape at the proper point (the spike line is usually the top of the rope lock). Such markers are easier to apply but harder to see under the dim light at the locking rail. Old spikes should be removed or they may confuse the operator.

High trim marks usually are installed only if it is not feasible to take the line set out to its farthest limit. In some cases it is critical that a piece not be raised more than just enough to clear sight lines lest it foul another set. Such marks must be scrupulously observed.

RUNNING THE SHOW

Riggers tend to lead a life of extremes; they are either desperately busy or doing nothing. Normally, they will work during shifts, and rest while the actors work. Occasionally moving drops or other elements become part of the business of the play, and the riggers then find themselves taking live cues in which speed, synchronization, and rhythm of movement are essential. They have become a part of the "cast." In any case, working the lines is a highly responsible job, but it is not necessarily a job for potential football linemen. What is needed is some strength, but more than that, a sense of timing, a cool head, and a great desire for accuracy. Speed of movement is not usually needed. The counterweight system makes it possible to put tons of scenery into motion at the pull of a rope. Remember that the faster this moves, the harder it will be to stop. A gentle overhand pull that produces a speed of a foot or so per second is sufficient *at the fastest*. Continued acceleration is dangerous. Slow stops and starts are essential to prevent swaying and fouling of other lines. Banging of the drops into the floor is inexcusable. They should float gently into place.

SOME SAFETY RULES

1. Never straddle a batten when it is down; it may go up suddenly causing injury.

2. The stage should be clear of all bystanders when lines are being hauled in or out. If lines are worked during a production while actors are on stage, the actors must be carefully disciplined to play well away from the moving parts. A careful watch should be kept by the stage crew for any out-of-place persons, so that the riggers can be warned to slow or stop.

3. NO ONE except those qualified should try to operate the locking rail or other parts of the rigging. This can be exceedingly dangerous.

4. If two line sets foul (tangle together), do not try to force them free unless all else fails. Then clear the stage because parts may be knocked loose. Gentle easing of the lines plus guided swinging of one in relationship to the other will usually unfoul them. Seek the help of the technical director.

5. No rigger should hang anything in the flies that he is not completely willing to work under himself. Every hanger should be double-checked and the entire system should be inspected frequently.

6. Storage of items in the flies (other than draperies used often) is a poor practice. Old drops and pieces of scenery are particularly hazardous because they are tied up by lines of unknown age and allowed to hang for years in the vain hope that they can again be used. Take them down and store them somewhere else.

7. Never release the rope lock on a set of lines without checking the tension of the operating line to determine if there is an unbalance. After checking, release the lock slowly while holding the hauling line, and be prepared to relock it if you detect movement you feel you will not be able to control easily. If a line set is marked with a red flag or tied with a snubbing line, do not release it without instruction and then only with assistance. Do not trust a rope lock to hold more than a few pounds of unbalance.

8. Never try to haul a heavily unbalanced line set without enough assistance to be sure that you can control it, nor try to handle a heavily loaded rope set without help.

OPERATING PRACTICES

The following ideas will contribute much to the smooth operation of the production. They also relate to safety.

1. If possible, the operators should be able to see the scenery as they are moving it. This is why the pin rails for rope set theatres (hemp houses) were placed high on the stage house wall. Most locking rail operators have had to depend on the eyes of others to tell them what the scenery is doing, but that day is passing. Closed-circuit television is now both economical and sensitive enough to make it possible for the riggers to view their work. This is particularly important when the moving scenery is a part of the action of the play.

2. The use of a set of cue lights operated by the stage manager will often facilitate working the rigging. For example, a blue light serves as a "ready" cue and a red light means "go." This avoids the necessity for whispered cues that are often lost or hand signals that may be blocked by actors awaiting entrances.

3. Operators should develop a sense of the amount of operating line that has passed through their hands as they move a line set. They will know better when to expect the arrival of a trim mark. Overshooting a trim mark by a wide margin is inexcusable. A very slight overshoot or undershoot should be smoothly eased into place.

4. Enough operators should be available so that no one need try to operate more than one line at a time. In most cases, grips and/or property crew can be borrowed and trained to do the job at peak demand times.

5. If an operator senses more than normal resistance to the operation of a line, he should immediately stop and find out why. Forcing will only heighten the possibility that something will be torn loose and fall from the flies. In hauling a line out, extra resistance often means that the bottom of the scenery is caught under something. Drops may be torn or settings upset if force is applied.

SPECIAL RIGS

It is not the purpose of this text to itemize all of the many sophisticated hookups that are possible in rigging. However, motorized line sets are so common that a few essentials must be noted.

1. Motor sets are almost inevitably more powerful than hand sets; more weight can be handled with ease. Extra care must be taken.

2. A motor set provides no "feel" to the operator. Unless the operator hears the motor straining—and this is unlikely if it is on the grid—he may not know that the line is fouled until something tears loose. Use extra care to see that lines are clear. Likewise, a motor set will not sense that scenery is being lowered onto something else, a prop for example; it will keep on lowering until something gives.

3. Since motor sets can be operated remotely and are often run from several remote positions, it is very important to be sure that no personnel are in the way when the set is operated. This is especially true of lightly loaded sets which may run very quietly. It should be possible to lock off the motor control securely so that it cannot be operated while someone is working on or near it. If you find that a motor set will not work because its power switch has been turned off, do not turn it on and attempt to run it without first making sure that no one else is working on it, or that it hasn't been shut off because of a fault in the system.

PART FIVE

PROPERTIES

From Die Frau Vom **Meer**, *Ibsen. Photograph by Stefan Odry*

16
SCENOGRAPHY AND PROPERTIES

INTRODUCTION In the early stages of developing a design, the scenographer makes no distinction between scenery and properties. All elements are simply components in the evolving design. His concern is with large masses, general lines, and color. As the design takes form, distinctions begin to emerge and properties appear as accents, as actor movement centers, and as elements that give a certain richness to the evolving setting.

The logic in the above paragraph is compelling, but it may have little to do with the actual order in which a scenographer works out his design, however accurately it may seem to fit the end product. Designing is a matter of rearranging nondiscursive symbols in the mind. This is a process that evolves its own logic as it proceeds, and may never follow the same path twice. What makes these speculations important to an introductory chapter on properties is the possibility that some of the key elements in this symbol-juggling process may very possibly be properties. As the designer gropes about for ways to build that final symbolic transformation leading to the development of his own version of the master symbol, he often finds himself looking for an image, an *interim symbol* that will serve as a catalyst to bring the entire amorphous mass into focus. (Note how scenographers tend to work not only in nondiscursive but in nonverbal modes. Three- and four-dimensional imagery are the working tools of scenography.) A property, or some part of a property, may turn out to be exactly the catalytic interim symbol the scenographer is seeking. For example, a scenographer seeking to bring the design for *The Marriage of Figaro* (Mozart) into focus, may find that a portion of the filigree work of a baroque picture frame seems to catch exactly what he hears in Mozart's score.

Although in *The Marriage of Figaro* it

is quite probable that the interim symbol borrowed from the picture frame would be a major element in the final design of the opera, this is not always the case. An image may be musical or even poetic and not translatable into visual terms, or a visual image may become so abstracted or so stylized that it vanishes, leaving no visible trace of itself in the final scenography. It has still served its basic purpose, which is to aid the scenographer in bringing his work into focus. It is important to note that such interim symbols always follow the necessities of symbolic analogy—there will be an inherent analogical relationship between the symbol and its object which is vital to the artist, whether or not it is evident to others.

The use of a property or part of one as a design starter or even as a pervading motif is not the end of the scenographer's concern with properties. As the total design develops, he must spend a considerable amount of time working on details related to properties.

PROPERTIES AND THE ACTOR

We have already seen in Part One how closely related set design is to the movements of the actors. The design of properties is just as closely related. The size and structure of properties, especially furniture, determine what sort of positions the actor takes while using a property, what sort of movements he will make around it, how his action is motivated, and how his costume will relate to the property (Figures 16-1a and b).

Since movement is one of the main elements in the actor's expressive repertoire, it is vitally important that the scenographer devise properties that make appropriate movements not merely possible, but almost inevitable. He works very closely with the director in this matter; they often choose key elements of furniture together. If, for example, a sofa must be used in a setting, almost every detail of its construction will be important to the actors using it. Will they sink deeply into it when they sit? Is the back the right height for action that must take place behind it? Must it be barely wide enough for two, or must it allow at least 3 feet of separation between two estranged characters sitting on it? Should it express the outrageous taste of one of the characters, or should it reflect quiet but elegantly rich taste? The questions are almost endless, but the point is clear: not "just any sofa" will do.

The three-way relationship that exists between character, costume, and furniture is a typical example of the way all of the elements of a production interlock artistically. Both furniture and costume function in the stage design as accent elements. They are in prominent focus because they are used by the actors. Both aid in establishing the kind of an atmosphere with which the characters have surrounded them-

FIGURE 16-1a

Figure 16-1. (a) Scaling Properties to Actors. Although the tree here might be classified as either scenery or property depending on the view of the scenographer, it illustrates the principle of scale. Note how every part has been designed to accommodate actor movement, and to place the actors in the right degree of emphasis with relationship to the object. Scene from a production of As You Like It *(Shakespeare), Cologne, Germany. Scenographer: Kissuer. Director: Ciulli. Photograph by Stefan Odry. Photograph courtesy Helmut Grosser. (b) Properties and Acting. Note how the bed has been sloped and foreshortened to make the action on it more visible. From* Morn to Midnight *(Kaiser) performed at Cologne, Stadttheatre. Scenography: Habben. Director: Ciulli. Photograph by Stefan Odry. Photograph courtesy Helmut Grosser.*

FIGURE 16-1b

selves. In this sense, they are extensions of the virtual human beings the actors are creating. For example, if a character has poor taste, chances are that both his costume and his furniture will show it. On the other hand, if he is in another character's house, the poor taste of his costume might contrast obviously with the elegant taste of the other character's furniture (Figure 16-2).

There are also mechanical relationships between furniture and costumes. For example, if the actresses are wearing hoop skirts, they will be able merely to perch on the edge of a small chair; an overstuffed sofa would be ridiculous. It is interesting to note how the furniture design of a period meets the needs of the costumes of a period. Our very casual contemporary costumes are reflected in our furniture which allows almost any position a person wishes to take; a beanbag chair is a good example of this.

Figure 16-2. Furniture and Costumes. This is another scene from the production in Figure 16-1a. Note the relationship between the chair and the costume on the left. The seat of the chair is high and has been made even higher by stiffening the upholstery causing the actor to sit upright in a stiff-backed pose which is part of his character. The texture of the upholstery and that of the costume form a unifying element of the design. Production: From Morn to Midnight (Kaiser). Scenography: Habben. Director: Ciulli. Photograph by Stefan Odry. Photograph courtesy Helmut Grosser.

PROPERTIES AND THE SETTING

The concerns about actor movement, interrelationship between character and properties, character and setting, and the like, are only part of the scenographer's concern with properties as they relate to the setting. There are also general design considerations. Properties, not only because of their interrelationship with characters, but because of their ability to carry bright colors, interesting lines, and textures, usually form the accents in the entire design. We have already seen how a key line of a filigree can become a design motif. (A *design motif* is a symbolic device made up of such things as line, form, mass, color, and texture. It is usually used repeatedly, sometimes with variations, to give unity to a design.) Even if the scenographer does not choose to follow this route, he will use properties to complete his design. For example, if he has determined that a Louis XV period is proper for the play, and has designed such a room, he will feel that it is complete only when filled with Louis XV furnishings.

At this point the scenographer distinguishes between two categories of properties: *set props* and *hand props*. Set props are those placed on the stage mainly for design reasons; they are set decorations. Hand props are required for use by the actors. The distinction is not as clear as it may seem because there are many properties, including most of the furniture, which serve both functions. Nevertheless it is a useful distinction because it enables the designer to set priorities. If a property is clearly a hand prop, its first function must be to satisfy the needs of the actor using it. If it is clearly a set prop, design is its main function. If it falls between these extremes, the designer must arrange to satisfy both needs.

Set properties provide accents, finish off the period quality of a setting, contribute to its mood, or follow through on a motif (Figure 16-3). Their selection usually begins with the scenographer who may or may not consult with the director depending on the latter's wishes. Some directors consider the selection of set properties entirely a scenographic matter. Others (including such famous people as Bertolt Brecht) consider the choice a vital part of the entire master symbol and insist that they be party to every selection. Crew members will have to determine the wishes of their scenographer and director and act accordingly.

As the scenographer sketches properties, whether for ultimate construction or for acquisition, he concerns himself with their value as symbolic elements in the production. This value will be a function of their line, form, color, and texture as well as their proposed use in the virtual world of the scene. If, for example, the scenographer is considering a chandelier whose function in the scene is to be the virtual light source in the room, he must also consider the following:

1. Line Is it elaborately curled or starkly simple?
2. Form. Is it a heavy, massive chunk of metal or a light, airy thing of indefinite outline?
3. Color. Is it darkly metallic or light pastel?
4. Texture. How would it feel if one touched it—hard, soft, cold, etc.?

FIGURE 16-3a

FIGURE 16-3b

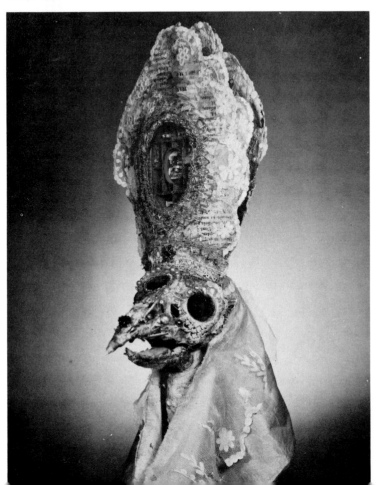

Figure 16-3. (a) Properties and the Setting. This set for Long Day's Journey into Night *(O'Neill) designed by Van Phillips of Purdue University illustrates the close interrelationship between setting and properties. Note how the diamond weave in the settee has been repeated in the balcony rail. The turned spindles of the balustrade are echoed in the turned legs of the chairs center. Director: Carl Williams. Photograph courtesy Van Phillips. (b) A model of a setting for* Orfeé *(Stravinski) designed by Andrej Majewski. Photograph courtesy Andrej Majewski. (c) A finished property for the setting in Figure 16-3b. Note the detail work. Photograph courtesy Andrej Majewski.*

FIGURE 16-3c

SYMBOLIC UNITY

Underlying the scenographer's concerns for the way in which properties meet the needs of the actors and how they blend into the design of the setting is the absolutely essential necessity of creating artistic unity. Without unity there will be no art. Thus the ultimate test of the usefulness of any property will be its evaluation as a part of the master symbol—an entirely nondiscursive process whose results cannot always be explained in discursive language. This may account for some of the frustrations encountered by property crews that bring prop after prop to the scenographer who rejects each one, saying only, "It does not fit." The scenographer should be able to provide such nonverbal aids as sketches or pictures of acceptable properties.

PERIOD PROPERTIES

"Period" refers to the historical time in which the object was made. This does not mean merely the date of the manufacture, although that is also relevant, but the era of which the piece is thought to be typical. An Empire period property would be one typical of the Napoleonic Empire. Although the actual dates of the Napoleonic Empire were 1804–1815, the Empire period as it related to furniture and costume may encompass a considerably longer time. Any piece that is typical of the period will be designated "Empire," without regard to the date of manufacture. If it comes from the historical period encompassing the Napoleonic Empire and some years surrounding that period, it would be termed "genuine Empire" and command a high price. A modern reproduction of such a piece of furniture would still be called Empire furniture, but would not be as highly priced. As far as scenography is concerned, the genuineness of the article is of little concern. In fact, a genuine piece of Empire furniture would probably be a liability because of its fragility and high value.

Beginning scenographers should be cautioned not to be too literal about periods. The scenographer's work is not the same as that of a museum curator, who must vouch for the authenticity of every piece in his display. The scenographer may seek exactly the opposite effect. He may, for example, wish to create a virtual environment for the characters which, while dated in 1940, suggests that they have surrounded themselves with relics of time long past. Moreover, periods are never "pure" in real life. It is only in museums and in books on furniture collecting that one gets the impression that everyone who lived during a given period had furniture typical of that period, wore clothing of the period, and decorated his dwelling in that style. Common sense tells us that leftovers from past eras linger on for a long time. Architecture is the most durable. There are many buildings in Europe exhibiting remnants of architecture from the Roman era all the way to the present. In fact, the problem of the art historian is to find a "pure" example. Furniture and other interior features also linger far beyond their period.

The job of the scenographer is to use the lines, form, and the aura of period properties as a part of the virtual world he is creating. A mixture of several eras will often work better than textbook purity. Catching certain lines or forms from a period and devising the setting and properties from them, may be more effective than seeking to reproduce the period environment in detail.

Stylization from a Period Motif

We noted in the beginning of this chapter how an element from a period property might form an interim symbol for the scenographer as

Figure 16-4. Stylization. This picture from a production of Ghosts *(Ibsen) performed at the Stadttheatre in Cologne, Germany, demonstrates the use of strong, almost mechanical lines to reflect the unyielding atmosphere of the play. Such architectural elements certainly have little realistic relationship to nineteenth-century rural Norway, but they have much to say about the world in which these characters live. Scenography: Muntner. Director: Grieff. Photograph by Stefan Odry. Photograph courtesy Helmut Grosser.*

he develops his design. And we noted that in some cases the scenographer might use such an element as a motif. It is necessary now to pursue this process somewhat further. The scenographer may seize on a line or element that is typical of a period, simplify it, and then repeat it with variations throughout the setting and properties. He might, for example, begin with a picture of a Gothic arch as it exists in stone. From this picture he might abstract merely the line of the arch, ignoring the thickness that the stone must have if a real arch is to hold itself up. This abstraction could exploit the weightless quality of Gothic architecture. The scenographer might repeat the Gothic line with variations in many forms in the setting, properties, and even in scenic projections.

It is only a step from the adaptation of a period element for stylization to the creation of one's own motif which can then be used in the same manner. However, caution is necessary. These processes can easily deteriorate into mere mechanical repetitions of the chosen motif which result in design that can only be praised for its consistency. The secret of successful stylization lies in the scenographer's ability to find analogue relationships between the import of the script and the lines or forms that he has chosen as motifs. If each repetition of the motif somehow brings new insight into the entire dramatic symbol, stylization is a successful design technique (Figure 16-4).

17
THE
PROPERTY
CREW

DUTIES OF THE PROPERTY CREW

The following list outlines the general duties of the property crew:

1. Acquiring or making properties needed for production
2. Supplying and taking care of rehearsal props
3. Handing out hand props to actors going on stage and receiving them from actors coming off stage during production
4. Shifting set props during production
5. Providing storage for props during production
6. Making minor repairs on props during run of production
7. Returning properties if borrowed or rented, or placing them in storage areas after show closes
8. Handling petty cash involved in the purchase of props

In addition to the above, the property crew is often expected to assist the grips and riggers during periods of peak activity. These people are, in turn, expected to help the property crew during shifts, particularly with heavy props.

ASSEMBLING THE PROPERTY LIST

The first job of a property crew is to obtain a complete property list. Generally crew members will assist in the preparation of this list. Work begins with the script itself. Someone, either an assistant to the director or a member of the property crew, goes through the script noting every property indicated in the stage directions or required by the lines. This list is then checked by the director and the scenographer.

The director goes through the list

with his script in hand checking the props noted against those he plans to use at each point. He makes changes, additions, and deletions based on his concept of the production. Frequently there will be property decisions that he is not able to make at this early stage in the direction. He should indicate alternatives if possible, and in any event, alert the crew to the fact that additions will appear later.

The director's main concern will be with hand props and with furniture and set props that have direct bearing on the action of the play. He may or may not check the other set props.

The scenographer, like the director, goes through the property list with the script to catch any items relevant to the appearance of the scene that may have been missed. He also adds to the list those set props that are necessary to the complete design of the production, and fills in all other props from a design point of view.

The comments of the director and the scenographer may conflict at certain points. For example, the scenographer may want a small-scale sofa while the director wants one that will seat four people. The property crew must study the checked-over lists, determine areas of confusion or conflict, and help to resolve them. This chore usually falls to the crew chief, who does not make artistic decisions, but instead, tactfully points out to the director and scenographer that they are not in agreement or that details are not clear. This is expected of property chiefs, and they will be faulted if they allow the confusion to persist.

The detailed property list will include sketches or even pictures of the desired properties. In some cases it will be up to the property crew to find pictures of potentially useful props and submit these to the director and the scenographer, although this may be a frustrating process. In spite of all the checking, the prop list cannot be considered completely final until dress rehearsals. Technical rehearsals will often reveal additional members in the chorus, or the crew will suddenly discover that a prop which comes offstage left is immediately needed stage right. This necessitates a duplicate.

The various methods of obtaining properties are discussed below. However, it should be noted that the final selection of key props usually is made by the scenographer (often accompanied by the director) in person. The property crew locates the most likely props and directs the scenographer to them.

REHEARSAL PROPERTIES

While the various stages of property acquisition are taking place, rehearsals will be going on. The director and actors will find that they cannot progress beyond a rather rudimentary level without some form of rehearsal props. It is, for example, hard to rehearse a sword fight without some kind of sword. To meet this need, a rehearsal prop list is prepared, frequently by the director's assistant, and the property crew is asked to obtain the props on that list. Rehearsal props need be only suggestions of the final ones. They should approximate them in size and weight but need not be more than moderately close. For example, sticks often substitute for swords. Usually the theatre prop room plus the shop will be able to provide rehearsal props almost immediately. If the list of rehearsal props is extensive, or includes valuable items, the property crew chief will probably assign one member of the crew to attend all rehearsals and control these props.

As regular properties are gathered for the show, some of them may be used in rehearsals. This is a good way to determine if a property is exactly right for the action. When it has been declared correct, it is returned to the shop for any finishing touches. Property crews, with the approval of the technical director, may have to restrict the use of certain valuable or fragile props until late in the rehearsal schedule. This is a particular problem with such things as swords that are used in fight scenes. The early stages of working out such scenes are likely to be uncontrolled, and thus more apt to damage or break the swords than the more controlled, later rehearsals.

OBTAINING PROPERTIES

There are a number of ways to get properties, depending on the location of the theatre, its budget, its educational needs, and even its standing in the community. They may be obtained in the following ways:

1. Renting from a theatrical property house. Where it is available, it offers an almost unlimited supply of properties. Money is the only limitation.
2. Renting from nonprop sources. This is often the only recourse in areas that do not have specialized property rental houses.
3. Borrowing from such sources as above.
4. Purchasing properties from commercial or specialty sources.
5. Manufacturing properties in the theatre shop.
6. Using properties from the theatre's stock.
7. Utilizing furniture and property items that are a part of the theatre organization.

As a member of the property crew, you may be involved in any or all of the above transactions, and this may include considerable travel on your part. You should check in advance with your crew chief to see what arrangements, if any, have been made for compensating your travel costs. At the same time you will want to find out all of the details concerning purchase, rental, or borrowing procedures. Since you may be acting in a legally responsible way with regards to the theatre, you will want to know exactly what your rights and obligations are.

THEATRICAL PROPERTY RENTAL HOUSES

If you are the harried property chief of a realistic show, nothing is quite so reassuring as the presence of a large theatrical property rental house. Your only concern will be money. Given enough of that, you can satisfy the most fastidious scenographer-director combination with ease. Moreover, if you rent all your properties from the same source, you may realize substantial savings over what you might spend renting props a few at a time here and there.

The procedure in dealing with such a rental house is simple, but must be followed carefully. Properties must be selected and reserved well in advance. Once a reservation has been made and the price agreed upon, the house will hold the properties for you no matter how many offers it may get from more lucrative renters. There will be a large savings if you agree to rent all of the properties for the production, less any that it cannot provide, from one house. (Most houses will direct you to the source of items which they do not have.)

In addition to the ready availability of almost anything needed, the great advantage of renting from a theatre rental agent is that he is familiar with theatre usage of props. He expects hard use and will often tolerate alterations in the rental items that a nontheatrical dealer would not even understand. Repainting, reupholstering, and the like are common practice. Since reupholstering is merely covering over the previous upholstery, it is common for a renter to pull up a corner of the upholstery to see if a better fabric is available underneath. If so, the dealer may agree to stripping the furniture down to that layer.

As a crew member, you will find that a trip to a rental house to assist in the selection of props is an exciting theatrical experience. You will be examining props used by professionals and may even see sets of furniture you will recognize as the background of a favorite film or TV show. You will also come to know the various furniture periods by observing rooms full of props arranged by period and type. A rental trip is time well spent.

OTHER SOURCES OF PROPERTY RENTALS

Unfortunately, only a few large theatre centers in the United States have theatrical property rental houses. In other locations theatre workers will have to seek out substitutes. These may be far inferior to the rental houses, but they will be the only sources available. The following are likely rental sources:

1. Dealers in secondhand furniture of high quality
2. Antique dealers
3. Furniture stores handling new furniture

Of these, the only source that may have its furniture organized by period will be the antique dealer. Antique dealers, however, especially those familiar with the details of furniture periods, will deal in items far too valuable and fragile for theatrical use. A 260-year-old Louis XIV chair might be precisely right for a production of a Molière comedy as far as its looks are concerned, but the slapstick action of the players might very well ruin the chair at a cost of many hundreds of dollars, and the eternal ill will of the dealer. If an antique dealer can be interested in the theatre and assured of continuing business, he can sometimes be persuaded to accumulate a stock of period furniture reproductions which he sets aside largely for theatre use.

Secondhand furniture dealers usually have a vast stock of almost totally unorganized furniture, most of it vaguely recalling some period or periods of the past. They are a good source of furniture for such plays as *Come Back Little Sheba,* or even some of O'Neill's works, but any production requiring clearly established style will probably exceed their capacity. Since secondhand stores are interested in sales, they will usually be reluctant to rent. They may be more amenable to a sale with a buy-back arrangement after the production. Since the stock of any secondhand store is a sometime thing, prop crews will spend large amounts of time going through the holdings of various stores to find the few items they can use. Store clerks will be of little assistance because they seldom know much about furniture styles. Beware of a sales clerk's assurances that a piece of furniture is "really a good imitation of Louis XVI." Check it out yourself against a furniture encyclopedia.

The foregoing should make it obvious that seeking out properties for rental in an area not supplied with theatrical property rental houses is a frustrating, time-consuming process. If the props are rented from a nonprofessional, the theatre should make some clear-cut advance arrangements concerning liability and insurance.

BORROWING PROPS

Occasionally a friend of the theatre who has exactly the style of furniture and bric-a-brac needed for a production may offer a loan of the furniture. Also you will occasionally find new furniture in a store that fits your needs, and may be able to work out a loan arrangement in turn for advertising in the program, etc. Such borrowing is risky business because the loaners usually have no idea how hard theatres are on furniture and other props. This is particularly true of amateur or educational groups where actor body control and discipline are still in the learning stages. Stage business tends to get rougher as time goes on and the props often suffer. A loaner, politely provided with tickets to the performance, may be shocked to witness a treasured sofa being jumped on by a 200-pound actor, or a prized table thoroughly soaked with spilled drinks during a bit of violent business. Such experiences tend to end all further chance of borrowing, and even worse, all support for the theatre group. Even furniture borrowed from the director's own house may get mistreated, leaving the theatre with a moral if not legal obligation to spend hard-earned funds for replacement.

Protection for Loaners and Borrowers

Whenever props are acquired by borrowing or renting from any source other than a theatrical prop rental house, the theatre group should seek to make the nature of the usage completely clear from the beginning, and to protect all concerned from losses. The following steps should suffice if carefully followed:

1. A clear statement, in writing, describing the nature of the use to which the borrowed equipment will be subjected, should be given to the lender.
2. The value of the items should be established at the time they are borrowed, and recorded in writing. Values tend to rise rapidly after an object has been damaged.
3. A careful description of each item, including its condition at the time of borrowing, should be prepared and made available to each party.
4. The theatre should take out insurance to cover any claims of loss or damage to borrowed or rented properties. If the owner of the property agrees to carry the insurance instead of the theatre, this should be part of the written rental agreement.
5. The theatre group should make every effort to satisfy promptly any claims against it, even if the individual responsible for the damage is no longer with the group. Failure to do this can so deteriorate the reputation of a theatre company that it will not be able to function in the community.

BUYING PROPS

Buying is a good policy, particularly for items likely to be used repeatedly. For example, a theatre group that makes a practice of producing drawing-room comedies, may find that it can save both money and time by buying several sets of furniture that suggest various periods of furniture style.

As a crew member, you will probably assist in the purchase of large props, but the final decision will be made by the technical director and the financial staff of the organization. Small hand props are commonly bought by crew chiefs. For example, a number of scripts call for dishes to be broken during every performance. A source of cheap, breakable dishes must be found and enough purchased for the entire run. Numerous other items and parts for making props will be handled in the same way, normally using petty cash for the purchases.

MAKING PROPS IN THE PROPERTY SHOP

Given the time and the skills, the ideal method of obtaining props is to make them in the shop (Figure 17-1). The scenographer can get exactly what he wants because he can supervise construction. Costs will be low and as many items as are needed can be made. The problem is that prop making is time-consuming work; production deadlines will not wait. Multiple items, such as swords for an "army" or jewelry for a "harem" can grow into a mass production project that will take over most of the available shop time and space.

The skills of the property maker should be numerous: woodworking, metal working, plaster casting, papier-mâché, plastics, even electrical and chemical techniques are common. As a crew member, whatever skill you may have will probably be used, and you will also learn some new methods. A beginner's text such as this cannot hope to detail all of the technical crafts of the master prop man. As problems arise during your crew duties, you can look up the techniques of whatever craft is needed in the library. These techniques can then be adapted to the needs of the theatre under the guidance of your crew chief and technical director. For example, you may need to reupholster some furniture. The basic tools will be the same as those used by professional upholsterers—heavy thread, curved needles, gimp, and the like. The techniques, however, are far less demanding. Instead of removing the old upholstery and reworking from the frame up, you merely baste the new fabric on over the old and cover the raw edges with braid or gimp. It may be necessary to finish only those portions of the furniture that will be in sight of the audience. If you must repair a chair, you will use far less padding and build it up on a base of solid wood, instead of using the materials of a professional upholsterer. The chair will be hard, but it will play better than if it were soft and professionally done.

Similar procedures will be followed in most other cases. Hobby materials (e.g., rub-on gilding) can often be used in a "quick and dirty" way instead of following the details of the instructions on the box. These methods work better on stage than finely detailed workmanship (Figure 17-2).

Figure 17-1. (a) Making Properties. These silhouettes have been cut on a band saw and then base painted. Detail painting will be the next step. (b) Comic mask. This mask, derived from traditional Commedia del Arte style, has been so constructed that the beard stands out horizontally no matter what gyrations the actor performs. Note how mask and costume blend to make the style consistant. Courtesy Cologne, Germany Stadttheater.

FIGURE 17-1a

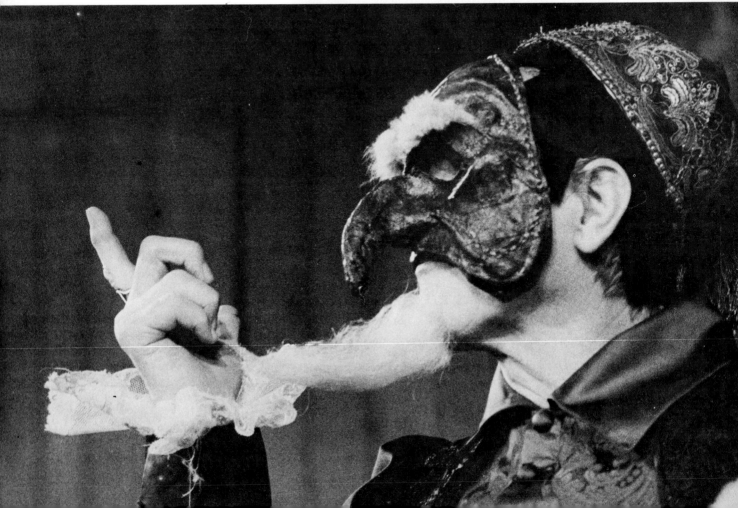

FIGURE 17-1b

FIGURE 17-2a

FIGURE 17-2b

Figure 17-2. (a) Gilding and Jewels. These two standards, which are about 2 feet high, were made by cutting masonite shapes, decorating with hot glue, and adding cast plastic jewels. The textures were then highlighted with rub-on gilding. Photograph courtesy California State University, Long Beach. (b) Stage jewelry, made in the theatre shop from commercial costume jewelry by rearranging and restringing to satisfy the needs of the designer. Courtesy Cologne, Germany Stadttheater. (c) Realism in properties. This head of John the Baptist for the opera Salome (Richard Strauss) has been built around a core of foamed plastic using latex, stage hair, and carefully applied paint. Courtesy Cologne, Germany Stadttheater. (d) This sturdy property was made by building up layer upon layer of glue-soaked paper and allowing it to dry. The result is a durable property which can be painted and finished as needed. Photograph by Michal Heron. Property courtesy Westport Country Playhouse.

FIGURE 17-2c

FIGURE 17-2d

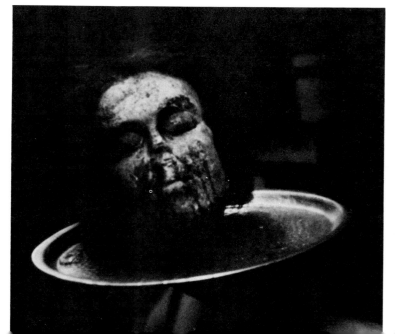

No property specialist can be worthy of that title unless he knows how to make properties using modern plastics. These same techniques also apply to scenery construction, the making of costume parts and masks, and a variety of other theatrical specialties, and are therefore treated separately in the next chapter.

THE PROPERTY SHOP

Most property shops, when they exist separately from scenery shops, are fitted out for relatively light wood and metal work. If special or heavier tools are needed, the resources of the scenery shop, the metal shop, or the electric shop are utilized.

Power Tools for the Property Shop

TABLE SAW   The property shop table saw is a smaller version of the tool mentioned in Chapter 8, "The Scene Shop." It will often be a table saw retired from the scene shop in favor of a much larger one. If one is to be purchased, the typical home hobby table saw will be adequate.

DRILL PRESS   A small bench drill press is adequate instead of the more powerful pedestal type shown for the scene shop (see Figure 8-14). Since it will be used a great deal, it should be equipped with its own supply of bits and with a drill vise.

JIG SAW   The jig saw (see Figure 8-10) may not be found in the scene shop. It is especially designed for small, precise cutting of irregular shapes. Although it will make heavier cuts than a Cutawl, it is not as rugged as a band saw.

SANDER   The small disk/belt sander is similar to that used in the scene shop (see Figure 8-13). However, it will not be convenient to try to make one sander serve both functions because of the special needs of making props.

$\frac{3}{8}$ INCH ELECTRIC DRILL   A $\frac{3}{8}$ inch electric hand drill is almost a necessity even if the bench drill press is available. Several of these handy tools, equipped not only with drill bits but also with various rotary files and cutters to aid in shaping properties, will be even better.

HOT GLUE GUN   The hot glue gun will disappear into either the costume shop or the scene shop unless each has its own. It facilitates near-instantaneous fastening of fabrics, wood, leather, some plastics, and other materials. It can also be used to form fine scrollwork on surfaces by laying down a bead of the glue and allowing it to set. Buy the glue in quantities at wholesale prices.

STAPLER   Although the scene shop should have a power stapler and several staple guns (see Figure 8-19j), the property shop should have its own machine with a good supply of staples.

POP RIVETER   The pop riveter is a handy tool for making moderately strong fastenings between pieces of leather, flexible plastics, thin metals, etc.

SOLDERING AND BRAZING EQUIPMENT   A soldering gun and a heavy electrical soldering iron are minimal requirements in a property shop. A small brazing torch such as those sold to model makers is also a great help.

AIR COMPRESSOR   If the theatre plant is equipped with compressed air, a line should be run to the property shop and provided with its own regulator so that the pressure can be adjusted to the needs of that area. Compressed air will be used for operating small paint guns, cleaning and drying parts, etc.

Safety in the Property Shop

All of the general rules of safety in the scene shop mentioned in Chapter 6 apply equally in the property shop, but one extra caution is needed. Almost inevitably there will be a wide variety of activities taking place at one time in the property shop. Some of these may be incompatible in terms of safety. For example, operation of the brazing torch will require the removal or secure covering of all glues and solvents, which are flammable. Of special concern are the common spray cans of paint, adhesives, and the like. The spray from these cans is usually violently flammable (have your local fire inspector give you a demonstration). Such spray cans should *never* be used near any open flame. Fumes from these cans and from many of the glues and solvents used in making properties are also dangerous. Use only with adequate ventilation.

Plastics and Properties

Chapter 18, "Plastics in the Theatre," will open a wide variety of new materials and techniques for making properties. This work will probably be done either in the scene shop or in the property shop unless the theatre is one of the very few plants having a separate plastics shop. The special safety precautions mentioned for working with plastics must be observed.

PROPS FROM THE PROP ROOM

A well-established theatre will probably have many props in storage. Since no theatre ever has enough storage space, they may be scattered over the entire plant in every available corner. They should be catalogued, in much the same manner that flats are catalogued. Pictures of the item will help if they can be made. You may be instructed to seek out various props from storage and bring them to the stage area for inspection by the scenographer and/or the director. They may be used as rehearsal props, or reworked in the shop and used in the show. If they are not useful, they go back to the prop storage. Such items should be checked out of and back into storage carefully so that their whereabouts will always be known. A lost prop is valueless; it merely takes up space somewhere.

USING THEATRE PLANT FURNITURE

Occasionally the furniture from the theatre building itself may serve as props. If, for example, office furniture is needed, it can sometimes be borrowed from the theatre offices—but not without careful advance arrangements. As a crew member, be sure that someone with authority far greater than yours makes arrangements before the box office desk vanishes into the wings. The wrath of the business office is awesome.

PROPS AND SPECIAL EFFECTS

Traditionally, the prop man was also the sound and optical effects man. He provided the coconut shells for the sounds of horses' hooves and the squeaking hinges for the mysterious door in the darkness. Much of this has changed. Most sound effects are now the province of the electronic sound man who takes them from tapes or records and plays them on cue. In some cases, theatres with highly sophisticated sound equipment make their own effects, recording them on tape. Optical effects have evolved into complicated projection apparatus requiring a specialist.

However, some effects still fall to the prop man. Gunfire and smoke are two examples. The discussion below merely covers some of the more common problems that may confront the prop crew. Some reasonably typical solutions are given, although many experienced theatre workers will have other methods of producing the same effects. Of course, no amount of ill-placed enthusiasm for a grand theatrical effect should be allowed to overshadow concern for safety.

GUNS AND GUNFIRE

Guns are always a special problem in the theatre even if they are only carried on stage and displayed. If they must be fired, the problem increases. Some of the difficulties have to do with theatrical techniques, but there is also a nontheatrical problem of security whenever firearms or what appear to be firearms are handled. Guns are notoriously susceptible to theft. The public display of a firearm on a stage advertises the fact that it must be stored somewhere backstage between performances. This increases the risk. Real firearms, whether in working order or not, create the greatest risk. Such weapons should be carefully stored in a highly secure area, preferably a safe, except for those short periods of time when they are needed on stage. When the gun is in the stage area it should be under the constant supervision of a responsible person, who will keep the gun on his person except when it is in the hands of an actor. If the gun is a real one, even though it has been made inoperative, its serial number should be recorded so that it can be traced if it is stolen. Your local police department may be a valuable source of advice both for security and proper handling.

Firearms are commonly fired both backstage and on stage. Blank cartridges are fired either from regular guns or starting pistols like those used in athletic events. Starting pistols have the advantage of being incapable of firing a regular cartridge. However, even blank cartridges are dangerous when fired. They eject a considerable amount of wadding and powder residue with enough force to blow a hole in draperies or, if fired at close range, to force the material into human skin. Therefore, users should never aim a stage gun so that anyone is in the path of this flying material nor should it be allowed to strike drapery or scenery. If a regular gun is fired, the residue comes out of the muzzle. If a starting pistol is used, it comes out of the sides of the gun at right angles to the line of sight. Regular guns being used to fire blanks in sight of the audience must be pointed upstage of other actors or into a clear space where the flying material will do no harm. Only powder loads barely large enough to produce the desired sound should be used.

Because blank cartridges often misfire, it is good theatrical practice to provide a "cover gun" backstage, whether the gun is to be fired on stage or off. A second person (usually a property crew member) stands by with the cover gun and follows the business closely. He watches as the actor squeezes the trigger of his gun; if nothing happens, the standby gun is fired. The actor is instructed to continue to pantomime the firing of his gun until the cover gun goes off. Actually, this process can be used quite successfully to simulate the firing of a gun on stage if it is felt that this practice will be dangerous (for example, if business requires that the gun point toward the audience). It can be so successfully done that members of the audience will assert that they "saw the flash," although the gun that went off was actually backstage.

The duties of the property crew will include caring for the guns, loading them before performances, cleaning them, and securing them. Prop crew members should have special training for these tasks unless they already can demonstrate their familiarity with firearms.

Backstage "explosions" are sometimes handled by the firing of guns. For example, a large explosion can be simulated by firing a *lightly* loaded shotgun into a barrel. This process, however, is hard on ears and equipment backstage. Electronic methods are highly recommended as a substitute. The use of explosive fireworks backstage to simulate explosions is usually illegal because of fire hazards, and it is not recommended.

SMOKE AND FOG

Two special effects are called for frequently, and the prop crew may have to provide them. The distinction between smoke and fog is blurry, although billowing clouds of vapor are usually read by an audience as smoke, and an atmosphere evenly laden with vapor appears to be fog. The distinction must be made clear by the lines and actions of the actors. Several materials are used to produce smoke and fog depending on the effect wanted, the quantity needed, and the availability of materials and equipment, as well as the relationship of the effect to the actors.

CO_2 "Smoke"

One favorite way to produce a smoke or fog effect is to utilize the vapors produced by evaporating solid carbon dioxide. When this gas is compressed and cooled, it forms a solid known as "Dry Ice," a white material that tends to maintain a temperature of about −70 degrees F. It absorbs heat from its surroundings and evaporates. The extremely cold temperature causes whatever water vapor is in the air in its vicinity to condense, forming fog. If the air is moist, the effect will be that of billowing clouds of water vapor which tend to sink to the lowest points on the stage and hang there for a while. This is the commonly seen effect of a layer of fog or "clouds" concealing the feet of actors or dancers as they move through a fantasy scene. Huge quantities of fog are produced by passing the steam coming from boiling water over baskets of Dry Ice (see Figure 17-3). On a smaller scale, releasing carbon dioxide gas from a cylinder in which it is contained in a liquid form can produce a similar effect—a puff of fog billowing outward and settling downward. This can be done by operating a CO_2 fire extinguisher. If an extinguisher is used for this purpose it should not be one "robbed" from its proper place on stage—it should be an extra one provided to

obtain the effect. After use, it must be completely recharged before it can be returned to duty as a fire safety device. If a larger and cheaper quantity of gas is needed, a cylinder of compressed CO_2 can be obtained from a soft drink supply house. Hoses and fittings can also be obtained to lead the gas to wherever it is to be released. In *Finian's Rainbow*, for example, it may be necessary to provide several outlets for the gas at various points in the setting. Such plumbing will ice up and stop functioning if operated for long intervals. Short spurts of gas will give it time to warm up between uses.

HAZARDS IN USING CO_2 Carbon dioxide is an odorless, noncombustible, nonpoisonous gas at low concentrations. However, it can suffocate by depriving its victims of oxygen. Therefore, care should be taken that CO_2 fog effects are operated in well-ventilated places (not enough to destroy the effect, but enough to dissipate the gas and avoid hazards). It will have a tendency to settle into low, enclosed places and force air out. Thus, a poorly ventilated orchestra pit or a depression in the setting that forms a "tank" could be dangerous. There is no warning—the victim simply passes out and will die unless promptly removed to fresh air.

Another hazard, not deadly but important, comes from the intense cold of Dry Ice. It can freeze the skin, causing an injury like a burn. This can come from handling Dry Ice or from being exposed to the cold fumes close to the nozzle of a gas cylinder. Since property crews will be handling the Dry Ice and operating the cylinders, they should be aware of these dangers. It is preferable that Dry Ice be handled with gloved hands and as little as possible.

In the theatre, Dry Ice is best for fantasy effects. It can also produce the blast of "smoke" for sudden appearances or disappearances but with the accompaniment of considerable noise. Actors find CO_2 relatively easy to work with because it makes no noticeable change in the air they breathe. The only possible distraction is the cold, if they get close to the outlets.

Oil Smoke

When large quantities of smoke are needed, and the smoke must endure for a considerable time and rise instead of settle, oil smoke is used. This is produced by vaporizing oil over a heater, which is usually an electrical element much like that found in an electric range. The result is a dense smoke made up a particles of oil finely dispersed in the air. Since it is warm, it tends to rise. The smoke will endure until it is dispersed through the building's ventilating system. Such smoke is most easily produced by the use of a commercial smoke generator like that in Figure 17-3. This generator contains a heater, the oil, and a pump mechanism to spray small quantities of oil over the heater as needed. One smoke machine can fill an entire stage with smoke in a few minutes.

Property crews should rent or purchase a smoke machine if none is available at the theatre when smoke is needed. Devising your own smoke generator is not for beginners. Commercial machines are sometimes provided with double chambers, one for oil, and the other for distilled water which can be used to produce quantities of steam for use with Dry Ice to make the low-lying fog effect. Quantities of steam produced are small, however, compared to the amount of smoke produced by using the oil.

Special "fog juice" should be used in these machines as specified by their manufacturer. A gallon of it will last a theatre company a long time, so the cost is minimal. Smoke dispersers are also available and can be dispensed with a second generator. They are used to dispel the smoke after it has served its purpose.

PROBLEMS WITH OIL SMOKE   Perhaps the biggest problem with oil smoke is that actors tend to hate it. It does not smell good and may irritate the eyes and noses. Oil smoke is especially irritating to those wearing contact lenses; many such persons cannot work in the smoke at all. Of course, these same problems will be transferred to the audience if the smoke moves out into the house. It will do this if the ventilation is not carefully controlled.

Another hazard from oil smoke is that it comes from the nozzle very hot and it can burn at close range. It also has a tendency to coat the floor and props near the nozzle with a film of oil, making a very slippery floor. The hazard is lessened by preheating the machine thoroughly before operating the oil dispenser, thus reducing the amount of unevaporated oil sprayed from the nozzle. Operators should be cautioned against using a fog machine that has been used to disperse insecticide (the same machines commonly are utilized for this nontheatrical function).

A new, much less irritating type of "fog juice" is now available in Europe in three types that produce varying degrees of smoke density. The smoke contains no irritating oil and is completely safe.[1]

Small Amounts of Smoke

Occasionally the prop crew will be asked to produce the effect of smoke coming from a recently extinguished torch or the "magical" effect of smoke rising from a container when opened (the genie from a bottle). There is a chemical known as titanium tetrachloride ($TiCl_4$) that can produce these effects with ease. When exposed to air it smokes quite generously without becoming hot or setting fires. It is, however, highly corrosive, and the vapors are dangerous. The fumes consist of hydrochloric acid (highly corrosive as either a vapor or a liquid), and titanium dioxide, an irritating solid. $TiCl_4$ should be handled only in extremely small quantities, kept in a glass-stoppered bottle until needed, and never used in such a way that anyone is apt to inhale the fumes. Very small amounts may be obtained from chemistry labs along with instructions as to its use. When used with care, it produces remarkable effects.

If the effect of a boiling kettle is desired, warm water can be put in the vessel and a chunk of Dry Ice added just before the prop goes on stage. The bubbling sound and the "steam" will be effective, but the "steam" will tend to sink instead of rise.

Although seldom found on small stages, low pressure steam from heating lines often is used to produce magical effects such as the "magic fire" in the *Ring of the Nibelungs*. It simply is released into the atmosphere, where it rises as it evaporates. Naturally it is very hot, and actors must avoid the outlets. Steam is perhaps the least hazardous of all smoke effects because nothing is added to the air except moisture —something helpful to the voices of actors and singers.

THUNDER AND LIGHTNING

These effects now belong to the electronics department. Thunder is available in realistic splendor on recordings, and lightning can best be

1. Safex nebelfluid (smoke fluid) is available from Safex, D2000 Schenfield, Bez. Hamburg, Kampweg 10, West Germany. Its cost is about $14.40 per liter.

produced electrically by various flash-tube devices. The old-fashioned sheet metal thunder sheet should be relegated back to the tin shop. Open electric arc lightning devices should be outlawed as fire hazards. A theatrical strobe light or even a photographer's unit can make better, safer lightning.

FIRES

Most large fire effects are now done by projection devices. However, the property crew may have the task of providing a campfire, a fire in a fireplace, or even the fire in the stove where Hedda Gabler burns the manuscript. Such visible fires call for the combined talents of the property and the lighting crews.

A "campfire" can be built up on a base of plywood and moved into place as a unit. The same technique can be used for the fire in a fireplace. The base of the fire should include a couple of sockets wired to take colored bulbs, usually one red and one amber. Over this base are placed chunks of heavy glass (bought at a fireplace supply house which handles the chunk glass for nontheatre artificial fires). Several colors of glass will add realism. Then partially burned pieces of wood or pieces of wood cut and painted to appear partially burned are added. This will produce the effect of a fire burned down to a bed of coals. If flames are needed, a small fan must be worked in under the "coals" and strips of colored silk or clear plastic such as Mylar can be attached so they will blow upward in the air from the fan. The addition of lighting from above and onto the faces of those actors near the "fire" will add still more realism. If "flames" are to be seen through an opening such as the inside of a stove or furnace, sheets of clear Mylar can be lightly stretched between supports and moved by turning a fan on them. Suitably lighted, this will produce a realistic effect of roaring flames.

Candles, Torches, and Lanterns

Hand-held light sources that would realistically contain fire are always a problem. Candles, in particular, present a problem because they are much used by actors and the effect of a real, flickering candle flame is hard to achieve. Furthermore, most directors and actors see no reason why a lighted candle should not be used—it has been and still is used frequently. The first step is to determine fire laws in your theatre. This should be done on a show-to-show basis because such laws are rapidly changing. What was legal (or overlooked) last year may not pass this year.

If an open flame may not be used, or if the "flame" is to be partially concealed in a lantern, electrical simulation will be standard procedure. This can vary from commercially made "flickering candles," which almost defy detection, to simple flashlight adaptations which only glow when turned on. The latter are common in torches or lanterns (see Figure 17-4). The property crew usually builds up the lantern or torch, leaving room for the batteries and lamp. Then the electrical crew will wire it. The prop crew will finish the job of decorating the prop, and will be responsible for replacing batteries during the run. Extra props should be on hand in case the original refuses to work.

The brightness of lanterns, torches, etc., should be held as low as possible, keeping within the needs of the scene. Since they are apt

Figure 17-4. Chandelier with Electric Candles. A chandelier such as this may be made by cutting thin metal with a torch to make the design. The metal holders can be welded on, and the candles built on them. "Flames" can be simulated with small electric lamps wrapped with pieces of plastic color medium to simulate the shape of a flame.

to be used by minor characters whose presence in the scene should be only felt, a too-bright lantern may upstage the scene. You may find it is necessary to reduce its brightness late in the rehearsal process. This is best accomplished mechanically, instead of electrically. Add another layer of semitransparent material to the openings in the prop, or dry-brush some paint onto the plastic already there. Test it under stage conditions and get the approval of the director or scenographer.

ACTORS AND PROPERTIES

Actors must, of course, be familiar with the properties they work with and satisfied that they can use them as the script requires. However, the design and working parts of a prop are the concern of the scenographer and the director, not the actor. Therefore, property crew members should be cautioned about making alterations in the design or operation of properties at the request of actors. Such requests should come to the crew by way of the director or the scenographer, not directly from the actor. Repairs are a different matter. If a prop is broken, the best way to find out how this happened and to fix it so it will not happen again, is to deal directly with the actor who uses it.

18
PLASTICS
IN THE
THEATRE

WHAT ARE PLASTICS?

Plastics are entirely synthetic construction materials not found anywhere in nature. The first plastic was Celluloid, a solid made from a nitrate of cellulose and camphor, originally used to make such things as combs. Soon after the invention of Celluloid came the invention of Bakelite, followed by literally hundreds of materials. Techniques for developing plastics have so improved that it is now possible for chemists to begin with a set of specifications and design a plastic to meet them.

Most of the materials called plastics today are *polymers,* formed by chemically linking together many molecules of a simple compound to form a solid of predictable and useful characteristics. Polymerization usually takes place under the influence of a material known as a ''catalyst.'' Technically, a catalyst is a chemical that facilitates a reaction taking place without becoming a part of the finished product. Actually most of the catalysts used in the polymerization of plastics do not meet this definition very closely, but for all practical purposes may still be called catalysts. We need to know about this chemistry because some of the plastic materials used in the theatre are polymerized on the spot by adding a catalyst and awaiting the results. Heat is a common part of these reactions, and we must be aware that it can be generated suddenly, causing fire or explosion if we do not use care. Mixing plastics may seem a simple operation, but in the hands of the unwary it can be dangerous.

COMMON DANGERS IN WORKING WITH PLASTICS

Heat of polymerization is the first danger encountered in the use of plastics. *Dangerous fumes,* the second hazard, fall into two categories: fumes from materials used in the polymerization process, and fumes formed during various shaping techniques such as cutting plastics with a hot wire, shaping them with flames, or etching them with chemicals to form textured surfaces. All of these operations are common to the theatrical use of plastics. In some cases, the dangers involved from the polymerization process are severe.

The third danger in working with plastics is *fire*. The chemicals used in the polymerization process are frequently highly flammable. Finished plastics vary in flammability from dangerous to completely flameproof. Of course, the latter will be desirable in the theatre. However, even flameproof plastics may involve the use of dangerously flammable materials during their forming stages. They become nonflammable only after the chemical reaction has become complete.

The above discussion might seem to indicate that the theatrical use of plastics is too hazardous to be worthwhile. This is probably true for some kinds of operations in some theatres. However, the results in terms of new potentials for theatrical artists and time-saving ways of doing things can be spectacular. Entirely new and fascinating possibilities are opened when the theatrical worker masters certain plastics techniques. Furthermore, wood is becoming increasingly costly —in fact it is already more expensive than metal or plastics for many applications. It is clear that economics as well as artistic necessity is going to push the theatre into greater use of plastics.

SURVEY OF PLASTICS FOR THEATRICAL APPLICATIONS

Table 18-1 gives some of the common categories of plastics, indicates some of the forms in which they are found, and suggests some of their possible theatrical applications. Because the number of available plastics and the possibilities for applications are constantly growing, this table can be no more than a suggestion of what may be possible.

SPECIFIC THEATRICAL APPLICATIONS OF PLASTICS

The processes below are outlined to give the beginner some idea of the sort of things that can be done with plastics. Actually they represent a very small portion of the potential for plastic in the theatre. Creative experimentation seeking new ways to do old things and new things to do with these artistically flexible materials should be happening in every theatre shop. Many artists who work in three-dimensional forms are using these materials, as are experimenters seeking further plastics application in industry. Theatre workers will do well to seek out these people and to exchange information with them.

Table 18-1

Type of Plastic: Common Name If Any	Form of Material and Light Transmission	Fire Rating[a]	Possible Theatrical Uses

Polyester
casting resin
	Liquid with catalyst
	Clear, can be colored
		S to SE
		or
		CFR
			Property jewelry, stained glass.
			Laminate with fiberglass to make
			  strong forms.
			Many boats and surfboards are made
			  of this material; Many other uses.

Epoxy	Liquid and catalyst Clear	S to SE	Very strong, fast setting adhesive. Tremendous possibilities for experimentation.

SOLIDS
Acrylic:
  Plexiglas,
  Acrylan,
  Lucite
	Rods, bars, sheets,
	  extruded shapes
	  Clear or colored
		Slow or
		CFR
			Window "glass" properties.
			Transparent weight-bearing surfaces.
			Entire settings.

Polycarbonate	Rod, bar, sheet
	Clear
		None to SE	Highly resistant to impact (used in
			  riot helmets).
			Use as above where additional
			  strength is needed.

Polystyrene	Bar, rod, sheet Clear	S to SE	About same as acrylics.

Polyvinyl
  chloride
  (PVC)[b]
	Bar, rod, sheet
	  Clear, opaque,
	  translucent
		S to SE	Good vacuum forming stock.
			  Easily formed with heat gun.
			  Wrought iron, intricate shapes.
			  Moderate strength.

Cellulose acetate	Bar, rod, sheet
	  Clear, opaque,
	  translucent
		Slow burning	Color medium, heat-forming stock.

Polyamides:
  Nylon
	Bar, rod filament
	  Fabric
		S to SE	Very strong in solid form, casters,
			  bearings, sliders.
			  Many uses for fabric.

Fluoroethylene:
  Teflon
	Bar, rod, sheet
	  White, opaque
		Does not
		burn
			High strength, great resistance to
			  chemicals.
			  Bearings, sliders, etc.

[a] S, slow burning; SE, self-extinguishing; CFR, can be manufactured as flame retardant.
[b] Polyvinyls may create dangerous gases if overheated. They should be heated with care and used only when safer substitutes are not available.

Table 18-1 (continued)

Type of Plastic: Common Name If Any	Form of Material and Light Transmission	Fire Rating[a]	Possible Theatrical Uses
Polystyrene: Styrofoam	Blocks, billets, boards	Inflammable to slow-burning CFR	Carve or hot wire form to make rocks, cornicing, props, entire settings. Much used in the theatre.
Urethanes	Slabs, blocks, sheets Rigid and flexible	S to SE or CFR	Rigid material used much like polystyrene but cannot be etched or cut with hot wire. Flexible form used as cushions, padding, parts of costumes, curved moldings, etc.
Urethanes	Two-part liquid	S to SE or CFR	Molding of properties, parts of settings, heavy texturing. Many theatrical uses.
LARGE FLEXIBLE SHEETS Polyvinyl chloride (PVC)[b]	By roll in 72 inch or more widths	S to SE or CFR	Projection sheets, costumes. May be too flammable for settings if not specially compounded.
Polyester: Mylar, Gelutran Roscolux	Very thin sheets Clear, colored, metallic	S to SE CFR	Color medium, light-weight mirrors, props, decorative surface materials.
SILICONES Silicone	Sprays, liquids	None to slow	Lubricants, parting agents.
Silicone rubber	Rubber	None to slow	High temperature electrical insulation in lighting instruments.

[a] S, slow burning; SE, self-extinguishing; CFR, can be manufactured as flame retardant.
[b] Polyvinyls may create dangerous gases if overheated. They should be heated with care and used only when safer substitutes are not available.

CASTING RESIN

Casting resin is available in every hobby shop along with the catalysts, colorants, parting agents, and even molds. These products are designed for the use of the home hobbyist who wants to try plastic casting, but they can also be used in the theatre. The resin is almost invariably a polyester, highly refined to produce crystal-clear castings. The catalyst is commonly methylethyl ketone peroxide (MEK). Mixing instructions are on the packages. However, more than a little judgment will be involved in deciding exactly what mixture, within the range given, will work best for the project at hand.

Safety Considerations

The resin itself is a sticky, strong-smelling liquid that is not particularly hazardous to store. The catalyst is a powerful oxidizer that is both flammable itself and capable of starting fires if it comes into contact with certain organic materials such as oils. It is also potentially explosive, especially in large amounts. Fortunately the MEK used for casting resin is quite weak and usually sold only in small containers. It should be stored and handled with care. Mixing of resin and catalyst should be done in a well-ventilated room.

If the instructions on the container are followed, there should be no danger of adding so much catalyst to the mixture that overheating and fire could result. Nevertheless, totally careless mixing of sizable batches could cause a violent reaction and even a fire. Experimentation with resin-catalyst proportions should be carried out on a very small scale.

Once the resin has hardened, it will be inert and only moderately flammable. If the casting must be able to meet a flameproofing test, chemicals may be added to accomplish this, but at the cost of some reduction in transparency and purity of color. Materials may also be purchased with the fire retardants already added.

Molds

A wide variety of materials may be used for molds. Hobbyists often use PVC molds purchased at hobby stores. These have been shaped by vacuum (see below) to form a negative mold. A completely equipped theatre plastics shop will be able to make its own molds in this fashion. Simple molds may also be made of such material as modeling clay, putty, or plaster, or cut from wood or fiberboard. The modeling clay will serve as its own parting agent; the wax in the clay will prevent the resin from adhering. Other molds should be greased, or better still, sprayed with a silicone parting agent. Molds should be designed with an eye to getting the hardened resin out. Unless the mold is flexible, or can be broken away, no undercuts should be allowed. If the casting is to be a broad, thin object, the mold may consist of a wooden cutout sealed to a sheet of glass with modeling clay. The glass should be treated with a parting agent (wax, grease, or silicone).

Mixing and Pouring

The resin and catalyst should be mixed in a throw-away container. Some of it will inevitably harden in the container and will be extremely difficult to remove. Tin cans or waxed paper cups work well. The proper amount of resin should be added first. Then the catalyst is added a drop at a time up to the proper amount, stirring while adding. You will note a change in the color of the mixture and some heat through the sides of the container. If the right amount of catalyst has been added, the mixture will remain a thick syrupy liquid for twenty minutes or more, then set into a heavy jellylike consistency. This gel will soon harden into a rigid piece of plastic. Heat will be given off during the entire process. If too much catalyst has been added for the job, the mixture will heat more rapidly and set abruptly. Assuming it has been poured into the mold in time, this does little harm unless the casting is thick. If it is, it may crack or warp as it hardens. If too little catalyst has been added, the mixture will be very slow to set. It may even take more than twenty-four hours.

Determining the Proper Amount of Catalyst

A number of factors determine how much catalyst is right for a given job. The key is heat. The heat generated in the mix also accelerates polymerization. Thus casting in a high temperature area or under circumstances that tend to hold the heat into the mix, such as a thick casting, will speed the reaction. Conversely, a cold room or a casting that is very thin and dissipates heat will slow things down.

Other factors also affect setting time. The addition of colorants, flameproofing materials, or extenders tend to slow the mix down. The solution is to increase the amount of catalyst or the application of heat. Any of these reactions may be speeded up with heat. A microwave oven is ideal.

Epoxy resins may also be cast by similar processes. Auto body putty (used to fill dents) can be forced into molds and cured to make properties of incredible durability. The molds can be taken by vacuum forming from original pieces of costume jewelry, scrollwork, or the like.

These casting processes will result in clear, glasslike surfaces if the material is allowed to level before setting. Any desired surface may be worked into the bottom of the mold. After the mix has jelled, it may be quickly trimmed of any excess while the material is easy to cut. Other than this, the solidifying mix should not be disturbed if maximum strength is desired.

LAMINATING WITH RESIN AND FIBERGLASS

The familiar process for coating boat hulls, surfboards, and a myriad of other objects is laminating with resin and fiberglass (Figure 18-1 and Plate XIII). The resin to be used is much like that used for casting processes, although it is chosen more for its strength and durability than its transparency. Catalysts and also safety precautions are the same.

In this process, resin and fiberglass are built up layer by layer on the outside of some sort of form. After the object has been formed and allowed to set, it is removed from the mold. More coats may be added if desired. If the laminations are built up to as much as $\frac{1}{4}$ inch thickness, an exceedingly strong object can be constructed.

Resin for lamination is always applied in thin layers. Therefore it is mixed with somewhat more catalyst than resin to be used for casting. This tends to reduce its "pot time"—the time before it sets. The mixed resin should be rapidly painted over the mold and a layer of fiberglass pressed into it. Then a second coat of resin is applied over the fiberglass and worked into its crevices to make a solid coating. The entire layer is allowed to set, smoothed if necessary, and the process repeated until sufficient layers have been built up. Some interesting variations can be worked on this process by draping the fiberglass and painting it with resin. This works much like the fabric and plaster system for making props but produces a far stronger object.

Cleaning Up Resin-Working Equipment

Acetone is the best solvent for unset or partially set resin. It can be used to wash the resin out of brushes and other objects. Once the resin has set, it is slightly soluble in acetone, but not enough to clean out a brush.

HEAT-FORMING ACRYLICS

Acrylics are thermoplastic materials. This means that they can be softened or even melted if heated sufficiently. When acrylics cool they harden back into the same clear materials they were before. They also display a remarkable trait: "memory." If a piece of acrylic is cast from liquid in a certain form, allowed to harden, and then heat softened and warped out of the original shape and allowed to cool, it will retain the new shape. However, if it is again heated to the softening point, it

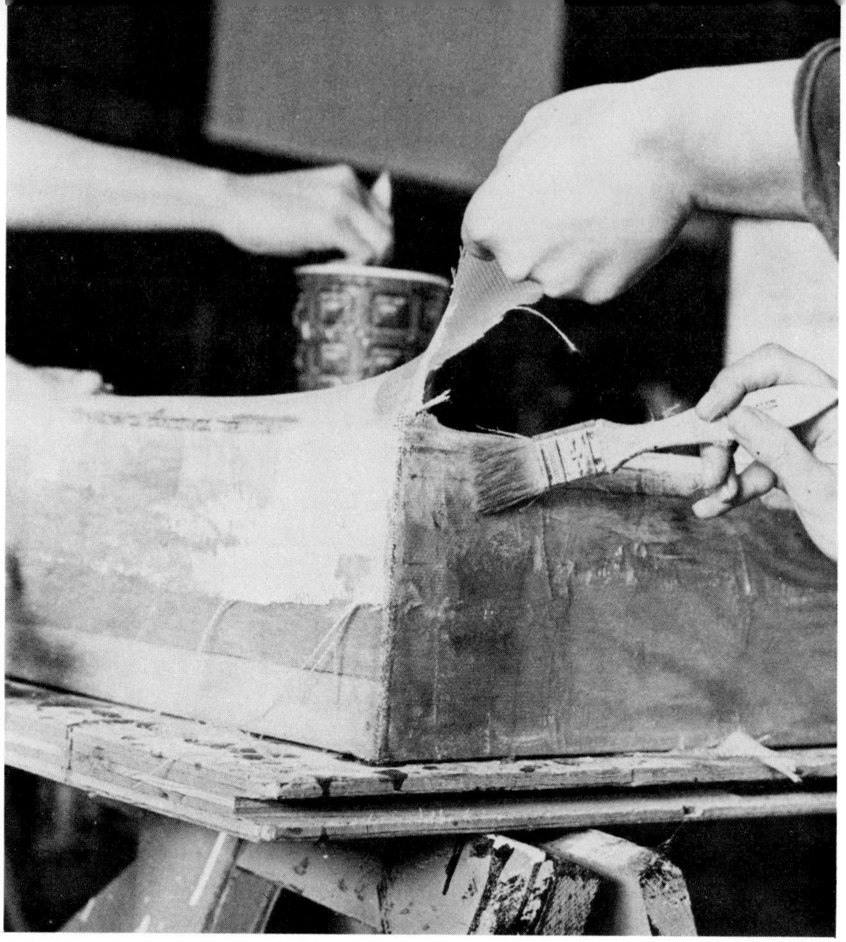

Figure 18-1. Laminating with Resin and Fiberglass. This example shows a lid to a lightly constructed property "trunk" being reinforced by laminating it with resin and fiberglass. The resin is rapidly painted onto the surface and the fabric worked into it. Additional resin is applied to the top. The finishing here consisted of sanding the surface to smooth it and staining it with thin paint.

will return to its original cast shape. This process can be repeated several times, and each time the material will return to its cast shape.

Shaping acrylics by heating requires some means of applying the right amount of heat to exactly the right place in the material. If too much heat is applied, the plastic may blister or even melt. Too little heat may cause cracking when a bend is attempted. In order to bend acrylics, they must be heated to between 240 and 340° F. A heat gun (see below) or an electric heater are two good ways to do this. The material may also be heated in an oven. The process is simple: the acrylic is heated until soft, then bent, and held in the new position until cold. If it is reheated, it will return to its original shape unless held or bent to a new shape. Plastics manufacturers will supply on request a booklet giving details of this forming process and some suggestions for heaters.

Drape and Blow Shaping

Draping and blow shaping may be performed on the thermoplastic plastics such as acrylics, vinyls, polyethylenes, and cellulosics (cellulose acetate). The material is brought to the softening point and allowed to settle into a mold of its own weight (draping) or blown into a bubble-like shape by forcing air under it. The material is then cooled in the newly formed shape. Draping is handy for making simple plastic containers, and can be used along with a heat gun to make free-form sculptures.

Vacuum Forming

A more complex and more flexible variation on the above methods is vacuum forming. It requires a rather complicated piece of machinery. Vacuum-forming machines can be purchased at high cost or built in the theatre for a modest outlay and considerable shop time. Instructions for building one are available (see the Bibliography).

A vacuum-forming machine consists of two major parts. The first is the *oven,* an electrical heater used to soften the sheet of plastic to the proper temperature for forming. When the sheet is sufficiently soft it is transferred rapidly to the *forming table* where it is draped over the mold and pulled down tightly into the mold by a vacuum. It is held against the mold until cool and is then released. Commercial machines are equipped to do these steps automatically, producing parts rapidly. These expensive machines pay for themselves under commercial conditions where a great number of pieces will be made from the same mold. In the theatre, where only a few dozen pieces will probably be needed, a new mold setup will frequently be required. Since the set-up time is the major share of such a procedure, the rapid-sequence operation of a professional machine is of little value. The homemade machine is operated manually and is fast enough for most theatres (Figure 18-2).

Figure 18-2. (a) A Shop-Made Vacuum-Forming Machine. This machine can be made for a fraction of the cost of a commercially available machine. Although it is incapable of the rapid production rates of the commercial machine, it is quite satisfactory for theatre work. This view shows the "oven," an electrically heated area, where the sheet plastic is softened. (b) The Forming Table. This part of the machine, which is partially visible in Figure 18-2a, is where the plastic is actually formed. The heated plastic sheet is transferred quickly from the oven to the forming table and manually forced down over the object and into close contact with the edges of the table. The vacuum is then drawn through the many small holes in the top of the table, and the object held in place until it cools. Two molds are shown on the table.

FIGURE 18-2a

FIGURE 18-2b

Vacuum forming is an ideal way to make repeated copies of filigree work for set decorations, duplicates of statuary (made in halves and put together), molds for casting resins (see above), duplicate props, and a wide variety of other decorative and useful items (Figure 18-3). Cost of operation, once the machine is on hand, is small. Any thermoplastic sheet material which meets OSHA safety regulations can be used in a vacuum-forming machine.

Heat Gun

An adjunct to all of these heat-forming processes is a *heat gun,* a hand-held tool consisting of a powerful electric heater installed in a tubular housing with a fan to blow air through it and out through a nozzle. It is somewhat like a hand-held electric hair dryer but produces much hotter air. This machine can be used to hand form strips of heavy vinyl to make "wrought iron work," or to spot treat plastic being vacuum formed, draped, or blown into shape.

FIGURE 18-3a

WORKING WITH PLASTIC FOAMS—CUTTING

Plastic foams are commonly bought in billets or slabs, and cut to shape as needed. Straight cuts can be made with a saw, but a hot wire cutter is better because it not only cuts the plastic, but seals the surface. Most

FIGURE 18-3b

Figure 18-3. (a) Drawing a Mold from a Part. This cast aluminum cornice piece was bought from a supplier and duplicated, using vacuum-formed molds. The part was laid on the forming table and surrounded with clay filler to hold the plastic to exactly half the depth of the metal. A mold was formed in thin plastic. The original was turned over and the process repeated. The result was an exact negative mold of the original which was then used to cast repeated copies for stage use. (Such copies may be cast in plaster, acrylic, or auto body putty.) (b) Molds and Formed Parts. This illustrates some of the many possibilities for forming details by use of the vacuum-forming machine. Note the mask. The negative and positive molds are cast from plaster and treated with release agents before vacuum forming. Also note the mold for the panel of bricks. It is made by cutting and placing pieces of carpet to form the mold for the faces of the bricks. (c) and (d) Cast Properties. These jewelry items were made by vacuum forming molds from originals and using these to cast duplicates. (c) The medallion was cast from acrylic resin. (d) Most of the items here were cast using automobile body putty (a pastelike resin originally made for filling dents in auto bodies). After casting, the parts were polished and finished with gilding where appropriate. All properties Courtesy California State University, Long Beach.

FIGURE 18-3c

FIGURE 18-3d

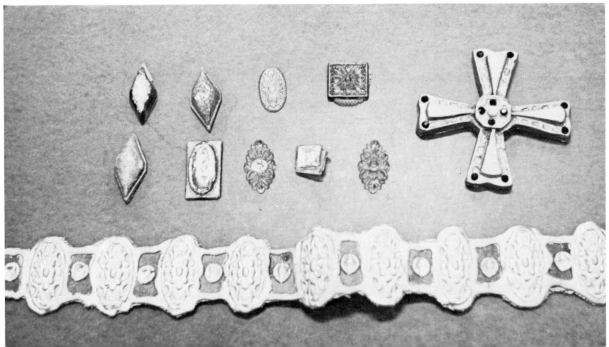

FIGURE 18-4a

of the plastic foam worked in this manner will be polystyrene. One commonly known brand is Styrofoam. This material can be bought at reasonable prices in fire-retardant form for theatrical use. It offers a wide variety of possibilities.

Hot wire cutters are pieces of electrical resistance material bent to whatever shape is desired for the cross section of the cut, heated to a dull glow, and passed through the foam (Figure 18-4b). The heat of the wire destroys the foam next to the wire and melts a layer of foam material into a skin over the cut surfaces, making a surface that takes paint easily. The only danger in hot wire cutting is that the fumes from the heated plastic are somewhat toxic. The process should be carried out either outdoors or in a very well-ventilated room.

A particularly spectacular time-saver is the use of hot wire cutting to make fancy cornices. They can be made in one piece by bending a hot wire cutter into the shape of the cross section of the finished cornice, and passing billets of foam past it (see Figure 18-4b). Both the positive and negative cuts will be useful. Be sure to pass the foam at an even rate past the wire without stopping until the cut is finished.

A hot wire cutter may easily be made in the shop. All that is needed is a heavy-duty step-down transformer. A small AC electric welder or "buzz box" is ideal. Moderate-sized step-down transformers are also available from electronics supply houses, but they will not handle very heavy currents for large cutters. Be sure to note that the variable autotransformers (powerstats) which are used to control the voltage to the transformer cannot be used to run the cutter directly. To do this is to risk electrocution!

Another interesting variation on the hot wire cutter can be made by altering a heavy-duty electric soldering gun. A piece of rigid nichrome wire (heater wire), or even a piece of a coat hanger, can be formed into a cutting loop and installed in place of the soldering tip. This gun can be used to hand cut all manner of filigree work, fantastic properties, and the like (see Plate XVI).

Texturing Foams

Polystyrene foams can be given surface textures in a variety of ways. One is to partially *burn the surface* with a torch. This dangerous work should not be done indoors because the fumes are toxic. Work only outside in the wind or in a forced ventilation space like a spray paint booth. The results can be varied to resemble rock, corroded metal, molten metal, or a number of other things. Working metallic paint and color into these surfaces makes them still more interesting.

Another method of texturing polystyrene foam is to *etch it with chemicals*. Acetone will do the job, but should be used with care; it is volatile and as flammable as gasoline. Its fumes are also toxic.

FIGURE 18-4b

Besides acetone, another etching material is "banana oil," amylacetate. It is used in crude form to make up lacquers for application of metallic powders. The technique is simple: brush it on until you get the surface you want. An interesting variation is done by brushing metallic powders (gold or bronze, for instance) into the foam along with the banana oil. This carries the metallic powder into the foam as it etches it, and bonds the powder to the surface. The result looks like etched metal. This work too should be done in a well-ventilated area.

Gluing Foams

Gluing one piece of foam to another can be a problem. Many glues, such as airplane glue or contact cement, are made with solvents that destroy the plastic, making a large hole where the user wants a joint. Water-mixed glues, such as white glue, work over small areas but may take months to dry when the joints are deep within a large object. A special clear glue sold for gluing Styrofoam is available at hobby shops. It is satisfactory, but expensive.

Figure 18-4. (a) Carved Styrofoam Statuary. This statue was carved from a block of Styrofoam using simple sculpting tools. It will be painted before use. Although the statue is about six feet high, it can be easily lifted with one hand. This technique works rapidly, takes sufficient detail for theatrical purposes, and produces lightweight, flame resistant properties. Courtesy the Cologne, Germany Stadttheater. (b) A Jig for hot wire cutting. This device was rigged to make repeated cuts of foam plastic molding. Note how the wire—actually a bent piece of electrician's "fish tape"—has been formed in the cross section of the molding to be made. In operation, the wire would be heated by passing current from a heavy-duty transformer such as an AC arc welder until almost red hot. The plastic is then pushed past the wire. Either rigid or flexible foam may be cut.

Another satisfactory method of gluing rigid foams together is to flow heated paraffin over the adjacent surfaces and immediately press the parts together. This produces a joint of good strength which has the advantage of not showing under hot wire cutting. Billets made up of paraffin gluing may be turned on a lathe without the joints becoming obvious. Hot paraffin, however, is dangerously flammable and can cause burns if spilled on the skin.

Casting Foams—Polyurethane

Although foams can be bought in billets and sheets and cut into almost any shape imaginable, these are not always convenient for every theatrical application. Another possibility is to make the foam on the job. Polyurethane foams are commonly used for this purpose. They are often used in industry for insulation in, for example, refrigerators. The liquid simply is squirted into the space between the walls and allowed to rise and solidify. The same materials can be used in the theatre.

There are two ways to use polyurethane foam ingredients. One is to buy packages or kits containing the ingredients in pressurized cans and equipped with mixing nozzles. The material is ready for use. Pressing the lever releases the materials, mixes them at the nozzle, and pours them into whatever mold or onto whatever surface you wish. The foam rapidly expands and hardens into a brown mass with a skinned surface ready to paint. The problem with this method is that it is too expensive for any but the smallest applications. The opposite extreme is to rent professional mixing machinery which consists of special pumps and a gun that mixes the material as it exits from the nozzle. This is production-line equipment, capable of pouring out many hundreds of gallons of foam in an hour. It is apt to clog if stopped too frequently. The rental cost of such equipment may run over $100 per day. However, the cost of bulk chemicals is much lower than that in kits, offsetting much of the rental cost. This process can be used to advantage if an entire setting is to be coated with foam, perhaps to create a fantastic or surrealistic setting. Respirators and protective clothing should be worn and good ventilation supplied for this process.

For very small applications such as making props, small quantities of the foam ingredients can be bought in cans and mixed by hand. If they are rapidly stirred together and immediately poured, they can be handled in this manner. Follow instructions; the process produces heat much like casting resin and could overheat.

Once hardened, polyurethane foam is one of the most inert of plastics. It is nearly flameproof in its natural state and can be made entirely flameproof when necessary. It is affected little by water and most solvents. It can be sawed or worked like wood if it is mixed to a heavy consistency. The mixture of the chemicals determines whether the foam is soft, light, and even flexible, or hard, dense, and as strong as wood. The latter is very expensive.

HAZARDS The ingredients used in making polyurethane foams can be dangerous. One of the two materials used is a member of a family of chemical compounds known as "isocyanates." These chemicals can cause severe allergic reactions if they get on the skin or are inhaled. The effect is cumulative, ultimately reaching a saturation point at which the victim can tolerate no further exposure. Admittedly this is more of a hazard in a factory where day-to-day exposure is the rule, but precautions taken in a factory are apt to be more rigorous than in a theatre shop where only occasional exposure occurs. Special masks should be worn when working with this material, and care should be taken to keep it off the skin.

Theatre workers seriously interested in using plastics and experimenting with potential new applications should not be without the book, *Plastics as an Art Form* by Thelma R. Newman.[1] It is a thorough treatment containing details on all of the processes listed here and many more, plus one of the most complete collections of information on plastics for artists to be found anywhere.

It is hoped that this brief discussion of some of the things that the theatre can do with plastics will encourage imaginative but informed experimentation with these materials. Their potential is only beginning.

---

1. Rev. ed. (Radnor, Pa.: Chilton Book Company, 1969).

PART SIX

COLOR IN THE THEATRE

From the Santa Fe Opera production of Le Rossignol *(Stravinsky). Photograph by Adam Woolfitt, courtesy of Woodfin Camp and Associates.*

INTRODUCTION

Concern for color permeates every aspect of scenography, and is seldom far from the technician's mind as he does his work. This part of the text represents an attempt to bring aesthetics and the theoretical and practical aspects of color together into one treatment. It will enable the reader to grasp better the various interrelationships among color as an aesthetic device, color as it is used by the scene painter, and color in lighting, than if these aspects were treated separately.

19
COLOR AND SCENOGRAPHY

INTRODUCTION   Color is a part of visual experience for all but those few sighted people who are completely color blind. As far as the art of the theatre is concerned, it is one of the many stimuli making up the raw material of an audience member's perception of the production—that is, part of the sensory data. Color must be abstracted by the perceiver and fitted into the artistic symbol.

Our present concern is to discover what color means to the scenographer. It is one of the elements he uses as he creates the virtual space/time world of the production. As such, it deserves considerable attention. To the scenographer, color is a very subjective thing, one that repeatedly appears during the dreamlike state of creative activity, sometimes as an aura or "sense," other times as a key *interim symbol*, i.e., a symbol that comes to signify all or a large part of the concept the creative artist is developing. Thus a scenographer might say, "This is a *blue* play," meaning that, in his mind, blue has come to stand for the play. In spite of this, blue might never appear in his design— it is an interim symbol.

The relationship between envisioned color and the virtual emotions that the scenographer is trying to create is a highly nondiscursive thing. Scenographers, like all visual artists, tend to think in form, color, line, and texture; in images, not in words. If we could pursue color through the creative process, we would probably find that it, like other elements, can be said to exist as an analogue for "felt" experience. The rightness or wrongness of a color choice depends upon the artist's inherent ability to find and develop analogues which will ultimately be expressive to others.

305

HOW DOES THE SCENOGRAPHER USE COLOR?

It is, of course, not possible to write discursively about a nondiscursive matter. Nevertheless, some generalizations can be made that may help the beginning scenographer organize his efforts.

COLOR AS A SYMBOLIC ELEMENT

Textbooks on general design—usually related more to the graphic arts than to theatre—traditionally list line, mass, form, texture, and color as the basic elements of design. The four-dimensional nature of theatre would certainly force us to add "change." However this list is composed, artists both in and out of the theatre manipulate these elements (with little concern for theorizing) into symbolic devices, and ultimately, when they are successful, into art works having the unity of a single but very complex symbol.

Our immediate concern is to investigate some of the symbolic capabilities of color as a part of the theatrical art work. Our discussion will be more complicated than that found in the graphic arts because color is a much more variable thing in theatre—it is not only a function of the various dyes and pigments applied to surfaces, fabrics, and even human skin, but it is also a function of lighting. Of course lighting is a determinant of the way any art work looks. Art museums spend fortunes on adequate lighting. But it is normally assumed by graphic artists to be a constant. This is not so in the theatre where lighting is one of the major variables, and color is one of the most important elements in that variability. Therefore, in the discussion that follows, the reader must understand that whenever "color" is mentioned, it cannot be assumed that this means pigment or dye. Just as often the color may be produced by the lighting, or it may be a combination of the effects of colored light on colored objects.

What are the capabilities of color as a symbolic element within the master symbol? Of all of the elements of stage design, color often is said to impinge most directly on the emotions. Whether or not this is true is open to question. However, it is obvious that powerful color splashed over a setting will engage most of the field of vision. It will be a strong stimulus demanding a strong reaction. Violent color contrasts, heightened by high light levels designed to augment their visibility, are also strong stimuli. They too demand a strong reaction.

This ability of color on the stage to stir the senses has often led to the development of theories of "color language." Lists have been developed asserting that "red means fire and passion," and "white stands for purity and innocence," etc. Such lists are usually self-contradictory and meaningless, although there is something to be learned by studying the reason for their existence. Color as a symbolic raw material does not have the specificity of words; it cannot "mean" as words do. There is no general dictionary for colors.

This does not mean that color is not powerful symbolic material. Rather it means that color is a kind of symbolic material different from words; it works differently and produces different symbolic effects.

The key to the symbolic function (including color) is in the concept of the artistic analogue. While it is evident that colors do not have "meaning" or carry emotions per se (if they did, we could make a dictionary of color meanings), they can become important analogues for the scenographer. Red, for example, does not automatically mean "hell fire." But if the scenographer and the director want it to mean this for the duration of the production, they have only to indicate to the audience at the first introduction of red that this is what they have in mind. From then on, the meaning will be automatic—too automatic, in fact, if the import does not increase. Note the qualification, "for the duration of the play." This is the distinction. Color symbolisms are not general; they are specific to the context in which the color is used. No audience would assume that because red meant "hell fire" in last night's production of *No Exit*, the same hue is anything more than the afterglow of a burned-down fire in tonight's drawing-room drama.

Symbols generally are established in the theatre by a number of indications given to the audience that the symbol is to be associated with the given referent. The most important indicator is *actor reaction to the symbol*. If an actor treats a display of red light like hell fire on its first appearance, the symbol will be established. Similarly, if the symbol is to grow in import with its next use, it will usually do so only with the assistance of the actors.

Color analogies, like all other artistic analogies, are not arbitrary. There must be an inherent experiential link between the potential symbol and its proposed import. Thus a block of ice would be an unlikely symbol for hell fire. The genius of the artist might be said to be in his ability to create analogical links where the ordinary eye could not see them, and to exploit what might appear to be a tenuous connection into a means of startling insight. For a symbolic connection to be artistically successful it needs two elements: (1) a base of experiential relationship between symbol and referent, and (2) the artist's ability to build upon that base to create a startling insight.

What are the symbolic potentials of color in this context? The answer is twofold: (1) colors provide an experiential sense of warmth and coolness, and (2) colors (particularly on stage) have an immediacy about them that makes their symbolic value powerful, but fleeting.

The sense of warmth or coolness engendered by color has been psychologically established. Those colors containing a large proportion of blue or green tend to lower our psychological estimate of temperature and to have a sedating effect on the emotions. Colors strong in red and yellow have the opposite effect. Intermediate colors such as yellow-green or blue-violet are ambivalent. They are "warm" or "cool" depending on what is placed in comparison with them.

The overpowering effect of a large field of color on stage has already been mentioned. Strong colors tend to be direct and immediate in their effect under any circumstances; the scale of theatre tends to enlarge this. But there is another aspect: the nature of our visual perception apparatus (see Chapter 20) is such that the eye tends to neutralize color perceptions if they are sustained for any great length of time. Although color contrast techniques can alleviate this to a considerable extent, the emotional impact of color, especially subtle color, is a fugitive thing.

Reaction to color as a symbolic device seems to be characterized by simplicity. Artists have great difficulty building the import of color into a complex, ever-growing thing. Instead its effect is inclined to be immediate, and sometimes stunning, but it soon exhausts itself. If, for example, a scenographer were to set out to use red light on the set every time the literary symbol "red" appears in *Macbeth*, he would run into serious trouble. As a literary symbol, "red" appears over and over again in the script. To the reader, who may fill in his own imagery at each instance, the effect is cumulative and contributes much to the total artistic impact. But converted into the symbolic use of red light on stage, the symbol becomes ridiculous. It would probably provoke laughter long before the end of the play. The reason is clear. The color itself is not capable of the same degree of symbolic complexity as the literary symbol. On the other hand, the judicious use of red light at the climax of *Macbeth* could be a great stroke of theatre. The power and immediacy may be just what the production needs to raise the climax to the level of tragic fulfillment.

ATTRIBUTES OF COLOR

Texts and theories of color that focus on the problems encountered when one attempts to bring together the various factors that influence color harmony (mainly in the area of pigment color) list three basic attributes: hue, value, and chroma. Since these terms will be important throughout the discussion to follow, they are defined below.

Hue

Hue determines which of the color sensors in the eye react, and to what degree. Thus it may also be defined as that characteristic which distinguishes the color from a gray of the same value (brilliance). A physicist might define "hue" by noting that each separate mixture of wavelengths which is perceptible by the eye is a hue. We may also say, somewhat loosely, that hue is what causes the normal eye to distinguish red from green or blue from violet.

Value

Value may be somewhat scientifically described as the total reflectance of a color, including all wavelengths in the visible spectrum. Actually, since these terms are all relative to what the normal human eye sees, the sensitivity variations of the eye to different wavelengths must also be taken into account. Value often is described by painters as an indication of the amount of black or white mixed with a pigment.

Chroma

Chroma refers to the intensity of a color (hue) within a given value. For example, a red of constant hue may have the same value (reflectance) through a wide range of chroma, from a brilliant red through red-gray to pure gray of the same reflectance. (Remember that reflectance in this sense refers to the sum of *all* visible wavelengths present.) Chroma is the property that allows us to say, "This red is redder than that red."

Ignoring certain effects which dimming has on the output of white light, one might say that operating a dimmer changes the chroma of a light. By contrast, dimming in or out another instrument which produces white light over the same area would change the value of the lighted surface. Changing gel would, of course, change hue.

MUNSELL SYSTEM

Because of the hopelessly tangled mass of popular color names that may refer to several different colors at the same time and may have different meanings to different people, those concerned with accurate indication of color such as decorators, paint manufacturers, fabric makers, and specialists in illumination design, have resorted to the development of complicated graphs which interrelate the three attributes of color to each other and thereby make it possible to indicate any color accurately by means of reference to the coordinates of the graph. The best known of these is the Munsell system.

This system is based on the creation of a "color solid," sometimes also called a "color tree" because of the treelike appearance of a typical three-dimensional arrangement of sample color chips according to the system. Unfortunately for the theatre, the Munsell system has not been developed with lighting in mind. A standard color tree almost inevitably leaves off most of the stronger readings, which are apt to occur in lighting, because the color chips are pigments that depend on their ability to reflect incident light for their maximum value readings. The Munsell color tree is valid only when viewed under certain well-specified color temperatures and levels of light. Chroma, in particular, is limited in its indication on the color tree by this fact. Theoretically chroma could be extended to infinity by simply adding more and more light. Practically, there are limits beyond which the human eye will cease to see increase in chroma. Value may be similarly extended.

Neither suppliers of lighting filters (gels) nor suppliers of theatrical pigments have paid much attention to the accurate notation that the Munsell system offers. Theatrical pigments are referred to by their traditional names such as "burnt sienna" and "ochre." Color media are sold by a system of names and numbers that are not standardized from manufacturer to manufacturer. Any comparison with the Munsell system (or extensions from the Munsell system) must be made by the user. Nevertheless, the way in which the Munsell system organizes the relationships between the attributes of color will be helpful to the student learning the art of mixing paint.

FOCUS OF ATTENTION AND BALANCE

As the scenographer works with color, he wants variations on the above three attributes. In doing so he seeks two things simultaneously: *focus of attention* and *balance*. Focus of attention is important because scenography is an interpretive art; the scenographer must work with the actors and the director to bring the script into artistic fulfillment. One of the keys to this process is to cause the audience to be looking at the right character or characters at the right time.

Balance is a more abstract consideration. It is a sense of repose or equilibrium produced by causing the eye to move with equal effort in every direction about the center of vision, and in the case of color, to exert approximately equal energy in its perception as the eye moves. A broad field of low-value color will be balanced, although it may be dull. A considerable area of moderate-value color may be balanced by a much smaller area of more intense color further from the center of vision.

Since the scenographer is working as a dependent artist (he depends on the actors and other elements to complete his "picture"), his color scheme will be unfinished until the actors are on stage. Thus his color scheme may provide the background elements which will be accented by costumed actors and further developed by the lighting. Color balance is inextricable from both acting and lighting because the scenographer is not creating a static picture in which he can arbitrarily arrange accents or counterbalances. The actors will be the accents, and the precise focus of attention at any given second will be controlled by actor position and lighting. The setting provides the large masses of color, line, and form within which the accents work.

This concern with accent and focus is where the scenographer's concern with costumes originates. Although many scenographers will not do the details of the costume design themselves, they must maintain close control over costume color if it is to function in proper relationship to the total color scheme. Of all the areas of color, costume is perhaps the easiest in which to work out color symbolism. This is because the key to the symbolic meaning is the actor. The very fact that a character wears a given color establishes a symbolic relationship for the duration of the play. Thus if a kingly character wears purple while wearing a crown and being treated like a king, and later wears purple with no other clues as to his present identity, the purple will continue to symbolize royalty. The same purple worn by a character not established as a king would probably not carry the same meaning.

Color Harmony

Balance and harmony are closely interrelated. *Color harmony* results when masses of color are so arranged and the colors so chosen that the relationships between the hues are pleasurable. Given the eye of an artist, no colors may be said to be incompatible — it is a question of how they are used. There are some categories of color harmony worth mentioning for the beginner because they will explain terms he is apt to hear, and perhaps provide a starting place in the study of color balance. They are not rules, but merely categories of color interrelationships that often work well.

MONOCHROMES   When only different values of the same hue are used in a setting, it may be described as *monochromatic*. The stage looks as though only one color plus black and white were used, and that the black or white was tinted with the chosen color. As stage designs, monochromatic schemes may be striking, but like many other color efforts, the effect may be fleeting. The human seeing apparatus tends to see all of a color as none of a color. Hence monochromatic settings often are accented by a color harmonious with, but different from, the general color. This removes them from the category of pure monochromatic (the skin tones of the actors also do this if one wants to be precise about the category), but makes for a more interesting picture.

RELATED COLOR SCHEMES   Analogous or related color schemes are those worked up from two or three hues which are very close to each other on the spectrum or on the color wheel. For example, one might work in a set of yellow-orange, orange, and orange-red. By varying the value and chroma of these three colors, an elaborate and potentially interesting color scheme might be worked out.

COMPLEMENTARY SCHEMES   In their simplest and most powerful form, complementary colors produce opposite reactions in the eye. If their sensations are mixed in the eye, white results. If one is presented by itself, it tends to form afterimages matching the other. If complementary pigments are mixed, they neutralize, producing gray or black. These pairs serve to heighten each other, each appearing brighter in comparison with the other than it would by itself. An example of complementary colors would be green and magenta.

Other combinations, not as directly opposite, but still far from related are possible. For example, one might choose two colors that are analogous and then combine them with their two complements. This would be a *double complementary* harmony. Another possibility is to choose colors about a third of the way around the traditional color wheel (Plate XI), such as red, yellow, and blue, or green, orange, and purple. These are called "triads."

It should be obvious that the mere choice of these colors in no way guarantees color harmony. Proportion of color, texture, location on the setting, and relationship to accents are all part of what determines success or failure.

20
PHYSICS AND PHYSIOLOGY OF COLOR

INTRODUCTION In this chapter it is our purpose to understand how color is related to light as a physical phenomenon, how our color perception apparatus works, and how the working of this apparatus determines the way we manipulate color on stage. To make these subjects clear, we will have to clarify some of the confusion that results from color names that are used indiscriminately to refer to quite different colors. We begin with some definitions.

DEFINITION OF COLOR

Color is a sensation produced by the human seeing apparatus (the eye, optic nerve, and the brain) under the stimulus of certain wavelengths of light. These wavelengths fall in a narrow band in the middle of a vast array of radiant phenomena known as the "radiant energy spectrum." This spectrum contains forms of energy ranging from miles-long electrical waves to extremely short X-rays. All of these have the property of moving through space at an extremely high speed, and exhibit characteristics of both wave motion and particulate (discrete particles) radiation. Only a tiny band of these radiations can be seen by the human eye.

Light travels through a vacuum at a speed of about 186,280 miles per second; it moves only slightly slower in air. It can also travel through other materials such as glass, plastics, water, and the like, but at lower speeds. Physicists commonly refer to light by its "wavelength," given as an actual measurement. Wavelengths for visible light range from 4/10,000 of a millimeter (blue) to 7/10,000 of a millimeter (red). Other color sensations are produced by intermediate wavelengths and by combinations of wavelengths.

If we arrange a display of all visible light according to wavelength, we will get what looks like a segment taken from a rainbow. It is known as the "visible spectrum."

313

HOW WE SEE COLOR

Examination of the seeing apparatus instead of what is seen will reveal the explanation of some things we have long taken for granted. The eye is equipped with two categories of sensors, known as "rods" and "cones," because of their appearance under the microscope. The rods sense the presence or absence of light without regard for wavelength. They are highly sensitive and can detect very minute amounts of light. The cones, which are less sensitive, produce color sensations. This explains why color vision deteriorates in near-darkness; only the rods are sensitive enough to operate in these conditions.

Much careful research has revealed the fact that there are three kinds of cones:

1. Red sensitive cones are sensitive to wavelengths ranging from the deepest visible red through those known as yellow
2. Green sensitive cones are sensitive to wavelengths ranging from yellow through green and including blue-green
3. Blue sensitive cones are sensitive to wavelengths ranging from blue-green through to the deepest visible blue

The sensitivity of each kind of cone varies in a bell-shaped curve peaking at red, green, and blue respectively. All of our color sensations are derived from stimuli produced by one or more kinds of cones acting at the same time.

If all three kinds of cones are stimulated at the same time and to roughly the same degree, the subject sees "white." The following are other important sensations:

Red cones only = red sensation
Red cones plus green cones = yellow sensation
Green cones only = green sensation
Green cones plus blue cones = blue-green sensation
Blue cones only = blue sensation
Blue cones plus red cones = purple or magenta sensation

COLOR TERMINOLOGY

Before we examine the ways in which these sensations may be generated, we must deal with a problem of terminology. Otherwise our discussion will be impossible to follow. Physicists have little doubt about what we see or what wavelength(s) produce the sensation. They have exact instruments that can analyze light down to a fraction of a wave-length, determining exactly what wavelengths are present in what quantity. However, the names nonphysicists give to these sensations are a quite different matter. The eye can distinguish perhaps as many as 7.5 million hues. There are at least that many names for color sensa-tions, and they often are applied carelessly to several somewhat similar sensations. For example, what comes to mind when the word "red" is mentioned? This word may refer to any color from red-orange to red-purple, and in a wide variety of value and chroma. Even the names we recall from childhood are not exact. How many good "primary reds" have you seen in a paint store? If our discussion of color is to succeed, we must dispel some of this confusion. The only solution is to resort to the spectrum and to actual samples of the colors we are talking about—names alone will not do the job.

To make good sense of the following discussion you should have at least one of the following sets of theatrical primary color filters avail-able (see Table 20-1). These filters should be observed by looking through them at a clean white surface illuminated with light from a theatrical spotlight lamp. Your instructor can help you make these arrangements.

Table 20-1

Additive Primaries	Roscolar	Roscolux	Cinemoid	Gelatran
Red primary	923	—[a]	6	08
Green primary	974	91	39	53
Blue primary	963	80	20	64

[a] No good red primary available.

You will note, if you have more than one brand of primaries available, that the hue and saturation of the various reds, greens, and blues do not exactly match. A number of good primary sets can be selected because the eye does not peak sharply on a single wavelength, but instead re-acts to a rather wide band. The saturation variations depend on the manufacturer's estimate of a reasonable compromise between effi-ciency of the color filter (how much light it allows to come through) and the purity of the color.

If possible, compare the above colors with a good set of painter's primaries named "red," "yellow," and "blue." You will find that al-though the names "red" and "blue" refer to both light filter colors and the painter's primaries, the colors are far from the same. The light filter colors in Table 20-2 closely match painter's primaries.

Table 20-2

Subtractive (painter's) Primaries	Cinemoid	Roscolar	Roscolux
Red	13	937	45
Yellow	1	908	12
Blue	16	962	76

It will seem almost a coincidence that the painter's "yellow" matches a light filter yellow of the same name.

ADDITIVE AND SUBTRACTIVE SYSTEMS

Having examined all of these colors and noted how they match up, despite the discrepancy in names, we can begin to summarize the results. The red, green, and blue filters are primary colors that match the sensitivity peaks of the three color receptors of the eye. These are sometimes called the "light primaries" or "additive primaries." The word "primary" in color terminology refers to a set of colors from which all other colors can be mixed, but the primaries themselves cannot be made by mixing other colors within the system. The painter's "red," "yellow," and "blue" are often called "pigment primaries," "painter's primaries," or "subtractive primaries." Since opaque painter's colors are harder to manufacture in pure form than the dyes used in materials such as Cinemoid, Roscolar, or Roscolux, mixtures of paint colors do not follow theory closely; they have a tendency to produce muddy results instead.

In order to standardize our terminology, when color names are used in our discussion hereafter, they will refer to additive system terminology unless the qualifier, "painter's" is used. That is, "red" will refer to the color within the range of the reds listed in Table 20-1; greens to those in Table 20-1, etc. If we refer to "painter's colors," we will be referring to those in Table 20-2.

With terminology under control, we are ready to proceed with our explanation of how the various sensations happen and how we use this information on stage. The three simplest color sensations are those produced by exposing the eye to narrow bands of wavelengths that match the peaks of the sensitivity curves for the three types of cones. A band of red wavelengths will produce a sensation, "red"; a band of green wavelengths will produce "green"; and so on. This is the only way these sensations can normally be produced, a property that meets the definition of "primary." Other color sensations are more complicated, involving the stimulation of two or more types of cones. As mentioned above, the approximately equal stimulation of all three varieties of cones causes the sensation of "white." This can be accomplished in two ways: by exposing the eye to three bands of primary wavelengths at the same time (red, green, and blue), or by exposing the eye to a mixture of all visible wavelengths of approximately equal strength. The result will be "white," and the eye will not be able to tell the difference between the two types of stimuli without help.

Still other sensations occur when the eye is exposed to mixtures of two primary bands at the same time. They are as follows:

Red plus green = yellow
Green plus blue = blue-green
Blue plus red = magenta

The entire set of relationships between the stimuli and the results can be diagramed in the form of a triangle (see Figure 20-1).

Note that the diagram reveals how the colors referred to in the two "systems" (additive and subtractive) really interlock into one system when terminology is clarified. This becomes even clearer when we examine the way in which pigments or dyes function. First, however, we must note certain important aspects of the color sensations and the wavelengths that produce them. Examination of a visible spectrum (e.g., a rainbow) will reveal that there are wavelengths that produce

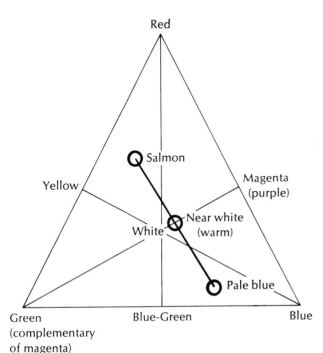

Figure 20-1. The Color Triangle. This simplified diagram of additive color relationships is adequate for most theatrical purposes. Mixtures of colored light may be plotted and the resultant determined as follows: (1) Locate each color on the triangle by estimating its color content. A pale blue and salmon are shown in the example; (2) Draw a line between the colors. This line will represent all possible mixtures of this pair of colors; (3) Bisect the line if you are determining the resultant of mixing equal (to the eye) portions of the colors. In this case the midpoint will represent the resultant color. Other mixtures can be determined by dividing the connecting line according to the amount of each color in the mixture—e.g., if there are two parts of salmon for each part of blue, the resultant will be found approximately at the point two-thirds of the way toward salmon.

sensations ranging from red through orange, yellow, yellow-green, green, blue-green, to blue. No single band can produce the sensation "purple" or "magenta." Only a combination of the stimuli, red and blue, can do this. We therefore call this color a "nonspectral" hue because it cannot be produced by a single segment of the spectrum. There are other nonspectral hues but the same sensation can also be produced by combinations of spectral bands. The two of importance to us are yellow and blue-green. Both of these sensations can be produced in two ways as follows:

Yellow—single band of yellow wavelengths or roughly equal quantities of red and green

Blue-green—single band of blue-green wavelengths or roughly equal quantities of blue and green

Unless assisted, the eye cannot distinguish between spectral and nonspectral hues. We will have occasion to use both types of color sensation on stage.

As we have seen, "additive" and "subtractive" refer to the effects of different kinds of color mixing. *Additive mixing* involves the blending of sensations in the eye. This can be done in several ways. The one we have discussed so far is the simplest and the most common in stage lighting; the eye is presented with both stimuli at the same time over the entire field of vision. Another method is to present the eye with tiny dots of color representing the two stimuli. If the dots are small enough, the sensations blend. This is the method of pointillism that painters use, and is also the basis of some systems of color printing. A third method is to present the eye with the sensations in rapid sequence. Because the eye retains its sensations for a moment, this causes them to blend. Color television works on a combination of the last two methods. A fourth method, handy to the lighting man, is to present one color sensation to each eye. Try this by holding a sample of pale blue color medium over one eye and a sample of pale straw over the other. Look at a white surface. They should blend to make a near-white if your eyes are of equal strength. The blend may fluctuate from one color through the mix to the other color or it may remain stable. This depends on the individual's eyes.

Subtractive mixing is what you have probably been calling "color mixing" all of your life. It is most commonly done by stirring two colors of paint in a bucket. Since this paint-mixing process is complicated somewhat by certain characteristics of opaque pigments, the process will be easier to understand if we first consider another type of subtractive mixing—that which takes place when two transparent filters of good purity are superimposed.

Plate IX. Additive Color Mixing. Three pools of light overlap on a white screen; regular stage-quality filters (Cinemoid) were used to produce primary colors. The white light is synthesized by mixing stimuli produced in the eye by the three primary colors. Adding stimuli causes the brain to respond as though the eye were stimulated by all wavelengths in equal (to the eye) portions. The secondary colors are synthesized by the combination of stimuli from two of the three primary colors mixed in equal (to the eye) portions. This realistic reproduction illustrates what may be expected from mixtures of stage-quality primaries rather than light filtered through the best-quality (and most expensive) filters. These cyan and yellow secondaries are not exact matches for their spectral counterparts because of the impurity of the filters. (Lamp color temperature was approximately 2950° K.) Photography by William Huling.

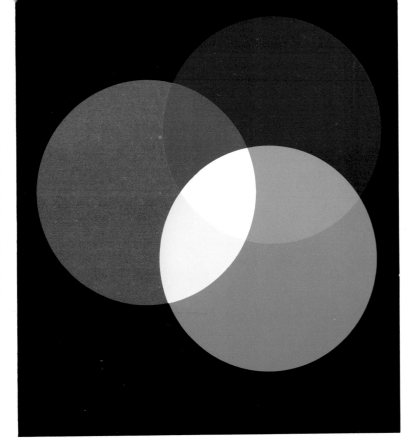

Plate X. Subtractive Color Mixing. This plate shows the manner in which pigments operate by selective transmission and absorption. It reproduces an artist's rendering of what will be seen when three filters, each capable of transmitting two of the primary colors, have been overlapped. These filters, which match the secondaries formed in Plate IX, are ma-genta (transmits red and blue), often called "red" by painters; cyan (transmits blue and green), often called "blue"; and yellow (transmits red and green). These pigments, usually under the names "red," "blue," and yellow are the familiar primary colors of painters. Note that the mixture of all three pigment primaries results in black, the absence of light, the consequence of blocking out or subtracting of all wavelengths.

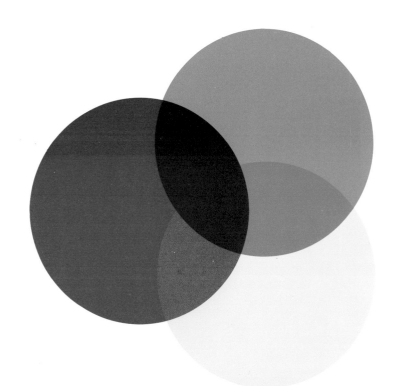

Plate XI. A Painter's Color Wheel. This color wheel has been based on frequently used scene paint colors which are available from a number of manufacturers in either dry pigments or as premixed pastes. Color names will not always be consistent from supplier to supplier. Color harmonies may be worked out on this chart. For example, numbers 5, 3, and 16 might form a related scheme. Courtesy Oleson Company, Los Angeles, California.

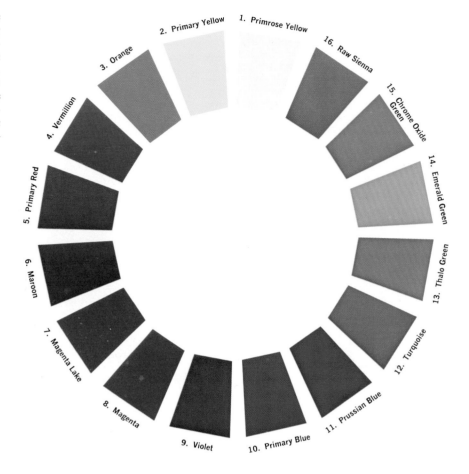

1. Primrose Yellow
2. Primary Yellow
3. Orange
4. Vermillion
5. Primary Red
6. Maroon
7. Magenta Lake
8. Magenta
9. Violet
10. Primary Blue
11. Prussian Blue
12. Turquoise
13. Thalo Green
14. Emerald Green
15. Chrome Oxide Green
16. Raw Sienna

Plate XII. The Mikado. This production at Northern Illinois University, DeKalb, was designed by Richard Arnold. Note the airy quality of the step units which are supported by special pipe arrangements. Photo courtesy Richard Arnold.

Plate XIII. **The Automobile Grave-** *yard (Arabal). This production at California State University, Northridge, utilized laminated plastic as the main scenic material. After lamination the plastic pieces were stained with aniline dyes to obtain the rich color. Director: George Gunkle. Setting: Lawrence Lester.*

Plate XIV. Laser Interference Pattern Projection. This is one of an infinite variety of images possible. It was made by combining interference patterns from laser light. Such images have no depth of field, but vary in nature with distance from the laser projector. Courtesy Wolfgang Bergfeld and Gerhardt Winzer, Siemens Corporation, Germany.

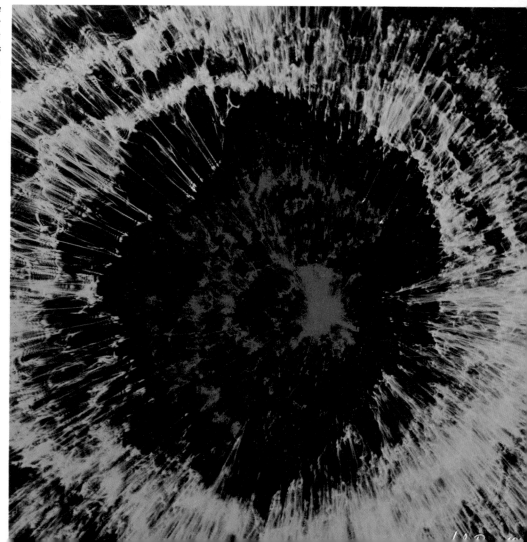

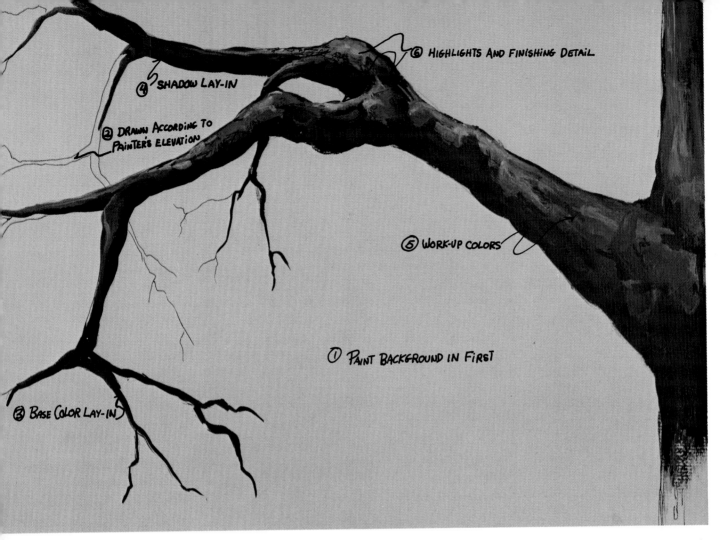

Plate XV. Detail Scene Painting. This plate shows the various stages in the development of a finished piece of detailed scene painting. Note the stages indicated. Painting by Kate Keleher.

Plate XVI. The Rake's Progress (Stravinski). This setting was modeled entirely from Styrofoam. Large stacks of glued blocks were cut with a hot wire. The surfaces were then etched with amylacetate and metallic powder. Production at California State University, Northridge. Director: David Scott. Scenography by author.

Consider what would happen if we selected two pieces of theatrical color medium, one a match for a painter's blue primary and the other a match for painter's yellow primary. If we were to examine the transmission characteristics of the painter's blue with a spectroscope,[1] we would find that the material transmits blue light, green light, and blue-green light. A similar analysis of painter's yellow would show that it transmits red, yellow, and green light. We might diagram the painter's blue filter as follows:

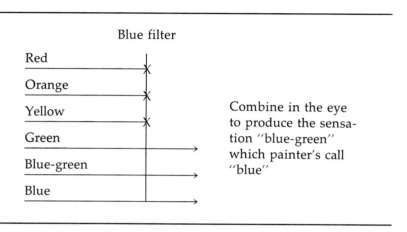

A yellow filter, similarly analyzed, would come out as follows:

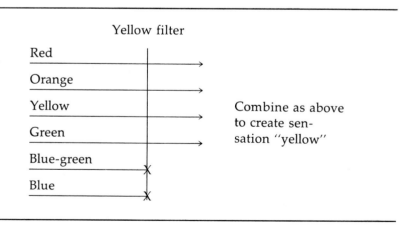

1. A spectroscope is an instrument that breaks light into its component wavelengths. It makes a spectrum.

If we superimpose the two filters, we combine their absorptive properties:

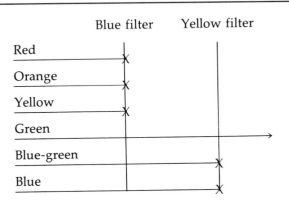

Note that it makes no difference if you interchange the filters. We have subtracted wavelengths until only green remains—thus, the *subtractive system*. All pigment or dye mixtures can be shown to work in the same manner.

Opaque and Transparent Colorants

Paints, dyes, and similar materials may be termed "colorants." They have the property of altering the wavelength content of light which either passes through them or is reflected from their surface. Those that function by allowing some wavelengths to pass while others are absorbed are termed "transparent" or "translucent," depending on whether or not the waves of light are also diffused in passage. If they are diffused, the material is translucent. Of course opacity and transparency are not totally separate phenomena. The most transparent material reflects some altered light back toward the source, and many opaque materials allow some light to pass through them. However, materials that generally are used for their selective transmission are categorized as "transparent" or "translucent," and those normally used for their selective reflective ability are "opaque."

We have already examined the way in which selectively transparent materials sort out wavelengths; we must now investigate how opaque pigments work. The varnished top of a desk will serve as an example of a typical opaque surface. As you examine this surface, you will find that there are two phenomena happening at the same time. First, light is being reflected off the surface of the varnish just as it might be reflected off the surface of a clean piece of clear glass. Note that such light is not changed in wavelength content. It retains its original color. This is the way highlights appear on all shiny surfaces whether satin fabric, metal, or painted. This surface reflection may be prominent as in glossy surfaces, or it may be nearly nonexistent as in the case of a surface coated with matte paint or a soft fabric.

The second phenomenon is the one that commands our attention. Much of the incident light passes through the surface of the varnish and penetrates into the wood or colored layer below. This light, as it penetrates, is filtered by the same process that causes selective absorption in transparent materials. Eventually some part of the light is reflected upward and escapes the surface (see Figure 20-2). This light is said to have been "colored" by the opaque pigment. It has been selectively reflected. Note that the process actually depends on a certain degree of transparency on the part of the flakes of pigment, which act as tiny color filters. Obviously the more efficient this filtering and reflecting process, the greater the reflectance of the surface.

The only difference in the effect of combining pigments is a bucket as opposed to superimposing filters is that the remaining light passes *through* the filters, but is *reflected back* in the case of pigments. The effect on the color of the incident light is the same in either case. It is also quite obvious that neither opaque nor transparent colorants have the power to add anything to the light present. These filtering effects always result in less light passing through the object or being reflected from it than striking it—hence the term, "subtractive mixing."

"Transparency," "translucency," and "opacity" are all relative terms, each really blending into the other. A film of material may transmit part of the light striking it, filtering it as it passes, and partially diffusing it to give a mixed effect of transparency and translucency. Some of the light may also be reflected from the film, both as surface reflection that will experience no color change, and as selective reflection that will alter the color of the light so reflected.

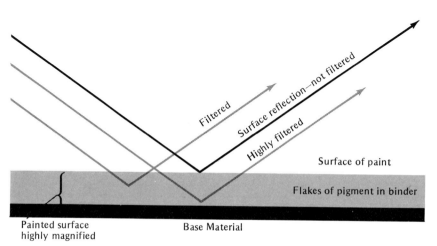

Figure 20-2. Selective Reflection. This diagram shows in a simplified manner how pigments selectively reflect certain wavelengths and absorb others.

Filtered

Surface reflection—not filtered

Highly filtered

Surface of paint

Flakes of pigment in binder

Painted surface highly magnified

Base Material

COLORED LIGHT ON COLORED OBJECTS

The color triangle plus your knowledge of the nature of pigments will tell you what the effect of a colored light will be on a colored object. Actually most of the information is in the triangle itself. We have noted that the painter's primaries reflect light as follows:

Painter's red—reflects light primary red, and light primary blue
Painter's yellow—reflects light primary red, light primary green, and spectral yellow
Painter's blue—reflects light primary blue, light primary green, and spectral blue-green

Pigments matching the light primaries reflect only those colors. Table 20-3 summarizes this information. Given this information, which may be inferred from the triangle, the observer can closely estimate the reflectance of many other colors and work out the result of illuminating them with various hues of light.

Table 20-3 Colors Resulting from Colored Light on Colored Pigment

| | | Incident Light Colors | | | | | |
		Red	Green	Blue	Yellow	Magenta	Blue-green
Pigment Colors	Red	Red	Black	Black	Red	Red	Black
	Green	Black	Green	Black	Green	Black	Green
	Blue	Black	Black	Blue	Black	Blue	Blue
	Yellow	Red	Green	Black	Yellow	Red	Green
	Magenta	Red	Black	Blue	Red	Magenta	Blue
	Blue-green	Black	Green	Blue	Green	Blue	Blue-green

THEORETICAL AND PRACTICAL RESULTANTS

The reader may have noticed that no allowance was made for the fact that painter's pigments are not chosen for their ability to reflect selectively only those colors that they theoretically should reflect. The transparent filters used in lighting, while intended to be as pure as economically possible, also allow wavelengths to pass that are not intended, particularly red wavelengths. Thus there will be two answers to a "colored light on colored object" problem: theoretical and practical. The theoretical answer assumes that all filters and selective reflectors are pure. Theoretically, red light should cause a painter's blue pigment to look black. The practical answer would take into account the faults in the colorants. Red primary filters are usually quite pure although some leak a little blue light. On the other hand, few painter's blue primaries absorb all the red light that strikes them. The practical result would probably be a dull reddish brown representing the red reflected by the paint.

When the colored light merely is tinted instead of filtered to a deep hue, the effect of the light on a pigment will be merely a trend. A pale red tint would "take down" (reduce the chroma) of the painter's blue pigment.

Those working with color problems must remember that pigments never add to the color of a light, they can only take away. Thus a coat of red paint can add no red to a setting illuminated by light devoid of red.

ACCENTING AND DEEMPHASIZING

It is frequently necessary to change the attention-getting power of colors on stage by adjusting the lighting. This is usually easier and cheaper than reupholstering or redyeing. The rules are simple: to accent a color, give it more of those wavelengths that it reflects best, but give its surroundings enough of the rest of the spectrum to maintain color contrast. Thus one might add more red light to an already warmly lighted stage if one wished to "bring forward" (accent) a red costume.

Reducing emphasis works in the opposite way: remove from the pigment to be deemphasized those colors it reflects best. Thus, reducing the red light on stage would reduce the emphasis on the red costume mentioned above.

SEPARATING OR INTEGRATING COLORS

The same theory of color can be used to control the contrast between two rather closely related colors. It may be necessary, for example, to bring the color of an upholstered chair and that of a costume closer together to avoid what the scenographer feels is an unpleasant color contrast. This can be done by choosing a tint of lighting that both colors reflect equally well. If an orange-red and a blue-red must be brought together, they should be lighted with a tint of pure red, a color they both reflect well.

Separating pigment colors works in the opposite way. Choose a light color which one of the pigments reflects significantly better than the other. This will then become the emphasized color at the expense of the other. Thus, lighting the above combination with yellowish tints would emphasize the yellow-red over the blue-red.

COLORED LIGHT AND MAKEUP

The above methods of emphasizing and deemphasizing relate to makeup as much as they do to pigments on canvas or in cloth. Moreover, the makeup artist must consider the natural color of the skin as another pigment. One frequently hears complaints that the lighting "sucks the red out of the makeup." This is a rather crude way of saying that red light is reducing the contrast between skin and rouge. If the light has been chosen as a design necessity, the makeup must be increased in contrast.

In cases of extremely strong color in the lighting (a romantic "moonlight," for example) the makeup artist may find that the light is so deficient in red that rouge looks black. Usually this can be remedied by using bluish-red makeup and sneaking a bit of purple light into the moonlight.

There will be nothing mysterious about lighting and makeup if the color content of the light and the reflectance of the makeup are analyzed just as other pigment-light relationships should be. With this understanding of the physics and physiology of color, we are ready to investigate how the scenographer uses subtractive color mixing as he mixes paint colors.

**21
SCENE
PAINTING**

INTRODUCTION Scene painting is one of the oldest theatrical crafts. During the nineteenth century it was almost synonymous with scenery itself; the wing and drop settings of that era were little more than surfaces to carry painted images.

Late in the nineteenth century illusionistic scene painting fell into disrepute, and the wing and drop setting all but disappeared. Adolphe Appia pointed out that actors are three-dimensional objects who move through three-dimensional space. Painted illusion, which follows the rules of linear perspective, is two-dimensional—there is no way that a live actor can enter parts of a room painted on canvas or sit on a painted chair. Moreover light that is satisfactory for painted illusion should be as shadowless as possible. All shadows have already been painted into the scenery, and real shadows will only reveal defects in the painted surface. Lighting the actor presents the opposite situation. Directional light is needed to reveal the real contours of the actor's face and body. Without revelation of these contours, the actor's expressive value is diminished. Thus the nineteenth-century purpose of scene painting—the creation of the illusion of space through the art of perspective—has fallen into disuse. With it has gone what might be termed the "golden era" of the scenic artist. Nineteenth-century painters prided themselves on being as capable of creating vast scenic illusion as their compatriots, the landscape painters of the period. They were artists in their own right whose work often vied with that of the actors for the attention of the audience. A few examples remain at such places as the Royal Theatre in Drottningholm, Sweden.

More recently, as the result of the writings of Appia, Craig, and others, scene painting has at times been looked upon as existing mainly to provide suitable reflective surfaces for stage lighting. Craig's concept of "painting with light" is an extreme example of this approach: the only purpose of paint is to provide a surface of the proper reflectance for the lighting which provides color and pattern. Unfortunately painting with light tends to "paint" the actors with the same light as the set, or vice versa.

After the first effects of the revolution against painted illusion died down, the art of scene painting regained some of its lost prestige. In the current eclectic mode of theatrical design, images are created on stage in a wide variety of ways, one of the most important being scene painting. However, the modern scene painter no longer works with artistic abandon ignoring the effects of lighting, nor with the goal of stunning the audience with effects so powerful that the actors disappear in the background. In brief, there is no substitute for the artistic contributions that scene painting can make to the modern stage, but painting is no longer a substitute for three-dimensional space.

Sometimes painting results in the illusion of three-dimensionality where only two dimensions exist, but this occurs only on parts of the stage, particularly in semishadowed space and *not* in conflict with the actor. At other times the painting serves to finish surfaces whose main function is to reflect light. At still other times (much to the satisfaction of master painters), the once serious intent of fooling the eye into believing that three dimensions existed where only two were present, has been treated as a stylistic element. Olio drops, wings, fancy ground rows, and other paraphernalia of the nineteenth century are reproduced. But they are no longer intended to fool the eye. Rather, they serve to set the style and era of the theatrical piece. The audience is asked to accept them for what they are, a theatrical device—a part of a virtual world.

Modern theatre technology offers a scale of virtuality to the scenographer. The most mobile of images available is that made by scenic projection. Such images may move, blend, fuse into each other, or they may be made to exist in three dimensions in space. Somewhat less mobile, but still highly flexible, are the images created for the audience by three-dimensional objects such as abstract sculptured elements, ramps, steps, and the like. These also may move, albeit more ponderously than projected images. Finally, there are painted images which are firmly fixed to the surface that carries them. Such surfaces may move, but the relationship between their movement and the painted images they carry is a mechanical one.

Each of these image-making techniques carries its own special virtuality. *The expressive value of painting grows out of the close and visible relationship between the surface and the painted image.* The special "permanence" of the painted image as it is related to its surface is at the foundation of the aesthetic of scene painting. Given acceptance of the image-surface interlock, the development of the illusion of the third dimension proceeds within the special virtuality thereby created.

In this chapter, we shall examine the tools and techniques by which scene painting is accomplished.

THE PAINT SHOP

Like the other shops described in this text, the paint shop will probably be combined with the scene shop in most theatre plants. The requirements will be the same as far as equipment is concerned, whether combined or separate. But painting takes a lot of space—a fact that cannot be rationalized away. If this space is not available in the paint or scene shop, it will have to be found elsewhere. Often it will be found on the stage itself. This poor compromise results in a messy stage and in many conflicts over usage.

The ideal space for scene painting should be large enough to allow crews to lay entire walls of settings or large drops out flat on the floor and nail them down (this implies a wooden floor). It should be well lit, preferably with light of the same color temperature as stage lighting (2950–3200°K). There is no real advantage in providing daylight, although this is often done. In any case, there should be facilities for providing stage lighting of whatever color is predominant in the final design.

Because more and more settings are being made of three-dimensional units, the paint shop should have a ceiling high enough and a floor large enough to allow the scenery to be set up for painting. There should be easy access from this shop to the stage. Since painting is a relatively quiet activity, theatre architects may be reminded that the painting area often makes a good buffer zone between a noisy scene shop and the stage. There is also good logic in the flow of materials: lumber into the scene shop; the constructed scenery to the paint shop; finally, the finished product to the stage. A well-equipped paint shop will contain the major tools and equipment discussed below.

PAINT FRAME

Although not an absolute necessity, a paint frame (Figure 21-1) will save time and make work easier, and is preferred by many scene painters. Much but not all scene painting can be done with the flats or drops mounted vertically on this frame instead of lying on the floor. A paint frame is a movable framework upon which the items to be painted are mounted. It moves up and down through a slot in the floor, allowing painters standing on the floor to reach all parts of the scenery without climbing. The paint frame usually is equipped with counterweights and driven by a simple winch arrangement. To be completely effective, the frame should be somewhat larger than the largest drop to be painted on it. This dimension will be determined by the size of the

Figure 21-1. Paint Frame. This framework is counterweighted much like a batten on stage. Set pieces are attached to it, usually by means of double head nails. The frame is then moved up or down into a well in the floor to gain access to whatever part the painter wishes. Ideally, the paint frame should be sized to handle the largest drop ever needed on stage. Some professional paint frames consist of two units identical to this, operating back-to-back in the same well.

proscenium opening and the depth of the stage. A smaller paint frame, while not useless by any means, will limit the painting of full stage drops. Most painters will prefer painting the drops on the floor to the difficulties encountered when an attempt is made to fold over part of the drop in order to do it piecemeal on a frame that is too small.

The well into which the paint frame lowers should be accessible to allow cleaning and recovery of dropped tools. The slot in the floor should be wide enough to allow the passage of flats with three-dimensional trim, but not wide enough to form a hazard.

Although it takes a lot of space, a painter's "boomerang," a multilevel scaffold on wheels, can be devised to allow the painting of drops placed against a wall or even hanging from battens on stage. It is, however, an inferior substitute for a paint frame.

PAINT MIXER

Scene paint can be entirely mixed by hand, although it is a tedious process. Another method is to attach some type of mixing tool to a variable speed electric hand drill and use it to mix the paint. This tends to throw paint if the drill is run too fast, and often results in the mixer striking the sides of the bucket, an occurrence that will tend to twist the drill out of the operator's hand. Finally, using a hand-held electric device to stir water-mixed paint in a metal can while the painter stands on what inevitably will be a damp floor constitutes a potential shock hazard. Good grounding and proper use of high-quality equipment will help to reduce this hazard, but a better method is to use the paint mixer (Figure 21-2). It operates from a compressed air line which eliminates the shock hazard. Since it is firmly mounted in place, there is far less chance of the impeller touching anything but paint. Its speed is easily and consistently adjustable by means of the air valve, which is not susceptible to sudden jerks from the operator's hand. It is powerful enough to mix the heaviest paint.

TINTER-MIXER

A tinter-mixer is a standard item in most commercial paint stores. It allows accurate formulation of paint by means of a metering device which adds precisely measured tiny amounts of concentrated color to the mix. The tinting stocks are usually kept in special containers which are part of the tinter-mixer.

SPRAYING EQUIPMENT

Spraying equipment, like the paint mixer, depends on the presence of a supply of compressed air in the plant. If such a supply is not available,

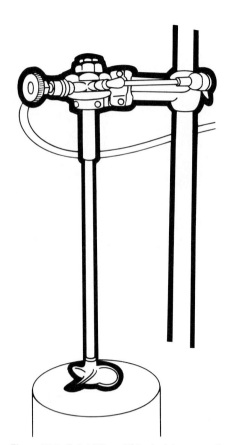

Figure 21-2. Paint Mixer. This air-driven propeller device will mix a large bucket of paint in moments. A still more efficient version has two propellers operating in opposition to each other.

a portable compressor may be purchased, although this means that there will be one more piece of machinery moving around in what will inevitably be a crowded shop.

Spraying is a fast labor-saving way of performing a number of otherwise tedious chores such as flameproofing, coloring translucent materials, applying base coats, etc. In addition, spray techniques provide the scenic artist with a range of subtle blending possibilities almost impossible to achieve with brushes or rollers. There are several types of sprayers, each with its own special purpose.

Flameproofing Sprayer

The simplest device of all, a flameproofing sprayer consists of a long siphon tube and a control gun. The tube is dipped into a bucket (or barrel) of mixed flame retardant solution and the material is sprayed onto the scenery. A huge area can be completely covered in a few minutes. Moreover, the pressure of the gun will force flameproofing into fabrics that might otherwise have to be dipped to get adequate treatment. Since dipping takes far more flame retardant, this saves material and shortens drying time.

A regular paint sprayer (see below) can be used to spray flame retardant, but its limited pot capacity will necessitate frequent refills. Furthermore, the delicate parts of regular sprayers are unusually susceptible to corrosion damage from flame retardant chemicals. Therefore, if the regular sprayer is used in an emergency, it must be cleaned immediately.

Regular Paint Sprayer

A commercial sprayer can be adjusted to spray scene paint (Figure 21-3). Since scene paint is rather heavy, pressure feed usually is used. The paint is forced from the cup to the nozzle of the gun by air pressure. Siphon feed, which creates suction at the nozzle to draw the paint upward, can be used for light paints and dyes. Most commercial guns can be adjusted to either type of feed by minor alterations. See the instructions for your particular gun.

A handy variation of the regular paint sprayer is the pressure pot. Here the paint is held in quantity in a large container from which it is fed to the gun by air pressure. This is particularly handy when a large job must be done with a single color of paint. Pots are usually equipped with stirring devices to allow the operator to keep the paint stirred while still sealed under pressure.

Figure 21-3. Paint Sprayer. This figure is typical of the many varieties of paint guns or sprayers available commercially.

Spatter Gun

The spatter gun has a special nozzle which produces an adjustable spray of droplets instead of a fine mist, an advantage if large areas are to be spattered. The flameproofing sprayer above can be utilized as a spatter gun, but it may dribble when adjusted to throw droplets instead of a coarse spray.

Pressure Tank Sprayer

A handy device that is the solution to spraying problems in small theatres without compressed air is the pressure tank sprayer. It also offers the utmost portability in any shop. It is not really a theatre tool, but an insecticide sprayer put to theatrical use. It is a simple device consisting of a sturdy tank containing the liquid to be sprayed and, when in operation, a head of compressed air above the liquid. This air is forced into the tank by means of a hand pump built into the top of the sprayer. The air serves only as a source of pressure to drive the paint, as in a regular spray gun. The nozzle is a simple device which allows adjustment from a rather strong stream of liquid (even useful for fighting small fires) to a fine spray. The hose connecting the tank with the spray nozzle is short, the whole assembly being intended for carrying or being slung over the shoulder while spraying plants. Some shops may want to substitute a longer hose, making it possible to leave the tank on the floor while taking the nozzle up a short ladder. (Too much difference in elevation between tank and nozzle will impede operation.)

A pressure tank sprayer is a fine tool for applying flame retardants and for producing rather fine spatter effects. This spattering is best done with the scenery in a vertical position where care may be taken to avoid allowing any drips from the nozzle to strike the setting. Covering wide areas with a flat coat of paint is usually beyond the capacity of this sprayer. Since the sprayer was originally made for spraying insecticides which may be corrosive, its tank is made of galvanized steel and its nozzle of brass. This makes it more resistant to corrosion than some commercial spray guns made of aluminum. Nevertheless, a tank sprayer may be ruined by leaving flame retardant in it overnight. All sprayers should be cleaned promptly after use.

Care must be taken not to overfill these sprayers. About one-third of the total tank volume should be left to hold the compressed air. When pumping up the sprayer for use, there is no need to pump beyond the point where the air pressure offers some resistance; more pressure may rupture the tank or hose, especially if the sprayer is old.

Airless Sprayer

A relatively new tool that some advanced paint shops may wish to try out is the airless sprayer. Unlike the spray painting tools above, this machine uses no compressed air. Instead the paint is pumped to the gun at very high pressure and ejected from the gun by pressure alone. Since it is not mixed with air, there is little overspray (the dusty cloud of partially dried paint that floats over everything in proximity to most spray paint operations).

Those trying airless sprayers should heed the warning that should be mounted on every machine: the high pressure stream of paint issuing from the nozzle is dangerous at close range. Its force is so great that it can be driven right into human flesh or through objects of considerable strength. At the proper spraying distance it is not dangerous.

GLUE POT

A glue pot will be needed only in shops using the now rather outdated animal glue binder system for mixing paint. Glue solution must not be allowed to get hotter than boiling water or it will burn, creating a terrible odor. This can be accomplished by rigging a double boiler out of two buckets. The outer one contains water and the inner one the glue. The whole setup is heated on a gas or electric stove, and requires constant attention to make sure the supply of water does not run dry. A thermostatically controlled electrical glue pot is a far better solution to the problem.

OPAQUE PROJECTOR

An opaque projector can usually be borrowed from the audiovisual department if the theatre is associated with a school. However, if much magnification from drawings is to be done, the shop should have its own. Sketches, details of scrollwork from manuals of style, and any other material printed or drawn on paper can be placed in this machine and enlarged to allow direct tracing onto scenic surfaces. In fact a considerable amount of distortion can be worked into drawings to fit them to the required surfaces if the scenographer can supervise the tracing setup.

These projectors usually are equipped with the most powerful lamp the housing will allow. This may be as high as 1000 to 1500 W. Such wattages are allowable only for very short periods per projected image. If the material remains in the projector for longer periods, which is inevitably the case when tracing, it is apt to char or even catch fire. Good books can be ruined and artist's originals destroyed. The solution is to decrease the lamp wattage to 500 W or less. In most cases lamps available for spotlight service will serve this purpose well. Of course the image will not be as bright, but the projected material can be left in longer.

Since these machines are made for short-throw projection under classroom conditions, they will usually provide the magnification needed within the throws available in the shop or backstage. If not, it may be possible to have someone familiar with the applications of lenses to scenic projection fit the projector with an auxiliary or alternate lens of shorter focal length.

PALETTE TABLE

There is wide variety in the manner in which rolling palettes are constructed. Each painter will have his preferences. The table should have a surface of metal (or some other impermeable material) suitable for mixing small quantities of paint directly on its top. After use, it must be possible to scrub the table clean with no injury to the surface. In addition to the mixing surface, there should be adequate space for buckets and cans of paint, brushes, chalk, straight edge, compass, and other paraphernalia. The whole table should roll easily around the shop.

PAINT SHOP SINK

Although it is technically a part of the building, a few notes are necessary about the paint sink. This should be a large double sheet metal sink deep enough to take large buckets and equipped with mixing faucets fitted to accept a standard garden hose. Enough hose should be supplied to facilitate filling buckets and tubs some distance from the sink. The sink trap should be oversized and easily cleaned. Dead glue, pigment, spoiled paint, and all other sorts of debris will accumulate there. Near the sink should be a soap dispenser, towels, and a place for hanging brushes, rollers, and such.

HAND TOOLS FOR THE PAINT SHOP

The following are tools most commonly found in a paint shop. Each experienced painter, however, will have his own tricks and techniques for which he has developed special tools. He may guard these jealously under some professional circumstances.

PAINT BRUSHES

Although sprayers, rollers, and special tools offer the painter an expanded range of techniques, brushes will still be the most commonly used tools in the paint shop. Older texts on scene painting stipulate that nothing but the best bristle brushes should be used. Such bristles once came from China where hogs were allowed to grow to a ripe old age producing long, supple bristles for paint brushes. These bristles are practically unavailable today; the few that are imported command prices far beyond those most paint shops are willing to pay. Therefore, synthetics, mostly nylon, have taken over. Some old-timers will assure you that they cannot hold paint the way bristles did, but they are reasonably effective and are available at prices the theatre can afford.

A good brush made of modern materials will have nylon bristles (larger sizes) which have been treated to produce split ends on the bristles. This makes the brush hold paint better. The bristles should be set firmly in rubber or some plastic material impervious to water. The bristles should be long and full, depending of course on the use for which the brush is intended. The following brushes are commonly used in scene painting.

Primers

Primers (Figure 21-4), the largest brushes found in most shops, are used to coat scenery with the first coat or two of paint applied to new fabric. They can also be used to apply flame retardant. (Spraying is a much faster way of flameproofing.) Wherever a wide surface must be evenly covered with paint primers are needed. Most primers are 6–8 inches wide with long supple bristles. Even when made with nylon bristles they are expensive and deserve the best care. Only in the direst of economical emergencies should cheap sisal fiber paste brushes be substituted for good primers. The fiber brushes wear out so rapidly and make painting so difficult that they are a very poor investment.

Lay-in Brushes

Lay-in brushes (Figure 21-4) are 3–5 inches wide with bristles about as long as those found in primers. In most cases these bristles will also be nylon. A well-made lay-in brush should produce very accurate work while having considerable paint-holding capacity. Cheap brushes will not enable the painter to produce sharp lines, and will hold so little paint that he will constantly be dipping the brush.

Liners

Liners (Figure 21-5) include a wide range of medium to small brushes used for detail work. Many may still be found in genuine bristle instead of nylon because they do not require such long bristles. Small liners are often cut to wedge shapes for greater accuracy in painting small lines. Many experienced painters will have a set of liners of their own cut to the shapes they like, and selected for those working qualities the painter finds most useful. Such brushes are seldom for loan, but be-

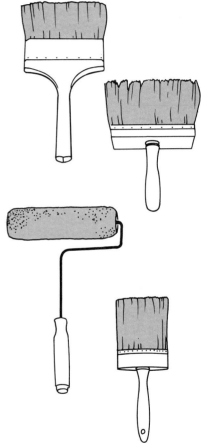

Figure 21-4. Tools for Flat Painting. These brushes and rollers are used to cover large surfaces rapidly in order to produce an even coat of color. Top left: 1 by 8 inch primer. Top right: 2 by 8 inch primer (preferred by many painters to the 1 inch thick brush because it holds more paint). Left center: 8 inch paint roller. Useful for coating hard scenery, painting floors, and texturing. Lower right: 4 inch lay-in brush.

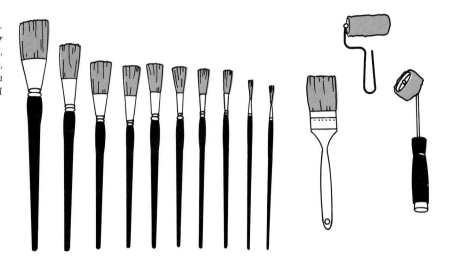

Figure 21-5. Detail brushes (Liners) and Rollers. These precision tools are used by the master painter. Brush sizes are (left to right): 2 inches, $1\frac{1}{2}$ inch, $1\frac{1}{4}$ inch, 1 inch, $\frac{7}{8}$ inch, $\frac{3}{4}$ inch, $\frac{5}{8}$ inch, $\frac{1}{2}$ inch, $\frac{3}{8}$ inch, and $\frac{1}{4}$ inch. At the right are a 2 inch brush and two special rollers (3 inches and 1 inch).

ginners may learn much by watching the master painter and asking him about the brushes he uses.

Foliage Brushes

Foliage brushes are also called "decorating brushes." They are larger than liners, being about 3 inches wide, and are used for a wide variety of detail painting. A sash brush, which is a standard item in a commercial paint store, often substitutes for a foliage brush though it is not as good.

Good quality house painting brushes of appropriate size can be substituted for theatrical brushes with fair success if the budget will not allow the purchase of the more expensive types. Some extra trimming and shaping will often improve the performance of these substitutes.

Note that, except for primers, most special brushes for scene painting are made with relatively long handles. These handles are frequently extended by painters with pieces of bamboo split and taped to the brush handles. This is especially handy for floor painting or to enable the painter to stand farther from his work and control the brush better.

Painters often treasure old lay-in brushes which have become too stiffened and warped to be of any further value for lay-in work. Such brushes may actually be better for dry brushing or graining operations than new ones.

A well-equipped paint shop will also have a variety of utility brushes for scrubbing, cleaning up, and other odd chores. Although it is possible for an experienced painter to clean up a brush well enough so that it can be used alternately in oil-base and water-base paint, it is a better idea to reserve certain brushes for those times when oil-base paints must be used (where a durable waterproof surface is needed). These should be commercial painter's brushes instead of the more expensive theatrical ones.

ROLLERS

Although many painters will prefer brushes, a quite adequate job of prime coating and base coating may be done with a regular paint roller designed for water-base house paint. Moreover a number of blending and texturing techniques may be worked out that produce unique surfaces not as easily achieved by the use of brushes. Rollers (Figures 21-4 and 21-5) are cheaper than priming brushes and frequently faster because of their greater width. They may use more paint but, in the hands of a beginner, coverage will probably be better with a roller than with a brush. The standard roller handles and rollers can be adapted to a wide variety of texturing tools. Tight-napped rollers may be wrapped with fabric, cut or abraded, partially coated with latex, or otherwise altered to produce pattern-making tools.

OTHER TEXTURING TOOLS

In addition to the texturing rollers mentioned above, sponges, both natural and synthetic, special short-bristled stippling brushes, and a variety of fabrics such as burlap, netting, etc., will be needed for working out assorted textures on scenery.

OTHER EQUIPMENT

In order to lay out detail work on scenery, the painter must have a variety of marking materials. Most of these should be capable of being easily removed from the surfaces after they have served their purpose. Stick (vine) charcoal, soft chalk, and cheap dry color all meet these needs. For more permanent lines the various felt marking pens are much used where old-timers used aniline dye in gum arabic.

Two tools are needed to apply long straight chalk lines. The first is simply a container holding a quantity of powdered chalk, charcoal, or pigment, and a reel of twine. As the twine is withdrawn from the container, it is charged with color and ready for snapping. The second (see Figure 21-6) is a bow whose string can be chalked with a piece of colored chalk and then snapped to produce a short line segment without the aid of an assistant.

Pouncing is a process by which powdered color is forced through small holes punched in paper to form an outline of a design on the

Figure 21-6. A bow-type chalk line also known as a snap line is used for short lines, which requires only one person to operate it. It is usually charged by rubbing with colored chalk or charcoal.

scenery underneath. For this process a pounce wheel and pounce are needed. The wheel is fitted with sharp points like the rowel of a spur. It is drawn over the design which has been laid out on heavy paper. Moving the wheel over the paper cuts a row of small holes. The paper then is held firmly against the scenery, and the pounce bag, a small bag of cheesecloth-like fabric containing dry pigment or powdered chalk, is patted over the holes, forcing some of the color through.

After the lines or marks have served their purpose, their remains are flogged away from the scenery by means of a stick to which some strips of fabric have been tied or wired, as in Figure 21-7.

All paint shops will have a constant need for a wide variety of pots, pans, and buckets. Some of these will be available if prepared paint is used and white glue is purchased in 5-gallon buckets. Others may be begged from restaurants where wholesale quantities of food are purchased. Small coffee cans should be saved.

Figure 21-7. Flogging Out a Line. This simple tool can erase lines snapped in chalk or dry pigment.

AUXILIARY PAINTING MATERIALS

The choice of pigments, dry and prepared, that will be needed in a paint shop will be discussed later. There are, however, a number of other materials used as colorants or surface treatments that the shop should stock.

DYES

Dyes are powerful colorants, mostly chemical derivatives of aniline, which are soluble in water or in water and alcohol. They produce transparent colors of great purity that work much like watercolors. Theatrical dyes are many times more powerful than the commercial products available in small packages for home dying of fabrics. In a pinch, these commercial dyes may be used, but much more dye will be needed.

Since dyes have greater purity than pigments, they can be mixed more predictably and with less tendency to go muddy; thus, fewer colors need be stocked. A set of primaries will actually make most other colors, but it will be advantageous to have a wider selection such as these:

Red	Black
Yellow	Brown
Blue	Green

Denatured alcohol should be stocked with the dyes to aid in dissolving them. It is also useful for encouraging some dry pigments to go into suspension.

GLAZES

Glazes are materials that impart a shiny surface to scenery. The original glaze was a stronger-than-normal size water, a solution made of eight parts warm water to one part strong glue. However, much better products are available today. Water soluble vinyl glaze, one of the best, can be used not only as a glaze but as an adherent for dyes and thin washes of color, or to hold down dyes or pigments that are being picked up by a coat of paint intended to cover them.

METALLICS

Metallics, materials that give the illusion of a metal surface, come in a wide variety of colors including silver (aluminum), bronze, gold, copper, and colored metallics such as red, green, etc. Metallics may be purchased either as powders or as premixed lacquerlike paints in cans or spray cans. Except for very small applications to properties where maximum shine and good wearing quality are required, the powders should be used. They are much cheaper, not flammable when mixed, and not as apt to result in the destruction of a valuable paint brush by drying into it.

Metallic powders may be mixed with the glaze mentioned above with good results. The mixture must be kept stirred. They may also be mixed into heavy size water or diluted white glue. Prop builders who want to gild small areas to the highest sheen should be directed to the commercially available gilding pastes which can be rubbed on with a cloth and burnished. These waxy materials should be used only where there is no intention of trying to cover them later with water paint. Pastes of this type are too expensive for anything but property applications, though they are spectacularly effective there.

WATER AND WEAR-RESISTANT PAINTS

Regular scene paint using glue size is not waterproof. Some premixed scene paints are relatively impervious to dampness but may not have very good wearing qualities. Where surfaces such as stair banisters or mantle pieces are going to get wear and perhaps be exposed to purposely spilled drinks and such, commercial water-resistant paints must be used. Acrylics or exterior latexes are good for this use, and have the advantage of being water soluble while on the brush. Thus cleanup can be done without having to stock flammable paint thinner. However the maximum durability will come with the use of enamels, which are paints that use mineral spirits or (now rarely) turpentine as vehicle. They dry more slowly than water-based paints, but last much longer.

TEXTURING MATERIALS

A wide variety of texturing materials can be added to scene paint to produce various rough textures. Sawdust, vermiculite, and sand are the most common. Spackle, a commercial patching compound, is also used frequently along with such standard shop commodities as whiting.

SPECIAL BINDERS

Special binders include such materials as polyvinyl alcohol, commercially prepared binders, and glues. If the shop wishes to mix its own paint from powder, but does not wish to use animal glue as the binder (see below), one of these products may be stocked in large quantities as the standard paint binder.

SPECIAL SOLVENTS

Most paint shops will want to have on hand small quantities of acetone, mineral spirits, and alcohol. They are all flammable and should be stored in compliance with local fire regulations. It is usually legal to keep very small quantities in the shop in special containers. Larger amounts will have to be stored elsewhere.

HOW PAINT IS MADE

Paint has three ingredients:

1. *Pigment* is the selective reflection material discussed above. Such materials are found in nature as ''earths'' (natural

chemical mixtures having the desired color values) or are manufactured in chemical laboratories. Pigments may interact chemically when dissolved or suspended in water; this may produce color changes not predictable in terms of subtractive color mixing, and may also result in violent changes in consistency.

2. *Binder* is the material that adheres the pigment to the surface. It changes from liquid to solid by a combination of chemical reaction and drying action. The result may be a permanently insoluble adherent or one that may be redissolved with additional vehicle.

3. *Vehicle* is the liquid that enables the paint to flow. In its simplest form vehicle merely evaporates, leaving the pigment and binder behind. More complicated vehicles enter into chemical reactions that result in their becoming part of the binder. This reaction usually involves combination with oxygen from the air.

A fourth ingredient, filler, is found in some paints. It is material added to increase the volume of the paint, and may be used to reduce the price of the paint per gallon, to change the consistency of the paint, or otherwise to produce special qualities. The cheapest and most common filler in theatrical paints is whiting, a chalk-base material.

Theatrical paints differ from ordinary house paints mainly in their cost and durability. They are relatively simple mixtures of pigment, binder, vehicle, and filler—each ingredient being chosen for economy, high color value, flexibility (will the paint allow the painter a variety of application techniques?), and relatively limited durability. The pigments used are much the same as those in regular paint except that those pigments whose main virtue is durability are seldom used. The vehicle is almost always water instead of oil or synthetic solvents, thus reducing cost, fire hazards, and fumes. Binders are chosen for simplicity, ease in working, and low cost. Although some are chemically similar to those in commercial paints, they do not usually have the same durability and high cost. (This is changing somewhat as the cost of synthetic binders drops.)

BINDERS

Binders for theatrical paints tend to be relatively simple low-cost materials. All are soluble in water at least until they have undergone a hardening action. The most common binders are animal glue, the traditional binder of the theatre painter for many years; casein, the most common binder in modern premixed theatrical paints; and certain other chemicals such as polyvinyl alcohol, synthetic rubber derivatives known as "latexes", vinyl acrylics, and similar substances which are developments of the plastics industry. Occasionally, refined gelatine, a variation on animal glue, is also used as a special binder.

Animal Glue

A now somewhat outdated binder for scene paint, animal glue comes in the form of glassy brown flakes or as a yellowish meallike material. It must be prepared by soaking the dry glue in enough warm water to cover until it forms a thick jellylike mass, a process that usually takes at least twelve hours. The glue is then cooked in a double boiler or a thermostatically controlled glue pot until it forms a heavy, syrupy solution known as "strong glue solution." In this form it is ready for gluing together wooden parts. This was its original application and accounts for its other name—"carpenter's glue." (Most carpenter shops have long since given up using animal glue for this purpose because there are many better products now available.)

Periodically, the strong glue solution must have water added to it to make up for evaporation. If it is allowed to cool, it will congeal into a very stiff jelly which can be reheated into a liquid. If allowed to sit around the shop for a few days in a warm place but not on the cooker, it will spoil, giving off a putrid odor.

Strong glue solution is almost never used straight from the glue pot, but rather diluted with warm water (16 to 1) to make size water. "Strong" size water is about twice the strength of normal; that is eight parts water to one part glue. Since the strength of each batch of strong glue will vary, the experienced scene painter tests the viscosity of the size water by rubbing it between his thumb and forefinger until he feels a "tackiness," and declares it too strong, too weak, or just right. Only experience will teach one to do this.

Casein Binder

Casein is the phosphoprotein portion of milk and is obtained by separating milk into its various components. When chemically treated to make a special solution in water, casein can be ground with pigment to produce an excellent theatrical binder. The process is best accomplished in a special plant; therefore casein binder paints come premixed in the form of heavy pastes or very syrupy solutions which are diluted for use.

Casein paint will gradually harden to a nearly waterproof coating if it is allowed to age for several days. When it has not yet aged, it can be quite easily redissolved in hot water.

Latex Binders

Latex binders are chemical relatives of synthetic rubber. Like casein, they must be manufactured into paint in a factory, not in the scene or paint shop. Latex paints tend to be rather tender for several days after application, but eventually harden into waterproof, scrub-resistant finishes. They are commonly used for interior household painting. These paints will form a flat finish, durable surface that blends well with regular scene paint. They are, however, usually too expensive for general theatrical use.

Vinyl Acrylic Binders

Synthetic materials, a product of the plastics industry, vinyl acrylic binders are found in a variety of paints including scene paint (see below). These water-base paints harden into a durable water-resistant surface. Furthermore, these binders have physical properties that favor the maintenance of high color brilliancy, a desirable property for scene paint to have. The cost of vinyl acrylic binders is relatively low because their adhering power persists even when they are diluted with many times their volume of water.

GLUE BINDER SCENE PAINT (DISTEMPER)

Glue binder scene paint has been standard in the theatre for a very long time although it is presently being replaced by more modern premixed paints. The steps in its preparation are given below:

1. Prepare *strong* size water and keep warm.
2. Mix the dry pigments together to get the proper color. Test the color by rubbing the mixed pigments between thumb and forefinger to get a complete mix, and compare with the sample supplied by the scenographer. This matching process will be complicated if one or more of the colors comes in the form of a "pulp" or paste. In this case, mix the entire batch into paste, as in step 3, and test the color match by smearing a bit of the mix (be sure that the colors have been completely mixed) onto a scrap of muslin. Carefully dry the test strip over a stove or an incandescent lamp.
3. Make a smooth paste of the pigment, using a little warm water. If the pigment will not go into suspension easily, add a little alcohol and stir. A paint mixing machine is ideal for this process, although it may be done by hand. Be sure all lumps are gone. A lump of unmixed strong color will make a surprising change when mixed in later, or it may streak if carried to the scenery on a brush.

4. With strong size water, dilute the paste to the consistency of coffee cream. Exact consistency will depend on the painting technique to be used.

This paint must be kept warm or it will gel. If this does happen, it can be reheated. The paint also changes color with storage. If a close match is needed over the period of two or three days, the job should be planned so that stopping points come at logical breaks in the setting, such as corners. Be sure you have mixed enough of each color for the entire job as batches of paint are nearly impossible to match (unless only one pigment was used in the beginning). If several buckets are needed, mix them together frequently by pouring from bucket to bucket ("boxing") and stirring well. Always keep the paint well stirred.

Distemper will spoil rapidly if stored in a warm place. If it must be kept for more than a day or two, add a *few* drops of carbolic acid or formaldehyde to each bucketful to retard bacterial action. Use care— too much may change the color of the paint.

This simple paint has been used in the theatre for many years. It is a flexible, relatively economical material capable of producing colors of very high brilliance, and it can be easily adjusted to fit the needs of individual painters. However, it is messy to make, consumes large quantities of shop time, spoils quickly (even with carbolic acid or formaldehyde), and often requires two coats to cover. It is also quite apt to pick up and stain later coats of paint placed over it because the glue weakens with age and will go into solution again if the fresh coat is warm enough. For these reasons simple glue binder scene paint is becoming obsolete in the theatre.

VINYL ACRYLIC SCENE PAINT

A relatively new category of scene paints is presently being manufactured as a two-part paint system by the Roscoe Laboratories.[1] Similar binders are also found in some premixed paints (see below). The Roscoe system consists of the following basic ingredients: concentrated colorant, a clear binder, and a white binder. The colorants, which are highly intense pigments, are mixed with either the clear or the white binder and varying quantities of water to produce paints of great brilliance. When dry, these paints are completely water resistant and will tolerate a great deal of scuffing and abuse without scaling or rubbing off the surface. Note that the paint becomes sufficiently water resistant to be painted over in a half hour. This is an advantage to the scene painter, but also makes it necessary to clean brushes soon after use.

---

1. Roscoe Laboratories, Inc., Port Chester, New York and Studio City, California. This product was developed by Nick Bryson.

Since the colorants used in this system are entirely the product of the chemical industry, no compromises have been made in the color purity of the pigments. Primary and secondary colors are almost exact matches for their theoretical equivalents in the additive system and mix much more predictably than most dry pigments or other premixed paints. Therefore, names of the pigments have been adjusted to reflect this. The result is a system that relates quite accurately to the additive color triangle. Those used to this scientific method of describing color mixing will find that the system is easy to comprehend and that it fits logically into their understanding of the physiology of color. Those used to conventional descriptions of the mixing of the earth colors and to the necessity for stocking special expensive "lake" colors to achieve certain brilliant effects may find this system quite different, but once learned, simple and logical.

Cost of Roscoe paints as shipped is high. However the net cost when mixed and ready to apply will often be as low or lower than that of other paints. This is because the pigment and binders withstand great dilution while maintaining color value. They do, however, become increasingly transparent with dilution. Thus, the system works best on scenic surfaces that have been carefully primed with a cheaper paint that completely obscures previous finishes. The white binder can be used for this purpose (tint to resemble the final color to be applied). To save cost, a base coat of either glue binder and whiting or of premixed paint may be used. The latter is preferable if maximum water and wear resistance is necessary. Such paints can be had with binders similar to those used in the Roscoe system. Of course the transparent quality of the mixed Roscoe paints is often an advantage. For example, translucencies may be painted with an effect similar to that achieved with dyes but without bleeding.

Spoilage is a serious problem with glue binder paint and sometimes with premixed paints left standing open. The Roscoe paint, however, is highly resistant to spoilage. It contains a small amount of mineral oil in suspension which rises to the top of the mixture when it is allowed to stand, and which prevents evaporation or the entry of air into the paint. This and the inherent preservative quality of the binder makes the paint last for long periods even when standing in open containers in a warm place.

Since the binder in this paint is chemically related to a wide variety of plastic substances, it adheres well to most of them. The concentrated white binder may be used as a one-coat base paint on Styrofoam, urethane foams, Plexiglas, polystyrene, polyester, and untreated polyethylene. It binds thoroughly if two days is allowed for complete water evaporation. Another way to bind this paint to plastics offers unusual opportunities to the scenographer. The paint can be applied to sheet plastic to be vacuum formed. As soon as the paint is dry to the touch, it may be heated and formed. The heat will complete the bonding process, and the paint will stretch along with the plastic, carrying the painted design over the newly formed shape of the plastic.

Roscoe paint is designed to dry absolutely flat to avoid unwanted reflections from the painted surface. If a gloss surface is needed, a water-base gloss medium is available. It produces a durable gloss surface on fabric, wood, and the like.

Roscoe two-part paints using vinyl acrylic binders can form a major part of a scene paint shop's inventory. They perform particularly well where the brilliancy of glue binder paints is needed without the disadvantages of that paint. However, the cost and the transparency of these paints will make it necessary for most shops to stock additional premixed paints of some other type for base coating and for applications where opacity and low cost are desirable, but brilliance of color is not essential.

PREMIXED PAINT

Premixed scene paint consists of the same ingredients as any paint: pigment, binder, and vehicle, plus filler when appropriate. The pigments are essentially the ones that a shop might buy as dry pigments for making glue binder paint. Instead of being bagged and delivered to the consumer, these pigments are ground in a paint mill with binder and vehicle (water) to make a paste. The grinding process assures that there will be a minimum of lumps. This paste is screened further to assure that nothing in the paint will clog a spray gun. A preservative is added, and the paste packaged and sold in 1- and 5-gallon containers.

Binders in premixed paints are usually derivatives of casein or vinyl compounds. These vary in resistance to water depending on their composition and how long they have dried. Users should consult the various manufacturers for specific details. The thick paste from the manufacturer should be further diluted with water to reach painting consistency. It will resemble the consistency of thick cream for most purposes. One may expect to get 2 to 4 gallons of paint from 1 gallon of paste. Naturally the amount will depend on the way the paint is to be applied. The preservatives mixed into premixed paint at the factory are considerably more effective than either carbolic acid or formaldehyde in glue binder paint. Nevertheless, the paint will eventually spoil if left in its dilute form in a warm place. It will develop a bad odor, and may not adhere properly.

Theatrical quality premixed paints are available in a wide range of colors, including some very high value expensive ones which should be used sparingly. Earth colors, black, and white are relatively economical. Some manufacturers also carry a line of very high-brilliancy tinting colors in shades which are so expensive and seldom used that it would not be economical to stock them in 1-gallon sizes. Dry or paste pigments in unusual or high-brilliancy colors may also be blended with these paints in small quantities without adding additional binder. The palette is just as extensive as that available to dry pigment users.

Color mixing with premixed pigments is no more complicated than mixing dry color when a paste or "pulp" color is used. Colors are mixed wet and test strips dried over a stove or hot lamp to get true colors. Color matching is neither more nor less difficult than with dry pigments.

The viscosity of premixed paints can be adjusted over a wide range, with the added advantage that since the paint need not be heated, viscosity will not change with temperature. In spite of the wide range of possible viscosity, some master painters may find that there is a different "feel" (it is more or less slippery) while brushing premixed paints. This may require minor adjustments in their technique. Beginners learning from the start with premixed paints will experience no difficulty that can be attributed to the paint.

The only special care that must be taken when using premixed paint stems from the fact that its binders tend to set up more permanently than glue binder paint. This means that brushes, sprayers, and utensils must either be immersed in water or cleaned immediately. If the paint is allowed to set, hot water will break it down unless enough time (a day or so) has elapsed to allow the binder to reach its completely insoluble state. However, such cleaning efforts are tedious and can be hard on brushes or rollers.

This same feature, permanence, will turn out to be an advantage when working on old scenery. The premixed paint used in previous coats will be completely hard and show little tendency to lift and stain the new coats.

The covering power of most premixed paints is superior to that of glue binder paints. Thus one coat will often serve where two would otherwise be needed. Nevertheless, thin wash coats of paint can be made when needed.

The possibility that a prime coat can safely be mixed with flame retardant is about the same for premixed paints as for glue binder paints. A test batch should be tried first in either case. Some paint manufacturers will advise about the compatibility of their paints with flame retardant compounds.

Preparing Fabric for Painting with Premixed Paints

The superior binding power of premixed paints and the superior characteristics of white glue over animal (carpenter's) glue offer the shop a wide variety of procedures to follow to prepare newly covered flats:

1. The flats may be treated in the three steps used with glue binder paint: (a) Flameproof the muslin and allow to dry. (b) Size the muslin with white glue size containing a small amount of whiting or other pigment to reduce glazing. Stains from glue will not be a problem. (c) Base paint with premixed paint.
2. The steps may be combined: (a) Treat muslin with combined sizing and flameproofing. (Test for compatibility.) (b) Base paint with premixed paint.
3. Further combination: (a) Flameproof. (b) Base paint, allowing binder in premixed paint to serve as size. This has the advantage of avoiding any flameproofing interactions with other materials, saves material and time otherwise used to make size, and produces as good a surface as any other method.

Similar alternative methods are available when preparing old scenery for reuse:

1. Glaze with white glue and whiting mixture.
2. Glaze with vinyl sizing. Cut with some pigment if the glaze is too smooth.
3. Repaint with premixed paint.

In most cases, simply repainting will suffice. The other alternatives are useful when working over hard-to-cover materials.

PIGMENT MIXING

Up to this point we have discussed the various components of scene paints and how they are combined to make paint that is ready to apply. We must now examine the process by which the proper colors are determined and mixed. Color information comes from the scenographer who has worked out paint colors as a part of the total design. Chances are great that the colors he has chosen will look quite different under stage lighting and may change frequently under that lighting. Thus the appearance of the painted set in the shop may give only a hint of the final effect. It will be helpful to beginning painters and student scenographers for the paint shop to be equipped with lighting instruments that enable those working to occasionally examine the setting under light approximating that which will be used on stage. In some cases it is sufficient to supply a couple of samples of the acting area color media that can be held, one over each eye, while viewing the painted set. In other cases where textures and three-dimensional settings are in use, several spotlights on rolling stands equipped with proper filters will be needed. Experienced theatre workers will probably be able to visualize the finished effects without these lamps, but their importance to beginners should not be underestimated.

What Information Does the Paint Shop Get from the Scenographer?

Information from the scenographer will vary depending on the complexity of the show, the methods of the scenographer, and the amount of time he plans to spend in the paint shop. Usually a painter's elevation (a special color rendering to guide the painters) will be prepared. It may be supplemented by special color patches and even by full-scale samples of certain techniques. This will seldom appear the same as a rendering showing the appearance of the finished set under stage lighting. A model may be substituted for the rendering or elevation. In any case, supplemental material will be needed and may accompany the original submission.

Beginning scenographers should be cautioned to do their painting of renderings or models in tempera, not watercolor, because the former closely approximates the color and texture of scene paint. This is especially important when the setting is to be painted by beginners who will find it far easier to match colors and techniques worked in tempera than in watercolors. A master painter can work from almost any medium the scenographer chooses to use with no more information than the rendering itself; those less experienced will appreciate a list noting the various stock colors that went into the mixes.

Most scenographers will want to maintain very close supervision over the painting processes and may want to do some of the finish work themselves. This is because the expression of visual images in reduced scale is difficult. Moreover, the scenographer may find that his concept of certain details of the painting process changes as the setting develops at full scale. Therefore, paint crews are cautioned to get approval of color samples, painting techniques, and detail work before moving toward completion.

Mixing Pigments to Match Color Samples

Color matching is perhaps one of the most difficult jobs that the novice may encounter in the paint shop. He may watch the paint shop supervisor, a master painter, casually glance at a rendering and then with seeming abandon toss several quarts of one paste color into a bucket followed by a couple of dips each of some others. The beginner will then be instructed to mix the batch thoroughly, adding a little water, and to take a sample and dry it for examination. When the sample has dried, the master tosses in a small dab of additional color, the testing process is repeated, and the result is an exact match! Such a show of skill is the result of much experience. The beginner will be well advised to try to match the feat using a small can and tiny amounts of the colors.

Subtractive Color Mixing

We have already noted that pigments work by filtering the light that passes down into them and reflecting some of it back out. Thus the basic tendency of all pigments is to reduce the amount of light that is reflected. This leads to the most basic of color mixing rules: *Mixtures of pigments always tend to produce less reflective results than the individual components, i.e., all pigment mixtures tend to move toward gray or black.*

Neither pigments nor dyes are capable of producing spectroscopically pure light. In fact, only certain exotic light sources or an expensive device known as a "monochromator" can do this. Instead of spectroscopically "pure" light, pigments reflect a rather wide band of wavelengths centered about their nominal color. This gives them their hue. In addition to these wavelengths, pigments usually reflect other wavelengths that have the effect of diluting the "purity" of the light they reflect. Note that no pigment is 100 percent reflective. It is equally true that no pigment is a perfect absorber of all wavelengths, although some blacks reflect only a tiny portion of the light that strikes them.

An important effect of the "impurities" in light reflected from pigments is that simple three-primary-color theory will not predict exactly how the pigments will mix. One must first determine the theoretical result of a mixture on the basis of the nominal color of the pigments, then calculate the effect of mixing the various "impurities," and add this result into the total effect. For example, theory indicates that mixing yellow paint with blue paint will make green paint. If the pigments were "pure," this would be true. However, if the yellow actually reflects some blue (in addition to red, green, and spectral yellow), the resulting "green" will actually also reflect some blue light.

Such "impurities" also effect neutralization. Where theory indicates that a completely neutral gray (ideally black) should appear, a brown, gray-green, or gray-purple will often be the result. Although these departures from simple theory are used to advantage by the experienced painter who exploits them to get desired colors, they may confuse the beginning color mixer. The practical result of this characteristic of pigments is that it is not advantageous to try to mix all needed colors from the three primary ones; a much more extensive palette is desirable.

COLOR WHEEL   As we seek to describe a practical palette, we find that the best way to organize it is in the form of a color wheel. This is an arrangement of color samples that serves to explain their relationship to each other as they are used in design, and also to explain approximately how they will mix. Given the number of pigments available today, a large number of color wheels representing the favorite palettes of various master painters might be assembled. The one illustrated in Plate XI was prepared by a group of painting experts seeking to offer guidance to those beginning the process of learning scene painting. It is adaptable to a variety of dry or premixed colors.

The color wheel (Plate XI) provides two kinds of information: how colors relate to each other and how they mix with each other. These relationships are shown on the wheel by the arrangement of the colors. Those colors opposite each other on the wheel are *complementary*; they have the greatest contrast with each other, and offer the designer or scenographer combinations of high attention value. This complementary relationship also describes how the pigments mix: they tend to neutralize each other. This means that their selective absorbencies cancel, resulting in no color at all. Theoretically the result should be black (the absence of light), but actually it will be gray, sometimes with a hint of color from "impurities."

Colors adjacent to each other on the wheel are known as *related* or *analogous* colors. Analogous colors, when mixed, change to a chroma between the two samples, but with a value lower than either component. All other relationships on the wheel fall somewhere between these two extremes.

Note that the color wheel is only a sampling device. Extended to its fullest form, it would be a huge color map in which each color blends imperceptibly into all of its neighbors. Such a map would be gray in the middle. Furthermore this map could be extended into a three-dimensional double-cone-shaped solid with black at one point and white at the other. All hues, values, and chromas would fall somewhere in this "color solid."

PIGMENT NAMES The names used on the color wheel reflect the history of the development of pigments. Early pigments came from two sources: minerals that were found in the earth and crudely ground and screened before mixing, and plant matter that was extracted and used as dye. Most plant-derived materials are now obsolete. The mineral pigments have survived to the present and still retain their generic name, "earth colors." Such colors are the browns, yellows, and reds. An example is "ochre," originally a clay from France, that contains a small percentage of iron oxide which gives it its distinctive color.

Today many pigments, including some of those originally found in nature, are made in the chemical plant. Unless such colors are substitutes for mineral earth colors, they are termed "chemical colors." Modern chemistry has added a great many colors to the original list of those found in nature, many of which are improvements over the earlier colors.

MIXING PIGMENTS   Ultimately all mixtures of pigments can have one or more of the following effects: change of hue, change of chroma, and change of value. Practically, almost every mix results in some change in all three characteristics. Thus the art of pigment mixing consists of juggling these three variables simultaneously. Discussing them one by one may help the novice sort out what is happening in his paint bucket.

Changing Hue   Changing hue means that we are changing the wavelengths or combination of wavelengths reflected by the pigment. If we stir blue paint into yellow paint, we combine the absorptive qualities of the pigments. Although the two components separately reflect a wide portion of the spectrum, the mixture reflects only green plus whatever "impurities" the pigments may have had. Note that it is impossible to change the hue without a reduction in value. Less light is reflected by the now-green mixture.

Changing Chroma   Reductions in chroma are best accomplished by adding some complementary pigment. This is easier to control if the value of the added color is about the same as that of the original pigment. The effect of adding a complementary is to move the chroma down the scale toward a neutral gray.

   Increases in chroma are effected by the addition of pigment of the same hue but higher chroma than the original paint. Within the range of available pigments, there are absolute limits beyond which higher chroma cannot be achieved. This means, for example, that the highest chroma red will be the purest high-reflectance red pigment available. Anything added to such a pigment will tend to reduce its chroma. No such limitation exists in lighting where chroma may theoretically be extended indefinitely.

Changing Value   The value (overall reflectance) of a pigment may be increased by adding white or a higher value pigment of the same hue, and decreased by adding black or a lower value pigment of the same hue. Theoretically hue should remain the same although chroma will inevitably change because of the effects of dilution.

TINTS AND SHADES   *Tints* are generally defined as colors whose value is above middle gray on the Munsell scale. This means that they reflect more than 50 percent of the light that strikes them. Commonly, tints also are described as colors that have been generously mixed with white. Although whiting is used for this purpose, it is not very effective because it is rather transparent. Other more opaque white pigments such as zinc white will increase the value of a color without increasing the volume of the paint as much.

Shades are the opposite of tints. They are colors whose total reflectance is below middle gray. Shades generally are described as mixtures of black.

"TAKING DOWN" AND "BRINGING UP" COLORS Two operations are called for repeatedly at all stages in color work, from original mixing all the way to last-minute adjustments. A color is "taken down" by reducing its value and chroma. Thus it reflects less light and its chroma is less apt to call attention to itself. "Bringing up" a color increases its value and chroma. Painters have several methods of taking down and bringing up colors, depending on whether the paint is still in the bucket or has already been applied. While still in the bucket, a color may be taken down by any of the following methods or combination of methods:

1. Adding a complementary color
2. Adding a color of the same hue, but with lower chroma and/or value
3. Adding black

The results of each of these methods will not be the same. Since it will often develop that the scenographer may want a change in hue in the process of taking down, the added color may also be chosen to shift the hue slightly.

"Bringing up" a color results in increasing its attention value. This may be accomplished by one of these methods:

1. Adding color of higher chroma
2. Adding pigment of same hue but higher value
3. Adding white

The above lists are not intended to reflect any special preference of one method of alteration over another. Preferences will most likely depend on the individual painter's style.

Once the paint has been applied, methods of alteration change, although the principles remain the same. The addition of pigment to alter the reflectance of the painted surface may be done by means of a thin "wash," a watercolorlike coating, or by means of a partial coverage effected by methods such as spattering or dry brushing.

Another variation on color alteration that emphasizes the effect of partial coverage as a means of taking down color, is the use of dark or black netting to take down costumes or pieces of upholstery fabric. It is also possible to accomplish taking down or bringing up by means of changes in lighting. See the section "Accenting and Deemphasizing" in Chapter 20, p. 323.

PALETTE MIXING   Instead of mixing paint in containers, a needed color may be mixed as it is used. The painter works with small containers of paint into which he dips his brush; he then mixes the paint in the brush itself by working it against the metal top of the paint table. Sometimes the colors are completely mixed together; sometimes the two or more components are purposely left partially separated in the brush, making it possible for the painter to lay down a variety of colors in the same brush stroke. Another variation on this technique, especially adaptable to premixed paint, is to work from dollops of paste laid out on the palette table, picked up on the brush, and mixed together as needed. This resembles the manner in which artists use oil colors. A can of water is kept handy to thin the mixed paste to a consistency suitable to the painter. These mixing techniques simply apply subtractive color theory "instantaneously" to small quantities of paint instead of to bucket-sized quantities.

HINTS ON MIXING PIGMENTS   There are some common sense procedures which may spare the beginning paint mixer the embarrassment of mixing far too much paint for the job.

If the color specified is of high value, begin with the lightest component to go into the paint, and work cautiously down to the value sought. This usually means starting with white and tinting it until the proper color is reached. Beware of hasty additions of strong color and lumps of color not yet mixed into the entire batch. It is amazing what a small dab of a strong color such as Prussian blue will do to a large bucket of near-white paint. Add small amounts and mix thoroughly before adding more.

The contrary situation prevails when mixing dark colors. Begin with the darkest hue and work cautiously upward. Be especially wary of white added to deep browns such as Van Dyke brown. A tiny amount may make the entire batch chalky. It is often better to work more cautiously up the value scale by adding lighter but less chalky colors than white.

Remember that water-base paints dry much lighter than they look in the bucket. The only sure test is to carefully dry a sample painted on a piece of the base material that you intend to coat.

Large batches of paint should be "boxed" (poured from bucket to bucket) to assure an exact mix. Such batches should be applied all in one painting session, or the work so planned that any delay comes at a corner of the setting where a color change will not be noticed. Remember always to keep the paint well stirred, especially if it is glue binder paint.

Texture and Color

Most scene paint will be applied to muslin, canvas, or wood. However there will be occasion to paint many other materials. The texture of the material will affect the apparent color of the finished product. In general, the smoother the material, the lighter the appearance; the same paint applied to a very smooth wood will appear lighter than if it were applied to muslin. In turn, muslin will appear lighter than canvas, and canvas lighter than material such as monk's cloth. Old, painted muslin makes colors look lighter than new muslin. For these reasons it is common practice to cover most wood surfaces with muslin or canvas before painting them. Otherwise separate batches of paint may have to be mixed, and the probability is that surfaces still will not match since the texture difference will remain evident.

The base material also affects coverage. The more nap or texture, the more paint will be needed in covering it. Some materials present the opposite situation. Gauzes, scrims, and netting take relatively small amounts of paint if the objective is merely to coat the fibers, not fill in the interstices between the weave. Such painting is usually best done with a sprayer.

APPLICATION OF SCENE PAINT

The art of scene painting is about equally divided between the mixing of pigment and the application of the paint to the setting. Although the most refined techniques of applying paint take years to learn and are to a considerable extent the result of individual styles developed by master painters, many of the basic techniques are easy to learn, and can produce very effective settings. We will discuss these techniques as nearly as possible in the order in which they occur in the painting process. However the reader should note that there are no rules which require that painting be carried to any particular degree of coverage or finish. If freshly sized, but otherwise uncoated muslin satisfies the needs of the scenographer, the set is finish-painted when the sizing has been applied.

SPECIAL SIZE COATS

Since regular sizing, using dilute glue solutions, is covered in Chapter 9, "Soft Scenery," we need only mention special sizes here.

Starch size is a special fabric filling size used when the fabric is to be painted as a translucency; for example, to represent a stained glass window. It is made by diluting about a cupful of cooked laundry starch to make about a 2-gallon bucket of size. Some theatre workers may wish to experiment with various dilutions of commercially available liquid starch. Starch size produces a smooth, semitransparent fabric that takes dye well. Some dye may be added directly to the starch if an overall color is desired.

Older glue binder paints have a tendency to chalk off and stain subsequent coats of paint. Sometimes an alum size is used to harden these old coatings before repainting. One-half cup of alum in about 4 gallons of water is sufficient. This will seldom be needed if premixed colors with relatively permanent binders are used.

Another method of holding down older glue binder paint is to treat the surface with white glue sizing and allow it to dry thoroughly. Add a bit of pigment to the white glue, mixed about 16:1 with water.

All such size coats may be applied by brushing evenly with a priming brush, or better, by spraying onto the surface. They are not normally intended to leave much, if any, pigment on the fabric. We will begin our discussion of painting techniques with the first coat containing any substantial amount of pigment.

PRIME COAT

The primer may somewhat inexactly be termed the "base coat" because prime coat may also serve as a base coat when starting with new fabric. In this case, the prime coat can serve its principal function, the filling of the pores in the fabric with pigment and binder, and at the same time it can form a base coat that will be the foundation on which the rest of the paint design will be built.

Pigments used in prime coating are normally chosen with an eye toward economy unless the primer is to serve also as a base coat. Whiting, the cheapest filler-pigment on the palette, is usually used. Another possibility, if available, is to box together the remnants left from other paint jobs, and base coat with this random color. A little color in the primer makes it easier to get good coverage.

Beginning painters will frequently be asked to apply the prime coat when it is to be completely covered with subsequent coats. This is the simplest of all painting processes. The work is most commonly done with large primer brushes that are dipped rather deeply to get a full load of paint, and carefully wiped against the edge of the bucket on both sides to avoid dripping. Brush strokes are applied in a cross-hatch motion to avoid any directional brush marks on the fabric. The object is to lay down a smooth, even coat, equal in color and coverage over the entire surface. The work must proceed rapidly to avoid lines developing where partially dried paint has been overcoated with later brush strokes. To further prevent this from happening, the edges of the work should be "feathered," that is, the margins of the portion being painted are tapered out by painting with a nearly dry brush, leaving the fabric in this area only partially covered (see Figure 21-8).

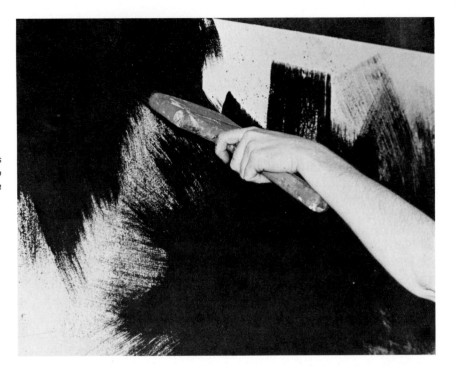

Figure 21-8. Base Coating. Note how the paint is applied in a cross-hatch pattern and feathered to improve the lap with the next row of brush strokes.

Feathered zones are then blended into invisibility as the next portion of the flat is painted. The goal is an even layer of paint over the entire piece of scenery with no indication of which areas were painted first.

Some shops have had success with applying prime coats with rollers. This is more feasible with drops lying on the shop floor, or with flats whose fabric is very tightly stretched. Otherwise the roller will tend to leave marks on the surface as it passes over toggle rails, braces, and the like.

Prime coats may also be blended or scumbled. Since these techniques are more common to base coats and are identical in either case, they will be discussed below.

BASE COAT

The base coat is planned to provide the foundation color and sometimes the foundation texture that will be part of the finished paint job. In its simplest form it is a coat of paint applied in the same manner as the prime coat, but whose color has been mixed to form the foundation of the design or texture to be painted on the scenery. If the scenery is to serve mainly as a colored reflecting surface for lighting, the base coat may be the only painting treatment it gets.

Blending

The objective of blending (Figure 21-9) is somewhat like that of a grad-uated wash in water colors. A gradual color change is painted onto the surface by working with two or more closely related colors and two brushes. Working rapidly while the paint is wet, the two colors are brushed together and mixed on the fabric to get an even blend of inter-mediate colors graduating from one to the other. Extra care must be taken that no portions dry before the blending has reached the stage desired. Sometimes it will even be necessary to spatter a bit of water or size into the drying paint.

Blends can also be accomplished by developing the feathering technique into a much more extended tapering of color. The second color is then feathered into the first. This technique probably more properly belongs under "dry brushing," which is discussed below.

Figure 21-9. Blending and Scumbling. This figure illustrates both techniques. Those portions where the paint has mixed in such a way that no line of demarcation between shades remains, may be said to have been blended. Those where demarca-tions exist meet the definition of scumbling. The scenic artist works with two or more brushes.

Scumbling or "Puddling"

A more elaborate version of the wet blending technique described above is known as "scumbling" (Figure 21-9). The intent is to produce a surface that has greater variety of color than blending; an effect that might be called "mottled," but is on a larger scale. Scumbling often serves as the base for painting techniques intended to suggest aged plaster, stained wallpaper, and the like. It can also be simply an abstract color variation.

Scumbling is best accomplished when the scenery is lying flat on the floor. High humidity that slows drying also helps. Painters work rapidly with two or more brushes, at least one for each color of paint used in the process. A layer of paint is put onto the fabric, and other colors partially brushed and partially dribbled into the wet paint. The color is mixed directly on the fabric to get the degree of mixture and separation desired. Sometimes parts of the surface are allowed to dry before other colors are worked over them.

Obviously scumbling is a highly individualized process in which no two workers will get exactly the same results. It will probably be necessary for the scenographer to supervise the first stages of a scumbling job so that he can make clear to the crew members exactly what sort of an effect he wishes to achieve.

CARTOONING

If a definite design or image is to be painted on the scenery in any but the most freehand of techniques, it will be necessary to draw (i.e., "cartoon") some type of guidelines on the surface. These may vary from a freehand sketch drawn directly on the surface of the fabric by the scenographer to minutely detailed outlines of architectural details, decorative scrollwork, etc. Transferring detailed drawings from the small scale of a scenographer's sketch or a picture involves considerable magnification. Most scenic artists do not trust themselves simply to begin at one edge of the scenery and draw the design. They use one of the two processes below.

Magnification by Squares

In one of the oldest techniques for enlargement, the original is squared off into a grid of lines representing relatively small segments of the finished scenery in scale. For example, each $\frac{1}{2}$ inch square on the drawing may represent a 1 foot square on the final work. (Squaring may be done on an overlay of acetate to avoid ruining fine originals.) The scenic artist then transfers the details from each square onto the scenery, sometimes by freehand, sometimes by taking scale measurements to determine the location of objects in the square. The entire layout is thus somewhat tediously but accurately transferred to the full-scale drawing on the scenery (see Figure 7-3).

Magnification by Opaque Projector

The second method requires more space and necessitates that the area be in semidarkness, but it is somewhat less tedious than the squaring method. It also offers the chance to make distortions in the original by projection techniques that may make it possible to fit a design into an area not exactly in the same proportions as the original. For example, handbooks of style are filled with details of decorations from various periods. A scrollwork design may be precisely what the scenographer would like to have, but may be too narrow or too short. By placing the projector so the line of projection is at an angle to the surface of the scenery, the image can be distorted. If it goes out of focus in some parts, try tilting the original to make it more parallel with the projection surface. Once the image has been fitted into the space intended for it, it is traced onto the surface in whatever detail the scenographer requires. Tracing may be done with chalk, stick charcoal, or with a felt-tip pen if more permanent lines are needed.

LAY-IN

Once the design has been transferred to the surface to be painted, the job begins in earnest. The first step is lay-in (Plate XV, numbers 3 and 4). This consists of filling in the outlines of the design with whatever color is to form the background of that part of the design. This is done with lay-in brushes which must be capable of laying down paint right up to a line without spilling it over. Lay-in work is not for the careless or those with bad eyesight. It must be done with precision. However, it is not particularly difficult, and beginning paint crew members can master it with a little practice. Draw your own design on an old flat, and practice until you can prove to your crew chief that you can do the job.

Correcting errors made in lay-in usually requires redoing the base coat in that area. This may change the texture of the fabric enough to make a permanently visible area in the design.

DETAIL WORK

After the lay-in has been completed, the myriad of refined techniques of the master painter come into play. All of these fall under the general heading of detail work. Although an almost endless variety of techniques could be given under detail work, many of which are the special techniques of various master painters, it will be sufficient for the beginner to consider the examples below. He will learn many more from practical experience in any paint shop that has the services of a master painter at its disposal.

The process of imitating three-dimensional objects on two-dimensional fabric is really a study in perspective and light-and-shade. A tree branch, for example, will almost inevitably have a highlighted portion where light strikes it, a more neutral area where the light tapers toward shadow as the light strikes at an increasingly oblique angle, and a shadowed area where only reflected light strikes. In real life these areas blend imperceptibly into each other where the branch is smoothly cylindrical. The scenic artist will probably exaggerate these areas by increasing the contrast between them and by painting each area with a definite edge. He may also increase the amount of color in the shadow over what it might be in real life (see Plate XV).

Lining

Lining is a technique used to create the illusion of architectural detail, to indicate separation between stone work, bricks, etc. It is done with special liner brushes designed to lay down an even, narrow line of paint. If the lines are to be straight, the liner is loaded with paint and drawn along a slightly tilted straight edge as in Figure 21-10. Curved lines may be drawn along a bent piece of wood or they may be drawn freehand. For detailing architectural items, lines are usually painted in multiples in order to imitate the pattern of shadows that forms at the edge of a molding or cornice. A fairly dark line forms the principal line. This may be highlighted on one side and shadowed on the other as in Figure 21-11, or simply provided with a secondary shadow line. More detailed line patterns are used to suggest elaborately formed cornicing. Such lining is usually done in variations of the "local color" —the base or lay-in color in the area being painted. Highlights will be lighter than local color, and lines usually darker, with shadows still darker.

Foliage Work

A special brand of detail painting is used to suggest foliage on borders, drops, and the like. After scumbling in the general tones of green as a background, details of the leaves are added with a special foliage brush which can leave a leaf-sized dab of paint with each stroke. A master painter will often charge the foliage brush with two colors, one on each side of its flat-oval shape, and proceed to paint "leaves" which have highlights and shadows, all in one stroke per leaf. Another, less exact method of doing foliage is to load a feather duster lightly with paint and tap it gently against the surface, leaving leaflike dabs of paint.

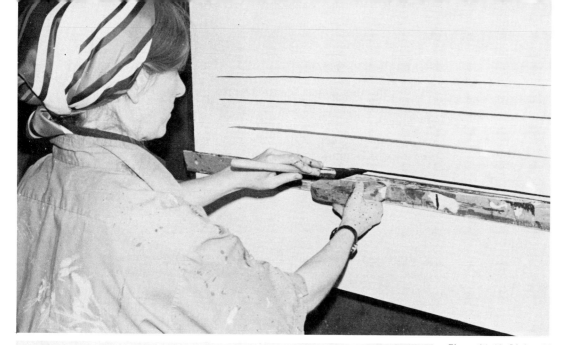

Figure 21-10. Lining. Note that the straight edge is slightly tilted to prevent paint from running under it. A smooth stroke produces an even line.

Figure 21-11. Lining and Shadowing. This illustrates the way a master painter would detail a cornice. The basic lines are determined from the cross section of the cornice as outlined in the middle of the illustration. Highlights and shadows are determined by assuming that the light is coming from an angle above the viewer's head and applied accordingly. Illustration by Kate Keleher.

SURFACE TREATMENTS

The techniques discussed below may be used as finish steps or as means of blending or taking down underlying designs. All of these methods have on thing in common: they result in only partial coverage of the surface underneath. They suggest textures, increase interest, and serve to hide or minimize the sometimes all-too-visible fact that the scenery consists of flat paint on flat fabric. Most of these techniques are easily learned.

Spattering

Spattering consists of partially coating the surface with droplets of paint. As the contrast in color between base and spatter and between various colors of spatter increases, the roughness of the texture increases. Thus the effect of a spatter job can vary from a slightly roughened but subtle surface to a very rough finish. Since the appearance of a spatter job can be controlled even further by adjusting the color of the light striking it (follow the rules for accenting or deemphasing colors), spattering is a flexible technique.

Spattering is done by dipping a brush lightly into paint and flipping or tapping the brush so that the paint flies off in droplets and lands on the scenery. (The latter method is shown in Figure 21-12.) Both methods are tiring if done for a long time. The size of the droplets is controlled by the viscosity of the paint, the amount of paint taken onto the brush, and the number of spatter strokes taken between loadings. When the paint is thin, and the brush heavily laden and shaken violently, the spatters tend to be large. When the paint is thick and the brush nearly empty, the spatters become smaller even with violent action of the brush. A little practice on an old flat will enable you to control the size. Hint: Shake the brush once at the floor or a piece of paper after each dip.

Spattering often is done in several colors, some lighter and some darker than the base. It may even be done in the three light primaries (red, green, blue), somewhat muted, to allow for great variation in lighting without dulling the surface. Spattering also is used to aid in focusing the attention downward toward the actors. For this purpose the set is shaded, making upper and corner areas considerably darker than the center and lower portions. Such shading increases the apparent depth of the setting, in addition to focusing attention.

Perhaps the greatest single value of spattering is that it can rapidly break up the rather flat, chalky appearance of much scene painting. It is a rapid-working, easily altered technique that usually is done as a last step, often after the set is on stage and under lights. Errors are easily corrected except for large dribbles or splashes of paint from an

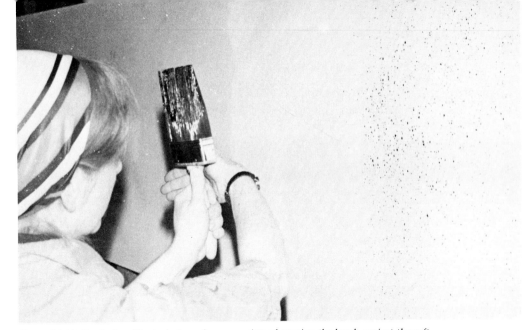

Figure 21-12. Spattering. The technique shown consists of tapping the brush against the soft part of the hand not holding the brush. Use care and experiment on unimportant scenery until the technique is mastered.

overloaded brush. If the spatter texture is a bit heavy, spatter over it with a light treatment of base color. Even minor splashes can be subdued with base coat spatter. Of course, if it has been used over fine detail work, such as foliage, errors will be harder to correct because every additional spatter will tend to obscure more of the detail painting.

Dry Brushing

Dry brushing (Figure 21-13) is also an easy technique for beginners to master, although its finer applications in detail work take years to learn. A specially treasured old lay-in or primer brush often is used for dry brushing. But the ideal brush is just the opposite of a good lay-in brush. Its fibers should naturally separate into small clumps each of which leaves a line of paint when dragged lightly over the surface. If the brush is very dry and the paint heavy, the streaks will be blurry and short. If thinner paint is used, lines resembling wood grain can be drawn. If the object of the dry brushing is to produce wood grain (Figure 21-13b), colors are chosen, and the brush moved to suggest the actual grain pattern of the kind of wood being imitated. Study a piece of real wood to get an idea of how it looks.

Dry brushing is far more than a wood graining technique. It can be used to produce blends (feathering) or a wide variety of textures, depending on the color of the paint and the direction of the strokes (see Figure 21-13a). It often is followed by a spatter coat to improve shadowing of the entire setting.

FIGURE 21-13a

Figure 21-13. (a) Dry Brushing. Two variations are shown. The top brush stroke was made by pressing firmly against the surface producing a smudgelike appearance. Such strokes are used for shading, taking down too-bright areas, and antiquing. The second brush stroke has been done lightly with the brush loaded more heavily with paint. This stroke is used for wood graining and similar applications. (b) Wood Graining. This is an adaptation of dry brushing where slightly more paint is used and details are added.

FIGURE 21-13b

Stippling

A tedious but more precise method of providing texture than either of the above is stippling (Figure 21-14). It consists of tapping the paint-coated surface of some irregularly shaped material against the scenery. A wide variety of materials can be used—almost anything that will carry paint and produce the desired texture on the surface will do. The most common stippling "tool" is a sponge. A natural sponge can be trimmed and, if necessary, sculptured to produce the texture needed. It is then dipped into the paint, squeezed out slightly, and the wet sponge patted against the fabric. Viscose (artificial) sponges can be used in the same way to produce a different pattern, as can rags, various heavy fabrics, the end of an old dry brush, and even wads of paper. For special details in relatively small areas, such textures as the ribbed surface of corduroy or sculptured carpet can be charged with paint and used as stippling tools.

Figure 21-14. Stippling. This stipple with a viscose sponge is one of many textures possible. Coarser textures can be produced by a natural sponge; still coarser ones by a rag or wadded paper.

Roller Texturing

It is only a step from patting the surface with a sponge or rag to rolling with a very lightly charged paint roller to leave a pattern instead of a smooth coat of paint (see Figure 21-15). Some of the possibilities of this method will be evident to anyone who has feathered the edges while using a paint roller. Other possibilities are almost innumerable. For example, a roller can be wrapped with cord; the nap can be partially cut away; it may be covered with special fabric; or it may even have odd bits of material fastened to its surface. Once the roller has been prepared and a technique worked out that satisfies the needs of the scenographer, texturing will proceed very rapidly. Of course multiple colors can be worked into this system just as they can in spattering or ordinary stippling.

Another method, somewhere between stippling and stenciling (see below), consists of purchasing special rollers with soft surfaces. These surfaces can be carved to produce accurately printable designs. Once the roller is prepared, this method is much faster than stenciling, and can produce many of the same effects.

Since these rollers are not available everywhere, some may wish to experiment at making their own by casting flexible foam around cores. See Chapter 18, "Plastics in the Theatre," for foam-casting information.

Figure 21-15. Roller Texturing. An old paint impregnated roller often works better for this purpose. Charge the roller lightly and apply light pressure.

STENCILING

Stenciling (Figure 21-16) makes possible the repetition of complicated designs in multiple colors over a large area. It is simply an elaboration of the familiar process of forcing paint through a cutout.

Designs for theatrical stenciling usually are cut from special stencil paper, a rather heavy cardboard that has been treated to make it water resistant. Thin cardboard of approximately the thickness of standard index cards may be substituted if it is heavily treated with shellac or clear plastic spray both before and after cutting. Another material that makes good stencils, although it is not available in as large sheets as stencil paper, is the thin aluminum sheeting used as backing for certain offset printing plates. This material is much more durable than the heaviest available aluminum foil and can often be begged at no cost from local print shops.

These stencil materials can be cut with a sharp matte knife, a risky process if the cutter is not careful. Patterns should, of course, be laid out in such a manner that all "islands" in the design are supported by thin strips of the material. If the "islands" must be completely

Figure 21-16. Stenciling. A typical setup for applying a stencil utilizing a spray gun. The cut stencil is held in place while the paint is gently sprayed through the openings. The complicated pattern is built up with multiple stencils. Photograph courtesy Theatre Arts Department, University of California, Los Angeles.

free of any visible support, they may be supported in the stencil frame by bobbinet. If multicolor work is planned, the complete design must be broken down into separate stencils, each of which must be capable of being registered properly with the others.

After the stencils are cut, they usually are framed to support the paper and to provide a handle. Any burrs or minor irregularities in the cut edges can be removed with sandpaper. If extensive use of the stencil is planned, it may be worthwhile to make two or three so that one can dry out while the other is in use. The stencil paper absorbs some water from the paint, in spite of all precautions.

Applying the Stencil

There are three common methods of applying paint through the holes in the stencil: brushing, stippling, and spraying. Brushing is best done with a special short-bristled stencil brush. Brush strokes should be away from the edges of the cutouts to prevent forcing paint under the stencil. An ordinary paint brush can also be used but should not be heavily charged with paint. After each use, the back of the stencil should be wiped to remove any paint that has managed to get between the stencil and the scenery. Minor smears on the set are best left to dry and then touched up by hand.

It is probably easier to stipple rather than brush most stencils. This technique also offers the possibility of developing further texture within the larger areas of the design, and provides quite subtle control over the contrast of the design against the background. The scenographer may require that the strength of the stenciled design be varied to aid in focusing attention. The flat surface of a regular stippling sponge is fine for stenciling. It should be well squeezed to remove surplus paint, and care should be taken to avoid pushing paint under the edges.

The fastest way to paint with a stencil is to use a paint gun set to spray a small area at a time. If the gun is aimed exactly at 90 degrees to the surface of the setting, and paint is not allowed to build up and run, this method is least likely to force paint under the stencil. Spraying also provides subtle control over the contrast between stenciled pattern and background.

Ready-made Stencils

A variety of coarsely woven materials may provide ready-to-use stencils for spray patterning. For example, agricultural netting, a coarse, square-woven jute material, can be placed over scenic elements and sprayed to produce patterns. If the material is offset a bit and the spraying repeated with a different color, very unusual effects may be achieved. The netting itself is useful for a wide variety of textures on stage.

SPRAYING AS A DECORATING TECHNIQUE

A paint gun offers the scenic artist about the same range of subtlety as an air brush offers a commercial artist. The results are usually subtle blends, almost invisible retouching, and foglike effects over wide areas. If it is necessary to paint clouds onto a backdrop (they are frequently better projected), a spray gun will provide the soft edges needed. If the lines of a painted setting are to be blurred, fogging with a paint sprayer may be the ideal solution.

In general, the applications of spray blending techniques to scenic painting turn out to be too soft for general use. The results are so subtle that they vanish completely in most theatrical situations. Nevertheless, when appropriate, spray techniques are fast and easily controllable.

DYES

Unlike scene paint which is most frequently mixed to get maximum opacity, dye is used whenever maximum transparency is desired. Dyes work on scenery much in the manner that watercolors work on a painting. They change the color of whatever is under them, following subtractive mixing rules, but do not obscure patterns (although each layer of dye will darken the surface). Since dyes have very little body, they do not fill the pores of the fabric. If they are applied to an open-weave fabric, they will adhere to the fibers of the weave causing light that strikes those fibers to be changed in color. However, light that passes between the weave will remain unchanged. For this reason dyes are the most desirable colorant for gauzes, scrims, and other open-weave fabrics.

When dyes are painted onto fabrics, they tend to soak through the fabric somewhat like ink through blotting paper. This leaves soft, fuzzy edges with each brush stroke. The degree to which this spreading takes place can be controlled by the amount of liquid applied, the dampness of the fabric, and the application of sizing to the fabric. Actually painting with dye can be likened to the Oriental art of Sumi-e, a painting technique using inks in which each brush stroke must be correct because there is no chance of obliterating mistakes. If freehand work will not suffice in laying in dyes, the edges of the area to be dyed can be treated with a resistant material such as glue or rubber cement to prevent spreading into unwanted places.

GAUZES AND SCRIMS

Gauzes and scrims are intended to be at least partially transparent. If they are heavily painted with pigment, they become nearly opaque, which defeats their purpose. Thin washes of scene paint can be used, but dye is usually preferable. It is best applied with a sprayer that will force the dye into the fabric and keep the pores open. Blends and wash techniques can be used to make elaborate and subtle color variations.

Since any technique that completely wets the fabric will tend to wash out flameproofing, it may be necessary to reflameproof after the dye has been applied, or to include flameproofing in the dye solution itself.

DYE AS A FINISHING TREATMENT

It is often necessary to "age" or partially stain a painted surface after detail work has been done. Sometimes thin washes of pigment are used for this, but they may tend to produce a muddy effect. Clear dye solutions, possibly mixed with a little glue or glaze as binder, will produce transparent "stains." The dye can be worked over either a wet or dry base, depending on the effect desired. The technique is much like that of doing a watercolor wash on a grand scale.

TRANSLUCENCIES

A translucency is a piece of scenery intended to diffuse light passing through it so that whatever is behind the scenery is obscured. Theatrical translucencies often imitate such things as stained glass windows or silhouettes of city skylines in the evening, or to suggest mysterious and magical backgrounds.

A translucency usually begins with a clean drop of lightweight muslin. If this material is merely treated with flame retardant, it will become somewhat translucent. If it is starched, its translucency increases. After the starch treatment, dye may be applied to the surface to give color to the light as it passes through the fabric. Since the starch also fills in pores, dye will be held in, and little unfiltered light will pass through the fabric. Opaque parts of translucencies are painted on the front of the fabric with scene paint, especially chosen for its opacity.

SPECIAL PROBLEMS

There are several operations requiring paint shop techniques which may take place either just after the scenery is built and sized, or as late as the end of detail painting. Since they involve materials and techniques peculiar to the paint shop, they are discussed next.

APPLYING DUTCHMEN

The best way to make joints between flats invisible is to design the setting in such a way that all joints are hidden in corners, behind panels or moldings, or otherwise mechanically blocked from audience view. However this is not always possible. When a joint must be in view of the audience it is usually covered with a dutchman, a piece of fabric glued over the joint and painted to match the surrounding area to make it invisible. The time when dutchmen are applied depends on the way in which the setting is to be handled. If the setting is to remain in one place on stage, or only needs to be shifted into a backstage area without breaking down the joint, the dutchman will be applied after the setting has been sized or base coated and its parts hinged together. It may be glued on with dilute glue or by means of scene paint. If glue is used, the dutchman must be considered a permanent part of the flat because it cannot be removed without risk of tearing the fabric off the flat. Such dutchmen may be applied with either diluted carpenter's glue or white glue, depending on shop practice.

If plans require the dutchman to be removed without damage to the flats, it must be adhered to the flat surfaces with a weak adhesive such as scene paint. This is done near the end of the painting process but before detail work is added. The most extreme situation calling for temporary dutchmen occurs when a show must tour and the dutchmen must be removed to disassemble the setting for shipping. After detail painting, the dutchmen are carefully stripped from the flats, rolled for shipment, and eventually reattached to the flats. This regluing is done with special gelatine glues that facilitate repeated removal and reattachment of the dutchmen at each touring stop.

Dutchmen normally are made from narrow strips of scene muslin—often trimmings from covering flats. However when it is necessary to dutchman two older flats together it is better to use an old dutchman or a piece of muslin salvaged from an old flat. Thus the surface of the dutchman will better match that of the adjoining flats.

PATCHING

Even in the best-run theatres, a flat will occasionally be torn or punctured. The patching technique is much like that of installing dutchmen; the patch fabric must match the fabric on the flat in terms of number of coats of paint. Patches normally are applied to the back of the flat by painting the area around the hole with scene paint or glue, pulling the torn edges of the break as close together as possible, and sticking the patch, paint side toward the front of the flat, to the back of the flat fabric. The back of the patch is then given a coat of paint and allowed to dry. After the patch is completely dry, retouching can be attempted on the front, although the result will never quite match the original. Paint usually is used to attach patches applied under pressure during the run of the show. Glue is used when reconditioning flats preparatory to base painting them for a new production. Flats needing more than very minimal patching should be recovered.

PAINTING ROLL DROPS

Although olio curtains are now primarily used to suggest the style of a past era, there are many occasions when a piece of unframed soft scenery must be rolled or even loosely folded. If the fabric has been painted with ordinary glue binder scene paint, the paint will crack and eventually flake off. If the paint has had a very small amount of glycerin added, it will remain flexible. Gelatine glue is also more flexible than regular animal glue. Premixed paints with synthetic binders are usually flexible enough unless applied in several heavy coats.

COVERING OLD PAINT

One or two coats or base paint will normally cover almost any design painted with glue binder scene paint. If premixed paints are in use, one coat is usually sufficient. However, certain painting materials such as metallic paints change the texture of the painted surface in such a way that the outline of the design shows through the base coat even though the color is completely obscured. In the case of glue binder paints, some colors may "bleed" (dissolve and penetrate the wet paint on top), causing stains. Either of these conditions can be alleviated by the application of a coat of size or glaze before applying the base. However, metallics in vivid designs are so hard to cover completely that the best solution is to choose flats due for recovering to carry the metallic design. After this final use, the cover is removed, and new fabric installed.

If dye dissolved only in water has been generously applied over a coat of premixed paint, a coat of glaze may be required to fasten the dye down before a new base coat is added. If the dye has been originally applied with glaze, a new glaze coat should not be necessary.

CARE OF PAINT TOOLS

Good housekeeping is essential in the paint shop. It is particularly important that tools be cleaned as soon after use as possible. In the case of sprayers and other tools used in flame retardants, cleaning must be done *immediately*. Most painting materials will be soluble in warm or hot water as long as they have not been allowed to dry.

Brushes and rollers should be thoroughly washed in warm water and mild soap. The brushes should then be carefully shaped to match their original contour and hung up to dry. A brush should never be allowed to rest for more than a few moments on its bristles either in or out of the paint bucket.

It is particularly important when using premixed paint that it not be allowed to dry even partially on the brushes and rollers. Cover them with a damp cloth whenever they are not in use.

Sprayers should always be cleaned according to instructions. Delicate parts of valves must be cleaned carefully and reassembled without stripping threads or forcing the assembly.

Partially used cans of premixed pigment will have less tendency to harden or scum over if a tiny amount of water is placed on the surface of the remnant before closing the container. This water can be either poured off or mixed into the paint when it is next used. Such precautions are not necessary for overnight storage but will save paint when it is stored for longer periods. Label all remnants.

PART SEVEN

LIGHTING

From a production of Hamlet *done at California State University, Northridge. Photograph by Mike Elliot.*

Figure 22-1. Light and Scenography. This series of production photographs has been reproduced to illustrate the close interrelationship that exists between lighting and the other visual elements of scenography. (a) As You Like It *(Shakespeare). Staged at the Stadttheatre, Cologne, Germany. Scenography: Kisseur. Direction: Ciulli. Photograph by Stefan Odry. Photograph courtesy Helmut Grosser. See also Figure 16-1.* (b) Cyrano De Bergerac *(Rostand). Produced at A.C.T., San Francisco, California. Set by Robert Blackman. Lighting: F. Mitchell Dana. Photograph by Dennis Anderson.* (c) Oberon *(Weber). Produced at the Bayrische Staatsoper, Munich, Germany. Scenography: Josef Svoboda. Direction: Rudolf Hartmann. Photograph courtesy Josef Svoboda.* (d) Idomeneo *(Mozart). Staged at the Stadtoper, Cologne, Germany. Direction and scenography: Ponnelle. Photograph courtesy Helmut Grosser.* (e) A scene from Don Giovanni *(Mozart) as staged at the Cologne Stadtoper. Direction and scenography: Ponnelle. Photographs courtesy Helmut Grosser.*

FIGURE 22-1a

FIGURE 22-1b

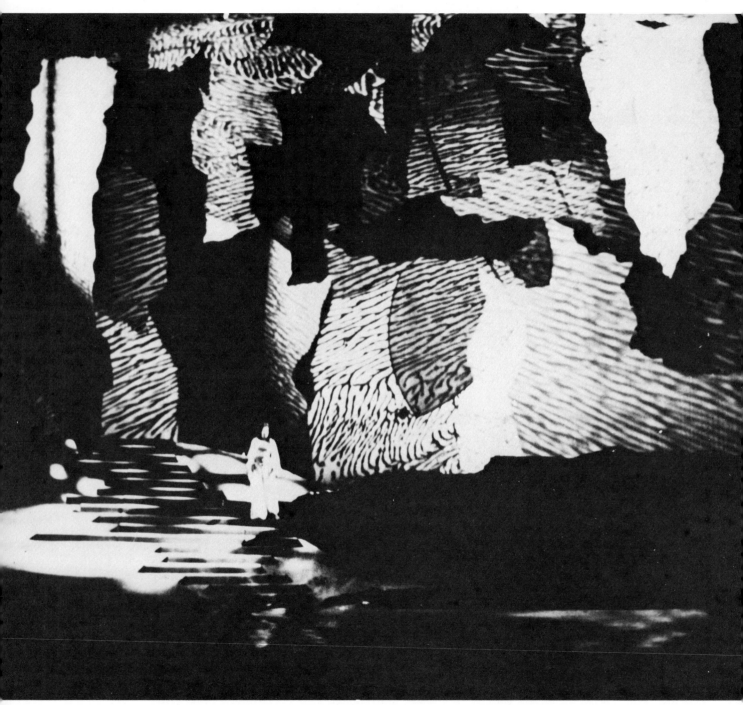

FIGURE 22-1c

FIGURE 22-1d

FIGURE 22-1e

22
LIGHTING
AND
SCENOGRAPHY

INTRODUCTION Lighting, like all other aspects of scenography, begins with the development of concepts by the scenographer and is at that point not distinguishable from other elements. However, as the scenography develops, light soon takes on expressive values of its own and becomes a distinguishable element. As the architecture of the setting is developed, bringing the basic structure of the virtual space into being, variations within that space begin to evolve. Such variations are largely a function of lighting. For example, the spatial value of a run of steps will be variable depending on how light and shadow play over them. As the scenographer mentally tests the expressive value of the proposed steps, he will imagine them under various directions and qualities of lighting. The final design of the steps will be a combination of the physical dimensions of the steps (shown in working drawings) and a variety of lighting angles and intensities that will eventually be expressed in the light plot and lighting cues. Such thinking on the part of the scenographer reinforces once again the folly of trying to separate the design of lighting from that of setting—neither can be thought about successfully without the other.

In the later stages of the design of a production the peculiar mobility of light begins to dominate the scenographic process. We have noted that scenery can be "choreographed." Such movement is ponderous compared to the continuous and subtle movement possible with lighting. Of all of the visual elements of theatre, including the actor, light is the most mobile (Figure 22-1).

LIGHTING, ACTING, AND DIRECTING

As the scenographer begins to concentrate on lighting he finds that he is one-third of a complicated triangular relationship. The moving actor, uttering his lines, is the pivotal figure. The mobility and expressive potential of light must work through him. Without the benefit of his words and pantomine, light is reduced to artistic generalities. His movement and the manner in which he delivers his lines are concerns of the director who must relate them to those of other actors. As the director considers such relationships, he must make moment-to-moment decisions about the focus of attention. One of his first concerns is *clarity*, which requires that the audience be focusing on the right character(s) at the right time. He has several ways to control focus of attention, but the most powerful is lighting. Not only will lighting determine where the audience is looking, but how they are seeing. It can make facial expression highly visible, giving prominence to those expressions that denote strong emotion, or it can reduce faces and figures to two dimensions.

The director must communicate to the scenographer his intentions concerning the flow of attention and the variations in seeing conditions needed from scene to scene. This seems almost mechanical as described, but another, almost completely nondiscursive element enters the picture: the aesthetic result of the flow of lighting over the stage, which is generated by the changing focus of attention, can be far greater than the mere sum of mechanical parts. Because of the powerful ability of light to alter space—making it larger, smaller, sharply defined, or nebulously vague—the moving, changing light takes on symbolic significance all its own. If the artists work together properly, what seemed a somewhat mechanical job of "putting the light where the main focus is" turns into an expressive element of major importance. The lesser, more mechanical functions are not lost; they are instead raised to new expressive levels by becoming a part of one of the major symbolic devices of theatrical art.

Thus it is possible to think of the combination of actors, setting (which forms the base on which the movements are made), and light, as forming a kind of "four-dimensional sculpture." This sculpture relates artistically to the vastly significant symbolic material of space/time we discussed in the introductory chapters. Superimposed on the space/time structure built up by these elements are the artistic capabilities of color and texture, which are both a function of lighting and of setting, costume, and makeup. We have already investigated this interrelationship.

HOW DOES THE SCENOGRAPHER PROCEED WITH LIGHTING DESIGN?

The scenographer starts with his knowledge of the script, the artistic information garnered from a number of conferences with the director, from witnessing some early rehearsals if possible, and from concepts developed during the design of the setting. From all of this he develops a concept of the lighting for the production. He will consider several artistic questions:

1. Where should the focus of attention be at each moment?
2. What is the rhythmic structure of the play?
3. What moods can be established or aided by lighting?
4. What naturalistic elements (weather, time of day, etc.) are needed?
5. How much space should the audience imagine at each moment in the play?
6. How are the characters related to each other? Are they in "separate worlds" or closely related?
7. How do the colors he has designed into the setting and costumes relate to the lighting?

Obviously this list is far from complete. Each production will generate its own special problems and artistic questions. It is up to the scenographer to work out each problem as it arises. He thinks in terms of lighted space and of light striking actors in that space. He considers highlights and shadows, murky moods and bright moments. Most of all, he considers changes, how they will be paced and rhythmically structured. As his ideas develop, he will begin to think in terms of light coming from various locations in the theatre—from the stage right end of the light bridge, or from directly overhead on a batten.

As these ideas become concrete, he begins to sketch out the lighting. He starts with a simple sketch of the stage in plan (that is, seen directly from above without perspective) with the barest outline of the setting, and the permanent features of the house on it. On this basic plan the scenographer marks the location of the lighting instruments that will provide the kind of light he wants at various places on the stage. He makes his choices purely on the basis of the light direction that will produce the right shadow pattern on the actor's face. He follows no rules; there is no set of absolutes dictating that any particular instrument may or may not be used in any location. The only limitations are those imposed by the physical nature of the theatre and by safety. Of course there are commonly used solutions to commonly met problems, but these have none of the rigidity of "law."

THE LIGHT PLOT

When the scenographer has finished his work, he will have produced a *lighting plot* (Figure 22-2). This is a formal version of the drawings that he made as he worked out his ideas. For a simple production it may consist of one or two sheets with a plan of the stage showing the light-

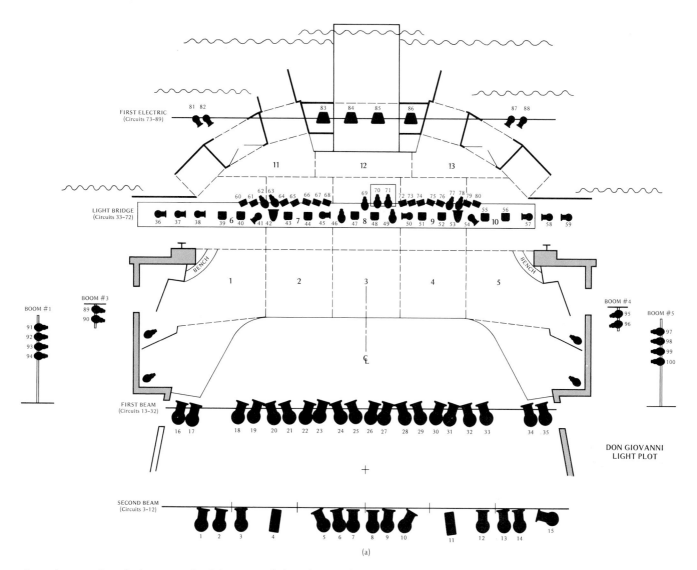

FIRST ELECTRIC
(Circuits 73–89)

LIGHT BRIDGE
(Circuits 33–72)

BOOM #1

BOOM #3

BOOM #4

BOOM #5

FIRST BEAM
(Circuits 13–32)

SECOND BEAM
(Circuits 3–12)

BENCH

BENCH

DON GIOVANNI
LIGHT PLOT

(a)

ing plot, sectional views worked in around the plan to show elevations, and schedules of equipment, color media, and circuitry. For an elaborate production, the plot alone may consist of several overlays or separate plans, each carrying the lighting for one act or one lighting condition. Elevations and schedules may be similarly complicated. The following information will normally be found on a light plot:

1. The location of each lighting instrument to be used.
2. The type of instrument, wattage, color medium, auxiliary parts, and the like, necessary to enable the crew to install the right combination of parts.

Figure 22-2a. A Lighting Plot. This plot is typical. There are many variations depending on the style of the scenographer and the equipment available to his draftsman. The shapes of the various instruments used in this drawing are taken from a commercially available template. Such templates vary in the exact outline designated for each type of instrument. The instruments are often drawn in outline with the color numbers or wattages entered within. Plot by Owen W. Smith.

3. The general area to be lighted by the instrument. This is an approximation to be refined by the scenographer during final angling.

4. The circuitry necessary to operate the instruments, or at minimum, information showing which instruments will operate together.

5. Any other details necessary for the electrical operation of the lighting. For example, if a fixed electrically operated wall fixture is needed, this will be shown on the light plot. (A portable torch is a prop and will be on the prop list although the light crew will probably wire it.)

The scenographer will usually accompany the lighting plot with a number of "schedules." These are itemized lists of various types of equipment needed for the production. They emphasize the technical details needed to assemble the equipment, particularly if it must be obtained outside of the theatre by rental or purchase. In an educational institution with an adequate supply of equipment or a community theatre that is well provided, the preparation of schedules is

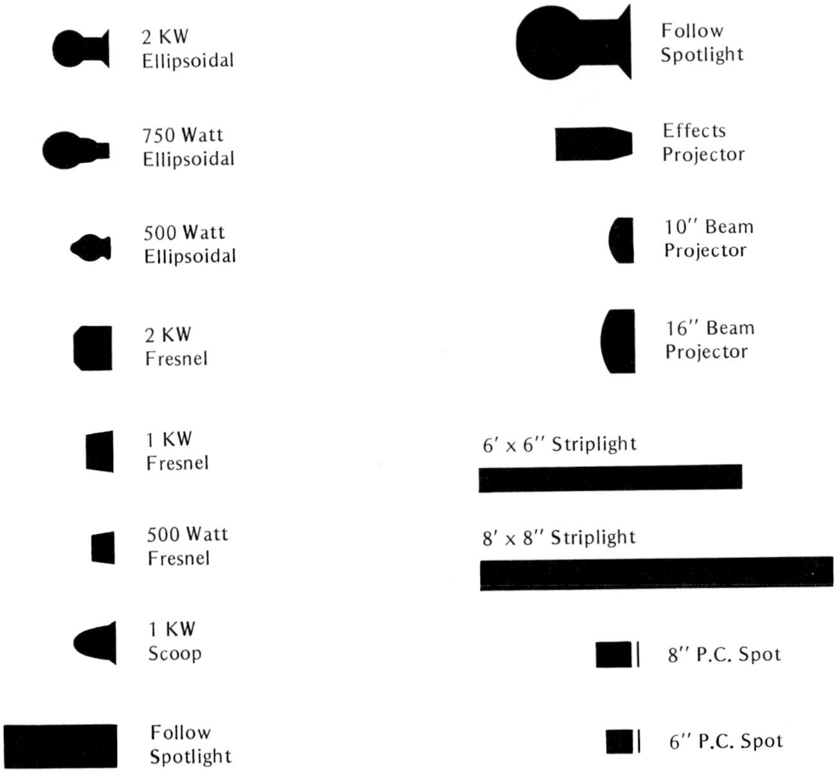

Figure 22-2b. Legend For Lighting Plot in Figure 22-2a. Note that the size of the diagram provides a rough indication of the power of the instrument. The items listed in the left column are those used in the lighting plot in Figure 22-2a. Those in the right column are other symbols commonly used but not on this particular plot. Note the discrepancy in the symbol for "follow spotlight." This is a common sort of variation.

2 KW Ellipsoidal

750 Watt Ellipsoidal

500 Watt Ellipsoidal

2 KW Fresnel

1 KW Fresnel

500 Watt Fresnel

1 KW Scoop

Follow Spotlight

Follow Spotlight

Effects Projector

10'' Beam Projector

16'' Beam Projector

6' x 6'' Striplight

8' x 8'' Striplight

8'' P.C. Spot

6'' P.C. Spot

frequently left to the lighting crew so that they can familiarize themselves with the lighting as they gather the necessary information from the light plot.

The light crew will prepare and mount the equipment under the supervision of its chief and the technical director. The scenographer then supervises the final angling and focusing of the instruments. Only he knows exactly what he wants. He does this in a series of work sessions during which he walks about the stage checking the light produced by each instrument, and calling instructions to the crew members as they make adjustments.

After the instruments have been angled, focused, and circuited, the scenographer is ready to "cue the show." (It is assumed that the set, costumes, makeup, and actors are ready.) He may provide written cues in advance of the cuing sessions, or he may simply call a series of rehearsals during which he calls for various light settings, makes changes until satisfied, and finally gives the word, "Write it." Such sessions may deceive the crew into thinking that the scenographer is ad-libbing his way to the lighting design. A poorly prepared scenographer might be doing this, but a well-prepared one will have done a lot a creative thinking about the possibilities that he will want to try out during these rehearsals. Even later there will be many changes — all the responsibility of the scenographer.

WHAT DOES THE TECHNICAL DIRECTOR DO?

In consultation with the scenographer the technical director concerns himself with problems such as the following:

1. How much equipment will be needed?
2. Have I the electrical power and the control apparatus available to do the job the scenographer wants?
3. Is there enough money in the budget to do the job? Can I save money without compromising the design?
4. What special electrical hookups are needed?
5. What special parts or apparatus must I order? Can I get them in time?
6. How many operators will I need? Do they already know, or can they be trained to do, what is expected of them?
7. Is everything safe? Will it pass inspection?

The operative word in the technical director's title is *technical.* The scenographer refers all technical matters to him, but communicates artistic changes directly to the lighting crew who execute them.

The above list is incomplete but it gives some idea of the scope of the technical director's job. Every show generates new problems.

Inventiveness is necessary. Some of the greatest scenographers today are also technicians and engineers. For example, Josef Svoboda, the European scenographer, is the inventor of a number of ingenious staging devices. Artistic success often depends on the artist's ability to create a machine that will make his concept possible.

WHAT DOES THE LIGHTING TECHNICIAN DO?

In the academic theatre the lighting technician is frequently a graduate student. He works as an assistant specializing entirely in lighting. This leaves the scenographer and technical director more time for other aspects of the production. He may assist the scenographer in the preparation of light plots. If he is a student learning the art of lighting design, he will be present at the conferences between the scenographer and the director, he will attend early rehearsals, and he will participate in planning sessions. He may even have total responsibility for some phase of the design, if the scenographer feels that he is capable. He is likely to take complete charge of the job of working out the patching of the control board, the circuiting of the lighting, the training of the crew, the preparation and repair of equipment, etc., under the supervision of the technical director. He will serve as the crew's main source of information about the lighting and will be able to answer most questions. During those sessions in which the scenographer is setting light cues, the technician serves as his assistant, keeping written records of the cues, solving circuiting problems as they occur, and preparing lists of changes to be made before the next rehearsal.

WHAT DOES THE LIGHTING CREW CHIEF DO?

The lighting crew chief is the immediate supervisor of the crew members. He may be a student or a volunteer. It is the policy in many theatres to choose him from among the crew members after a few work sessions have shown who can handle the responsibility. In other theatre situations he is appointed from those who have had more experience in lighting.

The crew chief is the administrative leader of the crew. He decides who will do what job if this has not already been determined by the technician or technical director. He makes sure that call schedules are clear, that rotating assignments have been properly worked out, and that crew members are present at the proper times. He serves as the intermediary for the crew in all personnel matters.

During the production run he is in charge. He is responsible for preshow lighting checkouts and has the right to request that the stage manager hold the curtain if trouble develops in the lighting system. Ideally, he should know the job of each crew member well enough to step in in case of an emergency.

If there is paper work such as time cards to be signed, it is the crew chief's responsibility. He will carry a set of keys to the control area, the console, the lighting equipment storage areas, etc. He must know where the cue cards or cue book are kept and have access to that area. He supervises minor repairs such as the replacement of burned-out lamps and reports larger problems when they arise to the technician or technical director.

As a crew member, you should treat the crew chief as your immediate supervisor and try to obey his requests. Do not be surprised, however, if there are many artistic and technical questions that he cannot answer. These are not his responsibility.

23
LIGHTING POSITIONS IN THE THEATRE

INTRODUCTION In our discussion of the various types of lighting equipment, it is necessary to refer to the locations in the theatre where they are commonly found, since these locations have determined the nature of the lighting instruments. However, the architectural form and the names of lighting locations vary from theatre to theatre. This must be clarified.

CATEGORIES OF LIGHTING POSITIONS

The two broadest categories of lighting instrument locations are front of house (FOH) and on stage. These terms, like almost all others discussed in this chapter, come from the proscenium theatre. FOH refers to any equipment location on the audience side of the curtain. The only exception is the footlights which are considered part of the stage. In all theatres, proscenium or otherwise, FOH refers to positions that provide light on the stage that comes from the direction of the audience, from above, behind, or slightly to their sides. Such locations result in long *throws.* The throw is the distance from the instrument location to the area on the stage that must be lit. A long throw is considered to be any distance more than 30 feet. FOH locations require that the instruments light only the area on stage, not the audience. This means that FOH equipment has to be designed to produce very little *spill light,* light coming from an instrument that strikes places that should not be illuminated. A poorly designed or misused instrument may flare light over a wide area or spill puddles of light in odd places.

On stage refers to all possible lighting equipment locations found behind the curtain in a proscenium theatre. In the case of the thrust stage or theatre-in-the-round, on stage refers to instruments mounted over the actors as opposed to over the audience.

FOH POSITIONS

There are several possible ways of mounting equipment in FOH locations. Since they vary in accessibility and in the effect they have on the lighting coming from them, we must examine them individually.

Balcony Front

This was probably the first FOH position for unattended instruments. The very first FOH instruments were limelights or arc lights installed at the top and back of the house which were used to follow the stars about on the stage. As soon as incandescent lighting equipment became powerful enough, a new innovation was added. Norman Bell Geddes claims to have been the first to use spotlights hanging from the front of a balcony to light actors from the front. Previously only footlights or follow spots provided front light for those on the apron. The balcony front was the obvious choice because it was accessible, a reason still valid in many theatres. New theatres are often built with lighting ports worked into the structure of the balconies (see Figures 3-3 and 23-1). If there are several balconies, at least one and sometimes all will have places for balcony front lights.

The instruments used for balcony front lighting must have long throw, be quite powerful and reliable, and be exceedingly safe to operate since they hang directly over the heads of audience members.

Figure 23-1. Balcony Front Position. A typical arrangement for temporary installation of balcony front lighting in a theatre where such arrangements have not been built in. Compare this with the built-in arrangements shown in Figure 3-3.

Beam or Ante-pro Positions

Other positions have been designed to do a better job of area lighting than most balcony fronts can provide. Ideally these positions are determined by the proper lighting angle for good area lighting and then worked into the structure of the building. Actually they often are tucked in wherever they will fit. The names come from a common theatrical architectural practice of providing a false beam in the ceiling of the house whose hollow interior conceals lighting equipment. Occasionally a real architectural beam serves the same purpose, although sometimes it does not conceal the equipment. The name "ante-pro" is a shortened form of ante-proscenium ("before the proscenium"), which explains where the lights are located.

Good beam locations have the great advantage of being accessible from above by means of walkways. The equipment can be reached during the run of a show for repairs and gel changes (see Figure 23-2). Note that such positions are provided with safety screening to prevent equipment from falling on the audience below. There are, however, all sorts of makeshift beam positions. They may be nearly inaccessible, requiring hauling of heavy equipment up teetering A-ladders. Such locations are obviously inaccessible during production.

Equipment designed to be used in beam positions must meet the same requirements as that used in balcony front locations. Additionally, it should be easy to work on and highly reliable, especially if it must be used in a makeshift beam. Because beam locations often provide little ventilation for instruments, a wattage lower than rated maximum should be used so that parts and lamps will not fail prematurely.

Side Ports

Side ports are locations in the sides of the auditorium, usually near the front. In a well-designed house, they are a part of the architecture of the building. In other cases the side ports are makeshift mounting positions worked into whatever space is available (see Figure 23-3). The most makeshift of all consists of portable towers of pipe placed in the side aisles of the theatre, a practice usually frowned on by firemen.

ON-STAGE POSITIONS

The main on-stage lighting position is the first electric.[1] This location, just upstage of the main curtain, has many other names: light bridge,

---

1. The complete name would be "first electric batten," but it is always shortened to "first electric." Electric battens, like regular carpenter battens are numbered from downstage to upstage.

Figure 23-2. Walk-in Beam Positions. These lighting positions provide space to walk behind the instruments for servicing. Note the follow spotlight installed in the first beam. The faces of the beams are provided with protective steel mesh.

Figure 23-3. Box Boom. A typical makeshift arrangement used to convert a side stage box from a poor seating area to a useful lighting position. A scaffoldlike structure has been installed to hold the lighting instruments, and temporary wiring has been run to the position. Such structures tend to remain in location for many years.

first pipe, concert border, No. 1 pipe, and more. Whatever its name, this is the most used and most important lighting position backstage. The purpose is to throw light into the areas upstage of the curtain line. Thus, the position is highly desirable not only for area lighting, but for all manner of special instruments, and should be provided with as many independently controlled lighting circuits as possible. Preferably, it should be accessible during production, hence a light bridge is the best form of mount in the first electric position (Figure 23-4). Older theatres often are equipped with a borderlight of ponderous dimensions at the first electric position (Figure 3-16). This will provide satisfactory lighting for concerts and the like, but will only get in the way of equipment installed for area lighting.

Lighting equipment for the first electric position needs to be designed for relatively short throw. It should be small in physical size because space is limited. Spill light is not a problem; in fact a certain amount of controlled spill will aid in blending the lighting areas together. The equipment need not have the power required of instruments in FOH positions; adaptability and small size are more important.

From the point of view of crew workers, the ideal arrangement of this location is a lighting bridge operated by a winch so that it can be lowered to the stage floor for work sessions. The bridge should be accessible in its working position by ladder. This working position should vary depending on the designed height of the proscenium opening.

Figure 23-4. Light Bridge. A lighting bridge for a medium-size theatre shown in lowered position. It is also accessible when raised into working position behind the teaser.

The problem is that such lighting bridges take up a lot of very valuable space at the proscenium opening, space used not only for lighting, but for scenic devices, sound equipment, motion picture sheets, inner prosceniums, and the grand drape. The result is that the light bridge, if there is one, may be forced upstage into a less desirable location.

The FOH positions and the first electric form the backbone of the lighting locations. Those discussed below are of great importance in a well-equipped theatre, but they would be of little use if FOH and first electric were unavailable.

Lighting Battens

"Light pipes" or "electric pipes" are numbered progressively from the first electric or light bridge upstage. The farthest light batten upstage is a special one—the cyclorama pipe (see Figure 23-5). It normally is equipped with the heavy apparatus designed to light the cyclorama. This may be a special borderlight unit or it may be a set of scoop floodlights. In either case, it will be heavy and bulky.

FIGURE 23-5a

Figure 23-5. (a) Lighting Batten. This batten is provided with a number of outlets, each with 5 feet of cable ending in a double connector. A set of portable borderlights hangs from the upper pipe, and spotlights hang from the lower one. (b) Cyclorama Pipe. A "cyc" pipe equipped with large scoops that are normally fitted with red, green, and blue filters, and angled to give smooth coverage.

FIGURE 23-5b

In a modern theatre each of the lighting pipes will be equipped with a number of electrical outlets and a sturdy counterweight system to handle heavy loads. Specific instruments are added according to the needs of each show. Old-fashioned theatres were equipped with borderlights at each light pipe. These originally were intended to illuminate painted wings, borders, and drops. Borderlights serve little purpose for dramatic lighting, although they do provide good lighting for full stage orchestras and similar events.

Equipment mounted on light pipes will vary widely depending on the scenographer. Almost any instrument may be found there. Demands are so varied that it is impossible to generalize.

Tormentor Lighting Positions

The tormentor positions are the areas just upstage of the sides of the proscenium arch. These are favorite locations for stage entrances and are subject to heavy traffic during scene shifts. They are also useful as lighting positions, producing light much like that from side ports. It is a position vitally important to many scenographers.

Equipment for side lighting must be powerful and low in spill light because the beams of light must sweep across the stage reaching from the near to the far side, not spilling out onto the apron or into the house. Adjustable beam shape is highly desirable.

Ladders

These may be found in the tormentor location or anywhere in the wings. They are ladderlike frameworks of pipe supported from above. Instruments are mounted on them for side lighting and special purposes such as suggesting moonlight (see Figure 23-6). Portable wiring usually is supplied to ladders because they must sometimes be completely removed to clear the space for shifting.

Floor Stands and Boomerangs

There are a number of commercial and homemade devices for supporting lighting equipment near floor level. The telescoping floor stand is the most common (Figure 23-7). Crew members should use caution when adjusting the height of the stand. If the loosened inner pipe is allowed to drop under the weight of the instrument mounted on it, the light may be damaged and parts of the hand smashed. Homemade floor stands do not usually telescope. They are heavy bases—perhaps a large block of concrete or an automobile wheel rim—with a vertical pipe attached. A boomerang is a scaffoldlike stand, sometimes

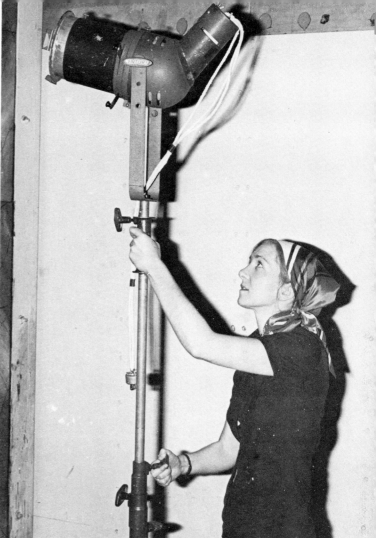

Figure 23-6. Lighting Ladder. Note the space for additional lighting instruments.

Figure 23-7. Focusing from Floor Positions. A typical telescoping, rolling floor stand. Use care when raising or lowering it; if part of your hand becomes caught in the telescoping mechanism, painful injury can result. Support the weight of the instrument when loosening the telescope screw.

equipped with a platform for an operator, that is intended to support a number of instruments.

Footlights

Rows of lamps, with or without reflectors, edge the apron. These foot-lights are now seldom used for acting area type stage lighting. A few small lamps may be installed near the center to soften shadows. However the footlight trough is a useful location for small, but powerful instruments used for special effects. They can be powered on their own circuits if the theatre has been equipped properly or a footlight circuit can be adapted for the purpose, necessitating that all other lamps in the foot circuit be removed.

Another type of footlight may be provided to light the bottom half of the cyclorama. It is located in a floor trough some distance in front of the cyclorama. When not in use it is covered with removable trapdoors. Instruments used here can be portable footlights or border-lights for cyclorama lighting or any others that the scenographer wishes. Be sure that no lighting instruments can be turned on while the covers are in place over the trough. Heat might build up and cause a fire.

Temporary Locations for Lighting Instruments

Any batten on the stage can be equipped to temporarily handle lighting instruments. The special technique involved in this will be discussed later. Other common temporary positions are found within the setting itself. Pipe flanges may be screwed to the wooden frames of the setting and short lengths of pipe added. Lighting instruments then are clamped to the pipe or attached directly to the flange. In either case the entire weight of the lighting instrument and its auxiliary equipment is borne by the screws. A stage carpenter should check out such mountings to make sure they are secure. A safety line should be installed if the set is to be shifted while the lighting instrument is hanging, or if there is any business that might jiggle the mount. Care must also be taken that no hot lighting instrument parts touch the wood or any flammable part of the setting, and that no portion of the beam that may be hot enough to cause fire, strikes the setting. Finally, setting-mounted lighting instruments must be out of the paths used by actors during entrances and exits. If not, the actors will cast large shadows as they pass near the lights, and they may hit the instruments themselves.

Cables running to temporarily mounted lighting instruments are a constant backstage hazard. If at all possible, they should be run away from highly traveled paths, or else they should be covered with tacked-down rugs, special cable covers, or even wooden decking. Whenever possible, cables should run overhead until they are in the vicinity of the control board or floor pocket, and dropped directly to where they plug in.

When lighting instruments are mounted on sets that must be shifted, it is the responsibility of the light crew to check them during the shift, move them if they must be moved, and check their operation before word is given to start the next scene. In theatres with back-of-house lighting control, at least one crew member commonly stays back-stage to attend to these duties and take care of any other problem that may arise.

24

ELECTRICITY AND ELECTRICAL SAFETY

INTRODUCTION Almost all of the light used in the theatre is made by conversion of electricity into heat and then into light. We control this process by controlling the amount of electricity that is supplied. This, in turn, controls the amount of light ultimately produced, although much energy is lost in the conversion process. This chain of events is so common in the theatre that we seldom think about it. We speak of "controlling the lights," although we are really controlling the electricity to make heat which makes light.

Electrical energy can be a dangerous form of energy. It can shock, kill, and maim, or it can generate heat so violently that explosion or fire results. Even if electricity does not get violently out of hand, it can go astray, interrupt a production, and cause expensive damage to the theatre's equipment. Therefore we must understand how electricity is generated and how it is controlled, in order to protect life and property and to maintain the integrity of the production.

WHAT IS ELECTRICAL CURRENT?

Exact scientific usage reserves the term "electricity" for phenomena related to charges and the term "electrical current" for those related to the flow of electrons. In common usage, which will be followed in this text, the terms are usually interchangeable. Thus we can say that electricity (electrical current) consists of a flow of electrons. Electrons are negatively charged detachable parts of atoms. When they are attached to an atom, they are held in place by the attraction of "protons" which remain in the nucleus of the atom and carry a positive charge.

When electrons are detached from atoms and moved about by the application of energy, they are said to flow, and this flow is described as an *electrical current*. It may be thought of as crudely analogous to a stream of water being pumped through a closed piping system. Once a pump gets the water moving it will be possible to extract energy from the pipe containing the moving water by passing the water through a water motor (a water-wheellike device that gathers mechanical energy from the moving water). As long as the pump keeps putting energy into the stream of water, the motor or motors can take energy out up to the amount the pump puts in, less whatever friction loss there is in the system. A stream of electrons can be made to do much the same thing.

HOW IS ELECTRICITY MADE?

Any device that will force electrons away from their normal balanced condition in an atom and propel them through a path might be called a source of electrical energy. Light beams striking a solar cell will detach electrons from the metal of the cell and cause them to flow. Thus a solar cell is a source of electricity. If you scuff across a carpet on a dry day, heat energy generated by the friction of your movement may separate electrons from their atoms, building up a collection of excess detached electrons on your body, thereby causing you to carry a negative charge. When you touch an object that allows the excess electrons to flow back to a condition of balance, they do so suddenly, and to your displeasure —you get a shock. You yourself are the source of the electrical energy in this case. Note that in each case there must be some source of energy for the conversion. Electricity is never made from nothing.

Batteries

A common electrical source is known as a "battery"—a container within which there are chemicals that react to produce electricity. As they combine to form other chemicals, energy is released in the form of electricity. In the case of the common dry cell (which is not really dry, but moist inside) the chemicals are put into the cell and are allowed to react, giving up their energy. The cell is thrown away when no more electricity is available from it. In other cases, such as the common lead-acid battery used in an automobile, the chemical reaction is operated in both directions. If we start with a charged battery, we can extract energy from it, perhaps to start the car. Later, when the car engine is running and we have energy to spare, the reaction in the battery can be reversed. It then absorbs electrical energy and is in readiness for another use. Such batteries are rechargeable.

Batteries are important to the theatre for a number of reasons: they serve as electrical sources for portable lamps, torches, and other portable props, and they may also form the reserve electrical system for emergency lighting.

Generators

Except for small amounts of emergency and property lighting provided by batteries, almost all of the electricity used in the theatre and in most other day-to-day uses comes from *generators,* machines that convert mechanical energy to electrical energy. They do this by an electro-magnetic process which takes advantage of the very complicated relationship that exists between electricity and magnetism. Fortunately we do not need to know the details of this process to understand the use of electricity in the theatre.

Most generators are huge machines that make millions of watts of electrical power. To do this they need large sources of mechanical energy such as water falling from the top of a hydroelectric dam or the energy from a steam turbine that in turn gets its power from expanding steam from a boiler. Presently atomic power is also being used to generate steam.

A generator may be thought of as a huge pump driving electrons through a vast electrical distribution system. Their energy is taken out of the system wherever needed, or, when things go wrong, wherever it manages to break loose. Since the total power in the system may be huge, so is the potential for damage.

Alternating and Direct Current

There is a further distinction between the current produced by a battery and that produced by a generator. All batteries produce *direct current* (dc) (see Figure 24-1a). This means that the flow of electrons proceeds continuously in the same direction from the connections of the battery. Electrons flow from the pole marked "minus" (negative charge) toward the connection marked "plus" (positive charge) as long as the circuit is complete (closed) and the chemicals in the battery have the power to react. On the other hand, most large generators produce *alternating current* (ac) (Figure 24-1b). This means that as the coils in the generator turn, they produce a current that rises from zero to a peak one-quarter of the way through the turn, then diminishes toward zero, reaching it at the halfway point. As the generator continues to turn, the voltage swings negative, reaching its most negative reading at the three-quarter turn point, and returning toward zero as the revolution is completed. The process then repeats for each turn of the generator. If the generator turns 60 revolutions per second, the result will be 60 complete sets of change (cycles) per second. This is known as 60 cycles/second or 60 Hertz alternating current (abbreviated 60 Hz ac) and is the standard current in United States power distribution systems. Many systems in Europe have standardized at 50 Hertz.

The constant change in the voltage value of ac alters power formula calculations because the average current is not the same as the

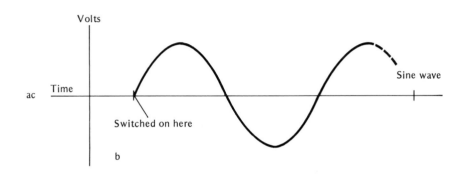

Volts

dc   Time

Switched on here

a

Volts

ac   Time

Switched on here

Sine wave

b

Figure 24-1. These drawings show the difference between direct current (a) and alternating current (b) in terms of the way these currents vary with time.

peak current. However this causes little trouble in most calculations because ac ammeters and voltmeters have already been calibrated to adjust for the difference. Therefore calculations of lamp loads using the power formula can proceed as if there were no difference as long as the voltage and current readings have been adjusted for ac average values. Although it will seldom be necessary to make such adjustments, it may be interesting to note that the peak voltage of an ac circuit must be divided by 1.41 to convert it to the equivalent dc value.

There are very important differences between ac and dc when it comes to motors and dimmers. Most modern dimmers, for example, work only on ac. The near-obsolete resistance dimmers work equally well on either kind of current. Fortunately almost the entire United States is supplied with 60 HZ ac, with the exception of a few theatres in New York City.

HOW DOES ELECTRICAL CURRENT FLOW?

The path that a stream of electrons will take in its rush to regain balance with protons will vary depending on the electrical pressure that is applied by the generator. If enough electrical pressure (voltage) is applied, the electrons will even jump through a vacuum or through air. They can, in fact, be driven through almost anything if the voltage is raised high enough. However, many materials will allow their passage only at the expense of being destroyed by the flow. These materials prevent the substantial flow of electrons at anything less than a voltage that will destroy the material. Such materials are known as "insulators." Conversely, there are materials that allow the electrons to move through them with ease. These are known as "conductors." A third category will allow electrons to flow through without damage to the materials, but at the expense of giving up a considerable share of their energy. These are known as "poor conductors," or sometimes as resistance materials. (See Table 24-1.)

Table 24-1

Common Conductors and Insulators in the Theatre

Insulators
    Plastics
    Rubber
    Dry wood
    Glass
    Ceramics
Good Conductors
    Gold (in console parts)
    Silver
    Copper
    Aluminum
    Brass
    Mercury
    Lead
Resistance Materials
    Tungsten
    Nickel-chromium-iron alloys
    Carbon

If one wants to construct a useful path for a stream of electrons one may provide a path of conductors through which they may flow to wherever we wish to extract energy. Another easy path must be provided for them to return to the electrical source to be pumped around again. Note that the path (Figure 24-2) is closed; it must be complete including the return path to the source, or energy cannot be extracted because no electrons will flow. There will be electrical pressure but no movement. To keep the electrons in this useful path, we surround it with insulators. As long as the voltage produced by the source is less

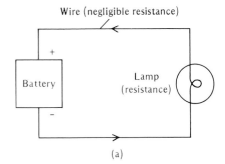

Wire (negligible resistance)

+

Battery

Lamp
(resistance)

−

(a)

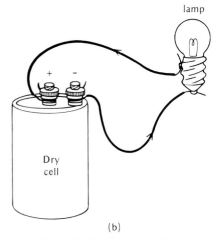

lamp

+ −

Dry
cell

(b)

*Figure 24-2. The Simple Circuit. These diagrams
show a simple circuit in schematic (a) and pictoral
(b) form. Note the direction of electron flow and
the closed nature of the circuit.*

than that which would cause the insulators to break down and let the electrons through, they will not allow the electrical current to leak away.

ELECTRICAL TERMINOLOGY

We have already defined one of the terms related to the flow of electricity:

Voltage (E) refers to the electrical pressure placed on the electrons by the electrical source. The unit is the *volt* (V).

There are other key terms:

Electric Current (I) refers to the quantity of electrons flowing through a circuit. It actually refers to a discrete although very large number of electrons flowing each second past the point of measurement. The unit is the *ampere* (Amp).

Resistance (R) refers to a characteristic of materials that can be described as the opposition that a material offers to the flow of electric current. Resistance depends on the type of material used, its length, diameter, and temperature. For example, iron has more resistance than copper. Therefore a piece of iron wire of a given diameter and length would have more resistance than a piece of copper wire of the same dimensions. On the other hand, a thicker piece of iron wire might have as little as or even less resistance than the piece of copper wire. Resistance is measured in *ohms*.

Power (P) refers to the rate at which an electrical circuit does work. In its instantaneous form it describes the amount of energy being produced at any given moment. The unit is the *watt* (W). 746 W is equivalent to 1 horsepower.[1] If we want to know the total amount of energy expended over a period of time, we must multiply average power (watts) by time. The unit then becomes the *watt-hour*. Since a watt-hour is a small unit, the *kilowatt-hour* (1000 watt-hours) is the commonly used term. This is the unit used to figure electric bills.

These various terms may be combined into simple mathematical formulas that describe what happens when electricity flows. The most fundamental formula is known as Ohm's law, after its discoverer. It describes the relationship that exists between voltage, current, and resistance in any simple electrical circuit. A *simple circuit* is one that provides only one path for the electrons to take from generator through whatever is taking the energy out (load), and back to the generator. Although it is rarely necessary in routine stage lighting applications to

---

1. Theoretically perfect energy conversion. A practical 1 horsepower motor will use 1000–1500 W, wasting the extra watts mostly as heat.

use Ohm's law, it is mentioned here because it forms the basis on which the electrical mathematics that is common in the theatre is constructed.

$$\text{Ohm's law: } E = I \times R$$

E refers to the voltage, I to the current, and R to the resistance. These letters are standard forms of denotation in physics and electrical engineering. If any two elements in this formula are known, the third can be found mathematically.

THE POWER FORMULA

Although Ohm's law will seldom be used in stage-lighting calculations, it ultimately forms the basis for the power formula:

$$P = E \times I$$

"Wattage equals voltage times current."

This formula makes up the backbone of most theatrical calculations because manufacturers have already applied Ohm's law to their products and have rated them in either watts or amperes. To make things still simpler, voltage is rather well-standardized in the United States and usually is treated as a given term (110–120 V).

The following list of common theatrical electrical gear indicates the term usually used to rate the equipment. The power formula can be applied to any two of these terms to find the third. For example, if power and voltage are known, current can be determined.

Lamps—rated in watts at standard voltages, e.g., 1000 W, 120 V.

Dimmers—rated in watts at standard volts, e.g., 2000 W, 120 V.

Wire—rated in amperes at a maximum voltage (depending on the type of wire insulation), e.g., 20 Amps at 600 V. Note that the voltage rating of the insulation is always much higher than the standard 120 V.

Fuses—rated in amperes at maximum voltage, e.g., 20 Amps at 250 V.

Switches and connectors—rated in amperes (or watts) at maximum voltage.

Lighting instruments—rated in maximum lamp wattage to avoid overheating.

Lamp holders, sockets—rated in watts and voltages well above standard.

Note that in the case of those items with voltage ratings above the standard 120 V, the higher voltage rating reflects a safety factor in the insulation or the heat load they may safely carry. It is important to note that operating them at lower voltages does not increase the number of amperes they can safely handle.

ELECTRICAL SAFETY

Safety comes before anything else. You may not have realized it, but the voltage and current available at a wall outlet in a home is far more than enough to kill or injure, and the stage uses electrical currents many times as powerful as those available in a home. In addition to the dangerous currents, you will be exposed to great quantities of electrically generated heat. Fire is a constant danger. Burned fingers, while not fatal, are unpleasant. We must learn what hazards are involved in stage lighting and how to cope with them.

ELECTRICAL SHOCK

Electrical shock can be fatal; it can maim; or it can merely ruin your nerves for a time. What actually happens when you get a shock depends upon several things.

1. How high was the voltage? If it was less than 30 V, there is little chance that you could get a serious shock. Anything more than 30 V is considered by safety experts as potentially dangerous and most stage lighting equipment uses 120 V, which can be deadly. Even higher voltages are commonly found inside lighting control boards, dimmer racks, etc.

2. How much current flowed through the victim? Anything more than a tiny fraction of an ampere can be too much. An ampere is approximately the amount of current that flows through a 100 W lamp when it is turned on. This is much more than enough to kill if the circumstances are right. Actually a few thousandths of an ampere can be deadly if flowing through the heart or brain.

3. Through what part of the victim did it flow? If the electricity flowed in through one finger of the hand and out through another of the same hand, the probability is that the victim was only slightly burned and felt a sturdy jolt. Of course, a jolt can also be fatal if it knocks you off the top of a 30 foot ladder. Use care. If the electrical current flowed through vital parts of the body, the victim may be knocked unconscious,

killed, or severely injured. Such shocks frequently paralyze the breathing apparatus. For this reason, first aid to shock victims calls for artificial respiration the moment the victim is free of the electrically live parts.

4. How dry was the victim's skin? This has much to do with how much current flows. Dry, calloused skin is a fairly good insulator and has saved many people from otherwise fatal shocks.

Obviously the point of the rather gruesome discussion above is simple: *Do not get in the path of an electrical current.* To avoid this we need to know how electrical circuitry is arranged.

Grounding

Electricity flows from the electrical source through conductors, passing through various devices that use the energy of the electron flow to produce other forms of energy (see Figure 24-2). If one manages to substitute oneself for a part of the conductor system, something unpleasant may happen. One way to do this would be to attach yourself to the outgoing and return conductors of a generator at the same time. This would involve making contact with two separate wires at once, something not impossible but relatively unlikely to happen. You probably know already from sad experience that you can sometimes get a horrible jolt by touching *one* electrically live part. This brings out an important complication in the flow of electric current as it is designed by engineers who must make our nation's electrical system work reliably and efficiently.

Electricity usually is made where huge sources of energy are available, for example at Niagara Falls. It must then be "shipped" over miles of transmission lines to the cities where it is needed. Here one of nature's electrical sources—lightning—enters the picture. A lightning bolt is a mammoth electrical current flowing between a cloud and the earth. (Occasionally bolts flow from cloud to cloud, but this does not concern us.) Lightning energy is measured in millions of volts and the current in hundreds of amperes. An electrical transmission line dangling from insulators designed to handle perhaps 100,000 V on towers 100 feet above the earth will be a good, short path to the earth for the lightning bolt. Without proper measures, lightning-induced current surges might damage the transmission system or the generators.

Obviously, engineers must do something to avoid this possibility. The solution is to make it easier for the lightning to pass to the earth without going through the generators. This is done by *grounding* one of the conductors of the electrical transmission system. The conductor is attached to the earth both solidly and frequently. This grounded conductor is attached to the earth at practically every tower in regions where lightning is prevalent.

In addition to the grounded conductor, the engineers provide traps that prevent any stray current surges from passing through the generating equipment.

The earth therefore becomes one of the conductors in the electrical system. *If you are electrically connected to the earth, you are already "holding" one lead from the electrical source.* It will only take one more connection to make you a part of the circuit. This is why you can often get a shock by touching only *one* electrically live part. It is also the reason that wearing rubber-soled shoes is a good idea when working on electrical apparatus. The shoes can serve as insulation to disconnect you from the earth if you happen to be standing on some grounded object.

Here is a list of objects commonly found on stages that are apt to be grounded (i.e., connected electrically to the earth):

> Concrete floors.
> Water pipes.
> Gas pipes.
> Steel framework such as gridiron parts.
> Pipe battens.
> Metalwork covering electrical apparatus. This is required to be grounded by law so that if a live wire touches it, a fuse will immediately blow, warning of trouble. Floor pocket covers are grounded for this reason and should be especially noted because you handle them while plugging cables into their sockets.
> The earth itself (outdoor theatre).
> Rigging and counterweight system parts.
> Steel parts of the building structure.

Two conditions must exist before an object may be considered to be grounded: it must be a conductor, and it must be electrically connected to the earth either directly or via other conducting materials. Obviously the safest course is to consider every potentially conductive object (such as a concrete floor) as grounded until you know otherwise. This may cause you to take some foolish precautions, but at least you will be safe.

Nevertheless, working with electricity in a properly constructed and maintained theatre is probably safer than using it in your home. There is no need for abject fear; reasonable caution will suffice. There is no truth to the stories you may hear about some people "attracting electricity" or others being "immune to it." Carelessness is sufficient attraction, and dry calloused skin is the only immunity, though a poor one at that.

What Is a Live Wire?

The practice of grounding one conductor of an electrical system leads to the distinction between "live" and "dead" electrical parts. Electrically live parts are those having a voltage relative to the ground. Dead parts are either carrying no electrons or they are at ground voltage. When you touch a grounded part while you are electrically connected with the earth, nothing happens because there is no voltage between you and the earth. If you touch a live conductor a voltage between you and the earth exists and *you provide the path* for current. You may handle a grounded conductor safely, but if you cut it or undo a connection, you may get a shock because you have ungrounded it. Grounded conductors are safe only while they are securely grounded.

HOW DO YOU IDENTIFY A LIVE WIRE? There are two ways to identify a live wire. First, you should assume that any internal conductor in a connected and working piece of electrical apparatus is live. This pertains to the working parts of all sockets, connectors, the interior of cables, parts of switches, dimmers, etc. In brief, if it works by electricity and is either on and working or off but connected, its internal parts are probably dangerous. (Note that this is particularly true of the inner metal parts of radios and televisions which may be at full line voltage even when switched off.) However, if a piece of electrical apparatus such as a spotlight is completely disconnected from its electrical source—the plug has been pulled and you can see the loose end—you can be certain that the interior of the spotlight is dead. You should note again that this may not be true of certain electronic apparatus such as TV receivers because they can store up an electrical charge, but it is true of all stage lighting apparatus. In brief, the first way to identify electrically live parts is by reasoning—if the part is connected and/or working, it is probably live.

A second method of identifying a live wire is to test for it. To do this you need a test light such as the one shown in Figure 24-3. You also need a ground that is known to be firmly attached electrically to the earth. Preferably you should use a cold water pipe or the grounded frame or conduit which encloses the electrical apparatus. The first step is to test the ground itself. This is done by attaching your test light between a conductor that is known to be live (i.e., a lead to a lamp that is operating) and the probable ground. Try both wires sequentially—one will be live. If your test light operates at half brilliance, you will know you have a satisfactory ground. If the test light merely glows, or does not light at all, look for another ground. Incidentally, these preliminary tests also assure you that the test light itself is in working order. Figure 24-3 shows the test light operating at full brilliance and at a satisfactory ground.

Figure 24-3. Pigtail Tester. The tester is made by connecting and insulating one of the leads from each of two pigtail sockets. Such sockets are available at any electrical supply store. The remaining free ends form the test leads. The sockets should be equipped with lamps of equal wattage less than 30 W apiece. If necessary for attachment to a distant ground, additional wire may be added to one of the leads. Operation: This double test light will operate at full brilliance only if you connect it to 220–240 V. Such a voltage is occasionally encountered and is the reason for the double lamps; a single lamp might explode. The picture on the bottom shows this full brilliance condition. The picture on the top illustrates the usual condition when the test light is attached to the ground or electrical neutral and a live wire. Be sure you touch only the insulated portion of the test light when making tests.

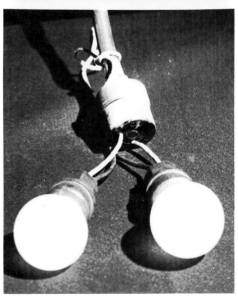

Attach one lead of the test light to the now-assured ground. You are now ready to seek out electrically live parts by touching them with the other lead of the test light. When you do this there are three possible conditions which you may encounter (in stage lighting situations):

1. The unknown part will be live and the test lamp will light up to half brilliance or to some lesser brilliance if the circuit is on dimmer. In any case, if the light glows at all, it means that the part is dangerous.
2. The test light will not light at all because the part is grounded.
3. The test light will not light because the part is not electrically connected to anything.

It will be necessary to distinguish between the last two possibilities because you must be sure that the part which tested "dead" will not come on unexpectedly. To distinguish between the second and third situation, reattach one lead of the test lamp to the previously established live wire, and touch the other lead to the part that tested dead. If the unknown part is really a ground, the lights will go on; if it is not connected to anything, the lights will remain off.

A test lamp is a source of assurance as well as safety. Do not be afraid to use it repeatedly to reassure yourself about anything on which you are working. However, as a beginner your best assurance of safety should be the fact that the equipment is completely disconnected from any source of power, and that the disconnection is plainly in your sight. Never simply turn off a piece of equipment at the control board and begin working on it. Some "helpful" person may note that a lamp is off, and turn it on while you are handling its working parts.

As a beginner you should not be asked to work unassisted on live lighting apparatus or on apparatus which cannot be disconnected by simply pulling a plug. However, you may encounter faulty apparatus or parts that appear to be dead and actually are not. For example, in many old theatres it is possible for the entire outer body of a spotlight to be live even though the instrument is still working. It is also possible for it to be live although the lamp is burned out or missing from its socket. These dangerous conditions happen when equipment is mounted in such a way that it is not grounded via the batten, pipe stand, or whatever is holding it up. If a piece of equipment shows any signs of irregularity, such as flickering, sputtering, not working, or smelling of hot parts, disconnect it before you examine it. This is particularly important if you know that the equipment is not grounded, and that *you are* while you are working on it.

Modern safety laws are designed to remove the risks mentioned above. Unfortunately, they apply to new theatres and to renovated older buildings, but not to theatres built before the laws were passed. The modern law requires that each piece of portable lighting equipment be provided with a *third* lead-in wire which does nothing but ground all noncurrent-carrying parts of the instrument the moment it is plugged in. When this wire is in operation, there is no chance that the entire spotlight, for example, can become "hot." If a live part touches the now-grounded case, a short circuit is formed which immediately blows a fuse. This shuts down the entire circuit and warns that trouble is present. The third wire is known as an *equipment ground;* it is costly but highly desirable.

ELECTRICAL HEAT

Although shock is certainly the electrical danger that strikes terror into most of us, the fact is that electrically generated heat causes damage and injury more frequently than shock. Heat is a form of energy—one easily converted from electrical energy. It is almost impossible to avoid converting some of the energy in every electrical circuit into heat. Whenever electricity flows through a conductor, except under rare and exotic conditions, heat is formed. Of course, heat is deliberately sought in many cases—in an electric heater, for example. The problem is that unwanted heat will be formed whenever too much electricity flows through a circuit or whenever the electricity flows through a loose connection. This heat can cause fire or even an explosion. It can destroy equipment gradually or instantly, and it can burn those handling the equipment.

The amount of heat produced in an electrical circuit varies according to the following formula:

$$H \text{ (in calories/second)} = 0.24 \ I^2R$$

While we need not concern outselves with all of the details of the heat formula, we do need to note two important things.

1. Any increase in resistance at a given point in a circuit will tend to produce more heat at that point. Thus a loose connection will heat up because R has increased. The effect interacts cumulatively making it almost diabolic: As the loose connection heats up, its parts begin to oxidize because of the additional heat. Metallic oxides are poorer conductors than pure metals. This increases R still more, resulting in more heat, which results in more oxide. The process spirals upward until the conductor is destroyed or fire breaks out. This vicious circle has destroyed the connections of many theatrical dimmers, making them useless although the rest of the dimmer remains in good order. The same vicious circle is responsible for many of those mysterious residential fires that break out at three o'clock in the morning. (This does not usually happen to theatres because their electrical circuitry is generally shut off when the theatre is closed for the night.) A hot connection somewhere in an attic, slowly spiraling its way to flames, is not a pleasant thing to contemplate.

2. The second implication of the heat formula has to do with overloads. In this case, I is altered in the formula. *Note that doubling* I *results in quadrupling the heat.* This is the reason that electrical overloads are so dangerous. The heat increases by the *square* of the current, not simply in direct ratio. This means that a stage cable designed to carry 20 Amps will get four times as hot if the current is doubled (perhaps by plugging in extra lamps in an attempt to avoid running more cable). It also means that the all-too-common practice of increasing the fuse rating to prevent blowouts from overloads rapidly increases the potential amount of heat that may be generated in a conductor. Such heat has a cumulative effect on the insulation. It gradually bakes the rubber or plastic until it becomes brittle and breaks down.

SHORT CIRCUITS

The most spectacular demonstration of the potentalities of electrically generated heat occurs in a *short circuit,* a situation in which a path of extremely low resistance is accidentally created in a circuit. Electricity takes the path of least resistance. Almost all of the electrons flowing in the entire electrical system will attempt to flow through the short circuit on their way back to the electrical source. In a well-wired stage circuit this may amount to many thousands of amperes. The heat increases by the square of this already large figure, and the result is that the conductor is heated so fast that it literally explodes, throwing molten metal and burning insulation in all directions. Fire is the usual consequence unless the explosion is contained in a nonflammable metal structure such as a conduit.

There is no sharp line of demarcation between overloads and short circuits as far as the effect is concerned. Briefly, in an *overload,* a controlled but too-large flow of electrons takes place, while in a short circuit the only controlling factor is the capacity of the system to deliver electrons or the ability of the system resistance to limit the current. However, the effects of a very heavy overload can be identical to those of a short circuit: explosion and fire.

Fuses and Circuit Breakers

Shorts and overloads can be prevented from causing great damage by the use of "overcurrent devices." These devices shut off the current when it increases beyond a predetermined amount. The simplest of these is the *fuse.* A fuse is a weak link purposely inserted into a circuit. It is designed to destroy itself and thereby shut off the flow of electrons before any damage can be done by overcurrent. Once it has served this purpose, it must be replaced. A *circuit breaker* performs exactly the same function but does not destroy itself. It can be reset when the excess current situation has been remedied. Fuses and circuit breakers commonly found on stage are shown in Figure 24-4. Although a circuit breaker looks much like a switch, it is not designed to serve as a switch on a regular basis, and it will be harmed if so used.

Circuit breakers, if they are of reliable quality, are desirable for stage lighting use because they can be easily reset after trouble has occurred. Fuses, although simpler and cheaper, take more time to replace and can easily be replaced by others of the wrong size. Unfortunately, common plug fuses (Figure 24-4) are mechanically interchangeable in sizes from 6 to 30 Amps. This often causes an uninformed buyer to assume that he is getting the best bargain in the largest, because they all cost the same amount. Of course, the right size is the one engineered into the circuit from the beginning. Inserting a larger fuse, say a 30 Amp one where a 20 Amp size is required, removes much of the protection against overloads for that circuit. If the erroneously inserted larger fuse is loaded to capacity, 2.25 times the heat will be generated in the circuit compared to the heat that would be generated before the opening of a 20 Amp fuse (20^2 compared with 30^2). The presence of a larger fuse only makes possible the larger current; it does not automatically cause it to happen. The final effect still tends to be automatic,

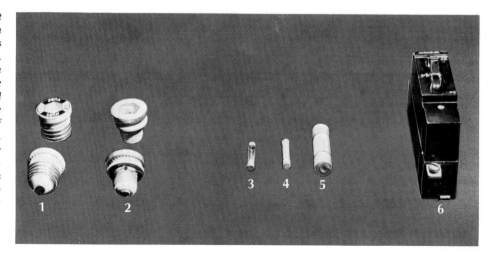

Figure 24-4. Typical Fuses and Circuit Breaker for a Stage. The photograph depicts only a few of the many types of fuses and circuit breakers available. These few usually are encountered in stage lighting. (1) Typical plug fuse used to protect circuits of 30 Amps and under. (2) Fusestat used in the same way as plug fuse. But the Fusestat of each rating fits only its special socket, defeating any attempts to alter fuse size. (3) Miniature cartridge fuse occasionally found in small stage circuits and often in control circuits. (4) Ceramic miniature fuse occasionally used to protect small dimmer circuits. (5) Standard cartridge fuse for heavy-duty circuitry. Fuse shown is usually available up to 60 Amps. Larger sizes have larger housing and blades to fit socket at each end. (6) Typical top quality thermomagnetic circuit breaker; these are excellent for stage use and come in a wide variety of current ratings. Photograph by Herbst.

however, because people are apt to load a circuit to whatever the fuse will take before checking into the safety of this procedure. By the time the oversize fuse blows, dimmers may have been damaged, wiring overheated, and fires started.

It should be obvious that the illegal practice of bypassing a fuse or circuit breaker, even temporarily, is exceedingly dangerous. A penny inserted under a fuse makes it the *least* likely instead of the *most* likely link in the circuit to open in case of a short circuit. This removes all protection against both short circuits and overloads.

Those who must use plug fuses instead of circuit breakers, usually because they work in older theatres, do gain one advantage. Examination of a burned-out fuse will often tell the observer what caused it to open. A slight overload (a common occurrence in theatres) will result in a fuse whose window remains clear. Inside you will be able to see the melted ends of the fuse wire, and if you are handling the fuse just after it has opened, the fuse will be hot. A short circuit will blacken the entire window, and will usually happen so fast that the fuse body will have no time to heat up (see Figure 24-5).

Fuses should occasionally be tightened in their sockets and circuit breakers should be checked for loose connections. Note that there is no such thing as a fuse "wearing out." If a fuse blows, there is a good reason for it. The reason should be found and remedied before a new fuse is inserted. The practice of inserting fuse after fuse in a faulty circuit in the hope that the trouble will go away or on the theory that the fuses are faulty, is foolish. Determine the trouble, fix it, then restore the circuit. (Circuit breakers will not allow the above foolishness. When they open, the handle becomes loosened from the mechanism, and will not allow resetting until the circuit is fixed.)

Figure 24-5. Blown Plug Fuses. This photograph will aid the reader in distinguishing between plug fuses opened by an overload and those opened by a short circuit. The upper fuse was opened purposely by subjecting it to a slight overload until it blew. Note that the central portion of the fuse wire melted out, leaving a clearly visible break. The lower fuse purposely was subjected to a simulated short circuit. This sudden surge exploded the fuse wire, blackening the entire face of the fuse. The break cannot be seen. This condition is typical of fuses opened under short-circuit conditions. Photograph by Herbst.

SUMMARY

Common sense and some basic knowledge of electrical flow should make the theatre a safe place in which to work. If the operator will take every precaution to avoid getting into the path of an electrical circuit; if he will seek out well-made and well-maintained equipment; if he will observe the loading limits of the equipment as specified by those who designed it; then he should encounter a minimum of difficulties, and those which do occur should be minor annoyances, not disasters.

25
PRODUCING AND USING LIGHT ON THE STAGE

INTRODUCTION In Part Six we discussed the phenomenon of color as a physical concept and a physiological process. We must now consider how light is made in the theatre, how it is filtered and controlled, and how we apply it to the stage. As previously stated, light is a form of energy made by conversion from other forms of energy. The usual device for making light in the theatre is the incandescent lamp (which will be examined in great detail shortly). However, other ways of making light are used occassionally in the theatre.

GASEOUS DISCHARGE LAMPS

All gaseous discharge lamps, a large family of light sources, work on the same principle: Electricity is forced through a tube containing gas. The gas is ionized by the electrical energy and light is emitted. The amount and color of the light produced will depend on the pressure of the gas, the kind of gas, and other factors.

Although the physics involved in the production of light in a gaseous discharge lamp is very complex, a simplified explanation may be of interest. Electricity is, as we know, a stream of electrons flowing under electrical pressure from the generator. As this stream is driven through the gas, the energy causes electrons attached to gas atoms to be raised to higher energy orbits than they normally follow. As these electrons "fall" back to their normal orbits they emit energy in the form of photons (light). Since these are discrete units of energy, their value depending on the atomic structure of the gas, the result is a narrow range of wavelengths which the eye sees as color. If, for example, the gas in the tube is neon, we will see the typical red glow associated with neon signs. Argon produces a bluish light, and mercury a cold bluish-white light. In addition to visible light, these gases, particularly mercury vapor, also give off large amounts of energy in the ultraviolet region of the spectrum. This is light of shorter wavelength than visible light. It is the ultraviolet in sunlight that causes the sunburn.

STROBE LIGHTS

One frequently used theatrical adaptation of the gaseous discharge lamp is the strobe light, which consists of a glass tube containing a small quantity of xenon gas. Electrodes are sealed into the ends of the tube. When a pulse of high voltage electricity is forced through the gas, it ionizes and produces a very brief but intense flash of white light. Although under proper circumstances, the flash can be as brief as a few millionths of a second, such brief flashes are shorter than necessary for theatrical use. Also, it is harder to produce high intensity flashes this short. The average theatre strobe probably produces flashes a few ten-thousandths of a second in duration. These brief flashes can be repeated as often as the high voltage power supply can provide pulses of electricity.

The thing that makes the strobe light such a spectacular theatre device is the ability of the flashes of light to "stop" motion. The flashes are so brief that the eye appears to see stationary images of a moving object, one for each flash. The result is the now familiar series of jerky images associated with strobe lights in discotheques.

Modern strobe lights can be controlled to produce flashes at varying frequencies, and if multiple strobes are available, they can be controlled to fire in a predetermined sequence. The addition of color filters to some of these strobes makes possible a series of flashes in varying colors in any sequence set by the operator.

Some precautions should be taken when using strobe lights. Since the flashes are of such short duration and reach their maximum intensity almost instantly, the normal reflexes of the eye, which cause the iris to close to protect against overbright light, cannot function before the flash is over. Thus a strobe light tends to promote eye strain, especially in those who must look at the bright lamp. For this reason, they should not be used for extended periods of time in total darkness.

Certain frequencies of bright flashes apparently have deeper effects on the human nervous system. Frequencies in the neighborhood of ten flashes per second may cause persons susceptible to epileptic seizures to have an attack. This frequency appears just a bit slower to the eye than the flicker of a silent movie and is usually too fast for the wanted theatrical effect.

Remember that the high voltage supply for strobe lights is potentially dangerous. Do not attempt to tamper with the interior of this unit unless you are qualified.

FLUORESCENT LAMPS

Ultraviolet light (UV) from a mercury vapor gaseous discharge is important to the theatre because it forms the basis for the fluorescent tube. It produces visible light as follows: (1) Electricity is passed through mercury vapor at a pressure adjusted to cause the maximum light output at the far ultraviolet region. (2) This light is absorbed by *phosphors* (the white powdery coating seen on the inside of the glass tube). (3) The phosphors reemit the energy in the form of visible light. The wavelengths of the visible light depend on the chemical makeup of the phosphors. These are normally chosen to produce red, green, and blue light in about equal portions, causing the eye to see white. Although this process is complicated, it is efficient. The average fluorescent tube produces about twice as much visible light per watt of power as an incandescent lamp.

Fluorescent lamps cannot be used as light sources for lens systems because the size of the source is too large. They can, however, serve as excellent sources for floodlighting applications such as cyclorama lighting. Recently the television industry has adopted fluorescent lighting to background lighting (analogous to cyclorama applications in the theatre) with excellent color rendering and great savings in energy. Tubes used for this are designed to produce red, green, and blue light, rather than white light from a single tube. Such cyc lighting seems likely to be used in the theatre soon.

Black Light

Black light effect (fluorescence from ultraviolet illumination) has been common in the theatre for many years, and has been used in discotheques and for home decoration. Effects may range from bizarre, often dazzling displays, to subtle accents which form part of the total scenographic palette. Of the three common sources of black light for the theatre, two are gaseous discharge lamps. These are the *mercury vapor lamp,* and the *black light fluorescent tube.* The mercury vapor lamp (Figure 25-1) is a gaseous discharge tube (much shortened) in which the pressure of the vapor has been adjusted to produce a maximum of the near-ultraviolet light. Such light is used to produce on-stage fluorescence. (Note that the UV produced in a normal fluorescent tube is far-ultraviolet. It has much shorter wavelengths and would be dangerous if allowed to irradiate a room. Near-UV, the "black light" variety, is not dangerous. These lamps, which must be operated from special current-limiting apparatus known as ballasts, require a warm-up period, and may not be dimmed. They produce, however, a controllable pool of UV light very useful for black light effects. The lamps and their associated equipment are moderately expensive.

Figure 25-1. Mercury Vapor Black Light. This instrument consists of a type PAR mercury vapor lamp in a rugged housing that contains the ballast to control electrical flow. When fitted with the black light filter as shown, it produces only a faint visible glow. Without the filter, it is an efficient source of cool blue-white light.

The fluorescent tube black light lamp operates in any standard fluorescent fixture. It is simply a regular fluorescent tube with a different mixture of phosphors and a filter on the outside. The phosphors are chosen to absorb far-ultraviolet light and emit near-ultraviolet light instead of visible light. Unfortunately such phosphors also emit quite a bit of visible light which must be removed by the filter if it is to be prevented from masking out the fluorescent effect on stage. The great advantages of fluorescent tube black light sources are their low cost and high efficiency. Fluorescent light fixtures are common everywhere and low in cost. All one needs are the black light tubes to make a satisfactory black light source.

ARC SOURCES OF BLACK LIGHT   While not exactly a part of this discussion of gaseous discharge lamps, it is appropriate to mention the third source of ultraviolet light for the stage. This is the *carbon arc lamp*, which consists of two pieces of carbon (rods) between which an electric arc (spark) is induced (Figure 25-2). A complicated mixture of incandescent and gaseous discharge reactions takes place that produces huge amounts of visible light and considerable ultraviolet. The source is small and well suited to use with lenses and reflectors. Carbon arcs (arc lights) are used in the theatre as light sources for large *follow spotlights,* which are often used in musical comedy and vaudeville-type productions. If a theatre already has a follow spotlight equipped with an arc source, it also has a highly controllable source of ultraviolet light. One simply adds a special filter that removes by absorption all visible light, leaving a controllable pool of UV. This filter will get very hot because it must absorb huge amounts of energy, but the effect on stage will be good. Ice shows often use this method for black light spectacles.

SHORT-ARC LAMPS

A relatively new category of light source has entered the theatre mainly for scenic projection and as a substitute for the carbon arc. Short-arc lamps are really a highly concentrated version of the gaseous discharge lamp. The gas is placed in a strong enclosure under high pressure. Then electricity is forced through the gas by passing the current between two sharply pointed electrodes made of tungsten. The result is an intensely brilliant point of light. Unlike the carbon arc which operates in air that causes the carbon rods to burn, no tungsten is used up in the process. All of the light is produced by discharge reactions in the gas (except a small amount from the hot tungsten electrodes).

Short-arc lamps presently are produced in two categories although new developments continue almost daily. The oldest and most used is the *xenon lamp,* filled with pure xenon gas (a rare gas found in minute quantities in the air). It produces a cool white light at effi-

Figure 25-2. Carbon Arc Burner. Although this is the burner from a motion picture projector, those found in follow spotlights are nearly identical. The set of carbon rods shown is approximately half used up.

ciencies considerably above those of the fluorescent tube and is usable with lenses. The xenon lamp is now a standard source for motion picture projection and in some follow spotlights. It is, however, dangerous. The lamp itself is filled with such highly compressed gas that it is explosive. The arc produces dangerous far ultraviolet radiation which is, at best only partially confined by presently available bulbs. Such radiation causes the oxygen in the air around the tube to change partially to ozone, a poisonous gas. In spite of these handicaps, the xenon lamp has gained wide acceptance (see Figure 25-3).

A still more recent development is the *HMI lamp*. It is constructed about like the xenon lamp, except that its gas is at much lower pressure. The gas is a carefully contrived combination of elements designed to produce a wide range of wavelengths that add in the eye and are perceived as white light. It is almost incredibly efficient, capable of producing about five times as much light per watt as an incandescent stage lamp. This is about three times the efficiency of the fluorescent tube, and over twice that of the xenon lamp. Moreover it is much less hazardous to use. The HMI lamp promises to gain wide acceptance as soon as its cost comes down and it becomes established as a reliable source. Both the xenon and the HMI lamps are expensive, costing hundreds of dollars per lamp. However, their efficiency compensates for these costs.

INCANDESCENT LAMPS

Perhaps the key device in all of modern stage lighting is the incandescent lamp. Certainly without it there could be no stage lighting as we know it. It has been in use for well over 100 years, but it is still being improved—particularly those lamps intended for high-efficiency uses.

HOW THEY WORK

The principle of the incandescent lamp is easy to state in a few words, but very complicated if you want to know the physics involved in the energy conversions that take place in a filament. We will settle for a simple description: Electrical energy flows through the filament (a thin wire made of tungsten metal) and is partially converted into heat as the electricity forces itself through the tungsten. When enough energy is converted into heat to make the filament very hot (near the melting point of tungsten), some of the heat is converted into light. This light radiates away from the filament, and we say that the lamp is "lit." It is a misnomer to say that the lamp "burns." Burning refers

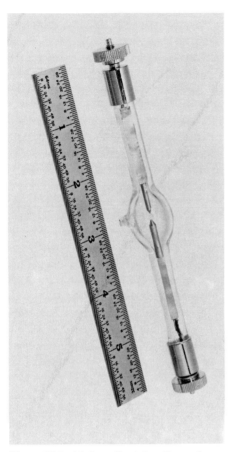

Figure 25-3. Modern Short-Arc Xenon Lamp. This one is typical of the xenon lamps used in the theatre. Photograph courtesy of Optical Radiation Corporation.

to the oxidation that takes place in a fire—the way a candle generates heat. In a tungsten filament lamp nothing oxidizes; it cannot because there is no oxygen inside the glass bulb. The heat is electrically produced. Also to say that a lamp has "burned out" is a misnomer unless it has suddenly fogged up with yellow-green tungsten oxide because oxygen got into it.

Incandescent lamps fail because the tungsten sublimates, gradually reducing the size of the filament wire until it breaks apart. The break stops the flow of electricity and prevents the formation of heat. The lamp goes out. *Sublimation* is a physical process by which a solid converts directly to a gas without first melting and going through an intermediate liquid phase. Ice, for example, may gradually disappear from the ground during the winter although the temperature remains far below freezing.

Sublimation increases in rate in porportion to increasing temperature and decreasing vapor pressure on the surface of the material sublimating. Thus the conditions inside early electric lamps were ideal for rapid sublimation. The temperature of the filament was high and the vapor pressure was near zero (a vacuum). Later it was found that an inert gas could be introduced into the bulb to increase the vapor pressure and slow the rate of sublimation. This increases lamp life and makes it possible to operate the filament at higher, more efficient temperatures. Still more recent improvements have been made, but since easily half of the lamps we use in the theatre today are of the simple gas-filled type (termed "conventional lamps"), we will discuss them first.

CONVENTIONAL INCANDESCENT LAMPS

All modern lamps of either specialized nature or common household types are conventional incandescent lamps. Almost all of these are filled with inert gas if their wattage is over 30 W. Below that wattage most are vacuum lamps. Lamps used in theatrical borderlights, footlights, and floodlights are little different from home lamps, except that many of them are larger in wattage. However, lamps designed for use with lens systems must be made differently.

The Concentrated Filament

The development of the incandescent spotlight lagged far behind the development of the incandescent lamp because early lamps had large nonhomogenous filaments. Such filaments will not produce an even pool of light when used with a lens. Instead they produce an out-of-focus image of the filament. In the early 1920s metallurgy finally developed to the point where it was possible to coil a tungsten filament into a small space producing the first concentrated filament lamp. This in turn made the first incandescent spotlight possible. From that early beginning with a low-wattage concentrated filament, development has progressed to the point where now 10,000 W concentrated filament lamps are produced routinely. Incandescent spotlights are made to utilize these monsters, especially for the movie industry.

Parts of Incandescent Lamps

Figure 25-4 shows a typical stage service incandescent lamp with most of the parts indicated. Not all lamps will have exactly the same parts in the same locations. The following list of parts and their functions should make identification easier:

> Lamp—the entire device but without the socket.
> Bulb—the glass part that keeps air out.
> Filament—the wire that gets white-hot and makes light.
> Lead-in wires—the wires that hold up the filament and carry electricity to it. Note that there may also be other supporting wires besides the lead-ins.
> Base—the metal and insulation fastened to the lamp to hold it up and make electrical connection to the socket.
> Socket—the mechanism made to mate with the base and hold the lamp in place. It also feeds electricity through the base via the lead-in wires to the filament, and provides the return path necessary for an electrical circuit.

The term "lamp" is not universal. Hollywood studio electricians call lamps "bulbs" or "globes." The engineering problems involved in supporting conventional filaments and in causing the sublimated tungsten to deposit where it can cause the least harm have led to categorizing these lamps into rather narrowly defined proper operating positions. Therefore, stage lamps are grouped into two types: "burn base down to horizontal" and "burn base up" (see Figure 25-5). Any significant departure from these burning positions may cause the lamp to fail prematurely.

Color Temperature

Although all incandescent lamps can be said to produce white light they do not all produce the same kind of white light; some are warmer, i.e., more yellowish, than others. Since this really reflects a difference in the amount of each wavelength making up what the eyes see as white, and since we will eventually want to determine how much of each wavelength we can filter from this white light, it is necessary to investigate the color content of the output of incandescent lamps more closely. Scientists have provided this information in the form of a *color temperature* rating, a scientific method of expressing the color content of light produced from incandescent sources (or sources that produce similar radiation). It is based on complicated physical theory of atomic structures having to do with the conversion of heat energy into radiant energy. Since heat is the basis of this process, the scientists

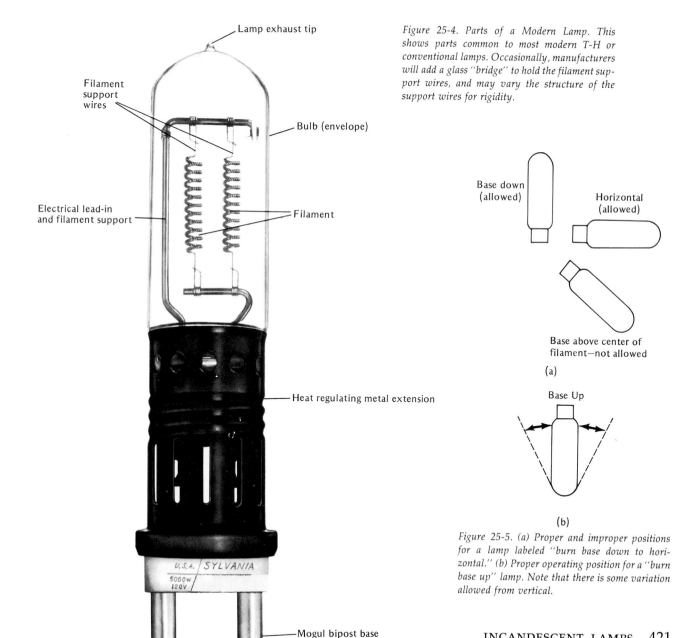

Lamp exhaust tip

Filament support wires

Bulb (envelope)

Electrical lead-in and filament support

Filament

Heat regulating metal extension

U.S.A. SYLVANIA
5000w
120V

Mogul bipost base

Figure 25-4. *Parts of a Modern Lamp. This shows parts common to most modern T-H or conventional lamps. Occasionally, manufacturers will add a glass "bridge" to hold the filament support wires, and may vary the structure of the support wires for rigidity.*

Base down (allowed)

Horizontal (allowed)

Base above center of filament—not allowed

(a)

Base Up

(b)

Figure 25-5. *(a) Proper and improper positions for a lamp labeled "burn base down to horizontal." (b) Proper operating position for a "burn base up" lamp. Note that there is some variation allowed from vertical.*

use an absolute temperature scale that counts up from the condition of no heat at all. This point, measured in centigrade (Celsius) degrees, occurs at about −273°C. Thus 0°C (the freezing point of water) reads 273°K (Kelvin) on the absolute scale. This scale has been named after a famous physicist, Lord Kelvin. Color temperatures are therefore stated in degrees Kelvin; e.g., 2950°K represents the color temperature of a conventional stage service incandescent lamp.

Although scientists refer to the Kelvin scale from zero up to astronomically high numbers, we are interested mainly in the range that refers to visible light from the point where a filament begins to glow (about 600°K) up to the coolest (bluest) white light commonly produced by stage sources (about 6000°K from a xenon lamp).

One of the standard items in rating a stage lamp is its color temperature. Note that this number describes the color content of the light, not the quantity produced. Thus a 100 W lamp and a 5000 W lamp might have identical color temperatures. However, there is a connection between the light output and the color temperature of any given lamp. When a lamp is dimmed, two things happen simultaneously: the quantity of light produced drops, and the color temperature of that light is lowered. The effect is that as the lamp goes out, it gets first yellower, then redder until only a reddish glow remains. In conventional lamps, there is also a relationship between color temperature and lamp life. Since the color temperature reflects the actual temperature of the filament (although not directly), as the color temperature of a lamp is increased, the filament becomes hotter and the sublimation process speeds up. The result is that lamps with high color temperature ratings tend to have short lives. They are also more efficient.

At this point we encounter another example of the perversity of color terminology. We commonly describe yellowish or orangish light as "warm," and bluish light as "cold." This reflects their psychological effect. However, the physics of color works in the opposite fashion. Yellowish light has a *low* color temperature, and bluish light a *high* color temperature.

With the introduction of new tungsten-halogen lamps (discussed later in this chapter) we have the possibility that the stage may be equipped with lamps of several different color temperature ratings. These different color outputs will affect the color produced by the color filters, thus a lavender gel in one instrument may not produce the same color as it does in an instrument equipped with a different type of lamp. This complicates life for crew members who must occasionally change lamps and match up gels to maintain the color balance specified by the scenographer. No simple conversion tables are available to tell the crew what gels to select when changing from conventional to tungsten-halogen lamps or vice versa. Careful observation of the color produced and subtle adjustment of gels are necessary.

Lamp Life and Light Output

As we have already noted, light output and color temperature increase with the temperature of a lamp filament. Sublimation also increases, with the result that lamp life tends to decrease. This has been the problem of lamp engineers since the first lamp was made. High efficiency has produced short life, and long life has meant low efficiency. Adding inert gas to the bulb helped but did not solve the problem. Concentrating the filament made it more efficient, but caused shorter life, creating the present condition of conventional stage lamps. Unlike household lamps which are designed for rather long lives (700–1000 hours), stage lamps have short lives—mostly under 200 hours. Fortunately they are somewhat more efficient than home lamps. However they cost much more, with the result that operation of lamps on stage is a very expensive proposition compared to home service. Moreover, failures are much more common because of the short life of the lamps.

TUNGSTEN-HALOGEN LAMPS

Recently the impasse over life and efficiency has been broken. Scientists found that adding a bit of the element iodine to the atmosphere surrounding the filament does some very helpful things. The iodine combines with any tungsten that has condensed on the bulb to form a gas (WI_2). When this gas passes the much hotter filament, it breaks down and deposits the tungsten back onto the filament. The bulb never blackens and the tungsten is replaced on the filament as fast as it leaves. This sounds like a "perpetual" light source. Actually it is not, because the tungsten is not necessarily put back exactly in the same spot from which it sublimated. Thus thin places develop in the filament and it eventually breaks. Also the bulb has to be so hot that regular glass cannot be used. For a time only fused quartz could be used to make bulbs for these lamps; now hard glass also is used. The heat continues to cause problems at the lead-in wire seals which often oxidize and cause the seal to break, ruining the lamp.

Since early lamps of this type were made with quartz bulbs and iodine atmospheres, they were called "quartz-iodine" lamps. Later, other chemical relatives of iodine (halogens) were used and the name became "quartz-halogen." Now quartz is no longer consistently used —hard glass has been made that is cheaper and easier to handle. The name now seems to be standardized to *tungsten-halogen* (abbreviated T-H).

You will be able to distinguish T-H lamps from the conventional types with ease: they are smaller in size for their wattage. In some cases, the base has been designed to fit bases previously made for conventional lamps, and will be as large or larger than the bulb. In other cases, they are being used in a completely new line of bases designed especially for them. If the lamp is operating, you *may* be able to tell by the color of its light, i.e., its color temperature. It will appear a bit bluer than a conventional lamp of the same wattage at the same dimmer setting.

Categories of T-H Lamps

There are two broad categories of T-H lamps available. The first category consists of lamps made to take advantage of the long life now possible. For example, a common T-H lamp for Fresnel spotlights (described in Chapter 26) is supplied in a type that has a life rating of 2000 hours. It still is almost as efficient as its conventional equivalent and maintains that efficiency throughout its life—something the conventional lamp could not do. The second category consists of T-H lamps which can be made to perform with very high efficiency at life ratings comparable to those found in older lamps, but at higher color temperatures. Here are examples of these two categories of T-H lamps:

> 500 W T-4 base 2000 hour life 10,000 lumens 3000 degrees K

> 500 W T-4 base 500 hour life 12,000 lumens 3100 degrees K (compare with conventional 500 W T20/60 200 hour life 11,000 lumens 2900 degrees K)

The choice of categories will depend on a number of considerations, including the ease or difficulty of relamping instruments, the need for maximum light output, cost of operation, consequences of early failure, and the like. You may find that your theatre is still trying various types and life ratings to see what type(s) fits its needs best.

Problems with T-H Lamps

Although the T-H lamp represents a distinct improvement over the conventional incandescent lamp, it is not without problems. It requires special handling. The halogen cycle makes it very difficult to estimate the life remaining in a used lamp. The cost per lamp is much higher than that of conventional lamps, and its small bulb size and high bulb temperature have caused some color medium problems.

HANDLING   T-H lamps are delicate and expensive. There is also a problem involved with the bulb. Because it is made of special material and because it operates at a very high temperature, it is subject to cracking which destroys the lamp. This does not usually occur unless something has etched the surface of the bulb, usually perspiration from human hands. Therefore, *do not touch the bulb with your bare hands*. Furthermore, if there are any fingerprints or smudges on the bulb, clean it carefully and completely with alcohol and a soft cloth. Handle it with a cloth, or better yet, with the protector shipped for this purpose with new lamps.

ESTIMATING REMAINING LIFE   The very thing that gives the T-H lamp its long life and high efficiency makes it difficult to estimate its remaining life. Unlike the conventional lamp in which the bulb blackens roughly in proportion to its age, the T-H lamp remains completely clear to the end of its life. Examination reveals nothing about its remaining life. If they were operated only at full line voltage, it would be relatively easy to estimate their life by keeping track of time used. However stage lights often are operated for extended periods of time at reduced voltage, which increases the life of the lamp. If T-H lamps blacken at the reduced voltage, they will promptly clean up again when run at full voltage.

Another factor that determines the life of T-H lamps is lead-in failure. See Figure 25-6 for an example of the appearance of a lamp that failed because of this condition. Lead-in failure tends to recur since it is a symptom of overheating at the socket connections. Overheating causes socket springs to weaken and socket contacts to overheat. Both of these conditions, in turn, increase the chances that the lead-ins on the lamp will overheat still more.

COST   The cost of T-H lamps is much higher than the cost of conventional lamps. However when one figures the cost per unit of life and output (commonly stated as cost per 1 million lumen hours, which is about the entire life of a common 100 W home lamp), the T-H lamp turns out to be the least expensive.

LAMP WATTAGE AND HEAT   There has been some controversy generated over heat produced by lamps since the introduction of the T-H lamp. It has been asserted that the T-H lamp is "hotter" than the conventional lamps of the same wattage. Evaluation of this statement depends on what is meant by "hotter." If it means that the lamp produces more heat per minute of operation than conventional lamps, the statement is untrue because heat varies in proportion to wattage and lamps of equal wattage will produce the same amount of heat regardless of any other factors. Thus 500 W of energy will produce the same amount of heat no matter what sort of conversion device is used as long as *all* of the energy is converted to heat. Actually, since the T-H lamp produces about 10 percent more light per watt than a conventional lamp, it produces somewhat *less* heat per watt.

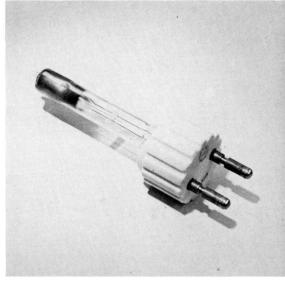

Figure 25-6. Failed Seal. This lamp displays the typical evidence of rapid failure due to seal breakage. The lamp failed within moments of the time it was turned on. In some cases, if the lamp is full on, the interior of the lamp may fill with yellow tungsten oxide instead of a smoky silvery deposit such as the one shown.

However, "hotter" may also refer to the temperature of the bulb itself, which is indeed hotter in the T-H lamp—it must be if the halogen cycle is to function. The very hot bulb, combined with the tiny size of T-H lamps, has produced some problems. Fixtures have been manufactured to take advantage of the small size of the lamp without taking into account the high heat levels encountered close to the bulb. There are floodlights available that cannot be fitted with any color medium at all except special slotted glass, and even this is subject to failure. These lamps are not producing more heat than conventional lamps; but it is too easy to get the color medium too close to the hot bulb.

TYPES OF LAMPS AND BASES

There are hundreds of thousands of types of lamps in the master catalogue of a major manufacturer such as General Electric, and new varieties are constantly appearing. The stage makes use of several hundred types.

Perhaps the most obvious characteristic of a lamp is the shape of the bulb. Household lamps are mostly pear shaped, which leads to one of their common catalogue designations: "PS." In other catalogues they may be designated type "A." At one time most stage lamps were globular and the designation was "G." Now most of them are tubular, "T" types. The diameter of the bulb is given in eighths of an inch. Thus a "T12" lamp has a tubular bulb $\frac{12}{8}$ of an inch in diameter, i.e., $1\frac{1}{2}$ inches.

Bases and Sockets

Variations in bulb shapes have become less significant with the introduction of the T-H lamp. All T-H lamps are so small that the bulb will fit an instrument housing without difficulty. On the other hand, the high bulb temperature of T-H lamps and its attendant seal problems, has produced an entirely new line of bases and sockets to fit them. These have been added to the list of conventional lamp sockets already on the market. We will discuss the conventional sockets first, then the new T-H types.

BASE-SOCKET COMBINATIONS FOR CONVENTIONAL LAMPS These bases and their sockets have been a part of the lighting market for a long time (see Figure 25-7). They overlap into the household and commercial market as well as being the "old standard" in the theatre.

The *screw base* is standard on all household lamps in the United States. It comes in four standard sizes: mogul, medium, candelabra, and miniature. Common household lamps have medium screw bases. The screw base is too inaccurate in terms of filament alignment for

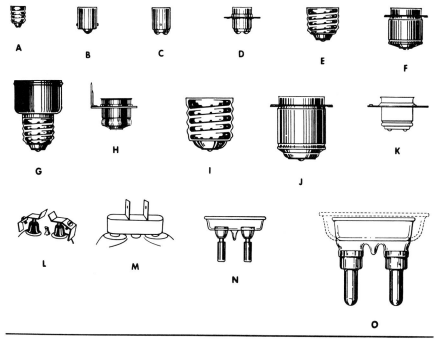

Figure 25-7. Common Lamp Bases. These bases are commonly found on conventional lamps for the stage and on retrofit lamps. Prefocus and bipost bases will be most common. Courtesy General Electric Company.

A — CANDELABRA
B — SINGLE CONTACT BAYONET CANDELABRA
C — DOUBLE CONTACT BAYONET CANDELABRA
D — CANDELABRA PREFOCUS
E — MEDIUM
F — MEDIUM PREFOCUS
G — MEDIUM SKIRTED
H — INDEXING RING

I — MOGUL
J — MOGUL PREFOCUS
K — DOUBLE CONTACT MEDIUM RING
L — SCREW TERMINAL
M — END PRONG
N — MEDIUM BIPOST
O — MOGUL BIPOST

any on-stage use except in borderlights and footlights where standard 100–500 W lamps are often used (see Figure 25-7, items E, G, and I).

The *prefocus base* was devised when it became necessary to make concentrated filaments "two-sided" rather than circular. A flat side had to face the lens if the instrument was to work efficiently, and a screw base would not assure this. Hence the prefocus base is cylindrical, but instead of threads, it has two fins, one larger than the other. It is inserted into its socket by lining up the fins with slots made to take them, pushing downward and turning clockwise about 90°. The lamp clicks into place and the filament is properly oriented. To remove, reverse the procedure—push down a bit, turn counterclockwise, and remove. The prefocus base also comes in the sizes mentioned above (see Figure 25-7, items F and J).

You may encounter problems with this base. For instance, if only one of the fins gets into its slot, the lamp will turn and click but remain at an angle to the socket. In this position the lamp makes a poor electrical contact and is out of alignment with the lens, causing poor light control. It is also possible that the stop in the socket can be broken, in which case the lamp will continue to turn instead of stopping with the filament facing the lens. The cure is to replace the socket, but you can use the instrument temporarily by carefully aligning the filament yourself so that it exactly faces the lens. When removing a lamp from a damaged socket be sure that the correct fin is coming out of the wide slot.

Still another problem with the prefocus base/socket combination is in the lamp itself. Many of these lamps made for spotlight service have the base attached to the bulb with cement that will not withstand much more temperature than the best conditions provide. If it gets a little too hot (for example, if the spot is operating in a poorly ventilated light beam), the base loosens. This usually does not cause trouble until the lamp is handled. Then the base twists off and remains in the socket while the bulb comes free. This, of course, destroys the lamp. Use pliers to remove the base from the socket and discard it. (Remember to disconnect the instrument before working on it.)

Lamps often are removed from instruments before they burn out. They may need cleaning or it may be necessary to change the wattage of the instrument. When the crew member grasps the lamp, turns it, and finds that he has twisted the wires in the base, he may be tempted to quietly return the lamp to its original position and reinstall the instrument. Crew members should understand that such base failure is, unfortunately, a common thing. The damaged lamp should be removed and discarded. Never leave a lamp with twisted lead-ins in an instrument—this is a short circuit waiting to happen.

The *bipost base* was devised when lamp sizes grew larger and currents to supply them became greater, and it became evident that the prefocus base could not carry the heavy current needed for 5000 or even 10,000 W. It has since been applied to many smaller lamps because it is also more mechanically reliable and avoids the loose-base problem mentioned above. It is the simplest of the three bases. The posts are a mechanical extension of the lead-in wires and are bonded directly to the glass of the bulb. No cement is used. There are two types of sockets: clamp and twist. The twist type operates almost like the prefocus socket. The lamp is inserted, depressed, and turned. However in this case, you turn only a short distance and the lamp clicks into place. Reverse the procedure to remove it. Do not use too much force or you will break the posts out of the glass and ruin the lamp. The clamp-type socket is even simpler. A screw device is loosened, the lamp base inserted, and the device tightened. Bipost bases allow the lamp to be inserted in either of two ways; both are equally satisfactory as far as alignment is concerned (see Figure 25-7, items N and O).

RETROFIT BASES FOR T-H LAMPS   As their name suggests, retrofit lamps (Figure 25-8) are made to be used in instruments originally designed for conventional lamps. However, these lamps have proved so successful that some manufacturers have designed new spotlights around them. The critical factor involved in fitting a new lamp into a previously designed instrument is that the filament be in exactly the same position as that of the old lamp and of about the same size. Filament location in both conventional and T-H lamps is determined by a dimension called "light center length" (LCL). This figure, measured in inches, indicates the distance from the center of the filament to either the tip of the base or the flange on the base, depending on type.

Retrofit lamps consist of conventional prefocus or bipost bases fitted with tiny T-H bulbs that have been elevated to bring the filament to the proper position. Since T-H lamps are immune to the problems of burning position, any lamp of proper LCL and filament dimensions can be installed in any instrument.

NEW BASES FOR T-H LAMPS   Most modern lighting instruments are being designed around the small physical size and the filament shapes of T-H lamps. These lamps come in two general base types and many sizes and configurations (Figure 25-9).

From the beginning, the T-H lamp has naturally taken the form of a tube. Early T-H lamps were tubes 6 inches or longer in length with the filament extending the entire length of the tube. These would not work in spotlights at all. Then short, tightly packed T-H filaments were invented and the T-H lamp was ready for lens application. The bulb, however, was still tubular. This natural shape plus the problem of overheated lead-in seals, caused engineers to continue to make double-end T-H lamps, which have a connection at each end and are held into their sockets by spring pressure. Since socket pressure determines not only good electrical conductivity, but also heat conductivity, you must be very careful not to destroy part of its spring tension.

You should also be on the lookout for sockets that have been overheated and whose parts are burned to a bluish color. These will overheat rapidly and burn lamp seals if they are used further. They must be replaced.

Pitting may also occur at the point where the lamp and socket make contact. This condition will worsen until both lamp and socket fail. The only satisfactory solution is to replace *both* socket and lamp. Either a pitted lamp or a pitted socket will continue to pit the opposite parts if it is left in service.

Although some spotlights have been designed around the double-end T-H lamp, most new instruments use the single-end variety. These lamps have now been perfected to the point where they are just as dependable as the double-end type. The simplicity of installa-

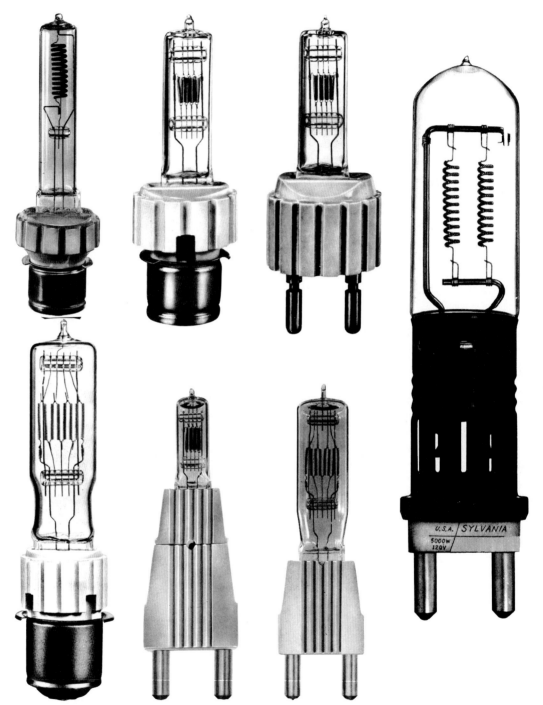

Figure 25-8. Retrofit Lamps. These were originally designed to allow owners of instruments designed for conventional lamps to convert to T-H lamps. However, new instruments have also been designed around these lamps making the distinction between retrofit lamps and modern special-based T-H lamps academic. Courtesy Sylvania Electric Products Inc.

Figure 25-9. Common Bases for Tungsten-Halogen Lamps. These bases have been especially engineered to control the operating temperature of the lamp seal and the base itself. Type TP-4, center, is most commonly found in modern spotlights using single-end T-H lamps. Courtesy Sylvania Electric Products Inc.

tion and socket construction seems to make them more suitable than the double-end type for spotlight service. Floodlights continue to use the double-end variety of lamp.

COST OF OPERATING INCANDESCENT LAMPS

Theatre lighting is expensive. Large amounts of electricity are used in expensive lamps to produce highly controlled and often highly filtered light. It is not uncommon for all but a fraction of a percent of the light made by the lamp to wind up wasted as heat, either at the lamp, in the instrument, or in the color medium. This is the price we pay for the flexibility of being able to change color and have tight control of our light.

However, we also pay in another way: short-lived lamps fail more frequently. To avoid such failures, we often remove a lamp before it has served to the end of its life, running costs still higher. With all of this in mind, you should heed the cry, "Save the lights!" by taking down the dimmers to a reading between 6 and 8, or even turning most of the lamps off entirely. Also, avoid using stage lamps for work lights, particularly at full brightness.

We now move from the study of how light is produced to the subject of how it is gathered from the lamp and directed to the stage in a controlled manner.

CONTROLLING THE LIGHT FROM A LAMP

Light radiates from the filament of a lamp in an essentially spherical manner. Therefore the total output of the lamp may be thought of as a constantly increasing sphere of light. *The intensity of this light will vary inversely with the square of the distance from the source,* because the constant amount of light from the filament must cover the rapidly increasing surface area of the sphere. This statement, describing the manner in which light decreases in intensity as it emanates from a point, is known as the "square law."

It is obvious that light from any source will dissipate rapidly if the light is allowed to disperse according to the square law. This is the reason that so much engineering has gone into the design of lighting instruments. Without this engineering little light would ever reach the stage.

The crudest way to control light from a lamp would be to block off all light not striking the stage area to be lighted. To do this effectively and get a pool of light with a sharp edge, one must start with a lamp whose filament is so small that it approximates a mathematical point, i.e., the concentrated filament lamp mentioned earlier in this chapter. If one encloses this lamp in a box with a round hole in one end, and if the box is painted flat black on the inside to absorb the unwanted light, one can produce a round pool of light on stage. Moving the lamp toward the hole will make a larger pool, and moving it away will make a smaller one. Such a device would meet the definition of a spotlight, but would be very inefficient because it does nothing to improve on the square law dissipation of the light.

SPHERICAL MIRROR

One simple way to increase the amount of light striking the desired spot on stage is to install a spherical mirror behind the lamp in our black box. If the mirror is so placed that its center of curvature is at the filament, its reflective characteristics will be such that it will catch the light emanating toward it from the filament, and return it (see Figure 25-10). This should theoretically double the intensity of the light striking the stage. Practically, the filament itself blocks some of the returning light, reducing the gain to about 60 percent, still well worth the price of the mirror.

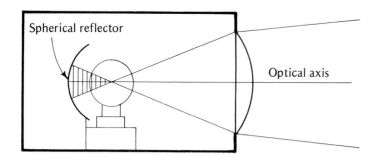

Figure 25-10. The application of the spherical reflector to the spotlight is illustrated. Light saved by the reflector is shown by shaded angle. Efficiency is increased.

LENSES

What is needed if we are to make any large improvement over the simple box spotlight is some method of catching a larger share of the light emanating from the lamp and directing it toward the stage. The device that does this is a *positive lens,* a curved piece of glass whose optical arrangement is such that it bends rays of light toward each other as they pass through it.

Plano-convex Lens Spotlight

If a lens (called a "plano-convex lens" because it is flat on one side and convex on the other) is placed at the hole in the box, the pool of light will become smaller and brighter. Then it will be possible to move the lamp toward the lens to get a pool of the same size as before, but with brighter light (see Figure 25-11). Note the dotted lines indicating the cone of light which would have been wasted without the lens. We can think of the light striking the lens as a cone of illumination. The larger this cone is, the better the efficiency of the instrument. As the cone of illumination striking the lens is increased in diameter, the cone striking the reflector may also be increased.

   This process would seem capable of producing a very efficient instrument if the lens could be made large enough to catch a wide cone of light and be matched by an equally large reflector. Within limits this is possible and the plano-convex lens spotlight is indeed a useful

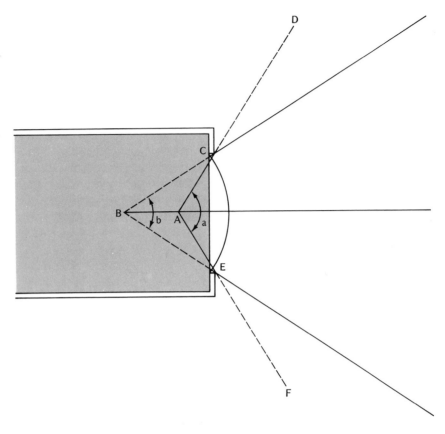

Figure 25-11. Increasing Efficiency with Plano-convex Lens. In this simplified spotlight, point B indicates where the light source would have to be placed to produce a beam with the same spread if no lens were used. Point A indicates the actual location of the filament. Note that the angle representing the cone of illumination is greater in the case of A than of B. This indicates a significant increase in efficiency. The dotted lines CD and EF indicate where the edge of the beam would be with the source at A, but without a lens.

instrument. However, its efficiency is limited to a rather low figure because of difficulties encountered in making plano-convex lenses of high light-bending power and large diameter. If we understand this problem, we will be well on our way to understanding how the plano-convex lens has been improved. The bending power of the lens is determined by the way light must pass through the two surfaces separating air and glass. One of these is the flat surface and the other the curved one. The greater the curve, i.e., the shorter its radius, the greater the bending power of the lens. The geometry is very simple: If one increases the diameter of a lens and retains the same curvature, the center of the lens thickens rapidly. Ultimately, if one increased the diameter enough, one would have a half sphere of solid glass. But trouble begins long before this. As the glass gets thicker than about 1 inch, it becomes very susceptible to breakage from heat which it begins to absorb in significant amounts from the lamp. Such lenses crack under the heat at the front of a spotlight.

Fresnel Lens Spotlight

The problem of designing an efficient spotlight did not arise until the development of the concentrated filament incandescent lamp. However the similar problem of designing an efficient lighthouse lamp was encountered much earlier in history. The two problems have much in common—both seek to gather as much light as possible from a source and to send it outward in a rather narrow beam that will not dissipate rapidly. In about 1800 Augustin Fresnel (pronounced "Freh-nell"), a French physicist, applied his ingenuity to this problem and came up with a solution. Since the bending power of a lens depended on the angle between the flat side of the glass and the tangent to the curved side, would it not be possible to remove much of the glass at the thick center of a lens and still retain the bending power? It proved to be true. Fresnel invented the Fresnel lighthouse lens which is still in use today. The principle of the lens is illustrated in Figure 25-12. Note how the curve is stepped back to keep the glass thin, but the angle is maintained. Such lenses can be made in any diameter with no concern for thick glass.

However, a price is paid for this improvement. The lens no longer has the optical precision of an unaltered plano-convex lens. This is not a major problem in many cases and actually turns out to be an advantage in certain stage applications.

A spotlight equipped with a Fresnel lens can have a short, wide body because the lamp will always be very close to the large lens. It will be an efficient instrument producing a pool of light with soft feathered edges that gradually blend into darkness.

FRESNEL LENSES FOR SPOTLIGHTS   Although Fresnel's original lighthouse lens was a marvel of optical precision in which each segment of the lens was ground and polished to fine tolerances, the modern stage lens is simply a molded piece of glass. Since the light will be soft (blurry edges) anyway, the flat side of the lens is dappled to make sure the light is distributed evenly. The focal length (a figure that expresses the light-bending power of the lens—the shorter the focal length, the greater the bending power) will usually be nearly one-half the diameter of the lens.

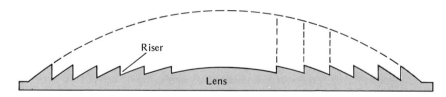

Figure 25-12. Development of a Fresnel Lens. The radius of the curved surface of each ring section corresponds to that of a thick plano-convex lens (dashed line).

Oval Beam Lenses Some modern Fresnel lenses display a double application of the Fresnel principle. The front is molded in the usual Fresnel pattern, and the back in a special cylindrical Fresnel pattern that bends light rays in one plane only. The result is that this lens produces an oval-shaped pool of light when the instrument is aimed straight at a plane surface. Such a pool is frequently very useful in stage lighting.

Step Lenses Another variation on the Fresnel principle consists of altering the flat side of the glass instead of the curved side. This results in a lens more easily ground to an accurate curve and is used to produce short focal-length lenses of higher quality for more advanced spotlight applications.

Further extensions of this principle have led to lenses so formed that they have the effect of a double convex lens, both sides being applications of the Fresnel lens. Most of these relatively refined lenses also have flatted risers to minimize spill light. "Flatting" risers consists of coating the vertical portions of the glass between each curved section with flat black ceramic enamel that minimizes reflection.

ELLIPSOIDAL REFLECTOR SPOTLIGHT

Although the Fresnel spotlight is an efficient instrument, it is not suited to operation in places where the soft edge and spill light produced by the Fresnel lens are objectionable. These places are the very locations in the theatre where a high efficiency instrument is most needed: FOH positions. These beam and balcony-front positions require long throws, powerful beams, and minimum spill. To achieve this, lighting instrument engineers took a different approach to the problem of collecting light. Instead of depending on a lens as the primary collector, they designed a much more effective reflector and used the lens in a totally different manner (see Figure 25-13).

Figure 25-13. Simplified Optics of Ellipsoidal Reflector Spotlight. Note that the principal light-collecting device is the reflector, not the lens system. The light from the point source (filament) comes to a focus at point P and then diverges. This diverging beam is collected by the lens system and focused on the stage as an image of the aperture. Thus the instrument is a crude lens projector, and any object placed in the aperture will be imaged on the stage.

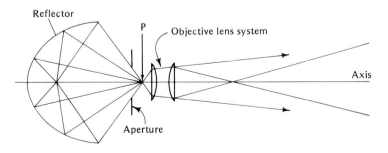

The Ellipsoidal Reflector

The efficiency of this instrument depends on the *ellipsoidal reflector* which gathers a large share of the light from the lamp and directs it to a focal point. As the light emanates from this focal point, now concentrated into a small cone of light, it is caught by the lens system and directed to the stage. Only a rather small cone of light passes directly from the filament to the lens. The efficiency of this instrument, when operating at optimum adjustments, is greater than that of the Fresnel spotlight. However this efficiency is only one of the advantages of the ellipsoidal reflector spotlight. Others are the absence of spill light, the adjustable beam shape, and its potential usefulness as an image projector.

Students of mathematics will note that an ellipsoid is a solid form created by rotating an ellipse around its axis. It has two focal points which are so related to the inside of the surface of the ellipsoid such that any wave motion originating at one focus must pass through the other if it strikes the inner surface. Lighting engineers arrange the parts of the ellipsoidal reflector spotlight so that the center of the lamp filament is at the focus of the ellipsoid which lies near the closed end of the reflector. (The ellipsoid is cut off at about its midpoint.) If the filament were a true mathematical point, all light striking the reflector would pass exactly through the second focal point, which lies somewhere outside the plane formed by the cut face of the reflector. Since the filament is much larger than a point, the reflection is not perfect. To correct for this unavoidable error, engineers often break the surface of the ellipsoid into planes, each of which aims a portion of the light more exactly at the focal point. Such reflectors are known as *flatted* reflectors. They are found in better quality ellipsoidal reflector spotlights.

The Aperture

At a point near the second focal point (this varies with the different types of instruments) is found an apparatus known as the "aperture" (see Figure 26-9). It consists of a metal plate with a round hole in it just slightly larger than the cone of light that is to pass through it. This hole will be seen on stage as the edge of a round pool of light if no objects are allowed to intrude into the hole. However this is the point where the other advantage of this instrument appears. If another shape is given to the hole, this shape will be projected onto the stage. Thus if metal plates with straight edges (shutters) are inserted part way into the aperture hole, the beam of light will take the shape formed by these shutters. If a metal plate with a simple design cut into it is inserted into the aperture, its image will appear on stage. The spotlight operates as an image projector. The difficulty is that the temperature at the aperture is so high that only designs cut from heat-resistant metal or painted on mica (a transparent, heat-resistant material) with heat-proof paint, can endure. Also the lens system is designed for maximum efficiency in transmitting light, not fine optical precision. Thus the image will be rather crudely focused.

This adjustable beam characteristic makes it possible to angle an ellipsoidal reflector spotlight toward a doorway, for example, and to adjust the edges of the beam so that only the doorway opening is lighted. This cannot be done as easily with any other stage lighting instrument. Standard equipment on most ellipsoidal spots consists of four framing shutters which may be pushed into the aperture to shape the beam. Other shaping devices such as iris shutters (like the iris in a camera), and special "gobo" holders are also common. A gobo is the theatrical term for the cut metal design or painted slide mentioned above (see Figure 26-10).

The Lens System

The lens system of an ellipsoidal spotlight may consist of one or two lens elements. It must have great light-bending power (short focal length) to converge the rapidly diverging cone of light coming from the second focal point to the point where it can form an image. One standard lens configuration consists of two plano-convex lenses installed in a metal tube with the curved sides facing each other. The entire tube is moved back and forth in the housing to change the focus of the instrument.

Another lens arrangement consists of one step lens installed in a similar tube. The step lens has a focal length short enough to equal that of the combined lenses in the two-lens arrangement.

Both systems have their advantages and disadvantages. Generally the two-lens system produces a sharper focus and a somewhat smoother distribution of light, while the single lens weighs less, is somewhat less susceptible to breakage, and is more efficient.

FOCUSING   Readers will recall that moving the lamp in relationship to the lens in a plano-convex spotlight or in a Fresnel spotlight makes major changes in the size of the pool of light produced. This is called "focusing." (There is now on the market one Fresnel instrument in which the lens moves instead of the lamp.) In the case of the ellipsoidal reflector spotlight, movement of the lens in relationship to the aperture (and thus the second focal point) determines whether the image of the aperture is in sharp focus or is fuzzy. To the extent that a fuzzy image will be larger than a sharp one, the size of the pool of light will be changed. This is a slight change, however. If greater change is needed, the size of the aperture must be altered by moving the shutters.

If full aperture opening still produces too small a pool of light, another instrument with a wider beam must be substituted, or in the case of some modern instruments, a different lens assembly installed.

SUMMARY ON CONTROLLING LIGHT

These three instruments, the plano-convex lens spotlight, the Fresnel lens spotlight, and the ellipsoidal reflector spotlight, provide the chief methods of gathering and controlling light on the stage: (1) cutting off unwanted light, (2) directing light by reflectors, and (3) directing light with lenses. The plano-convex lens spotlight is almost obsolete in the United States today; however, it is still much in use in Europe. Both the Fresnel and the ellipsoidal spotlights are the workhorses of modern American theatre.

In addition to controlling where light goes on stage, it is also necessary to control the color of that light and ultimately its intensity. Thus, our next topic is the means of producing colored light and using it on stage.

HOW COLORED LIGHT IS MADE ON STAGE

There are many ways to make colored light; the most efficient would be to make only those wavelengths needed in the quantity needed. At the present time the only practical application of this method is the use of special red, green, and blue fluorescent tubes for cyclorama lighting. There is no method of producing easily controlled point sources of colored light that may be varied at will from wavelength to wavelength.

Therefore we make colored light on stage by a simpler but much more wasteful process. We start with white light from an incandescent lamp. This light appears white to the eye because it contains substantial amounts of all visible wavelengths. These amounts are by no means equal, but they are sufficiently so to cause the eye to read "white."

Having made the white light, we filter it. We call our filters "color media" and choose them more for efficiency and economy than purity. They work by removing and converting to heat those wavelengths not wanted. This is wasteful—extremely so in the case of primary blue which may waste all but about one-half of 1 percent of the light from the lamp—but it is very flexible and it calls for no complicated equipment. Since the white light contains all of the wavelengths visible to the eye, they are instantly available, needing only the proper filter to sort them out.

COLOR MEDIA

Color medium is the generic term for any filter material used to sort out those wavelengths of light that are wanted on stage. "Gel" is a common stage synonym for color medium. It is a shortened form of the word, "gelatin" which refers to one of the earliest sheet color mediums used in the theatre. Gelatin, now improved, is still in use today although it seems to be in the process of being superceded by plastic materials. Following is a brief review of each of the major color media used on the stage to gel the instruments.

Glass

Colored glass is one of the oldest media to have been used in the theatre. It predates electric lighting by centuries. (There are records indicating that colored glass bottles were placed in front of oil lamps to make patches of colored light as early as the medieval days.) The color is part of the glass itself, chemically created as the glass is made. It will remain as long as the glass endures, which can be a very long time. Thus glass is considered to be a "permanent" color medium. It is also usually a very pure color medium because chemically it is relatively easy to make pure glass filters.

The problems that glass present are easy to anticipate: it is fragile, heavy, expensive, and rather low in efficiency. *Efficiency* in a filter is measured in terms of the percentage of wanted light transmitted as compared with the amount of that light available in the source. For example, a primary red filter that passes 75 percent of the red light available in the lamp is said to have a transmission factor of 75 percent, and is of course, 75 percent efficient. Note that the efficiency figure has no theoretical relationship to the *purity* of the filter which indicates how well it eliminates wavelengths not wanted. Practically, however, the greater the purity, the lower the efficiency, at least in stage quality filters.

The fragility and cost of glass has just about ruled it out for use in instruments such as spotlights which are moved about frequently. Glass filters commonly are found only in such seldom-moved instruments as borderlights and footlights. Even in these already heavy instruments the round glass filters, known as *roundels,* add considerable weight.

A recent application of colored glass is its use in floodlights equipped with tungsten-halogen lamps. These lamps are very small and operate at a very high bulb temperature. The housings of the floodlights built around these lamps are so small that they bring the color medium very close to the lamp; thus no material except glass will endure the heat. Even here, the heat is so severe that only narrow strips of thin, colored glass will serve. These strips are fragile and expensive.

Roundels are not as fragile, but they are expensive. If a roundel becomes chipped, it is likely to break under the stresses set up by the heat from the lamp behind it. Roundels should be carefully handled and washed gently with soapy water, like good chinaware. They should be securely inserted in their mounts—a roundel falling 30 feet is dangerous!

Gelatin

Gelatin is chemically the same as the famous dessert and also the same as old-fashioned woodworker's glue. It is made from the hides and hoofs of animals and is mostly protein. For theatrical use, dye is added to a solution of gelatin, and the mixture is poured onto sheets of glass, allowed to dry completely, and peeled off. In this simple form it can be used for stage purposes, but it has become common practice to treat the sheets chemically to somewhat reduce their susceptibility to humidity changes. Gelatin crumbles when it gets too dry and changes to a gluey mass when it gets too wet. Overdry gel can be salvaged by storing it in a closed container with a source of water vapor, such as a dampened sponge. There is no way to salvage overwet gel.

Gelatin's greatest advantage is its price—it is the cheapest of temporary color media. It is available in a wide variety of colors and its efficiency is higher than that of most other materials. Its disadvantages are its rapid fading, susceptibility to humidity changes, fragility, and vulnerability to water. It is not uncommon to have to regel instruments every other performance when using gelatin. This is a time-consuming and costly operation that may move the instruments out of alignment if not done with great care. If the show is in an outdoor theatre, a heavy dew may ruin the gels, and a rainstorm will wash them away.

Plastic—Cellulose Acetate

A number of synthetic materials have been developed as improvements over gelatin. Most of these have been based on cellulose acetate, a common and easily worked plastic material. This brings up a problem that no one worried about when gelatin was the only color medium except glass: flammability. Gelatin will burn, but so slowly that it is not a fire hazard. Untreated cellulose acetate burns vigorously. However, modern media made of this material have been treated to resist flame, and should pass a standard test for fire retardancy.

All plastic media are completely waterproof, resistant to fading under hot lights in most colors, and cost considerably more than gelatin. These plastic media eventually fail because the plastic itself succumbs to the effects of heat. The surface of the material becomes rough and the sheet warps out of shape. The result is that the medium tends to diffuse light, producing spill where none is wanted. It must be replaced when these conditions become intolerable. Any of these plastic materials will smoke and eventually melt if they are subjected to the intense heat of a misaligned ellipsoidal reflector spotlight. Dense blues and greens are particularly sensitive because they absorb the most heat. The cost of these materials runs two to three times that of gelatin but this is easily offset by their long life.

The colors are more exact. The range of colors available is about as broad as that in gelatin; however, many colors are available in plastic that are not available at all in gelatin. Colors of similar name do not match from manufacturer to manufacturer. For example, there are several "special lavenders" available from the different manufacturers; this becomes an advantage because it results in a broader palette available to the lighting artist who stocks media on the basis of color range, not manufacture.

An interesting and handy feature of these acetate sheets is that they are soluble in acetone. This makes it possible to use acetone as "glue" to join pieces of medium together. The joint warps somewhat but becomes quite strong when dry. This method can be used to simulate "stained glass," to make crude slides for Linnebach projectors (see Chapter 29), or to make varigated color media for use in spotlights to produce mottled effects. Still another possibility is to dissolve scraps of cellulose acetate material in acetone to make a syrupy solution to be used in painting slides for projections. Work in a well-ventilated room; acetone fumes are flammable and somewhat toxic.

MYLAR COLOR MEDIUM   A still more recently developed color medium is made of a plastic chemically related to Mylar. It is quite expensive, costing two to three times as much as acetate. However it has advantages which compensate for its high cost: It is highly efficient, transmitting a greater percentage of the desired wavelengths than other plastic materials, while maintaining reasonably high purity. It is exceedingly durable. Under favorable conditions, it will outlast an acetate medium by a factor of three or four times. These characteristics make it desirable in locations such as cyclorama scoop lights where long life is an advantage. Such scoops are usually gelled in red, green, and blue and are not regelled until the gels fail. Blue acetate, in particular, is subject to failure because of the heat that it absorbs. Obviously Mylar will not pay for itself in spotlight applications where the gel is changed long before it reaches the end of its life.

ACTING AREA LIGHTING

The theory of acting area lighting, although really a part of lighting design, is important enough to warrant separate consideration. Crew members will find it easier to do their job if they know at least the outline of the theory of acting area lighting color (Figure 25-14).

The basic purpose of colors used in acting area lighting is to enhance the visibility of the expressions on the actor's face. It also contributes to mood, costume emphasis, and to the final color of the setting. But most important is the way the light strikes the actor's face. While no scientific studies have been made to prove it, it seems safe to say that two principle sources of aesthetic information on stage are the spoken lines and the expressions seen on the actor's faces. Lighting determines the effectiveness of these expressions in at least two ways: it determines where the focus of our attention will be on the stage at each moment (aided by blocking), and it governs the plasticity of the figures. "Plasticity" refers to the three-dimensional quality given by shadows to the objects seen on stage. Lighting that is highly plastic is sometimes also said to have a "sculptural" quality. It may even be referred to as "Rembrandt" lighting, paying homage to that artist's ability to render figures as three-dimensional.

The only difference between a smile and a frown is the location and shape of the shadows cast by the bulges and hollows on the actor's face. The actor provides the bulges and hollows; lighting must provide the shadows and highlights if the audience is to see them. Much of this is accomplished through the careful use of color.

"ACTING AREA" DEFINED

Unfortunately, the term, "acting area" has two meanings. It refers both to the entire space occupied by actors at one time or another while they are within sight of the audience and to a specific unit of space defined by lighting and used as a stock element in building up lighting on stage. For the purposes of this text, the term "acting *space*" will be assigned the first meaning, and the term "acting *area*" will be restricted to its narrow meaning. Thus, an acting area is a unit of stage lighting designed specifically for the purpose of lighting actors. It forms a standard building block in the design of the acting space lighting. We are indebted to Stanley McCandless for the concept of the acting area. He developed it many years ago as a means of producing more natural or at least more effective light on actors through the use of spotlights.

An acting area (defined in terms of the proscenium theatre) consists of as much stage cubage as can be conveniently lit by two spotlights placed above and in front of that area. It will usually be referred to as "an area." If the lighting instruments available to the sceno-

Figure 25-14. Lighting and the Actor. This series of production photographs has been chosen to demonstrate the interrelationship between the actor, the character he is creating, and the lighting. (a) Rigoletto (Verdi). This close-up of Bruno Pola in the lead role shows how the lighting can aid in developing the plasticity of the actor's face and in establishing the directionality of the scene. Taken from a production of the opera performed at the Stadtoper, Cologne, Germany. Scenography: Pint. Direction: Anton Müller. Photograph by Stefan Odry. Photograph courtesy Helmut Grosser. (b) Idomeneo (Mozart). Note how the lighting has been used to focus the scene toward the figures at right center, and to establish the high directional quality of the scene. Staged at Cologne Stadtoper. Direction and scenography: Ponelle. Photograph by Stefan Odry. (c) Morowitz Hamlet (Charles Morowitz). Produced at Purdue University. Scenography: Van Phillips. Direction: Dale A. J. Rose. Photograph courtesy Van Phillips. (d) La Traviata (Verdi). Produced at Purdue University. Note the subtle blending of area lighting to maintain focus without sharply defining the area. Scene design: William A. Lorenzen, III. Lighting: Van Phillips. Direction and costumes: Carl Williams. Photograph courtesy Van Phillips. (e) King Richard III (Shakespeare). Produced at A.C.T., San Francisco. Scenery: Robert Blackman. Lighting: F. Mitchell Dana. Photograph by Dennis Anderson.

FIGURE 25-14a

FIGURE 25-14b

445

FIGURE 25-14d

FIGURE 25-14c

FIGURE 25-14e

grapher are sufficiently abundant and powerful, the acting areas can be any size that suits his needs. Usually the largest-sized acting area measures about 9 feet deep and 12 feet wide at *actor head height.* An acting area is not a puddle of light on the stage floor; it is three-dimensional—the space within which the actor works while illuminated by the two instruments. It is formed by the elliptically shaped intersection of two conical beams of light. A "standard lighting area" is produced by locating two equally powerful spotlights above and to either side of the actor so that one is illuminating him along a line extending upward at 45° to the horizontal plane of his eyes and 45° to the left of his line of sight to the center of the house. The other instrument will illuminate him along a line symetrically 45° to his right. See Figure 25-15. In actual practice, the vertical angles (Figure 25-15b) may vary from about 35° to 48° and the horizontal angles (Figure 25-15a) even more (about 30° to 50°); the area will still be termed standard. Note that areas produced by light located even farther from "standard" are equally useful; they simply fall outside the generally accepted definition of standard.

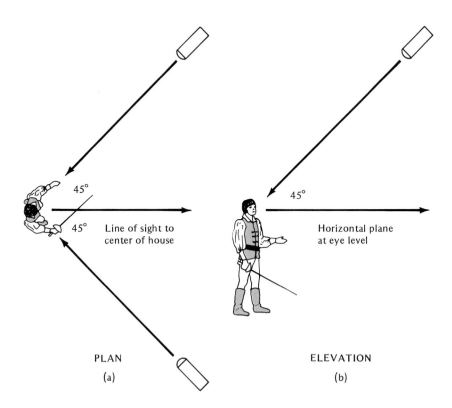

PLAN
(a)

ELEVATION
(b)

Figure 25-15. "Standard" Lighting Area. These drawings show in plan and elevation the approximate locations of the two lighting instruments which comprise a normal lighting area. Note how an actor whose head is in the center of such an area will observe the two instruments above and to his right and left as he faces directly toward the audience. The actual location of the two instruments may vary over a considerable range and the area will still be termed "standard."

In a standard area the light striking either side of a front-facing actor will be of equal intensity until color media are added or one of the instruments is dimmed more than the other. The highlights where both lights strike are roughly double the intensity of the sides of the face. This makes the sides read as shadows, but illuminated shadows in which details can be seen clearly. The result is that even without any color medium, the actor's face is seen three-dimensionally. Expressions are much clearer than they would be if the actor were lighted by border-lights which would cast no visible shadows at all.

Although any arrangement of acting areas that meets the needs of the scenographer will be acceptable, most lighting arrangements for the proscenium theatre tend to be variations of the two shown in Figure 25-16. After the scenographer has determined the number and arrangement of the acting areas, he designs the color scheme for them; all this will appear on the lighting plot. He may, of course, use any combination of colors he wishes. However, there are certain schemes that tend to be repeated, with variations, by most scenographers. In order to understand these more easily, they will be divided into categories. The categories have no artistic relevance; they are simply an aid to our understanding of the various types of acting area color schemes. They are:

1. Single tint acting area lighting
2. Related tint acting area lighting
3. Complementary tint acting area cross spotting

SINGLE TINT SYSTEM

The word "tint" is the key to this and the other color schemes. A tint is a pale color made by diluting a pure hue with white. Tints used in acting area lighting are almost always very subtle and have little apparent effect on the color of the actors' faces. Commonly used single tints are pale lavender ("special lavender"), pale rose, pale blue, pale salmon, and occasionally pale straw or amber. All of these colors favor the skin tones of the actors.

Single tint systems are the essence of simplicity: all acting area instruments receive the same gel. They are relatively easy to arrange because minor angling and focusing errors do not manifest themselves in pools of color.

Actors and makeup artists find single tint systems easy to work with because any compensation for "washing out" of facial color, usually reds, can be made with no fear that another color will undo the correction. Single tint systems are more economical because they allow bulk purchase of a single gel color. If instruments are in short supply, the scenographer can economize by using only one instrument, angled down from front center, for little-used areas.

Small stages (25'–35' proscenium opening):

This is known as a "6 area stage"

Large stages (to 50'–60' proscenium opening):

This is known as a "15 area stage"

Figure 25-16. *Arrangement of Acting Areas. These two sketches show common arrangements of acting areas on stage. The 6-area plan is usually found on small stages. The 15-area plan is used on large stages, but may be reduced to a 10-area plan if the situation warrants. This is done by removing the upstage row of five areas.*

There are, however, several disadvantages. Most important is the fact that a single tint will do little to increase plasticity. Contrast between shadow and highlight must depend only on intensity of light, not on color. Any mood effects created by the single tint will soon vanish because the audience' eyes will adapt to the color and cease to see it. There is no possibility of refreshing their color vision by a change in color—there is no other color. The single tint can be chosen to accent one color range of costumes over another (orange tints over purple tints, for example), but if there is a considerable variety of costume colors that must have equal emphasis, the single tint will not offer the necessary color range to make this possible.

RELATED TINT SYSTEM

Related tints are found near to or even adjacent to each other on the color wheel. There is a gradual blending from related to complementary as the colors get farther apart on the color wheel—no sharp demarcation exists. When related tints are applied to area lighting, one tint normally is placed in all of the right-hand instruments for acting areas, and the other in the left-hand instruments. Since one of these tints will inevitably be a gel of higher efficiency, an intensity difference is created along with the color difference. Advantages are as follows:

1. Related tint systems tend to enhance plasticity. Both color and intensity contrasts are created. The color contrast tends to heighten the perceived difference between shadows and highlights without producing dark shadows.
2. Potentialities for mood change and color adjustment are increased. If the right- and left-hand instruments are on separate controls, the contrast and intensity can be altered to suit each moment.
3. Color values for a variety of costumes can be more easily maintained. However single color corrections are not as easy as with single color systems.

These are the disadvantages:

1. This system tends to pile up color in the up-right and up-left corners of the setting.
2. The system absolutely requires the use of two instruments per area unless the scenographer is able to find a tint for single instrument areas which matches the combined results of the other areas — and this is unlikely.
3. Angling and focusing will require a higher degree of precision to prevent building up pools of varying color.
4. Dimming may deteriorate the effect by removing the contrast between the tints as the lamps move toward red.
5. Gels may fade at different rates causing one set to be changed long before the other.

Definition of Key Light

Before we can proceed with our discussion of complementary tint acting area lighting, we must clarify the term, "key light." This term, which comes from photography, refers to the light or lights that produce the brightest highlights on the actor' faces. These highlights tend to establish for the audience the predominant direction of the light striking the actor. Key light takes on a strong dramatic value when it is in high contrast to the rest of the lighting on the actor's face. This remainder is called "fill." It should be clear that a key light need not be a special instrument; it is simply the one that is producing the brightest highlight at that moment. It may be replaced by some other instrument at the next dimmer change, and become a fill.

The built-in intensity difference produced by related tint lighting tends to produce an automatic key light. The most efficient gel makes its instruments keys. This effect is much more pronounced when complementary tint lighting is used.

COMPLEMENTARY TINT ACTING AREA CROSS-SPOTTING

The third lighting system was first perfected by Stanley McCandless years ago. It consists of arranging the acting area instruments as nearly in the 45 degree pattern as the architecture of the theatre will allow, and then inserting tints of complementary colors into the gel holders. As in the related tint system, all left-hand instruments are gelled alike as are all right-hand ones. This produces three distinct color areas on the face: (1) a highlight which is near-white—this is the additive result of the two tints; (2) a warm shadow on one side of the actor's face — the highlight and the warm side tend to combine to form the key light; and (3) a cool side.

There are several advantages to this system:

1. A very high degree of plasticity is produced without heavy shadows.
2. A potential for a wide variation in color change for mood change is available.
3. Color values of costumes, makeup, and the like are enhanced.

The following are the disadvantages:

1. The system inevitably deteriorates toward a related color or even a single color pattern as it is dimmed. This is not disabling, and can be compensated for if the scenographer plans for it.
2. The system requires great precision in angling and focusing. Errors invisible in other systems manifest themselves as color patches.
3. A maximum of equipment is required if the system is to be exploited to its fullest. No single-instrument areas can be used, and there should be a dimmer for each side of each area.
4. The tendency to pile up color in the upstage corners of the setting, which was mentioned under related tint lighting, is aggravated. The scenographer will have to plan for this color variation from the beginning.

Obviously there is no sharp demarcation between related and complementary systems. As the colors chosen move away from exact complementary pairs, color contrasts diminish and the additive result of the mixture of the tints moves away from white. However, these shifts may be slight. The eye accepts a wide range of colors as "white" and rapidly adapts to those tints that are not at first read as "white." The result is that many color schemes which are categorized by their scenographers as complementary will be seen by others as related. This problem is academic; it makes no difference what the system is called if it does what the scenographer wants it to do. Very frequently the off-white quality of the additive result is exactly what he wants.

MIXED SYSTEMS

You may be asked to hang more than two instruments per acting area; the scenographer may contemplate shifting from one color scheme to another. He may even use both schemes at the same time. There is literally no end to the possibilities in combinations of color and contrast patterns that may be contrived by the scenographer, if he has the equipment and the time to work them out.

ACTING AREAS ON NONPROSCENIUM STAGES

Although McCandless developed the acting area system with the proscenium stage in mind, and it has been discussed in those terms heretofore, it is equally effective in various other forms of theatre. However, as the audience is wrapped further around the playing space in thrust staging or totally encircles the playing space as in arena staging, more instruments will have to be added to each acting area. The "standard separation" for instruments in a McCandless acting area is about 90 degrees. This angle can be increased up to about 120 degrees before a noticeable shadow area develops at the dividing line on the actor's face. Therefore, thrust stage areas usually consist of three instruments so placed that the horizontal angle between their beam center lines is less than 120 degrees. An angle approaching 90 degrees is much better. For theatre-in-the-round, four-instrument areas commonly are used, although three instruments 120 degrees apart can be used if they are so arranged that the view of the shadow at the separation area falls in aisles.

Color schemes for these three- and four-instrument areas usually follow one of the schemes above. However warm/cool relationships will shift from left to right and back as one moves around the area, and therefore cannot be so effectively tied to realistic motivation such as lamps or windows.

26
LIGHTING
EQUIPMENT

INTRODUCTION This is the spotlight era in the dramatic theatre. About 80–90 percent of all lighting is done with spotlights whenever they are available in sufficient quantities. Because of this, we will begin our discussion with the two main types of spots used today—the Fresnel lens spotlight and the ellipsoidal reflector spotlight. It is probable that most of your time on crew will be devoted to working with these instruments. After studying spotlights, we will take a somewhat shorter look at some of the other equipment usually found on modern stages: borderlights, footlights, floodlights, and the like.

Historically, lighting equipment has been categorized into two groups: specific and general. These were sharp, meaningful distinctions when they were developed. Specific lighting equipment was designed to light a sharply defined and rather limited area of the stage. General equipment did what the name implied; it flooded the entire stage with light. The equipment was not interchangeable. Today the terms are no longer meaningful because there are single pieces of equipment that can do both jobs. For example, there are focusable floodlights, and spotlights powerful enough to cover the entire stage area. If categories are necessary, the most meaningful are directional and nondirectional lighting.

DIRECTIONAL LIGHTING

The term "directional lighting" refers *not* to the equipment, but to the use to which it is put. Any equipment that is being used in such a way that it produces light which has a directional quality as seen by the audience may be considered as directional equipment while it is serving this function. Spotlights will fall into this category almost all of the time. Floods may be used in this manner or nondirectionally. The key to the distinction is that the equipment must produce shadows that are visible and meaningful to the audience.

NONDIRECTIONAL LIGHTING

Equipment being used in a nondirectional manner produces a presence of light on stage without a sense of direction. Borderlights and footlights usually work this way. Floodlights, particularly when used in rows, can produce this kind of light. Occasionally a "wash" of nondirectional light will be produced by means of a row of spotlights. Shadows must be invisible to the audience.

PROCEDURE FOR DISCUSSING EQUIPMENT

We will now take up specific pieces of equipment and discuss the following questions:

1. How do I identify it?
2. How do I prepare it for mounting?
3. How do I mount the instrument?
4. What auxiliary equipment may be added to it?

Note that not all questions will apply to every instrument. In some cases—cleaning procedures, for instance—the same explanation will apply to more than one instrument.

The answers to the preceding questions should supply you with enough information to do your work, but will not give you the fullest possible education. If you are at all curious, you will wonder why the scenographer choses one instrument over another, or why he insisted on a hood or barn doors, and many other details. He may order lens changes or even lens removal; he may insist on one lighting position which seems ridiculously hard to work in compared to another easier one nearby. While this text cannot answer all of these questions, it can provide some information about what a scenographer finds desirable and workable in certain equipment, and what characteristics make certain equipment useless in some situations. What follows is designed to help you reason out the answers to many questions that might seem simple to the advanced lighting technician. We will try to discover not only how an instrument is handled, but what sort of light it makes, how much light it spills, how much power it takes, what its mounting limitations are, and many other characteristics that determine where the scenographer will use it. With this knowledge you should be able, to some degree, to discover much for yourself about the art of lighting.

THE 6 INCH LENS FRESNEL SPOTLIGHT

IDENTIFYING THE INSTRUMENT

You are almost certain to encounter the Fresnel lens spotlight at your first crew meeting concerned with evaluating the lighting plot and assembling the equipment needed to light the show. It will probably be designated on the lighting plot as follows:

½ inch = 1 foot   ¼ inch = 1 foot

Be sure to check the plot to see if oval beam (OB) or regular Fresnel lenses are designated. The "zigzag" in the diagram is intended to represent the distinguishing feature of the Fresnel lens spotlight—its lens. Refer to the discussion of lenses in the previous chapter. Note the lenses shown in each of the Fresnel spotlights pictured in this chapter. They all reveal a ringlike formation of ridges on the outer face of the glass. These rings are the evidence of the structure of the Fresnel lens.

The identifying characteristic of the Fresnel spotlight is its lens and the cylindrical shape which is determined by the lamp and spherical reflector found inside. You will find a lens closely related to the Fresnel lens on certain types of ellipsoidal reflector spotlights. This is the step lens that has the ring pattern on the back; the front is curved in the form of a spherical surface.

Most 6 inch lens Fresnel spotlights will have a wattage rating of 500 W, so the instrument is often referred to as a "500 watt Fresnel" (Figure 26-1). However, the introduction of the T-H lamp has led at least one manufacturer (Kliegl) to produce a 6 inch Fresnel with a rating of 750 W.

PREPARING THE INSTRUMENT FOR MOUNTING

Except under emergency conditions, no instrument should be taken from storage and mounted without preparation. Even in an emergency, it is wise at least to plug the instrument in to be sure that it works, and to quickly check the wattage of the lamp before using it. Ordinarily you should take the following steps before mounting a Fresnel lens spotlight:

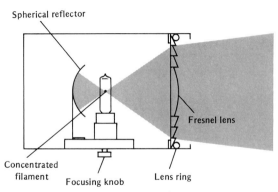

Figure 26-1a. A simplified sketch of a Fresnel spotlight that shows the main parts and the path that light takes from filament to lens.

Figure 26-1b. A Fresnel Spotlight.

1. Test for operating condition.
2. Open the instrument and remove the lamp.
3. Check the electrical system.
4. Check for mechanical and optical faults.
5. Clean the instrument and lens.
6. Clean and install the lamp.
7. Close, operate, and test for alignment.
8. Align the reflector.

Each of these steps will be examined in detail below.

1. Test for operating condition. This step is simple; plug the instrument into an outlet you know is working and see if it comes on. There is one risk, however, that you must take into account or you could get a bad shock. It is common practice to return faulty lighting instruments to the shop for repair. Since the shop is often also the instrument storage area, this can result in a faulty instrument going back into storage inadvertently without being repaired. Beware of equipment that has been returned because faulty wiring made the entire instrument electrically "live." This is a common occurrence in older theatres. If the instruments are equipped with three-wire cable and equipment grounds (see Chapter 24, "Electricity and Electrical Safety"), there should be little problem; older theatres, however, are seldom so equipped. Therefore, if the instrument has only two wires going into it, proceed as follows: Either ground the instrument by placing it firmly in contact with an electrical ground before turning it on, or place it on an insulating surface (perhaps a dry wooden table top) and turn it on without handling it. Then, while it is on, test it as you would test for a live wire. If you ground a faulty instrument before turning it on, it will cause a short circuit and open a fuse or breaker. Obviously, if the instrument turns out to be faulty, you will seek out the trouble during the electrical check to follow, and either repair it or see that it gets repaired before you turn it on again.

2. Open the instrument and remove the lamp. Most Fresnel spots open from the front. The lens and the entire front of the spotlight hinges downward when a catch at the top front is lifted upward and/or unscrewed (see Figure 26-2). Do not force the catch.

Removing the lamp depends on the type of lamp and socket in use. Refer to Chapter 25, "Producing and Using Light on the Stage" for details. If the lamp is of the T-H variety, be careful to handle it only by the base or use a cloth to protect it from your hands. Discard burned-out lamps and those with loose or burned bases. In the case of T-H lamps also discard those with pitted contacts.

3. Check the electrical system. The first things to look for are frayed lead-in wires. The problem lies at the point where the leads pass through the instrument housing on the way to the lamp socket.

Figure 26-2. Opening the Front of the Instrument. Note the catching device at the top.

Until very recently all stage instruments were wired with asbestos-insulated wire (called "motion picture wire") because no other type of insulation would take the heat generated by the lamp. While asbestos resists heat well, it resists abrasion poorly. Every time an instrument is moved or focused, the wires are rubbed at the point of entry. This often leads to the condition illustrated in Figure 26-8. When the copper touches the housing, electricity flows into the housing and it becomes "hot." If the faulty equipment is in a modern theatre, it will have an equipment ground that will cause a fuse or breaker to open the moment power is turned on. But older theatres seldom have this protection. The older the equipment, the more rigorous your inspection should be. Use extra precautions wherever there is no equipment ground.

The space age has produced an improvement on motion picture wire. It is silicone-rubber-insulated wire that resists heat and abrasion much better than asbestos. In addition to this, the wires may be further protected with a tubular shield of either fiberglass or more silicone material in order to cut down on failures of the wiring at the lead-in point. Regrettably, motion picture wire will still be around for a long time in older equipment. When you find an instrument with frayed lead-ins, seek the assistance of your supervisor to remove the leads completely and replace them with new wire.

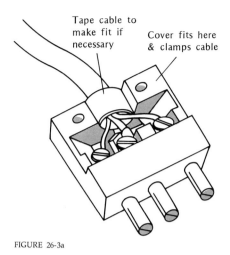

Tape cable to make fit if necessary

Cover fits here & clamps cable

FIGURE 26-3a

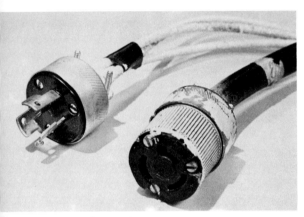

FIGURE 26-3b

Figure 26-3. Common Connectors for Spotlights. (a) A pin connector. This connector provides a third connection for the equipment ground. Note the wiring that has been shown by removing the connector cover. Replacing the cover forms a clamp around the cable to avoid strain on the connections. (b) Twist-Lock connectors. Although this has now been replaced by a more modern type less likely to be interchanged with similar connectors carrying different voltage configurations, there are still many in use.

A second likely place to look for trouble is at the socket. Wires have a way of burning off right where they attach to the socket. The standard test for this is to grasp each lead firmly and give it a pull. If it is so worn that it pulls off, it must be repaired. Of course you should exercise some moderation in pulling at the socket leads but they should withstand a firm tug of 3–5 pounds. Remember that you have to pull from *inside* the housing. Each wire is either knotted or fitted with a clamp to prevent the pull of cables from straining the socket connections while in use. As you are checking the socket leads, examine the socket itself. Its parts should be the color of brass or nickel plating, not the typical burned-blue look of overheated parts. If there is evidence that the socket has been hot, seek the assistance of your supervisor.

At the opposite end of the wires from the spotlight will be the connector—one of several types; the two most common are shown in Figure 26-3. If it is a pin connector, it should be possible to give the wiring a good hard pull without detaching it. If it comes loose, the connector should be opened up, the wires recut, and the insulation removed for about $\frac{1}{2}$ inch to allow the copper conductor to be first twisted into a tight "rope," and then wrapped around the terminal screw in a clockwise manner. If you wrap it this way, it will pull under the flange on the screw as you tighten it and make a good connection. Note that there should be no frayed ends of copper wires sticking out from under the screw when you finish. If there are, they may cause a short circuit. When both wires have been reworked, insert the asbestos wires into their slots and install the cover/clamp. Tighten very firmly and test by pulling hard on the wires. The plug should hold. It is less likely that you will have to repair a pin connector on a spotlight equipped with the new silicone-rubber-insulated wires, but if you do, follow the same procedure with the addition of enough tape (if needed) to build the diameter of the wires up to where the cover/clamp will hold securely.

The pin connector has one feature that has endeared it to electricians for decades: it offers easy and rapid repair of loose connections that may develop as a result of wear in the pins. Each pin is slotted down its middle most of the way to the fiber block insulator body. If the pin is loose, it can be spread slightly by inserting the blade of a knife into the slit and pushing until the pin fits snugly into its mating hole (Figure 26-4). Then the pin is scraped or sanded clean.

If it is necessary to rewire a Twist-Lock connector like the one in Figure 26-3b, it is best to follow the procedure listed on the side of the connector box. Note that on the Twist-Lock connector you will have a clamp at the back of the connector to tighten. It prevents extra strain on the wiring. When properly wired and tightened, a Twist-Lock connector should take a pull of several hundred pounds—more than you can exert in testing it. Give it a good hard pull before you declare it secure.

4. Check for mechanical and optical faults. Having gone over the electrical parts of the instrument, you should check it mechanically. The lens should not be cracked or broken. Minor nicks around the edge often are tolerated although they may eventually cause the lens to break. However major nicks and missing pieces usually cause light to spill off in odd directions, and the lens should be replaced if at all possible.

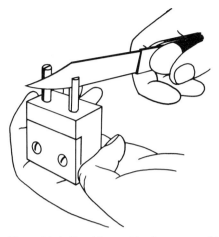

Figure 26-4. *Repairing a Pin Connector. This operation will tighten the electrical connection between line and load connector, reducing the chance of heating. Scrape the pins clean at the same time.*

The front of the spotlight will probably hinge down in order to allow you to reach the lamp (see Figure 26-2). Its catch should be secure. Some older spotlights develop weak catches that allow the instrument to pop open, spilling its color frame and any barn doors or hoods that may be in the color frame holder. This is dangerous. The catch should be fixed immediately, or, if this is not possible, the front of the instrument must be held in place temporarily by wire. Under no circumstances should a dangerous instrument be installed where it might dump parts on someone's head.

The apparatus for mounting the instrument must be secure. Mounting equipment usually consists of a U-shaped metal strap (yoke), attached to the instrument by two bolts, which is, in turn, attached to pipe battens by means of a C-clamp. The latter is held to the yoke by a bolt which should be very secure. It holds up the entire instrument, often under conditions of twist and vibration. Preferably the C-clamp should consist of two parts, a stem to which the yoke is bolted, and the C-shaped clamp itself which rides on the stem and cannot drop off (see Figure 26-5). Pivoting then is controlled by means of a small set screw at the side of the stem. With this pivoting arrangement, it should never be necessary to loosen the large bolt that holds the stem to the yoke in order to turn the spotlight. On the other hand, loosening the support bolt is the only way to pivot an instrument on a one-piece clamp. The moral is obvious: The bolt holding the entire weight of the instrument must be in good condition (and have no stripped threads) and it should be firmly screwed into place. The small pivot-locking bolt (if present) should be in working order and loosened in preparation for hanging the instrument. Never tighten the pivot lock extremely tight with your wrench. If you do, you are apt to twist the top right off the bolt, making it impossible to unlock the pivot. If you discover such twisted-off bolts during your inspection of spotlights, take the clamps to the shop where someone will have to drill out the remains of the broken bolt.

There should be no loose parts or missing screws. The lamp-socket-mirror assembly (Figure 26-1a) should move smoothly back and forth pulling the wiring along as it moves, and should not leave light-leaking slots at various positions. It should be possible to tilt the instru-

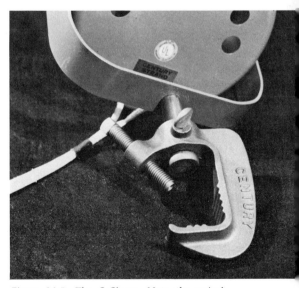

Figure 26-5. *The C-Clamp. Note the swivel screw on the side of the stem. This screw locks the rotation of the yoke. It should be set only tight enough to prevent movement.*

FIGURE 26-6a

FIGURE 26-6b

Figure 26-6. (a) A Poorly Adjusted Spherical Reflector. (b) A Properly Located Spherical Reflector.

ment in the yoke to any angle and hold it there with the tilt-locking screw(s) on the side.

The spherical mirror (Figure 26-6) should be bright and shiny, or in the case of some T-H instruments, bright and pebbled. It should show no evidence of overheating or corrosion. If the mirror has been damaged, it should be replaced. If the mirror is.dirty, it should be wiped with a clean grit-free cloth; if the dirt is greasy, it may be necessary to carefully wash the mirror in water and a little mild detergent. Be sure that it is throughly rinsed and completely dried. At no time should any abrasive scouring powder or the like be used in an attempt to clean a mirror. It has a rather delicate optically treated surface that thrives best on only an occasional dusting. Mechanically, the mirror should be supported rather firmly behind the lamp in such a position that the center of curvature of the mirror is at the center of the filament. If it appears to be out of adjustment, bend the support bracket slightly to bring it into the best position you can by observation (Figure 26-6). You will finish the alignment job after the instrument is completely assembled and turned on.

5. Clean the instrument and lens. In cleaning the mirror, we have already begun this process. If the instrument is exceedingly dirty and if the socket-mirror assembly needs further checking and possible repair, you may wish to remove this assembly from the interior of the spotlight. In many instruments this is accomplished simply by removing the focusing screw completely and lifting the socket assembly out through the front of the instrument. It will remain attached to the lead-in wires, but you should have enough slack to do whatever work is necessary. Empty any dirt out of the socket and double check it for signs of overheating.

While the socket is out, turn it over and visually check the wiring at the bottom. There should be no sign of burning, overheating, or any other malfunction. If there are screw connections they should be tight. This inspection will confirm your findings when you tugged on the lead-in wires to check them.

Carefully wipe out the entire interior of the spotlight housing, keeping an eye out for bits of broken glass from past violent lamp failures. If there is any such glass or other debris, shake it out and wipe the interior clean. Clean and check the mirror as described above.

Carefully remove the lens by pinching on the lens ring. If the lens is mounted with clips, remove the screws noting how they are installed so you can put it back together. Once the lens is out, double check it for chips, cracks, etc. If it is in satisfactory condition, wash it gently in either warm soapy water or in diluted ammonia solution, then rinse and dry.

Clean the outside of the instrument by dusting, if necessary. Reinsert the socket assembly and fasten it loosely with the focusing screw. Do not attempt to tighten the focusing screw until you have inserted the lamp again. Once the socket is in place, put back the lens, trying to avoid marking it with fingerprints. (Be sure the rings face the stage.) It should fit into its slot behind the lens ring rather loosely, allowing for expansion when it gets hot. If it is mounted with clips, these should also fit loosely. After the lens is mounted, wipe it again to remove any fingerprints. The instrument is now ready for the lamp.

6.   Clean and install the lamp. Refer to the previous chapter for details in handling lamps. If your Fresnel instrument is more than a few years old, it will have been fitted for conventional incandescent lamps and you will probably be using it either with such a lamp or a retrofit T-H lamp. This may either be the lamp you removed from the instrument, or another. If the surface of the bulb is at all dirty, it should be cleaned. A conventional lamp can be cleaned like a lens—be sure the base is completely dry before inserting it. If it is a T-H lamp, it must be washed in an alcohol solution provided by your supervisor. *Do not touch the bulb with your bare skin after it has been washed.* If you do touch it accidentally, wash it again, even if you see no perspiration mark.

No instrument should be used at a wattage larger than that specified by its manufacturer. To do so is to risk overheating the instrument and damaging the lens, reflector, and the lamp itself. In fact, overheating may occur anyway if the instrument is operated in a location with little or no ventilation. Evidence of overheating may be burned-off paint, cracked lenses, or swollen lamps, which fail prematurely.

An instrument may be used with a lamp of wattage smaller than the maximum stated by the manufacturer. The only requirement is that the filament be in the same location with regard to the reflector-lens system. This means the light center length (LCL) must be the same. After the lamp has been installed and the instrument front closed, it is ready for final check, and if necessary, alignment.

7.   Close, operate, and test for alignment. Attach the instrument to a live circuit and aim it at a blank wall. Move the focusing mechanism from spot to flood (narrow beam to wide beam) and back, noting any evidence of misalignment of the reflector. The pool of light should be circular and even, with no off-center bright or dark areas. If at any point in the focusing movement you detect evidence of two overlapping pools of light, alignment is probably necessary. If in doubt, ask your supervisor. If there is evidence of considerable misalignment, open the instrument while it is off, and double check the lamp to be certain that it is properly and completely inserted. If it is, proceed to step 8.

8.   Align the reflector. This procedure is most easily and safely carried out if the instrument is operated from a dimmer which is set at a reading just high enough to enable you to see the pools of light formed by the lens and the mirror. The object is to superimpose these two pools so they merge into one. Note where the dim pool (from the

mirror) is in relation to the brighter one. Because the light is passing through the lens, you will have to move the mirror in a direction opposite to that indicated by the location of the dim pool. If, for example, the dim pool is to the left of the bright one, bend the mirror toward the left (directions are given as if you were facing the same direction in which the beam of light is traveling). A slight movement will make a big change. Tilting the mirror forward or back will adjust for vertical errors.

It is more unlikely that the dim pool will be too large or too small in relation to the main pool because the reflector bracket usually fixes the distance from the mirror to the lamp. If this distance is adjustable, moving the mirror toward the lamp makes a larger pool, and moving it away makes a smaller pool.

If simple and minor adjustments of the mirror will not align the spotlight, seek the assistance of your supervisor. Once aligned, the spotlight is ready to mount, and should be stored in a clean place until it is put into use.

OTHER FRESNEL EQUIPMENT

We have discussed the 500 watt Fresnel spotlight in great detail because it is the instrument you will probably use most. Actually it is only one in a family of Fresnel instruments, and a rather small one at that. Most manufacturers list Fresnel spotlights in wattages from 100–10,000 W. The tiny ones are called "inkies," a name the movie industry conferred on them. The larger sizes are usually 1000–2000 W, sometimes called a "junior" in film and television where they are used in great numbers. Still larger are 5000 W "seniors" and 10,000 W "sun spots." These are found almost exclusively in motion picture and television work or on very large theatre stages. They are monsters with lenses up to 15 inches in diameter and housings the size of an ash can—a name also used sometimes. The 1000–2000 W Fresnel spotlights are very useful in medium to large theatres. You will probably be mounting some of them during your crew work. Mechanically they work almost exactly the same way as the 500 W instrument.

There is another class of Fresnel spotlights not usually found in theatres. These are made for photographic use, especially in motion picture studios. They are made more precisely with lenses of much higher optical quality. They cost from two to four times as much as theatre-quality instruments and can be used for many FOH purposes that a theatre-quality Fresnel spotlight cannot fulfil. However, you are not likely to find many of them available to you. The amount of money which one of them costs will buy several ellipsoidal reflector spotlights, which will do the theatre more good than one motion picture-quality Fresnel spotlight.

MOUNTING THE FRESNEL SPOTLIGHT

If a modern Fresnel spotlight is equipped with a T-H lamp of the size stipulated by its manufacturer or smaller, it may be mounted in any position as long as it is where it can get satisfactory ventilation. Your supervisor will know if there are locations where overheating has been a problem, and will probably instruct you to use smaller than normal wattages in these locations.

Lamp operating position must be base-down-to-horizontal if conventional lamps are in use. Other than this restriction, the only concern is that the instrument should not be in a position that will allow the color frame or any other equipment in the color frame slot to fall out. If there is any doubt, use safety chains or wires.

THE 6 INCH LENS ELLIPSOIDAL REFLECTOR SPOTLIGHT

The ellipsoidal reflector spotlight and the Fresnel lens spotlight are the two main instruments used in lighting small- to medium-sized theatres today. Both are usually rated at 500 W, although 750 W ratings are not unusual. Also, 250 W lamps are available when needed.

The complete and accurate name for the ellipsoidal instrument is "ellipsoidal reflector spotlight." Since this is somewhat long, there have been attempts by the makers to shorten the name and promote a trade name at the same time. Kliegl, who introduced the ellipsoidal spotlight in the late 1930s, used the name "Klieglight," which became synonymous with the bright lights of show business for many years. Century Lighting Company,[1] not to be outdone when they brought out a version of the instrument, termed theirs the "Lekolight." This was soon shortened to "Leko," which seems to have won the nickname contest because of its shortness. If you want to be impartial, call it an "ellipsoidal spot."

IDENTIFYING THE INSTRUMENT

All of the photographs used to illustrate this section of the text show ellipsoidal reflector spotlights. Some show the latest equipment available, others show earlier equipment that is still likely to be in service. Note that with the exception of Figure 26-7c these instruments exhibit the same external characteristics: They have a rather long tube in front which houses a lens or lenses. These lenses may be simple plano-convex lenses (Figure 26-7a) or a step lens (Figure 26-7b). Behind the lens tube is a bulbous housing which contains the

---

1. Now Strand Century Inc.

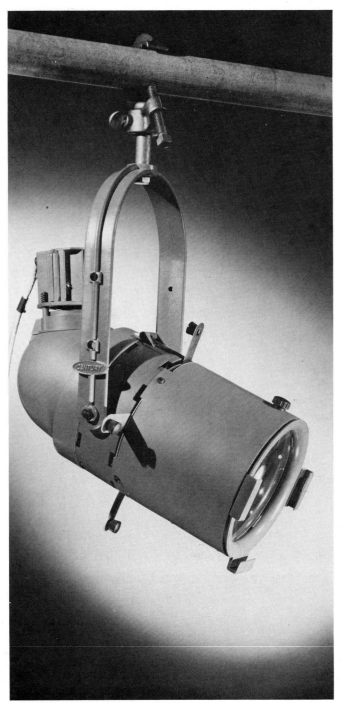

FIGURE 26-7a

FIGURE 26-7b

Figure 26-7. (a) A modern ellipsoidal reflector spotlight. Photograph courtesy Strand Century. (b) Modern ellipsoidal reflector spotlight. Photograph courtesy Kliegl Brothers. (c) An ellipsoidal reflector spotlight which does not reveal the outline of the reflector. Photograph courtesy Electro Controls. (d) Simplified sketch of an ellipsoidal spotlight that shows main parts and path of light from filament to lens.

FIGURE 26-7c

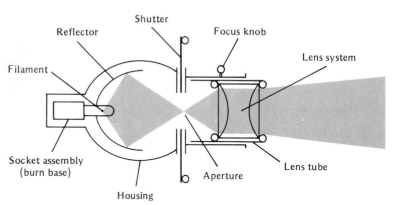

FIGURE 26-7d

lamp socket and wiring. Generally, when the instrument is mounted, this socket tube or "burn-base" will be upward, allowing the lamp to operate in base-up position. However this requirement is not necessary in the case of the T-H lamps.

On lighting plots, the ellipsoidal spot is usually designated as follows:

|← ½" →|

When it is in use, it is distinguished by the relatively sharp edge of its beam, and the variety of shapes that the beam can take.

PREPARING THE INSTRUMENT FOR MOUNTING

Ellipsoidal spotlights are as likely to be encountered on your first examination of the lighting plot as are Fresnel spots. They must be readied for mounting in much the same manner. The following discussion of this process assumes that the reader has already mastered those procedures such as checking the connector, which are common to both the Fresnel and ellipsoidal spotlight. It therefore concentrates on those things that are different.

1. Plug in the instrument—check for operation. The same precautions prevail as in the case of the Fresnel spotlight.

2. Remove the lamp from the instrument by releasing the latch that holds the burn base to the housing, and carefully withdraw the lamp assembly. Occasionally the lamp will be so bulged from overheat-

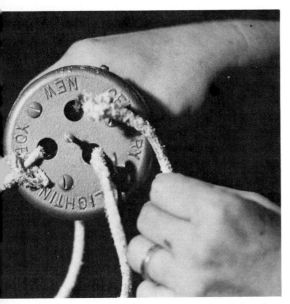

Figure 26-8. Checking the Wiring. This burn base from an ellipsoidal reflector spotlight has a frayed wire. This could cause a short or make the entire body of the spotlight electrically live. Such wiring should be replaced.

ing that it must be broken to remove the assembly from the reflector housing. Seek help if you encounter this condition. Remove the lamp from the burn base and set both parts aside for later inspection. Then open the instrument by releasing the latch near its midpoint, and hinging back the lens-aperture assembly from the reflector assembly. Check the latch itself to make sure that it is not damaged or weakened, and likely to open unexpectedly.

3. Examine the electrical system (Figure 26-8). This will actually be easier to do than in the Fresnel spot because the socket is more accessible. Fraying of lead-ins is also less likely because there is no movement of the wiring during focusing operation of the ellipsoidal spot. While examining the socket, note the condition of its mechanical mount. If it is loose, seek assistance or return the instrument to the shop for expert repairs.

4. Examine the spot for mechanical problems. Begin with the lens tube, checking the color frame holders for distortion and for weak springs, if springs are used. If the lenses are obviously dirty, remove them for cleaning. This operation is much like that in the Fresnel except that with double-lens instruments, there will be a spacer between the lenses which must be removed to get the second lens out. Be sure to keep the lenses in the same order in which they were installed. Some older instruments were equipped with a heat-treated lens only at the rear lens. If the lenses are inadvertently interchanged, the back lens may crack under heat. There are normally no markings on the lenses themselves to identify them. The lens tube offers little in the way of mechanical problems unless it has been dropped and bent, in which case, it should be replaced.

Examine the aperture assembly carefully. It will need frequent mechanical attention. The four framing shutters are susceptible to damage from heat inside the instrument and from bending and twisting from the outside. Note that when they are fully withdrawn from the aperture to produce the maximum beam size, they protrude from the outside of the instrument in such a way that they are easily bent or twisted. For this reason it is standard procedure to store all ellipsoidal spotlights with the framing shutters completely closed and thus protected inside the instrument. However, when the instrument is operating, whatever part of the framing shutters protrudes into the aperture is heated by the intense beam of light from the reflector. If they are closed all the way, the entire heat output of the lamp is trapped in the instrument where it rapidly overheats everything inside. Thus framing shutters are opened immediately after mounting an ellipsoidal spotlight to make certain that it will not be turned on with them closed.

No matter how carefully framing shutters are treated, they will be subject to failure. Whenever they are partially inserted into the aperture to shape the beam, they are heated to a high temperature.

This destroys the temper of the steel, warps it, and causes it to rust. Manufacturers have taken two different approaches to this problem. One group has sought to provide very durable shutters of heavy steel which are designed to last the life of the instrument. They are built into the instrument in a manner that makes them hard to replace when they do fail, which ultimately happens, in spite of the manufacturer's precautions. The other approach is to treat the shutters as expendables, making them of thin metal that is cheap and easy to replace routinely every few years. These thin shutters are held in the instrument only by friction and the small wooden handle attached to their outer end to insulate the operator's hand from heat. Once this handle has been removed, the shutter may be pulled out through the center of the aperture, and replaced (see Figure 26-9).

FIGURE 26-9a

If the aperture of the spotlight has been equipped with a gobo at some time in the past, you may find it still in place when you check out the instrument. Remove it unless you are instructed otherwise. It may simply be resting in a special slot made for this purpose at the front of the aperture, or it may have been slipped in between the framing shutters, if the spotlight was not equipped with a gobo slot (Figure 26-10a). If the aperture is equipped with an iris, use great care not to bend the blades, which are delicate (Figure 26-10b). If the iris does not work smoothly and easily, carefully clean it by blowing out all dust and grit.

Inspect the burn base assembly (socket, socket holder, and wiring) for mechanical problems. The latching device may be a troublemaker. Some types depend on a small twist-latch that is extremely hard to work and easily bent out of shape. If these become so badly damaged that they cannot be replaced, a bolt and wing nut may be substituted. In any case, no instrument should be operated with the burn base insecurely attached.

FIGURE 26-9b

5. Clean the lens(es) and reflector. Lenses are cleaned in the same manner as Fresnel lenses. The reflector should be cleaned and handled like a spherical reflector.

6. Clean and install the proper lamp.

7. Close, operate, and test alignment by aiming the instrument at a distant smooth surface. Pull all shutters except one all the way out. Focus the image of the remaining shutter carefully on the test surface, and then pull it out. This should put the instrument into its sharp-focus position and give the best beam formation possible at the test throw.

Figure 26-9. Apertures. (a) Aperture of a Kliegl Ellipsoidal Reflector Spotlight. Note the relatively heavy durable shutters used to shape the aperture. They are difficult to replace although they seldom wear out. (b) Aperture of a Strand Century Ellipsoidal Spotlight. (c) Shutter Plate from the Above Aperture. Note that these shutter plates are designed for easy replacement.

FIGURE 26-9c

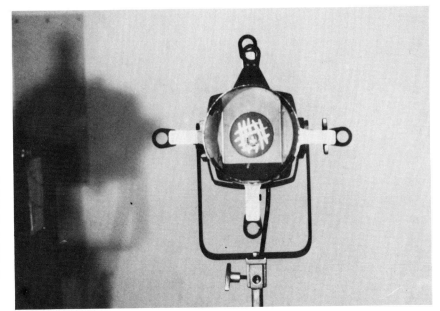

FIGURE 26-10a

Figure 26-10. (a) An Aperture Equipped with a Gobo Slot. Any simple image material that is designed to withstand the intense heat present in the aperture may be inserted into this slot and projected onto the stage. The image thus formed will be bright but not of high optical quality. (b) An Iris. This well-made unit has been working for many years. Such devices deserve careful treatment. Courtesy Berkey Colortran, a division of Berkey Photo.

FIGURE 26-10b

Examine the lighted field. It should be symmetrical and the light should be relatively evenly distributed. Do not expect an absolutely even field; the ellipsoidal spotlight has been designed to sacrifice optical perfection for efficiency and reasonable cost. However, there should be no dark patches and the beam should be symmetrical if the shutters are all the way out. If the field is not satisfactory, double check to make sure that the socket assembly is properly seated and locked, and that the lens(es) is properly inserted. It may also be necessary to ascertain whether the lamp is the proper one for the instrument.

8. Align the instrument. If all of the above things check, adjust the position of the lamp in relationship to the reflector by turning the adjustment screws slightly first one way and then the other while watching the lighted field (Figure 26-11). If the field improves, continue turning in the same direction. If turning makes it worse, reverse direction. You should get visible results in about one-half turn. If one or two turns produces no results, seek help. Do not drive the adjustment screws more than a couple of turns in any direction if you are not getting improvement, and never run them all the way in or out. Move by small increments and watch the results. It may be necessary to compare the field of a satisfactorily adjusted instrument with that of the one you are working on until you get the sense of what to look for. In some instruments there will be a screw in the center of the three that adjust the socket tilt. This is a "locking screw" which must be backed out a couple of turns before starting adjustment, and then turned in until it seats firmly when you have finished.

After the instrument has been aligned, it is ready to mount. The shutters should be closed immediately after finishing alignment, and should remain closed until the instrument is mounted.

You may occasionally open an instrument which is not working properly (the beam is lopsided and dim) and find a loose lamp rattling around in the reflector in addition to the one in the socket. This happens when the lamp is not properly inserted—and tightened if necessary—into the socket. If the lamp has been poorly mounted, vibration may cause it to drop out because it is hanging socket-up. When it is noticed that the instrument no longer works, someone checks it by removing the lamp/socket assembly, notes that there is no lamp in the socket, and inserts another. Of course the first lamp is still inside and remains there until someone checks the instrument thoroughly or notes the strange nature of the beam. The moral is simple: check for loose lamps before inserting new ones.

OTHER ELLIPSOIDAL REFLECTOR EQUIPMENT

Like the Fresnel, the ellipsoidal reflector spotlight is made in a wide variety of sizes. There is a tiny 100 W instrument which is handy for small pools of light that must come from tight locations, and there are giant instruments capable of 200 foot throws. There is also a special category of ellipsoidal spotlights designed as follow spots. These

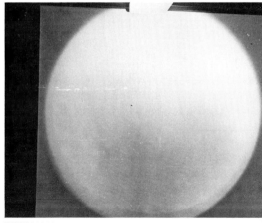

FIGURE 26-11a

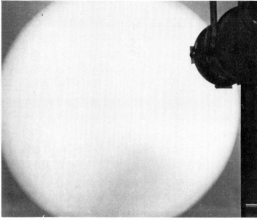

FIGURE 26-11b

Figure 26-11. (a) An Improperly Aligned Ellipsoidal Reflector Spotlight. Note that the bright spot is off center and the light is unevenly distributed. (b) A Well-Aligned Ellipsoidal Reflector Spotlight. The bright spot, if present, should be in the center. A certain amount of shadow from the lamp holder is inevitable in many spotlights. This is such a spot.

Gel holder

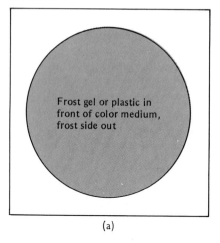

Frost gel or plastic in
front of color medium,
frost side out

(a)

Gel holder

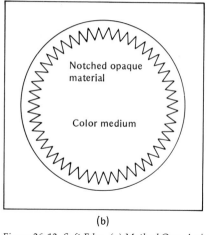

Notched opaque
material

Color medium

(b)

Figure 26-12. Soft Edge. (a) Method One. A piece of frost gelatin or plastic is installed in the color holder with the frost toward the stage and in front of the color medium. The frost then is wiped from the center of the exposed area using water on a cloth if gelatin has been installed, or acetone if plastic was used. (Use care—acetone is flammable and its fumes are somewhat toxic.) The degree of softness can be controlled by the amount of frost removed. (b) Method Two. A notched ring of opaque material is installed along with the color medium. It should be on the stage side of the color holder. The depth of the notches and their number control the soft edge; thus only a portion of a beam may be treated.

powerful instruments are equipped with special beam-shaping controls and with color changers.

MOUNTING ELLIPSOIDAL EQUIPMENT

Ellipsoidal spots equipped with conventional lamps must be mounted so that the lamps operate near base-up position. Those with T-H lamps may be mounted in any position as long as ventilation is good.

OTHER INSTRUMENTS THAT PRODUCE POOLS OF LIGHT

Although about 90 percent of the lighting in most theatres will be done with spotlights of either the Fresnel or the ellipsoidal reflector type, it is quite possible that you will encounter some other instruments. They are treated briefly below.

PLANO-CONVEX LENS SPOTLIGHT

As mentioned in the previous chapter the plano-convex lens was the earliest spotlight developed for use with the incandescent lamp. Since some of these now nearly obsolete spotlights are still in use in older theatres, we must know how to maintain them. Maintenance of plano spots is about the same as that of a Fresnel lens spotlight. Operating conditions are also similar. One special problem may be encountered if it is necessary to use plano spots for acting area lighting where blending is vital. The essentially sharp edge of this instrument is difficult to soften. Two techniques are shown in Figure 26-12. Neither produces the smooth blend that is naturally a part of a Fresnel lens.

BEAM PROJECTORS

Beam projectors (Figure 26-13a) are actually baby searchlights. They have the same optics as the large units now used mostly for advertising. While the light source in the large ones is a carbon arc (see below), the stage variety is powered by a 1000–2000 W lamp. The parabolic reflector is the operative part of the instrument. It gathers the light and forms it into a near-parallel beam. This beam often is used to imitate sunlight or moonlight on stage. It also serves to create the dramatic "pillar of light."

Maintenance of these beam projectors is simple. Clean the metal reflector with a dry, grit-free cloth, and check out the electrical system as you would that of a Fresnel spotlight. Do not attempt to polish the reflector—it is electrically polished aluminum and cannot be improved by hand.

FIGURE 26-13a

FIGURE 26-13b

Figure 26-13. (a) A Beam Projector. The spherical device in front of the lamp is merely a shield to prevent stray light, not a spherical mirror. (b) A Modern Follow Spotlight. This instrument is made in two types: one is equipped with a T-H lamp, and the other with a HMI lamp. Both are extremely efficient because of the highly refined optical system. The version with the HMI lamp rivals the highest current carbon arc follow spotlight in light output. Photograph courtesy Berkey Colortran, a Division of Berkey Photo.

FOLLOW SPOTLIGHTS

If you have attended an ice show or a major musical or variety show you have seen follow spotlights in action. These are the huge and powerful devices that are moved about by an operator to follow the leading actors with an intense, sharply focused pool of light. The power is usually so great that all other lighting on the stage is reduced to the status of fill light (Figure 26-13b).

Most of these instruments are powered by a carbon arc, which was discussed in the previous chapter. The light from the arc is gathered up optically and directed to the stage. However, the arc burns away the carbon rods, and they must be constantly readjusted if the arc is to be maintained. Normally this is done by an operator who also directs the light where it is needed, changes color media, etc.

Unfortunately the electric arc produces some dangerous by-products: carbon monoxide and ultraviolet radiation. Carbon monoxide is an odorless, poisonous gas—the same as that found in an automobile exhaust. It can kill or produce serious illness. To prevent this, all carbon arc sources must be provided with ventilation that will carry the carbon monoxide safely away from the operator and others who might be endangered. It is especially important that you be aware of this if an arc follow spotlight is rented for temporary use in a musical show. *Be sure that these deadly fumes are safely removed.*

The ultraviolet radiation is not dangerous to performers because the glass in the lenses of the instrument filters it out. However the operator must be cautious about exposing himself to the direct rays of the arc if he opens the lamp house while it is in operation or if it can leak out of the housing. This light is especially dangerous to the eyes.

There are also some small, incandescent lamp-powered follow spotlights. These are much easier and safer to use for small theatres. They work either on the optical principle of the ellipsoidal spotlight or that of the plano-convex lens spotlight, but with much more elaborate optical systems in either case. Get detailed instructions on follow spotlights from your supervisor and from the supplier if you are renting or buying.

The manipulation of a follow spotlight, as opposed to its technical operation, is relatively simple but requires a lot of attention. You will be expected to anticipate every move of the performer you are following, so that he will always be in the pool of light. When two or more performers are on stage and you have only one follow spotlight, it should be clearly established by the director which performer should be followed, or whether the beam should be spread to encompass both of them. If you spread it a great deal, you will weaken its effect considerably. The spotlight should be moved smoothly and unhesitatingly when necessary or otherwise held stationary. A jiggling follow spot during a solo is distracting.

You will have to plan on periods of time every so often that allow you to change the burned carbons for a new set. The burning time of a "trim" of carbons, as a set is called, will vary from about twenty minutes up to about forty-five minutes depending on the make of the arc light. The carbons will be red-hot and must be handled with pliers when you remove them.

The recently developed xenon and HMI lamps appear to offer a powerful light source without the constant adjustment required for the carbon arc. The xenon lamp has already taken over most motion picture projection operation for these reasons. Professional 35 mm motion picture projectors formerly used a carbon arc source almost identical to that found in many follow spotlights. Several manufacturers are presently making follow spots using HMI lamps.

"MAKE DO" SPOTLIGHTS

There are many small theatres, particularly community theatres, which have few if any spotlights if we count only instruments made by stage lighting manufacturers for that purpose. The rest of the lighting is done with lamps which are built in such a way that they produce a relatively narrow beam of light. Such instruments are known as "reflector lamps." They come in a wide variety of types and sizes with both conventional and T-H filament structures. In all cases the filament is permanently aligned in front of a reflector which gathers the light and directs it into a nonadjustable beam. They are highly efficient and relatively cheap, particularly the long-life varieties. They really amount to a lamp which has incorporated into it all of the functions usually found in the spotlight instrument itself.

These lamps are variously known as PAR lamps, bird's-eye lamps, type "R" lamps, etc. Many of them are fitted with conventional screw bases which must be operated in heat-resistant medium screw base sockets. The sockets usually are fitted with friction devices to hold the aim of the lamp after it has been moved into position. Another category of reflector lamps comes with simple screw connections such as an automobile headlight (which they closely resemble) and is intended to be fitted into a special holder. Either type is available in several beam spreads, the narrowest usually being about 15 degrees. This figure determines pool size at various distances because there is no way to change the spread at the lamp itself except by substituting another lamp. Wattages vary from 75 to 1000 W or more.

Operators of these lamps should be aware that they get intensely hot. They are quite capable of setting curtains on fire. For this reason, neither gelatin nor plastic color medium can be mounted directly at the face of the lamp. Only glass will take the heat, and it must be specially made for the purpose. The lamps are also breakable, particularly the "R" types made of thin glass. If they are struck by a piece of scenery, or if they come in contact with something cold, they will shatter, throwing hot glass around.

In spite of all these difficulties, these lamps produce more light and a reasonable degree of control for less money than anything else available. At a throw of 10–15 feet they produce a workable lighting area. Also they do not draw as much current as an equal number of conventional instruments producing an equal amount of light.

Reflector lamps are usually illegal to use (unless enclosed in a housing) in any structure considered by the safety authorities as a theatre. The reason they are found in small theatres is that these buildings are not legally "theatres." They must meet much less stringent fire and safety codes. However even under these more relaxed legal conditions, one must be careful. Reflector lamps should not be wired with ordinary household cord, especially the brown or white wire known as "zipcord." Its insulation is far too susceptible to heat and its conductors too small for safety. Four 150 W lamps will add up to 600 W, the theoretical maximum current for zipcord. But this maximum was not calculated for use next to a bank of high temperature reflector lights. The safe and reasonable thing to do is to use wire made to take heat, such as heater cord. It costs more, but will last longer and be safer.

EQUIPMENT NORMALLY USED FOR NONDIRECTIONAL LIGHTING

All of the instruments to be discussed in this section have one thing in common: they *ordinarily* do not produce the kind of light that the audience can interpret as directional. That is, these instruments, as ordinarily used, throw shadows which cannot be seen by the audience. This broad group of equipment may be subdivided according to the mechanical arrangement of the instruments. The first category is *floodlights,* consisting of a single lamp and reflector with the necessary mounting equipment. Although they may contain very large lamps— 2000 W is common—they are easily portable. The second category is *multiple reflector equipment;* it consists of *striplights, borderlights,* and *footlights.* These instruments consist of a row or strip of mechanically connected reflectors, each with its own lamp. In most cases the lamps are wired in periodically repeating circuits. When a strip of such reflectors is made long enough to extend all the way across a stage and is mounted behind cloth that masks the borders, it is commonly called a "borderlight." If the strip of lights is short enough to be considered portable—however awkward that may be—it is termed a "striplight." Footlights may be constructed approximately the same as borderlights but installed at the front edge of the apron (see Chapter 3, "The Proscenium Theatre"), or they may be made up of portable striplights identical to those used above the stage.

FLOODLIGHTS

The name tells the function in these instruments designed to produce a powerful flood of light. There is little or no control over the area covered except by adjusting the distance from the instrument to the lighted area, and even that provides little control. An exception to this is a line of "focusable floods" recently introduced. Edges of the lighted area are usually not very sharply defined, gradually feathering off into darkness.

These instruments can be very efficient because they depend only on a reflector to gather up the light and throw it in the direction of the stage. There are no lenses. Optical requirements are simple and it is presently quite easy to make good reflective surfaces for floodlights that are durable and highly efficient.

Scoops

The name, "scoops" has come to us from television, where it refers to the ellipsoidal reflector floodlight developed for lighting in TV studios. This is the logical development of the olivette (an early and now obsolete floodlight) from an instrument made in a sheet metal shop to one made in a metal-spinning factory. Efficiency has increased and the instrument has become easier to mount. The reflector has become the housing of the instrument itself. It is simply a heavy piece of aluminum that has been formed and surface-treated into an ellipsoidal reflector which gathers the light from a general service lamp, and reflects it to the stage (see Figure 26-14). Scoops come in several sizes from a 10 inch diameter to about 18 inches. Wattages vary from 100 to 2000 W. Color frames are something of a problem because scoops were designed for TV studio use without color media. The frames give the appearance of being an afterthought on the part of the equipment designer who found that the instrument would sell to theatre people if he added a color frame. It is almost always necessary to add a safety chain or wire to prevent the frame from falling.

In spite of this handicap, scoops are highly efficient and often are used instead of borderlights to light cycloramas. The advantage of scoops for this purpose is that they are easily portable. They can be removed or installed without the assistance of several people. (Cyclorama borderlights are usually not easily removable.) The only problem is that scoops take more space in the flies than borderlights, and the light from the instruments requires more distance for color mixing and blending.

Scoops are also used for lighting alcoves and hallways. In this case they serve the purpose once served by the "backing striplight" discussed below. Usually the smallest sizes of scoops will do for this purpose. They are often mounted on a metal flange screwed to the back of the scenery. A small C-clamp may also be used. Because they are efficient and cheap to operate compared to spotlights, scoops are often mounted on battens, light bridges, and on beams as rehearsal and work lights.

FIGURE 26-14a

Figure 26-14. Scoops. (a) An 18 inch scoop suitable for use as a floodlight. Photograph by Joseph Getzoff, courtesy Strand Century. (b) A row of large scoops arranged as a cyclorama borderlight.

FIGURE 26-14b

T-H Floodlights

Recently a new type of floodlight has come on the market, powered by the tubular T-H lamps which are exceedingly small for their wattage, and which produce huge amounts of light. These floodlights were developed first for the photo and movie industry and later adapted to the stage. They brought their movie name—"broads"—with them. The term refers to the flood of light that they produce. As stage instruments these devices have one drawback: they are so small that it is impossible to put any conventional color medium in the slot provided in the front of the instrument. Actually the slot is intended for a diffusing medium made of spun glass which is much more resistant to heat than color media. Some manufacturers do supply glass color media which can survive the heat of these instruments, but it is expensive and breakable under stage conditions. At their present stage of development, these instruments will probably serve best where color is not needed.

Reflector Floodlights

The counterpart to the reflector spotlamp is the reflector floodlight. Actually there is no sharp dividing line between these types of instruments. If the "R" lamp produces a relatively broad flood of light, it is a "flood"; if the pool is small and more well defined, it is a "spot." As in the case of reflector spotlamps, the floodlamps are highly efficient, run very hot, are breakable, and produce a lot of light for a low price. They are usually illegal on stages where the building is rated as a legal theatre unless they are operated in specially designed fixtures (see below). They may be found in small community theatres where laws are not as strict and budgets are tight.

MULTIPLE-REFLECTOR EQUIPMENT

All of the instruments discussed below have multiple reflectors and/or lamps. They are actually descendants of the gas lighting era of the theatre when similar units were made up of gas jets arranged along pipes.

Footlights

Footlights are the very "trademark" of the theatre. Strangely, the name has endured longer than the instrument itself. There are many theatres today with not the slightest provision for footlights. Others use them only rarely because modern FOH lighting has largely made them obsolete except as a design motif for nineteenth-century shows and occasional shadow control. Where there are footlights, however, they may be of several types.

TROUGH TYPES The oldest and simplest of footlights consist of a crude metal trough, painted white (at one time) and equipped with a row of sockets for lamps. Color first was provided by dipping the lamps in lamp dip, a colored lacquer much like nail polish. However as lamps became more sophisticated, the bulbs ran too hot for the lacquer, and "natural glass" lamps were used. These had the color manufactured into the glass, but are now prohibitively expensive. If color is needed in foots of this type there are presently two possibilities: (1) Use lamps that have the color permanently adhered to the outside of the glass; these are low in efficiency and high in cost. Also the colors are not pure nor are they available in wide variety. (2) The footlights can be lamped with low wattage vacuum lamps (consult the manufacturer's catalogue to find the largest size vacuum lamp). These may be dipped in the modern version of lamp dip which is still sold for this purpose and for painting projection slides.

INDIVIDUAL REFLECTOR FOOTLIGHTS The next development after the open trough consisted of rows of individual spun-aluminum reflectors, one reflector for each lamp. Wattage usually is limited to about 150 W per socket. Each reflector is equipped with a holder for a round piece of colored glass, known as a "roundel" (discussed in the previous chapter). Reflector footlights are much more efficient than troughs and are also more expensive. They run rather hot because the lamp is enclosed tightly in the reflector-roundel assembly.

Footlights are still made today in three types: (1) portable, (2) permanent disappearing, and (3) permanent nondisappearing. The portable units are essentially the same as portable borderlight units and are often interchangeable (see Figure 26-15). They consist of rows of lamps and reflectors 6–10 feet long, often equipped with hangers for borderlight use and floor mounts for footlight service. Some of them have holders that will allow the use of either roundels or regular color media in them. They are heavy, bulky instruments that usually require two people to handle.

Mounting them as border lights is a matter of attaching two C-clamps per unit or wrapping a piece of chain twice around a batten and hooking it. The chain hanger is cheaper and easier to operate but likely to slip if you try to direct the instrument anywhere but straight down.

Maintenance of portable footlights is simple. Electrical parts must be checked occasionally for frayed asbestos wire or loose connections. Sockets need checking for dirt or loose connections, especially at the point where the base of the lamp connects to the socket center contact. Reflectors and roundels must be kept clean if the instruments are to work at top efficiency.

DISAPPEARING FOOTLIGHTS Disappearing footlights are found throughout the country, particularly on high school and community center

Figure 26-15. Modern Portable Borderlight. This unit may serve as either borderlight or footlight. It is fitted with pipe clamps to provide a secure mount. Note the individual spun aluminum reflectors which are covered by roundels during use. The reflector makes such a borderlight an efficient unit.

stages, which are intended for a wide variety of uses. They are set into the floor near the edge of the apron and usually faced with hardwood so they will match the hardwood stage floor when closed. They are opened by inserting a tool such as a screwdriver into a socket and turning. This releases a latch and the unit turns over revealing the footlights. The footlight unit itself resembles a portable unit except that it is made to be permanently fastened to the pivoted floor section. It will usually be equipped with roundels. Better-quality disappearing footlights are fitted with a switch that prevents the lights from being turned on when the footlight unit is closed. This avoids the possibility that the lights will be left on for extended periods of time and perhaps cause a fire.

Operation of these footlights is simple. The principle hazard is that they may be turned on when closed, unless they are protected as above. Another problem is mechanical: if the latch holding the foots closed is not completely turned, it may give when someone steps on it and cause injury. When open, the footlight unit requires the same care as the portable unit described above.

Permanently installed nondisappearing footlights are common in old theatres. They are custom-made units that are bolted into a trough at the front of the stage apron. This usually forms a lip at the edge of the stage which restricts sight lines from the first few rows of the audience. It is likely that these footlights were planned for an era when they were the only source of light downstage of the curtain except a follow spotlight. Thus they will run from far right to far left, and if lamped at their rated capacity for the full length, throw a huge flood of light over the entire stage and the front of the house. Chances are, if they are used at all, only the center portion will be operated at much reduced wattage. Maintenance is the same as described for other footlights.

FOOTLIGHT CIRCUITRY   Footlights and borderlights usually are wired in three circuits, and occasionally in four. In older theatres these circuits were provided with either colored lamps or roundels in red, white, and blue. This combination provided what color change was necessary for variety show lighting with a follow spot and did so with reasonably high efficiency. Efficiency was important because there was no other source of FOH lighting. Today things have changed; there are powerful FOH sources, and footlights usually are used as fill light to soften facial shadows. Color changing is more vital than high intensity, and the best color combination for roundels is red, green, and blue (see Chapter 25, "Producing and Using Light on the Stage"). If the footlights can be fitted with gels, any color stipulated by the scenographer can be used.

Borderlights

As we have already noted, borderlights (see Figure 3-16 and 26-15) are long rows of reflectors built as a unit and hung over the stage. The first one, directly behind the proscenium opening, usually is known as the "concert border," or the first border. There may be several others at intervals of 5–8 feet measured upstage from the concert border and ending with the cyclorama border. Actually for modern dramatic lighting the only borderlight that is somewhat necessary is the cyc borderlight, and even this can be dispensed with in favor of the more easily handled scoops. Of course, open stages without prosceniums seldom have need for any borderlight. In more modern theatres the borderlights may be the portable units hung and circuited as needed.

Lamp wattages in borderlights tend to run higher than those in footlights, even if the same instruments are being used. They may range from 150–500 W per socket, depending on the stage size and the needs of the show. Color circuitry is similar to that of the footlights except for the cyc border, which should have two circuits of blue for each circuit of red or green.

Maintenance is nearly nonexistent; merely keep the borderlight reflectors and roundels clean and the lamps tightly screwed in place. When relamping, be sure that you do not overload the circuits feeding these instruments.

CYCLORAMA LIGHTING   Cyclorama border lighting often finds a place in regular dramatic productions. The need for sky effects or for a color field as a background is frequent. We will give some consideration to this application of borderlights. There are special problems of cyclorama lighting. (1) There should be a large, evenly distributed field of variable color. (2) Often this field should be brighter near the stage floor than at the top. (3) Much of the time, this field of color should be some shade of blue, which is the hardest color to produce on stage.

The main lighting instrument, the cyclorama borderlight, usually is mounted only about 6–8 feet in front of the top of the cyc. This means that there is a tendency for the top of the cyc to be much brighter than the bottom. To equalize this, engineers have devised reflectors that distribute the light more evenly over the entire cyc surface. However they must be properly angled and mounted with respect to the cyc. Similarly, if cyclorama footlights are used, they too should be specially engineered to distribute light from the bottom to the top of the cyc. Since a complete cyc (as opposed to a sky drop) is generally cylindrical in shape, the light must extend around the sides with no noticeable change in intensity.

Lighting such a curved cyclorama requires either specially fabricated and very expensive space-consuming curved borderlights, specially mounted portable borderlight strips, or specially mounted scoops (Figure 26-14b). The scoops are probably the easiest and most economical solution. They are easy to mount and may be used for other purposes when not needed as cyc lights.

In any event the cyclorama lighting will constitute a very heavy electrical load, the blue circuits being the heaviest. If cyc lighting is portable, loading must be carefully controlled because of the ease with which overloads may be built up.

BACKING STRIPLIGHTS   Although these instruments have been largely superceded by small scoops, they are still useful if available. They consist of short sections of striplights, usually three or four lamps per section, which are used to light alcoves and backings. They produce a very soft light—softer than that of a small scoop. Since this soft light is less apt to produce noticeable shadows, it is desirable for these applications.

27
LIGHTING CONTROL

INTRODUCTION The "instrument" upon which lighting is played is a complex combination of lighting equipment, wire, the various lighting positions in the theatre building, and the control board. The control board might be thought of as the "keyboard" of this vastly complex system; it controls what lights are on at what intensity and in what relationship to each other. Electrically, it may also be the only visible part of a very complex array of electrical apparatus. We have examined the lighting equipment that is attached to this keyboard, but we have not yet examined the keyboard itself. We shall now do so, first taking a brief look at the job that must be done on that keyboard, then at some of the forms that it has taken in the past, and finally at some of its present manifestations. Regretfully, we will have to note that no two lighting "instruments" (in the sense of the total array of lighting apparatus assembled for a production) are more than vaguely alike, and that two keyboards seldom resemble each other.

OBJECTIVES OF A LIGHTING CONTROL SYSTEM

The purpose of any lighting control system is artistic in spite of the fact that many of them seem to have been designed by engineers who had not the slightest idea about the art of theatre. The control system and its operators will be asked to perform a very complex interpretive task that will in a significant way determine the total artistic effectiveness of the whole production. As far as the control board operators are concerned, this may be divided into a two-part process with the understanding that progress should be made toward accomplishing both parts at the same time. In the first part of this process, the operators must gradually learn what operations to perform and how these are artistically related to the production as a whole. This is much easier to say than to do. The transmission of apparently mechanical instructions from scenographer to light crew such as, "Take areas I, III, IV, and VI down to out, as everyone x upstage but Macbeth," seems simple and straightforward. It is not. The pacing of this cue, planned to gradually narrow the focus on the solitary figure of Macbeth as he takes the scene and establishes by his stance and facial expression the attitude of "tomorrow and tomorrow and tomorrow. . . ," is a matter of sensitive judgment on the part of the crew. No mechanical count or clock time can catch the subtlety of it. Only trial and error and finally a "That's it" from the scenographer will establish that the crew has caught the cue. Even then, what they have come to understand is not mechanical timing, but a sense of how they should take their cue from the subtle variations of each performance as it happens. This is something no cue system can record. Thus lighting rehearsals will be a study in communication of nondiscursive material, most of it in skeleton form as cues.

The second part of the interpretive task consists of learning the subtle traits of the control instrument itself. Just as a pianist must learn the "feel" or "touch" of the particular instrument he is playing, the crew must learn the characteristics of the control board they are using. First they must learn where the "keys" are, and how they are related to each other and to the lights they control. Some control boards seem to be almost diabolically designed to hide any relationships between the control device and the groups of lighting instruments which must work together artistically. Others offer the crew some chance of grouping related functions into adjacent controls. This enables them to design the "keyboard to match the music."

Learning where the keys are, and if possible, organizing them into what seems to be a rational arrangement, is only part of the process. Lighting controls, like parts of musical instruments, have eccentricities of their own. Some of them start making significant changes in the lighting the moment they are touched, while others lag. Some provide a rather evenly distributed degree of control over their entire sweep, while others vary markedly. The same control board may have several varieties of control within it. Operators must learn to adjust their touch as they shift from one type of control to another.

Obviously a well-designed lighting control system should make both of these learning processes as easy as possible. Ideally it should fit itself so automatically into the interpretive needs of its operators that it is almost invisible to them. It should present no more impediments to the performance of the lighting than a Stradivarius violin does to a master violinist. Seldom, if ever, has this goal been achieved. Most control boards are reluctant helpers in the difficult task imposed upon their operators.

CONCEPT OF DIMMING

We already know that the incandescent lamp makes its light from heat which has been produced by passing electricity through the filament. The more heat, the more light and vice versa. We control the heat by controlling the supply of electricity. When we reduce the average amount of electricity that flows through the filament, we reduce the amount of heat produced and ultimately the amount of light produced. It would be nice and also much simpler if these reductions and increases were all proportional, each increment of change in the amount of electricity making a like change in the light produced. But it does not work out that way. The changes are interrelated, but in a very complicated way. To make matters worse, the human eye—the ultimate object of all of the change—varies in sensitivity. A change that would seem monumental when taking place on a darkened stage might be unnoticed when accompanied by normal stage light. These facts and many others have led to a great deal of electronic and mechanical "juggling" aimed at producing a change-making device of reasonable cost which will make controllable and predictable changes in the light output of a lamp.

All of these change-making devices are called "dimmers." They all alter the light output of a lamp *gradually,* although they vary a great deal in accomplishing this. Those who are technically informed will note that there are dimmers that actually turn the current on and off at rapid intervals to effect the change; others change on a continuous basis. We need not concern ourselves here with how they work, but we must know what to expect when we operate them. With this in mind, we will summarize the operating characteristics of the major types of dimmers to be found in the theatre today. This is an unfinished list; new equipment is being developed all the time. At the end of this chapter we will illustrate and briefly describe a few of the "latest" control board developments.

DIRECT CONTROL DIMMERS

There are two general categories of dimming apparatus: direct control and remote control. *Direct control* means that the handle the operator moves is mechanically attached to the electrical device that controls the power going to the lamps. There are no intervening electrical devices. Since direct control dimmers must handle the entire load of lamps attached to them, they are large, electrically dangerous devices. They often generate heat in the process of controlling their load, and therefore must be well ventilated. Since they are large, their moving parts have considerable inertia and are subject to friction. It usually takes a great deal of physical effort to move them. Once moving, they may tend to coast instead of stop.

Control boards made up of direct control dimmers tend to be large, unwieldy affairs whose shape, size, and organization are determined by the engineering requirements of the dimmers and the heavy electrical currents they handle. These same heavy electrical currents require that the control board be placed as near as possible to the load that it controls to avoid long costly runs of copper wire. For this reason, most direct control apparatus are installed backstage—not the ideal position for the operators.

RESISTANCE DIMMER

The first direct control dimmer was the resistance dimmer, a device which is now obsolete although some are still in use. Resistance dimmers were load sensitive, which means that their operating characteristics changed according to the lamp load imposed upon them. They also became very hot during normal operation. See Appendix I for a more detailed discussion of these dimmers.

AUTOTRANSFORMER DIMMERS (ATD)

Chances are that the first lighting control device a beginner operates will be an autotransformer dimmer. It was invented in the 1930s and installed by the thousands in schools, in community theatres, and in professional theatres wherever direct current did not prevent its use. There were also many homemade control boards constructed with these relatively cheap, versatile units. The operator will recognize ATD's by the fact that they are utterly insensitive to load changes. If you examine the dimmer mechanism, you will find something like that shown in Figure 27-1. The working part of the dimmer is a coil of copper wire, plainly visible if not in a housing. The unit does not get hot even under continuous use at full load. It hums slightly, reflecting the fact that it operates on alternating current *only*.

The operating characteristics of ATD's are almost all the same and somewhat unique. This is the consequence of their electrical nature; they are voltage-setting devices that can vary the voltage evenly from full line to zero voltage. The light produced by an incandescent lamp does not vary in this fashion. As the voltage rises, the lamp filament has to heat up considerably before any visible light is produced. Then the light output increases slowly at first, and more rapidly as the voltage approaches full. The lower curve in Figure 27-2a diagrams exactly the operating characteristic of an ATD.

Once the operator gets used to the operating characteristics of

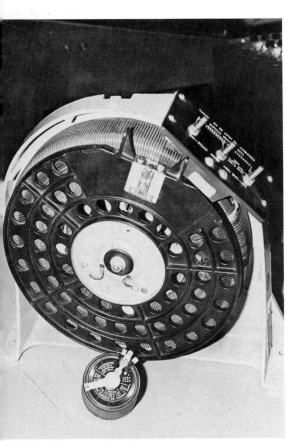

Figure 27-1. Autotransformer Dimmers. Shown are two of the many sizes and types of autotransformer coils. All such dimmers consist of copper coils wound around a heavy iron core. Some part of the coil is bared of insulation and a movable contact arranged to move over it.

ATD's, they are easy to use. The subtlety with which tiny changes in reading can be made at the low end of the scale—usually on a dark stage—is helpful. The same slight change at the low end has saved many beginners from a jerky and perhaps early start in operating a cue. At the top end, it is easy to slow down the movement slightly when necessary. The consistency of the ATD's operating characteristic is something more modern, sophisticated dimmers could do well to emulate.

MULTISLIDER AUTOTRANSFORMER DIMMERS

It is possible that you may encounter autotransformer dimmers with only one coil but four or six sliders (Figure 27-2b). These are an adaptation of a dimmer arrangement long known in Europe as the "Bordoni dimmer." Electrically the dimmer is about the same as those already discussed, but with one exception: load calculation must be based on a clear understanding of what the device is. As an example let us take a common configuration: The coil is rated at 4000 W. It is equipped with six sliders, each capable of a maximum wattage of 1500 W. What you must understand is that this is *not* the same as having six 1500 W dimmers. Any one or more of the sliders can be loaded up to 1500 W, but the *total* load on the entire unit cannot exceed 4000 W however it is distributed on the sliders. You could, for example, load two sliders

Figure 27-2. (a) Dimmer Control Curves. This graph illustrates the relationship between dimmer reading and light output which may be expected in various dimmers. The lower curve, marked "linear curve," shows the output to be expected when using almost all ATD's. The "square law curve" and many variations nearly like it are found on electronic dimmers. (b) Multislider Autotransformer Dimmers. This wall-mounted panel contains five dimmers, each with five sliders.

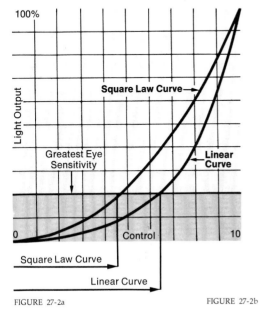

FIGURE 27-2a

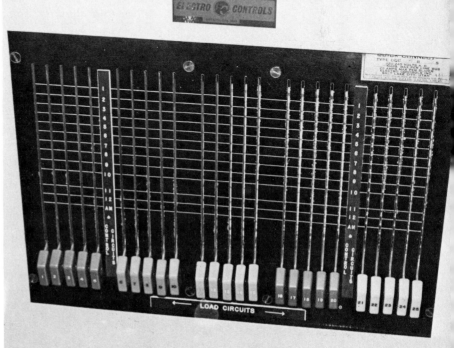

FIGURE 27-2b

to capacity—1500 W each. There remains only 1000 W capacity, however it is distributed on the remaining sliders. If a dimmer of this type is installed properly, there will be a set of breakers or fuses to protect the individual sliders *plus* a larger breaker or fuse to protect the coil itself. In case of an overload on a slider, only the breaker protecting that slider will open; in case the entire coil is overloaded, the coil will be cut off, making *all* the sliders inoperative.

PORTABLE CONTROL BOARDS

In spite of the size and weight of resistance and autotransformer dimmers, and the equipment necessary to protect and operate them, portable control boards have been manufactured throughout most of the history of electrical stage lighting. Resistance dimmers have been built into heavy wooden enclosures containing a main switch, a number of dimmers usually equipped with mechanical interlocks, and the necessary outlets, fuses, etc. Such boards have been until very recently the mainstay of traveling professional companies who usually start their journeys from a New York stage powered with direct current. Direct current systems are now almost totally obsolete, but these "piano boards" (so named because they look like a crated upright piano) still persist. They are heavy and awkward to operate, but exceedingly durable.

As already noted, autotransformer dimmers are also made up into portable control boards. Such boards have not been adopted by the Broadway theatre because they will not work on direct current. They have become almost standard among school, community, and professional theatres not hampered by the limitations of direct current. Several such boards are shown in Figures 28-11 and 27-3.

Most of these portable ATD boards offer electrical proportional mastering.[1] Switching (or plugging) an individual circuit onto or off a master without creating a noticeable sudden change in the lighting calls for some strategy. One needn't worry about the circuits already on the master—it will hold them at a steady reading as long as no shorts or heavy overloads are created. However, the addition or removal of an individual circuit (e.g., a special light) may result in noticeable changes in the light output of that circuit. The ideal condition for adding or removing an individual circuit from the master is with that circuit at zero. It cannot flicker or "bump" at that reading. After it has been added to the master, it can be brought subtly to any reading up to that of the master. Another possibility somewhat trickier to handle, is that a circuit can be transferred at 10 (full up). This is true *only* if

---

1. Proportional mastering consists of changing the intensity of a group of lights in such a way that the ratios between individual lights remain essentially constant.

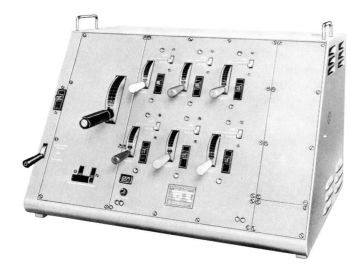

Figure 27-3. Autotransformer Control Board. This control board represents a typical configuration of dimmer control using autotransformer dimmers. The handle at the very lower left edge of the board controls the function of the master dimmer making it available as a separate dimmer when not needed for master dimming. Such autotransformer boards are rapidly being superseded by solid-state package boards, some of which now include simple memory facilities. Courtesy of The Superior Electric Company.

the master is also at 10 and the switching arrangement will work fast enough to allow the circuit to be transferred without any visible dip. These conditions are not difficult to meet, particularly if the stage is well lit so that any slight change in the light being transferred will not be seen.

Another difficulty with electrical mastering has to do with cue writing. If the control is distributed over two devices, it is very hard to record cue information while this condition prevails. If, for example, a three-color cyclorama setup is under the control of an electrical master, the following situation might prevail:

> Red — at 4
> Green — at 8 ——————— On master at 7
> Blue — at 10

These settings may be considered as percentages when using ATD's; e.g., the master is at 70 percent. Thus the readings at the lights will be the percentage equivalents of the combined settings. For example, the red will get a voltage equal to 70 percent of 40 percent, or 28 percent. If the line voltage is 120, this will come to about 33 V— just enough to produce a red glow from the lamps as filtered through red primary gel. Other readings will vary in the same manner. Note that the blue will get full 70 percent voltage because its own dimmer is set at full and thus makes no reduction.

These difficulties in writing cue information usually cause operators to be sure the master dimmers are at 10 whenever it is necessary to record cue information. Between cues, they can be at any setting desired.

Another application of the flexible dimming capability of portable ATD boards is a package consisting of six 1000 W dimmers fed from a 6000 W master dimmer (see Figure 27-3). This board offers the theatre the possibility of having a 6000 W house light dimmer which can be almost instantly converted into a 6000 W master dimmer after it has served its purpose in lowering the house lights. A typical sequence of operations follows:

1. (Before the show—theatre open.) Master transferred to house lights and brought up to prearranged reading. Six circuits of stage lights with feeder switches set on master. Dimmers are already at preset readings for the opening cue.
2. (On cue.) Fade house to out. With house light (master dimmer) in zero position, throw transfer switch to "master" position. (Curtain up.)
3. (On cue.) Bring up master with other equipment to begin the first cue of the act.
4. Continue running cues to the end of the act.
5. (End of act.) Fade master to zero. Transfer back to independent position, picking up house light feed. (Curtain down.)
6. Bring up house lights on cue for intermission.

Two or three control boards such as that in Figure 27-3 will do a very respectable job of controlling the lighting of a fairly elaborate production on a small stage. If the show requires many individual operations to take place simultaneously and at different paces, several operators may be needed. Such tricks as temporarily lashing two or three dimmer handles together may save hands.

One advantage of portable control boards is that it may be possible to locate them where the operators can see the effect of what they are doing even in theatres that have built-in provisions for such locations. This may involve long runs of cable and even some expense for relocating the power feeds for the boards, but it is well worth the effort.

OTHER EQUIPMENT ON CONTROL BOARDS

The words "switchboard" and "control board" often are used interchangeably. Such usage is not entirely correct since a switchboard should be exactly what the name says—an aggregation of switches. In the early days it was precisely this; the dimmers were mounted separately some distance from the switchboard. When dimmers, switches, and other related gear were brought together, the term "control board" was coined. It described exactly the function of the apparatus. However, one hopes that separate switchboards have receded into antiquity, and although the two names have become interchangeable in common usage, control board is preferred.

A lighting control board will probably contain a number of elements other than dimmers. There will almost inevitably be the switches controlling the feed to each of the dimmers. In the case of electrical mastering, these switches may be two-way or even three-way, enabling the operator to select from several sources (master I, master II, or line, for example) as he sets up his lighting. There will also be a number of "nondim" controls. These are provided for circuits that do not need any dimming because they only go on or off. These circuits also are used for such things as cooling fan circuits whose motors might be damaged by the reduced voltage from a dimmer. They can serve as signaling circuits, should the need arise. House lighting controls usually are found on the control board. These should consist of a switch controlling the house light supply, a dimmer(s) for the house lights, and a "panic" switch which makes it possible to transfer the house lighting to another source of power independent of not only the house lighting dimmer, but of the entire stage lighting feed. This provides house lighting in emergencies. Such controls usually are required by law to be duplicated in several accessible places on the stage and in the house. Work light controls and even such things as curtain motor switches and the like often are found on control boards. It will be the duty of the lighting crew to know each of these devices, and particularly to be informed as to what to do if there is trouble in the stage lighting circuits which can plunge the house into darkness.

REMOTE CONTROL OF STAGE LIGHTING

Modern technology is in the process of revolutionizing the entire stage lighting control industry. Resistance dimmers have been obsolete for many years. Autotransformer dimmers have now joined them in obsolescence. Although some are still being made, mostly as repair parts for existing equipment, economics of manufacture makes it clear that they will soon vanish from the marketplace. Early remote control dimmers (see below) are also out of date. The cause of all of this rapid change is solid-state technology. Tiny chunks of silicone are able to control more current with greater subtlety and at lower cost than any predecessor. Moreover, these devices have wide application throughout the electronics industry, which makes them even cheaper because of the advantages of mass production. Thus it is more and more likely that the newcomer to stage lighting will be doing work on modern portable remote-control equipment bought at a price lower than that of portable direct control equipment.

The next stage in this chain of development is the addition of memory devices to economically priced package control systems. Such equipment is already on the market and being touted as applicable to small theatres, even including those in high schools. Although such claims may be open to question at the moment, their validity in the very near future cannot be denied. In brief, the electronic age has arrived for stage lighting and the computer age is only moments away.

WHAT IS REMOTE CONTROL?

Remote control consists of signaling a distant device to do something. Electrically, this can be done by using a tiny wire and switch to tell a far-removed large electrical switch to open or close. On a more sophisticated level, it can mean using a tiny device to tell a large remotely located dimmer to raise or lower the intensity of lights. The same remote-control apparatus may signal several distant devices simultaneously.

The advantages of remote control are many:

1. Small inconspicuous devices may be substituted for large, noisy, dangerous ones.
2. Multiple control stations become feasible where they would not be possible with direct control.
3. Cost can be reduced by avoiding long runs of heavy expensive wire and heavy-duty enclosures at control stations.
4. Most important to stage lighting, vast and extremely flexible arrangements of control devices can be assembled at reasonable prices. These can be sized and arranged to the convenience of the operator instead of according to the needs of engineering.

REMOTE-CONTROL DIMMERS

Even early in the history of stage lighting, efforts were made to devise remotely controlled dimmers. These early attempts were not very successful. Various motor drives were tried, with the remote device telling the motor which way to run and at what speed. Lag and overrun plagued these early machines, and they received only minor acceptance. One exception is the motor-driven house lighting control which has become a standard system in multiple-use theatres in which it is necessary to control house lighting from a number of locations. Such systems commonly operate at a fixed speed. Each control station is equipped with an on and off button and an up and down button for dimmer control. They serve multiple-purpose functions well and dramatic performances poorly. Modern electronic dimmers have now made these rather crude devices obsolete.

Later more successful remote-control dimmers were developed. These utilize a tiny control current which may be altered to cause the dimmer to feed more or less current to the lamps. Variations in the control current cause the output of the dimmer to vary accordingly, making the dimmer "track" the control current. In theory, this should be a perfectly satisfactory system. In practice, early dimmers of this type often lagged significantly behind their controllers or displayed other difficulties. The first relatively successful remote-control dimmer was the *thyratron* dimmer. It used special electronic tubes which were perfected during World War II. It is now obsolete although a few are still in use. Next came the *magnetic amplifier* dimmer. It utilized rather complicated magnetic devices, closely related to transformers, to achieve control over huge amounts of current with a tiny control current. Its success was considerably greater than that of the thyratron dimmer, although it also is now obsolete, mainly for economic reasons. Many magnetic amplifier systems were installed and are still functioning satisfactorily. They may display a perceptible lag under some circumstances, although this is not a handicap to operation.

Modern remote-control dimmers all utilize a solid-state device known as a "silicon controlled rectifier" (SCR), or another very similar device known as a "triac." Both of these devices operate by what is known as "gating." They are really very high-speed switches which can be so controlled that they let a precisely adjusted fraction of each half wave of alternating current through to the lamp. The lamp averages the current, and produces light in proportion to this average. Obviously, the greater the percentage of the entire half wave the dimmer passes to the lamp, the brighter the light. Since the switching action of these dimmers is so fast that it must be measured in nanoseconds (billionths of a second), they are nearly instantaneous in response.

Modern remote-control dimmers have now become so dependable that operators seldom concern themselves with the dimmers at all. Of course they must still consider the capacity of the dimmer when loading it; maximum wattage must not be exceeded. There may also be a minimum wattage below which the dimmer may not be stable, but this will be a very small load, significant only in those rare situations where, for example, a 30 W property lamp must operate on a large dimmer. A small additional load hidden offstage solves this problem.

The advent of the remote-control dimmer has completely changed the nature of control boards. Even the name has changed. We now speak of a *console* instead of a control board or switchboard. Instead of containing dimmers, the console contains among other things *controllers*. A controller is a device that tells a dimmer what to do. The operator moves the handle of the controller and the dimmer alters the current to the light. Actually the controller allows a tiny amount of current (usually dc) to pass down a small wire (probably in a piece of telephone cable) to the dimmer. This tiny current may control thousands of watts of power going through the dimmer. The usual arrangement is that an increase in the control current produces an increase in dimmer output.

TWO CONTROL CONCEPTS

The following discussion of control moves from traditional to modern. It is an open-ended discussion because the computer era is upon us, leading the theatre again around that circle of development wherein a forward step in one area challenges the entire art. The challenge began with remote control which made feasible for the first time control devices designed for the needs of the operator. This has finally made possible many of the advances in lighting design longed for by such visionaries as Adolphe Appia. But the cycle is still in its beginning stages; the introduction of computer techniques has opened the way to still more sophisticated concepts than are presently in use. In fact, the computer probably has raised more artistic questions than it has answered. What remains is for the art of lighting to catch up to its technology and to direct that technology to provide the kinds of control it needs.

Note that a direct relationship exists between the arrangement of lighting control and the cuing of a show. Advanced students may wish to read the portions of this text on cuing systems (near the end of Chapter 28) immediately after reading this chapter.

Presetting

The concept of organizing lighting by presetting is so old and so ingrained that it is often thought to be the only way lighting may be handled. It developed out of the history of lighting, particularly vaudeville and musical shows, where the common practice was (and in many cases still is) to alternate large production numbers requiring the use of the full stage and complicated arrangements of lighting, with scenes "in one." A scene "in one" is done in front of the main or show curtain and lighted mainly by a powerful follow spot. The obvious advantage of this arrangement is that complicated setting and lighting changes can be made back of the main curtain while the audience is watching the scene "in one." The show moves continuously and can build effectively.

Presetting as it evolved from this situation means exactly what the word suggests: lighting controls were prearranged by throwing switches and adjusting dimmers while the curtain was closed and the power off. As the scene opened, the entire package was brought on at once. The lighting then remained in this condition until the end of the scene. After the curtain closed, a new arrangement was set up. It was not long before lighting designers were calling for changes to be made within each main scene. Some of these involved the operation of "specials," instruments hung and operated for one particular effect. Other changes were more elaborate, consisting of complete changes of the lighting, effected by using the mechanical interlocking system and as many operators as needed. Presently such operations are routinely being done on control systems that date back to this era.

Early remote-control systems were designed to facilitate this type of lighting. At first they consisted of rows of controllers, each row representing a "preset" which in its earliest form would have been set up while the curtain was closed and activated later by mechanical interlock and multiple operators. A cue could now be done by one person who operated a single small control lever known as a fader.

Although any degree of complexity in lighting could be done by the old mechanical and multiple-operator system, it is obvious that such cues became easier to run on a well-designed remote-control preset system. Thus they were more commonly used, and lighting tended to be more artistically sophisticated. This produced a demand for boards capable of handling as many as 10 or 20 presets, each controlling perhaps 200 or more dimmers. Simple multiplication reveals the folly of this sort of expansion—a field of 2000 controllers becomes impossible to work. The task of finding the one controller which is out of adjustment becomes almost hopeless under the pressure of rapidly sequenced cues (Figure 27-4).

The final stage in this chain of events has been the substitution of computer memory devices for the field of preset controllers. Computer devices can then be used to call up the proper "preset" (now really a name for a package of lighting settings stored in the memory) and to bring it into operation. Computer techniques can also be used to facilitate the finding of faulty individual settings without examining every controller.

But as these developments were taking place, lighting designers, especially those concerned with lighting for dance or with lighting as suggested by Appia, were finding progressively increasing difficulties with the preset system. While it works well in a show where the lighting falls into discrete moments of change followed by periods of inactivity, and while it can be carefully organized to provide a series of fast-moving changes in a short period of time (although with some difficulty), it breaks down almost completely when applied to a show such as a modern dance production where changes are constant and varied, each with its own rhythm, taking place simultaneously. Although it is obvious that such lighting can eventually be worked out using the preset method, the practical result is usually limiting. The

Figure 27-4. Large Preset Control Board. (a) This huge array of controllers approaches the limit. (b) The preset bank could easily overwhelm a harried operator trying to find a misset circuit. Photographs courtesy Berkey Colortran, a Division of Berkey Photo.

FIGURE 27-4a

problem is twofold: (1) The time required to convert such "constant flow" lighting into a series of presets that accurately reflect its character is enormous. (2) The mental process of slicing time into tiny static increments is at cross-purposes with the concept of the lighting. Both problems are severe enough to limit the artistry of the designer, and under pressure of professional schedules, frequently result in the artist settling for far less than he would ideally like.

Nevertheless, preset lighting is the standard in much of the theatre today. No student of lighting should be ignorant of its possibilities nor should he be incapable of working in that mode.

At this point of our discussion artistry and technique come together. As imaginative artists and engineers began applying computer techniques to lighting, they have rapidly come to see that merely substituting a "black box" for the rows of preset controllers is a travesty

FIGURE 27-4b

on the capabilities of computer technology. It is capable of things still unthought of in the theatre. Thus the challenge of a new engineering device has countered the challenge of those artists who found the preset system inadequate to their more complicated needs. Note, however, that these artists have no wish to abandon the preset concept when it is appropriate; they merely want a more flexible way of doing still more with lighting. The present stage in this development has been termed "pattern control."

Pattern Control

A "pattern" of lights may be defined as a set of instruments and their related controls which exists artistically as a significant element in the total scenography. For example, a set of instruments that provide cool, blue sidelighting from down stage left might be such a pattern. Another example might be a set of very high angle key lights directed onto center stage.

When a scenographer is designing while using pattern control he thinks of working out almost constant lighting changes in which patterns are "played against each other," much in the manner of musical melodies in a fugue. This is known as "counterpoint" in music —a name also applied to this type of lighting. More exactly, providing pattern control makes counterpoint lighting possible. We may also say that counterpoint lighting operates in both *space* and *time* since the patterns will change stage space as they vary and since the rate and nature of the changes will influence the audience perception of virtual or dramatic time.

The difference between counterpoint lighting using pattern control and preset lighting using preset control is first of all a matter of the thought processes of the scenographer. Preset lighting results from thinking of the stage as a series of essentially static "pictures," each of which blends or switches at some point into the next. Counterpoint results when the scenographer thinks in terms of a number of lighting elements—the patterns—which are almost continually varying with relationship to each other. As each pattern varies, it is convenient to think of it as a "time line." Such a time line might be graphed by plotting intensity settings against time, a process which can now be done automatically within a computer control device which can then assist in the operation of counterpoint lighting.

Although both preset and counterpoint lighting are capable of a tremendous range of artistic expression, it now seems likely that counterpoint has the greatest potential, one which largely remains to be developed.

It is obvious that a lighting control console originally designed for handling presetting will be a poor device for pattern control, although a skilled and ingenious technician can work wonders with such a control board, given time and insight into the design. What is needed is a console capable of handling a number of time lines at once and changing the patterns that exist in these time lines as needed. Computer technology is ideally suited to this challenge. It can "remember" as many patterns as the artist wishes. Given a suitable console arrangement, as many patterns as are needed can be brought out of memory and placed under the control of the operator for "playing." Automatic devices may be provided to assist the operator or operators in the "playing." Note that this system does not necessarily imply a single operator any more than one musician would attempt to play an entire string quartet. The single-operator concept has grown out of the presetting concept where there is little of interest to do even for a single operator once the settings have been arranged.

Given these two control concepts, it is now our purpose to examine some of the control devices presently available. We will begin with the relatively simple systems devised for portable use.

PORTABLE SOLID-STATE CONTROL

As noted above, solid-state dimmers have driven all other types from the marketplace. This makes it cheaper to build portable package systems that feature remote control than to make up the dimmers and their controllers in a single unit for an approximation of direct control. In addition to gaining remote-control possibilities, the purchaser of modern package lighting control gets genuine portability for the first time. Previous units were portable, but only at the expense of much muscular effort. They weighed hundreds of pounds, most of this weight in the copper and iron parts of autotransformer dimmers. In contrast, solid-state dimmers weigh only a few pounds each. Thus, a modern power pack containing six dimmers (the most common number) of perhaps 3600 W capacity each, may weigh about 60–80 pounds. The console will weigh much less—around 20 pounds (see Figure 27-5).

These portable systems usually are installed by placing the dimmer package backstage near the power supply, and locating the console where the operator can have a clear view of the stage. The heavy power cable feeds current to the dimmer pack. The load circuits are plugged directly into its output circuits backstage. A lightweight, low-voltage cable connects the pack to the console. Some types of consoles may require a 120 V supply for the small amount of power needed to generate control signals, operate pilot lights, etc.

Most basic consoles for these systems provide the possibility of two-scene preset operation complete with a fader. Other systems provide multiple-scene presets (see Figure 27-5a). In this particular system, the consoles can be patched together so that one fader will control several consoles allowing elaborate preset control. In some other systems a master console may be purchased which serves the same function. Obviously all of these systems are well suited to the theatre that wishes to gradually build up its lighting control capabilities as finances allow.

OPERATING PORTABLE CONSOLES

These portable units are an experience in miniaturization. They often contain a single row of controllers for "manual" operation analogous to the operation of a direct control board. However, the controllers are likely to be on 1 inch centers and to be about one-fifth the size of dimmer handles. They have none of the heavy, solid feel of a dimmer;

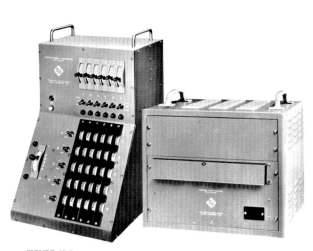

FIGURE 27-5a

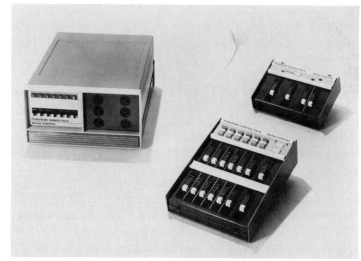

FIGURE 27-5b

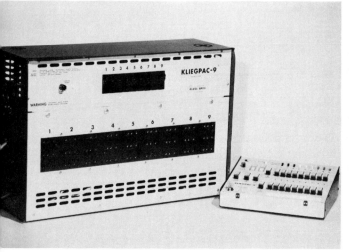

FIGURE 27-5c

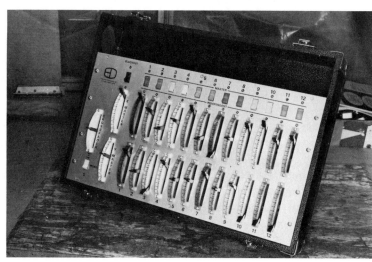

FIGURE 27-5d

Figure 27-5. (a) A Five-Scene Preset Six-Dimmer Board (1.8 kilowatts per dimmer). The fader is arranged so that several consoles may be plugged together allowing operation from one fader. Photograph courtesy of The Superior Electric Company. (b) Another Variation Consisting of Three Units. The lower right module is a two-scene preset console with individual preset masters. The upper right unit is a fader module capable of controlling a number of the two-scene preset consoles. At the upper left is one of several dimmer packs available with this system. They range from 1.8 kilowatts per dimmer to 3.6 kilowatts. Each pack contains six dimmers and the power handling equipment necessary for their operation. Photograph courtesy of Berkey Colortran, a Division of Berkey Photo. (c) This set of components provides nine dimmers and two-scene preset control. The dimmers are rated at 2.4 kilowatts each. Photograph courtesy of Kliegl Bros. (d) A Portable Scrimmer Console. This console provides two-scene preset control for twelve dimmers with cross-fader and scene masters. Photograph courtesy Electronics Diversified.

instead they move at a touch. The result is that at first they are harder to work without jerkiness. Transferring from manual controllers to the preset arrangement, if there is one, usually is accomplished by means of miniaturized switches with tiny handles. Use care or you will throw three when you intend to throw one. Once in preset mode, you will probably have to stay with it exclusively. It is not easy to carry control back and forth because controls have to be at matched readings to avoid jumps. In this regard, operation is similar to that of the electrical master dimmer, for good reason; the principle is exactly the same, but in miniature.

PERMANENTLY INSTALLED SOLID-STATE CONTROL

Until very recently this was the *ne plus ultra* of lighting control. Figure 27-6 illustrates a few of the many large systems now in use. Almost all of these systems are built around the presetting concept, and many of them carry it to the point of chaos. As dimmers have become cheaper, it has become the practice to install more and more of them. Theatre consultants now seriously consider the elimination of the patchbay in favor of installing a dimmer for every load circuit in the theatre. A preset board designed for such a system would be impossibly confusing. Computer-assisted control is the solution.

However, solid-state systems consisting of up to 120 dimmers are certainly feasible with manual presetting. Such boards offer the operator a tremendous potential for lighting control, particularly when combined with extensive power circuitry and a load patching system that enables operators to group circuits into rational packages for control. Such patching systems are shown in Figures 27-7 and 28-11. Note that these are *load* patchbays. They are a part of the dimmer output system, and as such, are arranged by the crew as they install and circuit the lights. A variety of rather sophisticated reload features are available to assist the otherwise touchy business of repatching during a show. Multiple outlets are provided for the dimmers, which are separately controlled by relays allowing the operator at the console to "repatch" the system by causing the relays to feed power to the proper patchbay outlets at the proper time. Note the double outlet sets on the lower part of the patchbay in Figure 28-11c. These are reload outlets, each pair feeding from the same dimmer.

MEMORY-ASSISTED LIGHTING CONTROL

Instead of depending on row upon row of preset controllers to electromechanically "remember" the many individual settings in each preset, a computer memory device can be given this task. The preset controls

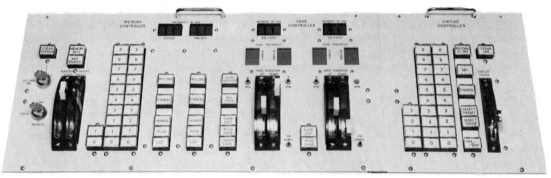

FIGURE 27-6a

FIGURE 27-6b

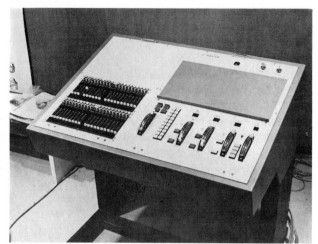

FIGURE 27-6c

Figure 27-6. Modern Control Systems. (a) This English-made modern memory control console is capable of memorizing and playing back hundreds of cues. It is possible to operate four time lines at once plus a fifth on the manual controls. Thorn Lighting, London. Marketed in the United States by Kliegl Bros., New York. (b) This memory system features a number of modules that can rapidly and economically be built up into a console to meet the particular needs of the individual. The number of time lines is variable depending on the modules chosen. Rank Strand, England. (c) This system is more modestly priced than the others, although it still offers a number of time lines and also individual control over each lighting circuit. Thorn Lighting, London. Marketed in the United States by Kliegl Bros., New York. (d) A modern memory system able to memorize fade times as well as dimmer readings. This system also uses rocker-arm setting devices that change rate instead of making direct intensity changes. Berkey Colortran, a Division of Berkey Photo.

FIGURE 27-6d

then vanish from the console, bringing its size and potential for confusion significantly downward (see Figure 27-6). In many of these systems presets are established on a manual bank and entered into memory when the scenographer is satisfied with the settings. This by itself is a great time-saver because the command, "Write it," can be immediately answered by pressing a record button. In fact, the crew will probably be ready to take the next set of readings before the scenographer is ready to produce them.

Presets are called up for use on stage by punching their assigned identification number into a keyboard much like that on a Touch-tone telephone. The information thus retrieved from memory is then assigned to a controller analogous to the fader on a nonmemory system and fed to the stage as needed.

No memory systems are being presently manufactured with the specific needs of pattern control in mind. However a number of advanced preset systems have been made so flexible that they allow the memory-assisted control of from four to eight time lines and manual control of a number of others. More modest memory-assisted preset systems offer control over a smaller number of time lines. Thus the needs of scenographers who wish to work in counterpoint lighting are beginning to be met.

As sophisticated as these devices appear to be, they are actually very primitive when compared to applications of computer technology

Figure 27-7. Slider Interconnect System. This system makes it possible to connect any of over 200 load circuits to any of 64 dimmers. The slider is simply moved to the proper dimmer bus and depressed, making the connection. Circuit load breakers are at the top and bottom of the panel. Photograph courtesy of Strand Century Lighting, Inc.

outside the theatre. The future seems likely to hold much more sophisticated consoles capable of handling patterns of lighting of almost infinite variety, and of responding to the commands of operators by means of advanced computer language specially developed for the theatre. (Present systems use only crude numerical commands.)[2]

"POOR MAN'S" LIGHTING CONTROL

There are available for installation in homes a variety of tiny dimmers that fit into a standard electrical switch box—a space $2\frac{1}{2}$ by $3\frac{1}{2}$ by 2 inches. Most of these units are rated at 600 W, incandescent lamps only. They are intended to replace the switch in the lamp circuit, and thus to always remain connected to the lamp. Under these conditions they can be expected to have a long life.

Many little theatre or community theatre workers have adapted these little dimmers to their needs. The price is low. Since the mode of operation is rotary, they limit each operator to two at a time, but this is no big handicap to a person who might otherwise have no dimmers at all.

The problems encountered with these small units, other than their limited wattage, arise from the fact that they were not engineered for the special risks they encounter in theatre service. The basic device in these little dimmers may be two SCR's similar to those used in theatre dimmers, or more likely, a triac. SCR equipped dimmers are extremely sensitive to both overloads and surges such as those caused by *hot patching,* the practice of ramming a plug into a hot receptacle, causing the lamp to come on almost instantly. It can generate a current surge up to five times the lamp load. Triacs are less sensitive to surges, but are still overload sensitive.

To economize on money and space, the SCR's or triac in these small dimmers are sized as close to the rated load as possible. There is little or no extra capacity. Furthermore, these units are made to operate in isolation from each other to avoid overheating. Instructions on the package usually indicate that the wattage rating of each unit should be reduced if more than one or two are mounted adjacent to each other in a wall. When adapted for theatrical use they should be well ventilated, preferably with a fan. Since they contain none of the expensive circuitry found in regular theatrical dimmers to protect them from overloads or surges, these dimmers should never be overloaded. In fact, it would be a good idea to avoid loading them to capacity.

2. For a much more extensive discussion of modern memory-assisted lighting control the reader is referred to Bellman, *Lighting the Stage; Art and Practice,* chap. 10. See the Bibliography.

28
PROCEDURES FOR LIGHTING CREWS

INTRODUCTION This chapter follows the work of the lighting crew from the time it first meets through the run of the show. It assumes that the crew members have already familiarized themselves with the basic information mentioned in previous chapters and that they are working under the guidance of a well-trained supervisor. (Their chief will be one of themselves, chosen during the preparatory stages of the production.)

In short, the job of a lighting crew may be described as analogous to that of a symphony orchestra. They set up their instruments, tune them, rehearse extensively, and then play the concert. A lighting crew must assemble and connect the lighting equipment, creating an "instrument" on which they will learn to "play" the lighting. They must rehearse until they are proficient and then they must run the show.

ANALYZING THE JOB

At the first meeting of the lighting crew it is desirable for crew members to have seen a run-through of the partially rehearsed production or to have read the script. The supervisor will make a copy of the lighting plot (see Figure 22-2) available to the crew and assist them in determining the extent of the job they have to do. If equipment schedules, hook-up (plugging) charts, and other necessary data (see Chapter 22, "Lighting and Scenography") have not been provided, the crew should prepare these.

A work schedule will have to be devised that assigns various parts of the job to small units of one or two people—it will not be efficient for everyone to work on every job at the same time. However, jobs should be rotated so that all members know how to do each of the main tasks.

503

TOOLS

Although the theatre shop will normally supply unusual tools used by the lighting crew, the following tools are needed so frequently that it is more practical for each member to supply his own:

1. A 6 or 8 inch adjustable end wrench (commonly known as a "crescent" wrench). A cheap one will do. It should be equipped with a loop of cord to prevent it from falling if it slips while the worker is on a ladder or other high place.

2. A pair of cotton or thin leather gloves to protect the wearer from hot instruments.

3. A pencil and note pad for jotting down assignments, circuiting information, etc.

CLOTHING

Being on a lighting crew is hot, dirty work that involves climbing ladders. Clothing should be loose-fitting and easy to clean. Shoes should be nonslip, preferably rubber-soled.

LIGHTING SHOP

The lighting shop is not related to the production activities in quite the same manner as the scene shop or painting shop. Since most of the physical activities involved in lighting consist of installation, circuiting, and adjustment of equipment on stage and over the audience, there is not the same concentration of construction and decoration activity as in other shops. In fact the lighting shop will usually be more of a repair and special equipment construction center than a regular workshop for crew personnel. It may, however, be quite an elaborate shop if devices for scenic projection are made and serviced there, and if it serves as the repair station for electronic apparatus such as lighting consoles, sound equipment, in-house video gear, and the like.

The lighting shop will usually be operated by one or more technicians who take charge of equipment brought in for repairs, maintain inventory, and assist in the development of special equipment. In some small theatres the lighting technician will also be the shop operator; in larger theatres there will be separate repairmen who run the shop. Crew members should not attempt to operate the test equipment or to make repairs in the shop without permission, which will usually be granted only after proof of familiarity with the tools and with the dangers of electricity.

Shop Equipment

Lighting instruments are made of metal—mostly sheet iron and aluminum. Fasteners fail, hinges bend, parts become overheated and must be replaced. All such activities require simple metal-working tools such as those described below.

VISE   A simple machinist's vise is used to hold parts while applying pressure, to straighten bent parts, and as an anvil to pound bent objects into shape. It should be firmly attached to a work bench.

DRILL PRESS   A drill press is usually found in the metal shop, but a separate drill press for the lighting shop is required if extensive work is to be done there.

WORK BENCH WITH TEST SETUP   An insulated work bench is essential to the safe, efficient testing and repairing of lighting equipment. It should have its own electrical supply. Preferably the fuse or breaker for this should be on or near the bench so that it can be easily reset as needed. The bench should be equipped with outlets for each type of connector in use in the theatre and should be capable of supplying power to the largest lamp commonly in use. There should be a load-type continuity tester (not the neon variety) capable of testing a circuit for continuity with at least 1 Amp (100 W) of current to detect loose connections. Since this is a dangerous amount of current, a good method is to provide two continuity testing lamps, one very small (5–10 W) and the other at least 100 W. Switches determine which is in use.

The work bench itself and the floor in its vicinity should be made of nonconducting material. This will aid in preventing shocks from faulty equipment.

The test bench should include lamp sockets (live) for each size and type of socket in use in the theatre. Outlets for hand drills, soldering irons, and other small tools should be provided. Spare parts should be stored nearby.

The work bench should never be allowed to become a storage place for lighting equipment. Any equipment on the bench should be assumed to be faulty and not available for use. In fact, a large theatre plant may find it advantageous to provide a special storage area for equipment found unfit for use and awaiting repair.

GELATIN CABINET   No matter what kind of color media is in use, the name "gel" still will apply. A gel cabinet is similar to a map cabinet and consists of a set of drawers large enough for flat storage of color media. Ideally each drawer should hold only one color. Since this takes many drawers, closely related colors often are stored together. The drawers should be clearly labeled with color name and number plus a sample of the medium itself. Manufacturer's color books should be handy. If the color medium in use is theatrical gelatin, there should be facilities for controlling the humidity, requiring a dehumidifier in some climates and moisture-emitting equipment in others. A cutting surface and large paper cutter should be adjacent to the gel cabinet. Either sample gel frames or templates of all cut sizes should be handy.

ELECTRONICS TEST BENCH   If electronic dimmers are in use and no other electronics test and repair station is available, the lighting room should include a bench with at least a volt-ohm-milliameter (VOM), a diode checker, and light wattage soldering equipment for soldering in the vicinity of solid-state equipment. If magnetic amplifiers are to be serviced, a special iron vane voltmeter will be essential for aligning them.

LIGHTING STORE   If the theatre keeps in storage all lighting equipment not actually in use, the storeroom will have to be large and equipped with enough racks to handle much of the equipment stock. If this is not the theatre's policy, the room will usually contain only the supply of spare lamps, spare parts, odd and seldom-used equipment, and equipment too expensive to leave hanging on stage (such as strobe lights). It may also include the gelatin cabinet, although many theatres purposely place this in the lighting shop. Crew members will usually be sent to the storeroom for a supply of lamps or for special parts needed for a production.

PREPARING THE EQUIPMENT

Preparation can be a lengthy process if the equipment is not in good shape. Each piece listed on the instrument schedule or on the light plot must be cleaned; checked for condition, alignment, and proper lamp type; and tested to make certain that it works, as discussed in previous chapters. Checked instruments are stored in a safe place until the next step.

HANGING THE SHOW

Mounting the equipment, circuiting it, and then gelling and rough-focusing it takes many hours of hard work. For most shows it will take several long crew calls and demand the exclusive use of the stage and house during these times. The stage itself must be clear of anything that will prevent the lowering of lighting battens or movement of ladders to gain access to the battens overhead.

MOUNTING THE EQUIPMENT

Mounting equipment consists of the following steps:

1. Determine the location of the instrument and its type.
2. Place it in position and secure it finger tight.
3. After making adjustments, clamp it securely in place.
4. Install safety chains if necessary.
5. Pull shutters in ellipsoidal reflector spots.

The location and type of each instrument will be shown on the light plot. Scenographers do not usually mark the dimensions showing the exact location of each instrument on the light plot. Instead, crews are expected to scale the locations by measuring from the center line of the stage marked on the plot. Final location will likely be determined by the exact placement of adjacent instruments on a crowded batten, so light plot location is only approximate. Once this location has been determined, the C-clamp is tightened finger tight until the crew is sure that all adjustments have been made. Then the clamps are set down firmly with a crescent wrench, but not to the point of twisting off the heads of the clamp screws (Figure 28-1).

After clamping, whatever safety chains law or common sense demands are installed (see Figure 6-1). If the instrument being mounted is an ellipsoidal reflector spotlight, the shutters are pulled wide open to prevent any chance of the lamp coming on unnoticed.

Not all stage locations will be as easy to work on as a light batten lowered to near the stage floor. In most cases instruments to be mounted in beam or portal positions must be hauled up ladders, through attics, etc. Furthermore instruments in these positions may have to be canted out from under the batten, placing strain on the C-clamp.

If instruments with conventional lamps or those that have been retrofitted with T-H lamps are being mounted, care must be taken to mount them so that the lamps burn in their proper positions.

Crew members should review Chapter 15, "Flying Scenery," to be aware of the special hazards of working counterweight systems be-

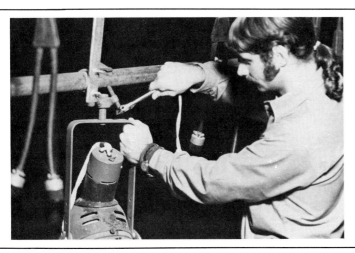

Figure 28-1. Mounting an Instrument. As soon as the instrument has been placed on the batten, its C-clamp should be tightened by hand to avoid any chance that the instrument will fall. When the instrument's location has been exactly determined, the C-clamp is tightened firmly with a wrench. Never lift a batten with instruments only finger tight.

Figure 28-2. Floor Pockets. Although most lighting circuitry will be found on overhead battens and in beam positions, floor connections also are needed. Floor pockets such as those shown are provided in well-equipped theatres. A pocket consists of an iron box set into the floor and equipped with connections for lighting circuits. (a) A pocket equipped to take three-pin connectors. (b) A pocket equipped for three-wire Twist-Lock.

fore attempting to move battens. Ideally this operation should be supervised by someone familiar with the rigging.

CIRCUITING

Circuiting consists of providing the electrical path to and from the lamp necessary for its operation. This can be simple or complex depending on the theatre. The simplest process is found in theatres with special lighting battens and floor pockets (Figure 28-2). These are provided with outlets at frequent intervals, and all that is necessary is to plug in the lead from the instrument. The outlet may be specified on the lighting plot by number. If not, record it on the plot or make up a hook-up chart (Figure 28-3) as you circuit the instruments. Theatres with light-

Figure 28-3. Plugging Chart. The information on this chart reads from the individual instruments toward the control circuitry. Compare with the dimmer loading chart in Figure 28-7 which reads from dimmer to load.

Hook-up (Plugging) Chart

Instrument	Wattage	Circuit	Dimmer
Bridge			
1	500	1	10
2	500	1	10
3	1000	2	11
4	1000	3	12
5 (Proj.)	5000	16	26
6	500	4	10
7	500	5	12
8	1000	6	10

ing battens usually will also have a patchbay where the individual circuits are attached to the dimmers as needed. However, as you circuit each instrument, it is good practice to first patch it into a nondim circuit (a circuit without a dimmer) and turn it on to see if everything is working properly. This avoids the chance that faulty equipment will impose a short circuit on a sensitive dimmer. After everything has been checked, the circuit is repatched into the dimmer that the schedule designates or the one requested by your supervisor.

Some older theatres may have no patchbay. The circuits run directly to the dimmers. In this case, you must take your chances on any malfunctions that might harm the dimmers.

Figure 28-4. Rigging a Batten.

Temporary Wiring

Some theatres have no permanently rigged battens for lighting or wiring to other lighting positions. In this case you must run stage cables for each circuit all the way from the control board to the equipment. You must do this in any theatre whenever you mount an instrument where there is no circuit for it. This takes lots of cable, and increases the weight on the battens, as well as the amount of work you must do.

Let us consider how to go about rigging a scenery or "carpenter" batten for a number of lighting instruments:

1. Lower the batten to working height and secure the assistance of a rigger in planning the necessary counterweighting after you mount instruments, cable, etc.
2. Locate the instruments in the usual manner and clamp them in place.
3. Beginning with the instrument farthest from the drop end of the batten, start running stage cable. The *drop end* is the end of the batten from which the cable bundle will drop to the stage floor and then run to the control board either directly or via outlets installed at floor level. It will be the heaviest end of the batten.
4. As you begin the cable run with the farthest instrument, coil about 5–6 feet of cable and tie it to the batten adjacent to the spotlight (see Figure 28-4). This will give you some slack if the scenographer later asks you to move the instrument, avoiding the necessity of rerigging the entire batten for one move. Use tie cord (small cotton line) to tie the cable(s) to the batten every 3–5 feet. Be sure not to allow the cable to contact any part of an instrument that will get hot or to hang below the level of the bottoms of the instruments.
5. As you reach other instruments, add the additional cables leaving a loop of slack at each instrument (see Figure 28-5). Tie the bundle of cables securely.

Figure 28-5. Detail Showing "Twofer" and Loop of Extra Cable.

Figure 28-6. Detail of Tie-off at Drop End of Batten. If the cable bundle is too large for such a knot, it must be securely tied with rope.

6. If two instruments operate together, you must run a short cable from the farthest to the nearest (reading from the drop end) and insert a multiplier (a two- or three-way connector, or "twofer") at the second instrument to enable you to attach both to the same cable. Leave a loop of slack at each instrument.
7. When you reach the drop end, make an extra secure tie (Figure 28-6) to support the weight of the cables. Attach enough cable to each circuit to reach the floor from working height plus the run to the control board.
8. Complete and test each circuit before raising the batten to its working height.

This system results in heavily loaded battens, particularly if the equipment is wired with three-wire cable. Have the rigger carefully balance the batten before you attempt to operate it. Even when balanced, the line set will be difficult to operate because as you lower the batten, the weight of the cable drop rests on the floor, unbalancing the system. The operating line may have to be snubbed to hold the batten in down position. As a temporary measure, the cable may be coiled as the batten is lowered, and the coil hung over the end of the batten.

Dimmer Loading

Whether the stage is equipped with permanent wiring or wired with portable cable, the final step in circuiting will be attaching the instrument (load) circuits to the dimmers. This involves checking the loading of the dimmers. No dimmer, old or new, should be overloaded. Most modern dimmers will operate equally well on partial loads although some have lower limits below which they are erratic. At any rate, you must determine what the proper load should be for each dimmer.

The mathematics of checking a lamp load is simple addition: add up the wattages of *all* lamps connected to the dimmer. This math is usually done as the plugging chart is made up.

DANGERS OF SLIGHT OVERLOADS   A slight overload is one that exceeds the capacity of the dimmer by an amount so small that it will not trip a breaker or blow a fuse except after the circuit has been on at full for a long period of time. Under some circumstances it may never trip the overcurrent device unless there is a slight line surge. Slight overloads usually are caused by careless checking of lamp wattages. A 750 W lamp may be operating in an instrument thought to have a 500 W lamp in it. If this lamp is part of the load of a large dimmer, the 250 W overage will represent only a slight percentage of the full load. Since fuses and circuit breakers operate very slowly on small overloads, nothing may happen for a long time. This is particularly true if most of the lighting for the show requires the dimmer to be set at less than full up. The danger in this situation is twofold: first, the circuit may fail at some point well into the production after a period of full-on operation (probably the middle of Act III), and second, the overload will overheat the dimmer causing it to deteriorate.

The best solution to this problem is to measure the current flowing through each dimmer with a clamp-on ammeter. This must be done by someone who knows how to translate the readings accurately into wattage figures.

Paper Work

As circuits are completed and dimmers loaded, the crew must keep a careful record of every connection at the electric batten and the patch-bay. If the scenographer has not prepared the plugging information for you (he will seldom do this in thrust stage theatres or theatres-in-the-round which are equipped with a grid of multiple outlet circuits over the entire theatre), you must make up a complete hook-up chart and dimmer-loading chart indicating what load circuits are used to feed which instruments, and how these load circuits are connected to dimmers (see Figures 28-3 and 28-7). Such charts are invaluable for trouble-shooting or for picking up where another part of the crew left off at the end of their work call. Eventually all circuiting information should be entered on the light plot as well as in the hook-up chart.

REPATCHING   If the lighting design is complicated in proportion to the dimming equipment available, it may be necessary to make some dimmers do multiple duty. This is known as *repatching*. It consists of attaching a set of lights to the dimmer for whatever period of time they are needed in the show, then removing them and operating other lights from the same dimmer for another period of time. This can be carried on for as many changes as time for repatching allows. Repatching will complicate the hook-up sheet because the circuits assigned to each dimmer will be grouped according to when they are to be used (see Figure 28-7). During the circuiting process, the circuits will have to be grouped on the dimmer for testing and then removed and tagged while other circuits are tested in the same dimmer.

INSTALLING COLOR MEDIA

The next major step in hanging the show will be rough angling and focusing of the instruments. However, it will save time if each instrument is equipped with its color medium at the same time that it is rough angled. (This is called "gelling" whether gelatin medium is

Figure 28-7. Dimmer Loading Chart. Compare
with Figure 28-3. The purpose of this chart is to
check for overloads and to enable the crew to
make a systematic check of patching whenever
necessary.

Dimmer Loading Chart

Dimmer	Load (watts)	Total Load (watts)	Dimmer (watts)
1	#1-500 #16-500 #73-1000	2000	3000
2	#2-500 #17-500 #74-1000	2000	3000
3	#3-500 #18-500 #75-1000	2000	3000
4	#86-5000	5000	6000
5	Red-cyc 2500 Red border-2500	5000	6000
6	Blue cyc-5000	5000	6000
7	A)#76-2000 #83-1000 (Repatch)	3000 (Repatch)	3000
	B)#5-500 #19-1000 #22-1000	2500	3000

used or not.) Therefore the color frames (gel holders or gel frames) must be prepared. Reference to the instrument schedule should indicate the number of each size frames to be made up. If a gel schedule has been prepared from the information on the light plot, all that will be necessary will be to identify the proper colors, cut them, and install them.

Color media should be indicated on the lighting plot by number and manufacturer. This is necessary because there is no uniformity among manufacturers as to color and color number. A sample book will be of great help to the beginner in this process. If theatrical gelatin is being used, samples in the book may not match those in stock because gelatin varies from lot to lot. Plastic color media are more uniform, but variations may be evident there also.

Media may be cut by using a scissors, a matte knife and straight edge, or a large paper cutter. Extra care is necessary when handling gelatin. If it gets moist from perspiration on your hands, it may stick together or be badly marred. If it has been allowed to get too dry in storage, it will be so brittle that it will be nearly impossible to handle without cracking it.

It is also a good idea to identify the colors in the holders by number and manufacturer. This can be written on the gel frame or on the medium itself with a grease pencil. Do not write on the portion that the light will pass through — it will probably cause the gelatin or plastic to burn.

Once prepared, the gel frames are taken to the stage and installed by the crew members as they rough angle the instruments.

ROUGH ANGLING AND FOCUSING

The next two steps consist of (1) determining the proper location for each pool of light as shown on the lighting plot, and (2) standing on the stage and directing other crew members to move each instrument and adjust its focus until the pool of light is adjusted properly. At least three people are needed to do this job: one on stage to determine the location of the instrument, one at the instrument being adjusted, and a third at the control board to turn various instruments on or off as they are being worked. Since instruments often are arranged in pairs to light the same area, additional crew members at various instrument locations may make the work go faster. Before you can begin to do this work you need to know that the circles on the light plot represent pools of light at actor head level, not on the stage floor. If the lighting plot indicates that an area should be illuminated by two or more instruments, each of these must be carefully angled to cover the entire area at head level.

Judging the Location of the Lighted Area

There are several methods of locating the lighted area depending on the power of the instrument being focused, local practices, and personal preferences. The most common way is for the person on stage to look directly at the instrument while he moves about in the pool of light. When he is exactly in the center of the pool, he will see an intensely bright spot in the center of the lens (see Figure 28-8). As he moves toward the edge of the pool, this bright spot will also move, vanishing as he steps out of the pool. This system is accurate but hard on the eyes, and may be harmful if one is angling very high-powered (3000 W or more) instruments. Dimming the lights down while angling will help, but it is not always practical.

Another way to determine where you are in the light beam is to turn your back to the light and observe the location of the shadow of your head on the stage floor. When the shadow is in the middle of the pool of light, your head is at the center of the pool. This system works best with a single light on at a time. When checking blending with many lights on, the shadow may be hard to see.

A practice sometimes used in Hollywood film studios is to focus the instrument to its smallest diameter, locating this pool precisely at

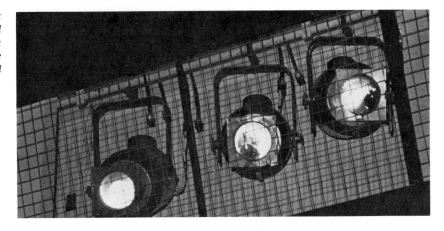

the center of the area to be covered. Then the instrument is flooded to cover the intended area.

How to Proceed

Equipped with the above information, the next step is to set each area separately. To do this the observer stations himself in the center of each acting area as shown on the plot, and has the two lights designated for that area moved until they center on him, and focused until they appear to be covering the proper area. All areas are thus roughed out. Each is done separately and then turned off while the others are being done. Then adjacent areas are lighted and the observer walks from one to another noting the bright spots in the lenses. Anytime he can see only one bright spot (one light only), he is in a dead spot and he calls for adjustments of angle or focus to eliminate it. Or, if he finds himself looking at three or more bright spots, he is in a hot spot and he adjusts this. Of course each adjustment tends to make changes in the other areas adjacent to the one under examination, and the process will be repeated many times before it is finished.

A combination of shouts and hand signals usually is worked out to tell the operators of the various instruments what to do. These operators may be hanging head-down in ceiling ports or false beams, or they may be peering through crevices surrounding the snouts of lights tightly fitted into holes in the ceiling, and therefore unable to see well or hear at all. Hand signals are then essential and should be carefully worked out in advance.

Installing Auxiliary Equipment

In addition to color media, you may be asked to equip some of the instruments with additional devices that control the light. The most com-

FIGURE 28-9a

mon of these are "hoods" (also called "snoots," "top hats," etc.) and "barn doors" (see Figure 28-9). Hoods reduce the spill from an instrument, sometimes also cutting beam size. Reduction of spill also has the effect of reducing flare from instruments visible to the audience. Barn doors have a similar effect, but only on the part of the beam they intersect. They are also used to shape a light beam, for example, to fit into an archway. These also are inserted into the color frame slots and usually require the use of a safety chain, even if color frames alone do not. Final adjustment of barn doors should be supervised by the scenographer.

FINISH ANGLING AND FOCUSING

Once all of the instruments have been rough angled and focused and all auxiliary equipment has been installed, it will be up to the scenographer or his well-trained and trusted assistant to supervise the final "tuning" of the lighting. Even after this is done, rehearsals will reveal many flaws and bring design changes which may result in moving equipment, reangling or focusing, changing colors, or the addition or removal of equipment. In fact, some scenographers purposely hang more instruments than they expect to use, holding part of it in readiness for additions. All of these alterations will be done by the lighting crew —often at the end of a long rehearsal session.

FIGURE 28-9b

Finish angling and focusing (Figure 28-10) follows the same procedure as rough angling and focusing except that the work will be much more precise. Often actors and the director will be needed to get things exactly right. It is important that crew members know the location and circuitry of every instrument so they can meet requests with dispatch, and that the person(s) operating the control board knows how to control the lights as needed. Thus it will be a good idea to begin the next step, "Practice sessions," after rough angling, if this is possible. If not, expect to be under a lot of pressure to know everything at once.

Figure 28-9. (a) Fresnel Spotlight with Hood. Note the safety chain on the far side of the instrument. (b) Fresnel Spotlight with Barn Doors.

LEARNING THE SYSTEM

Up to now you have been putting together a complicated "instrument" upon which you are now going to learn to "play." Of course it is not completely "tuned" yet and its nature may change a good deal as rehearsals bring up new problems, but you must start to familiarize yourself with it. The difficulty of this job will vary with the size and complexity of the lighting system. A simple high school control system in which almost all of the equipment is permanently connected to the

Figure 28-10. Focusing an Instrument.

dimmers offers little challenge. You will probably already know that dimmer No. 1 *always* operates the red foots—it is wired to them and it is nearly impossible to make it work anything else. As control equipment becomes more sophisticated the process of learning to "play" it becomes more difficult.

Patchbays (Figures 27-7 and 28-11), which are common in more elaborate systems, make it possible to group related controls together into some rational pattern. This usually makes operation easier. For example, all acting area controls can be grouped together in a pattern visually analogous to the arrangement of the areas themselves. Another advantage is that modern control boards are more likely to be placed where the operator(s) can see the results of their work and take cues directly from stage business. Other changes, however, may not be so helpful. For instance, as replugging is added to make a limited supply of dimmers go farther, the operators have to remember that the dimmer which controlled the "moonlight special" in Act I now controls the "fireplace special" in Act II. And it may control still another instrument in Act III. More sophisticated control systems may add complications far beyond these examples.

Let us focus our attention on the problems of learning to handle a control console of perhaps thirty dimmers with some repatching possibilities from control locations (1) backstage, and (2) at a position in the back of the house. In either case, the learning process will have already started by the time the lights are up and angled because at least some members of the crew will have had the task of running tests, bringing in and taking out areas and specials as they were being angled, and working out the details of the patching itself. If you make sure that you know what you are doing at each of these steps and realize that this is only the beginning of the most challenging part of a lighting assignment, you can learn a lot at these "menial" jobs.

BACKSTAGE OPERATION

Learning to run lights from backstage is something of a test in patience and imagination. You can usually see little or none of the results of your work, and the control board is likely to become a sort of mechanical monster for whom you do service in robotlike fashion. A lot depends on remembering how each of the lighting instrument's lights looked as you saw it finally angled and focused. It will help if you can spend some time in the house where you can see the results while others are running the board. It will also help if the controls are labeled in terms of the lighting function they control, e.g., "area I warm," "area I cool," etc. This will make it easier to understand instructions given you by phone from the scenographer as he sets the lights.

Probably the best way to learn the control board is to have someone sit in the house during rehearsal and call cues to you over a telephone while you attempt to follow them on the board. You will, of
course, be a couple of beats behind the moving actors as the cue caller
notes their movement, relays it to you, and you react. However you will
still learn the general flow of movement in the play and also the location
of each control on the board. Ultimately the real cues will have to be
timed to account for that lag so that the lights will do the right things at
the right time. A few practice sessions for each member of the crew
should ready them for the first "cue setting" sessions with the scenographer.

FOH Operation

If the control board is at the back of the house or where the operators
can see the stage directly, things go much faster and you get a better
grasp of lighting techniques. To get ready for cue-setting sessions the
supervisor will instruct you to "follow the action," keeping the portion
of the stage which you deem to be the center of focus some 3–5 dimmer
points above the rest. This has the advantage of teaching you the board,
the blocking, and the general nature of the production in one operation.
Most important of all, it gives you a sense of what the scenographer will
be doing as he subsequently designs the lighting to assist the director
and actors in controlling the focus of attention. It also gives the supervisor a good chance to size up the potential talent in his crew and discover who will make the best operators. Some people thrive on this sort
of challenge and display a sense of the rhythm of the movement of the
play very quickly. Occasionally a person will turn up who has not only
this sense of rhythm, but a kind of visual memory that enables him to
retain these patterns and "replay" them again on subsequent rehearsals. Such persons are the rare natural geniuses of lighting control
operation. At the other extreme are those individuals who seem to have
no sense of visual rhythm at all and who are terrified of the complexity
of the system. Only much rehearsal and considerable rote memory will
see them through as operators. Of course, the person who looks on the
whole thing as a game or a chance to catch up on casual conversation
with the crew, has no business in lighting — or anywhere else in the
theatre.

TERMINOLOGY

Terminology becomes important in learning the control board and in
the rest of the steps in lighting a production. It does not make a great
deal of difference what names you assign to certain lights. But no
matter what the names, all parties from scenographer to lowliest cue

FIGURE 28-11a

FIGURE 28-11b

Figure 28-11. (a) A Patchbay for Use with Portable Control Boards. (b) Patchbays Built onto Commercially Made ATD Boards. These offer the possibility of switching from one load circuit to another without repatching. (c) A Patchbay for a Permanent Installation. The load circuits terminate in the patch cords left and right. The dimmer and nondim outputs are located in the center. Note the lower center section where two groups of three outlets each are provided for each of nine dimmers. These groups of outlets are controlled by relays, making remote repatching possible.

FIGURE 28-11c

card turner must know what they mean and agree that they mean the same thing. For example, it will not do for the scenographer to refer to the lights coming from the stage left tormentor position as the "cool side lights," while the crew thinks of them as the "moonlight sides." Usually a shrewd scenographer will defer to the crew concerning the names of the various lighting functions since they will have to work with them the most.

SETTING THE LIGHTING—REHEARSALS AND PROCEDURES

Sessions in which cues actually are created and timed into the production are known as "lighting rehearsals." There are several types: (1) strictly mechanical sessions with only the scenographer, a couple of stagehands, and the lighting crew in attendance, (2) "technical rehearsals" in which not only lighting but all technical elements are somehow blended into the show, (3) rehearsals as in type 2, but with the cast on a standby basis (or stand-ins may be used) and technicians working through the show setting cues and using actors where they are required, and (4) rehearsals with full cast and setting where the actors move through the show without stopping, hardly realizing that lighting is being worked into the production.

Mode of rehearsal and involvement with other elements will vary from show to show because of script differences, and according to the practices of scenographers and technical directors. Some of the following considerations will apply in almost every case.

1. Communication must be clear between the lighting operators and the scenographer. This usually means some telephone arrangement or possibly an intercom or "squawk box" device. Additional communications to operators of follow spots, special effects devices, and the like will also be needed. If the lighting crew is working in a control booth at the back of the house and it is soundproof, there will also be a need for a "cue line" which feeds the sounds of the show to the lighting operators. This is often the same line that feeds sound to other parts of the theatre. There should be a back-up for these cue systems so that there is no likelihood of complete failure. Crew members should be sure that they know how to operate these systems. They may also have the responsibility of setting up the communications equipment in the house for rehearsals and storing it after each rehearsal. This house equipment often takes the form of a "rehearsal desk" with phones, intercom, lights for scripts, and other equipment. It is installed during rehearsal periods and removed for productions.

2. There may be prepared cues given to the lighting crew by the scenographer. Usually the warning and take signals for such cues will

come from the stage manager or an assistant, if the controls are back-stage. If the booth is at the front of the house, warnings and takes will vary, depending on policy and whether a visual cue is taken from the action. In any event, the cues that start each act beginning with, "House lights down," will always come from the stage manager.

3. The scenographer will ask for many settings and changes that he will decide not to use. Therefore as the rehearsal proceeds crew members should not record any change until they are given the command, "Write it." Then they should record the change accurately and rapidly, letting the scenographer know when they are ready for more changes. We will discuss methods of writing cues later.

4. The scenographer will often say, "Snap area X to full," or "Take area Y out fast." The controls should then be moved as fast as possible without banging them or damaging them. The scenographer wants to see the effect of the change quickly — usually before the actors have moved out of position.

5. The scenographer may ask you to "Run instrument Z up and down several times," or he may say, "Flash area Z." He is trying to identify a pool of light or a shadow which the rapidly changing light helps him to check. Move the controller rapidly up and down.

6. The scenographer may ask for a "normal fade." The term "fade" refers to any change in intensity whether upward or downward. A normal fade is in the neighborhood of four to six seconds depending on the pace of the production. It is the speed with which most changes can be made without calling the audience's attention to the fact that a light is being changed. Slower cues are given counts — approximately one second per count, or they may follow the stage business.

7. Dimmer readings will be given in a scale of 0–10, 10 being full up and 0 being black out. Depending on the dimmer and the equipment, a variety of control curves will be encountered. In almost no case will the change seen *on stage* be the same for all points on the scale. With autotransformer dimmers (commonly found in high school and small college theatres) 0–3 produce nearly no effect; 8–10 control about 40 percent of the entire light.

8. It will be necessary for someone to take notes about changes that must be made, instruments to be added, recircuiting, and many other things. They must be done before the next session takes place. This may mean staying late into the night or returning to the theatre early the next morning.

9. As the cues develop, they will proceed from general settings with long pauses between them toward continuous change. How far this process goes depends on the type of production and the style of lighting being designed. It will also depend on the ability of the lighting crew to execute cues. The better they are at timing and learning difficult combinations of operations, the more the scenographer will

feel he can add in the way of refinements. Of course there will be constant conferences between the director and scenographer. Occasionally an entire block of cues will be changed or removed because they do not meet the artistic needs of the director. He is the final authority and the scenographer will defer to him — usually after trying hard to make his case.

CUES

As the cues are developed and refined, crew members will have to arrive at a method of recording them so they may be learned and "played back" with accuracy. There is no completely satisfactory way of writing cues. Every scenographer and lighting supervisor has methods that have worked well for him and that he feels will work for others. As a beginner, you should try to learn as many of these as possible. Eventually, if you go far enough in lighting, you will develop tricks of your own.

The problem is that the instrument used to "play" the lighting has no standardized parts except the 10-point dimmer scale. Even it, as we have already seen, is subject to wide variations in its distribution of control. Thus the situation is much as it would be for writing music if every piano had a different keyboard, with a different scale and even varying numbers of notes. Moreover, since lighting exists in both time and space, it is more complicated than music when one sets out to list the variables that must be recorded in a successful notation. There is, therefore, no completely satisfactory cue system and no likelihood that one will appear in the near future. The best we can do is list some of the things we would like a cue system to do and not do.

The only successful system we will be able to devise consists of one or more artistically sensitive crew members who have memorized the rhythms of the show and the appearance of the lighting. They then depend on the faulty, but by no means useless, written cue system to aid their memory while they recreate what the scenographer has designed.

The Ideal Cue System

The ideal lighting cue system should have most of the following characteristics:

1. It should reflect graphically, and with little chance for reading error, the state of the lighting from moment to moment during the production.
2. It should provide sufficient warning before each change to allow the operator to organize himself to make the change. It should also give him the rhythmic structure of the change.

It should do all of this without requiring him to look away from the stage for more than a moment so he can constantly follow what is happening.

3. It should be capable of expressing changes within changes.
4. It should tell the operator about any electromechanical changes he must make to be ready for lighting changes to come.
5. It should relate itself directly to the script of the play so that its rhythmic structure reflects that of the script as interpreted by the director.

Practical Cue Systems

The above list could be extended considerably, but the point is obvious: any cue system we can devise will be little more than a "memory jogger" compared to demands such as those. The following are some of the practical possibilities for cue systems.

CARD CUES If the lighting of a production falls into distinct changes well-separated from each other by periods of inactivity, cue cards are a good system. Often a drawing-room comedy will call only for lighting changes at the beginning of each act, at the end of each act, and perhaps a change or two to represent time of day, or the effect of turning on or off room lighting. These changes can simply be written on a series of cards. The stage manager or other person responsible for giving the cues sets up warning points in the script well ahead of the changes, and the operators, when warned, check their cards for the operation and the cue line or business. Taking the cue is done on the line or business and backed up by a "Take" given by the stage manager. A count is provided if the cue is unusually long in duration. Such changes as these may be complicated. They may involve the efforts of several crew members if the control board is of the old manual variety, requiring one hand for each dimmer being moved.

Cues should be numbered on the cards and referred to by number: "Ready cue 10"; "Take cue 10 on John's cross"; and so forth. Cards should also be numbered and fastened together so that they cannot get out of order. On occasion it may be helpful to divide the cue information onto several cards, each with the same cue numbers on it, so the cards can be handy to several operators spread over a large manual control board such as that shown in Figure 28-11b. Each cue number should show on every card. When the cue requires no action on the part of a given operator, this should be noted so he will be reassured that no mistake has been made.

BOOK CUES Book cues are just what the name implies: cues written in the margins and empty spaces of the playbook. Warning cues are inserted where needed and take cues are written at exactly the word on which they are to be taken. Of course cues taken from business must be explained and related to lines that pinpoint the business.

Book cues work best when only one or two operators are running lights on a rather compact control board. Otherwise the difficulties of reading the book are insurmountable. Book cues must be written in pencil; they are subject (as are all cues) to repeated change. A relatively compact system of cue notation is necessary if the book is not to become so cluttered that it is illegible.

The great advantage of book cues is their close relationship with the lines and rhythm of the play. Subtle, constantly changing lighting can be recorded in this manner with considerable success. In fact, book cues are essentially what the scenographer uses himself as he designs the lighting. There are disadvantages, however: (1) only a very few cues are visible at a time and constant turning ahead is confusing, (2) only one or two people can follow the book at a time, and (3) repeated changes tend to destroy the book, often making cues illegible.

In spite of all this, the person who is both designer and operator will find book cues to his liking. They relate his artistic intentions closely to the information he needs to run the lighting, and he will usually memorize such large chunks of cues that the problem of turning pages will not bother him at all.

Book cues can be written in scripts as they come from the publisher, in ditto or type copies (with the advantage of blank page backs for additional space), or for complicated shows, a script made by dismantling a playbook and gluing it to cutout pages in the manner of a director's script.

BOOK-AND-CUE CARDS   A system that combines book and card cues will handle almost any degree of complexity, but it is worth the additional effort only when a show is so complicated and the control situation so arranged that several persons must be involved in running the cues. It combines the ready access to cue information of cards with the close relationship to the rhythm of the production provided by the script. A complete set of book cues is prepared during the design stages of the lighting. As soon as these cues reach enough stability to make it possible, the cues are assigned numbers consecutively from beginning to end of the show. All preparatory operations should also be assigned cue numbers. From the cue book, which now serves as a master cue list, cue cards are prepared either singly or in multiples depending on the number of operators and the problems they might have reading a single set of cards. These cards are arranged mechanically as described above in the discussion of cue cards.

The system during the operation of the cues is as follows: One person is designated as "cue reader." He *must* have a clear view of the stage, preferably somewhat like the audience's view—a back-of-house booth is ideal. This person reads warning cues that have been carefully placed in the book sufficiently in advance of each cue, to give the operator(s) time to check cue cards and ready the operation. They then await the "Take cue X," and perform the operation as instructed on the card. Each operator has an entry for *every* cue number even if it tells him that he does nothing. There is no confusion. Ideally, no one should have to do any talking except the cue reader.

The book-and-cue-card system works best when all operators have a good view of the stage and can follow business closely. Thus a card that reads, "Cross-fade from area I to area II to area III as John crosses left" (X fade I to II to III as J X L), will need no further elaboration. If the operators are backstage where they cannot see, the cue reader will have to break this down into a number of separate changes which he calls out as he follows the action. This is much more difficult, usually leading to poor synchronization between action and lighting.

The cue book will serve as a master book for all changes made during rehearsal. Afterward the crew can alter the cards to fit the changes. The sequence of numbers should be maintained. Where it is necessary to insert a new cue between two existing cues, for instance, cues 23 and 24, create a "cue 23A." If necessary, create 23B, 23C, etc., as far as you need to go. If a cue is deleted, simply abandon the number, noting that it is "dead."

GENERAL NOTES ON CUES   Crew members should resist the temptation to take the cue book and/or cards home to make a new set of cards for the sake of neatness and legibility unless the cards are almost completely illegible. Chances are that more errors will be made in recopying than came from illegibility. Generally speaking, cue cards and cue books should never leave the theatre. They should be stored in some safe place known to all members of the crew and to the supervisory staff. There is nothing quite as sure to produce panic as the realization that the one member of the crew who is late or unaccounted for also has the cue book.

The use of colored pencils or pens for emphasis is not a bad idea but be sure that the color of light you are using at the control board will allow visibility. Cues written in red pencil may vanish under a red light at the control board.

There is a very close relationship between the setup of the lighting control and the way in which the cues will be written. It is generally helpful to group together operations that are done on adjacent dimmers or controls. It is also a good idea to group together "up" movements and also "down" movements. Of course, if the control board is an old manual control system of huge dimensions needing several operators, operations will be grouped by operator—often on separate cards.

WRITING CUES

There are many systems of notation; each control system tends to generate its own. One principle seems paramount: *cues should be written in terms of lighting changes on the stage, not in terms of mechanical changes at the control board.* Thus we write, "area I cool up to 6," not "dimmer No. 5 up to 6." There are several reasons for this: (1) Operators, even when working blindly backstage, will be apt to do a better job if they know what effect they are having on the stage itself. (2) In any but the most primitive systems, the control device that handles a given instrument—in this case "area I cool"—may be changed. In fact, on a control board with a good patching system, it may change several times in the process of refining the setup. Such changes will necessitate no cue changes at all if all that is necessary is to move a label from one handle to another. (3) Such cue writing becomes even more significant when the operator is located where he can see the stage. In this case, he should be looking at the stage as he takes the cue. If he knows what change to expect, he will be able to catch many errors and rectify them before they are obvious to the audience. (4) Most important of all, the cue establishes a direct thought connection between the operation at the control board and the moving light on stage. This is vitally important when following the action with lighting—a process known as "follow focusing," which consists of raising and lowering the intensity of acting areas to control the focus of attention. It is analogous to the follow spotting technique common in European opera theatres, but provides far better control over lighting contrast and angle. It is a logical outgrowth of the McCandless system of acting areas.

The following system is one which has developed over many years of work with student lighting crews. It is offered here as an example of a system that meets theatrical needs relatively well:

1. It is graphic in terms of dimmer operation.
2. It is easy to read under panic circumstances, when information is most needed.
3. It is compact—the same system works well for the scenographer's records in his book.
4. It is easily adjusted to the special needs of any production.

As you examine the diagrams below, note how cues are grouped according to dimmer movement, and how the various numerical elements are separated to make misreading more unlikely. The system works equally well for backstage operation or for operation from a booth at the back of the house. Only one change is desirable. It derives from the fact that it is easier to visualize the arrangement of lighting areas if they are numbered in the usual left-to-right reading pattern. Thus it is best to number the areas from stage left to stage right when the operator is backstage, and from audience left to audience right when operating at the back of the house. These are the usual symbols used:

Roman numerals (I, II, III, etc.) — lighting area numbers
Arabic numerals (1, 2, 3, etc., if unmarked) — dimmer readings
Letters (A, B, C, etc.) or names — specials

↑	— move the dimmer up to	↓	— take the dimmer down to "out"
↓	— move the dimmer down to	④	— cue number four
		⑤	— perform the operation on a count of five
⟙	— raise the dimmer to full	HL	— house lights

Here are some sample cues using these symbols:

⑱   I, II, III   ↑8
     IV, V, VI ↓3

Cue eighteen: This would move the brighter area lighting from upstage to downstage if we assume a six-area plot. No timing is shown; use the "normal" 3–4 count.

Note that previous readings are not shown. You only need to know the new cue setting. Now we move from the setting in cue 18 to a tight focus on a single downstage area:

⑲   II ⟙ ④
     I, III, IV, V, VI ↓ ⑥

The oncoming area leads the outgoing areas, thus narrowing focus subtly.

We can now add a new key light (a special) to increase the dramatic effect of the scene:

⑳   A ↑ 8 ⑩
     II left ↓ 2 ⑮

Special A is raised to 8 (from out) and one of the two area lights is reduced to a slight fill. If special A is to the actor's right and at a high angle, strong contrasting facial lighting will occur.

Extended cues (which often have within them several other operations) are shown either as counts, as clock-timed cues, or by marking the page of script as shown in Figure 28-12. This same cue-writing system can be used whether simple cue cards, book cues, or book-card systems are used.

TAKING CUES

It often is stated that theoretically lighting cues are exact operations to be performed with the same precision we expect of a good record player.

But this statement is followed rapidly with the qualification—*if* the actors are playing the scene with consistency and accuracy. The governing word is "if." Actors are human and the very essence of living theatre is that there is a constant and constantly variable interplay between actors and audience. Any element that moves with mechanical relentlessness (a taped musical score, for example) is usually thought of as a terrifying detriment to artistic freedom. It is also terrifying from the mechanical point of view. Thus the idea of putting the entire operation of the lighting on some sort of memory device—a tape for instance —is not greeted with much enthusiasm. Incidentally, this idea is technically quite possible; it is just not desired.

Nevertheless a high degree of accuracy is demanded of lighting cues; the catch is that accuracy is not measured against an abstract time standard in the manner of the speed indicator on a record player. Instead the accuracy is measured against the equally rigorous but much more variable time structure of the production itself. To put it simply, cues must be *exactly* in time with the production, not with the clock. A light must come up to the proper reading at the proper moment in the lines or business and with the proper rhythm in the change, or it is wrong. The margin for error might be only a tenth of a second, but we are much more likely to say, "It was just a beat off," i.e., it was just perceptibly too early or too late *as measured with the rhythm of the scene.*

This kind of accuracy calls for concentration and sensitivity. You cannot run cues while carrying on a conversation. Although you may see "old timers" seemingly running a show out of the corner of their eye and casually making changes without a break in their conversation, you will note that they have memorized their cues and have developed the facility to do two things at once. Let something change the rhythm on stage by the slightest amount—e.g., an actor missing lines—and they are instantly all concentration.

What Variations Are Allowed during Operation?

If you are backstage and must work with counts for timing or from the sweep hand of a clock, there is very little room for variation. You must depend on the cue caller or stage manager for information that might change any cue in duration or reading. Your job is not to initiate change, but to work as instructed until told otherwise. Similarly some scenographers instruct their crews to follow the same rigid patterns even though they are where they can see the stage. However, most scenographers find that where the crew can see the stage, they can also take more responsibility. Obviously they can more easily and accurately follow business, timing cues to actor movements with precision.

It is only a small additional change in policy to allow crew members to make adjustments to account for changes that the actors make

As this SEGMENT BEGINS, THE ROMEO SPECIAL IS ALREADY AT 3½ AND
THE BALCONY SPECIAL IS AT 5.

BALSP↑6   BEGIN DAWN

Rom.   If my heart's dear love—
Jul. Well, do not swear. Although I joy in thee,
I have no joy of this contract tonight.
It is too rash, too unadvised, too sudden;   125
Too like the lightning, which doth cease to be
Ere one can say "It lightens." Sweet, good night!
This bud of love, by summer's ripening breath,
May prove a beauteous flow'r when next we meet.
Good night, good night! As sweet repose and rest   130
Come to thy heart as that within my breast!
   Rom. O, wilt thou leave me so unsatisfied?
   Jul. What satisfaction canst thou have tonight?
   Rom. The exchange of thy love's faithful vow for mine.

ROMEO SP↑4½

Jul. I gave thee mine before thou didst request it;   135
And yet I would it were to give again.
   Rom. Wouldst thou withdraw it? For what purpose,
      love?
   Jul. But to be frank and give it thee again.
And yet I wish but for the thing I have.   140
My bounty is as boundless as the sea,
My love as deep; the more I give to thee,`
The more I have, for both are infinite.
I hear some noise within. Dear love, adieu!
                                        [Nurse] calls within.
Anon, good nurse! Sweet Montague, be true.   145 (DAWN AT 1)
Stay but a little, I will come again.   [Exit.]
   Rom. O blessed, blessed night! I am afeard,
Being in night, all this is but a dream,
Too flattering-sweet to be substantial.
                         [Re-enter Juliet above.]

BALCONY SP↑7 [10]

Jul. Three words, dear Romeo, and good night indeed. 150
If that thy bent of love be honorable,
Thy purpose marriage, send me word tomorrow,
By one that I'll procure to come to thee,
Where and what time thou wilt perform the rite;
And all my fortunes at thy foot I'll lay   155
And follow thee my lord throughout the world.
   Nurse. (Within) Madam!
   Jul. I come, anon.—But if thou meanst not well,
I do beseech thee—

                                                                DAWN AT 2

Figure 28-12. Long Book Cues. These pages from a hypothetical cue sheet for Romeo and
Juliet *(Shakespeare) illustrate a method of recording extended cues. There is no way that such
cuing can reflect the actual rhythm of the operations; only starts and finishes can be shown.
Note that as the dawn is added to the scene, the lighting on the actors is increased to maintain
focus of attention. Although not evident within these two pages, the reader should assume that
there are additional lights on the stage which do not change during this interval until the "all
fade" at the end. Note that the cues should be written in pencil.*

Nurse. *(Within)* Madam!							160

Jul.					By-and-by I come.—
To cease thy suit and leave me to my grief.
Tomorrow will I send.

   Rom.					So thrive my soul—

Jul. A thousand times good night!			*Exit.* 165

   Rom. A thousand times the worse, to want thy light!
Love goes toward love as schoolboys from their books;
But love from love, towards school with heavy looks.

			Enter *Juliet* again [, above].

Jul. Hist! Romeo, hist! O for a falc'ner's voice
To lure this tassel-gentle back again!			170
Bondage is hoarse and may not speak aloud;
Else would I tear the cave where Echo lies,
And make her airy tongue more hoarse than mine
With repetition of my Romeo's name.
Romeo!							175

   Rom. It is my soul that calls upon my name.
How silver-sweet sound lovers' tongues by night,
Like softest music to attending ears!

   Jul. Romeo!

   Rom.		My sweet?				180

   Jul.				What o'clock tomorrow
Shall I send to thee?

   Rom.			By the hour of nine.

   Jul. I will not fail. 'Tis twenty years till then.
I have forgot why I did call thee back.			185

   Rom. Let me stand here till thou remember it.

   Jul. I shall forget, to have thee still stand there,
Rememb'ring how I love thy company.

   Rom. And I'll still stay, to have thee still forget,
Forgetting any other home but this.			190

   Jul. 'Tis almost morning. I would have thee gone—
And yet no farther than a wanton's bird,
That lets it hop a little from her hand,
Like a poor prisoner in his twisted gyves,
And with a silk thread plucks it back again,		195
So loving-jealous of his liberty.

   Rom. I would I were thy bird.

   Jul.				Sweet, so would I.
Yet I should kill thee with much cherishing.
Good night, good night! Parting is such sweet sorrow,	200
That I shall say good night till it be morrow.	[*Exit.*]

   Rom. Sleep dwell upon thine eyes, peace in thy breast!
Would I were sleep and peace, so sweet to rest!
Hence will I to my ghostly father's cell,
His help to crave and my dear hap to tell.		205
							Exit.

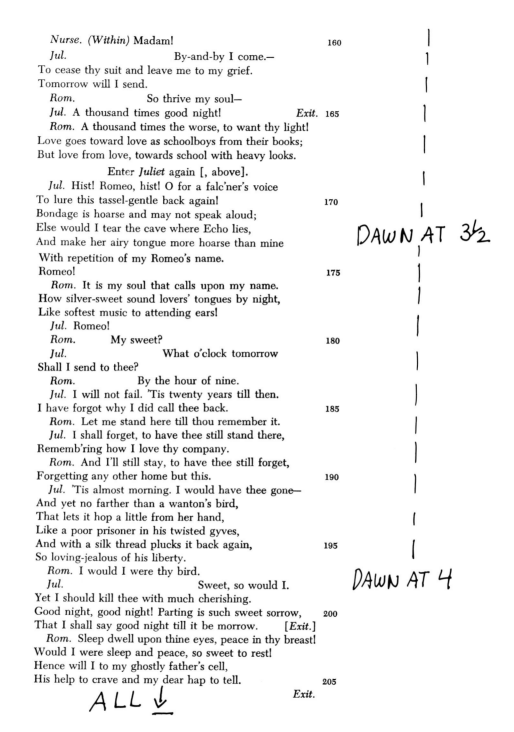

ROMEO SP ↑ 6

BAL SP^x ↓ and
EXIT

DAWN AT 3½

DAWN AT 4

ALL ↓

in blocking. For example, an actor blocked to cross left may normally move to area III. On occasion, for reasons beyond the control of the lighting crew, he moves to area IV (assuming a stage five areas wide). Lighting crews should normally be instructed to make adjustments so that the actor will not remain in the dark simply because he has missed his mark. However, this should not be converted into license for actors to wander at will and expect the lighting crew to make them look good.

The degree of responsibility for making changes that is allowed the lighting crew will be governed by two things: (1) the mechanical possibility they have for making such changes (e.g., then can do little from a blind position backstage), and (2) the amount of skill and sensitivity they develop as they are learning the show. The more they can display the skill and awareness needed to make such changes, the more likely they are to be given the opportunity to do so. This skill and awareness will show up as they run the cues as written with a sensitivity for the rhythmic patterns of movement and dramatic tension. No cue can be so subtly written as to catch the pace variations evidenced by a skilled actor playing Hamlet, for example. The person who can time lighting changes to this actor's movements will show a sensitivity worth encouraging.

"Winging It"

You will hear the term "winging it" early in your association with lighting operators. It means operating without cues and usually without rehearsal, or at least rehearsal of any useful sort. It is the thing that happens when you are told at 3 P.M. that you are going to light a dance recital at 8:30 P.M. Moreover no lighting has been designed or instruments mounted, but it is hoped you will be creative and make the dancers look good. This is no job for the beginner. However, beginners may be lulled into a dangerously casual attitude by watching an experienced control board operator perform one of these miracles. He hangs a set of instruments, angles, focuses, and gels them with casual precision and spends what time he can watching the dancers warm up. He asks questions about where key things will take place on stage, where entrances will be made, and the like. Then he proceeds to light the show. No one is ever in the dark for more than a moment; spectacular color patterns often appear; shadows seem to have meaning; etc. Many of his "cues" seem right on the beat as though he had worked with the group for weeks. What you are witnessing is a skillful application of the "tricks of the trade" plus the use of certain clichés of lighting that have grown up in the area of dance lighting. These are executed by an operator who knows his control board so well that he seldom looks at it—he plays it like a skilled pianist plays a piano. Moreover, the operator has probably lit a hundred or more dance recitals and knows the ways of dancers well enough to almost predict where they will move next. Watching an expert winging it is an experience well worth your time, but do not be deceived by the ease he displays. He is using every trick in the book.

CREW DISCIPLINE AND ORGANIZATION

It should be obvious now that the operation of lighting controls calls for a high degree of concentration. In fact, a show with continuous lighting change will call for more concentration on the part of the light crew than that required of the actors. Many an actor has found that nervousness which he thought he had learned to control came back threefold with his first turn at the control board. Clearly there should be no extra distractions. Visitors should not be allowed in control areas until the crew and the supervisor are certain that the crew is completely secure. Even then visitors are subject to ejection if they create any distraction. Also crew members who talk more than necessary should be asked to control their tongues or find another occupation. Of course these rules do not apply during moments when concentration is not necessary, but everyone, guests included, should be ready to drop conversation and make way for concentration at a moment's notice. Since the pressure is already high enough in a lighting control area, directors and even scenographers should stay out as much as possible.

Often the number of persons assigned to a lighting crew will exceed the number needed to get the job done, so some will get more and better experience than others. In most educational situations the supervisor will make an effort to see that every crew member gets a chance at every important part of the job. This includes sharing responsibilities for running the cues. However, the supervisor also has the responsibility for the integrity of the production. He cannot rotate crew members if they are not qualified, and he cannot be sure that cues will not be botched because a "new hand" is running the board. If you wish to learn to run cues during the production, you must show that you can do a good job. Practice on your own, volunteer to run cues during checkouts and extra rehearsals, and above all, *know the show*. Read it well in advance of your crew assignment and visit rehearsals as much as possible.

TROUBLESHOOTING

There is no such thing as a trouble-free lighting setup. No matter how carefully you test and repair, no matter how often you check, trouble will occur. Thus you should plan for it and be ready to take corrective measures.

PRESHOW CHECKOUTS

Checkouts are intended to spot trouble before the curtain goes up. Crew members test each instrument, turning it on, checking for electrical operation, alignment, angle, focus, gel color, and condition, and they see if anything comes on that should not when each instrument is turned on. This check should be made just before the house is opened to the audience—not early in the afternoon. Earlier checks leave the chance that someone will tamper with the equipment, especially the patching, while you are away. Never assume that just because you left everything in perfect order the night before, it is still in that condition twenty-four hours later.

In order to perform the kind of maintenance needed during checkout, the crew should have access to the following:

1. At least one spare lamp of each type used in the production —preferably several of those most used.
2. Fuses of the proper type and size, if these are used in the control system.
3. Access to keys to all fuse or breaker panels involved in the system.
4. Access to a supply of replacement cable, connectors, etc., to enable them to replace faulty parts. (Electrical repairs can then be made later under supervision.)
5. Lighting plot, plugging or hook-up chart, and any other paper work needed to assure a complete checkout and to track down trouble.

The crew chief should have authority to delay the opening of the house, if absolutely necessary, to complete checkout and repairs.

OUTAGES

Outage is the electrician's term for something going out unexpectedly. Usually it will be a lamp, but it may also be a circuit or even the entire system.

Lamp Outages

If a lamp outage is found during the checkout the lamp should be immediately replaced and the instrument rechecked completely for angle, focus, gel, and, if it is an ellipsoidal spot, alignment. Remember to disconnect any instrument before inserting a new lamp.

Lamps may also go out during the progress of the production. The crew may see a bluish-white flash of light as the filament breaks; sometimes a temporary short will occur. Since such shorts within lamps clear themselves, it is possible to restore the circuit immediately by resetting the breaker. If there are other instruments on the circuit with the blown lamp, the dimmer controlling the circuit should be taken to zero, the circuit restored, and the dimmer sneaked back to its original setting. As this is being done, the crew should try to bring up other instruments to cover the area darkened by the outage. Such crises test the crew's knowledge of the light plot and the hookup.

Insert a new lamp into the fixture as soon as possible. Sometimes this can be done immediately, or it may be necessary to await an act break when you can bring a ladder on stage. If so, notify the stage manager at once so he can plan for the additional time needed. Be ready to act fast but efficiently. In other instances, the light will be so inaccessible that you will have to wait until after the performance to do the job. In this case it may be possible to angle a spare instrument from some accessible location to the stage area lacking light. This will call for new circuiting and careful recuing. In still other cases you will have to get word to the cast that they must avoid a certain area until repairs are made.

Circuit Outages

The first problem is to distinguish circuit from lamp outages. If several lamps go out at once, odds are that the circuit has gone out. However, if one lamp of a group on the same circuit goes out and the rest remain on, the trouble must be in the instrument, its lamp, or its cable. Since lamps are the most common source of failure, these are usually checked first, but it may be worth doing a little thinking first. Was a repatch about to be performed? If so, perhaps the wrong plug was pulled. If it can be established that the lamp is functioning and that the fuse or breaker supplying the circuit is working, examine connections, particularly those in portable wiring leading to the nonworking instruments. Loose plugs or loose wiring in plugs often cause outages.

If a fuse blows or a breaker opens, there must be a good reason. These devices do not give false signals. The usual causes are shorts or overloads (see Chapter 24, "Electricity and Electrical Safety"). Shorts manifest themselves via smoke, sparks, etc. Overloads can be sneaky; particularly if the overload is slight, the breaker or fuse may last a long time.

Outages caused by dimmer faults are beyond the scope of a lighting crew as far as repairs are concerned. However you should know how to repatch to another dimmer or dimmers to get the lighting back into operation.

SMOKE AND FIRE

Occasionally you will hear, usually from a panic-stricken voice on a telephone, that something electrical is smoking or perhaps even glowing and burning. You have to think fast and try to get information in a hurry. Is it a gelatin in front of a lamp? Is anything else also smoking? If not, sooth the panicked person and tell him you will take care of it. Assure him that a gel with a hole burning in the middle of it is usually harmless. In most cases it indicates a lamp out of alignment in an ellipsoidal reflector spotlight. If you can determine which instrument has the trouble, you can dim it down a few points, which will alleviate the problem and also adjust for the light spilling through the hole in the gelatin.

A more serious problem is fire reported in the wiring or in a connector. The stage manager should be notified immediately and a crew member sent to determine if anything else is apt to catch fire. He should carry a fire extinguisher capable of handling electrical fires (CO_2 or dry powder). Power to the offending circuit should be either cut off completely or reduced, depending on the seriousness of the report and the importance of the circuit to the production. In any event the crew should be prepared for the imminent failure of the circuit and ready covering lighting. They should also be prepared to turn on the house lights if the stage manager decides that the problem is sufficiently serious to justify stopping the show. Supervisors should be notified as soon as possible.

AFTER THE PRODUCTION

It is seldom that a lighting crew will simply walk out of the theatre at the end of the last performance, leaving the equipment where they installed it. Some kind of a strike will be necessary. In some theatres it is the practice to remove all lighting equipment to storage between shows, leaving only work lighting. In others, a large share of the equipment will remain in position because there will be immediate use for it, or there is nowhere to store it. In any event, the crew will have to remove all specials, all equipment mounted on the setting or on the stage floor, and all temporary hookups to battens. Gels and auxiliary equipment will also be removed. If gelatin has been used, it will probably be faded and should be discarded. If plastic medium was installed, it may be returned to storage for future use.

Any instruments or cables that display faults should be held out of storage and directed to the electrical repair shop. An indication of what is wrong will aid the repairman.

Many theatres that operate a continuous schedule of events on the stage will have established a standard pattern of area lighting to be maintained between major productions. It will usually be a straight-forward six- or ten-area arrangement. Since such a pattern may also appear as part of a major production, it may remain at the end of the run requiring only minor adjustments and regelling to restore it. If not, the crew may have to hang, circuit, focus, and gel this pattern as part of the strike.

CRITIQUES

There are two kinds of critiques, those conducted by the crew themselves and those offered by others. It may be advantageous for the crew to meet a few days after the production has closed to consider what they did and how it came out. They should try to identify both the successes and the failures. In fact, it will probably be more profitable to examine why certain things worked well than to dwell on why others did not. If, for example, a certain sequence of lighting cues seemed to go smoothly every time in spite of their complexity, what made this happen?

It will be worth discussing how the crew felt their work related to the production as a whole. This will be particularly valuable if they were able to see the production night after night from a lighting booth. Was there a sense of the rhythm of the production evident in the lighting booth? Was concentration present at the time and to the degree necessary? What could have been done to make the lighting still more effective?

Most lighting crews will not suffer from a lack of external critical comment. Actors, classmates who were in the audience, stagehands, and student newspaper critics are all generous with their remarks. Unfortunately most of these will center on the most obvious blunders that have occurred—equipment failures, backstage and cast failures. Only rarely will such uninformed critics be aware of the subtleties of good lighting.

There is another category of critique to which the crew should listen with interest. These are the experienced students who have themselves operated many shows, the supervisors, and the various designers and scenographers who have seen the show. Of course there will also be the critical comments from the show's scenographer and the lighting supervisor. These are all important, but they are of a different nature—they come from those deeply involved in the production. Their best judgments may come three months after the show has closed.

Theatre is an art, a vastly complicated way of creating symbols which may enable us to penetrate to new insights into the human condition. Although the curtain comes down every night, this task is never finished.

PART EIGHT

SCENIC PROJECTION

Scenic projection designed by Annelies Corrodi.
Photograph by Elisabeth von Winterfeld.

INTRODUCTION

Scenic projection may be defined as any process that results in an image composed of light for use in the theatre. Thus it includes shadow projection, lens projection, such exotic phenomena as interference patterns produced by laser light, and images reconstructed from holograms. We will examine these forms later, but first we must determine how scenic projection relates to the work of the scenographer.

PROJECTION AND SCENOGRAPHY

In Chapter 21, "Scene Painting," we discussed the special fixed-on-a-surface quality of painted images in contrast to the images that can be created by arranging light beams. Scenic projection extends the scenographer's image-making ability, freeing him from the necessity of considering surfaces and images as interrelated. Not only can projected images be separated from their surfaces, they can move, blend, flow in and out of focus, change in size or perspective, and even exist in space with no surface at all. Of course, all of these possibilities are neither better nor worse than the potentialities of the painted image—they are merely different avenues of expression open to the scenographer as he goes about his symbolic transformation from master symbol to produced play.

SPACE-TIME AND SCENIC PROJECTION

Space-time is a difficult concept in the abstract. The potentialities of scenic projection as outlined below should make the concept concrete and illustrate the almost incredible flexibility of projected images. Consider this list of recent uses of projection techniques in the theatre:

1. A live television image of a character, magnified and in distorted perspective, was projected onto and surrounded the character himself.
2. Motion picture images of dancers were projected onto an elastic projection surface which was being moved in such a manner as to distort the images in a carefully designed time pattern. The images sometimes forecast what was going to be danced on stage; at other times they paralleled the action in

magnified and distorted perspective; at still other times they recalled action just past.

3. Images were suspended in space by being projected onto multiple layers of otherwise almost invisible gauze.

4. Images were projected onto multiple layers of scrim which also carried painted images. Thus part of the image seen by the audience was permanent, and other parts varied as the projections were cross-faded.

5. Laser interference patterns were projected onto a cyclorama and onto the bodies of moving dancers. Since such images are in focus at every point, but different in every plane, the effect was that of space filled with infinitely variable images, all of which had the special granular vibrant quality of coherent light.

6. Images were projected toward the audience by means of motion picture apparatus through a cloud of smoke. This created a 3-D image in space which included the members of the audience.

Such manipulations of space and time, particularly those in which two or more aspects of the virtual time of the production are presented at once along with multiple perspectives and magnification of the images, bring space-time into sharp focus. The theatrical potentialities of such expression have only been touched upon. These techniques represent new "tools" available to playwrights and theatrical artists who have yet to find dramatic purposes for them.

HISTORY

In spite of the newness of some of the techniques listed above, the use of projection is not really new to the theatre. Some shadow projection and lens projection devices go back into theatrical history for centuries. In the latter part of the nineteenth century there was great interest in the use of projection techniques for the production of spectacular theatrical effects which were much in mode at that time. For example, sophisticated lens systems and moving effects were developed for the production of Wagnerian operas, particularly at the Wagner Festspielhaus in Bayreuth, Germany. Some of these devices and the slides used in them are still to be seen there. They remain technically sophisticated even by today's standards. Thus the recent surge of interest in projection is only another high point in the rather long history of scenic projection.

Some of the modern developments in scenic projection—real breakthroughs that solve heretofore crippling difficulties—are technologically very sophisticated. They involve the crafts of the lighting specialist, the special technology of high power lamp systems, complicated electronic circuitry, and optical theory. Such things must be noted as important developments which will inevitably have great influence on theatre as it grows, but they cannot be treated fully in this text. However, there are numerous less complicated aspects of scenic projection that lend themselves to experimentation by the beginner. Much can be learned about projection without involving oneself in complicated technology and working with potentially dangerous equipment. These techniques can also be done at reasonable cost, something not possible in most of the state-of-the-art developments. In the following chapters some of these techniques and the equipment that goes with them will be discussed.

29
PROJECTION USING CONVENTIONAL OPTICAL SYSTEMS

INTRODUCTION   Compared to projection in a movie theatre or projection of slides in a classroom, theatrical scenic projection (see examples in Figure 29-1) must work against severe handicaps. Almost invariably, theatrical projection must work on a stage filled with acting area and set lighting. There is seldom the carefully prescribed throw which allows the projector to operate at an optimum distance from the screen with the line of projection at right angles to the plane of the screen. Finally, the "screen" is almost never a highly efficient specially prepared surface such as that found in a movie theatre.

Since the only way that scenic projection can be effective in the theatre is to be bright enough to compete with the rest of the lighting, scenic projectors must be made to produce very bright pictures. Recent developments in exotic light sources (such as xenon and HMI) and highly efficient lenses have for the first time made possible the production of images bright enough to compete with stage lighting without compromise. If projectors are to satisfy the needs of theatre applications, they must not only be efficient, but operate quietly, work safely, and be capable of remote control, including dimming. Such projectors are, even today, almost impossible to produce. Those that are available are exceedingly costly, bulky, and sensitive machines which utilize exotic light sources such as xenon or HMI (not necessarily safe to handle), and are capable of being dimmed only by special mechanical equipment (see also Chapter 25).

Fortunately for the beginning scenographer, not all theatrical demands for projection are so stringent that they need such highly sophisticated and costly equipment. Given some understanding of the limitations and some willingness to adjust the staging to accommodate projection, much can be done with lesser equipment.

In general, there are four methods of

Figure 29-1. Some Examples of Scenic Projection. In addition to the many illustrations involving scenic projection scattered throughout this text and the several in the color sections, the following examples are offered. (a) Projection with live television. Careful examination of the projected background reveals that it is composed of a live image of the performer at the piano. This image has been electronically combined with a number of videotape images of the same person. The effect is a strange telescoping of dramatic time. This photograph is taken from the first program of Laterna Magica, *a special display of projection effects, produced at Expo 58 in Brussels. It was designed by the late Alfred Radok. Photograph by Dr. Jarimir Svoboda; courtesy Josef Svoboda. (b) Projection as total background. This model and rendering for projections was designed by Analies Corrodi for Verdi's* Macbeth. *The projections vary and are superimposed to change the setting. Photograph by Hoffman; courtesy Analies Corrodi. (c) Multiple Projections. This production photo of* I and Albert, *book by Jay Allen, music by Charles Strauss, illustrates the use of multiple projections in a musical. At various times these projection surfaces were filled with separate images, at others, such as the scene shown, the slides were designed to blend into a single image. The production was directed by John Schlesinger, lighting by Robert Orubo. The projections were designed by Luciana Arrighi. Photograph courtesy Richard Pilbrow, Theatre Projects, London.*

FIGURE 29-1b

FIGURE 29-1c

producing useful images by scenic projection. The first two are common and can be used by the scenographer of limited means and experience. The last two (discussed in Chapter 30) are more unusual, but can occasionally be utilized by the informed and cautious experimenter. These are the systems:

1. Square law projection (shadow projection)
2. Lens projection
3. "Images" produced by the optical phenomenon known as "interference"
4. Images produced by holographic processes

SQUARE LAW PROJECTION

The principle of this process is well known: light travels in straight lines over reasonably short distances and radiates from a point source in an ever-increasing sphere. Anyone who has played shadow games with a tiny light source such as a flashlight, knows the tremendous magnification that can be achieved by placing an object near such a source and observing the results in a darkened room. If the source is small enough, the most minute detail can be magnified greatly. Furthermore, this magnification takes place in short distances because of the divergence of the light according to the square law. Unfortunately this same divergence also causes the brightness of the image to decrease with the square of the distance.

A square law projector for theatrical use is a simple device. All that is needed is a source of small size and great power, an enclosure to control the radiating light, and the image-producing material. The first square law projector in our modern era was known as the Linnebach projector after its inventor, August Linnebach. Linnebach projectors are still available today from theatrical supply houses. They are large, unwieldy devices utilizing spotlight service lamps. Because the filament size of such lamps is large, the slides for Linnebach projectors must also be large if the picture is to be at all sharp. The result is an awkward piece of equipment (see Figure 29-2). Such projectors can produce images of reasonable brightness, but the picture is almost invariably fuzzy. Practically, commercially made Linnebach projectors are limited to rather simple designs, mostly silhouettes.

An examination of catalogues to find lamps for use in square law projection can produce quite a list of potentially useful lamps if one is willing to sacrifice some brightness in favor of a sharper image. Since a sharper image tends to appear brighter than a fuzzy image of the same real brightness, this is a practical trade-off if not carried too far. Furthermore, if source size can be kept small, the same or better sharpness can be achieved with smaller slides, thereby reducing the bulk of the apparatus. (See Figure 29-3.) Note how the size of the source determines the size of the blurred area at the edge of sharply defined areas on the slide. Once throw distance is fixed, sharpness will be determined by the combined action of source size and distance from slide to source. Decreasing the size of the source or placing the slide at greater distance from the source will increase sharpness. Obviously, if the slide is to be farther from the source but the image remain the same size, the slide size will have to be increased. Also note that the image brightness is determined by the distance from source to screen and by source brightness. Location and size of the slide do not enter into the determination as such, although a muddy, near opaque slide will reduce picture quality, and a clear, sharply outlined slide will improve it.

LAMPS FOR SQUARE LAW PROJECTION

Although regular spotlight service lamps often are used for Linnebach projectors, other lamps are available which will produce better results within their power range.

Motion picture projection service lamps are highly concentrated filament lamps designed for use under forced ventilation in 8 and 16 mm motion picture or in slide projectors. If such lamps are provided with a well-ventilated housing, they can be operated without forced

Figure 29-2. Large Linnebach Projector. Photograph courtesy Kliegl Brothers.

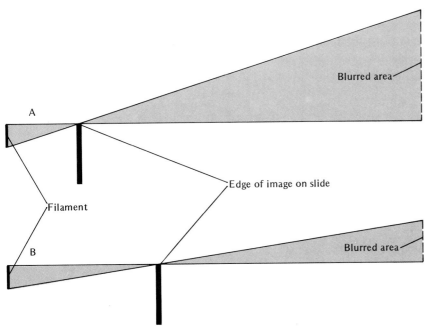

Figure 29-3. Image Sharpness in Square Law Projection. Drawing A shows an exaggerated situation that illustrates how the filament-to-slide distance determines image sharpness. Note how light from separate points on the filament will strike the screen at different locations, blurring the edge of the shadow image. (If the filament were a true point this could not happen.) Drawing B shows the effect of increasing the filament-to-slide distance. Sharpness is improved. Unless the size of the slide is correspondingly increased, the image size will be smaller. Decreasing the size of the filament will also improve sharpness, but small powerful filaments are difficult to get.

ventilation. The compact filament will produce sharper images than spotlight service lamps. Lamp life will be somewhat shorter than that expected from spotlight lamps.

Low voltage lamps are designed for automotive spotlight service and for marine applications. They have very small highly concentrated filaments which are much more rugged than their high voltage counterparts. Most of them are rated at 6 or 12 V. Instead of wattage ratings, they may be rated in candlepower, a figure not very useful to the stage technician. Current will either have to be measured or a more detailed lamp catalogue consulted to determine the rated current of each lamp being considered. For projection service these low voltage lamps may be operated considerably over rated voltage to produce much more light at a higher color temperature. This practice will shorten lamp life. However, these lamps have very long life ratings to begin with and are cheap to replace. The increased efficiency is well worth the reduced life. Note that the now common "sealed beam" lamps are of no use for scenic projection. Low voltage lamps with conventional bulbs are needed.

High-efficiency T-H lamps are made for photographic service. They have short life ratings and very high efficiency. They come in a wide variety of types of filament configurations, most of which are compact enough for square law projection. Consult a lamp manufacturer's catalogue of photo service lamps.

HOMEMADE SQUARE LAW PROJECTORS

Once the principles governing sharpness are clearly understood (a process best accomplished by experimenting on stage with some small lamps and slide materials), the planning and construction of square law projectors for specific stage uses are quite simple. The basics are to be found in Figures 29-3 and 29-4. Note that the most basic question to be answered is scenographic: Where is the image to be seen and how big should it be? The next question concerns both scenography and technology: Where can the projector be located? This will be determined by the necessities of stage design, the size of the device, its heat output, and the possibility that it may need attention during the production. Of course these are really interlocking questions. Location of the projector will be easier if it can be small, low in heat output, and if it does not require an operator. In practice, two or more small projectors, each equipped with a single slide and an efficient low-heat-output lamp, and run in sequence to avoid using an operator, may serve the show's needs better than one more complicated device.

Once the light source and the image have been located in scale on a plan and elevation of the setting, projection lines are drawn, and the actual design of the projector can be worked out. Since the enclosures of such projectors are cheap and easy to build, they are often

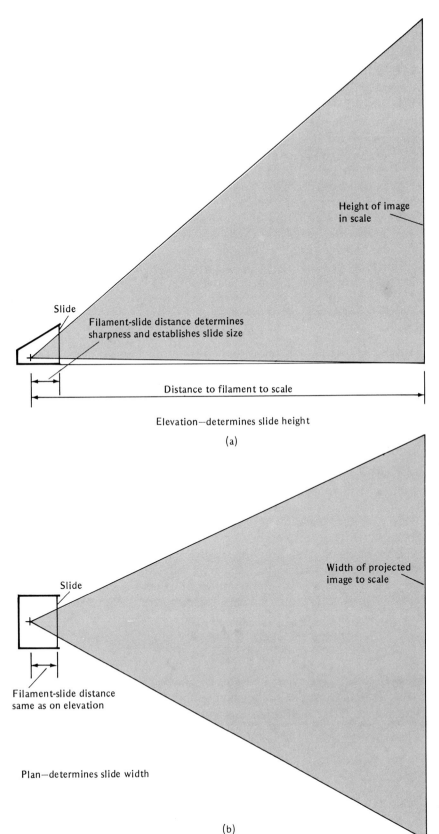

Height of image
in scale

Slide

**Filament-slide distance determines
sharpness and establishes slide size**

Distance to filament to scale

Elevation—determines slide height

(a)

Slide

Width of projected
image to scale

Filament-slide distance
same as on elevation

Plan—determines slide width

(b)

*Figure 29-4. Custom Designing Square Law Pro-
jectors. This sample set of elevation (a) and plan
(b) scale drawings illustrates the principle. Be
sure that all drawings are done to the same scale.
The establishment of the slide-to-filament distance will be dependent on the amount of image
blur that can be tolerated (see Figure 28-3). Make
slide larger than minimum size derived from these
drawings.*

SQUARE LAW PROJECTION   547

custom built for each show. Lamp bases, electrical apparatus, and the like are retained for repeated use. It is a good idea to make the enclosure slightly oversized to allow for last-minute adjustments in projector location. Making the lamp mount movable is also helpful in this regard. If the enclosure is made of wood, it should be carefully lined with asbestos and provided with ventilation. A simple sheet metal enclosure will be safer, but surrounding objects may need protection from heat.

Experimenters should note that the slide need not necessarily be physically attached to the lamp enclosure. As long as it intercepts the cone of light emanating from the housing, it may be placed anywhere between the lamp and the screen. This makes possible the use of multiple slides whose sharpness will vary in direct ratio to their distance from the lamp, creating an illusion of depth in the image because the fuzzier parts will appear to be in the distance. It also makes possible movement of parts of the image, color changes, alteration of some parts of the image in relationship to the rest, or any other manipulations which the ingenious scenographer can contrive.

Powering Low Voltage Lamps

Although the mechanics of constructing small square law projectors are quite simple, the electrical circuitry is more complex. It is assumed that the projector or projectors must be dimmed to allow cross-fading from one image to another. Low voltage lamps draw relatively large amounts of current that could be supplied by batteries as they are in an automobile. If so, resistance devices can be used as dimmers. This method is hazardous (because batteries large enough to power such lamps can produce dangerous short-circuit currents and cause fire) and removes the possibility of using regular theatrical lighting controls.

A better arrangement is to supply current to the lamps by means of step-down transformers, one per projector. These can be mounted near the projectors, eliminating need for long runs of heavy wire to handle large lamp currents. Such transformers tend to be expensive. They are available from large suppliers of electronic parts where they will be listed along with "filament transformers." There are also transformers on the market for operation of low voltage decorative outdoor lighting. These are expensive and do not offer the user the option of operating the lamps at increased voltage for greater efficiency. The ideal transformer is one that will produce about 15 V (assuming nominal 12 V lamps) at a current at least 1.5 times the rated current of the largest lamp likely to be used in projection.[1] Remember that lamps draw more current when operated at higher than rated voltage.

---

1. This can be worked out by following the example below:
    Assume a 12 V lamp which draws 10 Amp at rated voltage. It is planned to

TRANSFORMERS AND DIMMERS   Most transformers, unless they are of an expensive special design, will not operate satisfactorily on the output of electronic dimmers. They may not produce rated voltages and/or currents, may buzz or hum, and may overheat. For these reasons, the only practical dimmer for most home-built projectors is an autotransformer dimmer. If the control board is not so equipped, special dimmers will have to be supplied for the projector circuits. Fortunately autotransformer dimmers are often available secondhand at reasonable prices. They should, of course, be adequately protected against shorts by the proper fuse or breaker. Note that this will not necessarily protect the low voltage system from overloads, although a short circuit will usually be reflected back to the 120 V system sufficiently to open the fuse or breaker. If the step-down transformer is considerably oversize for the low voltage circuit and can thus provide a large overload current if one is demanded, a fuse should also be installed in the low voltage system.

Step-down transformers are rather heavy devices that give off some hum and a little heat. They are best mounted close to but not in the square law projector. They should be provided with either a totally insulated enclosure or with a grounded metal enclosure to protect workers from contact with the high voltage connections.

The 120 V Square Law Projectors

The above discussion should make it clear that there are considerable advantages in choosing a 120 V compact filament T-H lamp for the projector if the filament size can be tolerated. This eliminates all transformer and dimmer problems. Unfortunately the smallest filaments are still to be found among the low voltage lamps. Transformers and special dimmers will often be necessary.

HIGH-POWERED SQUARE LAW PROJECTORS

Although not for the beginner, light sources do exist which can provide square law projection of incredible power. These are the short-arc

---

operate the lamp at 15 V. What is the minimum rating for a transformer to safely carry this current?

Ohms law:	$E = I \times R$
(Substituting)	$12 = 10 \times R$
	$R = 1.2$ Ohms
(Substitute new voltage)	$15 = I \times 1.2$
	$I = 12.5$ Amp

The transformer must have a continuous rating of at least 12.5 Amps or 187.5 V-Amps (12.5×15). A 15 V, 200 V-Amp transformer would do.

lamps such as the xenon and HMI lamps discussed briefly in Chapter 25, "Producing and Using Light on the Stage." The xenon lamp has the greatest brilliance within a very small source size. Therefore, it is the very best source for square law projection. A single 4800 W xenon lamp was used to produce projections over the entire cyclorama in the Wagner Festspielhaus at Bayreuth, Germany. The projections were sufficiently bright to overcome full stage lighting.

The problems with xenon lamps have been outlined in Part Seven, "Lighting." Briefly, these lamps are explosive, produce dangerous ultraviolet radiation, and generate poisonous ozone gas. Safety regulations, both in the United States and in Germany, have now made the simple half-cylinder projectors sketched in Figure 29-5 illegal if they contain xenon lamps.

The HMI lamp seems to promise at least a partial solution to the difficulties of the xenon lamp. It is two to three times more efficient than the xenon lamp and has few of the other risks. The drawback for square law projection is that the HMI source size is considerably larger than the xenon and is not symmetrical. In a 4800 W HMI lamp the arc is 35 mm long and about one-sixth as wide. This shape will cause sharpness in square law projection to vary with direction. Lines at right angles to the longer arc dimension will be considerably blurred; those

Figure 29-5. Cylindrical Square Law Projector. This projector is based on the same optical principles as that in Figure 28-4, but is designed for approximately 180 degree projection. Distortion is prevented by keeping the slide and the projection surface parallel to each other or as nearly so as possible. The ideal source for such projectors is a xenon lamp, but current safety rules make it difficult to design a safe projector using this lamp. The same design may be used quite successfully in small theatres by installing a low-voltage small filament incandescent lamp in the cylindrical unit. It is interesting to note that German manufacturers make a cloud projector that produces moving cloud images by rotating a full cylinder around a concentrated source.

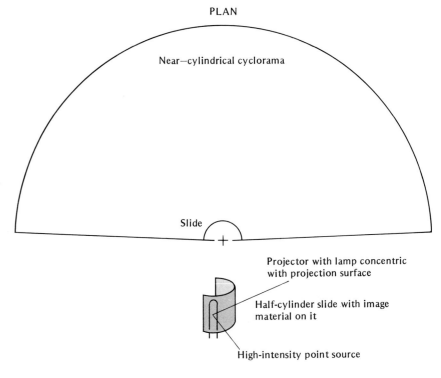

PLAN

Near—cylindrical cyclorama

Slide

Projector with lamp concentric with projection surface

Half-cylinder slide with image material on it

High-intensity point source

parallel to it will be much sharper. Color temperature of both xenon and HMI lamps is high, making projection of blue images efficient. The xenon lamp may be dimmed to about 10 percent of brightness with no change in color temperature. At lesser settings it goes out and must be restarted. The HMI lamp cannot be dimmed appreciably by electrical means.

SQUARE LAW PROJECTION WITHOUT PROJECTORS

One technique is so simple that it is often overlooked. It consists of placing objects in front of directional lighting apparatus in such a way that the shadows produced form a design. In some cases, the objects may also form part of the stage design; in other cases, only their shadows will be seen by the audience. A good way for experimenters to begin investigating this sort of projection is to remove the lens and reflector from a standard Fresnel lens spotlight. This leaves a well-ventilated lamp house that produces an adjustable wide angle cone of light. Any object placed in the cone of light at some distance from the lamp will produce a relatively sharp-edged shadow. If two or more instruments are arranged at a distance from each other so that their cones of light overlap, and they are equipped with gels of varying colors, the shadow patterns will be multiplied, and their color will vary with the additive result of the overlapping beams. These can be exceedingly useful to the scenographer. Those wanting the sharpest shadows from this type of projection will find that substituting a projection service lamp for the spotlight service lamp may improve resolution.

LENS PROJECTION

The key element in lens projection is a positive (magnifying) lens so mounted that it picks up the light passing through the slide and organizes that light as an image. Thus lens projection does not depend on the simple geometry of light radiation to determine image size. Sharpness does not depend on source size, but instead on the quality of the lens used and the general design of the optical system. Brightness of image, while ultimately dependent on the geometry of the square law, is no longer directly dependent on source-screen distance. Thus, lens projection is a much more flexible method of producing images. It can, under ideal conditions, be quite efficient. Its greatest advantage lies in the fact that brightness of the image is not limited by the need for very small source size, and the optical qualities of lenses add many new possibilities to the manipulation of images. In summary, lens projection is a more flexible, usually more powerful way of producing very sharp images with a wide range of variability.

PARTS OF A LENS PROJECTOR

The lens projector may be subdivided into a lamp house, light collection apparatus, the aperture and slide holder, and the objective lens system (Figure 29-6). It is necessary to examine each of these in some detail as they are found in theatrical projectors.

Lamp House

Since high power is the first consideration in most theatrical projectors, the lamp house is one of the most important parts. If incandescent lamps are used, they will normally be the highest-efficiency lamps available in the size rating designed for the housing. If the lamp is a conventional type, chances are it will be operated over its rated voltage to increase efficiency and color temperature at the expense of lamp life. If it is a T-H lamp, it will be chosen to have high output, high color temperature, and the short life will be tolerated. Note that such T-H lamps are seldom operated at overvoltage since they have the effects of overvoltage operation already designed into them.

Housings for incandescent lamps are almost invariably equipped with fans to remove waste heat. These are often noisy, but they are necessary to the operation of the equipment.

Many modern scenic projectors are being equipped with xenon or HMI lamps. If a xenon lamp is used, special safety precautions must be taken, both out of prudence, and to satisfy safety laws. The housing containing a xenon lamp must be light tight, ventilated to remove dangerous ozone, and capable of withstanding the explosive force of the largest lamp for which the housing is rated; it must also have a special lock to prevent the unwary from opening the housing. It must carry a warning against opening the housing until the lamp inside has cooled sufficiently to avoid danger of explosion from sudden temperature change.

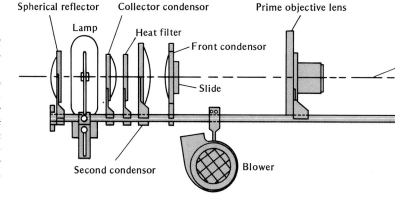

Figure 29-6. Working Parts of a Typical Scenic Projector. A typical arrangement of the main optical parts of a scenic projector. A blower is shown in position to cool the slide. Supplementary lenses often are added to the prime objective lens. The distance between the slide and the front condenser frequently varies greatly from this illustration. The mounting of all optical parts on heavy rods, approximating an optical bench, is a good practice. Courtesy of Universal Screen Company.

Although precautions for HMI lamps have not been completely formulated, it is obvious that they should be much more lenient than those for xenon lamps. However, it is necessary to protect operators against unfiltered light from HMI lamps. A single layer of glass (a lens, for example) will do this.

Collecting the Light

Collection begins with the installation of a reflector behind the lamp to gather light and direct it toward the aperture. Either spherical or ellipsoidal reflectors are used for this purpose, depending on the design of the projector. Since the collection system must converge the light first into the aperture and then into the still smaller rear element of the objective system, it is always necessary to install condenser lenses, usually plano-convex lenses of spotlight quality which are placed between the lamp and the aperture. Their location must be adjustable because slide size, distance to the back element of the objective, and the size of the rear element of the objective are all variable. In some commercially built projectors, condensers are supplied in sets to be used with specific objectives as a package. In other more flexible machines, the condensers are completely variable along an extension of the optical bench arrangement that forms the mechanical foundation of the entire projector. (An optical bench is a heavy, accurately machined metal bar on which optical devices are mounted to keep them in alignment for precision work.) Whatever the mounting system, condenser lenses should be kept to the minimum number necessary to converge the light. Each lens will inevitably waste nearly 10 percent of the light passing through it unless it has been optically coated, a process far too expensive for condenser lenses.

Aperture

The aperture is the hole through which the light exits on the way to the objective lens. It contains whatever image material is to be projected. Perhaps half of the time this image material will be a painted or photographed slide of glass or plastic. The other half of the time the aperture may contain complicated devices for creating moving effects. Ordinary slides usually are mounted in the aperture to allow easy change between the times when the lamp is on. A simple pull-across slide changer can handle two slides at a time. Other systems may be devised to handle an almost unlimited number of slides. Operators should be wary of changing slides while the projector is on. The slightest jiggle will be greatly magnified.

Following are some possibilities for moving effects, most of which are available commercially as attachments for high-powered projectors. Many of them can be devised in the theatre shop:

1. Fire effect. In its crudest form this consists of a rotating disk of glass (or plastic) on which flamelike dabs of paint have been applied (see Figure 29-7). As the disk rotates in the aperture, "flames" are projected. These will always follow the arc motion of the disk and will repeat frequently, giving a mechanical effect. A better fire effect is made by passing an endless band of film through the aperture so that one plane of the film is in sharp focus and the other somewhat out of focus. If the band is long enough, and the splice well made, a quite realistic effect may be achieved.
2. Water ripple. This is done by slowing moving two or three pieces of glass up and down in relationship to each other. Each is painted with wavy lines. The entire moving element is "seen" by the lens through a piece of irregular glass such as that sometimes used in shower doors. If the lens is thrown slightly out of focus the effect is realistic.
3. "Rain." Streaks of color intermingled with dark paint may be painted on the disk mentioned above to suggest rain. This should be run faster than the fire effect. The endless band may also be used.
4. Polarized light effect. The basis of this effect is two disks of polarizing film, one stationary, and the other rotating. The

Figure 29-7. A Scioptican. This relatively crude moving image device consists of a motor-driven glass disk in which a variety of images may be painted. Clouds are shown here, but this device may also be used to simulate flames. Speed is variable. Unit is shown without the objective lens that fits into the slots in front of the revolving disks.

image material is placed between them either as a stationary or a moving element. It may be made up of any material which is transparent, and has the property of influencing the polarization of light passing through it. For example, crumpled cellophane may be glued to glass to make up a random slide. As the polarizing disk rotates, a startling variety of images in varying colors will be projected. Ingenious scenographers will find hundreds of variations.

5. Crawls. A crawl is an extremely steady, variable speed drive used to move a variety of effects across the aperture area either vertically or horizontally. For example, a field of clouds can be moved slowly across a "sky," or a moon or stars can move to indicate passage of time. Either endless bands or simple rolls of film may be used.

These effects represent only a few of the many things which can be done with lens projectors. The experimenter will note that the same piece of film or the same slide may serve many purposes, depending on the focus of the lens, the angle of projection, and what other images and/or lighting effects are mixed on the "screen."

EFFECTS DRIVES   All of the effects devices listed above require some type of mechanism to move the image material. Because of the great magnification involved in scenic projection such drives must be extremely steady. Any jiggle or variation in speed will be magnified to the same extent that the image itself is magnified, and thus prove distracting to the audience. Fortunately there are available at surplus stores a number of low-speed motors which can serve as the basis of such drives. The experimenter will need access to a small machine lathe, a drill press, and metal-working equipment such as taps and dies, files, grinders, and the like. With these tools he will be able to fabricate parts for a wide variety of drive mechanisms. Even without such equipment a number of devices may be constructed using simple woodworking and metal-working techniques and belt drives instead of gears. These will not be as steady, but will serve many purposes.

Objective Lens System

The objective lens system can easily be the most expensive and delicate part of the entire projection system. It should be optically efficient, which means that a minimum of light should be lost in passage through the lens. It should have adjustable focus over a wide range, and capable of handling great quantities of light and heat energy without damage.

Generally speaking, short focal length objective lenses will be needed. However, provision should be made for altering the focal length of the objective system because throw distances and magnification will vary over a wide range. Some commercially made scenic projectors try to achieve this flexibility by providing sets of exchangeable objectives and condensers. Each set is designed to fit a range of throw distance and image size needs. Other projectors are fitted with an optical bench arrangement where a number of lens elements may be mounted to fit whatever needs come up. The latter is probably the best arrangement (see Figure 29-8). Experimenters with homemade projectors will be well advised to adopt the optical bench approach because it is by far the most flexible when working with a wide variety of lenses.

Objective lenses purchased for scenic projection work should have high efficiency. This means that they should have low "f" numbers. (The "f" of a lens is determined by dividing its focal length by its effective diameter.) Lenses with ratings of f 4.5 or less will be reasonably useful.

Those experimenting with lens projection will usually find that they have no objective lens available that will produce exactly the degree of magnification needed for the throw required. Sometimes slide size can be modified to adjust for this. A better solution may be to adjust the focal length of the objective lens by adding an auxiliary lens. This can be a simple plano-convex lens of spotlight quality if no better lens is available. Naturally this lens will degrade the image quality somewhat, but it will usually repay this loss with flexibility. The usual procedure in planning for an auxiliary lens is to begin with the first objective lens available whose focal length is *longer* than that needed. This means that the lens will produce too small an image.

Figure 29-8. Optical Bench Lens Holder for Projection. This is part of a commercially manufactured projector (no longer available), but the same system may be adopted by those building their own projectors. Photograph courtesy Background Engineering.

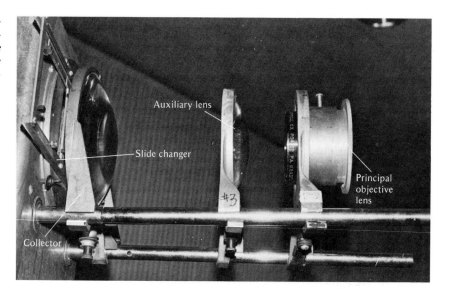

Set up the projection situation either on stage or in an area where the image may be magnified to full scale at proper distance. Focus the image sharply, and then move the objective lens slightly toward the slide producing a blurry but larger image. Experiment with plano-convex lenses (from ellipsoidal reflector spotlights or other sources) by placing the auxiliary lens between the regular objective and the slide, and moving it toward or away from the objective lens. A little experimentation will often find a location for the lens which will produce the image size wanted and a sharp focus. Both lenses may have to be moved. If no combination seems to work, try an auxiliary lens of different focal length. Actually all of these experimental adjustments may be calculated if one is willing to go to the trouble. Consult a book on optics for the necessary formulas if you wish to do this.

Once a satisfactory auxiliary lens has been found and approximately located, it must be mounted in the lens system. The easiest way to do this will be found in those projectors on which all lenses are carried on a solid bar or bars (an optical benchlike arrangement). In this case, a mount is devised for the auxiliary lens, and it too is mounted on the bars. The entire lens assembly will constitute a crude but effective "zoom lens" capable of considerable adjustment in focal length. It will probably serve a number of similar projection situations.

COLLECTORS Experimenters will often find that they cannot converge all of the light passing through the slide into the rear element of the objective lens, even with the help of an auxiliary lens. Whatever light misses the back of the objective is not only lost to the image, but will pass directly to the screen, degrading the image being formed. A shield may be devised to cut off such light. If a plano-convex lens of diameter sufficient to match the diagonal of the slide is available, it may be mounted flat side toward the slide, just in front of the slide. It will have only slight effect on the focal length of the objective system in this location, but will serve to converge the light from the slide into the rear element of the objective. It will, of course, exact a toll of about 10 percent of the light, but this may be far less than the amount of light lost otherwise. The collector may be moved slightly to aid in converging the light.

HOMEMADE LENS PROJECTORS

Given the information above, time, and ingenuity, an experimenter can devise a useful lens projection system for theatrical use. He will probably utilize an existing spotlight housing for a lamp house and fit additional condensers as needed to converge the light on the aperture. Some sort of optical benchlike mounting bar for lenses and aperture apparatus will be desirable. The projector in Figure 29-8 was professionally made, but it illustrates these simple principles well.

PROFESSIONALLY MADE LENS PROJECTORS

Although they are all expensive devices, often beyond the budget of experimenters, there are several projectors on the market designed specifically for theatrical use. Most of these machines may also be equipped with a variety of aperture devices that rotate the image material, allow use of bands of film carrying images, or provide special effects such as fire, rain, underwater ripples, etc. The special effects devices are almost always extra equipment not included in the base price of the projector. Therefore a scenic projector equipped with a reasonably adequate set of lenses (objectives and condensers), with a powerful lamp (lamps are always extra), and several effects devices may cost several thousand dollars. Moreover, at least two projectors will be needed if any cross-fades are to be used.

AUDIOVISUAL LENS PROJECTORS IN THE THEATRE— OVERHEAD PROJECTORS

Two types of commercial audiovisual projectors have been widely and successfully adapted to theatrical uses. These are the overhead projector and the 2 by 2 inch (35 mm) slide projector. The overhead projector is a classroom instrument designed to produce rather bright images at

Figure 29-9. Projection on the Operatic Stage. This production photo shows Lucia Di Lammermoor (Donizetti) *as designed by Analies Corrodi. The foreground, including the curved railing, is three dimensional; the remainder is projected. Courtesy Analies Corrodi. Photograph by Elizabeth von Winterfeld.*

short throws. It is equipped with a horizontal aperture area where a wide variety of image material may be placed. Audiovisual supply houses carry a large line of materials for use in preparing image material, plus a line of already prepared slides. Since images can be built up a layer at a time by laying transparencies on the projector aperture, variations in image are easy to make. The lens can be focused over a considerable throw distance which can be extended somewhat by relocating the lens in its holder.

Perhaps the greatest difficulty in the use of overhead projectors is that they produce quite a bit of spill light. They may also be noisy and too bulky for some applications.

Probably the most widespread theatrical use of overhead projectors was in the now outdated display of liquid projections in discotheques. Containers holding colored oils and water were placed in these projectors and moved in rhythm to music. The results were abstract, ever-changing images of the blobs of colored oil in water. This made an interesting but now overused effect. Other experimentation is possible. For example, an arrangement of counterrotating disks mounted at the aperture and provided with intersecting radial or spiral slits can produce a variety of flying spots on the screen that imitate fireworks, flying space ships, or whatever the imagination can conjure up.

The 2 by 2 Inch Slide Projectors (35 mm)

The 2 by 2 inch slide projector is a standard item in the audiovisual and home projection field. A number of brands have been highly developed, including the addition of special high power lamp houses for long throw, large screen projection. T-H lamps are standard and xenon lamps are not uncommon. One instrument, the Kodak Carousel, has been fitted with a line of auxiliary equipment, making it a flexible, powerful unit. This machine has been much used in small theatres, clubs, and similar locations. Used in multiples, it is quite capable of producing usable images.

This brings us to still another solution to the image brightness problem. Instead of one or two large projectors of high power, a considerably larger number of projectors of medium power may be used to get adequate image brightness. This will avoid loading almost impossible amounts of power into single housings, and imposing nearly impossible coverage requirements on lenses. Of course, one must pay for this subdivision of the image by designing images that will tolerate the degrading that vignetting together will inevitably cause. There are also some advantages that accrue. The most important is the possibility that one or more parts of the image may be changed by cross-fading to other slides in adjacent projectors. This offers the scenographer a flexibility not otherwise attainable. Figure 29-9 shows an image made by the multiple projector technique.

Probably the greatest difficulties to be encountered with Carousel projectors (or other similar types) is the noise made by the fans, the fact that lamp and fan are on the same circuit, and the lack of flexibility in lens and aperture. The solution to the first two problems is to rewire the projectors, bringing the fan feed out as a separate cord and plug. This need not be heavy wiring because the fans draw little current. Several fans can then be fed from a single line controlled by an autotransformer dimmer to reduce speed and noise. About 10 percent reduction in speed is usually possible if the projectors are operated in a reasonably well-ventilated space. This speed reduction will reduce noise greatly. The lamps, of course, will be fed from separate dimmer-controlled circuits if the projectors are to cross-fade independently of each other. Lamps should be inspected frequently when projectors are being operated with reduced fan speeds until the operator is assured that no overheating is occurring.

Lens problems can be solved only to the extent that special commercial lenses, including zoom lenses, can be used. If the scenographer is contemplating the use of moving aperture apparatus in 35 mm projectors, he may encounter difficulties. These machines have not been designed with this application in mind.

PROJECTION SURFACES

Obviously, if the image is to be projected on existing scenery or onto the figures of the actors, the image will have to be strong enough to be visible on whatever surface is available. However, in many cases the surfaces may be adjusted to facilitate projection. There are basically two types of projection surfaces: front and rear.

FRONT PROJECTION

Front projection commonly is used in most theatres because there is seldom enough space behind the setting to allow the throw necessary for rear projection. Moreover, front projection may be performed on any opaque object that has a reflective surface. For the purposes of good stage projection, any surface above middle gray will probably work well. Even darker surfaces can be used if lighting is adjusted to low readings. Of course the ideal surface for front projection will approximate a movie screen in efficiency. Unfortunately such a surface will catch almost every beam of spill light and make it painfully visible to the audience. Scenographers using such highly reflective surfaces should plan to have them constantly filled, either with images or with floods of color, to avoid this effect. The secret of good front projection on varied opaque surfaces is reasonably high reflectivity plus lots of power in the projectors.

Unless the scenographer wishes to have actor shadows be a part of the design, and to have parts of the front projection strike the actors and be seen on their bodies, there will inevitably be a "dead area" in front of the projection surface where actors may not go. The depth of this area will be determined by the projection angle. In many cases it may be 15–20 feet deep. Lighting angles will also have to be carefully calculated to minimize spill light or reflections from flat surfaces that might otherwise degrade the image to the point of uselessness.

REAR PROJECTION

Where possible, rear projection offers much flexibility to the scenographer and gives him several advantages over front projection. Perhaps the greatest advantage is that rear projection, if done with a properly designed screen, is less susceptible to high ambient light (too much acting area light) and to spills of light on the screen surface. The ambient light is controlled by designing the screen so that it allows light from the front to pass through and be absorbed by dark backgrounds behind the screen. The projected image passes through in the opposite direction to be seen by the audience. The great flexibility appears when one realizes that it is possible, under certain conditions, to utilize front and rear projection on the same screen at the same time. Very complicated and potentially expressive image patterns can be developed in this manner.

Unlike front projection, rear projection does not generate a "dead area," useless to actors, of any great depth. Obviously actors cannot cast shadows by intercepting a beam that is coming from upstage of the screen. However, it will be necessary to allow a relatively shallow "dead space" in order to avoid angling acting area lighting directly on the screen. Side lighting may be used quite close to the screen if carefully angled and if the actors are wearing dark costumes which will not reflect the side lighting onto the screen. Yet another advantage of rear projection is that it locates the projectors as far away from the audience as possible, eliminating much of their noise, and puts them in a location accessible to workers for slide changing and maintenance.

A good rear projection screen must transmit light relatively well but diffuse it thoroughly. If diffusion is too low, there will be a "hot spot" in the center of the image where the flare from the projection lens may be seen by the audience. Also, if diffusion is low, those seated at the sides of the house may not see any image at all, or only a faint outline. Commercial projection screens for rear projection may be ordered with prespecified diffusion angles. Theatrical applications usually require the widest angle available.

30
PROJECTION USING COHERENT LIGHT

INTRODUCTION This chapter will deal only briefly with some of the most advanced and fascinating developments in the entire area of scenic projection. Our treatment must be brief because the technology of these developments is incredibly complicated, and in many cases even casual experimentation is both expensive and potentially dangerous.

COHERENT LIGHT

Coherent light may be briefly defined as light which is all of the same wavelength (color) and which is radiating in such a manner that the wave motion is in the same plane and in phase. Such light has the property of making visible a number of optical phenomena ordinarily obscured by the action of noncoherent light. Unfortunately, theatrical sources of coherent light are almost entirely limited to expensive and potentially dangerous devices known as "lasers." Lasers, whose technology is far beyond the scope of this text, consume great quantities of energy in proportion to the amount given out as coherent light. Nevertheless, their output is so concentrated that any except the smallest lasers are dangerous. The light is emitted from a laser in a small-diameter parallel beam. The rays are so nearly parallel that this beam will widen only slightly over such a vast throw as the distance to the moon. So much energy may be packed within this tiny beam that it may be capable of burning holes in light-absorptive materials, performing cutting and welding operations, and, unfortunately, permanently damaging human eyes.

Most lasers are dangerous devices, although even the largest is far from the "death ray" lasers sometimes are said to be. Under no circumstances should experimenters allow an undiffused laser beam of more than a couple of milliwatts of power (the smallest available) to be reflected about in such a way that it might enter a human eye. Permanent damage could result. Low-power lasers, while not so dangerous to the eye, may create blinding afterimages that can cause dancers and actors to stumble or fall. Therefore, the eyes should also be protected against these sources.

Two methods of protection are available for those who must work where they may encounter laser light. If there is any risk that the light may enter the eye in dangerous quantities, the monochromatic quality of the light may be used to develop protection against it. The principle is that of subtractive color mixing. Filters in the form of protective contact lenses over the eyes are used to prevent the light from entering and causing damage. For example, a green filter will almost entirely block the pure red light from a helium-neon laser. Of course, such filters offer no protection against lasers powerful enough to burn the filter material itself, but there should never be any thought of using such dangerous devices.

Another method of protection is automatically available when it is necessary to disperse the beam, such as in the production of interference patterns or the illumination of holograms (see below). In these cases, the light is spread out until the intensity at any given location is reduced below the danger point. In any event, actors or dancers should not look directly at the source of dispersed laser light, particularly if interference patterns are being generated. It is the nature of interference patterns that the energy varies markedly from place to place. At least some filter protection to the eye is advisable if the source of the interference patterns is large enough to be dangerous.

LASER BEAMS AS DESIGN ELEMENTS

The remarkable parallelism of a laser beam makes possible repeated reflections with no perceptible increase in beam size. This property has fascinated artists in and out of the theatre for a number of years. For example, environments have been designed by experimenters in three-dimensional art in which a space is filled with varicolored laser beams that are reflected and rereflected through it. If a slight amount of smoke or fog is injected into this space, the effect is much more perceptible. Similar applications of lasers may be tried on stage if adequate precautions are taken to protect actors or dancers who must enter this space while the lasers are on. If the stage is sufficiently dark and the audience's eyes have been given time to adapt, these effects can be done with low-power, relatively safe lasers; afterimages, however, may still plague the actors. In such experiments, color will probably be limited to the red laser light typical of helium-neon lasers. If a krypton laser is available (they are rare at safe powers), special filters of dichroic material may be used to separate the green and blue light emitted. (Ordinary filters will not do; they will be burned out rapidly by the laser because they absorb energy.)

INTERFERENCE PATTERNS

Interference is a phenomenon apparent under many circumstances involving light. For example, it causes a thin film of oil floating on water to display varied color. Interference is also used as the basis for extremely precise scientific measuring devices. Theatrical applications of interference patterns (Plate XIV) demand a considerable quantity of coherent light. Practically, the laser is the only source of such quantities of light. Special image-making devices have been contrived that cause some parts of the coherent light from a laser source to travel a slightly longer path than other parts. This sets up a situation in which interference phenomena will be visible on any surface that the combined beams strike. Such images are different on every plane but are always "in focus" wherever they are seen. For example, if the variation in path is produced by an irregular piece of glass, a wide variety of fascinating patterns may be generated. Furthermore, if this light is reflected obliquely from a small mirror (a piece of aluminum foil will do) mounted on the face of a loudspeaker, and the speaker is activated with a musical signal, the images can be made to vary with the music.

In order to render the interference patterns safe and to make them visible over a large surface, the laser beam must be dispersed by a very short focal-length lens. A microscope objective often is used for this purpose. Experimentation with varying distances between the dispersion lens, the irregular glass, and the sound-activated reflector, if one is used, will produce an almost infinite variety of images. *All such experimentation must be done with low-power lasers.*

Some of the most fascinating theatrical applications of interference patterns are to be found when the patterns are generated on the surfaces of three-dimensional objects. Since there can be no depth of focus problems, the images may be made to flow over objects of great depth. The various parts of the image will be interrelated, but different in every plane. Any movement in the optical system will result in a new set of images over the entire space. All of these images will have the unusual "granular" or vibrant quality of coherent light. This quality is actually a localized interference effect caused by reflections within minute irregularities in the reflective surface. The effect is a "living" quality that defies still photography. For this reason, photographs of laser images are not the same as the images themselves.

HOLOGRAMS

The term "hologram" has been used to refer to both the film which contains the optical information, and to the image that it will display. To avoid this confusion, we will refer to the film as a "hologram," and to the image as a "holographic image."

Probably the most spectacular and most theatrically interesting application of laser light is in the making and reproduction of holographic images. This process is too complex for explanation here, but it results in images that have the same optical qualities as the three-dimensional objects from which they were made. Walking around a holographic image causes perspective to change exactly as it would in the real object. The image can be in full color and can give the appearance of being a solid object until someone or something passes through it revealing it as the illusion it is. A myriad of theatrical applications immediately comes to mind, one being Banquo's ghost in *Hamlet*.

Although developments are proceeding rapidly, holography is not quite ready as an effective theatrical tool at the time this text is being written. Efficiency is still incredibly low, and the cost of producing the original hologram very high. Most present holographic images are seen either as reflections from the surface of a hologram or as virtual images seen "through" it. It is possible to construct a holographic image in space, but the space must be filled with some reflective material such as smoke if the image is to be visible. The amount of energy in the form of coherent light from lasers to make such an image visible under stage conditions would be tremendous if one used the low-efficiency lasers commercially available today. (It would probably run into thousands of kilowatts of input power!) However scientists are producing more and more efficient lasers, and it should be possible in the very near future to produce stage-worthy holograms at more reasonable cost.

The process of making holograms is also becoming simpler and less costly. The original record is made by exposing extra-fine-grain photographic film to coherent light being reflected from the object, and from a reference source of coherent light. While the developed film appears to the eye to be merely fogged, it actually contains a record of the arrangement of light waves that made up the reflection from the original object. Making high-quality holographic films requires an optical bench mounted on an extremely steady base. Theatrical experimenters have found that under certain circumstances useful films can be made without such costly equipment. Some readers may wish to try to make their own after studying books on the applications of laser light.

Once the hologram has been made, it will display its information if illuminated with coherent light at the proper angle. Actually, any directional light from a small source (a pen light, for example) will display the image, but not nearly as impressively as coherent light.

At this stage of development, laser light is only beginning to be available as an artistic tool. It offers the scenographer-experimenter a chance to delve into the outer fringes of technology in search of new artistic tools and techniques.

APPENDIX I

OBSOLETE EQUIPMENT

Although the equipment mentioned below is obsolete, it is quite possible that the theatre worker will find it in many older theatres which have not been modernized. Such equipment is by no means useless, although every effort should be made to have it replaced by more modern instruments as soon as funds are available.

OLIVETTES AND BUNCH LIGHTS

Olivettes were early floodlights that date back many years but were actually preceded by a still more primitive instrument, the bunch light, now an antique. The latter instrument has a "bunch" of light bulbs in it instead of a single lamp because when it was invented, no single lamps were large enough to produce the amount of light needed. The outer structure was similar to the olivette.

The olivette consists of a simple sheet metal boxlike structure enclosing a single general service pear-shaped lamp, usually 1000 W in size (see Figure A-1). The origin of the name has been lost somewhere in the history of the theatre, although there are many theories about it. When the reflector is new and clean, the olivette is a rather efficient instrument. Usually the reflector has been allowed to deteriorate to a dirty gray and its light output is poor. Cleaning and repainting the reflector will work wonders. A highly reflective flat white paint is probably best, although aluminum paint also works well. Color frames for olivettes are large and should be equipped with crosswires to support the color medium when it gets hot. These wires are less necessary for plastic media than for gelatin, but still a good idea. The frames are often made of wood, built in the theatre shop if necessary.

Olivettes usually are found on stands —they were intended to work in the wings of a wing and drop setting. They can also be equipped with clamps and mounted on battens when necessary.

RESISTANCE DIMMERS

Resistance dimmers are obsolete. Except for a very few theatres supplied with direct current, there is no electrical reason why they should still be in service. However, they are a durable piece of equipment and many of them are still in service simply because they still work. They will be recognized by the heat they give off, and by the fact that they must be loaded to near-capacity if they are to be expected to dim the lights to black out. Most resistance dimmers look like those shown in Figure A-2.

These dimmers were frequently fitted with a mechanical interlocking arrangement to aid the operator in moving a number of them at the same time. This consists of a slotted shaft running horizontally in front of a row of dimmers (see Figure A-3). The pivot end of each individual dimmer handle rotates around this shaft as long as the metal "dog" (a rod shaped to fit into the slot in the shaft) is in its raised position. When this dog is released by rotating the dimmer operating handle to the left, a spring causes it to press down on the shaft. The moment the slot in the shaft aligns with the dog, the dog drops into the slot, locking the handle to the shaft. If the shaft is then rotated (by means of any single dimmer handle locked to it, or by means of a master handle permanently fastened to the shaft) all locked-in dimmers will move with it. This system sometimes is complicated further by providing a mechanical link between several rows of dimmers, and thus has the capability of running all dimmers on the system with a "grand master handle" (Figure A-4).

This system does make possible the movement of many dimmers at the same time, but only when all interlocked dimmers are at the same reading. Moreover, the sheer weight and friction of a large number of resistance dimmers being operated together will be enough to make the operator of the master handle use more brute force than subtlety, if he is to move it at all.

As you move a resistance dimmer from 0 to 10, assuming that it is properly loaded, you can expect some visible light within the first couple of numbers, then rather evenly divided changes as the handle is moved on upward. If the dimmer is not loaded to capacity, the change will begin sooner and progress much more rapidly, often finishing before you reach 10. As the load decreases still further, 0 will produce considerable light, and about 5 will be full up. Thus the operating characteristic of the dimmer changes with each change in load. Thus, to keep the dimmer operating properly, a "phantom" or "ghost" load is used, made up of extra lamps attached to bring the load up to the necessary minimum. These usually are mounted somewhere outside of the backstage area where their light will not interfere with the show, and the heat they create will dissipate harmlessly. Computing phantom

Figure A-1. Olivette. Although this olivette has been lamped with a G-type lamp instead of the normal type PS, it is typical of such instruments.

Figure A-2. Resistance Dimmers. These dimmers are typical of the round type found in most old installations. Note the ring of contacts set into the porcelain insulation. A number of very large wattage rectangular plate resistance dimmers also were made. Many of these are installed in old-fashioned "piano boards" still used in traveling shows.

loads is easy. Simply subtract the instrument load from the dimmer wattage, less 10–20 percent. The difference is the wattage needed as phantom load. Round off to the nearest larger available lamp size that will not overload the dimmer.

If a resistance dimmer has been overloaded and part of its resistance wire burned out, it will dim downward from 10 to wherever the break occurs. Then the lamps will suddenly go out. During a fade-up, the lamps will suddenly come on at the same point. The usual cure for such a faulty dimmer is to bridge the gap where the resistance wire has burned out by wedging a piece of metal (called a "jumper") between the contacts on either side of the break. This restores the circuit but eliminates a part of the resistance wire built into the dimmer. The result will be a jump in the otherwise smooth dimming action. A dimmer that has been repaired several times in this fashion is nearly impossible to operate without jerky lighting effects. A better repair may be effected by brazing the gap where the jumper would be inserted. Soldering will not work; heat of operation is too great.

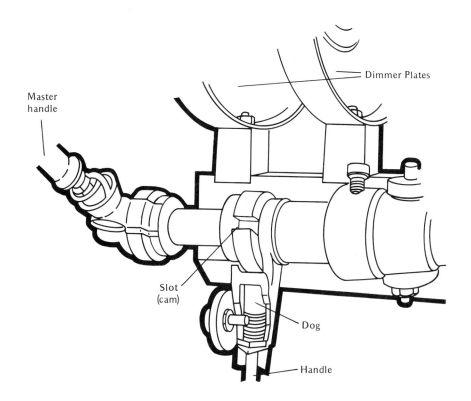

Master
handle

Dimmer Plates

Slot
(cam)

Dog

Handle

Figure A-3. This close-up shows one of the several simple dog-and-cam arrangements used for mechanically interlocking resistance dimmers.

PROPORTIONAL DIMMING

Proportional dimming consists of changing the intensity of a group of lights in such a way that the ratios between the individual lights remain essentially constant. Proportional dims usually take the form of a fade-in or fade-out of a number of dimmers at the same time. The idea is that the appearance of the stage should not be altered, except in intensity, as the change is made.

The best method of achieving proportional dimming is by some type of master dimmer which controls the power going to all of the individual dimmers. In direct control systems this means that the master dimmer must be as large as the total wattage of all of the individual dimmers. It is possible to achieve proportional dimming by the use of a large resistance-type master dimmer, but only if each operation of the master dimmer results in the end of the cue bringing the master to either full-up or black out, and if the load on the master dimmer is kept at more than about 70 percent capacity. If the master is left in an intermediate position, any adjustment of one of the individual dimmers will change all of the others.

Since most resistance boards were not equipped to perform electrical proportional dimming (the mechanical interlock is much cheaper),

Figure A-4. The Face of a Resistance Board. The handles aid the operators in determining whether or not the dimmer is set to interlock. Note the long master handle.

the only way it can be done well is by the use of one operator for every pair of dimmers, and much rehearsal.

The following system will offer a method of approximating proportional fade-outs with only one operator. It is applicable to resistance control systems or to autotransformer control boards fitted with mechanical interlocks instead of electrical mastering.

1. Before the fade-out, move the mastering handle to a reading equal to that of the highest reading dimmer(s) to be faded

out. In this position, it will be possible to lock this dimmer(s) to the master handle.

2. After setting the master handle, turn the hand grips of all the remaining dimmers to be included in the fade-out to the left so they will release the locking device. Since the slot in the mastering shaft is not in line with these dimmers, no interlocking will take place at this time.

3. On cue, move the master handle downward, bringing with it the highest reading dimmer in the cue.

4. Watch the other dimmer handles as you move the master. They should "lock in" sequentially as the slot in the shaft lines up with their locking devices. Expect the master handle to be progressively harder to move as it picks up additional dimmers. Be ready to individually operate any dimmer that does not lock in.

5. Continue the fade until you have moved the master handle to 0.

6. Immediately unlock all of the dimmers from the master handle so that they can be moved individually as needed in future cues. The only exception to this rule is the unlikely possibility that you will want to move all the dimmers upward at exactly the same reading on the next cue.

The reverse, a proportional fade-in, is nearly impossible. It will take as many people to release the various dimmers at their prearranged readings as it would to run each dimmer manually.

A resistance board will require several operators, well rehearsed and working as a team, if more than rudimentary lighting is to be done. Given such a crew, almost anything a scenographer can conjur up is possible. One of the tricks of the resistance dimmer operator that saves hands on difficult cues, is careful use of the *sneak*. A sneak is a dimmer operation performed so smoothly that the audience never knows it has happened. A shrewd operator, with the cooperation of the scenographer, can often simplify a complex operation by sneaking parts of it down (or up) in advance of the actual cue. The remainder then becomes much simpler to operate. The secret of successful sneaking is very smooth operation and careful strategy in the choice of instruments to be changed early. The most obvious are those whose light output is masked by the output of other instruments. Next is the output of instruments lighting parts of the scene well away from the center of attention. These require utmost subtlety.

Designing and running lighting on a resistance board usually is complicated further by the fact that these boards are almost invariably backstage where the operators can see little or nothing of what they are doing. Also the board gets hot as the show progresses, and ventilation is almost nonexistent.

APPENDIX II

PREVENTING FIRE IN THE THEATRE

Theory of fire prevention and control is the same in the theatre as anywhere else. The difference is that the special kinds of equipment and the special conditions of the theatre make it what firemen call a "high risk area." Many potentially flammable materials are gathered together in a heavily populated area under conditions favorable to the starting of a fire. Therefore theatres are closely watched by fire inspectors. History has proven them right; there have been a number of exceedingly disastrous theatre fires.

Three things must be present under the right conditions to cause a fire: Air, fuel, and heat. Fuel and air are almost everywhere in the theatre. Heat is also common in electric lamps, and it is potentially available in all areas of the theatre. When enough heat is supplied to a fuel-air combination an oxidation reaction starts. If conditions are right, the reaction produces enough heat to more than replace that lost into the surroundings, and the reaction continues getting larger and larger, starting a fire. To stop the reaction we must remove one of the components. We may cool the reaction by taking away the heat (apply water, for example) or separate the fuel and the air (e.g. smother the fire with foam).

KEEPING FIRE FROM STARTING

Obviously it is far better to prevent a fire from starting than it is to try to put it out. Prevention works by keeping the fuel-air-heat combination from becoming favorable to fire. Since air is everywhere in the theatre and heat is a necessary part of such things as electrical lamps, fuel is the usual point of attack. Two alternatives are available: We may choose materials that refuse to become fuel at any temperature encountered in the theatre, i.e., they are "flameproof." Such materials as concrete, asbestos, steel etc. will not burn at any temperature apt to be present in a working theatre. The other alternative is to treat potentially flammable materials in such a way that they will minimize the chance of a fire starting and spreading. Such treated materials are called "flame-retardant." If they will only burn under the effect of an externally applied flame they may also be called "self-extinguishing." Since the range of flameproof scenery-building materials is rather narrow for use in the theatre, we find it necessary to make many of our fabrics and other materials flame-retardant or self-extinguishing by special treatment. Such materials must be tested to guarantee the effectiveness of the treatment.

MAKING FLAMMABILITY TESTS IN THE THEATRE

"Exact" tests for flammability as specified in the National Fire Code involve complicated equipment and measurements. The relatively simple "field test" described in the code requires nothing more complicated than a box of kitchen matches. It can be performed by theatre workers to determine whether or not the materials they have flameproofed will pass inspection. It is done as follows:

Samples of the material to be tested should be at least $1\frac{1}{2}$ by 5 inches and should be completely dry. The test sample should be taken to a draft-free place and held over a safe surface such as a clean concrete floor or an empty metal trash container. The sample should be supported in a vertical position by means of a pair of tongs, a metal rod, or the like. A regular kitchen match must be used for the test. (A cigarette lighter or paper book match will not burn at a high enough temperature to equal the wooden match.) The match is lit and held one-half inch below the lower edge of the material near the center. It should be held there for 12 seconds unless the material is burning out of control by then. Be careful when making tests with materials of unknown type—some of them may burn very rapidly. After 12 seconds the match may be removed. The material should not continue to burn for more than 2 seconds. During exposure to the flame, the burned area should not spread more than 4 inches upward into the sample. If there are particles which break away and drop, they should not continue to burn after they reach the floor. Although the National Fire Code is not clear on this point, most fire inspectors will reject material that continues to glow for more than a few seconds after the match has been removed, particularly if the glowing area spreads. (See the National Fire Code, Section 701.)

TREATING FLAMMABLE MATERIALS—"FLAMEPROOFING"

"Flameproofing" is actually a misnomer: "flame retardant" is the proper term because treated materials can be burned although they will be self-extinguishing if properly treated. Materials may be purchased already treated, they may be flameproofed by the theatre staff, or a professional flameproofing company may be called upon to flameproof the finished scenery. Most theatres will use a combination of all three methods. Certain materials, scrim, for instance, are usually available from suppliers only in flameproofed form. Scene muslin or canvas can be purchased flameproofed or not. It is cheaper to purchase it untreated and do the job in the theatre shop because the labor involved can be absorbed into sizing operations that must be performed anyway.

Flameproofing chemicals must be matched to the material to be treated. The commonest and cheapest types are made to flameproof cotton fabric, paper, cardboard, burlap, and other similarly absorbent materials. These chemicals are not satisfactory for some synthetics, for moisture-resisting materials such as evergreen trees and most foliage, or for plastics. They are also not satisfactory for fine fabrics such as voiles or chiffons because they will ruin the texture or stain the fabric. Special compounds are available for fine fabrics and for high penetration applications. Many plastics cannot be flameproofed except during their manufacture.

There may also be legal considerations. A professional flameproofing firm must be licensed and will affix a certification tag to materials that they have treated; this automatically satisfies the fire inspector. Materials treated by the theatre group will have to be tested. If the group's relationship with the fire inspector is sufficiently bad, he may require that the setting be professionally treated by a certified flameproofer. Theoretically a member of any group could get training and certification. Practically, this is often a long and difficult process.

Given the willingness of the fire inspector to test the work of uncertified flameproofers, the treatment of most theatre materials is not difficult. State or locally approved chemicals must be purchased from a supplier, properly mixed and applied by dipping, spraying, or brushing. Sample swatches of the materials must be treated in a manner identical to the actual scenery and submitted for test. If they pass — and the theatre group should pretest them to be sure they will — and the inspector is assured that the scenery itself is also flameproof, the scenery will pass and the show goes on. If it does not pass, the group may treat it again and ask for another inspection, or it may call in a professional whose fees for a stage full of scenery may run into many hundreds of dollars.

Most flameproofing compounds are mixtures of boric acid, borax, and in some cases, ammonia-bearing chemicals. They are soluble in warm water, mildly irritating to the skin, and severely irritating to the eyes. They are also somewhat corrosive to metals, which means that sprayers, buckets, and other equipment used for flameproofing must be well-cleaned immediately after use. One common application tool is

Figure A-5. Pressure Tank Sprayer. This simple tool enables crew members to spray instead of brush flameproofing chemical solutions onto the fabric. It must be cleaned of all traces of chemicals immediately after use.

the pressure tank sprayer. Figure A-5. This is an efficient way of applying flameproofing. Some larger theatres and professional paint studios use siphon sprayers that work directly from a barrel of premixed flameproofing. See Figure A-6. These tools must be cleaned immediately after use.

Formulas for mixing your own flameproofing chemicals are available in the National Fire Code. However, some areas (e.g., the California) require that commercially mixed compounds be used. Since these premixed chemicals are not much more expensive than mixing your own and are certainly more convenient, they are desirable. These compounds usually come in 1 or 5 pound boxes in the form of dry chemicals or as concentrated solutions. In either case, one only needs to add the chemicals to warm water and mix well.

Flameproofing is not a permanent process, at least in the form that is applied in the theatre. Since most scenery is used for a relatively short time, this is not a problem. Draperies, however, may remain in the theatre for years. A well-flameproofed set of velours that passed a test 5 years ago may be highly flammable today. The flameproofing chemicals have mostly fallen off and been replaced by highly flammable theatre dust. The curtains may even be more flammable than they were before their original treatment. Cleaning, washing, or even heavy handling tend to destroy flameproofing. Drapes should be tested every few years and cleaned and retreated when necessary. Of course another solution is to use flame-resistant fabric from the start, but such materials still must be occasionally cleaned to remove flammable and unsightly dirt and dust.

Figure A-6. Siphon Sprayer for Air Line. This handy tool enables those shops equipped with compressed air to work directly from a large container of flameproofing solution, making the task of applying flameproofing simple. The sprayer has the advantage of being powerful enough to force the solution deep into the pores of heavy fabrics. Sprayer must be cleaned immediately after use.

What Must Be Flameproofed?

In general, all scenic elements and decorative materials such as artificial foliage must be treated. Costumes and properties are usually exempt, although there is movement to change this. Makeup items are not required to be flameproofed which leads to a potentially dangerous situation: Wigs made of heavily-lacquered artificial hair are common in the theatre and are violently flammable. While present day fire laws do not cover them, common sense should. Any stage business that requires an actor or actress to play near a candle flame while wearing such a wig should be reworked. The potential for severe injury is terrifying.

The distinction between properties and set dressings may be a source of contention. Fire inspectors do not always make the same distinctions that theatre workers make. Generally a few flammable plastic flowers or decorations will pass, provided they are surrounded by thoroughly flameproofed scenery and clear of any live candles or ash trays. The same material in larger quantity or near a flame will not be exempted. Since artificial flowers and foliage are standard in the theatre today and since most of these are made of flammable polyethylene, problems will continue to arise. Nonflammable flowers are not usually available and making them in the shop, while possible, is a time-consuming task.

CONTROLLING FIRE

It is obviously more desirable to avoid starting a fire than to face the task of controlling it. Nevertheless fire inspectors are realists; they know that fires will occasionally start even in the best-inspected, best-run theatres. Therefore, the next line of defense—control—is a matter of great concern. Control falls into two categories: (1) Controlling the spread of the fire itself, and (2) controlling the panic that may result in the audience from even a minor fire.

Controlling the spread of fire takes two major forms: Limiting the spread, and reducing or extinguishing it by automatic means that can operate before the firemen arrive.

FIRE BARRIERS

These are architectural features that tend to prevent the fire from spreading unless it reaches disastrous proportions. The most common, although least noticed in everyday use, is the *fire wall*, a wall of the building that has been specially constructed to resist the spread of fire.

Fire walls must have doors in them for convenience, but these doors must be as resistant to fire as the wall itself, and must be closed under fire conditions. The removal of such a door to facilitate scene shifting, for instance, may ruin the fire wall. Two types of *fire doors* are common in theatres: (1) Spring-loaded self-closing doors that remain closed except when someone is actually passing through them, and (2) counter-weighted doors that are normally open but close automatically when heat in their vicinity reaches a certain preset point. Both types must be properly used if they are to do their job. The spring-loaded type must not be blocked open for additional ventilation, for example, or to aid in moving and storing props. The counter-weighted type must not be blocked in such a way that it cannot close in case of fire. Workers in rooms protected by counter-weighted doors should be warned not to consider these doors as potential emergency exits. They may close just when they are needed, and they are usually very hard to open under emergency circumstances.

One of the most prominent fire barriers in a proscenium theatre is the *asbestos curtain*, discussed in Chapter 3.

CROWD CONTROL

In the case of fire or other disasters, one of the major concerns is that the audience be able to exit quickly and safely without panic. To this end a number of measures are taken:

Emergency lighting is provided
Exits are plainly marked and lighted
Audience circulation paths are maintained as unobstructed flow-paths.
Panic communications systems are installed.

Emergency lighting is discussed in Part Seven, "Lighting." The reader is referred to that discussion for details. However, everyone from beginner up should know how to operate the manually activated portions of the emergency system. Usually there are "panic buttons" which turn on the house lights no matter what the state of the stage lighting system. Everyone should know how to use this system.

PERMITS

A *fire permit* is a legal document issued by a fire inspector giving permission for performing special operations or for the use of materials or equipment which might be considered hazardous. For example, it is usually necessary to obtain a permit from the fire inspector if an open flame, such as a candle, is to be used on stage. In some circumstances even lighting a cigarette may require a permit, particularly in public school theatres. Such things as special platform construction which influences the operation of the asbestos will almost certainly require a permit.

The procedure for getting a fire permit will generally be as follows: The theatre seeks the general advice of the local fire inspector as to how a desired scenic effect can be safely achieved. This is often a good idea even if you are fairly certain that what you intend to do may not even require a permit. After getting this advice, the theatre staff devises the exact apparatus and works out a procedure for handling it on stage. Operators are trained and instructed in the safe operation of this apparatus. Then the inspector is invited to witness a rehearsal of the effect and to inspect the equipment. If he suggests changes, they are effected. If he refuses the effect entirely, another method is sought or the effect must be abandoned. Any attempt to feign abandonment and then insert the effect at the last minute will be an invitation to the fire inspector to close the show, or perhaps worse, to embark on a policy of absolutely rigid and rigorous enforcement of every detail of the fire code. There are so many technicalities and possibilities for what will appear to the theatre staff as harassment, that this kind of relationship with the safety inspector is deadly.

The permit should be displayed as required by the authorities—usually posting it on the stage manager's desk suffices. The theatre should expect occasional unannounced visits from the inspector to see that the conditions have not been changed during the run of the show. The key to the entire process is a respect for safety concerns and a willingness to involve the inspector in the development of effects so that he is not placed in the nearly impossible position of making last-minute denials.

A good procedure to follow is to seek the advice of the inspector whenever you plan anything which might conceivably need special permission. Ignorance of the law is no excuse. The following situations will usually require a fire permit:

> Open flames, flash pots, fireworks
> Spark effects such as lightning devices
> Gunfire using blanks
> Any obstruction of fire safety apparatus such as the asbestos, fire door, smoke traps, etc.
> Unusual installations over the audience, such as effects machines, special lights, etc.
> Changes in audience circulation that may affect their speed of exit.
> Use of unusual materials in quantity such as plastics. This may apply to both setting and props and sometimes even to costumes.
> Use of flammables during construction of stage props, sets, etc.

GLOSSARY

Act Curtain: The curtain used to close the proscenium during scene changes between acts. Usually the same as the grand drape.

Acting Area: (1) "Acting space." That portion of the stage space occupied or able to be occupied by actors. (2) (Preferred) A unit of stage lighting prepared exclusively for effective lighting of actors. Usually 9 by 12 feet or less at head level. Two spotlights at 45 degree angles horizontally and vertically compose a "standard" acting area.

Additive Color Mixing: Combining color sensations in the eye. Results in stimulation of more than one color sensor at a time. For example, R + B = Magenta.

Alternating Current (ac): Flow of electrons that reverses direction frequently. United States standard reverses direction sixty times per second. Produced by generators. Necessary to the functioning of transformers and transformer dimmers. Standard form of almost all current in the United States.

Alzak: Patented electrochemical process for surfacing aluminum reflectors. Types of "anodizing." Can produce highly efficient specular or controlled spread finishes.

American Plan Seating: Arrangement of seats in a house using vertical aisles and crossover aisles if necessary. Crowds flow from back to front of house and reverse. Side exits near stage right and left usually used only for emergencies. No row with more than fourteen seats.

Ampere: Unit of electrical quantity referring to the rate of electron flow. The current.

Analogical Symbolic Links: Symbolic devices in an art work whose most basic quality is that of an analogue. The artist builds on this analogue to gain insight.

Analogues: Two things similar in certain respects; different in others. The *combination* of similarities and differences is significant.

Animal Glue: A protein material extracted from hides, hooves, and other slaughterhouse remains. Crudely purified, it is glue; more refined, it is gelatin.

ANSI Code; ASA Code; ASI Code: American National Standards Institute code designating incandescent lamp types. This is a three-letter system that has been devised to describe lamps of different manufacture, but the same application. The letters have no relationship to lamp description, but the same letters always designate the same type of lamp.

579

Anteproscenium Light: See Beam. Any light placed in front of the proscenium for the purpose of FOH lighting.

Aperture: Opening at the front of the reflector of an ellipsoidal reflector spotlight through which all light from the reflector passes. Lens system is arranged to focus image of this opening on the stage. Framing shutters are found in the aperture. See also Gobo.

Apron: The part of a proscenium stage that protrudes in front of the act curtain. Also called the forestage.

Arbor: A heavy steel frame to carry counterweights when they are in use. May be attached to a T-track or guided by guide wires. Moved by operating the hauling line.

Arc Light: Powerful light source consisting of electrical spark formed by placing two pieces of carbon in a circuit, touching them together, and drawing them a slight distance apart. Incandescent carbon produces most of light.

Arena Theatre: A theatre-in-the-round. The stage of playing area is in the center of the room surrounded by the audience.

Asbestos; Asbestos Curtain: A fire safety curtain designed to close the proscenium opening automatically in case of fire. Normally located in front of the act curtain. Runs in smoke traps, which are slots designed to impede the passage of smoke from backstage to the house. Also called fire curtain.

Autotransformer: Electromagnetic device used to dim stage lights. Runs on ac only. Consists of a single coil of insulated copper wire around a laminated iron core. Slider taps off voltage from coil. Now obsolete.

Baby Spotlight: Obsolete type of small plano-convex instrument, usually 400 W. Consisted of simple box with lens and sometimes a spherical reflector. First incandescent spotlight.

Backdrop: A large sheet of canvas or muslin upon which designs may be painted. Used to enclose upstage portion of setting. Often seen through doors and windows in setting. A drop painted pale blue may sometimes substitute for a cyclorama.

Backing: Pieces of scenery (often a two-fold) set up outside a doorway or window to prevent the audience from seeing backstage. May resemble other walls or outside elements.

Backing Striplight: A small striplight, one color circuit only, used to illuminate entryways and small window backings. Now usually superceded by the 10 inch scoop.

Back Lighting: Light coming from above and somewhat behind the actor as he faces the audience. Used to separate actor from background, especially in television.

Balance (color): An arrangement of hue, chroma, and value within a design that produces a sense of equilibrium—i.e., no colored area commands attention to the detriment of the entire arrangement.

Balcony Spotlight: Any spotlight mounted on a balcony front to provide frontal illumination for the apron. Usually a powerful ellipsoidal reflector spot is used. Angle of illumination is usually low and position less desirable than beam position. Much used in older theatres and for portable applications.

Ballast: A device to limit the amount of electrical current flowing in a circuit with as little loss of energy as possible. Most ballasts consist of coils of insulated electrical wire wound around iron cores. A rather complex electromagnetic effect causes the current to be limited. Ballasts work on ac only.

Barn Doors: Adjustable metal flaps mounted on a framework that fits into color-holder slot of spotlight. Flaps can be hinged in or out of beam to shape it and control spill. Use with safety chain.

Batten: A piece of pipe, usually of $1\frac{1}{2}$ inch diameter, hung from above for support of scenery, lighting equipment, etc. Electrical battens generally are equipped permanently with wireways, outlets, and the like.

Beam: (1) The cone of light from an instrument capable of directing light into a relatively narrow angle of emission. (2) Abbreviation for "light beam" or "ceiling beam." A major mounting position for FOH lighting. Consists of a false beam built into ceiling or a slot in the ceiling. See also Anteproscenium Light.

Beam Projector: An instrument with a parabolic reflector (defined below) and concentrated filament lamp. Produces near-parallel rays of light. Highly efficient. Not adjustable. Simulates sun and moonlight or "pillar of light" effects.

Binder (paint): Material that causes pigment to adhere.

Black Light: See Ultraviolet Light.

Blackout: (1) A sudden removal of all or almost all light on stage, usually by means of a switch or "blackout button" which turns all dimmers to "off." (2) A short scene, usually comic, ending in a blackout.

Blending Light: Light "washed" over the stage to smooth out minor variations in acting area lighting and bring lighting together in a more realistic manner. Not much used in stylized productions.

Block: The metal or wooden framework that holds a sheave (defined below) in place.

Board: See Control Board; Switchboard.

Bobbinet: A near-transparent fabric used for haze effects. See also Scrim.

Book Ceiling: See Ceiling.

Boom; Boomerang: (1) A color-changing device attached to the front of a spotlight, usually one used as a follow spotlight (defined below). Color frames are moved electrically or mechanically, often remotely. Also called color box. (2) Vertical mounting for lighting equipment.

Border: (1) A scenic element consisting of a piece of drapery or a short drop running across the stage above the acting area to mask the upper portion of the stage house. May be part of setting representing foliage, parts of ceiling, etc. It may be a purely functional piece of dark drapery. (2) Also short for borderlight.

Borderlight: A striplight. A long row of lamps, usually in separate reflectors, equipped with color medium. Used to illuminate the entire stage or cyclorama with flat, shadowless light. Usually hung above stage on battens. May be dead hung.

Borderlight Cable: Large cable containing many individually insulated wires leading to equipment with multiple circuits, such as borderlights. Must be flexible in spite of its size and weight. Common neutral sometimes is used. One equipment ground only is needed for most applications.

Box Set: A relatively realistic setting consisting of three walls representing a room.

Boxing: Mixing buckets of paint together by pouring from bucket to bucket. Assures consistent color in large batches.

Brace: See Stage Brace.

Brace Cleat: A small metal plate attached to the wooden part of a flat to accept the hook at the top of a stage brace (defined below). Properly used, it prevents the brace from poking through the fabric of the flat. Occasionally used to keep flats in alignment.

Bridge: A narrow catwalklike platform mounted in first border position. Used for mounting lighting apparatus. Operator can reach equipment while it is in use to make adjustments. May be movable via a winch. Also known as lighting bridge.

Brilliance: That property of a color that denotes the lighting energy reflected or generated. Can be measured by a light meter. Also described as that property of color that enables it to be classified according to a gray scale.

Bulb: (1) That part of a lamp which encloses the filament to protect it from oxidation. Usually made of glass. (2) Synonym for lamp or globe.

Burn Base: The socket, its supporting assembly, and wiring in an ellipsoidal spotlight. It can usually be removed from the instrument as a single assembly.

Cable: Two or more insulated electrical conductors combined in the same outer covering. Insulating material is usually plastic, rubber, or Neoprene. Most modern stage cables have three conductors—hot, neutral, and equipment ground. Older stage cables had only two conductors—hot and neutral. See also Borderlight Cable.

Carpenter Pipe Batten; Carpenter Pipe; Carpenter Batten: Regular pipe batten fitted with trim chains and supported by either a rope set or a counterweighted line set. Normally used for the support and shifting of scenery but frequently rigged for lighting by use of portable cable.

Cartridge Fuse: See Fuse. Cylindrical fuse device. Fuse wire is contained in fiber cylinder equipped with brass contacts at ends. Comes in wide variety of sizes; mostly used for high current situations. Also see Instrument Fuse.

Catalyst: Chemical that is added to liquid resin (plastic) to make it harden (Polymerization, defined below). Generates heat in the process.

Ceiling: A large canvas- or muslin-covered frame mounted horizontally over the setting to approximate the appearance of a ceiling. May fold (book ceiling) or be demountable for rolling into transportable form.

Chemical Etching: Method of producing a textured surface on plastic foams by applying chemicals that partially dissolve the plastic. Should be done in well-ventilated space. Flammable chemicals frequently are used.

Chroma: An attribute of color. Describes the saturation of a hue (defined below). Makes it possible to say that one red is redder than another although both are of the same hue. Chroma is altered in pigments by mixture with black or white, a process that inevitably also alters value. Chroma in lighting is altered by dimmer adjustments (but with some hue changes).

Cinemoid: Plastic color media made in England. Much used because of its durability and wide range of color.

Circuit: A complete electrical path leading from a source of electrons through conductors, switches, dimmers, etc., to the lead (lamp) and returning to the source. Also refers to a complete path from supply point through control and load and return, although generator may be far distant from supply point.

Circuit Breaker: A device to protect against overcurrent situations. Opens circuit whenever too many amperes flow. Can be reset when trouble has been cleared. Size can be closely calibrated if necessary. Usually has some lag to prevent opening from harmless surges.

Clew: A heavy steel clamp designed to hold several ropes together so they may be hauled as one. Usually has eye for attaching sandbag. Standard item on pin rail (defined below).

Clinch Plate: A piece of steel plate used on the floor or workbench under a joint being nailed with clout nails (defined below). Causes nails to clinch (turn under) as they are driven through the wood.

Close-in Curtain: A drapery curtain on a traveler installed somewhere upstage of the main curtain to cut off some of the upstage portion of the playing area from the audience's view.

Clout Nail: A now relatively unusual way of fastening corner blocks and keystones to 1 by 3 inches. It is a tapered, chisellike nail made of soft steel, designed to clinch in use.

Code: National Underwriter's Code. Refers to model fire and electrical safety laws produced by the National Fire Protection Association. Often written into local laws to give it legal status. Also National Electrical Code.

Coherent Light: Light that is all of the same wavelength (color) and whose waves are all in phase, and polarized in the same plane. Such light is produced by lasers.

Color: Sensation arising from stimulation of the cones in retina of the eye as interpreted by the nervous system and the brain. It is partially dependent on wavelength of light causing stimulus.

Color Box: See Boomerang.

Color Frame: Color medium holder. Usually made of metal. Designed to support gelatin, plastic, etc., while in lighting instrument.

Color Language: Term referring to the aesthetically and psychologically unsupported notion that various colors have psychological meanings such as "anger," "mourning," and the like.

Color Medium: A transparent material that selects wavelengths, transmitting some and stopping others. A filter. Consists of glass, gelatin, acetate plastic or Mylarlike material.

Color Temperature: A temperature figure given in degrees Kelvin which describes the "whiteness" of near-white light. The higher the temperature reading, the cooler the light.

Color Wheel: (1) Device to effect rapid color changes on a spotlight. Consists of a large, unwieldy disk mounted on front of spot. Disk contains several color media mounted in holes the size of the spot lens opening. Rotating the disk brings various colors in front of lens. May be motor driven. (2) A chart of colors so arranged that it shows how the colors (pigments) mix and also shows interrelationships between the colors which are of interest to designers and scenographers.

Company Switch: A large supply switch provided for the purpose of attaching portable lighting control equipment. Usually consists of large switch, fuses or breakers, and hook-up terminals.

Complementary Colors: (1) Two colors of light that produce sensation of white when mixed in equal proportions. (2) Two colors of pigment that produce black or neutral gray when mixed in equal proportions. Complementary colors have greatest color contrast and tend to generate afterimages of each other, thereby increasing contrast still more.

Complementary Tints: A pair of tints selected because their additive effect approaches white.

Concentrated Filament: Tungsten filament engineered to offer the smallest possible dimensions to the lens system of the instrument. Makes possible the use of incandescent lamps in lens units. Increases efficiency and cost at expense of life.

Concert Border: Name sometimes applied to the first border (defined below).

Cones: Color sensing organs of the eye. There are three types.

Connector: A device for electrically attaching conductors. Must make secure attachment electrically and mechanically. May consist of

(1) fiber blocks with two or three pins (pin connectors), or (2) patented latching type which is turned slightly to lock, and reversed to unlock (Twist-Lock).

Console: A desklike assembly of remote-control devices for stage lighting. Contains controllers, submasters, pattern masters, faders, selector switches, and similar equipment.

Contactor: An electromagnetically operated switch used for remote off-on control of circuits. Usually handles large current. Small switch(es) is used to control contactor by controlling the current to its electromagnetic coil.

Continental Seating: A system of arranging a theatre that provides long, continuous rows of seats from one side of the house to the other. Audience enters and exits from numerous doors at sides of auditorium. So called because it is common in Europe.

Contour Curtain: A curtain that is drawn upward to form a scalloped profile above the playing area.

Control Board: Also see Switchboard. Assembly of dimmers, switches, breakers or fuses, etc., within a metal enclosure for the purpose of controlling stage lighting. Generally refers to direct control equipment as opposed to "console," which refers to remote control. Sometimes synonymous with switchboard.

Controller: Device for the remote control of a single dimmer or several dimmers treated as one. Essentially a tiny resistance element known as a "potentiometer." May also contain diode and pilot light to indicate when it is in use. May be a modular unit, removable for repair, or a built-in device.

Corner Block; Corner Plate: Triangle of $\frac{1}{4}$ inch plywood used to make a joint between two pieces of 1 inch by 3 inches, meeting at an angle, usually 90°.

Counterweight System: A system of lifting scenery vertically into space above the stage area. Weight of scenery is balanced by a like weight hung from ropes (wire or hemp) supporting scenery.

Cover Gun: In properties or special effects, an extra gun kept in readiness backstage to be fired in case gun on stage misfires in hands of an actor.

Crash Box: Sound effects device for approximating sounds of broken glass or falling objects.

Cue Sheet: Chartlike arrangement of data needed to run lighting for a production. Used to aid lighting operator's memory during the performance.

Current: See Ampere.

Curtain: Usually refers to act curtain, but can refer to any fabric hanging in fullness (as drapery hangs). Also known as front curtain, main curtain, main, house curtain, flag, or rag.

Curtain Line: (1) Imaginary line formed by act curtain when it is closed. Reference line for many stage measurements. (2) Last line spoken by actor as curtain closes.

Cut Drop: A drop with portions cut out to represent foliage or the like.

Cyclorama: A device to represent the sky, or to suggest limitless space. May be a partial sphere of plaster *(Kuppelhorizont),* a U-shaped drop of fabric, or (not very exactly) a set of drapery surrounding the acting space. Abbreviated cyc.

Cyclorama Footlights: Footlight apparatus installed at the base of the cyclorama to increase intensity of light near bottom of cyc. Often installed in trough in stage floor which is equipped with removable covers. Usually circuited for red, green, and blue.

Cyclorama Lights; Cyc Border: Set of lighting instruments hung near top of cyc some distance downstage of it designed to flood cyc with even illumination. Usually high-powered instruments. Normally gelled red, green, and blue for full color mixing.

Dead Hung: Rigging term applied to lighting or other apparatus mounted permanently above stage in such a way that raising or lowering it is extremely difficult. Batten usually is fastened by chains to ceiling structure. Lighting equipment is mounted on batten.

Diffuse Reflection: Reflection from every point on a surface as though each were a nondirectional source of light. For example, surface of blotter or piece of chalk.

Dim: To change the intensity of lighting either upward or downward.

Dimmer: Any device used to vary the intensity of lighting gradually. Modern dimmers are solid-state devices, known as Silicon Controlled Rectifiers (SCR, defined below).

Direct Current (dc): Flow of electrons that continues in one direction until cut off. Produced by batteries. Presence requires use of resistance dimmers. Very unusual in power supplied in United States today.

Dock; Scene: A storage space designed for flats. Sometimes any storage area for scenic elements.

Double Head: A special nail used in constructing scaffolds (in industry) and for temporary nailing of scenery. It has two heads, one below the other on the shank. The lower head prevents nail from being driven flush with the wood surface and makes removal easy.

Drape Shaping: A plastic forming technique where the sheet of plastic is softened by heating, and allowed to sag of its own weight into a hollow mold.

Draw Curtain; Traveler: A curtain that moves horizontally across to conceal or reveal a part of the stage.

Drop: See Backdrop.

Dutchman: A strip of material, usually fabric, used to cover the joint where two flats meet.

Electric: Refers to rigging or other materials used by the stage lighting staff. Often used as "first electric," "second electric," etc., to refer to battens reserved and equipped for lighting apparatus.

Electrician: Term used by professional theatre people to refer to those operating lighting and allied equipment. Generally refers to member of union. A designer is *not* an electrician in professional houses. Also known as a "gaffer" in Hollywood.

Elevation: A working drawing showing the vertical surfaces of scenery, properties, etc.

Elevator: A portion of the stage floor which is mechanically raised and lowered (usually by hydraulics). It may sink two or three stories below floor level and rise as much as two stories above it. Often installed in multiples to include whole playing area.

Ellipsoidal Reflector: A specular reflector in the form of a truncated ellipsoid. Has two focal points, one occupied by the filament, the other very near the lens system. It forms heart of highly efficient ellipsoidal reflector spotlight. Also used in matte finish form for scoops.

False Proscenium: Also, inner proscenium. A proscenium-shaped piece of scenery used to reduce the size of the architectural proscenium, and on occasion to alter its shape. May fly in or be permanently mounted.

Fan and Deluge System: A theatre fire safety system that eliminates the asbestos curtain. Consists of a very heavy set of sprinklers over the stage area which work in conjunction with a special powerful fan system at the top of the stage house. The sprinklers douse the fire, and the fan removes the smoke, preventing it from spreading to the house. Part of the new New York City Fire Code.

Filigree: Fancy scrollwork, usually of wood or metal, used to decorate various pieces of period furniture or architecture. Imitated in the theatre by use of less sturdy materials.

Filler: A material added to paint to extend it and/or alter its viscosity or covering power. Often used to reduce cost of paint.

Fill Light: Also, base light. Light that fills in shadows, preventing them from appearing black.

Fire Curtain: See Asbestos.

Fire Retardant; Flame Retardant: (1) Term referring to a material which has been chemically treated so that it will not *sustain* a flame. Note that treated material *will* burn if externally heated to a sufficient temperature. (2) Chemical mixtures for above.

First Border: Borderlight and/or its position immediately upstage of the teaser (defined below), i.e., just upstage of the top of the proscenium arch. Most used lighting position in the theatre.

Flameproof: (1) Refers to materials that will not burn at commonly encountered temperatures. Materials considered "flameproof" by the fire department are rare in scenic construction, with the exception of metal. (2) A misnomer for fire retardant.

Flies: The space above a proscenium stage where scenery, lights, etc., are hoisted to be out of sight of the audience. Term may also apply to similar space over any other theatrical space.

Flipper: A relatively narrow flat hinged to a wing. Often any narrow flat hinged to swing from a larger piece of scenery.

Float: (1) To allow a flat to free fall from the upright position to the floor. (2) A nearly obsolete term for footlights.

Floodlight: A simple boxlike or ellipsoidal enclosure generally treated to improve reflectivity, containing a single general service lamp (usually frosted). Produces a broad distribution of light, non-adjustable in most cases. Used to cover large areas such as cycloramas or a large drop.

Floor Cloth: Large piece of canvas or other durable material tacked to the stage floor to cover the acting space. Can be used to simulate earth or other nonwooden surfaces. Improves acoustical quality.

Floor Plan: Drawing of stage, including setting as seen from above without perspective. An orthographic projection. Usually simplified for use by director, lighting crews, and others. Also called ground plan.

Floor Pocket: A metal enclosure built into stage floor which contains electrical outlets for lighting apparatus. Usually arranged around perimeter of stage for operating side lighting, cyclorama footlights, etc.

Fluorescence: The property of certain materials to absorb light of certain wavelengths (usually ultraviolet, but not always) and reemit the light at other (visible) wavelengths.

Fly Loft: See Flies.

Flyman: Rigger who is operating line sets during run of show.

Focal Plane: A plane made up of focal points. An area in space, generally forming a plane, where an image is in sharp focus. Varies considerably with lens. Used in scenic projection to control image sharpness and in lighting to diffuse edge of ellipsoidal lens spotlight.

Focus: (1) To adjust the beam size of a spotlight to meet the specifications of the light plot. (2) A point at which light beams converge after passing through a lens (or being reflected by a curved mirror) and form a real image. A point on a focal plane.

FOH; Front-of-House: Illumination coming from the direction of the audience and aimed at actors on the apron. Once mostly footlighting. Now provided by beam, anteproscenium, and balcony lighting instruments.

Follow Spotlight: In the United States, a powerful instrument mounted in back of house and operated by an electrician who moves it about to follow an actor(s) with a bright, sharp-edged pool of light. In Europe, it often is operated from the beams or light bridge, soft-edged, and made nearly indistinguishable from the rest of the lighting.

Foot: To hold the bottom of a large flat or framed drop in place on the floor while the other end is being raised into vertical position. Done by placing foot firmly against edge of flat.

Footcandle: A unit of illumination (brightness). That amount of light found on a surface 1 foot from a standard candle.

Foot Iron: L-shaped hardware attached to the bottom of a piece of scenery to allow the scenery to be temporarily fastened with a stage screw to the floor.

Footlights: Striplightlike units mounted at front edge of stage to provide light for actors downstage of proscenium arch. Only source available except arc light before incandescent spotlight came into use for FOH lighting.

Forestage: See Apron.

Foul: Riggers' term for the tangling of scenery and lines in the flies. A dangerous situation.

Fourth Wall: The concept of theatrical style which tends to assume that the curtain line represents a "fourth wall" of a room in which the play is taking place. Actors treat the space as though the wall were still there. The audience "oversees" the action. More of a metaphor than actual fact even in the days of utter realism.

Foyer: That part of the theatre building where the audience congregates before entering the house and during intermissions.

Fresnel: (Pronounced Freh-nel). Type of spotlight named after the inventor of its lens. Lens consists of concentric rings which are segments of spherical portion of plano-convex lens. Large diameter possible without great thickness. In spotlight, lens produces soft-edge beam.

Funnel; Top Hat; Hood; Snoot; High Hat: A device shaped like a top hat without a crown used to limit beam spread and spill on spotlights. Normally made of sheet metal and painted dead black. Mount with safety chain.

Fuse: Safety device to prevent excessive current from flowing. Consists of fusible piece of metal adjusted to heat to melting point and drop out, breaking circuit when overloaded. Must be replaced when it opens. See Plug Fuse; Fusestat; Cartridge Fuse; and Circuit Breaker.

Fusestat: A variety of plug fuse (defined below) sized so that each current is noninterchangeable with all others. Prevents unauthorized increase in fuse size.

Gel: Verb used to describe installation of *any* color medium.

Gelatin: Color medium. Made of animal material dyed with analine dyes in wide variety of colors. Fades, drys out, and gets wet, but still cheap and efficient.

General Illumination: Light spread over a wide area of stage and not easily adjusted as to area. Term once applied to a category of equipment which was the only source capable of lighting entire stage at once (striplights, borderlights, floodlights); now general illumination is possible from other sources.

Ghost: Faint glow emitted from a lamp not quite dimmed to total black. May show on an otherwise totally dark stage.

Ghost Load: Also called phantom load. Electrical load (usually lamps) added to the load of a resistance dimmer to make the dimmer capable of dimming to black. Wastes power.

Globe: See Incandescent Lamp. Hollywood movie lot term for lamp.

Gobo: A cutout, usually of metal, placed in the aperture of an ellipsoidal reflector spotlight to project a simple pattern.

Grand Drape: Also called main curtain, main, rag, etc. The principal curtain used to close the proscenium opening. Usually designed to compliment architecture of the house.

Grand Master: Refers to both switches and dimmer handles. Device controls all other units including "masters." Often found as huge lever on mechanically interlocked switchboards.

Gridiron: Also called grid. The heavy framework of iron (early grids were made of wood) which supports the pulleys carrying the lines holding up materials in the flies.

Grid Winch: A relatively new device that takes the place of counterweight systems. Consists of a special electrical winch that hauls a single line up and down from the grid. Winches can be closely synchronized to haul large objects.

Grip: A stagehand whose work consists of moving scenery.

Grommets: Metal rings set into holes in fabric to reinforce the edges of the holes against wear from ropes passed through them. Often made of brass.

Ground Cloth: See Floor Cloth.

Ground Plans: See Floor Plan.

Ground Row: A piece of scenery placed upstage of the acting space to suggest items near the horizon. May be cut to suggest silhouette of trees, distant hills, distant buildings, etc. Usually painted on surface to increase the illusion.

Hand Prop: A small property whose primary function is found in the way in which an actor uses or handles it. May have secondary decorative function.

Hanger Iron: A piece of scenic hardware designed to allow secure fastening of hoisting lines to flats and framed drops. May be attached to top or near bottom of back of drop.

Hanging Plot: Drawing showing the arrangement of scenic elements in the flies. May consist of a special horizontal section of the fly loft showing battens and what they carry, or may be a longitudinal section of the loft. Both often are used to clarify details.

Hard Edge: Beam of light with distinguishable border. Little light beyond that line.

Hard Scenery; (Old definition—any scenic element not framed, i.e., capable of being rolled or folded.) Scenery whose surface is solid to the touch, and which has acoustic properties approaching those of real walls.

Hauling Line: See Operating Line.

Head Block: A block with multiple sheaves (defined below) used to turn the lines coming from the loft blocks downward toward the arbor. Also may contain sheave for hauling line.

Heat Gun: An electrically operated hand tool consisting of a heater and fan. Blows heated air for heating plastics, drying objects, etc.

High Hat: See Funnel.

HMI; Hygerium Metallic Iodide: Refers to a very high efficiency point source lamp of the short arc variety. Useful for scenic projection, follow spotlight service, and for motion picture work.

Hood: See Funnel.

Horizontal Sight Lines: Imaginary lines drawn from the seats furthest from the center line of the house to determine what portions of the acting space will be visible to all the audience. Also lines from these extreme seats to opposite sides of the stage to determine masking.

Hot-Wire Cutter: Tool for cutting foamed plastics. Consists of length of electrical resistance wire fitted with insulating holder. Wire is heated by passing controlled electrical current through it. Hot wire is passed through the foam to make a cut. If wire is heavy enough, it may be shaped to make complicated cuts.

House: (1) That portion of the theatre building where the audience is seated. (2) Also refers to the audience itself.

House Lights: Lighting provided for the audience.

Hue: Property of a color that distinguishes it from gray of same brightness. Result of selective reflection in pigments.

Idler: Sheave (defined below) near floor on locking rail. Movable on weight to take up slack in operating line.

In One: Refers to a scene which is played in front of main curtain while other scenes are being set up on main stage area.

Inner Proscenium: See False Proscenium.

Instrument: Refers to a device for producing and controlling light on stage.

Instrument Fuse: See Fuse; Cartridge Fuse. A tiny cartridge fuse usually made of glass, designed to handle minute current. Often found in consoles. Automotive type for low voltages and high currents appears nearly the same.

Insulation: Any material that has high resistance to the passage of electricity—usually will not pass significant amounts without being destroyed if voltage forces itself through. Used to prevent electricity from going where we do not want it to go.

Intensity: Power of a light source measured in footcandles (defined above).

Interlock: See Mechanical Interlock.

Iris Shutter: A device used to vary the diameter of the beam of light coming from a spotlight continuously from large to tiny. Usually found on follow spotlights.

Jack: (1) A brace hinged or fastened to the back of scenery to make it stand upright. (2) A tool that enables one to raise a very heavy object.

Jackknife Stage: Special stage wagon pivoted at one corner and swung into or out of the playing area around the pivot in a motion resembling the movement of a blade of a jackknife.

Jig: A special tool made up to guide a drilling or cutting operation that must be repeated many times with accuracy.

Kelvin Scale: A temperature scale with Celsius (centigrade) size degrees that begins at absolute zero ($-273°C = 0°K$). Used to describe color temperature. Visible light begins around 600 degrees K.

Key Light: Light that gives a sense of direction to the audience's view of the lighting. Produces highlights and shadows which indicate its direction.

Keystone: Plywood joint reinforcement cut in the shape of a keystone. Used to attach toggle rails to stiles (both defined below).

Klieglight: Trademark name for ellipsoidal reflector spotlight sold by Kliegl Bros. Klieg is often used to refer to any bright source.

Lamp: See Incandescent Lamp.

Lamp Dip: Colored lacquer used to color small (under 60 W) lamps, and for painting slides for projection.

Lash: Method of temporarily fastening flats together by lacing a length of lightweight rope from one flat to the other over special hooks.

Lash Cleat: Piece of stage hardware used with the lash line to lace two flats together. It is attached to the inner edge of stiles (defined below) with wood screws, its end protruding beyond the inner edge of the wood to form a simple hook over which the lash line is placed.

Lash Line: Piece of soft rope used to lash flats together.

Lash Line Eye: Stage hardware used to attach top end of lash line to the upper corner of flat.

Lead-in Wires: Wires carrying current to filament in an incandescent lamp. They pass through the glass envelope (bulb) and must be sealed to it where they pass through in order to protect the vacuum. Lead-in wires may also serve as supports for the filament.

Leg; Leg Drop: Piece of drapery hung in the wings to mask the sides of the acting space much in the manner of an early wing. A number of legs plus a close-in curtain (defined above) and one or two cloth borders make up a drapery setting.

Legitimate; Legit: Term referring to live theatre as opposed to motion pictures or television. Now little used.

Lekolight: Trademark of type of ellipsoidal reflector spotlight sold by Strand Century Inc. Often shortened to "leko" and used as a synonym for any ellipsoidal reflector spotlight.

Lens: Transparent piece of material, usually glass, shaped to bend light rays passing through it. See Plano-convex Lens. Used to converge light and to form images in stage lighting.

Levels: Series of platforms made up of stock units usually rectilinear and modular in style. Levels are wide enough to afford playing area; steps are usually not.

Lift: See Elevator.

Light Bridge; Lighting Bridge: See Bridge.

Light Ladder: Frameworks of metal pipe ($1\frac{1}{2}$ inch diameter) suspended at sides of a stage, usually in tormentor position to facilitate hanging instruments.

Lime Light: One of the earliest point light sources used in the back of early theatre balconies to produce a moveable pool of light on stage. The light source consisted of a chunk of limestone heated to incandescence by a blowtorch.

Line Connector: Electrical device feeding current from supply source; thus it is live even when not being used. Has holes into which pins or hooks fit. Electrically live parts are recessed to prevent accidental contact when handling. Also called "female connector."

Linnebach Projector: A shadow-box projector using a point source of light and no lens. Produces large images in short throw. Projects only simple images.

Load: (1) Anything that uses electricity. (2) The amount of electricity being drawn from a source of supply.

Load Connector: Electrical device attached to anything using electricity. On stage, usually a lighting instrument. Has pins or hooks that insert into its mate, the line connector. Also called "male connector."

Load Sensitive: Characteristic of some dimmers that makes their operating characteristics change in proportion to load. For example, resistance dimmer must be nearly fully loaded or it cannot dim lamps to black out.

Lobby: The first inside area the audience usually encounters when entering a proscenium theatre. May house ticket booths or other areas that must be open to those not holding tickets. Opens into the foyer.

Locking Rail: Metal framework holding idler pulleys, rope locks, and associated hardware. Main purpose is to support rope locks. Must withstand upward strain of pull on operating lines.

Longitudinal Section: Detail drawing of the stage house (and sometimes the house itself) showing a section taken along the center line which is vertical to the curtain line. Used for planning rigging and for working out lighting.

Lumen: Unit of luminous flux. Light energy contained on 1 square foot of surface 1 foot away from a standard candle.

Luminescence: Property of material capable of giving off light as a result of stimulation, usually by an ultraviolet source. Often confused with phosphorescence (defined below).

Mask; Masking: Scenic elements placed behind entrances, doors, windows, and other openings in the setting with the purpose of preventing the audience from looking backstage. Usually consist of neutral draperies or flats painted in a dark neutral color. Installing such materials is known as "masking."

Mechanical Interlock: Arrangement of levers and cams to tie several dimmers together mechanically so that moving any one will more all of them.

Medium: See Color Medium.

Mercury Vapor Lamp: Gaseous discharge lamp that produces light by passing electrical current through gas — in this case vaporized mercury metal. Lamp produces large amount of ultraviolet light and visible light in the blue-green range.

Module: A dimension chosen as a "standard" for construction because of reasons of economy, availability of material, potential for multiple use, and convenience. The scenographer may strive to make as many dimensions of the setting come out on multiples of the molecule as possible without jeopardizing his design. Most common horizontal module is 4 feet because of the standard size of plywood (4 by 8 feet).

Monochromatic: A color scheme worked around varying chromas and values of the same hue. Produces marked stylization.

Motif: In scenography, a visual element carefully chosen and then much repeated to give style and unity to the design. Must have some analogical connection to the script.

Nichrome Wire: Electrical resistance wire made of nickle and chromium alloy. Has high resistance, high melting point, and good resistance to oxidation. Used in resistance dimmers and in electrical heaters.

Nonspectral Hue: Color sensation caused by the stimulation of more than one set of cones at the same time by more than one wavelength. A spectrophotometer (defined below) would not find any single wavelength able to produce the same sensation.

Objective Lens: Lens capable of converging light beams sufficiently to bring them to a focus. Actually any converging lens, but usually a highly refined lens made for the purpose of producing high-quality images.

Ohm: Unit of electrical resistance.

Ohms Law: Basic formula describing flow of electricity. $E = IR$, or voltage = current $\times$ resistance.

Olio Curtain: An old-fashioned main curtain made up of a painted drop rolled upward from the bottom on a special roll device. Drop was usually elaborately painted. May also refer to a drop which does not roll if it is painted to resemble such a curtain.

O.P.: British abbreviation for "opposite prompt." Prompt side is stage right, and opposite prompt is stage left.

Operating Characteristic: Applied to dimmers. Describes relationship between mechanical movement of dimmer control handle and light output of lamp(s) controlled by dimmer. This is seldom linear.

Operating Light: A work light provided to enable the lighting operator to see what he is doing. Often dimmer controlled.

Operating Line: Heavy rope that runs from top of arbor to sheave at grid height, returns to near stage floor, passes over idler sheave, and is tied to bottom of arbor. Used to pull loaded arbor up and down. Also called hauling line.

Operator: A person responsible for running lighting equipment. Also an electrician. May run control board, handle individual equipment, run projection apparatus, etc.

Orchestra: That part of the audience space on the main floor as opposed to the balcony. Term dates back to Greek theatre where the "orchestra" was a circular area in front of the stage used by the chorus. The term is now frequently misapplied to any main floor seat no matter what the house configuration. British equivalent is "the stalls."

Outlet: A device that facilitates making an electrical connection temporarily. A receptacle into which a plug is inserted to receive electrical energy.

Papier-mâché: Heavy paper material made of paper fiber and glue. May be made up in layers or as a pulp. May have considerable strength.

Parabolic Reflector: A specular reflector in the shape of a paraboloid. Has single focal point. Source placed at focal point tends to produce parallel rays if it is small enough. Used in beam projectors and searchlights.

Parallel: A stage platform consisting of a removable top and a framework that folds for storage when the top is removed. Usually built in modules and repeatedly used as a stock item.

Parallel Circuit: Electrical circuit in which several branches function independently, sharing current in proportion to resistance. Fault in one section does not affect others. This is the usual circuit used in stage lighting.

Parting Agent: A material applied to a mold to prevent whatever is being cast or formed from adhering to the mold. Often a greasy substance.

Period (style): A period of time in history, usually referred to by the name of a prominent figure (e.g., Louis XIV) used to designate a style of decor and architecture. Also used as an adjective to refer to any setting or costume designed to suggest such a period.

Phosphorescence: Property of material capable of giving off light without noticeable heat. Light is usually the result of chemical action.

Pigment: A chemical (often crude) having the property of selective reflection. Pigments usually are assumed to be opaque although many are somewhat translucent. Pigments are the most important ingredient in paints.

Pilot Light: A very small lamp used to indicate the electrical state of a piece of remotely controlled apparatus. Often colored.

Pin Connector: Older, simple stage connector consisting of fiber blocks with pins to make electrical contacts. See Connector.

Pin Rail: Heavy wood or steel beam with sturdy rods (pins) set into it at right angles to the beam. Ropes supporting hanging scenery are tied to the pins, thus holding up the scenery. Rail must be capable of supporting total load of scenery. The pins may be removable for quick release of the ropes.

Plano-convex Lens: Circular piece of glass flat on one side and having a spherical bulge on the other. Converges beams of light passing through it. Used in now-obsolete plano spotlights and in many ellipsoidal reflector spotlights. Also used to form images in projectors.

Plasticity: The shadow-producing quality of good stage lighting that enables the viewers to perceive the three-dimensionality of the actors and the setting.

Plug: (1) Any electrical device designed to fit into a receptacle and make electrical connection. (2) "Stage plug." A now nearly obsolete connector. A heavy piece of fiber with copper strips on two sides made to mate with large receptacle, usually in floor pocket. Carries large current. Still used in movie studios. (3) In scenery, a narrow flat used to fill in a relatively small gap.

Plug Fuse: Fuse in the shape of screw-in unit like base of home-type lamp. Normally comes in 3, 6, 10, 15, 20, 25, and 30 Amp sizes. "Window" enables viewing of fuse wire inside. See Fuse.

Pocket: See Floor Pocket.

Point Source: A lamp designed to approximate the mathematical point as nearly as possible by having its filament (if it has one) compressed into the smallest possible size. See Concentrated Filament.

Polymers; Polymerization: Most plastics are formed by a process known as "polymerization," in which many identical molecules of a chemical link together to produce a material, usually solid, with physical characteristics far different from those of the component molecules. The end products of such reactions are known as "polymers." Heat often is produced as a by-product of such reactions.

Portable Control Board: A lighting control apparatus made to be moved frequently from theatre to theatre. Often made in several units for convenience.

Pot Time: The time during which a plastic material (resin) remains liquid after the catalyst has been added. Pot time varies with temperature, amount of catalyst, and many other factors.

Power; Power Formula: Calculation used to determine the amount of work that can be derived from an electrical current. Power is stated in watts (defined below). Watts = amperes × volts.

Practical: Refers to a prop that must actually work in the manner in which it appears to be made. For example, a "practical" drawer in a cabinet will open and close as a real drawer might.

Primary Colors: A set of three colors from which all other color sensations can be mixed but which cannot themselves be mixed from other colors. Red, green, and blue are primaries when mixing sensations in the seeing apparatus. If pigments are mixed, primaries are red (magenta), yellow, and blue (blue-green).

Profile Board: Thin (approximately $\frac{1}{8}$ inch thick) plywood. Extra flexible and used wherever sharp bends must be made.

Projector: (1) A device for producing images in the form of light on a surface. (2) More accurately, beam projector (defined above).

Prompt Side: British term for "stage right." See Opposite Prompt.

Proportional Dimming: Changing the intensity of a group of lights without altering the intensity ratios between the lights in the group (unless the entire group is dimmed out).

Proscenium: (1) The architectural opening through which the audience views the play in a traditional proscenium theatre. (2) The style of production that clearly separates the audience from the play by interposing an opening in a wall that forms the dividing line between them.

Quartz-Halogen Lamp: See Tungsten-Halogen Lamp.

Quartz-Iodine Lamp: See Tungsten-Halogen Lamp.

Rail: (1) The horizontal parts of a flat frame. See Toggle Rail. (2) The pin rail (defined above).

Rake: (1) To angle away from vertical. (2) Angling the side walls of a setting to more closely follow the sight lines. (3) (Now seldom found as a permanent feature.) Slope of stage floor that increases elevation as one moves away from the footlight line. Originally part of the wing and drop theatre.

Receptacle: See Outlet.

Reflectance: Reflected light divided by incident light usually given as percentage figure. Figure indicates efficiency of reflective surface.

Rehearsal Props: Simple simulations of actual proporties provided to the actors for use in early rehearsals.

Related Color Scheme: Two or more colors chosen from near-adjacent locations on the color wheel. Produces harmonious relationship.

Resin: Liquid plastic material that can be hardened by addition of catalyst.

Resistance Dimmer: A now-obsolete device for dimming lights. Consists of a length of resistance wire capable of being variably inserted in series with lamps to decrease current flow and thereby decrease light. Load sensitive; produces much heat.

Return Piece: A small flat or a piece of lumber attached to edge of a flat to give the appearance of architectural thickness.

Reveal: A thickness piece. Often one on a false proscenium set at 45 degrees to the face of the unit.

Rheostat: See Resistance Dimmer.

Riser: (1) The vertical portion of a step. It determines how high the step will be. (2) A stock platform, usually a single step high.

Rods: The light-sensing devices in the eye that are sensitive to light but not to differences in wavelengths. The rods provide vision under low light levels.

Rope Lock: Clamping device attached to locking rail. Operating line passes through the clamp and may be held stationary against moderate pulls by closing the lock.

Saddle Iron; Sill Iron: Piece of strap iron (may be specially formed) attached to bottom of door opening in a flat to hold side pieces in place and strengthen the flat.

Saturation: That property of any color that distinguishes it from a gray of the same brightness. The "purity" of the color. The inverse of the amount of white mixed with a color of light. High saturation means little or no white light added to the color.

Scale Rule: A rulerlike device designed to simplify conversion of dimensions in feet and inches to reduced scale, or the reverse. An architect's scale is universally used for stage purposes.

Schedules (lighting plot): Charts listing equipment, color medium, hookup, and such, used to elaborate and clarify a lighting plot.

Scioptican: An image projection device made by adapting a spotlight. A slide carrier and objective lens are added. Usually the slide carrier is adapted to take moving effects devices such as rain, rippling water, and the like.

Scoop: A modern floodlight whose reflector is made of spun aluminum in the form of a parabolic or ellipsoidal reflector. It faintly resembles a scoop; hence the name.

Scrim: Semitransparent fabric that can be made to appear near-opaque when front lighted, and near-transparent when the only light is on objects behind it.

Secondary Colors: Colors made by mixing equal portions of two primary colors.

Section: A drawing that shows a "cut-through" view of an object.

Selective Reflection: A process similar to selective transmission (defined below), but where the remaining light is reflected from the medium instead of passing through it.

Selective Transmission: A process by which light passing through a material is filtered allowing certain wavelengths to pass and others to be stopped and converted into heat, or otherwise rejected.

Selvage; Selvedge: A specially woven edge on fabric which prevents raveling.

Series Circuit: An electrical circuit arranged so that all of the current flows through all portions of the circuit. Interrupting any part of the circuit cuts off the entire flow. For example, "indoor" (series string) Christmas tree lights. Resistance dimmers operate in series with the load.

Set Prop: A property chosen primarily for its appearance on stage as opposed to one which must function in some manner (hand prop).

Shade: A color whose value is lower than that of middle gray. Often produced by adding black to the pigment.

Sheave: The grooved wheel of a pulley.

Shop Grade: A grade of lumber suitable for general construction in a shop where occasional defects may be cut out. A medium grade.

Short Circuit: An uncontrolled flow of electricity. Control is so minimal that all of the available power in the system tries to flow through the shorted path. Usually causes explosion and fire. Fuses and circuit breakers are used as protection against short circuits.

Show Curtain: A specially designed main curtain intended to be a part of the setting of a particular show. Frequently the permanent main is opened to reveal the show curtain which then remains in view until the end of the overture.

Side Lighting: Lighting coming from the side of the actor and usually above head level as he faces the audience.

Sight Lines: Lines on a plan indicating the line of sight from the most extreme seats in the house. Determines placement of masking, rake of setting, location of entrances, and many other critical matters. See Horizontal Sight Lines; Vertical Sight Lines.

Silicon Controlled Rectifier (Thyrister, SCR): A solid-state electronic device that can be made to pass predetermined portions of each wave of ac, thus effecting control of total power flow. Forms heart of most modern dimmers.

Sill Iron: See Saddle Iron.

Size Water: Thin solution of glue used to fill in the pores of canvas or muslin and to shrink the fabric to a smooth fit.

Smoke Slots: Automatically operating trap doors in top of stage house designed to open with excessive heat to allow smoke from a fire on stage to escape. Also called smoke traps. Also slot in which asbestos curtain runs. It is designed to prevent smoke from a fire on stage from leaking into the house when it is down.

Snatch Line: Lightweight rope attached to a piece of scenery to allow operators to swing scenery while it is suspended.

Snub Line: A sturdy piece of line tied around operating line with a special knot, and secured to locking rail. Intended to reinforce rope lock in case of dangerously heavy out-of-balance conditions.

Soft Edge: Beam of light which has no distinguishable edge. Tapers off toward darkness. Desirable for blending lighting areas.

Soft Scenery: (1) Formerly, scenery that could be rolled or folded, i.e., unframed. (2) Now, scenery whose surface is soft to touch and acoustically near-transparent.

Spattering: Painting technique by which flecks of paint are thrown onto the surface of scenery by flipping the partially charged brush. Produces texturing.

Spectral Hue: A color sensation caused by exposure of eye to a single relatively narrow band of wavelengths.

Spectrophotometer: A very complicated and expensive scientific instrument which breaks light into its component wavelengths and accurately measures the amount of each. Usually makes a graph of its results, known as a spectrogram.

Spectroscope: Expensive scientific instrument that breaks beams of light into their component wavelengths.

Spectrum (visible): A display of visible wavelengths arranged according to their wavelength. Resembles a rainbow.

Spherical Reflector: A specular reflector, usually made of metal, in the shape of a portion of a sphere. The inside surface has the property of returning rays to their source if that source is at the center of curvature. Used to increase the efficiency of Fresnel spotlights by capturing light emanating away from lens.

Spill; Spill Light: Light emitted from spotlight that is not in the main beam. Tends to light areas not intended to be lighted by the instrument.

Spotlight: Instrument capable of producing a concentrated beam of light, usually adjustable.

Spot Line: A single line located at a particular place on the gridiron to accommodate a special object such as a chandelier. Usually a rope line.

Stage Brace: Adjustable wood or metal device with an eye at the lower end to accept a stage screw (defined below), and a hook at the top to engage a brace cleat (defined above). Length of brace is adjustable to set flat perpendicular to floor.

Stage Screw: (1) A large wood screw equipped with a handle to facilitate driving it into wooden stage floor. (2) A special threaded heavy machine screw with a handle made to fit into an adapter set into a hole drilled in wood floor. Also called patented stage screw.

Stenciling: Process of applying a repeating pattern to scenery by painting through a cut-out pattern.

Stile: Vertical portion of a flat frame.

Stippling: Process of applying texture to scenic surfaces by lightly touching surface with an irregular object charged with a small quantity of paint.

Stop Block: Wooden or metal block fastened to back of a flat near edge. Keeps another flat from sliding past the corner when the flats meet at an angle.

Strap Hinge: Scenic hardware. Crude iron hinge consisting of two V-shaped flat portions attached by a permanently installed pivot.

Striplight: Instrument made up of a number of lamps mounted in a line in a housing. Usually each lamp is provided with a separate reflector and color holder. Used for producing general illumination.

Strobe Light: A gaseous discharge tube or fluorescent tube designed to flash brightly at frequent intervals. Produces flickering "stop-action" effect with movement of actors.

Stylization: Design technique where a natural object, shape, etc., is exaggerated and often repeated to increase its attention value and emphasize its symbolic value.

Subtractive Color Mixing: Mixing of selective transmitting or reflecting media in such a way that the absorptive values are combined. Result always produces less light than the separate colorants could reflect or transmit.

Surge: "Glitch." A very short but often violent increase in current flowing through a circuit. Frequently caused by sudden turning on of large tungsten lamps or by starting large motors. Can also be sudden backward flow from turning off transformerlike devices. Dangerous to silicon rectifiers.

Switch: Device designed to make it easy and safe to open and close an electrical circuit. See Contactor.

Switchboard: Early term for a slab of insulating material (slate or marble) holding open knife switches used to turn lights off or on. Such boards contained no dimmers. Later, term was used to refer to device containing both switches and dimmers behind an electrically "dead" front panel. Synonymous with control board.

Teaser: Curtain hung at the top of stage opening to make height of that opening adjustable.

Template Table; Template: A carefully squared heavy table designed to facilitate construction of flats.

Thermoplastic: Term applied to plastics that can be softened or melted by heat. When cooled, the material regains its original solid state.

Thermosetting: Applied to plastic materials that are formed as a liquid or pastelike material which then is heated in the mold to cause solidification. Once solidified, the material cannot be softened by reheating.

Thickness Piece; Thickness: A piece of lumber or similar material attached to edge of a flat to give appearance of having thickness of a wall. Adds rigidity to flat.

Three-Dimensional Trim: Molding, scrollwork, and the like, attached to surface of a flat to give the appearance of panel work, etc. The effect is more realistic than painting the images of such decorations on the flat surface.

Three-fold: A set of three flats hinged to fold together much like a screen. Stores compactly and provides a manageable unit during shifts.

Throw: Distance from lighting instrument to area it lights up, or from projector to image plane.

Thyrister: See Silicon Controlled Rectifier.

Tint: A color low in saturation. Pale hue.

Titanium Tetrachloride ($TiCl_4$): A corrosive and potentially poisonous liquid that gives off dense white "smoke" when exposed to moist air. Used for magic smoke effects. Safe if used with care in small amounts.

Toggle Rail; Toggle Bar: A horizontal cross-brace in a flat frame. Prevents inward bowing of sides (rails) of flat, and provides solid point of attachment for items on front of flat.

Toning Light: Wash of colored light added for purpose of improving color of setting. Particularly effective with spattered set when spatters vary in color.

Top Hat: See Funnel.

Tormentor Light: Instruments hung in tormentor position, i.e., at sides of stage upstage of proscenium opening.

Tormentors: Curtains hanging at sides of proscenium opening. Usually adjustable to alter width of opening.

Translucency: A drop or curtain (usually of muslin) painted with dyes to allow it to be lighted from behind revealing the design in brilliant color.

Transverse Section: A kind of drawing showing the arrangement of parts as they would be seen if the item were cut along a designated plane.

Traps: Removable sections of stage floor that allow movement through floor when opened.

Triac: An SCR-like device also used in electronic dimmers.

Traveler: (1) The track on which a horizontally drawn curtain runs. Actually a heavy duty version of a home curtain draw rod. (2) The horizontally drawn curtain itself.

Triad: A set of three colors evenly distributed around the color wheel.

Trim: (1) (Verb) To adjust the height of a hanging object to specifications. (2) (Noun) Decorative material on set pieces.

T-Track; T-Bar: A bar of heavy steel whose cross section is T-shaped. This steel is attached to the wall behind a counterweight system to form a guide track for counterweight arbors in order to prevent swaying.

Tungsten-Halogen Lamp; Quartz-Iodine Lamp; Quartz-Halogen Lamp: Improved type of incandescent lamp that uses a halogen (iodine, bromine, etc.) in the atmosphere surrounding the filament to return sublimated tungsten to the filament, cleaning the bulb and extending the life of the lamp.

Turnbuckle: A hardware device for closely adjusting length of a wire or cable. Consists of opposing right- and left-handed screws so arranged that turning a center element causes shortening or lengthening.

Twist-Lock: Patented connector that locks together when twisted slightly. See Connector.

Two-fold: Two flats hinged to fold together for storage or shifting. Will stand free if not opened flat.

Ultraviolet (UV) Light: Light lying just beyond visible blue-violet on the spectrum. Capable of producing fluorescence. Sometimes used to produce bizarre effects on a darkened stage.

Vacuum Forming: A process by which thermoplastic sheet material can be formed by heating it to softness and then drawing it tightly over a mold by use of vacuum action. Material then is allowed to cool in its new shape.

Valance: A decorative header at top of a proscenium opening used to permanently reduce height of that opening. Often distractingly decorated and used to cover poor architectural design of proscenium theatres. Occasionally valance is movable, and is really a teaser (defined above).

Value: Term in the Munsell color system that refers to the reflectance of the surface with no concern for its color or hue. Often referred to as the equivalent gray which reflects the same amount of light.

Vehicle: Material in paint that causes it to flow, i.e., makes it liquid. Usually water in scene paint.

Velour: Fabric with a pile surface like velvet but more rugged.

Velours: A set of draperies made of velour used as a general purpose setting for concerts, etc. Black velours often are used to mask settings.

Vertical Sight Lines: Imaginary lines drawn from the highest seats in the balcony, the front seats in the house, and other key positions to determine what portions of vertical elements of the setting will be visible to the audience. Also used to locate masking.

Volt: A unit of electrical pressure.

Watt: Unit of electrical power. Watts equals voltage times current.

Webbing: A narrow strip (4–6 inches) of woven jute used to reinforce top of draperies, unframed drops, etc. It is sewn to top of fabric before grommets are installed for tie lines.

Winch: A heavy machine for hauling rope or cable. Usually electrically driven. Used for hoisting and hauling heavy objects such as large stage wagons.

Wing and Drop: A now-obsolete style of setting developed in the early proscenium theatre. All elements were flat, depending entirely on painting for three-dimensionality. Consisted of flat side elements (wings) and a back element (drop) which enclosed playing space. Could be rapidly shifted by complicated rope works.

Work Light: Illumination provided on stage for rehearsals, setting up scenery, and the like. Should be cheap to operate. Spotlight lamps are too expensive.

Xenon Arc Source: Very high-intensity, small-size light source produced by passing dc through high pressure xenon gas enclosed in quartz bulb. Dangerous; may explode. Produces noxious ozone and dangerous ultraviolet radiation. Used as projection source because of efficiency.

X-rays: Name given to now-obsolete type of borderlight which had ribbed glass reflectors, one for each lamp. Also applied at one time to concert border or first border.

BIBLIOGRAPHY

AESTHETICS

Appia, Adolphe. *La Musique et la Mise en Scène*. Available in an English translation by Robert W. Corrigan and Mary Douglas Dirks, entitled Adolphe Appia's *Music and the Art of the Theatre*. Coral Gables, Fla.: University of Miami Press, 1962. This work is probably the most important document for the modern scenographer. Appia establishes the aesthetic basis for modern scenography. The German translation of this same work, though faulty and long out of print, is worth seeking in a large library for its scenario of the staging of *Tristan und Isolde* (Wagner). This remarkable example of modern scenography remains to this day a challenge for lighting designers, not to mention designers of lighting control equipment.

Craig, Edward Gordon. *The Theatre Advancing*. Boston: Little, Brown and Co., 1919.

Craig, Edward Gordon. *Scene*. London: Milford, 1923.

Craig, Edward Gordon. *On the Art of the Theatre*. Boston: Small Maynard, 1925. The three books by Craig constitute another major reference source for modern scenography. Although the original edition is out of print and increasing in value, facsimile editions are available. Also, originals can be found in most major libraries. Craig, like Appia, is concerned with the unity and artistic integrity of the theatrical production, especially the visual production. His works and their accompanying sketches should be a part of the basic reading of every student scenographer.

Hospers, John. *Meaning and Truth in the Arts*. Hamden, Conn.: Archon Books, 1964. Aesthetician philosopher Hospers deals effectively with many of the basic aesthetic problems that underlie the work of the scenographer. He also deals incisively with the problems of art in society which lie behind our modern theatre movement and find expression in the activities of collective theatre groups.

Langer, Susanne. *Philosophy in a New Key*. Cambridge, Mass.: Harvard University Press, 1951; New York: New American Library, 1948. Langer is the most important of modern aestheticians for student scenographers. Her fresh treatment of the problems of artistic communication, especially that which takes place between artists during creative efforts, provides the background for much of the aesthetic statement in this text.

Langer, Susanne. *Feeling and Form*. New York: Charles Scribner's Sons, 1953.

SCENOGRAPHY

Burian, Jarka. *The Scenography of Josef Svoboda*. Middletown, Conn.: Wesleyan University Press, 1971. (Available in paperback.) A very important study of the work of the theatre's foremost scenographer. Profusely illustrated.

STAGE SCENERY AND PROPERTIES

Bay, Howard. *Stage Design.* New York: Drama Book Specialists, 1974. Focuses on professional design processes on Broadway.

Bowman, Ned. *Handbook of Technical Practice for the Performing Arts.* Winkinsbury, Pa.: Scenographic Media, 1972. A loose-leaf notebook compendium of techniques, tricks of the trade, new products, old (and otherwise forgotten) practices. Designed to be updated as new material is available. Also Part II, designed to be interfiled with Part I.

Burris-Meyer, Harold, and Cole, Edward C. *Scenery for the Theatre,* rev. ed. Boston: Little, Brown and Co., 1971. A revised and updated version of a standard text on conventional scenic construction.

Gillette, Arnold. *Stage Scenery,* rev. ed. New York: Harper & Row, Publishers, 1960. Another text for the advanced scenery builder and painter. Provides excellent day-to-day information on construction methods. Should be part of every scenographer's library.

Hefner, Hubert C., Selden, Samuel, and Sellman, Hunton D. *Theatre Practice,* 3d ed. New York: Appleton-Century-Crofts, 1946. General treatment of theatre technology. Now out of date.

Payne, Darwin Ried. *Design for the Stage: First Steps.* Carbondale, Ill.: Southern Illinois University Press, 1974. Focuses on process of design.

Selden, Samuel, and Rezzuto, Tom. *Essentials of Stage Scenery.* New York: Appleton-Century-Crofts, 1972. An update of the scenery portion of *Stage Scenery and Lighting.*

Selden, Samuel, and Sellman, Hunton D. *Stage Scenery and Lighting,* rev. ed. New York: Appleton-Century-Crofts, 1959. Detailed treatment of scenery and lighting. Now out of date.

Welker, David. *Theatrical Set Design.* Boston: Allyn & Bacon, 1969. Extensive treatment of modes of presenting design concepts.

LIGHTING

Bellman, Willard F. *Lighting the Stage: Art and Practice,* 2d ed. New York: Thomas Y. Crowell Co., 1974. Advanced aesthetics and practice of lighting.

Bentham, Frederick. *The Art of Stage Lighting,* 2d ed. London: Sir Isaac Pitman & Sons, 1968. Much information on British lighting practices.

McCandless, Stanley. *A Method of Lighting the Stage,* 3d rev. ed. New York: Theatre Arts Books, 1947. Contains the original bases for much modern stage lighting.

Pilbrow, Richard. *Stage Lighting.* New York: Van Nostrand Reinhold Co., 1971. The most up-to-date book on British professional lighting practices. Well illustrated.

Rosenthal, Jean, and Wertenbacker, Lael. *The Magic of Light.* Boston: Little, Brown and Co., 1972. A personal statement about the practices and atmosphere of the Broadway stage.

NEW THEATRICAL FORMS

McNamara, Brooks, Rojo, Jerry, and Schechner, Richard. *Theatres, Spaces, Environments: 18 Projects.* New York: Drama Book Specialists, 1975. Deals with the creation of existing spaces into theatre spaces for new theatre forms.

PLASTICS

Bryson, Nicholas L. *Thermoplastic Scenery for the Theatre, Vol. I— Vacuum Forming.* New York: Drama Book Specialists, 1972. Plans for a shop-constructed vacuum-forming machine for theatre use. Detailed instructions for using plastics.

Newman, Thelma R. *Plastics as an Art Form,* rev. ed. Philadelphia: Chilton Book Co., 1969. Profusely illustrated. Very valuable to the theatre worker.

PERIODICALS

Theatre Crafts. Rodale Press Inc., 33 East Miner St., Emmaus, Pa. 18049. Many articles for the beginner on theatre technology.

Theatre Design and Technology. Publication of U.S. Institute for Theatre Technology, 1501 Broadway, Room 1408, New York, N. Y. 10036. Continuing articles on theatre technology and reviews of books in this area.

Numbers in italic refer to pages on which the items cited are illustrated.

Tripping, 248
Tri-square, 143, *144*
Troubleshooting, lighting, 531
Tumbler, 227, *228*
Tungsten-halogen lamps, 423, *425*, *430*
Twist-Lock connector, *458*
Two- or three-way connector, 510
"Twofer," 510

U

UV (ultraviolet), 415, *416*, 418, 472
Unframed drops, 148

V

VOM, 506
Vacuum forming, *295*
Valence, 59
Value, color, 309, 351
Variations allowed in cues, 527
Vehicle, paint, 340
Vinyl acrylic binder, 341, 342, 343
Virtual, concept of, 21
Virtual destiny, theatre as, 22
Virtual space-time, 25
Virtuality, 20
Vise, machinist's, 505
Visible spectrum, 313
Voltage, 402
Volt-ohm-milliameter (VOM), 506

W

Wafers, 242
Wagons, stage, 63, 234
Walking up, flat, *223*
Wallboard, 173
Warm and cool colors, 307, 422
Warning, cue, 519, 520
Water ripple, projection, 554
Watt, 402
Watt-hour, 402
Wavelength, 313
Weight-bearing three-dimensional scenery, 184
Western red cedar, 151
Wet blending, *357*, 358
White glue, 137, 158, 346
Windows, 165
Wing and drop setting, 52, 118
"Winging it," 530
Wings, 52, 63
Wire guide system, *71*
Wire rope, 241, *242*
Wood graining, 363, *364*
Wood lathe, *141*
Work lights, 489
Working drawings, *123*, 126
Writing cues, 525

X, Y, Z

Xenon lamp, 417, *418*, 472, 541, 550, 552
Yellow pine, 151
Yoke, *459*
Zipcord, 474

77 78 79 80 81 7 6 5 4 3 2

DATE DUE

APR 2 8 78			
JAN 0 3			
GAYLORD			PRINTED IN U.S.A.